The Arabian Mission's Story

In Search of Abraham's Other Son

by

Lewis R. Scudder III

The Historical Series of the Reformed Church in America

No. 30

The Arabian Mission's Story

In Search of Abraham's Other Son

by

Lewis R. Scudder III

Wm. B. Eerdmans Publishing Co.
Grand Rapids, Michigan

© 1998 Wm. B. Eerdmans Publishing Co.
255 Jefferson Ave. S.E., Grand Rapids, Michigan 49503 /
P.O. Box 163, Cambridge CB3 9PU U.K.

Printed in the United States of America

01 00 99 98   5 4 3 2 1

ISBN 0-8028-4616-5

Body text set in Adobe New Caledonia
Chapter titles set in Adobe Garamond
Typeset by Russell L. Gasero

To Nancy,
and to my children,
lovers and believers

The Historical Series of the Reformed Church in America

This series has been inaugurated by the General Synod of the Reformed Church in America, acting through its Commission on History, for the purpose of encouraging historical research and providing a medium wherein this knowledge may be shared with the academic community and with the members of the denomination in order that a knowledge of the past may contribute to right action in the present.

General Editor

The Rev. Donald J. Bruggink, Ph.D.
Western Theological Seminary

Commission on History

Gerald F. De Jong, Ph.D., Orange City, Iowa
The Rev. Sophie Mathonnet-Vander Well, M.Div.,Wynantskill, New York
Mr. Christopher Moore, New York, New York
The Rev. John Oquendo, M.Div, Paterson, New Jersey
The Rev. Jennifer Reece, M.Div., Princeton, New Jersey
The Rev. Jeffrey Tyler, Ph.D., Hope College, Holland, Michigan

Contents

Conclusion: Making Port is a Transition

Editor's Preface

by Donald J. Bruggink

The Historical Series had hoped to have a history of the Reformed church mission in the Arabian Gulf ready for its centenary. The consent of Edwin M. Luidens to author that work seemed ideal because of his participation in that mission and the relative leisure of retirement to accomplish the task. After the tragedy of his death, a new search for an author began and was consumated with the acceptance of Lewis R. Scudder III, of stellar credentials, to accomplish the lofty goals set for the work by Ed Luidens.

Lewis R. Scudder III was born in 1941 to RCA missionary parents in Kuwait. His father, a physician, served in Kuwait from 1939 (with a sojourn in Iraq from 1946 to 1949) until he died in 1975; his mother, Dorothy, a medical administrator and nurse, served until she died, still in active service, in 1991. Scudder lived in Arabia during a transition period between the time oil was first discovered and through the time when it was being fully exploited.

Scudder was educated in a missionary boarding school in South India from the age of seven through high school. In the footsteps of his father and elder sister he attended Hope College. After receiving an M.Div. from Western Theological Seminary in Holland, Michigan, he was ordained by the Classis of Holland. He and his wife, Nancy (child of Presbyterian missionaries in India), were commissioned by the RCA in 1966 as missionaries to the Middle East.

From 1967 to 1973 Scudder served in Lebanon, primarily in student work, and at the same time earned a masters degree in Middle East studies from the American University of Beirut. There, he focused his studies upon contemporary Arab affairs and the Arab response to the political and spiritual crisis of their defeat in the Six-Day War of 1967.

After a year with the Beirut office of the Ford Foundation, Scudder served as pastor of the English Language Congregation of the National Evangelical Church in Kuwait from 1973 to 1976. His mentor was the late Rev. Yousef Abd-un-Noor, the Arab pastor of the same church, a man of deep pastoral wisdom and keen insight.

At Abd-un-Noor's recommendation, from 1976 to 1980 Scudder did course work and successfully passed comprehensive examinations toward a Ph.D. in Islamic studies at McGill University in Montreal, Canada, focusing on Muslim-Christian relations. While employment prevented the completion of the thesis, the present volume has in large measure benefited from those doctoral studies.

In 1980 Scudder became the first Liaison Officer in the Gulf for the Middle East Council of Churches (MECC) and was based in Bahrain. His mandate was to help the expatriate churches of the region establish lines of communication with each other and between themselves and local society, and to provide the churches with resources to better understand more fully their presence and ministry in the Gulf.

Returning to the States in 1986, Scudder was able to accept the invitation to begin research for this volume. Unfortunately for the early completion of the book, the Scudders accepted a call to parish work in Istanbul, Turkey, with the Union Church of Istanbul. In 1993 Scudder was invited to return to service with the MECC to bear principal responsibilities for the council's English language publications. Supported both by the RCA and the Evangelical Lutheran Church in America, the Scudders have been stationed in Limassol, Cyprus, from 1994 to the present.

In addition to his responsibilities for publication, early in 1995 Scudder was asked by the newly elected general secretary of the MECC to be his personal consultant and confidential assistant. This position of assistant to the general secretary has become a full-time job with region-wide responsibilities.

Somehow, in the midst of the above myriad of responsibilities in one of the world's most troubled areas, the writing of this work has gone slowly forward, hampered not only by other demands, but by the exacting standards of the author. The completion of this work, which Ed Luidens would have seen as fulfilling his goals, is an accomplishment for which the church, and especially those who have served for over a century in the mission to the Gulf, may be justly grateful.

Donald J. Bruggink
General Editor

Foreword

by Donald A. Luidens

Some gifts of Providence have a long gestation period, perhaps because the magnificence of the gift takes time to reach its fullness. So it has been with this marvelous volume.

When Edwin Luidens, my father, retired from forty years of service to the world church, he announced his intention to embark on an ambitious plan. It was a plan born in his heart and nurtured by countless hours of notejotting (often on airplane stationary and stenopads as he traversed the globe).

I recall well the enthusiasm with which he outlined his project: he wanted, he said, to write a history of the Reformed Church in America's mission to the people of the Arab world, "but not a typical history." He wanted to do extensive interviewing with retired and current missionaries so that the human side of the history could be brought to life. So far, it was a plan with which I resonated.

But there was more, much more. He wanted to talk to academic missiologists in order to place into global context the entire sweep of the century since the first intrepid pioneers trekked forth from New Brunswick Theological Seminary to the sands of the Arabian peninsula in the late 1880s. He wanted to show how the theology of mission hd been reworked on the anvil of experience. He wanted to understand and include accounts of historic milestones, parallel events transpiring around the world at propitious moments in the narrative of the Arabian mission saga. He wanted to help his readers understand the multilayered impact on the Arabian Mission of the discovery of oil, the unequivocal support which the United States extends to the state of Israel, and the late twentieth-century revival of fundamentalisms—Muslim and Christian.

In all of this, Dad wanted a book that was accessible to the lay reader, the person in the pew who had long supported—sometimes with enthusiasm, but, increasingly as the church turned to counting conversions per dollars spent, with equivocation—the work of the church in what has become known as "the Middle East." I remained as supportive as I could be, but I found it hard to imagine that such a work could be produced.

One of the great losses I experienced when my father died in 1989 was the apparent demise of his ambitious project. Imagine, then, my rekindled excitement when Lewis Scudder, a family friend of long standing (as a wizened teenager, Lew was my beloved "chaperon" when I was an eightyear-old fledgling flying off to boarding school in India, 3,000 miles from my family home in Iraq), expressed a willingness to tackle the project that Dad had so involuntarily relinquished. Lew's skills as a writer and historian, his vast storehouse of missionary contacts and anecdotes, his heritage in Reformed church missionary service, and his personal experience as a missionary to a much transformed Arabian world all gave weight to his selection to take up the vision Dad had dreamed.

What follows is truly a gift of Providence to me and to my family. More importantly, it is a gift to the Reformed Church in America and to all those who are enriched when they learn about faithfulness in the face of adversity, persistence in the face of institutional skepticism and even acrimony, and an unyielding love for Christ and God's people, whatever the station of their lives. What follows is Dad's dream come to vibrant and fulsome life—and much more.

Let the words which follow sweep over you on several planes. They were composed by a poet-historian. Select passages to read aloud, and you will thrill to the sonorous tenor of the text. The words are rich with the narrative of exotic, far-away times and places. They are emboldened by personal sacrifice and conviction. They are humanized by failures of spirit and personal idiosyncrasies. Most lastingly, they are ennobled by the greatest commission to which anyone can commit his or her life, the call by Christ to preach, teach, and heal.

It is rare that we are treated to the gift of a dream. *The Arabian Mission's Story: In Search of Abraham's Other Son* is the realization of Dad's dream, it is a majestic gift to the Reformed Church in America and to Dad's legatees. Come, enter into these magical pages and relish the story with me.

Donald A. Luidens

Edwin M. Luidens on the eve of his
departure to the Arab World in 1943.

Author's Foreword

With Special Tribute to
Edwin M. Luidens

The Arabian Mission, an American Protestant organization, operated in the Arab Gulf[1] and southern Iraq. The mission was launched in 1889, adopted by the Reformed Church in America in 1894, and formally dissolved in 1973. Its successor institutions continue to exist in Kuwait, Bahrain, and Oman. This is the story of that mission.

Many people have contributed to what appears here. That does not mean that they are responsible for how it is presented and analyzed. But I owe them a great deal – especially my extended family, all my "aunts and uncles" and my "brothers and sisters" of the Arabian Mission in whose embrace (and sometimes at whose insistence) I grew up.[2]

In 1976, while on furlough in New Brunswick, New Jersey, I was privileged to assist two scholars who were then working on histories of the

---

[1]This term has been consistently preferred over the more archaic usage, 'Persian Gulf.' It is also more fitting to the subject matter, since the Arabian Mission limited its activities to the Arab side of the Gulf.

[2]I was born to Dorothy and Lewis Scudder II, Arabia missionaries who served in Kuwait from 1939 until their lives' ends. Given the close relationships between missionaries and opportunities throughout the years of growing up to visit and dwell in other stations of the mission, I have had the rich experience of enjoying the mission as an "extended family." And this theme is evident in the book. My birthright, if you will, is the mission, and that bias is present in what follows. I do not apologize for it.

Arabian Mission. One was my long-time friend, H. Conway Zeigler, now an officer in the U. S. Navy, who was at that time earning a masters degree at Princeton University.[3] The other was my friend, 'Abd-ul-Mâlik Khalaf at-Tamîmî, then a doctoral candidate in the School of Oriental Studies at the University of Durham in England, now on the faculty of Kuwait University.[4] While working with them my appetite was whetted, and both men have since encouraged me to pursue the topic beyond what they had been able to do.

A little more than ten years ago, while searching for a Ph.D. dissertation topic of my own, I entertained thoughts of writing the history of the mission myself, and I explored the possibility under the guidance of the prominent historian of the Arab Gulf, Professor Ahmad M. Abu Hakima,[5] a friend to many Arabia missionaries and intimately acquainted with the mission's history. For a variety of reasons, I put the topic aside, but Dr. Abu Hakima, in his patient and gracious way, continued to nourish and encourage my dormant interest whenever we met.

I have picked up the topic again now because of one very special person. He set out to fulfill this present task before me and would probably have done better at it. He was prevented from doing so. Edwin M. Luidens died

[3]H. Conway Zeigler, *A Brief Flowering in the Desert: Protestant Missionary Activity in the Arabian Gulf, 1889-1973* (Masters Dissertation, Near Eastern Studies, Princeton University, Princeton, New Jersey: February, 1977) [bound typescript in possession of the author]. The study has the virtue of being brief, but a great deal of the documentary evidence now available was not available when Mr. Zeigler was compiling his study.

[4]Abdul Malek K. Al-Tameemi, *The Arabian Mission: A Case Study of Christian Missionary Work in the Arabian Gulf Region* (Doctoral Thesis, School of Oriental Studies, University of Durham, Durham, England: November 1977). [Typescript in possession of the author.] This dissertation, somewhat revised, has been published in Arabic: 'Abd-ul-Mâlik Khalaf at-Tamîmî, *at-tabshîr fî mintaqat-il-khalîj il-'arabî: dirâsah fî it-târîkh il-'ijtimâ'î wa is-siyyâsî* [*Evangelism in the Area of the Arabian Gulf: a Study in Social and Political History*] (Kuwait: Sharikat-il-Kâzimah li-n-Nashr wa-t-Tarjamah wa-t-Tawzî', 1982). This study had a fairly clear orientation from the outset. Dr. Al-Tameemi is a Muslim and, while that is not an indictment, it is a conditioning factor evident in the study. His major conclusion is that the Arabian Mission, by and large, failed in its primary evangelistic purpose even though some of its activities (medical in particular) were beneficial to Gulf society. Again, many of the documents used in this present study were not available at the time Dr. Al-Tameemi did his work.

[5].See especially his *History of Eastern Arabia, 1750-1800, The Rise and Development of Bahrain and Kuwait* (Beirut: Khayyats, 1963).

in May of 1989. In the spring of the year when kings go forth to war he entered the last of his many battles, and perversely, as Christians do, he won through to the Resurrection.

I have known Ed virtually my whole life. From my memories of childhood in Iraq and the Gulf he was there. Children can be harsh critics, insufferably prideful when they have an edge on adults. We children of the mission grew up speaking Arabic fluently. But I remember that, among the stumble-tongued adults vainly trying to master the "Language of the Angels," he stood out as one of the few who did it right. It was not surprising to us, the young, that he became one of the mission's premier Arabists.

A child also remembers smiles, expressions of face, tones of voice. There was an authenticity to Ed Luidens. His smile was true, the affection he demonstrated heart-felt, and the understanding he showed genuine. He was insightful without having to be aggressive, a critic with a keen cutting edge but without the rasp to irritate. There was in him the intuitive gift of compassion, and his eyes were always asparkle with humor.

From childhood on into my adulthood, Ed Luidens was always somewhere accessible. And that was important. I counted on it. I was never disappointed. So, when he laid this work down, there was no question but that I would be willing to take it up. Again, I've not been disappointed. It has been a deep pleasure working with the materials he had been gathering. They were fragments, to be sure, and his penmanship was atrocious. He had not yet begun hammering the data into coherent shape. During the last few months of his life the pain of his illness and the always unsettling prospect of dying were preoccupations that could not be denied.

But the fragments – both recorded on tape and written – glisten with Ed's insights. His probing questions are there in the interviews he conducted. His long and broad view of the mission of the Church of Christ is evident in the few paragraphs he framed. These all enliven for me personal memories of long and earnest discussions on where the mission of Christ's Church is going and where it has been and why. We have worked closely together, especially recently, and I cling as best I can both to Ed's gift for charity and to his sometimes almost ruthless analytical ability. But I miss most his enthusiasm for the cause, his joy, and his happy confidence that God knows what he's about. And it is that happy confidence in God which permits me this pleasant digression: Ed typified the best of the Arabian mission. I could have chosen any of a dozen others who, as master builders, laid brick and mortar in my life – my father, for instance, who in many ways deserves the honor at least as much. But I choose Ed and I do not think I have mischosen.

Coming as it did out of a belligerent attitude toward other religions – and toward Islam in particular – the Arabian Mission has always swung between two poles: On the one hand, there is the "polemic" approach, the easily defined confrontational approach, witnessing with an intellectual and verbal cudgel; on the other hand there is the "irenic" approach, the hard road and the narrow, requiring the sacrament of Christian sacrifice. That road is the one which, at great cost, passes through walls of division and enmity, using the exposed soul as a key to open doors. Isaiah sang, "How beautiful upon the mountains are the feet of him who publishes good tidings, who publishes peace, who brings good tidings of good ...." That is the legacy of Ed Luidens and scores of others who worked in the Arabia field. If there is a legacy of the Arabian Mission that abides, it is the "gospel of peace" which Ed had the grace to learn from the best practitioners of the art and which he passed on to those of us who followed.

We examine the past so as to sharpen our judgment about the consequences of our actions for tomorrow. The past educates the present and points toward future. The past is where commitments were undertaken, implemented, and modified by circumstances and other course correctives day by day, case by case. It is not there to be reverenced, but neither is it given that we might distort it. When I took up the historian's mantle, it was to tell the story of the Arabian Mission so that the movement of its life and times might be seen to be consistent with its context, like a sailing ship drinking the wind and cutting the water; so that change and growth might be seen to be rooted in real soil; and so that the circumstances of the present appear not only plausible but are shown to be manageable. What we have in the present is something quite new; the stuff of which it is made is primeval.

Many people have helped make the research and writing of this book possible. And there may be those among them who will be disappointed by the fact that this history, at points, will speak bluntly about faults and human weakness, about policies misconceived and miscarried, and about the small and large evidences that missionaries and their enterprise exhibit human failings. The mandate I have, however, requires that I be rigorous with facts and as thorough as possible. It is not the purpose of this book to promote the Arabian Mission. It is intended to be a history that will allow the record of that mission to stand on its own merits. Paul notes, in another context of personal trial, God's pledge, "My grace is sufficient for you." If we cannot speak openly about ourselves then adversaries will take note and portray us as though they knew us better than we know ourselves.

The issue becomes particularly sensitive, of course, when the writing of history takes up current events and deals with living personalities. I have, myself, been a part of those events and I will be as clear as possible about where my personal involvement has colored my judgment and my interpretation. But if, having examined this portrait, a reader does not perceive a work of the Holy Spirit, then the fault is mine and not that of those who have faithfully borne witness.

Finally, I am indebted particularly to Donald and Peggy Luidens for their unquenchable enthusiasm for this project and for their personal support. Donald Bruggink, a mentor and a friend, has also been in the front rank of "note holders" and his editorial hand shall be evident in the crafting of the text. As we came down to the wire, and the book took final shape, two people actually became the linchpins of the wheels which carried the product into the form which you now hold in your hands. They are Laurie Baron and Russell Gasero. Laurie, first, my copy editor: there is none better. Our dialogue over months of intensive work gave us both a great deal of satisfaction, but I was the student much of the time and she my mentor. Much of her integrity and professional competence has been poured into this effort and, to date, she has been my closest and most thoughtful reader. To her I am, simply, grateful. For his part, Russell has taken the piece into its final form. Overworked and stretched as the RCA's archivist, he described the difficult task of laying out this difficult book as a "labor of love." And, indeed, that is evident. Those touches that have turned a manuscript into a book are his, crafting the essential index not the least of his contributions. And here too, my gratitude is only properly profound.

Dozens of people have been generous in their material and prayerful support of this project. My wife, Nancy, has been with me, a long-distance runner of exceptional qualities and endurance in this as in other tests of our marital mettle. And my children, too, have taken a hand in making my task a wee mite lighter, especially Thomas and Beth, who (for a small consideration) took it upon themselves through the summer of 1990 to sort through and organize piles of documents rescued from store rooms and files in Kuwait and Bahrain. And there was, of course, my mother, Dorothy Scudder of Kuwait, who is now with the Lord. Her deliberate ways over the years accounted for the preservation of invaluable documentary material from the waste basket's oblivion, and through the years of her motherhood she stood by her errant son with the smug assurance that, of course, he was after all her son. In other words, the Family Scudder have put in their licks one and all, and presumption need not preclude praise and thanks when the note falls due.

How Shall We Proceed?

Organizing this narrative has been a challenge. Treating the story of the Arabian Mission as a single narrative involves dealing with four (some might even say six) main locations, and in each of those locations there is a subnarrative. The solution to this has been, in part three, to treat the pioneer years as a single narrative, and then, in parts four through six, to take up the narrative in discrete thematic strands. Part seven picks up the relationship of the mission on the field with the home base. These five parts, in a sense, make up the meat of the Arabian Mission story as it is told here.

Parts one and two may appear to some to be "too heavy" and too academic. Part one treats those historical factors which shaped and guided the mind of mission. It might be a temptation for someone to skip over these matters and "cut to the chase." It would be a mistake (in my humble opinion), but it is a way of proceeding. The author surrenders ownership, in this respect, to the reader. Wherever possible or fitting, however, references to the Arabian Mission are to be found in this part, and they are significant.

Part two is, broadly speaking, the historical environment of the mission. This is broken down into the regions in which the Arabian Mission was most closely involved. Again, the hasty reader may be tempted to skip to part three. And again that person would lose out. Here, even more than in part one, the text contains notes on the Arabian Mission and its engagement which are necessary to a full appreciation of its story.

Several appendices have been added which were, to a large extent, part of the apparatus used in writing the narrative. Having been developed, it seemed a shame not to include them. Particularly significant are the time line and the chart giving the distribution of Arabian Mission personnel. These are places to which sauntering readers may turn from time to time in order to construct their own frames of reference as they move through the narrative.

What of the gargantuan footnotes, then? It is tempting to topple into an apology at this point. But, in fact, I rather enjoyed building them. Some, of course, are purely reference notes. But a good many (perhaps most) of these notes are actually the icing on the cake. The footnotes are digressions, by-ways of the mind, amplifications, and sometimes locations for critical appraisals. They are made for the saunterer who, like the casual hiker, likes to pause frequently to take a swig from his or her canteen. Again, the goal-directed may have little patience for these. They are invited simply to let the numbers in the text flash past and proceed on their way.

As I wrote this book (the first I have undertaken), I found myself caught in a dilemma. Am I a historian or a participant, a memorialist? Perhaps to the frustration of some, I have never quite made up my mind. What I have written is a book which is in many respects very personal. It is loaded with judgments and assessments which some may even find offensive. I have, to my knowledge, hidden no names (which has been part of the paranoia of Arabian Mission authors over the years) save three, and in those three instances it either seemed wise to do so, or I was under instruction to do so by the source of the information.

One point I have tried to cover and have done so inadequately: The partners and coworkers of the Arabia missionaries have not received the attention they deserved. In some cases, in terms of the mission's local impact, they were crucially significant, and in a few cases they remain the only intentional expression of the mission's tradition. In a few instances (I have noted some) these coworkers have been westerners. But overwhelmingly they have been indigenous citizens (a minority of whom were Christians), expatriate Arabs, people from other middle eastern subcultures and places, or (a great many of these) individuals from the Indian subcontinent. I mourn this failing, because it bespeaks a certain measure of rank ingratitude and arrogance. To say, truthfully, that these names are not easily found in the primary sources is, in the end, not a valid excuse. Where I have tried to remedy this failing, I hope people will take appreciative note of the gifts these people have placed upon the altar of the Arabian Mission's witness. Where I have failed to do so, I apologize. As a good many of these individuals will be readers of this book, I beg indulgence, and if opportunity comes to repair the shortcoming, I will endeavor to make amends.

Lewis R. Scudder, Jr.
Limassol, Cyprus
March, 1998

Arabic Transliteration

It seems that any book which deals with Arabic names and words and is written for those who are not members of the "cult of Arabists" feels duty-bound to include a note on transliteration. Over the years the quixotic discipline of Orientalism has left us with innumerable transliteration systems. Then, of course, there came the Victorians who just did things their own way, and systems proliferated. It was all a bit of a sport. Colorful terms like Medina, sheik, emir, and harem have found their ways into English dictionaries and that is quite apart from the Arabic loan words like algebra, artichoke, admiral, tariff, alcove, amulet, elixir, and lute, to name a few. In any case, here is yet another note for the note-weary to take note of:

The system of transliteration employed in this book is a simplified version of that being used in contemporary scholarly work. It has the inestimable virtue of making people say the words almost correctly. An approximate version of this system can be found in the grammar published by the British Foreign Service's Middle East Centre for Arab Studies – *The M.E.C.A.S. Grammar of Modern Literary Arabic* (Beirut: Khayats, 1965). The main departure here is that the diacritical marks on the "heavy" consonants – hâ', sâd, dâd, tâ' and zâ' (or dhâ') – have been omitted as a mercy to typesetters. The unique Arabic consonants, 'ayn and hamzah, the one a deep and the other a light glottal stop, are indicated by using apostrophes or single quotation marks – respectively ['] and [']. The heavy fricative, khâ', and the thâ', dhâl, and shîn are represented by the letter combinations "kh," "th," "dh," and "sh" respectively. The glottal catch, qâf, we represent by the conveniently odd Latin letter "q" without the conventionally trailing "u." The "q" in Qur'ân, therefore, is not to be pronounced in the same way as you would pronounce the "q" in "queen" but nearer to "k."

It is with the vowels that most irregularities in transliteration are encountered. This is not the fault of the Arabic, in which vowels are extremely regular, but of the English in which vowel sounds can be represented by many combinations. Arabic invariably has three short and three long vowels – kesrah (short "i"), fathah (short "a") and dammah (short "u"); and alif (long "â"), wâw (long "û") and yâ' (long "î"). In diphthongs the wâw is represented here by a "w" and the yâ' is represented by a "y." Diphthongs are formed either by doubling a long consonant or by combinations of a short vowel with a long. Although purists would like to see a long dash [-] over the vowel to indicate that it is long, we have availed ourselves of the French circumflex [^] for the purpose. (The English letters "e" and "o" ought never appear in a transliterated Arabic word.)

The word commonly encountered in English as "sheik" is a good case in point. The vowel combination "ei" in the conventional English spelling is itself an idiosyncrasy ("i" before "e" except after "c" or when pronounced "ay" as in "neighbor" and "weigh"). Because English speakers are incorrigible mispronouncers of their own language, "sheik" more often than not comes out being pronounced "sheek"! The Arabic diphthong is a fathah followed by a yâ' and is represented in this book by "ay," yielding the more representative spelling "shaykh" (pronounced very close to the English "shake").

With some words, especially place names, a grudging concession to established usage has been made. Thus what should appear as Sa'ûdî Arabia may appear as Saudi Arabia, Makkah is left as Mecca, Kûayt is left Kuwait, Bahrayn is left Bahrain, and Masqat is left Muscat. An exception among the mission's stations is made of Amarah. The traditional English spelling yields a mispronunciation that has been repeatedly pointed out to me by Iraqi friends. In this book it shall be spelled 'Imârah. *The Times Atlas of the World* (London: Times Newspapers, Ltd., 1973) attempts valiantly to set a new standard in such matters and its authors are to be commended, but I have not been as rigorous as they. The intention throughout has been to encourage a closer representation of the Arabic while making reading the text easy.

ARABIA
Stations of the Arabian Mission underlined

Mashhad●

●Teheran

●Qom

●Isfahân

IRAN

'Imârah

Khorramshahr
Abadân

Basrah

Kuwait

Busheir

Arabian
Gulf

Bandar
'Abbâs

Hormuz

Qatîf

Bahrain

Dhahrân

Râs al-Khâymah

Dubayy

BAHRAIN

●Riyâdh

Doha

Abû
Dhabî

Arabian Sea

Suhâr

Matrah
&
Muscat

QATAR

U.A.E.

Buraymi

Nizwah

Sûr

OMAN

Salâlah

SOUTH
YEMEN

Part One

The Makings of the Mission

The Modern Missionary Movement

The Arabian Mission was a late blooming flower of what has been called
The Modern Missionary Movement.[1] For convenience's sake, having as its
seed bed the English Free Church movement of the seventeenth century
with some cross-fertilization from individuals like Jonathan Edwards in the
United States, the Modern Missionary Movement is said to have begun with
the publication in 1791 by William Carey of *An Enquiry into the Obligations
of Christians to Use Means for the Conversion of the Heathen*.[2] This book
and Carey's personal eloquence stimulated the formation of the English
Baptist Missionary Society and, two years later, facilitated the launching of

[1] The Protestant missionary enterprise of the late 18th century trails by some four
centuries the efforts of Roman Catholic missionary orders like the Franciscans,
the Dominicans, the Jesuits, and the Carmelites. The Carmelites first and then the
Franciscans (especially in their Capuchin branch) are significant for the work in
Arabia.

[2] William Carey, born in the English Midlands on August 17, 1761, was the son of a
weaver. He grew into his mid-teens as a lackadaisical Anglican. In 1779, while
apprenticed to a shoemaker, his fellow apprentice persuaded him to join the
"dissenters." Pedantic and deliberate of mind, he moved from the Congregationalist
version of dissent to the Baptist, was rebaptized in 1783, organized a congregation
in the town of Hackelton, and became one of its preachers. He was fully ordained

3

Carey's own pioneer missionary work in northeast India.[3] The London Missionary Society (LMS)–an association of Congregationalists,

in 1786. In 1785 he began preaching in the village of Olney and then he went on to Moulton in 1787.

Self-educated, he earned part of his daily bread as a teacher. As teachers will sometimes do, he taught himself. He was an amateur entomologist and ornithologist. He developed a passion for languages and his interest in geography was insatiable. As Carey began to voice the opinion that a world of "heathen" deserved to hear the gospel and that Christ's commission to his disciples was still in force, he was rebuffed. The Baptist tradition in which he found himself took the title of "Particular." It had strong scholastic overtones, speaking of itself as Calvinistic. The gospel, Carey was told, was only meant for God's elect, and only God knew who *they* were. God would find them. Furthermore, righteousness ought not be expected from the unregenerate mass of humanity, nor ought they be exhorted to obedience. Five practical impediments were also voiced against his proposal: the heathen were too far distant, they were by nature barbarous, they would probably kill the first missionary they saw, among them the necessities of life would be difficult to find, and their languages were impossible to learn. In the course of his arguments, Carey wrote down his responses and by 1786 the manuscript of his *Enquiry ...* was complete. Through the gift of £10 from a friend he managed to get it published in 1792. It was not reprinted nor widely circulated until 1822, when it was reprinted as a pamphlet.

Carey's studies in geography led him to some interesting conclusions. The people for whom he was mainly concerned were those who lived in "pagan" or "heathen darkness." From these he specifically excluded Muslims, Catholics, Protestants, Armenian Orthodox, Greek Orthodox, and Jews. By inference, these had at least some access to revealed knowledge of the true God. In point of fact, sparing the Jews, he excoriated all the rest–the Catholics for their tolerance of idolatry, the Muslims for their depredations in the African slave trade, the Orthodox for their viciousness and hypocrisy, and most Protestants for their lack of holiness, many errors, and hypocrisy. His call, therefore, went out to individual Christians of pure conscience and devout heart who would band together in societies dedicated to the over-riding goal of converting the heathen.

On May 31, 1792, he preached a sermon at the ministers' meeting in Nottingham in which he coined mated slogans that have fed missionary enthusiasm for generations: "Expect great things from God. Attempt great things for God." His eloquence in that moment tilted his colleagues in his favor, and the movement toward forming his longed-for society was under way.

[3]This society first bore the awkward title of *The Particular [Calvinistic] Baptist Society for Propagating the Gospel Among the Heathen.* It was founded October 2, 1792. Carey was appointed a missionary on January 10, 1793, and set out on his trip to Calcutta on March 24. Delayed by his fellow appointee, Dr. Thompson, Carey, Thompson, and their families finally sailed from Dover June 13, 1793. His stormy and fruitful career in India is beyond the scope of this study. Suffice it to note that he set the themes of Protestant missionary aspiration and work for the future, and much of his agenda still has a curiously contemporary ring to it. He had a powerful influence on the young Henry Martyn, and had a less salutary encounter with John Scudder. He died in Calcutta June 9, 1834, a man full of years

Presbyterians, Methodists, and free-church Anglicans–was born in 1794.[4] The organization of the Anglican Church Missionary Society (CMS) in 1799 and others followed in short order.[5] Perhaps the Protestant society with the widest impact on the world stage was the American Board of Commissioners for Foreign Missions (ABCFM), formed in 1810 by agreement among a number of American denominations–the Reformed Church in America among them–but dominated by the Congregational church.

An early impulse to Protestant foreign missions grew out of Christian revulsion against slavery, particularly after the capture and shipping of slaves from Africa was intensified for the sake of the American colonies. Opposition to the massive and brutal African slave trade and to slavery in general had its first effective voice among British and colonial American Quakers toward the end of the seventeenth century. By the late eighteenth century, disapproval of the slave trade was powerful in the Western Hemisphere, and that disapproval was expressed largely in religious terms.

and honor. [The source for this and the previous note has been the excellent biography written by George Smith, *The Life of William Carey, D.D., Shoemaker and Missionary* (London: John Murray, 1885).]

[4]The most famous of the LMS missionaries was David Livingstone, whose career as a medical missionary in East Africa spanned from 1840 to 1872. This crusade against the slave trade in East Africa electrified the western world with his exploits, and his *Missionary Travels and Researches in South Africa* (published in 1857) as well as his *Journals* (published in 1874 after his death) became important sources for missionary thinking. It was partly due to Livingstone's work and that of other missionaries in East Africa that the Arabian Mission was, from its inception, sharply aware of the Arab investment and interest in the slave trade which operated primarily out of the island of Zanzibar, off and on a dependency of the Sultanate of Oman.

[5]For the Arabian Mission, the Church Missionary Society (CMS) was perhaps the most important society, especially in the early years in the Arabian Gulf. The CMS provided the Arabian Mission with its first strong support group on the field, and off and on throughout the years that old relationship has been revived. Predating the CMS, the Anglican Society for the Promotion of Christian Knowledge (SPCK) was founded in 1699, and the Society for the Propagation of the Gospel (SPG) came into existence in 1701. Both of these laid a foundation, particularly in missionary research, from which later groups benefited.

The antislavery movement kindled in western society a special kind of compassion for the disadvantaged and exploited "native," which grew stronger as the colonial ventures of Europe developed.

Henry Martyn was another prominent figure in the movement toward foreign missions. Martyn began his career as a chaplain with the English East India Company in Bengal.6 His stories, along with those of William Carey, nurtured infectious enthusiasm for "foreign mission" that spread quickly in Europe and in the United States, internationalized Protestant self-awareness, and gathered momentum well past the midpoint of the nineteenth century. But perhaps nothing may be given more recognition for infusing the movement with enthusiasm and optimism than the Student Volunteer Movement founded by John R. Mott in 1886.7 Mott targeted his

6Henry Martyn was born to a mine owner's family in Truro, England, February 18, 1781. While studying law at Cambridge, he was moved by the example of his sister and the preaching of Charles Simeon to abandon a hot temper and sharp tongue in favor of a call to humility and service. Upon graduation, he was ordained to the priesthood of the Anglican church, and became the curate at Holy Trinity Church in Cambridge under Simeon. There being no missionary society to which he could then apply, he leaped at the chance to become chaplain to the troops and civil servants of the East India Company. He took up his post in India April 22, 1806. He found little support among his parishioners. They considered his preaching to Indians politically dangerous and socially insulting to "the ruling race." He pursued work among the local population at his various postings but was constantly on the defensive before his fellow countrymen. Martyn left India at the end of 1810, bound for Iran and Arabia. He landed in Muscat, Oman, April 20, 1811, where he stayed for only a short time before proceeding on to Busheir in the Gulf and then to Shiraz. Ten months later, having evoked the ire of the local Muslim clergy, he went to Tabriz. He completed a translation of the New Testament and the Psalms into Persian. In failing health, he decided to proceed to Constantinople but died on the road in Tocat October 16, 1812, at the age of thirty-one. His achievements were not primarily in his translations into Arabic and Persian. He established no great institutions, nor did he move masses. His achievement was in his person as an example of what devotion to Christ could do to beautify the soul. His journals were read widely and inspired a growing interest in missionary work in Arabia and among Muslims in general. [For an enthusiastic and brief biography refer to Archibald McLean, *Epoch Makers of Modern Missions* (New York: Fleming H. Revell Company, 1912).]

7The Student Volunteer Movement for Foreign Missions began in 1886, at precisely the time when the three founders of the Arabian Mission — James Cantine, Samuel Zwemer and Philip T. Phelps — were in the midst of their seminary studies. Its slogan was "The Evangelization of the World in This Generation." Explaining that slogan in the book which remains the central testament of his career, John R. Mott said that the slogan meant "…to give all men an adequate opportunity to know Jesus Christ as their Saviour and to become His real disciples. This involves such

The Portuguese may be credited with the first colonial ventures, especially in Asia and Africa. With Shihâb-ud-Dîn Ahmad ibn Mâjid, a navigator from the Arab Gulf port of Ra's-ul-Khaymah, on board, Vasco da Gama sailed from Portugal July 8, 1497. His specific purpose was to find a way around the trade routes that had to pass through Muslim and Ottoman control. He rounded the Cape of Good Hope, and for a century and a half thereafter the Portuguese dominated the maritime trade route to India. Motivated by a strong anti-Muslim animus, their heritage from a day when Muslims dominated the Iberian Peninsula, they invaded Arabia, built forts in Oman and on the main island of Bahrain, and established a base at Hormuz, on the Persian side of the straits into the Arabian Gulf. Their main colonial stronghold was Goa, on the western coast of India. In the Gulf they lent encouragement and political protection to the Catholic Carmelite mission activities in Persia and Mesopotamia.[11]

Neill's *Colonialism and Christian Missions* (New York: McGraw-Hill Book Company, 1966). In his conclusion (pp. 412-425) he gathers together all the threads of missionary experience and finds, in the balance, that the missionary to foreign fields was inevitably caught in this ambiguous situation between culture and faith, between nation and church, and that the record of how missionaries dealt with this tension is a spotted one world wide.

In a sensitive article Paul Harrison, who walked a very delicate tightrope under careful British imperial scrutiny, confessed, "...deep down in his heart, the missionary too often believes that the only hope of the Gospel lies in its support by Western bayonets. Unless the protection of Western Governments, with their military power, is given to the missionaries, their lives will not be safe, and they cannot proclaim the Christian message. Unless that same worldly and un-Christian power is prepared to protect the lives of converts from Islam to Christianity, we shall never have any. To expose the converts to the rigours of persecution with no protection except that of God in heaven would be hopeless. To expect missionaries to live thus unguarded, outrageous" [Paul W. Harrison, "Christ's Contribution to the Moslem," pp. 323-337 in John R. Mott (editor), *The Moslem World To-Day* (New York: George H. Doran Company, 1925), p. 325]. Harrison goes on to argue that it is precisely upon such "hopeless" and "outrageous" foundations that mission must be built if it is to eventuate in anything permanent and worthwhile. He says, "It is possible to change the professed creeds of some men by physical force, and those of others by intellectual arguments, but coercion of any sort is utterly unable to introduce the divine life into a man's heart" [Harrison, "Christ's Contribution...," p. 336-337].

[11]See R. B. Serjeant, *The Portuguese off the South Arabian Coast: Hadrami Chronicles* (London: Clarendon Press, 1974).

The Portuguese Catholics were succeeded by Dutch Protestants under the Dutch East India Company (chartered in 1602). From then on the competition of western powers in the East had a strong subtheme of Protestant-Catholic rivalry. The English chartered their East India Company in 1600 to exploit the resources of the Indian subcontinent. For the time being, they left the East Indies to the Dutch, fellow Protestants with whom they were not yet prepared to compete.

The first British acquisitions in India by the company date from 1611. To protect their lines of communication, they destroyed the Portuguese base in Hormuz on the Persian coast in 1622. They acquired Madras in 1638 and Bombay in 1661. From 1664 the British also competed in the Orient with the French Company of the East Indies, and the French assumed from the failing Portuguese the mantle of patronage for ever more active Catholic missionary enterprises around the world.

Western colonialism began as a form of private enterprise. It operated upon the principles of mercantilism – the notion that control of resources meant inevitable national prosperity, and that prosperity was measured by the accumulation of gold and silver. The trading companies, therefore, were structured as monopolies. They dealt largely in finished products; all western commercial activity with the Orient was channeled through them up until the early years of the nineteenth century. Their colonial enclaves existed primarily for the profit of the shareholders. Beyond those enclaves the mercantile companies did not interfere in "native affairs" unless they felt forced to do so. Supported by their home governments, their land-based and maritime military structures were devoted to protecting those enclaves, maintaining lines of communication, and discouraging competition.

In 1776 Adam Smith published his *Inquiry Into the Nature and Causes of the Wealth of Nations*, in which he advocated free trade and governmental noninterference with private enterprise which, by its very nature, would pursue a policy of enlightened self-interest. Although his ideas did not influence policy until some fifty years later, they made common cause with other ideas such as those articulated in 1762 by Jean-Jacques Rousseau in his *Du contrat social*. Rousseau argued that free human choice was the foundation of the rule of law and of legitimate government. These ideas, much like those planted by Roger Williams in the American colony of Rhode Island, were already maturing in the mind of the young Thomas Jefferson and finding their way into the everyday speech of colonial America. It was an age of liberalism and liberation, both economic and political. It brought in a new age for the empire builders and set the stage for the earthshaking Industrial Revolution.

The Industrial Revolution of the nineteenth century radically transformed the economies of Europe, and patterns of trade had to change to match. A dramatic shift took place away from trade in gold, silver, spices, sugar, slaves, and marketable luxury goods produced in the Orient. Now colonial interest focused on new sources of cheap raw materials and on ways to develop foreign markets for finished machine-made products. The new doctrine focused upon vertically integrated control of the sources of wealth: from guaranteeing the supply of cheap raw materials, to assuring efficient means for producing finished products, and finally to developing, controling, exploiting, and expanding markets for those products. The companies began to understand that by linking all these various steps together they generated capital and controled wealth.

The colonial enclaves of the trading companies, which had long perched on the fringes of largely unaffected "native" societies, had to give way. Whole nations and cultures had to be transformed to respond to the new demands of an industrializing Europe. That meant a heavier hand and a more comprehensive colonial policy. Superior armaments, accelerated means of communication and transportation, and a more productive and efficient system of education gave Europeans the edge and permitted them to gain control over the means of production and effectively to dominate the economic and political systems in their expanding eastern colonies.

These were the economic and political currents that were stirring in western culture when the Modern Missionary Movement began. The West had seen Asian and Oriental societies as inscrutable and self-contained "worlds apart." Carey had been told by his old-world skeptical elders that, if God had wanted to convert the heathen, he would have done so quite on his own. It was a pre-Capitalist theological outlook. Now western thinking began to see in Asia and the Orient societies which must be transformed to meet modern needs and integrated into the new system. They were the primary source of cheap raw materials, and they must be developed as markets for the finished products of European industry. This implied education and development. This new perception opened the door to a great deal of literature on the condition of Asian society, its lack of modern knowledge and science, and its desired place in the interlocking relations among nations.[12] People began to think of humanity in global terms, to see it all under one administrative doctrine rather than as a fractured collage of small, separate worlds.

There were also people of conscience who participated in the colonial enterprise who found themselves distressed by this policy which enshrined exploitation. Carey himself ran headlong into the English East India Company's administration in Bengal and was, for a time, banished to the cultural traditions "established" state-managed churches were the order of the day. They might and *did* take up their work in regions where their governments and agents exercised control with little sense of ambiguity. Aggressive measures taken against western missionaries by indigenous authorities have frequently been the pretext for "gunboat diplomacy" around the world, and even the United States (as, for example, in China at the turn of the century during the Boxer Rebellion) has exercised that option.[13]

For the most part, though, *American* missionaries had a more open choice to make, at least until the late 1890s. The case in Syria and Lebanon

[12]The eastern culture that responded most vigorously to the new reality, of course, was Japan. By the turn of the century it was able to go toe-to-toe with Russian naval might, and it set about following its own colonial policy in the East, especially with regard to China. Japan, at the dawn of the twentieth century, was entirely different from other eastern societies. It was a society that never submitted (and was never exposed) to alien imperial supervision.

[13]The use of American muscle in this way has not always been appreciated by missionaries. James Cantine tells the story that, while studying in Lebanon when he first arrived in the Middle East, he went on a walking tour to Jerusalem and back with two other missionaries – a Scott and an Englishman. On his return to Beirut the Turkish authorities found an irregularity in his passport. He was, therefore, incarcerated in the guard house for a short time. He found the incident

illustrates the point: From the very beginning of American missionary work there in 1820, the missionaries (as was the fashion) heartily despised Ottoman authority. They advocated quite openly that Britain (if not America itself) develop proprietary interests over those regions of the crumbling empire. But the primary European patron of those regions had been France ever since – or so it was said – the days of Charlemagne. Republican France, although antiecclesiastical at home, habitually promoted Roman Catholic interests in its colonies. American missionaries, for their part, were fiercely Protestant, passionately anti-Catholic, and as Francophobic as any Victorian Britisher. Through major institutions like the American University of Beirut (first known as the Syrian Protestant College), American missionaries cultivated in the Arab intellectual milieu the ideas of nationalism and the dreams of autonomous self-rule against the Ottomans. When the First World War destroyed the Ottoman imperium, the governing authority became French, and all hopes of an American or British mandate under the League of Nations were dashed, the attitudes of American missionaries continued along much the same lines but with an openly anti-French bias.[14]

Conversely, in India during the Gandhi era[15] American missionaries found themselves in an awkward situation. While they felt sympathy for the

amusing and, in passing, mentioned the incident to the American consul in Beirut. The consul, incensed, then ordered Cantine not leave the city until an apology could be demanded and received from the Ottoman government. Cantine comments: "I have always been ashamed of the unwilling part I played in this scene, and it is not the only time my American citizenship has been used to support the dignity of the flag, rather than, as is so often reported, as an excuse for running to the flag for protection" [Cantine in Samuel M. Zwemer & James Cantine, *The Golden Milestone: Reminiscences of Pioneer Days Fifty Years Ago in Arabia* (New York: Fleming H. Revell Company, 1938), pp. 25-26.] [Note: This book is a compilation of articles written individually by Zwemer and Cantine. The appendix is comprised of the seminal article of John Lansing published in August 1889. Hereafter, this source will be referred to as follows: (author), *Milestone* ..., (page number).] Although this might reflect an honest sentiment, the mission had frequently to avail itself of diplomatic intervention. The British were willing to act *in loco parentis* for the Americans in the Gulf when political leverage seemed called for

[14]The leaders of the American missionary effort in Lebanon were avid "Wilsonites," they believed in the benevolence of the "American Way." In no community more than theirs was the sense of disillusionment felt when Wilson failed of his promise, and America returned to isolationism under the leadership of Senator John Cabot Lodge in 1920.

[15]Mohandas Karamchand Gandhi (born Oct. 2, 1869; assassinated Jan. 30, 1948) was known simply as Mahatma Gandhi, the leader of India's nationalist movement against British rule, politically active from 1919 until his death in 1948.

cause of India's independence, the habit of more than a century of close cooperation with British authorities was hard to break. As a result, arguing that missionaries ought not "get mixed up in politics," American missionaries in India as a rule refrained from expressing their feelings openly. When independence came their neutrality did not stand in their favor.[16]

In the particular case of the Arabian Mission, during the early years (not long enough after the War of 1812 so that all its wounds had been healed) British authorities in the Arab Gulf viewed the newly arrived Americans as potentially subversive, especially in view of the fact that the missionaries had established their field headquarters in Basrah, in Ottoman territory, and the Ottoman Empire at the time was coming under increasingly heavy German influence. (Always there were wheels within wheels!) American missionaries of the Arabian Mission, therefore, took pains to affirm to the British that they intended no subversion of British interests in the region. One observes, therefore, the extremely cordial relations that developed between British political agents in Iraq and the Gulf on the one hand, and the American missionaries, on the other.[17] Imperial recognition was accorded to Arabian Mission personalities like Stanley Mylrea (himself an American-educated British citizen), Paul Harrison, Harold Storm, and Lewis Scudder (Sr.).[18]

[16]While this observation needs little to justify it, the author was chiefly enlightened in this by J. J. DeValois, pioneer agricultural missionary of the Reformed church with the Arcot Mission in India. Mr. DeValois lived close to the soil and experienced the Gandhi phenomenon first hand from beginning to end. At the end of the remembered conversation he conceded the point that, yes, the missionaries' reticence to openly support the Indian hero (whom they unabashedly admired in private) had its bitter aftermath.

[17]In his introductory note to Zwemer's first book, *Arabia: The Cradle of Islam*, James S. Dennis sums up Zwemer's view of British imperialism in a nutshell: "It may not be out of place to note the hearty, outspoken satisfaction with which the author [Zwemer] regards the extension of British authority over the long sweep of the Arabian coast line. His admiration and delight can only be fully understood by one who has been a resident in the East, and has felt the blight of Moslem rule, and its utter hopelessness as an instrument of progress" [Zwemer, *Arabia: The Cradle of Islam* (New York: Fleming H. Revell Company, 1900), p. 3].

[18]Mylrea, Harrison, and Storm each received the Kaiser-i-Hind Gold Medal from the British Government of India; Mylrea and Scudder both received the Order of the British Empire from the British Government. Harrison, in what amounts to an act of penitence, related the following anecdote: "'Why don't we allow you to come and set up a missionary hospital here on the Pirate Coast?' The speaker was a Sharjah merchant. 'Because, if we admit you, just behind you will come the English with a telegraph office and a consulate. And we, after that? Nothing but vassals!' Nor was the man, in the bitterness of his hostility, a fool or blind, and the

It has been clear to the indigenous population of any foreign mission field that their western missionaries represented not only the power of the gospel but, willy-nilly, the power of the governments of their nations as well. The latter was something far more concrete (not to say intimidatingly persuasive) than the former. Foreign missions have found it virtually impossible to unambiguously illustrate the "other worldly" power of the gospel except in the lives of a very few pioneer missionaries (Henry Martyn, for instance) and proto-missionaries (of the ilk of the explorer, Charles Doughty[19]) who, through force of circumstance or by deliberate choice, laid aside the special privileges and immunities to which their western nationalities entitled them.

The World of Business and the Business of Mission

Locally, the Arabian Mission was not known by that name. It was known (as the American missionary work in Egypt, Syria, Lebanon, and Turkey *chose* to be known) as the "*American* Mission." Try though they did in later

justification for his attitude has been given, not by alien rulers, but by the missionaries themselves. Do they not associate with these rulers and cultivate their friendship at every possible opportunity? Do they not reckon a decoration by the alien power that rules the country as the achievement of a lifetime? A traveler returns home to announce that the greatest political asset of the colonial administrators in a certain province is the reputation of the resident medical missionary. Thus it is that the Gospel, in its appeal to the hearts of the Moslems, must carry on its back the whole evil weight of Western imperialism" (Harrison, "Christ's Contribution," p. 325).

[19]Charles Doughty is the author of the classic, *Travels in Arabia Deserta* (New York: Random House, 1921), which records his travels in the Hijâz, Najd, and the northern deserts of Arabia from 1875 to 1878. As Doughty himself warns the reader, it is a book which is not to be read by the flippant, because it is a serious and sensitive assessment of the Arab as well as of the Arabian environment. He was known as he wandered about Arabia simply as *an-nasrânî*, 'the Christian.' T. E. Lawrence, in his introduction to the third edition of the book, wrote, "They say that he seemed proud only of being Christian, and yet never crossed their [Muslim] faith.... He was the first Englishman they had met. He predisposed them to give a chance to other men of his race, because they found him honorable and good. So he broke a road for his religion" (p. xix).

Samuel Zwemer, spending a few days in London on his first journey to the Middle East in 1890, bought Doughty's books, only recently published (1888). "Those two volumes were to me a second Bible for many years, until I sold them at Cairo during the World War to Colonel Lawrence. But that's another story" [Zwemer, *Milestone* ..., p. 33.]. (We do not know that other story.)

years, the missionaries were not able shake off the label.[20] At first, however, it was seen to be convenient...even an asset. Even though Americans were known to be Christians (after all, what else would they be?), the Muslim of the Gulf found it convenient to express admiration for missionaries more in terms of national character than in religious terms. When, in its season, that national American character was seriously besmirched, then the missionaries were held up as examples of personal moral rectitude, models of what America *ought* to be and once *may have* been.[21] At times they were pitied for fighting a hopeless, rear-guard action against a manifestly corrupt America. The strictly *religious* impact upon Gulf society of missionary institutions such as hospitals and schools, therefore, was compromised by this "American" connection.

Not incidentally, but not quite intentionally either, this national label encouraged a second association that had an impact upon American missionaries. From the outset, a great deal of what missionaries employed in their daily work rested upon a base of relative material affluence and

[20]Henry Bovenkerk, in his "Deputation Report of Board Treasurer," submitted to the Board of Foreign Missions of the Reformed Church in America January 16, 1956 (document in author's collection), observed (p. 8): "The phrase 'American Mission' must, without a doubt, give the Islamic community the impression that the schools and hospitals located in their area are primarily benevolent projections of well-meaning Americans." He then asks, "Should not some terminology be adopted in the title of the organization which would have vivid meaning in the Arabic language and would describe the Church's schools and colleges as both Christian and universal and quite separate from any political terminology?"

[21]The image of America in the developing world hit its high water mark during the latter years of the Wilson presidency. It was on a high plateau through the Roosevelt years. But with Truman and his successors it has been an image much compromised by American internal political alignments, particularly those which express an uncompromising alliance with Israel. The partition of Palestine and the establishment of the State of Israel in 1947 marked the first tarnishing of the American image in the Middle East. Suspicion intensified during the subsequent Arab-Israeli War, in which the United States adopted an unblushing partisan policy in favor of Israel, a new and artificial entity which, in Arab eyes, had all the earmarks of a colonial venture, this time with a "made in America" label.

technological sophistication. The hospitals they operated were materially and technologically advanced over (if not to say alien to) the indigenous society. So too were the instruments they used in their educational institutions. Even the evangelists, with their "magic lanterns," portable "baby organs" and slick publications (and later their movies, radios, and tape recorders) bespoke impressive material and technological backing.

At the dawn of the twentieth century, missionaries quite blandly assumed that these things were simply the products of "Christian civilization."[22] Those to whom they ministered, however, could distinguish them as things that ingenuity could devise and affluence could acquire without a religious price tag. As the affluence/poverty ratio leveled out in the years following the Second World War, Arab individuals and governments did, in fact, seek after and buy those things for themselves.[23] The clear need for mission benevolence was blurred, and when Gulf society became wealthy beyond all expectations that aspect of the need was completely wiped out, a fact which seriously challenged the very existence of the Arabian Mission and certainly contributed to its eventual formal dissolution.[24]

---

[22]It was, after all, the Victorian Era with its bland assumption that European (and particularly Anglo-Saxon) civilization was the apotheosis of all things right, and that the changes western missionaries were introducing into Arab society were, by definition, good.

[23]Cornelia Dalenberg, in her memoirs, recalls a visit to Qatar as she prepared to retire in 1959. She wrote: "Years before, we missionaries had marched into Arab homes with an air of confidence, which was only natural because we came not only as ambassadors of Christ but as citizens of countries that were respected for their strength and knowledge. After the oil money settled into the Gulf, I must admit that things changed. We were still Christ's ambassadors, but now the nations of the Arab world were developing their own strength and using their wealth to acquire whatever knowledge they needed. We even felt a bit humble in the presence of the oil money" [Cornelia Dalenberg (with David de Groot), *Sharifa* (Wm. B. Eerdmans Publishing Co., 1983), p. 215].

[24]Collin Blair, an Australian with the Bible and Medical Missionary Fellowship (now Interserve) who had served in Afghanistan and Pakistan with his wife, Gladys, worked with the mission in Bahrain during the early 1980s. He moved on to serve the Bible Society in Hong Kong. He had the endowment of wisdom. Once, when speaking with the author about the difficulties of interpreting the missionary challenge in the Gulf to western constituencies, he commented: "It is too bad, but the church seems to have a vested interest in misery." It is a comment that has stuck verbatim, echoing even a decade and a half later, and that might have an application in this context. Perversely, those were good years in which to be a missionary.

American missionaries, with their clear national identity, also influenced the success of American business and industry in the Arab Gulf (and elsewhere as well). When the race for oil began in the second decade of the twentieth century, American companies already had available to them a large fund of good will built up by missionaries in the Gulf; unabashed, they drew upon it.25 The domination of the Arab Gulf oil industry by American companies in the teeth of heavy British political clout is not to be understood as having evolved simply because American explorers, negotiators, and businessmen were more competitive than their British counterparts.26

25Prominent among these was Charles Crane. In the next part of this book we will have opportunity to return to Mr. Crane.
26While American companies may have benefited most directly, British interests were also promoted.   C. A. P. Southwell, later knighted, the well-known managing director of Kuwait Oil Company (a joint Anglo-American venture), wrote to Everdine DeJong in 1952, expressing his condolences to the mission upon the death of Stanley Mylrea. He made the following revealing remark: "I had no greater regard for any man than for Dr. Mylrea, and the medical missionary work that he did in the Middle East made possible the early cooperation we [of the oil industry] had with our Arab friends" [in the author's document collection, letter dated 22nd February, 1952].
Sir Arnold Wilson was a British colonial administrator and later head of the AngloPersian Oil Company. As an observer and scholar in the Gulf, he had a marked impact upon developments there.   He wrote, "How far Christian missions have had a direct effect upon Arab thought and on the general trend of public administration and private conviction in the Persian Gulf must always be a matter of controversy. The writer is, however, convinced that their effect has been only less profound than that of the British political and mercantile agencies. Each has set, in the sphere of its respective activities, a high standard of personal conduct and public rectitude. British Political Agents or Consuls and Merchants have, by their personal dealings with chiefs and individuals, gained a respect and confidence which has given added weight to the precepts of missionary bodies, who themselves have not always appraised at its full value this silent testimony to the practical worth of the ethical system of which they are the devoted and worthy exponents.   On the other hand, the disinterested, but not dispassionate zeal, and the high qualities and personal ability of individual missionaries, has, beyond all question, permeated the Arab social and religious system, and has set standards of public conduct and personal rectitude which have been tacitly and indeed unconsciously adopted by an increasingly large body of educated men" [Sir Arnold T. Wilson, *The Persian Gulf* (London: George Allen & Unwin Ltd., 1928), pp. 248-249].   Arnold's observations here target specifically developments in Bahrain, but are intended to apply to the whole of the Arabian Mission. It is to be noted that they apply also to the time before oil when missionary, political officer, and merchant alike had to relate to a society living on the survival line and, therefore, had to meet standards of conduct higher than those expected during years of later affluence.

Even in Riyadh, the capital of the Sa'ûdî State, the reputation of the American missionaries was high; the term "American" bespoke high moral standards, honesty, altruism, and perhaps even a smidgen of gullibility. An anecdote is perhaps appropriate to illustrate the point:

In January of 1937 Wells Thoms, on one of his tours into Sa'ûdî Arabia from Bahrain, to pass the time in the evenings used to attend King 'Abd-ul-'Azîz's *majlis* or *diwâniyyah*. At such gatherings the ruler would sit at the end of a great hall. People would sit around the sides quite informally. The doors were open and people could come and go as they wished. From time to time a petitioner would come forward to the king and state his business quite openly. Occasionally the king himself would ask someone to come and sit beside him, a significant gesture of showing honor. On one particular occasion, the king called Thoms to come and sit with him and then he gave a short speech. Beth Scudder Thoms Dickason recounts the story thus:

> "Ya Thawmas," he pointed to Wells who was sitting at the end, "I want you to come and sit up here. I want to tell you why I gave my oil concession to the Americans."
>
> So Wells went up and sat down.
>
> He [the king] said, "Now I want all of you to know this." (That was the newspaper. Whatever went on there was the news. So he wanted to make sure that that was in the news.)
>
> So he said to the whole lot, "You know, the Japanese wanted our oil, but, in thinking about it I thought, 'Well, their emperor is to them God. So they worship a human being.' I don't want anything to do with that."
>
> He said, "The Russians wanted our oil, but they say there *is* no God, and I don't want anything to do with that."
>
> He said, "The Italians wanted our oil, and they say they love us, but they love us like a wolf loves a lamb. They came across, they went into Abyssinia, they've taken all of that territory, and we don't want any of that."
>
> He said, "The British want our oil. *Wallah, hum rajâjîl!* [By God, they're *real* men!] But," he said, "wherever they go they take over."
>
> He said, "Our experience with Americans has been nothing but good. They've helped us. They've come in here and served us. So I've given my concession to the Americans."

To the author's comment, "So in a sense the Arabian Mission paved the way for the American oil companies to operate in Sa'ûdi Arabia," Beth Thoms Dickason with a rueful chuckle added, "I don't know if that's any good or not."[27]

As this last comment indicates, these links – political, material, and commercial – had their drawbacks. The massive American presence that grew with the development of oil brought with it all types of people. Many of the early pioneers of oil exploration and development were remarkable individuals of strong moral character and high integrity – men like Frank Holmes (early explorer and negotiator), James MacPherson (ARAMCO

[27]Transcribed from a recorded interview by the author with Mrs. Ethel S. Thoms Dickason, Kalamazoo, Michigan, January 28, 1990.

Commenting on this story, William Brewer, son-in-law of John Van Ess and a distinguished American career diplomat in the Middle East, wondered at just what 'Abdul-'Azîz was really trying to do in making this rather striking public declaration. If, Brewer speculated, the American oil company which had been exploring for oil in the Eastern Province since 1933 had still come up with no results by January 1937, the king may have been trying to temper the impatience and de-fang the criticism within his own ranks for the slow progress being made by his chosen company. [Recorded interview by the author with Ambassador William Brewer and Mrs. Alice Van Ess "Van" Brewer, Falmouth, Massachusetts, July 5, 1990.] In point of fact, the first producing well in Sa'ûdî Arabia was brought in a year later, in 1938. But if Brewer's speculation is backed up by the sequence of actual events, it remains remarkable that the king would have held up a Christian missionary to symbolize his point before his rather religiously intolerant people.

In an article for *The Middle East Journal*, Joseph W. Twinam, once American Ambassador in Bahrain, wrote: "In the understanding of most Americans the Gulf Arabs were discovered by oil men, who brought an incredible bonanza of material things to a people who previously had to rely rather much on things of the spirit in search of the quality of life. It is therefore interesting, and not unimportant, that the first Americans to go after 'exploiting' the resources of the Gulf in a serious way were themselves people of the spirit – American missionaries seeking a harvest of souls.... [S]uffice it here to say that the missions came to convert, ran into the strength of Islam and stayed to heal. In the long and arduous process they created a firm impression that Americans were basically decent folk who want to help if they can. That perception, which many other Americans of more worldly interests also subsequently nurtured, has done much to develop and sustain the American position in the Gulf over the years" [Joseph W. Twinam, "America and the Gulf Arabs," p. 132].

It is interesting to note that, although ARAMCO, the Standard Oil-based American company which opened up the mineral resources of Sa'ûdi Arabia, employed as advisors and consultants individuals who had been associated with the Arabian Mission (Edwin Calverley, Louis Dame, and Robert Van Peursem, the second son of Gerrit Van Peursem, prominent among them), no recognition

and AMINOIL), Leland Jordan (Gulf/KOC), Wilton Gerhardt (Bechtel), and others. But the influx of personnel after production began was massive and less discriminating. When the Arabian American Oil Company (ARAMCO) began to negotiate for land on which to house its people, there is a plausible myth which suggests they were offered a choice by the Saʿûdî government: either liquor or churches, one or the other, but not both. As the story goes, the wise ones of the oil company went into a huddle and chose liquor, knowing the hard living habits of the American driller. The upshot was that they got neither, and since then duplicity in matters ethical and religious has been the order of the day.[28]

The point of the anecdote is that the reputation for high moral character the American missionaries enjoyed was compromised by association with their compatriots.[29] This all happened at the same time as Harry Truman, despising the advice of his State Department, chose to tie America's future in the Middle East to the fortunes of the fledgling State of Israel. The righteous indignation and outrage this fanned among Arabs was virtually unequivocal and in some cases, as in Iraq, led to violence from which the

of the mission's influence is made in the publications of the company. No doubt it is politically understandable that this kind of selective memory should be evident, but it does cloud the historical issue.

[28]The jury-rigged distilleries (which occasionally blew their operators into the next world) and bathtub breweries of Dhahran are legendary throughout the Gulf. Exploding stills or brews which produced deadly and blinding methyl rather than simply intoxicating ethyl alcohol led ARAMCO to openly circulate a handbook on how to practice this quaint "cottage industry" safely. Worshiping groups within the oil camps were dubbed "morale groups," and ordained pastors were admitted under the euphemistic title of "special teacher."

[29]In a thoughtful article entitled, "The Business Man and Foreign Missions," published in *The Arabian Mission Field Reports* (#82, July-September, 1912, pp. 3-5), Charles Shaw discussed precisely this phenomenon as it applied in the Arab Gulf. His conclusion was that the church must encourage Christian businessmen to work abroad and not leave so much to chance the matter of the quality of western Christian representation overseas. Shaw himself was one such experiment in attempting to establish a deliberately Christian business enterprise in the Arab Gulf. His efforts were not directly fruitful. [NOTE: The publication, *The Arabian Mission Field Reports* underwent several metamorphoses over the course of time: *The Arabian Mission Field Reports* (#1, January 1-April 1, 1892 to #26, April 1-June 30, 1898); *The Arabian Mission Quarterly Letters from the Field* (#27, July-September, 1898 to #40, October-December, 1901); *Neglected Arabia: Missionary Letters and News Published Quarterly by the Arabian Mission* (#41, January-March, 1902, to #215, Winter 1949); *Arabia Calling* (#216, Spring 1949, to #250, March 1962). Hence, the above would be noted thus: AMFR #82, July-September, 1912, pp. 3-5.]

mission was not immune. The double blow suffered by missionaries in consequence has been one from which the Arabian Mission never recovered, even though, as individuals locally, missionaries continued to be respected, even *highly* respected.

Orient and Occident

Another discussion is required for the setting of the stage. It has to do with the peculiar way in which the West has been conditioned to view the Middle East or, as the Germans quaintly call it, "The Land of the Morning" (*Morgensland*).[30]

From the days of classical Greece, as its wars with Persia were portrayed in literature, there was shaped in western heritage an image of the East which time has only elaborated and worked more deeply into the fabric of western culture. The East was the land of inscrutable mystery, gratuitous violence, capricious autocracy, legendary sloth, and decadent luxury. (Replace the adjectives in the last sentence with the word, "oriental," and the sense of it to the average western reader will remain unchanged.) The Orient was

[30]The shaping of western and Christian attitudes toward the Orient and Islam is a major study in itself, a field of inquiry that is still evolving. We do know, however, that the heritage left us by the nineteenth century had itself been deeply conditioned by a centuries-long hatred toward Islam and a supercilious attitude toward eastern culture generally and particularly toward the culture and society of the Middle East. A definitive, concise, and very readable study in the field is that of R. W. Southern, *Western Views of Islam in the Middle Ages* (Cambridge, Massachusetts: Harvard University Press, 1962). It is an insightful discussion of how western and Christian society shaped its attitudes about Islam from the seventh century to the dawn of the Renaissance. Building on that foundation is Edward Said's *Orientalism* (New York: Random House, 1978). Said's scope is broader than Southern's, perhaps. Said takes into consideration how ancient Greek authors set the stage, as it were, for the rivalry between East and West long before either Christianity or Islam were even in the picture, and he shows how those themes continue into later phases of the relationship between the two cultural and political zones. But his main concentration is upon cultural and scholastic developments which began in the late seventeenth century and continue to our day. Said's challenge to a whole tradition of ideological and scholarly work – Orientalism – demonstrates that western and Christian society exploited its rivalry with Islam and the East as a means for confirming its own vaunted self-image. The damage this has done to our present ability to truly see humanity as a whole has been extensive. For our consideration here, we must understand that the pioneers of the Arabian Mission were products of their time. They wore the same blinders everyone else did.

the enemy over against which the Occident came to define its own ideal self-image: its devotion to knowledge, its championing of justice, its rule of law, and its discipline of moderation – the Athenian ideal of the pure and elegant line.

Later, as the Roman Empire divided and declined into the Middle Ages, the West persisted in this tendency. The classical division was expressed in terms of the division between Rome and Constantinople, along which lines the church's most persistent division was drawn. The continued prosperity, arrogance, and high culture of Byzantium (which encompassed all the lands between Egypt and Greece) was seen by semibarbaric medieval and Catholic Europe as further evidence of the cosseted and effete nature of the Orient.

When, in the seventh century, Islam broke out of the deserts of Arabia and attacked the war-exhausted Byzantine Empire in its soft underbelly, the reverberations in the West were limited to some sense of inconvenience that now the places of high pilgrimage were under a new administration. But western pilgrims to the Holy City soon came to speak quite approvingly of the new Muslim management of the region, the honesty of the rulers, and their effective restraining hand against thieves and brigands. Christian political and military opposition to Islam was seen in the West as the business of the Byzantine state. That state managed to survive dismemberment, restrain the Muslim tide, and for five centuries hold the line roughly along what are the southern borders of modern Turkey. So impressive was Byzantium's achievement that among some Muslims it was felt that the fall of Constantinople would herald the Resurrection and the Day of Accounting.[31]

Islam ceased to be only a Byzantine problem when Muslim armies swarmed across the straits at Gibraltar and swiftly conquered the only recently Romanized Visigothic kingdoms of Spain. Then Islam became a western problem, too. We have been led to believe that, were it not for Charles Martell and his valiant champion, Roland, the whole of Europe might have been overrun. It was after the battles of Tours and Poitiers in 732 that the relatively dignified and intellectual anti-Muslim polemic of the eastern Orthodox champions of Christianity was popularized and elaborated in the West. The garish images from John's Apocalypse were added and, in

[31]Bernard Lewis, *The Middle East and the West* (Bloomington, Indiana: Indiana University Press, 1964), pp. 115-116.

the popular mind, Islam became the vessel of the Antichrist, a theme that has carried through to our day.

As Muslim culture developed its proud heritage of scholarship, science, literature, and art, especially in Spain, western scholars came to sit at the feet of Muslim learned men. Names like Averroes (Ibn Rushd), Avicenna (Ibn Sînâ), and Algezzel (al-Ghazzâlî) became common in western intellectual vocabulary. One would have thought that, as a result, a more accommodating attitude might have been cultivated as the seeds of the western Renaissance were thus precariously planted. But any hope of that was significantly offset by the enthusiasm and popular rhetoric that accompanied the Spanish *Reconquista*, the subsequent Inquisition, and Europe's rush into the Crusades in the eleventh century. The notion that the only antidote to Islam was the power of Christian armies became ingrained in the western mind during 400 years of Crusades,[32] and it was not until that movement began to degenerate

---

[32]The portrayal of one's enemy as The Enemy is a political activity which intends to motivate and mobilize, not necessarily inform; intellectual integrity has little to do with the matter. Through the mid-twentieth century the Crusades have mesmerized western romantics, and missionaries were, by and large, incurable romantics. It was (and *is*) an occupational malady. The modern campaign against Islam began as a continuation of the Crusades. Little wonder that Samuel Zwemer chose as his hero the fiery and militant martyr, Raymond Lull, rather than his irenic mentor, Francis of Assisi. During World War I, when General Allenby rode into Jerusalem December 9, 1917, at the head of the Egyptian Expeditionary Force which had "liberated" it from the Turks, he did so quite deliberately in the guise of a latter day Richard the Lion Hearted. And it would be quite in character were it true that he was overheard muttering something to the effect that "Here end all the centuries of the Crusades."

The Crusades fundamentally transformed Muslim-Christian relations not just between East and West, but more radically within the Middle East itself. Until then Arab Muslims and Christians lived together fairly casually. They shared the same social values, spoke the same language in the same way, and, for the most part, considered each other legitimate in their worship of the same God (even though they very energetically contested with each other the mode and mediation of that worship).

For his doctoral dissertation at the University of Utah, Harvey Staal, a career Arabia missionary, examined and provided a critical text of an early Arabic translation of the Pauline epistles — Romans, I & II Corinthians, and Philippians. Three scribes, he determined, had been involved in the transcription from between 876 and 1035 (or later). [Harvey Staal, *Codex Sinai Arabic 151: Pauline Epistles (Rom., I & II Cor., Phil.), Part II (English Translation)*, Vol. XL of *Studies and Documents* (J. Geerlings, ed.) (Salt Lake City, Utah: University of Utah Press, 1969), pp. 19 & 24.] The first two evidently wrote during the days of the 'Abbâsid Caliphate of Baghdâd in the ninth and tenth centuries, and the

and finally fail that western voices showing some real understanding of Islam began to be heard.[33]

Nonetheless, if the oriental Christian empire of Byzantium was finally destroyed in the wake of (and, to some extent, *because* of) the western crusading effort, that seemed to be of little long term consequence. The Orient had been Byzantium; now it was Islam, the Moor, the Saracen, the Terrible Turk. It remained the Orient for all that, a threat to the very soul of all that was precious and pure in occidental Christendom. The Reformation, when it came, had no effect upon this view of the world.

Constantinople's last defenses collapsed in 1453. Although the event failed to bring the expected world's ending, it did signal the end of oriental Greek power. In its stead rose the Ottomans. The Ottoman Empire

third during the middle or latter Crusades (some time in the eleventh or early twelfth century). As was the scribal practice, an invocation was written at the beginning of the manuscript with a piously expressed identification of the scribe, emphasizing virtues such as humility and devotion and such. The invocation was always a formula beginning with: "In the name of ..." In this case, the two scribes writing before the Crusades apparently "... felt no compunction about using what is called today, 'The Muslim formula,' 'In the name of God, the Merciful, the Compassionate.' This apparently was a common and acceptable practice of the Christians of the early Islamic centuries. However, with the passing of time, animosity began to build up between the followers of these two great monotheistic faiths, with the result that our third scribe no longer feels free to use the Muslim formula, but changed to the Christian formula, 'In the name of the Father, the Son, and the Holy Spirit'" [Staal, *Codex* ..., p. 25]. This evidence correlates closely with other evidence, such as conversion rates from Christianity to Islam in Syria, which rose sharply after the Crusades [Richard W. Bulliet, *Conversion to Islam in the Medieval Period* (Cambridge, Massachusetts: Harvard University Press, 1979)]. Arab Christian apologetic and polemic literature addressed to Muslims also sharply decrease after the Crusades. This evidence points to a phase during which Arab Christians, for a variety of reasons, set about deliberately to distinguish themselves linguistically, socially, spiritually, and intellectually from Muslims – a kind of mental ghetto. Muslims, for their part, came to view their Christian compatriots as constituting a potential fifth column.

[33]Christian voices of moderation and accommodation have, until recently, been small voices speaking against a wind of bellowing polemic. Paul of Antioch, Melkite bishop of Sidon, as early as the twelfth century spoke about a limited Christian recognition of Muhammad as a legitimate prophet to the Arabs [Paul Khoury, *Paul d'Antioche, Eveque Melkite de Sidon (xii s)* (Beyrouth: Imprimerie Catholique, 1964)]. John of Segovia and Nicholas of Cusa in the fifteenth century sought for peaceful approaches to Muslims in which Islam could be seen positively as a "tutor to Christ." But it was not until the twentieth century that these old voices found responsive listeners. (For a condensed and well balanced discussion of the evolution of western views of Islam during the Middle Ages, see Southern, *Western Views....*)

remained the nemesis of European ambitions through the early seventeenth century. But in 1683, when it failed for the second time to capture Vienna, the rising powers of Europe sensed that rot had set in under the Sultan's throne. The economic tides of the world were changing. Ottoman control of the Mediterranean was already a thing of the past. Cheap silver from the New World flooded the marketplace, devaluating the empire's currency. The route to the Indies no longer had to pass overland through areas of Ottoman control. The brittle feudal structure of the Ottoman state could not compensate, and corruption began to riddle its once lean and efficient bureaucracy.

By the dawn of the eighteenth century the Sick Man of Europe (as the Ottoman Empire came to be called) was being avariciously fought over by the young empires of Austria, Russia, Britain, and France, and they dismembered it piece by piece. First came Napoleon Bonaparte's invasion of Egypt in 1798. Then the empire lost Greece, then many of its holdings in eastern Europe, then its control of the Black Sea, then North Africa.

The French invasion of Egypt under Napoleon coincided with the rise of the Wahhâbîs in Arabia. From then on until the end of the First World War it was only jealous rivalry between western powers that prolonged the old empire's life.[34]

Although his military adventure in Egypt was cut short in 1801 by British sea power, Napoleon took with him to Egypt a team of scholars. He used them to study and assess the treasures of that ancient land. The influx of information and treasure this brought into the West gave new impetus to the traditional discipline of Oriental studies, a discipline devoted to elevating the western image of the Orient to the level of scientific respectability.

It was in this intellectual tradition that all Westerners addressing themselves to the Middle East were steeped, missionaries not excepted. They approached Islam and the East with the bland assurance that western values and western religion would prevail. Following the example of victorious Christian arms and enterprise, they expected that the Christian religion likewise would

---

[34]There are a variety of studies of the end of the Ottoman Empire. A good summary of the matter is M. S. Anderson, *The Eastern Question, 1774-1923* (London: Macmillan, 1977). See also Bernard Lewis, *The Middle East ...,* and his classic work, *The Emergence of Modern Turkey* (London: Oxford University Press, 1961); and Peter M. Holt, *Egypt and the Fertile Crescent: 1516-1922* (Ithaca, New York: Cornell University Press), pp. 149-163. Said, *Orientalism,* p. 81-88, portrays the cultural impact of the French venture.

inevitably overcome the stubbornness of the Muslim heart. All that was required was strong concentrated effort, dedication, and prayer.[35]

'Occidizing' the Oriental Church

This triumphal attitude did not only apply to Islam. It also applied to oriental Christianity. By the mid-nineteenth century the oriental churches were inbred, impoverished, ill educated, and governed by traditional leaders whose roles were defined more in political terms than in spiritual terms. For centuries the Ottoman *millet* system had conditioned them to isolation from each other, from their Muslim environment, and from the outside world and had deprived them of adequate educational resources and cultural outlets. From the time of the Crusades the Catholic church had maintained a vigorous effort in the region, finally alienating significant segments of Orthodox and heterodox communities from their traditional loyalties.[36] When they arrived on the scene, western Protestant missionaries,

---

[35]In a sensitive meditation, Cornelia Dalenberg, who represents the generation which followed the Arabian Mission's pioneers (she served from 1921 to 1961), wrote, "As I reread some of the books on missions that were written in the early part of this century, I am struck by the military terminology of some of the authors.... but it was at the core of our thinking in the early part of the century. We were Christ's soldiers in a foreign land, sacrificing ourselves in His service, and striving for spiritual victory. We believed firmly we were an advance arm of a campaign that would succeed" (Dalenberg, *Sharifa*, pp. 97-98). She noted that missionaries were cut off from amenities and the security of good medical care. They exposed themselves to some of the most hazardous environments then known. And the sense of being on "campaign" was an essential prop to their spiritual motivation. "Like soldiers entering a battle, any of us could be taken at any moment. We were fully prepared to sacrifice our careers, our well being, our health, and even our lives" (pp. 98-99).

[36]Catholic influence was not confined to drawing off membership. There was a heavy ideological and political influence as well. The interesting story of Cyril Lucaris, the Greek Orthodox Ecumenical Patriarch of Constantinople, is instructive. As a promising young priest he had been sent off to eastern Europe to counter Protestant influence there. He went on to travel in western Europe, imbibing Lutheran and Reformed ideas. After serving as bishop in Alexandria, he was elevated to the Patriarchal throne in Constantinople and, in 1629, he published his *Confessions*, a heavily Calvinistic work on church doctrine. It was heatedly opposed by Latin influences in the Orthodox church and condemned in the Council of Jerusalem (1673). Lucaris was strangled by order of the Ottoman Sultan Murâd IV on June 25, 1638. Whatever else might be observed in Lucaris's

lacking experience and perspective, saw only corruption and the lack of faith.[37]

A. L. Tibawi, in his careful study, *American Interests in Syria 1800-1901*, discusses this phenomenon in detail. The oriental clergy were known to the pioneer American missionaries in Syria as "the enemy." By 1826 open "warfare" against the oriental churches was accepted mission policy. Tibawi

stormy career, it shows that over a century before Protestants began working in the Middle East, the churches in the region had already developed a strong predisposition to oppose them. All the indicators are that this predisposition was cultivated as a by-product of the animosity between Catholics and Protestants in Europe. [For a detailed profile of Cyril Lucaris see Steven Runciman, *The Great Church in Captivity* (Cambridge: Cambridge University Press, 1968), chapter 6, "The Church and the Churches: The Calvinist Patriarch," pp. 259-288.]

[37]For the attitude of disdain for the ancient churches reflected by members of the Arabian Mission particularly see the comments of Amy Zwemer in *AMFR* #18, April-June, 1896, p. 4, where she discusses the beginnings of work for women: "We can only speak of the *possibilities* [*sic.*] of work amongst women in these parts, because of our recent arrival among them. The vista is a wide one, and needs to supply its need the army of women spoken of in Ps. 68, R.V. The ground is very hard and full of weeds, both of their own [Muslim] superstitions, and those of the Eastern Churches." Writing somewhat later, James Cantine made this revealing remark: "It should be remembered that we are the only mission in all this country, and except at Basrah, where we come in contact with *the old and debased Oriental churches* [emphasis added], we are the sole representatives of Christianity" (*AMFR* #48, October-December, 1903, p. 4). Speaking of the early contacts between Christians and Muslims, Mason and Barny summarize the effect of Islam upon the Oriental churches thus: "Conquering so many nominally Christian peoples by force of arms, the faith of the Crescent flourished side by side with that of the Cross in the large area adjacent to the eastern and southern shores of the Mediterranean sea, until its virus had poisoned the faith and life of the Christian churches and had gradually conformed the Christian world of Asia Minor, Syria, Mesopotamia, Arabia, North Africa, and other lands to the will of the Prophet" (Mason and Barny, *History ...*, p. 44).

This attitude toward Arabs in general and among them no less the Christians was augmented by what can only be identified as clear racial prejudice. The following remarks on the trials and tribulations of being a native colporteur by James Cantine are but indicative: "They naturally meet many more hard knocks than do we who are hedged about with the protection which comes from belonging to a superior race; and if our Western Christianity is what we claim, it must also have given us more strength, moral and spiritual, to endure and overcome" (*AMFR* #41, January-March, 1902, p. 10).

The legacy of proselytization among the Oriental Christians has left deep wounds in the ancient churches of the Middle East which are still tender, but they are healing. Although the Arabian Mission outlook was not different from that of the American Board with regard to the ancient Oriental churches, because its field of operation was mainly in a region where no churches existed, it did not

summarizes the point accurately when he says, "In the eyes of early missionaries, even Muslims were morally superior to eastern Christians."[38] The main thrust of this mission effort, therefore, was directed toward the oriental churches as much by choice as out of necessity. At least a virtue was made of the necessity. The Ottoman government forbade direct evangelism among Muslims by foreign nationals. The ban did not apply to Ottoman citizens who were Christian. The strategy adopted by the early missionaries (British and American alike) in Turkey, Syria, Lebanon, Palestine, Egypt, and Iraq, therefore, was to try to revitalize the indigenous Christian community. This was characterized as "indirect" evangelism of the Muslims by western missionaries.[39] The veteran missionaries in Lebanon expressed their amazement at the audacity of the two novices, Cantine and Zwemer, who intended *direct* Muslim evangelism in Arabia.

Given their conditioning, it isn't surprising that the first American and British missionaries to begin work in Ottoman territories never really considered identifying with the ancient churches but rather intended to convince them of the superiority of western Protestantism.[40] Those Arab Christians who accepted this premise became alienated from their parent communions, and new Protestant communities began to evolve.[41] In

directly participate in what those ancient churches felt to be the assault upon their people. In an ecumenical age, this has given scope for Reformed church involvement in cooperative work which is not as strongly tainted with ill will from the past.

[38] A. L. Tibawi, *American Interests in Syria 1800-1901* (Oxford: Clarendon Press, 1966), pp. 36-41.

[39] The recent study by Antonie Wessels, *Arab* and *Christian? Christians in the Middle East* (Kampen, the Netherlands: Kok Pharos Publishing House, 1995), is well worth examining. It is a disciplined examination of the fact that Christianity is indigenous to the Middle East, and every bit as "Arab" as Islam. In his eighth chapter (pp. 165-184) Wessels, speaking of the role of mission from the West, clearly discusses the ideological orientation and policies of western mission enterprises in the region and the rise of Arab Protestantism.

[40] Pliny Fisk and Levi Parsons, the pioneer missionaries of the American Board of Commissioners for Foreign Missions to the Middle East, disembarked in Smyrna, Turkey, January 14, 1820, with this mandate: "The two grand enquiries ever present in your minds will be *what good can be done* and *by what means?*" But they had already determined ahead of time that Christianity in the Middle East was Christianity "only in name" [Tibawi, *American Interests ...*, p. 15 (for the quotation) and pp. 12-19, for the larger discussion.] Beirut was first "occupied" by American Board missionary personnel, Bird and Goodell, November 16, 1823.

[41] Hovhannes P. Aharonian has argued forcefully that the phenomenon of the evangelical churches of the Middle East is not to be written off simply as the result

theory, the new indigenous Protestant communions would have the same zeal as their western mentors. They were to be the vanguard for evangelizing Jews, Muslims, and whatever chance "Pagans" (like the Sabeans of Mesopotamia) happened to fall in between. But this hope was, by and large, unfulfilled. Arab Protestants had to abide by the same social and economic constraints and were subject to the same social and political conditioning as their Orthodox coreligionists who had remained loyal to their ancient communions. Except for a few who were hired to work as colporteurs[42] under western missionary direction and protection, Arab Protestants shared with all other Arab Christians a vulnerability to Muslim censure and reprisal. They were no more anxious to court martyrdom than anyone else.

What western Christians failed to appreciate was the manner in which oriental Christian piety under Islam had evolved during its centuries of isolation from the rest of the church. Westerners found the ancient liturgies difficult with their elaborate lections, incense clouds, sacred icons, sonorous chants, and ornate vestments. But the heavy emphasis of the oriental churches was upon the Eucharist not simply as a rite but as the very

of "sociological, economic and even political factors. No doubt, these factors had their impact, but to ascribe the success of the Evangelical movement mainly to these factors would belittle the spirit of reform which right from the beginning of the Apostolic era has been the renewing and revitalizing element in the churches of the East....The spirit of reformation was there before the western missionaries arrived in this region in the beginning of the 19th century." He characterized the motive of the first middle eastern Protestants as a concern "to reform the church and make it 'Evangelical.' Separation was forced on them because of anathemas and excommunications. At this point the missionaries came to their rescue" [H. P. Aharonian in an address given before the founding assembly of the Fellowship of Evangelical Churches of the Middle East in 1974 and published in a collection of Mr. Aharonian's writings and speeches: H. P. Aharonian, *The Armenian Evangelical Church on the Crossroads* (MECC: Beirut, 1988), p. 287.]

[42]The term, "colporteur," is a curious one borrowed, as are a lot of curious words, from the French. It originally identified an itinerant book seller. Since the mid-1800s it has been used exclusively in English to describe a paid (usually indigenous) itinerant agent of a western religious organization whose work it is to sell especially Bibles and other religious literature. Colporteurs were not considered to be an integral part of the missionary contingent. The colporteur's foreign colleague was known as the "evangelist." In fact, these terms do not fairly recognize the colporteur's role. In many cases in the experience of the Arabian Mission, as in 'Imârah and Kuwait, they were actually the vanguard of the mission's initiative, and not infrequently in the early years they held stations with only light supervision by missionary personnel. Yet the distinctive and to some extent prejudicial term stuck.

substance of Christian witness and life. Unable to witness aggressively, Middle Eastern Christians saw their ministry to be one of presence and example, endurance and faithfulness. And it was in the Eucharist that the flesh and blood of the Great Example was renewed in them. Simple bread and wine were brought into the sanctuary, but when the celebration of the divine liturgy ended the incarnate flesh and blood of the Cosmic Christ walked out into the world borne in the bodies of his faithful.[43]

Western missionaries failed utterly to appreciate the power and tenacity of this peculiarly oriental spirituality, and they set forth on their task in roughshod and arrogant ignorance. The net effect was an overall demoralization of the Arab, Greek, Armenian, Suryani, and Assyrian Christian communities in the Middle East, an effect which is only now being painfully overcome. Only recently has a new appreciation of the deep spiritual resources of the ancient churches begun to develop among western Christians.

Western Protestant mission efforts were launched in the Middle East with a heavy load of baggage, much of it extraneous, a good deal of it hurtful. Shot full of idealism and a genuine desire to be faithful to the gospel, western Christians also fed philosophically at the same trough as did western imperialism. Their purpose to mediate the gift of salvation, therefore, was borne upon compromising vehicles of power and arrogance. Missionary attitudes toward the East were conditioned by a cultural bias that simply assumed their own religious, moral, and cultural superiority. Furthermore,

[43]See the unusually clear and concise statement of Orthodox "missiology" by James Stamoolis, "Eastern Orthodox Mission Theology," pp. 59-63, in *International Bulletin of Missionary Research*, vol. 8, no. 2, April 1984 (published by the Overseas Ministries Study Center, Ventnor, New Jersey). His concluding remark is worth quoting: "…if one is to understand and learn from Orthodox missiology, it is imperative to begin with a holistic approach to Orthodox theology. The framework of Orthodoxy provides the starting point for mission. The richness of the Orthodox tradition, obscured from the West by long centuries of theological isolation and historical separation, offers a vital contribution to Christian knowledge" (p. 62).

the Protestants entered the Middle East with a clear sense of contesting the ground with the Roman Catholic church. While their respective attitudes toward Islam were much the same, Roman Catholics and Protestants each saw the other as competing for the soul of the disadvantaged eastern churches. Both failed to appreciate the depths of wisdom that had been plumbed by the eastern churches during their centuries of isolation under Muslim rule.

It is tempting to attempt to absolve the Arabian Mission of this indictment. And it is true that the Arabian Mission thought of itself as primarily committed to encounter Islam in the heartland of Arabia where there were no indigenous Christians. In Bahrain, Oman, Kuwait, and Arabia's interior the ancient churches of the region had no established presence until after the age of oil began in the 1950s. Nonetheless, particularly in Iraq, there were intersections—especially with the Ancient (Assyrian) Church of the East and its Uniat counterpart, the Chaldean Catholic church. There was also contact with the Syrian Orthodox church, the Armenian Apostolic church and the Antiochene Orthodox. And it must be confessed that, while the main focus of the mission was southward, it too played a part in disparaging the ancient Christian presence in the region. Although it shied away from the preoccupation of the older missions with the shortcomings of the older churches,44 nonetheless, like the other missions, it had to struggle to understand its presence in the fuller context of the Middle East and to appreciate the resources which were already at hand.

The Muslim-Christian Interface

We have dealt with the conditioning of Christian mission to Islam in largely cultural terms, and those terms are important. But there is another

---

44F. M. "Duke" Potter, the secretary of the Board of Foreign Missions at the time, spoke at the funeral of James Cantine in July 1940. He made this remark: "It is easy to turn aside in a country like Arabia or Iraq, to work with the old Christian groups found there. When the Mohammedan will not hear the gospel it is a temptation to build up a church or a school among these other elements in the population. But, without any suggestion of swerving from the appointed task, Dr. Cantine insisted always, in both Missions [the Arabian Mission and the United Mission in Iraq], that however meagre the tangible results, the great object is to minister to the followers of the Prophet." [In a memorial brochure containing tributes by Potter, Samuel Zwemer, and Harold J. Hoffman, document in the author's collection.]

dimension that this discussion may not ignore. The church and the Muslim community have responded to each other as spiritual entities. The religious dimension was obviously linked to the cultural and political, but it was distinct in texture and significance.

Christian Assessments of Islam

The identity of the Muslim community[45] has always puzzled Christians. An aggressive people asserting a positive creed, and claiming close kinship ties to the church and to the Jewish people, the Muslim community, as it emerged during the seventh century, posed a problem. The Qur'ân links itself to the Torah, Psalms, and Gospel. It speaks of Muslims as closely related to Jews and Christians, sharing a common bedrock of faith and prophetic tradition. While it urges Muslims to tolerance as within a family, it has no cumpunction about addressing Christians and Jews with advice and admonition. From a Muslim point of view, Christians and Jews are inextricably part of Islam's spiritual dialectic.

[45]The term for community in Arabic is *'ummah.* The constellation of meaning involved in this word is quite vast. The root meaning would seem to be dominated by the notion of guidance or proper aim toward an ideal. In the noun form it can also bear the sense of the firm foundation of integrity, the root of one's being, and the focal point of one's existence. Thus: Mother. As an abstract or collective noun, it refers to a community which follows a certain religious path in obedience to God who has communicated his will by sending a prophet to them. Thus it becomes the communal focus of a person from which he gains identity and integrity. More loosely applied it can mean any kind of human grouping from one's own family to one's nation, or even one's particular generation. Following other lines of possible development, a single man who, for one reason or another, is an archetype, can be called an *'ummah.* Abraham is one of the most commonly referred to in this sense. Or *'ummah* can refer to the sterling features of one's stature or beauty of face. In a very abstract sense, it can also refer to a space of time, that is: a coherent sequence thereof.

The *Qur'ân* uses the word, *'ummah,* in the sense of focal community, even a fraction of a larger ethnic group, who respond to (or refuse) the call of a prophet. Thus an *'ummah* is not an *ethnos,* but more nearly a "fellowship," a *koinonia.* When discord arises an *'ummah* breaks down as in the dispersal of Babel (Sûrah 10, vs. 19). Such structures are finite and not created to last for ever (Sûrah 10:49 – each has its appointed time for existing), and many *'umam* (the plural form) have existed and are no more. Membership is, seemingly, fluid; those who belong to an *'ummah* may (and frequently do) stray (Sûrah 16:93). The individual, Abraham, as we have noted, is referred to as an *'ummah* (Sûrah 16:120). In this case I prefer to set aside the slavish literalism of the commentators and lexicographers and read "Abraham" in this context as a corporate personality, or

It is not to be wondered at, therefore, that as the Muslim armies moved into predominantly Christian Egypt and Syria, discussions between Muslims and Christians should have taken place. We have records of several formal encounters: (1) The interrogation of the Jacobite Patriarch, John I, of Antioch, by the famous Muslim commander, 'Amr Ibn-ul-'Âs, in 639 is among the earliest examples.[46] (2) The correspondence between the Byzantine Emperor, Leo III (717-741), and the Umayyad Caliph, 'Umar II (717-720), is preserved in an Armenian text of the tenth century.[47] (3) The debate between the "Nestorian" Catholicos, Timothy I, with the 'Abbâsid Caliph, al-Mahdî, somewhere around 781, is preserved in both Syriac and Arabic in the form of a letter.[48] (4) John of Damascus, the last of the Church Fathers, was an official at the Umayyad court in Damascus and out of his experience wrote a short description of "The Heresy of the Ishmaelites."[49] And (5) Theodore Abû Qurrâ, the "Nestorian" Bishop of Harran (740-820) appeared before the 'Abbâsid Khalif al-Ma'mûn to defend his faith.[50] As these events and experiences are all recorded by Christian pens, we are not

the core around whom an *'ummah* coalesces. One usage is of *'ummah* as a space of time given for repentance before judgment falls (Sûrah 11:8).

The sense of *'ummah* in Muslim religious thought is very powerful. It is a very large concept. In the *'ummah* all Muslims are bonded together in a brotherhood. It is not equivalent to any political or ethnic entity. It is far broader and less institutional. It is appropriate to translate the term, *'ummah*, by "mothering community." As we understand it in this way, it must also be in our awareness that it has within it not just the notion of nurture but also of direction and discipline.

For a disciplined (if somewhat controversial) treatment of the whole notion of *'ummah* and its implications, see W. Montgomery Watt, *Islam and the Integration of Society* (London: Routledge & Kegan Paul, 1961). Another interesting article dealing with the dynamics whereby the Muslim *'ummah* is integrated is that of G. E. von Grunebaum, "The Problem: Unity in Diversity," pp. 17-37 in G. E. von Grunebaum (editor), *Unity and Variety in Muslim Civilization* (Chicago: The University of Chicago, 1955).

[46]F. Nau, "Un colloque du Patriarch Jean," pp. 225-279 in *Journal Asiatique*, Vol. 11, No. 5 (1915).

[47]A. Jeffery, "Ghevond's Text of the Correspondence between 'Umar II and Leo III," pp. 269-332 in *The Harvard Theological Review*, Vol. 37 (1944).

[48]A. Mingana, "Timothy's Apology for Christianity," in *Woodbridge Studies*, pp. 1-162, Vol. 2 (Cambridge: 1928), and other sources.

[49]Daniel J. Sahas, *John of Damascus on Islam: the "Heresy of the Ishmaelites"* (Leiden: E. J. Brill, 1972).

[50]Alfred Guillaume, "A Debate between Christian and Moslem Doctors," pp. 233-244 in *Centinary Supplement, the Journal of the Royal Asiatic Society* (London: 1924).

given a full (nor a particularly fair) account of the Muslim position in these exchanges, but we can be sure that these early encounters stimulated the subsequently far better developed Muslim participation in the interreligious debate.

Because it pressed itself vigorously upon Christian awareness, and because it demanded special consideration, the church has endeavored to answer the question of Islam's identity in a wide variety of ways.[51] Initially, there were two classes of Christian response to Islam. Among those communities anathematized by the early ecumenical councils (as "Nestorians" and "Monophysites," primarily) and who survived on or beyond the frontiers of the Byzantine Empire, Islam was seen as the scourge of God upon wayward (Chalcedonian) Christianity. The scourge would be lifted if and when those Christians repented. In itself and as itself, Islam was not given really serious consideration.[52]

Following the lead of John of Damascus, Chalcedonian Christianity first analyzed the Muslim community as a revival of the Arian heresy. In its initial

[51]The endeavor of the church to identify the Muslim community has always been tinged with reluctance and with a certain sense of anxiety. This latter expresses itself in the need to reassert, in the face of Islam, the legitimacy of the church's existence and its continuing (if not occluding!) mandate.

Among the very earliest and most important expressions of this attitude and perspective is the ninth-century work of an author who calls himself 'Abd-ul-Masîh bin-'Ishâq al-Kindî [the Servant of Christ, son of Isaac, of the blue blood Arab tribe of al-Kindah], who is writing in response to a letter he received from a Muslim friend who is called (and the symbolism in the names can only be intentional) 'Abd-Ullâh bin-'Ismâ'îl al-Hâshimî [the servant of God, son of Ishmael, of the upstart clan of al-Hâshim from which the Prophet came]. The Arabic text is quite long but we have an English condensation: William Muir (editor/translator), *The Apology of Al Kindy, Written at the Court of Al Mâmûn (Circa A.H. 215; A.D. 830), in Defense of Christianity Against Islam*, Second Edition (London: Society for Promoting Christian Knowledge, 1887).

[52]The largest non-Chalcedonian community was the Coptic church of Egypt. Dessenters from the formula of faith expressed at Chalcedon, the Copts had been under the heel of the Byzantines (and their arrogant Greek Chalcedonian clergy) for many dreary years when, in 638, the Arab Muslim armies invaded, and the Byzantine era abruptly ended. The quick collapse of the Byzantine forces in Egypt is to be partly explained by the antagonism of the Coptic population. The Copts, as Aziz Atiya points out, were largely neutral toward Islam, having a long tradition of keeping their own counsel. [Aziz S. Atiya, *A History of Eastern Christianity* (London: Methuen, 1968), pp. 82-84.] In fact they benefited from the new Arab overlord in that Greek Melkite persecution ceased and the Copts were able to live their own lives in relative peace so long as they paid the Muslim-imposed "capitation tax" (the *jizyah*) regularly and with due humility on each

statements, therefore, the church addressed Muslims (or, more precisely, counseled its people to address Muslims) in the argumentative spirit typical of the spirit of early intra-Christian debates.[53] Interestingly enough, Islam was first known as "the heresy of the Ishmaelites." A similar term used to characterize the Muslims is "Agarenes," or the descendants of Hagar.[54]

By the ninth century, however, Christians had come to the conclusion that Islam emerged from a fundamental delusion. Christian writings on Islam became angry. Muhammad was being vilified and his followers were seen as little better than barbarians. Byzantine theologians coined the notion of Muhammad as an epileptic, and it became customary to portray him as a power mad, sex-obsessed deviant whose teachings were designed to sanctify his own perversities.[55] It was but a short step from there to forming the notion which held sway through the western Renaissance that the Muslims

adult male of their community. (This tax, as initially imposed, was actually lighter and easier to bear than the extortions of the Greek administration.) The Arabs, in need of bureaucrats to operate the machinery of the state (which they left pretty much intact wherever they went), engaged Copts in most positions and Coptic replaced Greek as the administrative language for many years. The point that is worth making is that the Copts viewed the Muslim phenomenon as transitory and paid little attention to it, exploiting to the full the respite that it offered, but returning very little to it in the way of interest in Islam as such.

The other non-Chalcedonian communities – the Syrian Orthodox church and the Ancient (Assyrian) Church of the East – were also of a similar mind, having come through similar experiences with the Chalcedonians and their Byzantine patrons (Atiya, ... *Eastern Christianity*, pp. 193-199 and 267-271). These communities, however, seem to have been far more ready to participate in the cultural flowering of Islamic culture. This especially applies to the Assyrians.

[53] See: Sahas, *John of Damascus*.

[54] See: James M. Demetriades, *Nicetas of Byzantium and His Encounter with Islam: A Study of the "Anatrope" and the Two "Epistles"* (Hartford, Conn.: The Hartford Seminary Foundation, a Ph.D. dissertation, 1972).

[55] Muir, *Apology*, pp. 44-55, and Demetriades, *Nicetas*, p. 94. These treatments of the problem of Muhammad have had lasting effect upon the perspective of Christian, be they western or eastern. By way of example we may cite two examples which may, on first view, seem at opposite poles of the intellectual spectrum. An early example of these is the highly influential polemical work of C. G. Pfander of the Basel Mission, entitled *The Balance of Truth [mizân-ul-haqq]* (London: The Religious Tract Society, 1910). There are fairly clear traces of the influences of al Kindî in the Pfander document even though Pfander's work is original to himself. It has recently been republished in both English and Arabic and is being circulated by The Fellowship of Faith for Muslims. Because it is an intense frontal attack upon the integrity of Islam and the Muslim community, it has aroused much Muslim reaction and elicited very little light.

were, in fact, the minions of Anti-Christ, Muhammad being his False Prophet.[56]

From the thirteenth century, however, there appear Christian endeavors to formulate an understanding of the Muslim community in a way that would allow peace between the two faiths and that would build an ideological framework for coexistence. Paul of Antioch, Bishop of Sidon, to whom we will shortly return, put forth the idea that Islam is a legitimate prophetic religion with the limited mandate of converting the Arab pagans to monotheism. Within that mandate, Christians ought to respect Islam, but they ought not to think that it has anything of substance to say to the faith of a Christian.[57] By the end of the Crusades and as Constantinople's fall drew near, some Christian voices spoke out advising that Muslims be approached through peaceful persuasion and acts of love.[58] Following Constantinople's fall Nicholas of Cusa came forward with the idea that,

The attacks upon the person of Muhammad, cleverly using Muslim sources, are particularly ruthless. The second example of a modern writer is the Marxist French author, Maxime Rodinson, in his biography entitled simply, *Mohammed* (Harmondsworth, Middlesex: Penguin/Pelican, 1971). Rodinson, who commands a great deal of respect in western scholarly circles, presents a very human portrait of Muhammad, but like the earlier polemic, he becomes fascinated with Muhammad's sex life and, in the end, loses perspective through becoming engaged in a pop-Freudian analysis of his subject. On this level, there is not much to choose between Pfander and Rodinson. The real classic western biography of Muhammad and one which is scholarly in the best sense is that of W. Montgomery Watt, published in two volumes entitled, *Muhammad at Mecca and Muhammad at Medina* (Oxford: Clarendon, 1953 and 1956). It is available in a one volume condensation entitled, *Muhammad: Prophet and Statesman* (Oxford: University Press, 1961).

[56]Demetriades, op. cit., pp. 96-97. See also the ruthlessly detailed and passionate book of Norman Daniel, *Islam and the West: The Making of an Image* (Edinburgh: University Press, 1960), and the cooler and briefer treatment of R. W. Southern, *Western Views of Islam in the Middle Ages* (Cambridge, Mass.: Harvard University Press, 1962). The evolution of the demonic image surrounding Muhammad is well presented and fully elaborated in both these works.

[57]Paul Khoury, *Paul d'Antioche, Évêque Melkite de Sidon (xiis)* (Beyrouth: Imprimerie Catholique, 1964).

[58]The most important voices raised in advocacy of a peaceful approach to the Muslim community are those of Francis of Assisi and Roger Bacon. That of Raymond Lull might also be cited here, but his attitude toward Islam went through several different stages, and toward the end of his life he was all in favor of calling for a new Crusade. The voices of Francis and Bacon were early voices. Later others joined them.

indeed, Christians might see in Islam a "tutor to Christ" and meet Muslims on grounds of mutual respect.[59]

From the fifteenth century onwards, the idea that Islam merited a degree of respect and that the approach to Muslims should be through the instrument of preaching rather than that of the sword gained ground. A high optimism developed in certain quarters that, through preaching, the gospel might penetrate the hearts of the Muslims and turn them *en masse* to Christ.[60] As Orientalism developed its portrait of Islam based upon the declining Ottoman and Indian Islamic cultures, the assertion developed that Islam was a religion of backwardness and Christianity one of progress and enlightenment.[61] By the time of the mid-ninteenth century there had developed a passionate conviction in certain circles[62] that God was preparing the Muslim world for its moment of fulfillment, and that the ancient promises to Ishmael would shortly be realized.[63] Islam would turn to Christ

---

[59]The notion of a "tutor to Christ" is an old one. With respect to Islam, it refers to the possibility of approaching the gospel using Muslim sources. This was the dream of John of Segovia and of Nicholas of Cusa in their hope to extract from the *Qur'ân* those points upon which a dialogue might be based which would lead, in the end to the conversion of Muslims. [See: R. W. Southern, *Western Views of Islam in the Middle Ages* (Cambridge, Mass.: Harvard University Press, 1962), pp. 86-94.] In a similar constructive vein we find the book of Abdiyah Akbar Abdul-Haqq, *Sharing Your Faith with a Muslim* (Minneapolis, Minn.: Bethany Fellowship, 1980).

[60]The early writings of S. M. Zwemer and of most of the pioneer missionaries of the Arabian Mission in their reports from the field expressed this high optimism. As an example: Not long before his death in Muscat on the 26th of June, 1898, the Rev. George F. Stone wrote to the Auburn Seminary *Review* and penned these lines: "I do firmly believe that the strength of Islam has been overestimated, and that if ever the church can be induced to throw her full weight against it, it will be found an easier conquest than we imagine – not but what it will cost lives, it has always done so, but I do believe that Islam is doomed" [*AMFR*, No. 30, April to June, 1899, p. 6].

[61]"The Koran has frozen Mahometan thought; to obey it is to abandon progress." [Fairbairn quoted in the anonymously authored *Papers for Thoughtful Muslims*, Nos. I-IV (Madras: The Christian Literature Society for India, 1900), p. 78.]

[62]See particularly S. M. Zwemer, *Arabia: The Cradle of Islam* (New York: Fleming H. Revell, 1900), pp. 391-408.

[63]In point of fact, the figure of Ishmael in Genesis is enigmatic. Antonie Wessels, *Arab* and *Christian?*, p. 208: "After speaking of his objections to Islam at a missions conference held in 1890 at Middelburg (The Netherlands), the renowned Calvinist, Abraham Kuyper, (died 1920), added that the mission of the churches should also build on the "true elements that have remained in their [i.e. Islam's] confession of Moses and the Christ." In his opinion one should honor and

if only the church would fulfill its role as preacher with wisdom and courage.[64]

During the nineteenth century and into the twentieth, the story of Christian missionary endeavors in Muslim societies give us a great deal to admire (and not a little to repent). We mark the work of W. St. Clair Tisdall, *A Manual of the Leading Muhammedan Objections to Christianity*, first published in 1904.[65] It is, by no means, the first of its kind,[66] but it attained a justifiably wide circulation as the most solid and concise statement of the principal themes of the Muslim rejection of Christian propositions. It is characteristic of the beginning phases of such scholarship that it should be oriented toward Christian missionary endeavors in the midst of Islam. While Tisdall's scholarship intended to direct the Christian to a deeper appreciation of and sensitivity toward the Muslim's outlook on Chistianity, its guiding motive is "Muhammadan controversy." Controversy was the norm and conversion was the object when Christians sought to establish relationships with Muslims.

Contrary to initial expectations, however, Islam did not crumble before the onslaught, and all western missionaries experienced with varying degrees of poignancy and frustration the deep (some would say stubborn) resolution

---

acknowledge the line "by which the Mohammadens are linked to Abraham. Ishmael was born of Abraham and was circumcised by Abraham. Christ saved Ishmael's life and indicated the refreshing spring. Mohammedanism has the worldwide call to be a bulwark against heathenism."

Kuyper's is an amazing statement for its day. The meditation upon scripture has continued. Jim Dunham, reflecting on this, asked the question of the theological link between Christians and Muslims which the covenant with Abraham established long before either existed. The author, in his work for the Commission on Theology, developed a study which was published in *Dialog* (Vol. 29, No. 1, Winter 1990, pp. 29-32, entitled "Ishmael and Isaac and Muslim-Christian Dialogue." In it he argued that the positive relationship between the two brothers, drawing upon their covenant companionship in their father, is a paradigm for what Muslim-Christian relations can be.

[64]Samuel M. Zwemer, *Islam: A Challenge to Faith* (New York: Student Volunteer Movement for Foreign Missions, 1907), especially its closing chapters IX to XII.

[65]W. St. Clair Tisdall, *A Manual of the Leading Muhammedan Objections to Christianity*, third edition (London: SPCK, 1915).

[66]For instance, see many of the works of Sir. William Muir, especially *The Mohamedan Controversy* (Edinburgh: T. & T. Clark, 1897); and Thomas Wherry, *The Muslim Controversy* (London: The Christian Literature Society, 1905).

of Muslims to resist the invitation to accept Christ on Christian terms.[67]
John Van Ess, writing in 1943, notes, "The Moslem would recite the
Apostle's Creed as follows: 'I believe in God Almighty, Maker of heaven and
earth. And in Jesus Christ, who was conceived by spirit from God, born of
the Virgin Mary, suffered, He ascended into heaven, and from thence he
shall come to be judged. I believe in the forgiveness of sins, the resurrection
of the body, and the life everlasting.'" He goes on to add: "This is, of course,
significant more for what it omits than for what it mentions."[68] To some
observers and even a few participants, this experience has suggested over
the years that either Islam is utterly to be condemned as a machination of
the Devil,[69] or else we are faced here with a serious challenge to the
Christian faith and a persistent mystery which demands profound theological
assessment.[70]

[67]The figure of Jesus is not strange or novel to Muslims. He is a prominent figure in
   the *Qur'ân* and a very important one for Muslim piety. For a discussion of this see:
   Geoffrey Parrinder, *Jesus in the Qur'an* (London: Sheldon Press, 1965). Kenneth
   Cragg has published a very thoughtful study of precisely this topic: *Jesus and the
   Muslim: An Exploration* (London: George Allen & Unwin, 1985). In his insistent
   manner, Cragg proposes that Christians take seriously Islamic Christology. For
   a shorter treatment giving a summary of Muslim perceptions of Jesus, see my
   article, "'We Wish to See Jesus' – Christianity Through Muslim Eyes," pp. 12-24
   in the *Reformed Review*, Vol. 36, No. 1, Autumn, 1982, especially p. 13.
[68]John Van Ess, *Meet the Arab* (New York: The John Day Company, 1943), p. 31.
[69]This notion, we have seen, is not novel. It was expressed very early on. But it is still
   current. See, for instance: Jans Christensen, *The Practical Approach to Muslims*
   (Marsielle, France: Mrs. M. Christensen and the North Africa Mission, 1977), in
   which the idea is central to the argument of the book. For instance: "We as the
   Church Militant have to come to grips with Islam, not as an interesting scientific
   problem, nor as a historical fact, but as the powers of darkness that struggle
   against the revelation of God in Christ" (p. 1). See also Zwemer, *Islam: A
   Challenge*; and George W. Peters, "An Overview of Missions to Muslims," pp.
   390-404 in Don McCurry (editor), *The Gospel and Islam: A 1978 Compendium*
   (Monrovia, Calif.: Missions Advanced Research Center, 1979). In this last we
   note the following remark: "I am inclined to stand in line with such men as
   Pfander, Zwemer, Freytag and others who see in Islam a 'supra-humanly
   designed' anti-Christian religious movement to offset and oppose the gospel of
   our Lord Jesus Christ" (p. 401).
[70]Here the work has been led by Kenneth Cragg in his several profound works
   dealing with bridge-building between Christians and Muslims, as well as with a
   Christian understanding of Muslim spirituality. In his courage and obvious
   integrity, Cragg is a pivotal figure so far as the discussion of this subject is
   concerned. He has demonstrated by word and life that a Christian need not lose
   his evangelical integrity simply because he takes the spirituality of another

The scholarly appreciation of Muslims' responses to Christianity continued to develop and was put on a firm footing with the publication of Erdmann Fritch's *Islam und Christentum im Mittelalter*.[71] Confining himself to the Medieval period, Fritch made good use of the bibliographical work done by other scholars, and brought to light many of the basic texts of the period, analyzing their content. The work of Arthur Jefferey between the mid-1920s and early 1940s in this regard is also extremely valuable.[72]

Although heavily dependent upon Fritsch for his analysis of the Medieval period, Harry G. Dorman, an outstanding heir to the Presbyterian missionary work in the Levant, substantially advanced the discussion in his *Toward Understanding Islam*.[73] Like Tisdall, Dorman specifically justified his work as a background study for the shaping of Christian mission policy with respect to Islam, but he went beyond Tisdall in many respects. For one thing, the format of the study is distinctively different. It is a historical and not a thematic survey of the dialogue/debate between Christianity and Islam as it was carried on primarily in the medium of Arabic. The summaries of arguments (both Christian and Muslim) are presented with refreshing objectivity and a relative lack of controlling glosses. The selection of representative statements shows a thorough familiarity particularly with the modern sources available. At this stage, Dorman's remains *the* text on the subject. Furthermore, *Toward Understanding Islam* is a historically significant book. By displaying the evidence of the "Muhammadan controversy" in a fully rounded manner, giving both sides of the debate and

tradition seriously and senses it with deep compassion. But for a critical assessment of Bishop Cragg and his understanding of Islam, see Andreas Felix D'Souza, *The Origin of Islam as Interpreted by W. Montgomery Watt and A. Kenneth Cragg* (Montreal: The Institute of Islamic Studies, McGill University, a Masters thesis, 1979).

[71]Erdmann Fritsch, *Islam und Christentum im Mittelalter* (Breslau: Muller und Seiffert, 1930).

[72]Arthur Jefferey, "New Trends in Moslem Apologetic," chapter 20 in *The Moslem World of Today* (edited by John R. Mott) (New York: George H. Doran, 1925); "Anti-Christian Literature," pp. 216-219 in *The Moslem World*, Vol. 17 (1927); "A Collection of Anti-Christian Books and Pamphlets Found in Actual Use Among Mohammedans in Cairo," pp. 26-37 in *The Moslem World*, Vol. 15 (1925); and "Present-Day Movements in Islam," pp. 165-186 in *The Moslem World*, Vol. 33 (1943).

[73]Harry G. Dorman, *Toward Understanding Islam: Contemporary Apologetic of Islam and Mission Policy* (New York: Columbia University Bureau of Publications, 1948).

assessing impact, Dorman is to be credited with bringing the traditional western missionary literature of "Muhammadan controversy" to a close while laying the groundwork for a new literature of Muslim-Christian dialogue.

The confrontational and dialogical strands of thought have often interpenetrated each other in positions which hold the grey middle ground as far as judgment upon Islam itself is concerned, but which remain insistent that the Gospel must be preached to the Muslim community and that the invitation to receive Christ ought not be withdrawn from them. The "how" of this and the spirit with which it is undertaken, however, are matters of lively debate.[74]

Muslim Initiatives and Responses

Operating with its own dynamic, Islam has always provided the Muslim individual and Muslim society with a powerful system of integration. Muslim life is not highly compartmentalized. A Muslim does not do religion here, profession there, politics in another place, and recreation somewhere else. Life, like Arabic stylistics, can be something of a run-on sentence. That is why almost any issue may become a religious one.

A second feature of Muslim response goes back to Islam's early mythology. Not unlike some of the gospels of success and progress that have grown out of American religion (Dale Carnegie and his religious disciples, Norman Vincent Peal and Robert Schuller, for example), Islam proclaims itself the spiritual vehicle for human prosperity. From the days of the Prophet Muhammad and for many centuries thereafter, Islam seemed destined to prosperity and vindication on the world's stage. Even when the Muslim state fell into decadence and intellectual life languished, this seemed to be the case because there was no alternative power to challenge it. When the challenge arose (as in the case of the incursions of pagan Turks and Mongols), it was quickly converted to serve Islam; it was religiously domesticated.

---

[74]The literature treating the methodology of mission to Muslims is intimidatingly vast. Islam as a point of Christian fascination has always provided good grist for the missionary mill, the more so since it baffles the most creative mission methodologists. McCurry, *The Gospel and Islam*, provides a healthy selection of a variety of contemporary evangelical opinion.

By the mid-ninth century, however, Muslim scholars and theologians had begun to sense a challenge in debating with Christians. The *Fihrist* of Ibn an-Nadîm[75] bears witness to the fact that almost every Mu'tazilite theologian worth his salt had to compose at least one refutation of Christianity. The exchange between Yahyâ bin-'Adî, a Christian, and Abû Yûsuf Ya'qûb al-Kindî[76] bears witness to a fairly brisk exchange on sophisticated topics between Muslim and Christian intellectuals during the early 'Abbâsid period.[77]

This is no accident or coincidence. The ninth century was the era during which the basic theological language of Islam evolved, and it evolved within the environment of apologetics.[78] Modern Muslim theologians and philosophers have a tendency to portray the Mu'tazilah as true free thinkers and the best examples of creative theological genius in early Islam.[79] It is also tempting for the Christian scholar to cheer him on when Harry Dorman says, "It is probable that the apologetic of the Christians, immediately on the defensive against a new heresy, widened the breach..., crystalized the opposition, and prevented such liberal movements as the Mu'tazilah from effectively softening the rigidity of orthodox Islam and introducing an appreciative understanding of the figure of Christ."[80]

---

[75]An extensive catalogue of Islamic writings of the classical period.

[76]Augustine Perier, "Un traite de Yahyâ Ben 'Adî, defense du dogme de la Trinite contre les objections d'al-Kindî," pp. 3-21 in *Revue de l'Orient Cretien*, Vol. 22 (Paris: 1920-1921).

[77]See: L. E. Browne, *The Eclipse of Christianity in Asia* (Cambridge: Cambridge University Press, 1933), and Dorman, *Toward Understanding Islam*, p. 42.

[78]The jury is still out on the question of the extent to which Islam is indebted to Christian influence for its theological vocabulary and for its choice of theological issues. For a positive statement of this see: Armand Abel, "La polemique damascenienne et son influence sur les origines de la theologie musulmane," pp. 61-85 in *l'Elaboration de l'Islam: Colloque de Strasbourg, 12-14 Juin, 1959* (Paris: Presses Universitaires de France, 1961), and C. H. Becker, "Christliche Polemik und islamische Dogmenbildung," pp. 175-195 in *Zeitschrift fur Assyriologie und Verwandte Gebiete*, Vol. 12 (1926). For a cautionary word on this issue see: W. Montgomery Watt, *The Formative Period of Islamic Thought* (Edinburgh: Edinburgh University Press, 1973), pp. 98-99.

[79]See, for instance, Muhammad 'Azîz al-Lahbâbî, *ash-shakhsâniyyah al-islâmiyyah [Islamic Personalism]* (Cairo: Dâr-ul-Ma'ârif, 1969).

[80]Dorman, *Toward Understanding Islam*, p. 116. Dorman's argument here, of course, is interesting in the fact that it contends that Christianity during Islam's first contact with it in the Middle East was too ardent, too dogmatic, too aggressively assertive of its own position. This argues in the teeth of those who

But this is to claim too much. Given its own rather intolerant dogmatic spirit, the movement of the Muʿtazilah, had it prevailed, would not have proved any more tractible from a Christian perspective. Although many of the terms of reference would surely have been different, it is doubtful whether the Muʿtazilah—transcendentalist unitarians that they were—would have done much by way of "introducing an appreciative understanding of the figure of Christ." Such a task within Islam remained for the Sûfî metaphysicians to take up.[81] But Dorman is probably correct in suggesting that the Aristotelian logic of John of Damascus and Theodore Abû Qurrâ and the polemical arguments which they deduced through it were formative factors in the Muslim response-in-kind.

The rigidity of Christian and Muslim positions *vis a vis* each other, and their seeming irreconcilability direct us to seek, not for disagreement in principle, but for a more fundamental attitudinal factor. Dorman is again correct, on the Christian side, in showing that apologetic/polemic tended not so much to battle through to a Muslim-Christian consensus on issues, but rather to vindicate Christianity against the threat of Islam.[82]

Cause and effect are difficult to assign in the matter, but it is true that certain issues (eg. the validation of prophethood through the evidence of miracle *a la* Theodore Abû Qurrâ and ʿAbd-ul-Masîh al-Kindî) were definitely introduced through the Christian polemic against Islam and quickly became keystones in the Medieval Muslim theological system. Other issues, such as argumentation on the divine attributes and their relationship to the divine essence, very much a concern of the Muʿtazilah, were also set up in the environment of the interreligious polemic. And it is difficult to see how history might have been replayed so as to avoid establishment of basic sets of intellectual barriers on both sides.

The fact is that they were indeed constructed. The problem is, what caused them to be built? Was it genuine intellectual dissonance? Were the issues themselves *the* issue, or was the real issue something else? The almost inescapable conclusion grows out of the historical demonstration that the

have long argued that middle eastern Christianity was lax and corrupt and weak and, therefore, easy prey for Muslims.

[81]See, for instance, Muhiy-ud-Dîn Ibn al- ʿArabî (d. 1240), *Fusûs-ul-Hikam [The Essences of Wisdom]* (edited by Abû-al-ʿAlâ ʿAfîfî) (Cairo: Dâr-Ihyâ'-il-Kutub il-ʿArabiyyah), pp. 138-142. [A risky English translation exists by R. W. J. Austin: *Ibn Al'Arabi: The Bezels of Wisdom* (New York: Paulist Press, 1980).]

[82]Dorman, *Toward Understanding Islam*, p. 11 and 115.

Aristotelian argumentative system was the same on both sides, it was used with the same self-satisfaction on both sides, but it achieved no cross-over results on *either* side. To the contrary, it only entrenched misunderstanding. The conclusion is that the basic factor on both sides was the appearance and subsequent nurture of a fundamental attitudinal dissonance, a sense of incipient enmity which fed suspicion and could turn vindictive.

If, during the period of the Mu'tazilah there existed a lively interest in Christianity *per se*, following the downfall of the Mu'tazilah and the rejection of the apologetic task by Muslim theologians, that interest became secondary. The sense that Islam constituted a world sufficient unto itself rendered the task of confronting the religious declarations of the outside world one that could conveniently be laid aside. Quite clearly, beginning with al-Ash'arî, pacesetter for the post-Mu'tazilah Muslim theologians,[83] the principal problem of the Muslim theologian became justifying the discipline to the now-dominant Muslim jurist. This fundamental shift in the orientation also shifted the nature of the Muslim concern with Christianity.

By the time of Ibn-Hazm (d. 1064)[84] and al-Bâqillânî (d. 1013),[85] in the tenth century, the shift in mood is pronounced and significant. It is no longer of interest to rebut Christianity as such. What is of interest is to condemn Muslim deviations as participating in the errors of Christianity. It may be worth pointing out that by the eleventh century the impact of Muslim isolation of Christian communities from full participation in cultural life had been having its impact, and Christian communities had become seriously depressed and in-grown. They were easy targets for the mockery Muslim polemicists directed their way. Thus the *portraiture* of Christianity became ever more significant, not for its depiction of Christianity, nor for the cause of debate with Christians, but rather for the background it provided to the major controversial issues being debated within Islam itself. With the

---

[83]Al-Ash'arî (874-936) was the pace-setter for the post-Mu'tazilah Muslim theological exercise.

[84]Abû-Muhammad 'Alî bin-Sa'îd Ibn-Hazm, *kitâb-ul-fisal fi-l-milal wa-l-'ahwâ' wa-n-nihal [The Book of Discernement Among Religions, Sects and Creeds]* (published in five volumes) (Cairo: alMatba'ah al-Ahliyyah [vols. 1-3], Matba'at-ut-Tamaddun [vol. 4], and Matba'at-ul-Mawsû'ât [vol. 5], from 1900 to 1904). This is far and away the most massive work of its kind, and is still very much in circulation.

[85]Muhammad Ibn-ut-Tayyib al-Bâqillânî, *at-tamhîd fî-r-radd 'alâ-l-mulhidah il-mu'attilah wa-rrâfidah wa-l-khawârij wa-l-mu'tazilah [Introduction to Refuting the Obstructionist Heretics, the Rejectionists, the Khârijites and the Mu'tazilah]* (Cairo: Dâr-ul-Fikr il-'Arabî, 1947).

exception of al-Ghazzâlî's (d. 1111) *ar-Radd ul-Jamîl*,[86] the heresiographical theme came to predominate.[87]

By the latter thirteenth century, however, the tractates of Paul of Antioch (in Arabic, Bûlus-ul-Antâqî), to which we have made earlier reference, had begun to circulate relatively widely in Muslim circles. What seems indicated by this phenomenon, and is further aided by the rather extensive citations in writings of the straight-laced Syrian jurist, Ibn Taymiyyah,[88] is that Christian apologists had found new scope for their own expression and more access to the Muslim population during the period of Crusader patronage in the Levant. Paul put forward what he hoped would be a reconciling compromise: He advocated that Muhammad was indeed a prophet and could be accepted as such by Christians. Although he was a prophet, Muhammad was one who had been pointedly sent to the Arab pagans. His mission, therefore, was a limited one and not universal; therefore, it did not behoove Christians to change their religious loyalties.[89] Al-Qarâfî, a predecessor of Ibn-Taymiyyah's, took heated exception to Paul's arguments and set about refuting them point by point.[90] Ibn Taymiyyah, some fifty years later, also devoted major attention to Paul's arguments. A third respondent to Paul in this period was the Sûfî, Muhammad Ibn-Abî-Tâlib.[91]

[86]Abû-Hâmid Muhammad al-Ghazzâlî, *ar-radd ul-jamîl li ulûhiyyat-'îsâ bi sarîh-il-injîl [The Elegant Refutation of Jesus' Divinity Based Upon the Explicitness of the Gospel]*, published as *Refutation excellente de la divinite de Jesus-Christ d'apres les evangiles* (edited and translated by Robert Chidiac) (Paris: Librairie Ernest Leroux, 1939).

[87]Among the more important heresiographies of this period which treats Christianity (as well as Judaism) in some detail is that of Abû-l-Fath Muhammad ash-Shahristânî (d. 1153), *al-milal wa-nnihal [Religions and Creeds]* (editor: 'Abd-ul-'Azîz Muhammad al-Wakîl) (Cairo: Mawsû'ât-ulHalabî, 1968). This too continues to be well read and much referred to.

[88]We note here particularly his still-current and very popular *al-jawâb us-sahîh li man baddala dîn-al-masîh [The True Refutation of Those Who Have Changed Christ's Religion]* (in four volumes) (Cairo: Matba'at-ul-Madanî, 1964).

[89]Khoury, *Paul d'Antioche*, pp. 59-83.

[90]Shihâb-ud-Dîn Ahmad bin-Idrîs al-Qarâfî, *al-ajwibah al-fâkhirah 'an al-as'ilah al-fâjirah [The Splendid Answers to the Disrupting Questions]* in the margin of 'Abd-ur-Rahmân Bâche-ji-zâdah, *al-fâriq bayn al-makhlûq wa-l-khâliq [The Distinction Between the Creature and the Creator]* (Cairo: Matba'at-ut-Taqaddum, 1904).

[91]Noted in Dorman, *Toward Understanding Islam*, p. 13.

What is interesting in this is that a measure of direct interchange between Muslim and Christian had been reestablished. A vital issue was debated between them. Although the arguments and terms of the debate were not particularly novel, the context was refreshing. Ibn Taymiyyah provides further illustration of this direct discussion in his short epistle to the king of Cyprus,[92] in which he argues eloquently for an attitude of tolerance and mutual respect between the proponents of the two faiths.

Even so, the heresiographical implications of the portrait of Christianity continued to dominate even in the writings of Ibn Taymiyyah and those of his disciple, Muhammad Ibn Qayyim al-Jawziyyah (d. 1350).[93] To their way of thinking, the vital issues of the day were the stagnation of Muslim scholasticism, the deviant speculative philosophies of the Sûfîs, and the perversions of true worship and piety manifest in the devotion popularly paid to Sûfî saints (a thing which smacked of paganism).

Between the fourteenth century and the beginning of the modern era there is a curious dirth of Muslim discussions on this topic. It is the more curious because this interstice also represents the period during which the population of Syria shifted from being dominantly Christian to being majority Muslim. In all fairness, however, the period held little political stability, and intellectual activity in the Middle East as a whole was at an all-time low. The Ottoman synthesis which followed in the fifteenth century was administrative and political, and it did not stimulate intellectual life.

Entering the modern era, on the eve of the Arabian Mission's founding, we witness a marked change.[94] Suddenly there is an explosive increase in

---

[92]Ibn Taymiyyah, *ar-risâlah al-qubrisiyyah: kitâb li sirjuâs malik qubrus [The Cyprus Epistle: A Letter to Sergius, King of Cyprus]* (Cairo: Huhibb-ud-Dîn al-Khatîb, 1974).

[93]Muhammad bin-Abî-Bakr Ibn-Qayyim al-Jawziyyah, *kitâbu-hidâyat-il-hayârâ fî ajwibat-ilyahûd wa-n-nasârâ [The Book of Guidance to the Perplexed As to the Answers to Jews and Christians]* (Cairo: al-Maktabah al-Qayyimah, 1977).

[94]At this point, it is enough to suggest the literature available: The short historical treatment by Bernard Lewis, *The Middle East and the West* (Bloomington, Ind.: Indiana University Press, 1964); the classical intellectual history by Albert Hourani, *Arabic Thought in the Liberal Age: 1789-1939* (London: Oxford University Press, 1962); a terse analytical treatment by Hisham Sharabi, *Arab Intellectuals and the West: The Formative Years: 1875-1914* (London: The Johns Hopkins Press, 1970); the very significant examination of the origins of the Arab-western meeting by Ibrahim Abu-Lughod, *Arab Rediscovery of Europe: A Study in Cultural Encounters* (Princeton, N. J.: Princeton University Press, 1963); a work which promises to become a difficult one to surpass is 'Abd-Allâh al-'Arawî,

middle eastern intellectual activity and in the amount of literature being produced by Muslims on the topic of Christianity. This is not difficult to explain. If the eleventh-century interest in Christianity expressed by Ibn Hazm and others had to do with the emergence of an organized and viable Christian opposition to Islam,[95] the dominance of western Christian power and the increased activity of, first, Catholic and, quite a bit later, Protestant Christian missionaries during the latter era of the Capitulations (1453-1937)[96] began to have a profound effect upon the Musilm intelligentsia in the eighteenth century. The external pressures eventually implied coming to grips with an internal crisis perceived as the stagnation of Muslim intellectual life and its loss of cultural initiative and political potency.[97]

The crisis had an added dimension. Christianity, which Muslims had conditioned themselves to look down upon for seven centuries, had suddenly

al-idyûlûjiyyah al-'arabiyyah al-mu'âsirah [*Contemporary Arab Ideology*] (Beirut: Dâr-ul-Haqîqah, 1970); the wide-ranging but sensitive survey of Islamic responses to the modern world by Kenneth Cragg, *Counsels in Contemporary Islam* (Edinburgh: Edinburgh University Press, 1965); no less wide-ranging but a bit more chatty and opinionated is Wilfred Cantwell Smith's *Islam in Modern History* (Princeton, N. J.: Princeton University Press, 1957), see especially pp. 93-160; a helpful background study, focusing particularly upon 'Abd-ul-Rahmân al-Kawâkibî, is Khaldun S. al-Husry's *Three Reformers: A Study in Modern Arab Political Thought* (Beirut: Khayats, 1966); the careful discussion of Erwin I. J. Rosenthal, *Islam in the Modern National State* (Cambridge: Cambridge University Press, 1965); and, bringing the matter closer to current concerns, there is R. Hrair Dekmejian, *Islam in Revolution: Fundamentalism in the Arab World* (Syracuse, N. Y.: Syracuse University Press, 1985).

[95]Antonie Wessels, *Arab and Christian?*, pp.209-210.

[96]The Ottoman government's grant of *Droit Capitulaire* or "Capitulations" began in 1453 (a special grant of immunity to the Genoese traders in Galata) and continued until the Convention of Montreaux was signed in 1937. Among the earliest beneficiaries of this system of foreign privilege was France, which asserted its right to protect and promote the Catholic community in the Ottoman Empire. Further rights eventually included the right of foreign nationals and their clients to appeal to foreign courts operated under the umbrella of diplomatic missions, exemption from Ottoman taxes, and a variety of other advantages. Eventually, by the nineteenth century, the Capitulations system came to absorb such activities as the publishing of periodical literature. The abolition of the Capitulations (reluctantly recognized in 1937) by the Republic of Turkey ended an era of western privilege in the Middle East.

[97]Among the most important documents we have giving this expression is Jamâl-ud-Dîn alAfghânî and Muhammad 'Abduh, *al-'urwah al-wuthqah* [*The Firm Grip*] (Beirut: Dâr-ul-Kâtib al'Arabî, 1970), an intellectual journal published by the Islamic revivalist and his reformist colleague in Paris between March and October, 1884.

emerged in alliance with an overwhelming powerful technological-scientific culture. Favored by political dominance, the polemical and apologetic literature produced by Christian agencies increased many fold and was widely circulated. It called into question the integrity of Muhammad as a prophet and claimed that the main doctrines of Islam were based largely upon deception and ignorance.[98]

This new aggressive literature of controversy elicited an equally vigorous response from Muslims. The issues at stake were best brought to a head in the fiery writings of Jamâlud-Dîn al-Afghânî and his less volatile but far more profound disciple, Muhammad 'Abduh. While these two pioneers replayed the classical themes, the new and more pressing issue for them was that of the link which Christian propagandists claimed existed between their faith and the prestigious aspects of western civilization—a link mated with the accusation that Islam was, in fact, a factor contributing to backwardness and stagnation.[99]

Both of these assertions were given heed by the new generation of Arabs and others (both Muslim and non-Muslim) who were intensely interested in appropriating the material and political virtues of western civilization. This gave rise to a kind of secularism. Being a Muslim became a bit of an embarrassment for some. Some Muslims (prominently, the founder of the modern state of Turkey, Mustafâ Kamal Atatürk)[100] began to believe the western propagandists who said that Islam was the root cause for Muslim society's backwardness. For them, to become a modern person meant to adopt modern garb in all its western meaning. Religion became a private affair, and if you were a modern Muslim you became almost secretive about

---

[98]See the introduction to 'Abd-ur-Rahmân Bâche-ji-zâdah, *al-fâriq bayn al-makhlûq wa-l-khâliq [The Distinction Between the Creature and the Creator]* (Cairo: Matba'at-ut-Taqaddum, 1904), and the rather more harsh study: Mustafâ Khâlidî and 'Umar Farrûkh, *at-tabshîr wa-l-isti'mâr fî-l-bilâd il-'arabiyyah [Missions and Imperialism in Arab Lands]* (Beirut: al-Maktabah al-'Asriyyah, 5th printing, 1973). See also: Dorman, *Towards Understanding Islam,* pp. 32-39.

[99]The most explicitly revealing document in this regard is that of Muhammad 'Abduh, *al-islâm wa-n-nasrâniyyah bayn al-'ilm wa-l-madaniyyah [Islam and Christianity: Between Knowledge and Culture]* (Cairo: Muhammad 'Alî Subhî, 1964). See also Jamâl-ud-Dîn al-Afghânî, *ar-radd 'alâ-ddahriyyîn [Refutation of the Materialists]* (Cairo: Dâr-Karnak, ND).

[100]For a profile of the extremely significant figure of Mustafâ Kamâl Atatürk see Lord Kinros, *Atatürk: The Rebirth of a Nation* (London: Weidenfeld and Nicolson, 1964), with special note of pp. 384-387.

it. On the surface, and to all intents and purposes, the new Muslim was a secular person. Matters of modern science and education and other outward signs of modernity were treated as though they had little or no religious meaning. As in many western societies, so too among some Muslims being clearly and openly religious became a mark of primitive culture. For the more traditionally committed Muslim, this phenomenon was extremely distressing.

The Muslim community in the early modern era found itself shocked by these signs of compromise and faith's erosion and on the defensive. It could only react to the initiative of others. In the wake of the First World War, the Turkish Republic took action to abolish the Islamic Caliphate (March 3, 1923), once viewed as a fundamental institution.[101] Beginning in the 1930s, however, Arab nations began to achieve at least formal independence. Imperialism, as a force, was weakening. The air came to be filled with dreams of Arab national unity, but they were dreams colored by many different ideological currents, some of which were blatantly secularist. Already, toward the end of the Ottoman period, the advent of printing and mass publication of journals, newspapers, and books (particularly in Egypt) had given Christian Arabs remarkable scope for participation in evolving the new perspectives. There was a renewed quest for a positive statement both of Arab identity and of the issues facing Islam. Not insignificant among these latter is the issue of how Christian Arabs fit into some form of inclusive national society.[102]

[101]See Malcolm H. Kerr, *Islamic Reform: The Political and Legal Theories of Muhammad 'Abduh and Rashîd Ridâ* (Los Angeles: University of California Press, 1966), pp. 153-186; 'Alî 'Abd-ur-Râziq, *al-islâm wa 'usûl-ul-hukm: bahth fî-l-khilâfah wa-l-hukûmah fî-l-islâm [Islam and the Foundations of Government: A Study of the Caliphate and Government in Islam]* (Beirut: DârMaktabat-ul-Hayât, 1966 [first published in Egypt in 1925]).

[102]See the interesting collection of articles by the founder of the Syrian Nationalist Socialist Party, the Christian, Antoine Sa'âdah, *al-islâm fî risâlatay-hi al-masîhîyyah wa-l-muhammadiyyah [Islâm in its Two Vocations, the Christian and the Muhammadan]* (Beirut: Syrian National Socialist Party, 1977—first written between 1941 and 1942), in which he argues that the Arab religious genius is one in two principal expressions, both of which are "muslim" in the lexical meaning of that word. That is, both of them are religions of surrender and obedience to the will of God. For him, of course, this is a political item that should promote the unification and integration of society throughout the Arab world, and it has been because of foreign interference that the ancient divisions have been maintained.

One expression of this search for an inclusive formula was a spate of Muslim meditations in the 1950s and early 1960s on the person of Christ. Muslim authors attempted to craft a portrait of Christ equally acceptable to both Muslims and Christians, or at least one which demonstrated to Christians that a Muslim might see Christ in a manner which offered scope for interreligious peace and understanding.[103] Another dimension in the contemporary discussion is the treatment of issues which concern the nature and destiny of the human being rather than the classical metaphysical focus of the debate, a trend which had already been set in motion by Muhammad 'Abduh. In the contemporary setting it found increasing momentum and sophistication.[104] A third approach by Muslim authors (and by Arab Christians as well) is to call for a moratorium on Christian Muslim polemic and work instead at building a coalition between Muslims and Christians in order to face common political, cultural, and even ethical challenges. This kind of literature transfers the discussion from the theological realm to ideological and political issues like materialism and atheism, a

[103] By way of example: 'Abbâs Mahmûd al-'Aqqâd, *hayât-ul-masîh [The Life of Christ]* (Cairo: Dâr-ul-Hilâl, ND), on whose cover appears a classic portrait of Christ, crowned with thorns; Muhammad Kâmil Husayn, *Qariyah Zâlimah [Tyranical City]* (Cairo: Maktabat-un-Nahdah alMisriyyah, ND), whose significance has been amplified by Kenneth Cragg in the introduction to his translation, *City of Wrong: A Friday in Jerusalem* (Amsterdam: N. V. Djambatan, 1959); Khâlid Muhammad Khâlid, *ma'an 'alâ-t-tarîq: muhammad wa-l-masîh [Together on the Road: Muhammad and Christ]* (Cairo: al-Hadîthah, 1965), very much in this same vein; and 'Abd-al-Hamîd Jawdat as-Sahhâr, *al-masîh 'îsâ ibn-miryam [Christ, the Son of Mary]* (Cairo: Maktabat-un-Nahdah al'Arabiyyah, 1977), upon whose cover is a scene of the Crucifixion, but whose content is largely a rewriting of *The Gospel of Barnabas*.

[104] The Moroccan Muslim philosopher, Muhammad 'Azîz al-Habâbî, writes primarily for a French readership, and his titles have been subsequently translated into Arabic. That, in itself, is an interesting vehicle for dialogue. A selection of his titles: *ash-shakhsâniyyah al-islâmiyyah [Islamic Personalism]* (Cairo: Dâr-ul-Ma'ârif, 1969); *min al-hurriyyât ilâ-t-taharrur [From Freedoms to Emancipation]* (Cairo: Dâr-ul-Ma'ârif, 1971); and *min al-kâ'in ilâ-sh-shakhs [From the Creator to the Person]* (Cairo: Dâr-ul-Ma'ârif, 1968). Another study which merits close examination in this regard is Muhammad Jalâl Sharaf and 'Abd-ur-Rahmân Muhammad 'Îsâwî, *sîkûlûjiyyat-ul-hayâh ar-rûhiyyah fî-l-masîhiyyah wa-l-islâm [The Psychology of Spiritual Life in Christianity and Islam]* (Alexandria: Mansha'at-ul-Ma'ârif, 1972). Another extremely significant contribution is by the Qur'ân scholar, 'Â'ishah 'Abd-ur-Rahmân (who bears the *nom de plume*, Bint-us-Shâti'), *maqâl fî-insân: dirâsah qur'âniyyah [The Doctrine of the Human Being: A Qur'ânic Study]* (Cairo: Dârul-Ma'ârif, 1969).

development foreshadowed in the writings of Jamâl-ud-Dîn al-Afghânî. Finally, there is a still-tentative but growing interest on the part of Muslims in pursuing dialogue with Christians. This is a formal activity which has begun to generate a new literature of self-assessment and mutual assessment on both sides. Although it is characterized by a great deal of mental reserve, it is still an encouraging development.

This new era of Muslim self-evaluation and engagement of Christian themes has witnessed also the disestablishment of the Muslim clergy class as the leading intelligentsia. There has also been a willingness to reassess the value and nature of Muslim Hadîth/Sunnah (traditionally, among the main sources of religious guidance). There have been some new and fresh commentaries written on the Qur'ân and its themes, at times even approaching it with a literary-critical method which would be strange to earlier generations.[105] A new religiously engaged, secular, educated class has emerged whose intellectual attitudes are not locked in step with the classical interests vested in the traditional Muslim fields of learning. Theologians, therefore, have had to accommodate their thought to new radical circumstances. What has emerged is a whole new environment within which Christianity itself is being reassessed from a Muslim perspective.[106]

This new environment has not come about without a struggle. The themes of the old Muslim-Christian face-off have not been abandoned. They are still very much on the agenda. Testimony to this is borne by the revival of interest in the polemical works of Ibn-Hazm, Shahristânî, 'Alî at-Tabarî,[107]

---

[105]Among the exciting modern scholars of the Qur'ân is 'Â'ishah 'Abd-ur-Rahmân, professor at 'Ayn-Shams University in Egypt, and disciple of Amîn al-Khawlî, who has moved into the field of qur'ânic exegesis with penetrating insight. We note: *at-tafsîr al-bayânî li-l-qur'ân il-karîm [The Explanatory Exegesis of the Glorious Qur'ân]* (volume 1) (Cairo: Dâr-ul-Ma'ârif, 1977).

[106]For a survey of modern Muslim voices and perspectives, see the study by Fr. Dr. Munîr Khawwâm, *al-masîh fî-l-fikr al-islâmî al-hadîth wa fî-l-masîhiyyah [Christ and Christianity in Modern Muslim Thought]* (Beirut: Mu'assasat-Khalîfah li-t-Tibâ'ah, 1983).

[107]'Alî bin-Rabban Tabarî, *ad-dîn wa-d-dawlah fî ithbât nubuwwat-muhammad [Religion and Destiny in Affirmation of Muhammad's Prophethood]* (Beirut: Dâr-ul-Âfâq al-Jadîdah, 1977). Tabarî, son of a rabbi (as his name suggests), was a Mu'tazilite apologist during the reign of the Caliph al-Mutawakkil (who is given credit as having helped in the book's composition). Tabarî died around 861, shortly after the book was composed, at the age of eighty-six.

Ibn-Taymiyyah and Ibn-Qayyim-al-Jawziyyah. There is increasing reference to *The Gospel of Barnabas*.[108] The writings of Abû Zahrah,[109] Muhammad al-Ghazzâlî,[110] Shalabî,[111] and Muhammad at-Tahtâwî[112] eloquently illustrate that the classical agenda still demands treatment and restatement. Interest in these writings, in fact, correlates with the rise of reactionary fundamentalism in Egypt, Sa'ûdî Arabia,[113] and the Indian subcontinent, an element which is both vigorous and self-confident.

Amid all of this, in the 1980s, there emerged the quiet voice of Husayn Ahmad Amîn, son of the nationalist reformer of the 1950s. His small

[108]Lonsdale and Laura Ragg (editors and translators), *The Gospel of Barnabas* (Oxford: Clarendon Press, 1907. Use of this document by Muslim apologists was first introduced by Rahmat-Allâh al-Hindî in the late 1800s [Dorman, *Toward Understanding Islam*, p. 55], and has become a standard feature in conservative Muslim anti-Christian argumentation.

[109]Muhammad Abû-Zahrah, *muhâdirât fi-n-nasrâniyyah [Lectures in Nazareenism (Christianity)]* (Cairo: Matba'at-ul-'Ulûm, 1942).

[110]Muhammad al-Ghazzâlî, *at-ta'assub wa-t-tasâmuh bayn al-masîhiyyah wa-l-islâm [Bigotry and Tolerance in Christianity and Islam]* (Cairo: Dâr-ul-Kutub al-Hadîthah, ND).

[111]Ahmad Shalabî, *muqaranat-ul-adyân – 2 – al-masîhiyyah [Comparative Religion – 2 – Christianity]* (Cairo: Maktabat-un-Nahdah al-'Arabiyyah, 1977).

[112]Muhammad 'Izzat Ismâ'îl at-Tahtâwî, *an-nasrâniyyah wa-l-islâm: 'âlimiyyat-ul-islâm wa dawâmu-hu ilâ qiyâm-is-sâ'ah [Nazareenism (Christianity) and Islam: The Universality and Permanence of Islam Until the Day of Reckoning]* (Cairo: Matba'at-ut-Taqaddum, 1977). In thought like that of Tahtâwî, we find a disturbing element: the effort by extremist Muslim polemicists to discredit not just Christianity but Christ himself. The thesis of the book is to knock out all the supports of Christianity (including some which exist within Islam itself, such as the teaching of Christ's return at the end of time), and to demonstrate that its proper and parochial mission to the Jews failed thus yielding the stage to Islam. In this line of thought, Tahtâwî is obliged to work hard to reduce the stature of all other prophets to ineffectual (noble but ineffectual) essays to which Muhammad is the completed master work. Under the circumstances, Jesus in particular is the target. He goes on to argue that Christ's ministry and that of his immediate followers was limited by divine command to the Jews, and that when (upon his disappearance) his mission failed, the subsequent phenomenon of gentile Christianity emerged as a fabrication in the mind of Paul, pseudo-John, and the venal bishops of their day. Hence, Christianity is fundamentally illegitimate. That is a new aberration which may have some connection to earlier arguments, but it has stepped over the brink beyond the Muslim sources themselves, especially the Qur'ân. The fact that it is a position taken in wrath against Christian missionary efforts is not surprising.

[113]Wahhâbism in the Arabian Peninsula, actually developed before the rise of the Usûliyyah and Muslim Brotherhood movements in Egypt. Although drawing inspiration from similar traditional Muslim sources, there is a clear distinction to be drawn even now.

collection of articles published in Beirut in 1983 (and banned in Egypt) has a title which, with tongue-in-cheek, speaks a world of meaning: *A Guide for the Muslim Distressed About the Need to Keep Pace with the Twentieth Century*. One would hope that his effort to administer a little "reality therapy" in the environment of Arab and Muslim culture is not being ignored.

A Connective Remark

The extent to which the Arabian Mission was linked into this swirl of thought, action, and reaction is difficult to document in detail. It is also true that few of the missionaries were conversant with the intellectual history which we have reviewed. From the side of the developing Christian literature, they were certainly informed and even involved. They had to deal with the Muslim reaction as it was translated into social attitudes and responses. The fact remains that the interreligious dynamic greatly conditioned their own outlook and the outlook of those among whom they were sent to labor.

Part Two

Arabian Sketches

The Environment

In Arabia, the dawning years of the twentieth century constitute a period when new political institutions and identities were in the bud. After a tumultuous eighteenth century and an unstable first half of the nineteenth century, the Ottoman grip on Arabia was quickly weakening. As the Ottoman presence atrophied and British imperial interest in the region grew stronger, new political forces emerged in the Arabian peninsula.

The region had severe economic limitations. It was dominated by a desert climate, so that even in the highlands of Najd only small towns could survive. Towns were built around permanent sources of water,[1] and people earned

[1]These were mostly wells, the drawing of whose water was accomplished by an ingenious device: A structure of beams leaned out over the well at the end of which was a pulley. A long rope was fed over the pulley and attached to a skin funnel whose lower opening was attached to a second rope that, as it was lowered

their livelihoods by modest trade, basic crafts,[2] a modest amount of herding, and agriculture – date gardens and whatever would thrive under the shade of the palms: vegetables, fruit trees of various kinds, and alfalfa for fodder. The great bedouin tribes held the balance of power in the interior and controled the routes of trade. They lived off their herds of goats, sheep, and camels; they raided each other and the townsfolk; and, in seasons when regional government was weak, they collected protection fees from merchant caravans and pilgrims alike.

Along the coast of the Arab Gulf were strung economically important port cities – from Basrah in the north to Kuwait, Qatîf, Dammâm, and Bahrain to Doha, Abu Dhabi, Dubay, and Ra's-ul-Khaymah and on to Sohar (reputed birth place of Sinbad the Sailor), Matrah, Muscat, and Sur on the shores of the Arabian Sea. By modern standards these were small towns which lived on commerce, trading between the desert and the sea. Some of them supported significant fleets of trading ships which ventured sometimes as far afield as China, but usually they limited their enterprises to ports of call in India and along the east coast of Africa where the export of slaves was a thriving business.[3] The ports of Kuwait, Bahrain, and Dubay supported large pearling fleets that went out in the warm intermonsoon doldrums season and injected the local economy with capital that fluctuated wildly according to the world market for pearls.

Southern Arabia was divided from the rest of the peninsula by ranges of rugged mountains. They rose up out of the utterly barren Empty Quarter

---

into the well, was drawn taut, lifting the lower extension of the funnel to its upper edge. This funnel was raised and lowered by an animal – customarily a donkey – walking down an inclined plane. When the skin funnel reached the top of the well, the second rope was released and opened the mouth of the funnel, spilling the water into the irrigation channels. Sometimes as many as four of these devices were mounted in tandem. Wells of thirty to forty feet in depth were efficient sources of irrigation. Where wells had to be dug deeper, gardening was not profitable. A few places had natural springs (as on the island of Bahrain and at some points in the Hasâ' Oasis complex).

[2] Tradesmen were mainly weavers, makers of clothes, brass workers, and an occasional gunsmith.

[3] See the remarkable narrative of Tim Severin in his *The Sindbad Voyage* (London: Hutchinson, 1982), documenting the successful modern voyage of an Omani dhow to China. A classic reference on Arab seafaring is David Howarth's *Dhows* (London: Quartet Books, 1977). Alan Villiers, *Sons of Sinbad* (New York: Charles Scribner's Sons, 1940) records Villiers last-of-its-kind experience, sailing with a Kuwaiti ship captain of the al-Hamad clan in the late 1930s.

and, after climbing to harsh wind-eroded peaks, dove abruptly into the Arabian Sea and Indian Ocean, forming some of the world's most spectacular coastlines and beaches. The desert and mountains provided a climatic and cultural, as well as political, barrier that from time immemorial has always divided Arabia into North and South.

Ancient Arabia: Christianity and Islam

Arabia is a harsh land whose people are almost without exception Muslim.[4] It had also once been home to many Christians.[5] Yemen and the Hadramaut were once part of a Christian kingdom, a client state to Christian Ethiopia. There were also several major tribes in the mountains of the Hijâz and among the desert rovers of the interior who wholly or in part espoused Christianity. Furtive archeology has identified the ruins of at least one Christian sanctuary near the ancient port of Qatîf on the shores of the Arab Gulf. Another has been discovered and quietly reinterred on the Qatar peninsula. Still another in the Emirates shows signs of once having been a monastery. There is evidence that some recognition of Christian sensibilities was built into the pagan sanctuary in Mecca which, to promote trade and the security of the Meccan caravans, was designed to accommodate all the tribal gods of Arabia. When Muhammad, the founding prophet of Islam, began his ministry in the early years of the seventh century there were individual ascetics, *hunafâ'* (singular: *hanîf*), who espoused monotheism, and some of these were Christian. One, Waraqâ bin-Nawfal, was the cousin of Muhammad's first wife, Khadîjah, and an early supporter of his.

[4]The Jews of the Yemen are perhaps the only exception, living in the urban concentrations of San'â' and the other main cities and surviving as artisans. This Jewish community was much reduced in the aftermath of the founding of the modern State of Israel in 1947, having been lured into an almost mass migration in an enterprise dubbed "Operation Magic Carpet." In recent years, however, as disillusionment with the Israeli experiment has grown within the disadvantaged Oriental (Safardî) Jewish community in Israel, some of those who left are quietly returning to their original homeland.

[5]See the interesting and informative chapter on early Christianity in Arabia by Ida Paterson Storm, "Religion in Arabia," chapter 2, in Harold Storm, *Whither Arabia? A Survey of Missionary Opportunity* (New York: World Dominion Press, 1938), pp. 31-51. Her conclusions concerning why Islam was finally supreme in Arabia match those of other Arabia missionaries: The church in Arabia was torn by divisions and corrupt and therefore no Christian witness could endure [p. 44].

To understand how Islam developed, it is important to remember that Arabia stood apart from the great empires of the day, Byzantium and Sassanian Persia – the one Orthodox Christian and the other Zoroastrian in religious character. On the fringes of these two empires were renegade (or "heretic") Christian groups who marched to their own drummers[6] as well as Jewish settlements of various tendencies and a variety of pagan communities. Ethiopia, dominated by a non-Chalcedonian form of Christianity associated with the great Coptic Orthodox Church of Egypt, held a strong position in southern Arabia. It failed, though, in its effort to expand its influence northward to Mecca in the closing years of the sixth century. But, for the most part, the Arab tribes stubbornly continued to espouse a religious attitude which exalted the power of fate and populated the land with a multitude of tenacious spirits and demigods – their sacred trees, holy stones, and enchanted places of sanctuary peppered the Arabian landscape.[7]

[6]It is difficult to summarize briefly the varieties of Christianity which existed in the Middle East. Historically, these are to be divided into those who participated in and concurred with the findings of the Council of Chalcedon (451) and those who did not. The Chalcedonian churches were those allied to the political power of the Roman Empire – the See of Rome (the stem of Protestantism in the sixteenth century) and the various patriarchates of the Eastern Orthodox church which recognized the See of Constantinople as the first among equals. The non-Chalcedonians included the Oriental Orthodox churches of Syria, Egypt, Armenia, and Ethiopia (which have been branded "Monophysites" by their detractors), and the "Nestorian" Assyrian Church of the East (whose main concentration is in Iraq). The intramural bickering of these churches, it was held by their latterday Protestant critics, undermined their evangelical zeal and was blamed for the failure to win Arabia for Christ before the advent of Islam. Such criticism, however, is cheap, superficial, and almost intentionally lacks understanding of the more profound factors which led to the advent of Islam.

[7]Although the Arabs formally adopted Islam, the magic-filled landscape did not vanish. Pagan shrines continued to be frequented, sometimes furtively, down to the most recent of times. One such was the shrine to Ashteroth on the island of Faylaka at the head of Kuwait Bay. The author observed the shrine in active use in the late 1960s. The taboo protecting the site said that the person who destroyed the shrine would die. One attempt on the part of the governor of Kuwait to demolish the small domed structure was abandoned when the man fell deathly ill. (He swiftly recovered his health when demolition work was ordered to cease.) Then the powerful magic of bureaucracy was brought into play. An order "went out" that the shrine should be destroyed, and Pakistani laborers accomplished the task in short order without any ill effects being observed. The lesson learned: In a properly functioning bureaucracy not even the gods can ascertain who is responsible.

Muhammad came to challenge this Arabian pagan spirituality. In the sophisticated urban center of Mecca, around 610 A.D., he began to preach a revolutionary message. Against the syncretistic pluralism of the day which Mecca's merchants manipulated to their profit, he proclaimed the uniqueness and singularity of God. His vision was of a God who demanded worship out of gratitude and close obedience to his *Sharî'ah*, his law. He rewarded the faithful with his bounty in this life and on the Day of Decision (*yom-ud-dîn*) – Judgment Day. The ungrateful and the hypocrites would find that day difficult to bear. The pantheon of Mecca, with its crowd of idols and shrines clustered around the central Ka'bah (and the Black Stone inset in its wall),[8] was a place Muhammad demanded be purified and devoted once again to the praise and worship of God alone. The model of that worship was the patriarch Abraham who, it is believed, rebuilt and dedicated that ancient Adamic shrine assisted by his son, Ishmael. And the Qur'ân, the sacred book which Muhammad recited to his followers and which they inscribed under his direction, spoke out against those who would compromise God's inimitable singularity by attributing to him a son. "Declare: He, God, is singular, God impervious; he neither procreates nor is he the product of procreation; and none has ever been his equal."[9]

Muhammad's career was controversial. He was persecuted by those of his own clan who held power in Mecca and spent twelve years of nearly fruitless preaching during which, with a few notable exceptions, he attracted mainly the down-and-out of the city.[10] Then he was approached by two tribes from the oasis city of Yathrib to act as a *hakam*, an adjudicator, in a controversy between them. After being assured that he and his followers would be granted sanctuary in consideration for his services, he and his people emigrated to Yathrib where he established a theocratic government. Muhammad's migration to Yathrib occurred in 622, and Muslims claim that

---

[8]English acquires its word "cube" from Ka'bah. The Ka'bah is a modest and featureless stone structure which may have housed a fertility deity at one time. The Black Stone, inset in the wall, was said to have been given to Adam by Gabriel. It is claimed originally to have been white, but after the eons of exposure to human sin and perversion it has turned black. Under Muslim devotion, the Ka'bah is covered with an elaborately embroidered cloth covering that is periodically replaced.

[9]*The Qur'ân*, Sûrah 112, entitled *al-Ikhlâs* (sincerity).

[10]Those to whom he could not personally extend protection, he encouraged to take refuge in Ethiopia where they were given sanctuary.

date as their genesis as a community. Working out of Yathrib as a power base, Muhammad was able to break the power of his Meccan antagonists in 630 and personally fulfill his desire to purify the sanctuary in Mecca for the worship of God. The city of Yathrib came to be renamed Madînah,[11] and Muhammad ruled there until his death in 632.[12]

Muhammad's character and habits were quite unlike that of one of his heroes, Jesus the son of Mary, the Messiah of the Christians. He cut a figure more akin to that of Moses, whom he strove closely to emulate. There was a magnetism about him and his message which permitted the Arabs to choose a monotheism which did not compromise their independence over against the Greeks, Persians, or Ethiopians, but rather reflected their own characteristics and strengthened their autonomy.[13] From 622, when Muhammad established the nucleus of the Muslim state in Madînah, the speed with which Islam conquered the Arabian peninsula was remarkable. The expansion of Islam after Muhammad's death beyond the borders of

[11]The name is a rendering of a longer title. It could be thought of as *madînat-un-nabî* [the Prophet's City] or as *al-madînah al-munawwarah* [the Light Filled City, by virtue of the Prophet's ministry there]. In either case it was more simply known as *al-madînah* [The City].

[12]The ancient Arabian calendar was lunar. In each third year or so it was adjusted to the seasonal rhythms of the solar year by the addition of a thirteenth month. The control of this addition was in the hands of the religious functionaries of the pagan sanctuary in Mecca. During Muhammad's sojourn in Madînah a *sûrah* of the Qur'ân was revealed which had wide-reaching impact. "The complement of months in God's book, from the day he created the heavens and the earth, is twelve. Four are holy. That is the religion of merit. Do not bedarken yourselves in this respect. Do battle with all polytheists just as they battle against all of you. Know that God sides with the pious" (Sûrah 9:35). The upshot of this dictum, of course, was to emancipate the Muslim calendar—with its holy months and religious festivals—from the rotation of the seasons. It constituted a clear break from pagan fertility rhythms. The solar year, regulated under the rubrics of what we know as the Gregorian Calendar, is approximately eleven days longer than the Islamic lunar year. [See G.S.P. Freeman-Grenville, *The Muslim and Christian Calendars* (London: Oxford University Press. 1963).]

[13]Paul Harrison, showing deep insight, observed that out of Muhammad's religious experiences "was born a religious system which was the best product of Mohammed's mind, and much more than that — it was the crystallization of the mind of a race." He adds, "It is because his thinking and feeling were the thinking and feeling of a great race that he stands out as one of the great men of the world." And further: "Probably not six men in the whole history of the world have made such a mark as he" [Paul W. Harrison, *The Arab at Home* (New York: Thomas Y. Crowell Company, 1924), pp. 188-190].

Arabia to encompass much of the known world is still an event without historical parallel.

Arabs have continued to be proud of that history, and – though the power of the wide-flung Muslim empire slipped from their hands within a space of less than 200 years – their Prophet, his Book, and their language have continued to shape the thoughts of the entire Muslim world from the Pacific to the Atlantic Oceans. As the Muslim empire developed and sprawled, however, Arabia remained distinct, chronically ungovernable by empire builders, the preserve of the inimitable Arab style of self-government, and uniquely the heartland of Islam.

During the early years of Muslim expansion, there were few instances of specific Christian populations in Arabia being forcibly relocated outside the peninsula. Some may have chosen (or been urged) to migrate northward. There is a Tradition[14] that, as the Prophet Muhammad lay dying, he said, "In Arabia there shall be but one religion." And certainly, because Arabia was the recruiting ground for the Muslim armies of conquest,[15] there was a

---

[14]*Hadîth*: The sources of Islamic authority are three: the *Qur'ân*, the *Hadîth* or *Sunnah*, and analogical reasoning, *qiyâs*. The first is paramount since it recites the very words of God without human admixture in their authorship. The second–the words or practice of the Prophet Muhammad recollected by reliable witnesses, meticulously recorded, and evaluated according to a more or less critical apparatus–is a supplementary source whose authority is based upon the doctrine that the Prophet was restrained by God from committing error ... immunized, as it were, against it. He was *ma'sûm min az-zalal*. What he said and did, therefore, was iconographic: it depicted divine truth in graphic form. The particular *Hadîth* in question is frequently quoted and shapes the policy of the modern state of Sa'ûdî Arabia with regard to the legal presence of non-Muslim worshiping groups in Arabia. *Qiyâs*, the use of analogical reasoning, however, is not universally acceptable, especially by the more conservative schools of jurisprudence. They view the gift of human reason with deep skepticism. These latter, therefore, have had to develop a far larger body of often questionable *Hadîth* to take up the slack.

[15]The campaign of Muslim expansion is described in Arabic by the term, *fath*. Literally it means the "opening up" of other lands to the saving message of Islam. Here we may be sensitive to the caricature of Islam as essentially violent and warlike. That sensitivity does not belong to the seventh century. The *futuhât* (plural of *fath*) rode on the wings of religiously ardent armies, and those armies engaged in very military conquest. There is some irony in the fact that the eleventh-century Christian Crusades owe something of their ideology to the Muslim concept. Where the Muslim model differed from the latter-day imitation was in the refusal of the victorious Muslim commanders to demand by force the conversion of subjugated peoples. Personal religious conviction was an individual

strong interest in encouraging all of its population to become Muslim. Marshall Hodgson, however, indicates that some Christian Arab tribes openly joined the early Muslim conquests of the Fertile Crescent and Persia.[16] But in the end, those Arabs who persisted in considering themselves Christian or Jewish were constrained for political reasons either to become Muslim or to migrate from the Arabian heartland northward and westward. Except for the Jews of Yemen, Arabia became entirely Muslim during the reign of the Caliph 'Umar (634-644). Richard Bell comments: "The Arabs within the Peninsula seem to have gone over from Christianity to Islam without much hesitation or regret."[17]

Arabia: From Modern Times to Oil

The transition from seventh-century Arabia to the Arabia of modern times may seem an incredible leap. But, with the notable exception of Iraq, the tides of history were stronger and more dramatic beyond the region of the Arabian Mission's primary activity. These historical tides began to ebb from the region when the Umayyads shifted the caliphate's capital from

---

matter. The qur'ânic saying, *lâ ikrâha fî-d-dîn* (There is no coercion in religion.) (Sûrah 2, "The Cow," vs. 256), continues to be a conscience-prod for Muslims and a watchword among them. The purpose of the *futuhât* was to bring an increasing portion of the world under Muslim administration (*Dârul-Islâm*) which, by implication, was the proper human expression of God's will in matters political.

A second term, more recognizable in the West, is *jihâd*. Its meaning is "the exercise of effort" or "struggle," a necessary characteristic of true faith. In that broad meaning, it is sometimes cited as one of the pillars of the Muslim religion. In Muslim usage there is some ambiguity with respect to *jihâd*. It was certainly an element in the motivation of a soldier of the *futuhât*. He was a *mujâhid*. The effort he expended in battle had a religious sanction. At times, therefore, *jihâd* is to be identified as the moral and spiritual mode by which *fath* is achieved. In this context, it can become a close approximation to the conventional English translation, "holy war." On the other hand, it is a term which has far deeper meaning. It describes a Muslim's religious posture. *Jihâd* is the day-by-day struggle of the Muslim to remain spiritually and morally faithful. But ordinary human beings are rarely profound, and when a Muslim religious leader declares *jihâd* against this or that political entity, it is the more superficial meaning of the term that is being used.

[16]Marshall G. S. Hodgson, *The Venture of Islam, Vol. I: The Classical Age of Islam* (Chicago: The University of Chicago Press, 1974), p. 229.

[17]Richard Bell, *The Origin of Islam in its Christian Environment* [London: Frank Cass & Co. Ltd., 1968 (originally published in 1926)], p. 182.

Madînah to Damascus.[18] The founding of the 'Abbâsid Caliphate in Baghdad (750 A.D.) marks the end of Arab control of the global dimensions of the Islamic movement, and the Arabian peninsula slipped into its own mainly parochial concerns.[19]

The centers of empire shifted over the centuries, coming to rest strongly upon Persia (Iran) in the east and Egypt (from 756 to 1492, also Spain) in the west. Baghdad finally fell to Hulagu's Mongols in the thirteenth century, and from then on the story of Islamic government became largely a Turkish one. A member of the caliph's family reputedly escaped, and a shadow caliphate was maintained under the patronage of the Slave Kings of Egypt (the Mamlukes) until the sixteenth century. The mantle of the caliphate was then assumed by the Ottoman sultans of Anatolia, a Turkish dynasty.

It was under the Ottomans that the last political barrier to an Islamic advance into Europe was finally broken down. Constantinople fell in 1453. At about the same time (1503) Shî'ah Islam was being established in Iran, and Muslim Spain, after a four-century battle, was tottering on the brink of expulsion during the last phases of the *Reconquista*.[20] That seriously

---

[18] Down through the centuries Muslims have bickered most fiercely among themselves over the question of the transmission of sanctioned authority. The word, "caliphate," is an anglicized version of the Arabic *khilâfah*. The caliph (*khalîfah*) was understood to be the deputy/successor of the Prophet Muhammad in his role as governor and administrator of the Muslim community. The genealogy and qualifications for this caliph absorbed Muslim theologians and legists for centuries. When the office was abolished by Mustafâ Kamâl Atatürk in 1924, it threw the Muslim world into a serious identity crisis from which it has yet to emerge.

[19] The exception to this are the Qarmathians. An off-shoot of the Ismâ'îlî Shî'ah variation in Islam, the Qarmathians emerged as a force from the ninth to the eleventh centuries. They formed a republican Islamic state in the eastern oasis region of Arabia. They threatened both the 'Abbâsids to the north and the newly formed Ismâ'îlî Fâtimid Caliphate of Egypt, terrorized the pilgrim traffic headed to and from Mecca and Madînah, and even for a time stole the Black Stone from Mecca (which they eventually returned). Never actually conquered, the Qarmathians were eventually contained and isolated. By the eleventh century Sunnî Islam had been reestablished in eastern Arabia. But it is interesting to observe that the detractors of the Wahhâbî movement of the eighteenth century note not only the geographical coincidence between the modern movement and the Qarmathians, but draw parallels to their ferocity and bigotry as well.

[20] The struggle for Spain, which the Muslims had invaded in the late seventh century and had controlled since the eighth century, attained the status of a Christian Holy War in the mid-eleventh century. The Kingdom of Castile reconquered Toledo in 1085; Granada, the last Muslim outpost in Spain, fell to the combined forces of Aragon and Castile in 1492.

disrupted the integrity of the Islamic world. With Iran in between, Islamic culture and political development diverged between the Indian subcontinent in the east and the Mediterranean Basin in the west. By the sixteenth century the western Islamic empire was Ottoman. On its western and northern borders stood a fragmented Europe beginning to coalesce into nation states; on its eastern frontier stood the antagonistic Shî'ah Safavid empire. Arabia, a south-dangling appendix, was not of much concern so long as control over the holy cities of Mecca and Madînah were not made a problem. Still containing those main symbols of the faith, Arabia was its own world, almost purely Muslim.

It was part of the audacity of the Arabian Mission that it was directed stubbornly toward that part of the Muslim world which seemed least vulnerable to the Christian message. But the mission took up its task at precisely the time when a new force, no less passionate and audacious in its own right, had revived in Arabia, insisting more fervently than ever that Arabia was the exclusive preserve of Islam.

The Wahhâbîs, as they were called by their enemies, were a purifying sect of Islam. In the mid-eighteenth century Britain was encircling Arabia with its influence, and the Ottoman Empire was falling into the grasp of foreigners. Around 1745, in the Najdî town of Dar'iyyah, near the modern Sa'ûdî capital of Riyadh, a controversial and headstrong religious teacher, Muhammad bin-'Abd-ul-Wahhâb (The Shaykh), allied himself with the amîr of Dar'iyyah, Muhammad bin-Sa'ûd. Between them they forged a strong alliance for a formidable spiritual, ideological, and political movement. It was motivated by vague anxiety over the inroads of western powers, but it was also aware that Muslims on their own account had strayed far from their roots in the pure message of the Prophet.

The Wahhâbîs knew themselves as "The Unitarians" (*al-muwahhidûn*) or, simply, "The Believers" (*al-mu'minûn*).[21] Theirs was a mission to purify

---

[21]*Al-mu'minûn* (the believers) is the term applied in the Qur'ân to loyal Muslims, contrasting them to hypocrites, *munâfiqûn*, who only feigned piety for profit. It

Islam of all the dross which the effete culture of the Ottomans had mixed into Muslim society. Their heroes and intellectual guides were the figures of Ibn Hanbal (died in 855) and Ibn Taymîyah (died in 1328), men who had defied caliphs and princes and upheld the strict cause of conservatism for the sake of the people's spiritual well-being. The Wahhâbîs opposed virtually all foreign-inspired innovations as corruption and, where they ruled, they enforced stern and often ruthless moral and religious discipline. Unabashedly militant, their initial success was dramatic enough to make the Ottoman throne tremble and even to trouble counsels as far away as London.

The Wahhâbîs were suppressed in 1818 by the then-rising power of Egypt under Muhammad 'Alî Pasha, but the house of Sa'ûd survived and continued to embody the pristine values of the old shaykh whose vision they had once so ably implemented. Through the years they retained a substantial foothold in Najd, remaining faithful to their seminal ideology. At the dawn of the twentieth century, they stood ready to emerge again as the dominant power of Arabia, always with the caveat, "God willing."

From the mid-1800s[22] until January 15, 1902, the fortunes of the Wahhâbîs and the house of Âl Sa'ûd were depicted as being in irreversible decline. The house of Âl Rashîd, erstwhile Wahhâbî lieutenants and then Ottoman clients, seemed to be in the ascendancy from their stronghold of Hâ'il in Jabal Shammar, ruling central Arabia.[23] Samuel Zwemer, in his first major book, reflected the wishful thinking of the time:

> In 1890 a final attempt was made by the partisans of the old [Sa'ûdî] dynasty to rebel against the [Rashîdî] Amir and secure the

was the Wahhâbî conceit that they were the quintessential Muslims, and that other Muslims were (for the most part) apostate.

[22]The death by cholera in 1865 of Faysal bin Turkî Âl Sa'ûd, the seventh Wahhâbî Imâm and grandfather of 'Abd-ul-'Azîz, marked the beginning of forty-odd years of indifferent leadership for the Wahhâbî movement.

[23]The Shammar tribal confederation formed an alliance with the Âl Sa'ûd when Faysal bin-Turkî sponsored the initiative of 'Abd-Allâh ibn-Rashîd to regain control of the fortress of Hâ'il some time around 1843. The alliance, however, was temporary. The Shammar had no particular taste for Wahhâbî discipline and ideology. With the death of Faysal in 1865 and his sons' struggle against each other for power, Jabal Shammar asserted its independence and the alliance ended. In early the early 1870s the Shammar became allied with the Ottomans against the Wahhâbîs.

independence of Riad. It was fruitless; and the severe defeat of the
rebels proved it final. 24

Within two years of the publication of these words the house of Âl Sa'ûd,
under the leadership of 'Abd-ul-'Azîz bin-'Abd-ur-Rahmân bin-Faysal bin-
Turkî bin-'Abd-Allâh binMuhammad bin-Sa'ûd (whom the world came to
know as "King Ibn Saud" or simply as "Ibn Saud"), had set in motion the
movement which in one blow displaced the Âl Rashîd and quickly gained
control of the Najd highlands. By 1910 the Wahhâbîs had ejected the last
vestiges of Ottoman rule from eastern Arabia, and by 1915 they had
established Sa'ûdî power on the Gulf coast, the amîrates under British
protection excepted. Building his empire, 'Abd-ul-'Azîz Âl Sa'ûd was in an
acquisative frame of mind. The British check on his ambitions was significant.

By 1917 the power of Britain in the region had also been openly asserted.
Under Sir Percy Cox,25 then British civil commissioner in Iraq, a conference

24Zwemer, *Arabia* ..., p. 201. The actual bid to revive the fortunes of the house of
   Âl Sa'ûd began in 1874 and ended in 1891. Zwemer was not the only one who
   prematurely announced their demise and that of the Wahhâbîs. Lady Ann Blunt,
   the wife and constant companion of a peripatetic British traveler, wrote around
   1894: "The power of the Ibn Sa'ud family in Arabia might truly be considered to
   have come to an end and to have passed to the Al Rashíd of Ha'il. Everything that
   was truly national in thought and respectable in feeling began to group itself
   around Muhammad Al Rashid, the great Amír of Ha'il and Jabal Shammar"
   [quoted in H. R. P. Dickson, *Kuwait and Her Neighbours* (London: George Allen
   & Unwin Ltd., 1956), p. 128].
      The Arabia missionaries often encountered Wahhâbî spokesmen and agitators
   in their work, and their frustration is reflected in Zwemer's overconfident and
   certainly premature prediction. For their part, the British were no great promoters
   of the Wahhâbîs either. They preferred smaller, less forceful, more biddable
   rulers and ideological systems in the lands they chose to dominate. The Sa'ûdîs
   were far too forceful. But when the inevitable appeared they learned to work with
   it, and the altogether admirable person of 'Abd-ul'Azîz Âl Sa'ûd eventually won
   over their sympathies (as he did those of many missionaries as well).
25After a start in the Indian Army, and a term as assistant political resident in British
   Somaliland (1892-1901), Cox entered service in the Gulf as the British consul in
   Muscat in 1901. From that base he traveled extensively in Oman and across the
   mountains into the Trucial (sometimes called the Pirate) Coast, devoting much

was convened in 'Uqayr, the purpose of which was to regularize regional relationships and draw in national borders between Iraq, Kuwait, and Sa'ûdî Arabia.[26] It was a British priority, and the Arab participants came prepared to mollify Cox while not taking the matter too seriously. It proved, however, to be one of those pivotal events, repercussions of which are still being felt.

Cox, trained in India, was a man of autocratic preferences. Through his long career in the Gulf and in Iraq, he won for himself a high reputation as a man of justice and fair dealing. He was an old-world British colonial officer and worked in all things to assert the authority of the Crown. But, as Harold Dickson, one of his young political officers and close associates, observed, he planted the seeds for the unpopularity of the British in the Gulf when, at the 'Uqayr Conference from 21 November to 2 December, 1922, he unilaterally dictated and imposed western-style national boundaries on Sa'ûdî Arabia, Iraq, and Kuwait.[27] The subsequent revolt of 'Abd-ul-'Azîz Âl

of his energy to suppressing the slave trade. He became Britain's political resident in Busheir in 1904. With the occupation of Southern Iraq by the British at the outbreak of hostilities in 1914, he was given the additional responsibility of chief political officer for the Indian Expeditionary Force in Iraq. In 1917 he became the first British civil commissioner in Iraq. Between 1918 and 1920 he was British minister to Tehran. When he returned to Iraq in 1920, he adopted the title of British high commissioner in Iraq and took up his residence in Baghdad [John Marlowe, *The Persian Gulf in the Twentieth Century* (London: The Cresset Press, 1962), pp. 64-66]. Cox retired in 1924, his last official act being to sign the protocol to the treaty between Britain and Iraq, which he had been a key factor in negotiating.

[26]A preparatory conference was held in the amîrate of Muhammarah, on the Shatt-ul-'Arab, hosted by its ruler, Shaykh Khaz'al from 3 to 5 May, 1922. In it the broader questions about frontiers between Sa'ûdî Arabia and Iraq were thought to have been settled.

[27]Dickson, *Kuwait...*, pp. 270-280. As one who observed the process first hand, participated in it, and had to live with its repercussions, Dickson is to be acknowledged as one of the most trustworthy reporters of this particular event. Dickson observed, "...I doubt if any other person in the world could have succeeded as he did, but he grievously harmed a great reputation for fair dealing among the Arabs, which he had justly acquired over a long period of years..." (p. 276). Dickson continued, "This arbitrary boundary of Western type between Iraq and Najd was, in my opinion, a serious error. It resulted ultimately in Ibn Sa'ud, almost for the first time in history, restricting the annual natural movements of Najd tribes towards the north." Dickson also felt strongly that 'Abd-ul-'Azîz Al Sa'ûd, while conceding that he had been outmaneuvered by Cox and the Iraqis, resolved to make the best of a bad deal. The boundaries would divert trade, which had heretofore been controlled by Kuwait, to the Sa'ûdî ports of 'Uqayr, Qatîf, and Jubayl. It would also allow him to isolate his people from contact with

Sa'ûd's Ikhwân generals in 1926, partly in reaction to the 'Uqayr Conference, was the first major convulsion of an era of radical realignment.

Cox's move in 1922 was designed to limit the ambitions of 'Abd-ul-'Azîz Âl Sa'ûd. As World War I came to an end, the Sultân of Najd turned the attention of his Wahhâbî followers toward the West. As the Wahhâbîs pictured it, the holy sites of Islam – the shrine cities of Mecca and Madînah – were governed by an unworthy man. Husayn bin-'Alî Âl Hâshim, father of King 'Abd-Allâh of Transjordan and King Faysal of Iraq, was that man.[28]

environments over which he had no control. "But," Dickson concluded, "natural lines of trade cannot thus be lightly interfered with or laid aside, and, as a result of his policy, we have seen nothing but trouble. Had Ibn Sa'ud left well alone, it is not improbable that we should not have had the Ikhwan rebellion of 1929-1930, or the friction between Iraq and Najd that preceded it, or the long-drawn-out fourteen years' agony of the Kuwait blockade" (Dickson, *Kuwait*, pp. 276-277).

[28]Husayn bin-'Alî Âl Hâshim was a descendant of the Prophet Muhammad's clan. As a person of symbolic standing, Sultan 'Abd-ul Hamîd had kept him in Istanbul, under close observation, and the young Husayn became adept at the devious ways required for survival at the Ottoman court. In 1908 the Young Turks came to power in Istanbul, and Husayn was appointed sharîf of the holy city of Mecca, a position of more prestige than power. In 1914 the Ottoman Empire entered the World War I in alliance with Germany against Britain, and during the following year Husayn engaged in a secret correspondence with the viceroy of Egypt, Sir Henry McMahon, in which Husayn bargained for his best advantage should he declare for Britain and urge the Arabs to rise in revolt. On June 10, 1916, Husayn declared the "Arab Revolt" against the Ottomans without knowing that Britain, France, and Russia had only the month before come to an agreement concerning the dismemberment of the Ottoman Empire which would cancel the painfully negotiated concessions he had gained. His role in the Arab Revolt was marginal, the main task being assumed by his third son, Faysal, assisted by the Englishman, Col. T. E. Lawrence. A year and a half after the Arab Revolt was declared, the British made another secret commitment, this time to the Zionist movement. The "Balfour Declaration" confessed the British Government to "view with favor" the establishment in Palestine of a "Homeland for the Jewish People." In the long term a more significant commitment, this further undercut Husayn's position. When the war ended in 1918 and all the secret agreements were aired, Husayn declared that he had been betrayed. Of course, he was right. The effort of Britain to compensate by establishing 'Abd-Allâh as king of Transjordan and, later, Faysal as king of Iraq did not mollify the old man. He became something

Husayn had assumed the title, King of the Arab Countries, in 1916,[29] and he declared himself the caliph – the spiritual and temporal sovereign – of all Muslims in March of 1924. Although none recognized these pretentious claims, they (especially the latter) provided the perfect pretext for the Sultan of Najd.[30] By October 1925 his Wahhâbî troops had conquered Mecca and Madînah, Husayn had retired to Cyprus,[31] and 'Abd-al-'Azîz had assumed the title of king for himself. The Kingdom of Sa'ûdî Arabia was founded.

Having realized his main political objectives in 1925, the new king of Arabia then tried to cool down his own inflamed army. This led to the revolt of a large and powerful group which knew itself as the Ikhwân, "the brotherhood."[32]

The Ikhwân, the radical point of the Wahhâbî spear, were stamped by a strong ideological focus, but they also represented a nationalist reaction to

of a laughing stock in the eyes of other Arabs, and his disdain for Wahhâbî teachings nurtured an enmity between him and the Sultan of Najd, Imâm of the Wahhâbîs, his neighbor in Arabia. The Wahhâbîs came to depict him as corrupt and venial and no fit guardian of Islam's holy shrines. They too, probably, were correct.

[29] Britain and France recognized him only as king of the Hijâz in 1917.

[30] 'Abd-ul-'Azîz Âl Sa'ûd was officially given the title of "Sultan of Najd" by an assembly of Najdî tribal leaders and religious dignitaries August 12, 1921. The formality was devised in order to give Najd and its governor international standing in the face of Faysal bin-Husayn's election as king of Iraq (Khaz'al, *Kuwait* 5.1, p. 45).

[31] Fleeing his Wahhâbî enemy, Husayn passed his kingly title to his elder son, 'Alî, who had no desire to hold it. 'Alî, for his part, took refuge with his younger brother in Baghdad. Husayn died in 'Ammân, Transjordan, in 1931, a broken and bitter old man, betrayed of all his dreams.

[32] The Ikhwân movement represents a resuscitation of Wahhâbism. According to Harold Dickson [*Kuwait...*, p 148ff], it had its birth in the teaching and preaching of Shaykh 'Abd-ul-Karîm al-Maghrabî who, in 1899, established himself in the town of 'Irtawiyyah in the Najd. It remained a small movement until 'Abd-ul-'Azîz Âl Sa'ûd took notice of it in 1914, following his reconquest of al-Hasâ' and the eastern provinces. In early 1916 he formally announced his approval of the Ikhwân and was adopted as their Imâm. It was a crucial decision. 'Abd-ul-'Azîz had mounted a steed difficult to control (Dickson, *Kuwait...*, p. 153ff.).

encroaching foreign influences. The movement aimed to preserve Arabia for the Arabs. 'Abd-ul-'Azîz Âl Sa'ûd found it a useful force which, in the end, immeasurably enhanced his power. He used the Ikhwân to attack Kuwait during the reign of Shaykh Sâlim al-Mubârak Âl Sabâh. But as on that occasion he was obliged to limit his ambitions, he increasingly found the Ikhwân a liability. Beginning in 1922 (from the time of the 'Uqayr Conference) he found himself struggling to keep control of his Ikhwân lieutenants, especially Faysal ad-Duwwîsh, paramount shaykh of the powerful tribe of the Mutayr, general of the Sa'ûdî forces which attacked Kuwait in 1920. The westward campaign which won the Hijâz for Sa'ûdî Arabia and 'Abd-ul-'Azîz his crown served as a temporary diversion, but it did not forestall the inevitable.

The Ikhwân resented 'Abd-ul-'Azîz's pretensions to the title, "king;"[33] his interruption of their traditional migratory patterns by agreeing to set state boundaries where none had ever existed; his adoption of modern innovations such as the motor car, telegraph, and wireless; his restriction of their plundering of the Hijâz after its conquest; his curbing of their seasonal raiding parties; his refusal to follow up on his obligation as their imâm to declare *jihâd* (holy war) on Iraq; and his efforts to settle them in villages and change their whole way of life. They came to know that he had used them for his own purposes, and in 1929 they raised the standard of revolt.

Out of 'Abd-ul-'Azîz's control, these battle-hardened and masterfully led desert troops moved to expand the holy empire in spite of their sovereign's reluctance. They began raiding northward. Their attacks on border tribes in Iraq were a direct challenge to the newly founded British authority there, and Britain (with the tacit blessing of 'Abd-ul-'Azîz himself) moved in with air and sea power, mobilizing the newly organized Arab Army of Iraq to guard the frontiers.

The rebellion of the Ikhwân also had a tragic impact upon the Arabian Mission. Western businessmen and representatives of oil interests had

---

[33]The word for king in Arabic is *malik*. It implies ownership beyond simple sovereignty. Among true Arabs, the motto has it, there are no kings.

begun to investigate the resources of the region. The Anglo-Persian Oil Company (later named Anglo-Iranian and still later British Petroleum) was launched in 1909 by William D'Arcy. The oil refinery in 'Abbadân on the Shatt-ul-'Arab went into production in 1913. In 1923 an adventurous New Zealander, Major Frank Holmes, negotiated on behalf of American interests the first oil concession with 'Abd-ul-'Azîz Âl Sa'ûd and carried on from there to do the same in Bahrain (1925) and Kuwait (1934).[34] The Kirkûk oil fields in northern Iraq also came into production in 1927, those in Bahrain in 1932; the fields of Sa'ûdî Arabia and Kuwait were established in 1938 with producing wells. The Gulf became the focus of blazing international greed.

Arabian Mission personalities like John Van Ess, Paul Harrison, and Henry Bilkert, among others, believed these new initiatives would introduce major destabilizing factors – western-fed Arab secular materialism and a jingoistic nationalism – more fearsome to them than Islam itself. Yet they aided and abetted the oil men as well. In 1908 John Van Ess himself helped organize the resources for George Reynolds and his friends, the first British group which headed into Iran to explore for oil and laid the foundations for the AngloPersian Oil Company.[35]

Among those who were seeking opportunities in Arabia was Charles R. Crane. A close friend of President Woodrow Wilson, he was an industrialist who had made his fortune in plumbing, an enterprising businessman, a one time diplomat,[36] and a philanthropist interested in religious causes. One of the two leaders of the King-Crane Commission, in the summer of 1919 he

---

[34]The remarkable career of Frank Holmes (1874-1947), who made many friends in the Arabian Mission and earned from the Arabs the name Abû-nNaft (Father of Oil), is sketched by his close friend and competitor, Archibald H. T. Chisholm, *The First Kuwait Oil Concession Agreement: A Record of the Negotiations 1911-1934* (London: Frank Cass, 1975), pp. 9395.

[35]Van Ess relates: "Something under forty years ago [writing in 1943] an Englishman, named Reynolds, came to my house in Basrah and asked me to hire forty mules for him. He said he was going across the border into Persia to prospect for oil. I got him the mules and the upshot of the expedition was that oil was discovered, and the net result was the Anglo-Iranian Oil Company, today one of the world's largest producers. I have since hinted subtly to the A.I.O.C. that they might have given me forty preferred shares, one for each mule, as a slight token of appreciation. But my hints have been non-producing, so to speak" (Van Ess, *Meet the Arab*, p. 137).

[36]He had served Woodrow Wilson as ambassador to China.

had investigated and reported to President Wilson the desire of the people of Greater Syria (including Palestine) for self-rule.[37]

Crane came to Basrah in 1929 to investigate economic opportunities in Arabia which, he said, would be pursued on Christian principles. As a favor to Crane and not in line with his other duties, Henry Bilkert, then field secretary for the mission, offered to accompany the businessman to Kuwait. On Monday, January 21, the two-car cavalcade was ambushed in the desert by a small party of Ikhwân marksmen, and Bilkert was mortally wounded. He received a bullet through the shoulder which passed through to sever his spine, paralyzing him. The cars raced back over the excruciatingly rough desert track to Basrah, but Bilkert died before they arrived. His death caused a ripple of shock to fan out not only among the missionaries but also throughout the larger expatriate and Arab communities. The deliberate nature of the attack on westerners in the desert was a unique event. None could adequately explain it, but it appears likely that it was a premeditated assassination intending Charles Crane or Henry Bilkert or both.[38]

[37]The report was buried during the final days of Wilson's failing health. It had no political effect.

[38]In 1990, the author spoke with Timothy Harrison, the son of Paul Harrison, a close friend of Henry Bilkert who later married Bilkert's widow, Monty. Harrison remembered his father telling him that some years after the shooting a group from Sa'ûdî Arabia came to the mission hospital in Bahrain for treatment. Among them was a man who was known to have been part of the raiding party that killed Henry Bilkert. Paul Harrison said to the Arab that he knew the killing was intentional but that the mission would not pursue the issue, since it was the Christian way to forgive. As in the case of the clearly deliberate assassination of Maurice Heusinkveld many years later in Oman, the mission refused to press for vengeance.

Cornelia Dalenberg, has this complementary commentary, erroneously placing the incident in Kuwait:

"Arab tribesmen going in and out of the mission hospital in Kuwait spoke of the incident with doctors there, and through word of mouth our doctors eventually had a pretty good idea of who was responsible for the incident. A few years later one of these same gunmen became ill and was carried by friends to the hospital in Kuwait. The doctors learned who he was when he was admitted.

"Since the law of the desert is 'an eye for an eye,' the gunman and his friends would not have been surprised if the hospital staff had refused treatment.

"The man was welcomed to the hospital, though, to the amazement of the tribesmen. He was given the same treatment as the other patients. It was truly an eye-opener for the Muslims to see that the people who embraced the Christian gospel were ruled by a different law than that of the desert" (*Sharifa*, p. 103).

The loss of Henry Bilkert at the age of thirty-five was a serious one. He had already shown his ability when he and his wife opened 'Imârah station for permanent mission work and then covered for James Cantine in Baghdad when the latter had to withdraw. He was a strong apologist for the case that evangelism should be given the same standing in the mission's program as medical work and education. Politically aware, outspokenly idealistic, good humored, and gifted with the ability to make friends among Arabs, as mission secretary he was an excellent spokesperson for the mission's cause

Jacob Chandy, a young bachelor physician serving with the mission hospital in Bahrain between 1938 and 1944, was deeply influenced by Paul Harrison. He later went on to a distinguished career as a professor of medicine at the Christian Medical Center in Vellore, South India. He notes, "One occasion impressed me greatly – the case of a Bedouin Chieftain. Dr. Harrison had been visiting him almost every day. From the day of his admission for treatment for chronic osteomyelitis Dr. Harrison had been asking me to pray specially for him. That Bedouin Chieftain was one of those people who operated on the borders of Iraq and the mainland of Arabia, carried on raids into towns, attacked travelers, plundering their goods and belongings. They often took people as slaves and sold them in the mainland market places. This Bedouin Chieftain had made such a raid and had killed Mrs. Ann Harrison's first husband, Rev. Becket [sic.] who was a close friend of the Harrisons. Dr. Harrison's wife had also died and he later married Ann. Harrison had recognized him as soon as he had come into the Hospital for treatment and that was why he had taken extra pains to show respect, kindness and love for him. We had operated on him three times to clear his osteomyelitis. During that evening Dr. Harrison was radiant with excitement and joy. He started asking the Chieftain to stop his usual activities of plundering and killings. During the conversation and pleadings he said that the Chieftain had killed his brother Rev. Becket [sic.]. The Bedouin Chieftain could not believe that Dr. Harrison would be so kind and good to him and would dispense such loving care to him knowing fully what he had done to Rev. Becket [sic.]. The Bedouin Chief broke down and cried and asked how Dr. Harrison could show such love. Then he talked to him about the love of his Master and Saviour. The Bedouin Chief promised to abandon his usual occupation. Such incidents inspired me" [Jacob Chandy, *Reminiscences and Reflections* (Kottayam, Kerela, India: The C.M.S. Press, 1988), pp. 21-22)].

Dorothy Van Ess (*Pioneers...*, p. 121) remembered that, at the time, the American consul in Baghdad was considering holding the Iraq government accountable for the tragedy, since they did not warn the Crane-Bilkert party that the Basrah-Kuwait road was dangerous. John Van Ess talked him out of pursuing that course, since any action demanding indemnity would smack of asking for "blood money," would damage relations between the United States and Iraq, would injure the goodwill which the mission had won for itself, and would belie the principles of love and forgiveness on which it had been founded. "This attitude," she observed, "which became generally known, made a deep impression on the Arabs of Iraq and Kuwait, as well as the tribes."

and one of its most promising young leaders. The abrupt and violent end to his life sobered his colleagues up and down the Gulf. Crane, in an act of remorse and compassion, offered to pay for the education of the Bilkert children. Monty Bilkert was at first reluctant to accept the offer but, persuaded by John Van Ess that this was not "blood money" but a genuine moral act, she finally accepted.[39] Crane himself continued to be fascinated by the Middle East, and Arabia in particular.

The revolt of the Ikhwân was finally suppressed in early 1931,[40] but not without serious loss. 'Abd-ul-'Azîz compromised his standing as the beloved and charismatic Imâm of a goal-driven religious and political movement[41] and had to be content with merely being the feared king of Arabia, ruling all of Arabia excluding Yemen, South Arabia, Oman, and those amîrates which fell under the protection of Great Britain. The fact that 'Abd-al-'Azîz Âl Sa'ûd was finally able to bring his rebels under control and to establish strong working ties with western powers did not diminish the lesson that the

[39]Related to the author by Alice Van Ess Brewer in an interview July 5, 1990. Mrs. Brewer was a close friend of Margaret Bilkert and was in Basrah at the time of the Bilkert assassination.

[40]The Ikhwân leader, Faysal al-Duwwîsh, surrendered to British forces January 10, 1931. The British, in turn, negotiated with 'Abd-ul-'Azîz on behalf of al-Duwwîsh and his colleagues. The final agreement was signed January 26, and al-Duwwîsh and his friends were sent to prison. Faysal alDuwwîsh, conqueror of Madînah, died in prison October 3, 1931 (Dickson, *Kuwait...*, pp. 285-330).

[41]"The 'Ikhwân rank and file now understood that Ibn Sa'ud had raised the cry of religion in 1914 for his own ends. They felt sore and resentful at having been played with, and so no longer had the desire to be loyal or even militant. They just wanted to be left alone. The King had ceased to be the popular hero and father of his people, and one found, even among loyal Shammar, Harb, Sebei', Sahúl and 'Awázim tribesmen, let alone those who had failed in their revolt against him, a spirit resembling deep disappointment. If asked to say why this was so, they were unable to give concrete or sensible replies, but distrust and disillusionment would seem to have been the root cause....As time went by Ibn Sa'ud's title of 'Imám was discarded by the Badawin world north and north-east of the Dahana sand belt...and he was widely known as Al Wahhábi, an epithet of opprobrium than anything else" (Dickson, *Kuwait...*, pp. 329-330).

intrusion of Western forces into the internal affairs of the region was not universally welcome. For the Wahhâbî power there is some irony in the fact that the one constraining force able to stand against 'Abd-ul'Azîz's ambitions was Great Britain, known to itself and to the world as a Christian nation.

We have already noted that from the late 1600s, when the English East India Company first entered the region, its primary motives were to protect the trade routes to India from encroachments by the Portuguese, the Dutch, the French, and Arab pirates and to suppress the slave trade. From strategically sited trade enclaves known as "factories" on both sides of the Gulf, and not averse to employing their navy to affect the complex balance between local powers, British commercial and political agents paid close attention to the developments in the amîrates of the "Pirate Coast,"[42] Qatar, Bahrain, and Kuwait, as well as the emerging local "superpower" of Sa'ûdî Arabia. They were also much involved in the Sultanate of Oman, whose days of imperial glory had faded.

The relationship between the fledgling Arabian Mission and the British was extremely important. By and large, personnel of the mission admired the British political agents and administrators. The sentiment was more often than not reciprocated, even though the British did tend at times to be leery about the American presence represented in these missionaries and would occasionally express annoyance at their political brashness. The British were also aware that several significant missionaries were not entirely in sympathy with Britain's overall colonial policies.[43] But the Arab

---

[42]This region was later known as the "Trucial Coast" or "Trucial Oman" after it had been pacified by British sea power, and it is now known as the United Arab Emirates (U.A.E.). The U.A.E. includes the city states of Abû Dhabî, Dubay, Sharjah, Ra's-al-Khaymah, 'Ajmân, Um-al-Qaywayn, and Fujayrah. Under British protection from 1892, they were granted independence in 1971, and the Union was finally formed in 1972.

[43]Paul Harrison, among the most colorful, productive, and widely experienced of the Arabian Mission's leaders, expressed his high esteem for the British as individuals but felt that, ostrich like, they denied the implications of their own enlightened policies. The most important of these implications was that, sooner or later, as

Gulf had its share of exceptional British political agents like William Shakespear,[44] Harold Dickson,[45] Arnold Wilson,[46] Charles Belgrave,[47] F. C. Leslie Chauncy,[48] and others who admired the missionaries as individuals and worked closely with the mission, at times directly advocating for its cause.[49]

Arabs became educated and aware of their potential, they would seek full independence. Looking at the "British Regime" as he knew it intimately in 1924, Harrison concludes, "The better educated the subject race becomes, the more determined it is to achieve self-government. Perhaps it is not too much to say that because of this fact British dominion is destined to disappear eventually, and certainly nothing would do so much to make the present situation acceptable to the Arab as a frank and unqualified avowal of its temporary character" (Harrison, *The Arab at Home*, p. 186. The whole discussion, pp. 178-186, is excellent).

[44]Indeed, this Shakespear was a distant relation of the great Elizabethan playwright, William Shakespeare, descending from the bard's uncle, Thomas. Thomas, it is said, was embarrassed by William's questionable social connections and dropped the "e" from the end of his own name to mark a discontinuity [H. V. F. Winstone, *Captain Shakespear* (London: Quartet Books, 1978), pp. 28-29].

[45]Harold Dickson, in his colorful career, and his wife, Violet, no less a personage in her own right, were close friends of the Arabian Mission throughout their long presence in Kuwait, which began in 1929 and ended with Dame Violet Dickson's death in 1990. Relations between their two children, Hanmer Saʿûd and Irene Zahrah, and the Scudder family continue to be cordial.

[46]Arnold Wilson, who previously held a diplomatic post in Iran, served as deputy political resident in the Gulf from 1912 to 1920. He became a good friend and strong advocate of the Arabian Mission. So close were Arnold Wilson's relations with the mission that, at one time, his name was strongly nominated as an honorary trustee. The suggestion was never acted upon, but the fact that it was made is itself significant. Wilson served under Cox until 1920. Thereafter, earning a knighthood in 1922, he worked for the Anglo-Persian Oil Company until he retired in 1932 to serve in the British Parliament (1933-1940). He was killed in action while serving with the Royal Air Force during the Second World War at the age of fifty-seven (Chisholm, ...*Oil Concession*, p. 91).

[47]Belgrave was actually not hired by the British foreign service but was directly employed by the shaykh of Bahrain as his government's top administrator. But his long tenure in office and the influence he had on British policy brings him into this group, as it were, through a side door.

[48]From 1949 to 1958 Leslie Chauncy was British political officer and then consul in Muscat, the capital of Oman. Following his retirement he continued in the sultan's service as his personal advisor. While Chauncy was a personal friend of the missionaries in Oman, in his official capacity he was at times something of an obstruction as well. But in the balance, the missionaries thought well of him and he of them. As a member of the inner circle of the old regime, he was encouraged to retire in 1971.

[49]Harold Dickson was quite unabashed to sing the praises of mission doctors whenever opportunity availed. Arnold Wilson, another prominent British civil servant, made no bones about his admiration. In a paper presented before the

Beginning in the early 1930s, Sa'ûdî Arabia became a focal point for the growing international grab for oil. No other factor was more powerful in

Royal Geographical Society January 10, 1927, he said, "There is no greater influence for good in the [Persian] Gulf than the Christian missions; no Europeans are so universally respected as are the missionaries, such as Zwemer, Van Ess, Harrison, and Mylrea, and those who decry foreign missions do less than justice to themselves and harm to our good name."

But for all the mutual esteem which pertained between the British administrators in the Gulf and the Arabian Mission, the British kept a pretty tight reign on the mission's ambitions. The mission was not able to pursue a policy independent of British policy no matter how it might have rankled. The net effect of this close oversight was to inhibit the mission from energetically pursuing any plans for expansion beyond the bases it had established before the First World War.

In a report he wrote in 1921, Paul Harrison expressed his firm conviction that the British had circumscribed his movements and contacts in the interior. Were it not for the British, Harrison argued, there would have been no impediment to the mission's establishing a hospital in al-Hasâ' and even in Riyâdh. At the end of 1920, Harrison noted, 'Abd-ul-'Azîz Âl Sa'ûd negotiated an agreement with Sir Percy Cox to the effect that the British would no longer hinder the visits of American medical personnel to Najd, provided they had been invited by the amîr. In an exaggerated burst of optimism, he concluded, "The gates of Nejd have never been more widely ajar. It is an indication not only that the Arab chiefs and townspeople want us, and that the British are willing to have us enter. It means that the fanatical Ikhwan are coming to desire the service we are able to render and to approve our residence among them. Above all, we believe that it means that God's day for the occupation of Nejd is at hand, even at the doors." ["Report on Inland Arabia" in *Special News Bulletin: Board of Foreign Missions - Reformed Church*, Number 14, July 12, 1921, New York. Copy seen in the collection of D. B. Scudder, now lost.] Harrison's optimism on this score was sustained by the mission for many years, but his dream never came to pass. What is clear, though, is that the good will of the British was recognized to be key.

The mission felt reticent even to express a difference of opinion with the British. Such expressions could precipitate reactions from the highest quarters and led to the invocation of the mission's policy that "missionaries should carefully abstain from all interference with the political affairs and institutions of the people among whom they labor." (Circular letter from James Cantine to the mission with reference to an article by Edwin Calverley discussing Kuwait-Sa'ûdî tensions. Letter dated March 7, 1921, in the author's collection now in the Archives of the Reformed Church in America, New Brunswick, New Jersey.) It is evident from Cantine's caution that, while missionaries knew what was going on politically, they were not to talk about it openly. Indeed, that is the way the British preferred it.

shaping the destiny of the Gulf. From 1859, when Edwin Drake drilled his first well in Titusville, Pennsylvania, petroleum began to emerge as a modest economic force. With the invention of electric lighting, the internal combustion engine, and the automobile at the turn of the century, however, the major role of petroleum in the world was forecast. Suspicions that the Middle East contained significant oil reserves were first explored by the British. On May 26, 1908, a British speculator, George Reynolds, made the first strike of oil in the Middle East at Masjid-i-Sulaymân in Ahwâz, Iran. Only a year later the enterprising William D'Arcy had launched the Anglo-Persian Oil Company (APOC), precursor to British Petroleum (BP). By 1913 APOC's refinery in the Shatt-ul-'Arab port of 'Abbadân was in production, proving itself a vital resource for British India and its energy needs.

From 1911 onward British political residents in the Gulf had as part of their brief the quiet acquisition of British rights to oil concessions. Along with the first motor cars imported into Arabia, oil became a vigorously treated topic of discussion in the Gulf's *diwâniyyahs*. The development of oil, however, was suspended as the world went to war, and the Middle East was caught up in that war from 1914 to 1920.

The change of pace was marked by the entry into the Gulf of a personality: Major Francis "Frank" Holmes. A New Zealander and a mining engineer, Holmes served during the war as a supply officer for the British army in Mesopotamia. After demobilization in 1920, Holmes, an enterprising forty-six-year-old, returned to Arabia representing a speculative venture known as the Eastern and General Syndicate Ltd. After a sojourn in Aden, he established his base in Bahrain in 1922, where he became a favorite of the missionary community.[50] His primary negotiations at the time were with

---

[50]Cornelia Dalenberg, recounting how Holmes discovered "something that was to change the course of events in the world," also recalled: "I smiled when I heard about Major Holmes' shenanigans, although I do not know if the account is true. Those of us in the mission who knew him were not privy to his business dealings. What we did know was that he enjoyed life tremendously and he loved telling a good story.

"In several history books, Major Holmes is now called 'The Father of Oil.' That was a term originally bestowed upon him by the Kuwaitis, I understand. Who would have thought that the short, fun-loving fellow who had sipped tea with us after tennis matches would someday wear that title?

"For all his work in opening up the largest oil fields on earth, however, Major Holmes did not make a personal fortune. He retired comfortably to a farm in

'Abd-ul-'Azîz Âl Sa'ûd, and he succeeded in gaining the concession in March 1923.[51] From then until 1934, when he retired, Holmes also succeeded in signing concession agreements in Bahrain (1923) and Kuwait (1934).[52]

Led by Gulf Oil, American companies began moving into the Gulf in 1927, capturing first the Bahrain concession and then that for Sa'ûdî Arabia's eastern province (1933). Except in Kuwait, the British had been displaced. And 'Abd-ul-'Azîz, quite amazed by his good fortune, turned a great deal of attention in his later years to eliciting higher payments and disposing of his new wealth in flamboyant acts of generosity. Holmes, negotiating from Bahrain, fell into disfavor with 'Abd-ul-'Azîz who was demanding £5,000 rent and accusing him of having defaulted on his concession.

It was in the middle of the Depression that Charles Crane reappeared. To what extent his new involvement was to put coals of fire on his enemy's head by loving him, it is difficult to say. Certainly he had not forgotten his experience as Henry Bilkert's companion when Bilkert was assassinated and would have been pardoned for thinking of the Sa'ûdîs as "enemies." But

Essex in 1940. I don't think he felt badly about watching the big oil companies reap billions from his pioneering work. I think he just loved playing the game" (*Sharifa*, pp. 77-78).

Harold Dickson, another close friend of the mission, also encountered and was charmed by Holmes at the outset of his Gulf career in 1922. Serving on special assignment for Sir Percy Cox in Bahrain at the time, upon the request of 'Abd-ul-'Azîz Âl Sa'ûd, Harold Dickson and his wife Violet were Holmes's first hosts on the island. Dickson was trying to move negotiations along for convening the 'Uqayr Conference on establishing national borders, and he strongly suspected that the Sa'ûdî sultan was awaiting Holmes's arrival to gain a better idea of what he ought to bargain for. Amusingly tight-lipped about his business in Sa'ûdî Arabia, Holmes did, in fact, show up at the 'Uqayr Conference among the sultan's entourage (Dickson, *Kuwait*, pp. 268-271). As proved the case, the readiness of Sa'ûdî negotiators to bargain hard for large parts of Kuwait's territory was inspired by the realization that it contained oil.

[51]Sir Percy Cox had urged 'Abd-ul-'Azîz also to consider a bid by the Anglo-Persian Oil Company to be presented to him by Sir Arnold Wilson, but Holmes had gained the inside track and the APOC's offer was never seriously entertained, APOC's close association with the British government not being a mark in its favor (Chisholm, ...*Oil Concession*, p. 94).

[52]When Holmes retired at the end of 1934, having successfully negotiated the oil concession in Kuwait, he spent the remaining years of his life as the London representative of Shaykh Ahmad al-Jâbir Âl Sabâh of Kuwait. He died in 1947 from a bladder disease he had contracted in Aden before embarking on his remarkable sojourn in the Gulf.

Crane returned, ostensibly seeking Arabian horses. He was given these as a gift, and in return he proposed to his Sa'ûdî contact in Cairo that he could help explore the possibilities of mineral wealth and water in the kingdom. No sooner had the offer been made than, finances ruling over Wahhâbî hesitations, 'Abd-ul-'Azîz invited Crane to meet him in Jiddah. Crane arrived there in early 1931. The outcome of the visit was that Crane provided a geologist/engineer who had worked for him, searching for water in Ethiopia and the Yemen: Karl S. Twitchell. Initially funded by Crane, Twitchell began his geological research in April of the same year. The American conglomerate, Standard Oil of California (SOCAL), that had retained the now-discredited Holmes as its negotiator, was quick to pick up Twitchell, who knew the land intimately. It was a move advocated by 'Abd-ul'Azîz's eccentric and egotistical British friend and advisor, Harry (al-Hajj 'Abd-Allâh) St. John Philby. Bidding successfully against the British Iraq Petroleum Company, SOCAL signed its agreement with 'Abd-ul-'Azîz May 29, 1933.

The first oil on the Arab side of the Gulf began to be pumped in 1932 in Bahrain. The refinery of the Bahrain Oil Company began producing in 1935 and was corporately linked to the venture being undertaken in Sa'ûdî Arabia. Only one month ahead of Kuwait, the first viable oil well was successfully drilled in Sa'ûdî Arabia in March, 1938. Again, after only a few tankers had picked up their loads, war delayed the enterprise. In 1944 oil shipments were resumed and the Arabian American Oil Company (ARAMCO, the successor company to SOCAL) began pumping oil in fabulous quantities, supplying the United States with extraordinarily cheap fuel for its post-war boom.

For Sa'ûdî Arabia, the last years of King 'Abd-ul-'Azîz were a study in cultural and economic chaos. A man who had always lived with limited means, he was the typical Arab shaykh, giving of his own with open-handed generosity in times of want. It was the foundation of his political reputation and popularity, and also a key to his own self-image. His practice of personal generosity continued to typify his style once the days of plenty had begun. Fabulously rash personal spending typified him and his family, causing palaces to spring out of the desert. But he did not invest in public works or general services. On the strength of personal extravagance, the Sa'ûdî debt suddenly skyrocketed with nothing to show for it in the way of development or nation-building.

The rising expectations of the people, the presence of increasing numbers of foreigners on Sa'ûdî soil, the king's own declining health and befuddlement all may have conspired to make the king finally reverse his previous stand and look on with passive favor when the Arabian Mission opened a base in the oasis area of al-Hasâ' in 1952. It was, perhaps, a sop to the people, but it made little difference in the end. Only a year later, with his economy in a shambles, the old king finally died in the hill resort of Tâ'if on November 9, 1953. He was succeeded by his son, Sa'ûd.[53] With Sa'ûd's ascension the modern development of Sa'ûdî Arabia began, but the mission's presence there ended in 1956.

Southern Iraq: The Mission's First Home

While the Arabian interior was the lode star of the Arabian Mission, its first home and resource was the Land of the Two Rivers, Iraq. To summarize the history of Iraq during the mission's sojourn there is not our purpose. It would be impossible, in any case. But it is important at least to give a flavor of the springboard of the Arabian Mission's work. Furthermore, as more recent developments have illustrated, Iraq had a heavy impact upon the Gulf, not least of all Kuwait.

Basrah, where the mission first took its stand, is situated on the ancient delta below the confluence of the Tigris and Euphrates rivers, where their union takes the name *Shatt-ul'-Arab* (the River of the Arabs). It was a city of date palms. All around it flourished the palm groves where the famous dates of Basrah matured in the hot summer sun and were then picked and

---

[53]Harold Storm in Hufûf, talking with some who had been near when the old king died, reported it thus: "… immediately upon the death of Ibn Saud, he, Amir Saud, called the brothers (thirty some) and said, 'Now choose you a King from among yourselves.' They all at once said, 'No, you are our King,' and all pledged allegiance. The new King then announced that his brother, Faisal, was to be the new Crown Prince. Thus a new regime started ere the old King was buried. Ibn Saud's body was then taken to Ryad for burial beside his father" (in a letter to "Dear Colleagues" dated November 20, 1953, a copy in the author's document collection).

The saga of Sa'ûdî Arabia's development is colorfully (and, for the most part, accurately) recounted in Robert Lacey, *The Kingdom: Arabia & the House of Sa'ud* (New York: Avon Books, 1981).

packaged as the staple goods of trade for much of the Gulf's commerce in the days before oil was discovered. Not far up stream are the ruins of Ur of the Chaldees from which Abraham set forth,[54] and the marshes at its back provided the reeds for building ships which once bore ancient seafarers to places as far distant as Mohenjedaro and Egypt, linking it to the ancient

---

[54]This observation is not flippant. The missionaries of the Arabian Mission were taken up into the romance of walking in the footsteps of Abraham, of living among those who replicated in modern times the setting of the Bible stories they had learned as children. Not atypical of others, Beth Scudder Thoms Dickason commented, "I think the Bible takes on reality (in Arabia), and you can experience what the Bible tells you. I don't know whether I could have done that had I been in this country (the United States) all the time. So many things in the Bible are *so Arab*" (in a taped interview with the author, January 28, 1990).

This sense of the Arabness of his faith was so powerful in a man like John Van Ess that, in the one instance when he experienced a personal encounter with the living Christ, Jesus presented himself to him as an unmistakably Arab young man. Van Ess related the incident in a sermon delivered in the United States during his furlough in 1934 entitled, "Rethinking My Task." He said:

"I saw Christ once. It was a blazing afternoon in August in Arabia and I was tossing on my bed in the delirium of a fever. Suddenly I saw a young Arab standing by my bed. He was dressed as all Arabs are, in the white tunic with the long sleeves covering his hands, and with the head-cloth and the camel hair coil about his head. As I accosted him he slowly raised his hand. The sleeve fell away and I saw a scar on his hand as of a nail. Then still very slowly he lifted the head cloth from his forehead which I saw all marred with gashes. I said to him in Arabic, 'Who are you Seidi? My Lord?' He only smiled and slowly, as I watched him, he faded away. Was it the delirium of a fever? I have come to think that I was never saner than at that moment. And now I go everywhere trying to find him again. As I see a common Arab on the street I think it may be He. The footfalls around my house at night I imagine to be His. It makes of every hut and tent a temple where I may find Him. Some day on some desert highway as I give to one whom I regard as a common Arab a drink of water, I shall see in the outstretched hand the prints of nails again, only he will say, 'My disciple, why have you been so long in finding me?'" (in the "Van Ess" box in the Archives of the Reformed Church in America, New Brunswick, New Jersey).

When the author queried John Van Ess's daughter, Alice, she said, "You know, he really had that vision. He told it to me, not just in a sermon. And he asked how I thought people would react. Well, I don't cry all that easily, and I was just ripped apart. And I said, 'Daddy, you really saw Jesus, didn't you?' And he said, 'Of course I did.' And he saw him in Arab dress....This is the vision my father had, and he (Jesus) was speaking Arabic in the vision. Oh, yes, he was speaking Arabic in the vision. He was dressed in Arab clothes with the *kaffiyyah* (head scarf) and the *'aqâl* (rope head scarf binder) and everything." (In a taped interview by the author with Alice Van Ess Brewer and her husband, William, July 5, 1990).

civilization of Dilmun.[55] It was a much fought-over city and vulnerable, having no natural defenses save the broad Shatt-ul-'Arab that flowed down beside it. The Arab tribes and their political configurations to the west and south were the single most important factor determining its fortunes.

From the days of the first Muslim caliphs, Basrah had been an intellectual center. It was the first home of Muslim Sûfî mysticism, the most famous figures being Hasan al-Basrî and Râbi'ah al-'Adawiyyah. It was also a center from which radiated the drive to internationalize Islam (the *shu'ûbiyyah* movement which fed into the movement of the *Shî'ah* branch of Islam). It was also more than likely the center from which emerged the liberal and speculative movement of Muslim theologians known as the *Mu'tazilah*. This movement, because of the vigor of its opponents, accounted as much as any other factor for Islam's later coming under the thrall of jurists. In the famous tales known as the *Thousand and One Nights*, Basrah was the home port of the legendary Sindbad the Sailor (although his birthplace is said to have been Suhâr in Oman). And down through the years it has served as a principal nerve center at the far end of the bow of the Fertile Crescent.

In the years prior to the arrival of the Arabian Mission in 1891, Basrah had passed back and forth between Ottoman and Safavid Persian hands several times.[56] The heterogeneous population of the city had learned how to survive (and connive) under whatever regime governed the land. Ribboned with tidal creeks, Basrah was the Middle East's equivalent of Venice in a variety of ways. It was a town which lived by its wits and survived with its robust sense of humor. But it also seemed to have a taste for violence that burst forth in sporadic outbursts. In the latter days of the glory of the 'Abbâsid Caliphs, the marshes above Basrah were the site of the great Zanj slave revolt (869 to 883 AD), and southern Iraq has always had the reputation of being a land difficult to govern.[57]

---

[55]Still the classic introduction to Dilmun is Geoffrey Bibby's *Looking for Dilmun* (London: Collins, 1970).

[56]The last Persian occupation of Basrah lasted from 1776 to 1779.

[57]In his inaugural speech, the Umayyad governor who ruled Iraq from 694 to 714, Hajjâj ibn-Yûsuf, characterized the people of Iraq as impious and factious, whose government could only be achieved by the sword. It is a speech still often quoted almost as a maxim [see: E. A. Belyaev, *Arabs, Islam and the Arab Caliphate in the Early Middle Ages* (trans. from Russian) (New York: Frederick A. Praeger, Inc., 1969), pp. 170-171)]. This was the same Hajjâj who, in 692, had reduced the holy city of Mecca using Syrian troops, ending the last serious opposition to Umayyad rule.

The population of Basrah was more cosmopolitan than that of any other settlement on the Arabian Gulf. From Basrah all the way to Baghdad were scattered settlements of people who presented themselves as followers of John the Baptist–the Sabaeans (or the Mandaeans).[58] There were also many Assyrian Christians, belonging to a tradition that had been cut off from the Christian mainstream since the Council of Ephesus in 431 and branded "Nestorian" by its detractors.[59] The Jewish population of the city, dating from the days of the Babylonian exile, was prosperous and significant. Although the land was ruled by Sunnî Muslims, the rural population and much of the town's was Shî'ah. The heterogeneity of the area was enriched by the fact that Basrah was a major port which welcomed ships from all over the world, and the foreign community brought its own colors and varieties.

In the days when the mission settled there, the dominant local figure was Khaz'al, the Shaykh of Muhammara, an amîrate down stream from Basrah on the site now named Khoramshahar in a region of Iran known as 'Arabistân, modern day Khûzistân.[60] Upstream from it were 'Imârah on the Tigris and Nâsriyyah on the Euphrates, both of which towns interested the mission. From Basrah the Ottomans extended whatever influence they could along the eastern shores of the Arabian Gulf, and political links tied

---

[58]In fact, the Sabaeans were devotees of an ancient philosophical religion with marked Gnostic and Manichean overtones. In the early years of the Muslim conquest of Mesopotamia, they identified themselves as those mentioned in the Qur'ân along with Christians and Jews as "scripturebearing people" (*ahl-ul-kitâb*), with a linkage to the prophet John the Baptist. This was, by and large, accepted at face value. In spite of a long history of persecution, the sect continues to exist in Iraq but is much diminished. In the early years of the Arabian Mission's work in 'Imârah, on the Tigris River, there was a substantial community of Sabaeans in the town who were well known for their truly remarkable skills in working in silver. Several women of this community were active "inquirers" at the mission, and the mission maintained cordial relationships with the leaders of the community. The 'Imârah Sabaean community has largely dissolved, but a group continues to exist in Baghdad.

[59]The Ancient Assyrian Church of the East survived beyond the boundaries of the Roman Empire with great vigor. It did not share in the three and a half centuries of intellectual development that designed for Orthodox and Catholic Christianity its theological terminology; rather, it moved on its own course. The product, as Protestant missionaries first saw it, was somewhat exotic. But judged by the substance of the Assyrian church's doctrine and practice, there can be little doubt today that it belongs solidly within the broader Christian community of churches.

[60]Shaykh Khaz'al played a critical mediatorial role in launching the mission's medical work in Kuwait.

Basrah to Baghdad, two days by steamer up the Tigris River. Basrah was a pivotal city; a well chosen site for the mission's first base.

In the twilight years of the nineteenth century, the Ottoman administration of Iraq was firmly in place, but it suffered from the overall decline of the empire. As western powers squabbled for control, two main influences came to dominate: Germany and Great Britain. Caught in the squeeze, on November 1, 1914, the Ottoman government chose Germany as its patron and ally. Anticipating the alliance, British India forces had been marshaled in Bahrain, and on October 31, 1914, the Indian Expeditionary Force "D" landed on the island of Fao, at the mouth of the Shatt-ul-ʿArab.

The American ambassador in Istanbul, Henry Morganthau, seeing that matters in Iraq would require a person of some sagacity, quickly appointed John Van Ess of the Arabian Mission to be acting American consul general in Basrah.[61] And when the British landed on Ottoman soil, it became quite evident that the Turks would not make their stand at Basrah.

As Ottoman troops and civil servants withdrew, the whole administrative and police structure of the town collapsed. Enthusiastic mullahs paraded in the streets at the head of noisy mobs proclaiming the virtues of holy war against the infidels. Large scale looting began. John Van Ess observed the city heading toward anarchy. Some form of civil administration had to be put in place quickly to check it. The British were the only viable alternative. He therefore sent a letter by one of his boatmen to Sir John Nixon, the British commander, urging him to make all possible speed in occupying Basrah.[62]

This set of circumstances had a significant effect upon the career of John Van Ess. As a diplomatic officer (if only for a short time) he was compelled to deal with political issues first hand, and his partisanship for the British was

[61]Dorothy F. Van Ess, *Pioneers in the Arab World* (Wm. B. Eerdmans Publishing Co.: Grand Rapids, Mich., 1974), p. 84.
[62]Van Ess, *Pioneers...*, pp. 85-87.

something he never afterward forswore.[63] Sir John Nixon and many of his staff[64] saw the value of this young missionary and his skills as an innovator. His knowledge of the situation in Iraq and his fluent command of its spoken dialect was as extensive as could be found anywhere. They therefore used Van Ess as their chief consultant in establishing the public school system in the areas Britain came to control in southern Iraq. They also commissioned him to produce his landmark text on the spoken Arabic of Iraq for use in training British officers.[65]

Politics in Iraq during the years from the First World War until 1958 were dominated by Britain, which was granted the mandate for Iraq by the League of Nations in 1920. Its style of government was set by the regal figure of the British high commissioner, Sir Percy Cox, and, after his retirement in May, 1923, the less magisterial Sir Henry Dobbs and his successors.

---

[63]"I am not British, nor do I have any British affinity, but any fairminded man will have to admit that in Mesopotamia Britain is today showing the world that she is trying to live up to her programme of justice, magnanimity, and civilization" (John Van Ess quoted in Van Ess, *Pioneers...*, p. 102).

[64]The staff which John Nixon gathered in Basrah sounds like the roster of most of the best informed people of the time. The names that Dorothy Van Ess recites in *Pioneers in the Arab World* are many. Among them are those of Reader Bullard (who was later knighted and served in Iraq and Sa'ûdî Arabia, concluding his career as British ambassador in Tehran, where he hosted Roosevelt, Churchill, and Stalin in 1943), D. L. R. Lorrimer (who published the exhaustive Gazetteer on the Persian Gulf, still a basic historical source book), Gertrude Bell (the Oriental secretary for the British mandatory authority, and known as "the Uncrowned Queen of Mesopotamia"), Percy Cox, and Arnold Wilson. In the period just before the outbreak of the Arab Revolt in Mecca, Van Ess even met with T. E. Lawrence. The Van Esses also became well acquainted with the eccentric H. St. John Philby, who became advisor to 'Abd-ul-'Azîz Âl Sa'ûd in the 1930s. There were many others. The Arabs whom they came to call friends included many of the cream of post-World War I Arab elite. The Van Esses knew these people very well and found themselves counselors to them on matters political as well as personal on many occasions.

[65]British officers and civil servants who successfully passed their language examinations in Arabic were said to have "VanEssed."

The British came to favor the establishment of a Hâshimite monarchy in Baghdad. This Van Ess opposed, favoring a more democratic form of government and the candidate from Basrah, Sayyid Tâlib an-Naqîb. When, in April 1921, the latter failed to consolidate his position and was exiled to Ceylon (Sri Lanka), Van Ess bowed to reality and cultivated his relationship with the constitutional monarch, Faysal bin-Husayn Âl Hâshim.

Faysal was the third son of the sharîf of Mecca, Husayn bin-'Alî, who had aided the British during the war by declaring the Arab Revolt in 1916. Faysal had become its field commander and was assisted by the legendary T. E. Lawrence. In the spring of 1919 Faysal was elected by the General Syrian Congress as constitutional monarch of Syria, but in July 1920 the new French mandatory authority deposed and expelled him. Having been unable (or unwilling) to successfully support Faysal's claim to Syria against the French at the Paris Peace Conference, the British nonetheless felt they owed him a debt.

After a formal referendum in July, the British enthroned Faysal bin-Husayn as constitutional monarch in Iraq August 23, 1921. Van Ess proceeded to establish very close ties with the king and with Iraq's perennial power behind the throne, Nûrî Pashâ as-Saʿîd, one of the Arab officers of the Ottoman army who had joined the Arab Revolt.[66] He had been a key figure in that revolt, and when Prince Faysal was driven from Damascus by the new French mandatory authority and installed in Iraq by the British, Nûrî as-Saʿîd moved with him. [67]

---

[66]Nûrî Pashâ had been held as a prisoner of war by the British in Iraq, and in the course of his internment had required funds. Van Ess had come forward to loan him money and, ever afterward, had refused repayment. From that time forward the relationship between the two men was extremely cordial.

[67]The story of Faysal's ejection from Syria and his enthronement in Iraq is to be found told and retold in many narratives. [See especially: Zeine N. Zeine, *The Struggle for Arab Independence: Western Diplomacy & the Rise and Fall of Faisal's Kingdom in Syria* (Beirut: Khayat's, 1960); and Stephen Hemsley Longrigg, *'Iraq 1990 to 1950: A Political, Social and Economic History* (London: Oxford Univ. Press, 1953).] It is also worth observing here that, although the relationship between John Van Ess and Nûrî Saʿîd served the mission well into the mid-1950s, when the monarchy fell to the violent revolution of Col. 'Abd-ul-Karîm Qâsim in 1958, the mission inevitably was held suspect.

Great Britain formally ended its mandate in Iraq in 1931, but it retained a powerful presence there.[68] In return for the privilege, Britain sponsored Iraq's application for membership in the League of Nations in 1932. But symbolic independence did not bring contentment. The Assyrians rose up in rebellion, ostensibly in order to reestablish the secular powers of their patriarchate, powers that had been recognized by the Ottomans. The massacres of Assyrians which followed left a bitter aftertaste and an aroused Kurdish population. Efforts on the part of King Faysal I to heal the millennial breach between Sunnî and Shî'ah Muslims proved unfruitful. He died in 1933, a deeply disappointed and troubled man. His son, Ghâzî, a flamboyant and erratic young man, succeeded to Iraq's throne.[69] The storm clouds of the Second World War were gathering.

Iraq was a very unsettled country. Many of its elite, with whom King Ghâzî was sympathetic, admired Germany's ability to shake off the yoke of Allied control and emerge from the Depression as a military power in Europe. They also admired Mussolini, and Italy's invasion of Christian Ethiopia in 1935 did no damage to Mussolini's prestige in Iraq. Ghâzî died in an automobile accident April 3, 1939. He left his minor son, Faysal II, as king under the regency of his uncle, 'Abd-ul-Ilâh, son of the ill-starred King 'Alî of the Hijâz. The king's death was popularly thought to have been arranged by the British. As war broke out in 1939, Baghdad was a hotbed of conspiracy and discontent.

Among those who conspired was the idealistic Rashîd 'Alî al-Gaylânî, a gifted man who had for a short time after 1924 served as minister of justice. He initiated a coup in May of 1941 that was partially successful. The royal family, with young King Faysal, managed to escape to safety in Transjordan.

---

[68]Among the stipulations in Britain's draft charter for Iraqi independence was a clause which stipulated that the Iraqi government would not hinder the work of foreign missionaries. In the version that was eventually accepted, that clause was removed at the insistence of King Faysal. The argument he put forward was profound: Such a clause reflected lack of trust and a demeaning assessment of the Iraqi people. They, the king said, were not against missionary work. They were grateful for it. They would encourage it. But in the end missionary activity in Iraq would have to be dependent upon the will of the people and not protected by political concessions. The mission was not at ease with this situation, but there was nothing they could do, and, of course, the king was quite right.

[69]Van Ess, *Pioneers...*, p. 123. Dorothy Van Ess here relates Faysal's last words to John Van Ess: "You are one of the few who have come to this land to give and not to get. By the milk of your mother, swear to me that you will always tell the Arabs the truth about themselves."

German and Italian technicians and aircraft landed in Mosul, and the British were forced to act. The British army managed to suppress the coup, and Rashîd 'Alî fled to sanctuary in Sa'ûdî Arabia. These events mark an important stage in the increasingly strong antiforeign sentiments of Iraqi society, sentiments which spread like an infection throughout the region.

The impact of these events upon the mission's stations of 'Imârah and Basrah was considerably less than upon the stations further north operated by the United Mission in Iraq. The popular James Moerdyk, during the summer of 1940, had held 'Imârah station all alone until he died unexpectedly. He was followed there by the saintly pair, Gerrit and Gertrude Pennings. The popularity of the mission there was unquestioned and unchallenged. John and Dorothy Van Ess in Basrah were a kind of royalty of their own. In Basrah George and Christine Gosselink were being groomed to assume major responsibilities. In the last few days before his formal retirement in 1949, John Van Ess died and was buried in the land that had adopted him. He was spared the brutalities that followed.

The period between 1952 and 1962 was a difficult one. The year 1952 marked the rise of Gamâl 'Abd-un-Nâsir in Egypt and the successive fall of post-colonial governments throughout the Middle East. It was also the post-Churchill period, during which Anthony Eden and his successors presided over the dismantlement of the British Empire. The rules were being rewritten; it was a time of radical and often violent change in what was beginning to be called the "Third World."

As war yielded to post-war reconstruction, United States foreign policy became militantly anti-Soviet. Senator Joseph McCarthy's brutal witch-hunt for alleged Communist sympathizers in American government and in public life shocked many Arabia missionaries.[70] Then came an event that hit the Arab world like a blow in the solar plexus. On May 15, 1948, the United

[70]The author, then a child, remembers driving across the United States, at times listening to radio broadcasts of the McCarthy hearings. Paul Robeson, the great American singer, was being tried at that time. There was a moment of stark revelation when the author's father, Lew Scudder, Sr., who rarely expressed judgment upon people, suddenly said of McCarthy with powerful intensity, "There's an evil man!"

States – and only two days later the Soviet Union – recognized the Zionist conquest of Palestine as the new State of Israel. This era also brought to power the harsh and battlesome Presbyterian figure of John Foster Dulles. It was he who insisted upon creating, in 1955, a circle of containment around the Soviet Union, forcing such diverse and individually unstable governments as those in Turkey, Iraq, Iran, and Pakistan (with Great Britain as the up-front sponsor) to join in an encircling wall of over-militarized and shaky states known as the "Northern Tier."[71]

Backlash to the United States' policy of containment in the Middle East came in the form of Arab nationalism, led by the fascinating figure of Colonel Gamâl 'Abd-un-Nâsir (Nasser) of Egypt.[72] As Nâsir, encouraged by Tito of Yugoslavia and Nehru of India, determined to play the role of a neutral in the Cold War, work for his nation's autonomy, and the control of its own vital resources, he became portrayed in the West as an enemy and in the Arab world as a hero. The Middle East was radicalized. British embassies, once seats of shadow governments, were placed under siege. American embassies likewise became targets for popular indignation, and the Soviet Union, bemused by its unearned good fortune, found itself happily backing the "good guys" of Arab public opinion.

[71]It was also known as the "Baghdad Pact." Iraq's accession to Dulles's demands in this regard on February 24, 1955, was a principal contributory element to undermining the Iraqi monarchy. America, the back-room sponsor of the pact, was not a credible ally of Arab governments so long as its main eggs for policy in the Middle East were in an Israeli basket. An intimate alliance of Iraq with the United States, therefore, was contradicted at its root, a factor which Dulles could never quite fathom. It can be argued that Dulles was one of those who set the stage for revolution in the Middle East, and he was certainly a stimulator of radicalism.

[72]Nâsir came to power July 23, 1952, at the head of the "Free Officers Movement" of the Egyptian army. It was the example of the revolution of Mustafâ Kamâl Atatürk, father of modern Turkey, which had inspired him. Working behind the figurehead, General Muhammad Nagîb, Nâsir emerged as first the prime minister (1954) and later (1956) president of Egypt. Along with Jawaharlal Nehru of India and Marshal Tito of Yugoslavia, at the Bandung Conference of 1955 he emerged as a world-class leader and advocate of nonalignment in the Cold War. Nâsir, having asserted Egypt's sovereignty over the Suez Canal, weathered the subsequent Sinai invasion by Israel, Britain, and France in 1956; the bungled attempt to form the United Arab Republic with Syria (1958-1961); and the debacle of his army in the war with Israel in 1967, and he emerged as the unquestioned symbol of Arab self-esteem, the Arab world's strongest leader since medieval times. He died September 28, 1970, of a massive heart attack.

For the cold warriors in Washington, the flirtation between Cairo and Moscow was sign enough. Egyptian applications for American aid to build the Aswan High Dam were rejected by Congress with loud and flowery rhetoric – little to the point but of strong effect.[73] Moscow stepped in to fill the vacuum and the deed was done. But Nâsir was cautious. His flirtation with Moscow never terminated in a seduction, much to the frustration of Russian strategists who tried at every turn to do the "right thing." They figured without one well-drilled Arab habit of mind.

From earliest history, Arabs have resisted becoming pawns of any foreign power. That is one of the more convincing explanations of why Islam came into being in the way it did, and it also explains why Islam continues to be a rallying point for national pride. It was over this issue of foreign domination that Nâsir found himself in direct contention with the Hâshimite regime in Iraq and its domineering prime minister, Nûrî Pashâ al-Saʿîd, who had made a strong American alliance. When, in October, 1956, the Hâshimites (in both Jordan and Iraq) refused to come to the aid of the Egyptians during the time of the Suez Crisis, Nâsir turned his full attention to undermining the Iraqi regime.[74]

[73]United States-Egyptian (and Arab) relations were irreparably damaged under John Foster Dulles. Nâsir, endeavoring to build up his military as part of his overall policy of strengthening Egypt's autonomy, had secretly agreed to purchase weapons from Czechoslovakia early in 1956. According to the Dulles doctrine, this was treachery to what he thought of as the "Free World." As a punishment, with the enthusiastic backing of Congress, Dulles, on July 20, canceled American participation in the Aswan High Dam project. The American example led to Britain's withdrawal from the project shortly thereafter. On July 25 Nasser announced the nationalization of the Suez Canal, with the notion that revenue from the canal might finance the building of the high dam. On October 29, without American participation or approval, Israel invaded Sinai and two days later was joined by British and French military occupation of the Suez Canal Zone. Strong American opposition to the initiative forced Britain, France, and Israel to withdraw (one of the few correct choices Dulles made in maneuvering American Middle East policy). As for the Aswan High Dam, the Soviet Union underwrote the project after the Americans and British withdrew, and the project was completed in 1968.

[74]Egypt had for many years been the intellectual capital of the Arab world. Its institutions of higher learning exported teachers in great numbers into Iraq and the Gulf, and these worked with zeal and to great effect for the aims of the Egyptian revolution. Posters of Nâsir became common sights throughout the Gulf in the mid-1950s, and the younger generation of Arabs were buoyed up and inspired to a new sense of their Arab dignity, common cause, and destiny. Egyptian agents had little difficulty organizing active subversive cells in Iraq and elsewhere at all levels of society.

One such effort was launched in February, 1958. Negotiating with the Ba'ath-supported government in Syria (which was under much pressure from Iraq), Nâsir convinced them that the ideal of Arab unity could become a reality. The United Arab Republic was the result, and much fanfare went into its founding.[75] With a base in Syria, more pressure was brought to bear on Iraq.

George Gosselink, walking out onto the Basrah school grounds in the early morning, would find them littered with dew-besogged "communistic" fliers and nationalist pamphlets. He was a more prosaic man than his predecessor and was conditioned, as were most Americans of his generation, to perceive the demonic workings of "international communism" in every aspiration for liberty and populist change. Agitators within the student body frustrated him; he did not know how to relate to them. Basrah society, the native Protestant church included, began to hold itself more aloof from the mission.

This was the second time in slightly over a decade when the missionaries felt themselves the objects of negative sentiments which they themselves had had no hand in aggravating. Giving to Caesar the things that are Ceasar's is never an easy judgment call. After all, in a world that was in the process of buying the American notion that power belongs to the people, who on earth *is* Caesar? And are there *really* any innocent bystanders in the game of nations? How does one cooperate with an unpopular government without somehow coming to be implicated in its unpopularity? How does one continue to stand with honor as a citizen of a foreign country whose actions are seen to be dishonorable? It was a tremendously confusing time; nobody was quite sure of anything.

Suddenly, in Baghdad on July 14, 1958, the boy-King Faysal II; 'Abd-ul-Ilâh, the regent; and Nûrî Pasha al-Sa'îd, his prime minister, were brutally slaughtered. The Hâshimites were violently ejected from Iraq, and a new republican regime installed itself under the leadership of Colonel 'Abd-ul-Karîm Qâsim and his more radical ally, Colonel 'Abd-us-Salâm 'Ârif. If these revolutionaries at first flirted with Nâsir, it soon became evident that Cairo and Baghdad almost inevitably represented poles of tension. Iraq never fell under Nâsir's spell; instead, it reacted to his patronization by charting an

---

[75]The UAR collapsed when Syria withdrew from the federation in September, 1961.

independent and far more violent course to become the military powerhouse of the Middle East.

The Iraqi Revolution of July 14, 1958, caught the mission by surprise.[76] There was little warning save the discontent which rippled below the surface of Iraqi society concerning Iraq's cooperation with Dulles's imperial adventure, and the embarrassment Iraqis felt when their Hâshimite regime failed to go to the aid of Egypt during the 1956 Suez crisis. The winds of conspiracy and political infighting that blew through Arab capitals after the rise of Nâsir and his fierce rivalry with Iraq's strongman, Nûrî Pashâ al-Saʿîd, largely passed by the American missionaries except, perhaps, as curiosities that had little to do with their day-to-day work.

When Colonel ʿAbd-ul-Karîm Qâsim launched his coup, therefore, nobody in the mission was really attuned to the fierce mood which had developed in the country. In any case, the Iraqi government seemed to be in control of the situation. The violence of the revolution, when it broke out, was breathtaking and terrible. The experience changed the mood of the mission. There was a clear heightening of anxieties. When Jacob Holler, who had been alone in Basrah when the revolution broke out, told of the terror in the streets and the massed anger of the crowds that boiled past his living room window, everyone knew that times had suddenly changed. Among the first blows struck against American interests in the newly realigned country was struck against the "American Mission Hospital" (the mission's Lansing Memorial Hospital which had been established in 1925) in ʿImârah. It was

[76]Jeannette Boersma [*Grace in the Gulf* (Grand Rapids, Mich.: Wm. B. Eerdmans Publishing Co., 1991), pp. 150-151] indicates that there was some warning. William Quandt, an anthropologist doing research in the Marshes, visited the mission in ʿImârah in the spring of 1958. He advised Bern and Jacque Draper to pack up their precious things in one suitcase that they could take with them at a moment's notice. He foresaw a crisis; things were not well at all in the Marshes at that time (Harvey Staal, in an interview with the author February 7, 1994). This warning was evidently memorable but not sufficiently weighty to provoke action.
[77]This event will be covered in more detail in part five.

expropriated, and the last missionaries left 'Imârah March 22, 1959.[77] Even though the mission's School of High Hope in Basrah continued to operate and even develop significant new facilities until 1967, it did so with the Sword of Damocles hanging over its head. The sword fell in 1968, when all Christian mission agencies were expelled from Iraq.

Kuwait: The Taste of Bittersweet

When the mission first appeared on the scene, the change in the fortunes of the Âl Sa'ûd was not predictable. In the northern Gulf, the dominant political force was Kuwait.

Kuwait was a town with a relatively brief past when compared with the ancient glories of Basrah, Bahrain, and Muscat. About eighty miles south southeast of Basrah, it was nothing more than a small fishing village at the dawn of the eighteenth century. Although it boasted one of the most remarkable harbors in the Gulf, settlement there was not attractive because it lacked a good and reliable source of fresh water. The only wells that produced marginally potable water were outside the town and were not to be counted upon. Notwithstanding, toward the end of the seventeenth century its uniquely dry climate attracted the interest of the paramount shaykh of the dominant tribe of eastern Arabia, the Banî Khâlid. There he built a small fort as a kind of resort and visited it occasionally.[78] Kuwait remained a sleepy sideshow of Gulf affairs until the middle years of the eighteenth century when, quite abruptly, its fortunes changed.

Outside of the eastern province of al-Hasâ', the only area of Arabia which might lay some claim to agricultural fertility and, hence, the region most heavily populated, was the plateau land of Najd. From time to time

---

[78]The word, *kûayt*, in Arabic is the diminutive of *kût*, the word for fortress. Hence, Kuwait meant "small fort."

Since the Banî Khâlid were Ottoman clients and ruled in the name of the sultan through the Ottoman governor of Basrah, this precedent has been cited as establishing Kuwait's belonging within the Ottoman region of sovereignty. As heir to the Ottoman regime in Mesopotamia, Iraq has employed this argument to justify its claims to Kuwait.

throughout history it has been a source of migrant populations. In the mid-seventeenth century, forced by drought and overcrowding, out of the Najd moved a group of clans belonging to the great tribal confederation of 'Anazah. They came to be dubbed collectively as the *'Utûb* (roughly to be translated as the "meanderers" or "peripatetic ones").

The 'Utûb settled first along the shores of the Gulf, especially in the port of Zubârah on the peninsula of Qatar, where they picked up skills as seafarers. They then scattered throughout the whole Gulf, finally coalescing as a group in Kuwait during the first two decades of the eighteenth century. The principal clans of this migration were the Âl Sabâh (eventually dominant in Kuwait), the Âl Khalîfah (later of Bahrain), and the Âl Jalâhimah (subsequently paramount shaykhs of Ra's-ul-Khaymah, presently one of the United Arab Emirates). Although these with other prominent families directed Kuwait's local affairs (such as they were), they acknowledged the rule of the Banî Khâlid amîrs of Al-Hasâ' and were, therefore, nominally Ottoman clients.[79]

Beginning in 1722, however, the Banî Khâlid became embroiled in internal struggles for succession, and tributary tribes, among them the 'Utûb of Kuwait, exploited the occasion to augment their local independence. The 'Utûb built Kuwait into a thriving commercial center, making it the port-of-call for caravans bound for Aleppo, linking northern Syria with India and the spice trade. Their wide-ranging merchant fleet began to rival that of Oman. They also developed the pearl fishing industry,[80] and established themselves as shipbuilders and mariners of high repute.

The problem of water was solved by developing a fleet of water tankers, locally built dhows of the *bûm* design[81] fitted with special tanks. The *dhows*

[79]As late as 1893 the British Government seems to have sustained Turkish claims that Kuwait was an Ottoman dependency [Husain M. Albaharna, *The Arabian Gulf States: Their Legal and Political Status and Their Internal Problems* (Beirut: Librairie du Liban, 1975), p. 41].

[80]The pearling fleet of Kuwait at the turn of the century numbered more than 400 captains and 10,000 divers.

[81]The term dhow is not Arabic and is of mysterious origin in English. The Arabs of the Gulf and East Africa and the shipwrights of western India share a common craft. The designs of their ships are various, depending upon the purpose. The *bûm* was the most common. A moderately large sailing ship, between sixty and a hundred feet long, the bûm was built with a sharp rather than a square stern and a simple unfigured stem. All the styles of dhow sported lateen rig. The sailing ship that appears at the head of each part of this book is a *bûm*. The author was once talked into writing a whimsical article on a Kuwaiti shipwright, 'Abd-Allâh

would sail up the Shatt-ul'Arab to where the water flowed fresh, fill their tanks, and then sail back to Kuwait. At high tide they were brought up and grounded on the shelf coral surrounding the town, and when the tide receded troops of donkeys would be burdened with filled water skins and run into a central distribution point whence other donkeys would take water to individual houses.[82]

By 1760 Kuwait was a walled city and had established its autonomy against the waning authority of the Banî Khâlid (who now had their hands full battling the Wahhâbîs under the newly risen family of Âl Sa'ûd, also a clan of the 'Anazah).[83] Around 1750 the Âl Sabâh had emerged dominant from among the three leading 'Utûbî families in Kuwait. The Âl Khalîfah and Âl Jalâhimah clans, finding themselves eclipsed by their cousins, in 1766 elected to migrate again back to Qatar and subsequently to Bahrain and Ra's-ul-Khaymah respectively.[84]

Kuwait, at the turn of the century, was a town elongated in shape, bent back around the crescent of the harbor and its busy port. It had no wall. The old eighteenth century wall had been dismantled as the town grew, and during his rule Shaykh Mubârak, with some justification, declared himself to be the town's wall.[85] The desert market – the Safât – formed in the

Marzûq al-Yûsuf, and the various types of Gulf-built ships: "A Boat-builder in Kuwait," pp. 27-29, in *Middle East International*, No. 36, June 1974 (London). The illustrations were drawn by the artist Penny Williams (Yaqoub).

[82]This very effective system continued in use well into the late-1940s. The *dhows* were first replaced by small modern tankers operated by the Kuwait Oil Company, and then, as natural gas became available, large desalinization plants were built. These also generated electricity. The first of these plants was located in the city's new port of Shuwaykh in the late 1950s.

[83]Ahmad M. Abu Hakima, *History of Eastern Arabia, 1750-1800, The Rise and Development of Bahrain and Kuwait* (Beirut: Khayat's, 1963), pp. 45-62. The Al Sa'ûd were also of 'Anazah descent, and so cousins to the Âl Sabâh and Âl Khalîfah.

[84]The Al Jalâhimah of Ra's-ul-Khaymah took up piracy as a means of livelihood and, for a time, served as the naval arm for the rising Wahhâbî power of the interior.

[85]Mylrea, *Kuwait...*, p. 39.

backward embrace of the built-up part of town. There the bedouin came to trade and buy, and there, in covered markets branching away from the square back toward the shore, the craftsmen plied their trades – gunsmiths, tinkers, weavers, tailors of bedouin apparel, sandal makers, makers of brass vessels, carpenters, makers of saddles, leather workers, jewelers, and all the support trades of a thriving market.86

It was a town of narrow streets and high-walled houses built cheek-by-jowl. Each house was built around an inner courtyard, and its facade was broken on the outside only by high barred windows and a great door of brass-studded teak with a smaller door inset – *al-khawkhah*, the little plumb. The lime plaster (*juss*) used on the walls made the city shine in the sun and reflect the heat back into the pale blue sky. It was a city reputed for its "good air" (except for when the sand storms blew), and, in truth, the sun served as an incinerator, drying to dust any garbage that might be left on the streets.87

The latter years of the nineteenth century in Arabia were dominated by the unique figure of Kuwait's shaykh, Mubârak bin-Sabâh bin-Jâbir Âl Sabâh, known in history simply as "Mubârak The Great."88 This sobriquet seems well deserved. Mubârak's personality is portrayed in H. V. F. Winstone's excellent biography of the shaykh's contemporary, Captain W. H. I. Shakespear, the adventurous British political agent in Kuwait and eastern Arabia.89 Mubârak ruled Kuwait from 1896 to 1915.

86*AMFR* #73, April-June, 1910, pp. 12-15.
87E. Calverley, *Days and Nights...*, pp. 12-20. It must be admitted, however, that in the most crowded alleyways there lingered a miasma of odor from latrines, and the shore was often dotted with fecal matter awaiting the flushing action of the next incoming tide.
88Mubârak came to power by assassinating his brother Muhammad May 17, 1896. Assisted by his two elder sons, Jâbir and Sâlim (both later to rule Kuwait), he also had his other brother, Jarrâh, murdered. The Kuwait population accepted the new order with some relief.
89H. V. F. Winstone, *Captain Shakespear: A Portrait* (London: Jonathan Cape, 1976), especially pp. 65-71. See also H. R. P. Dickson, *The Arab of the Desert* (London: George Allen & Unwin Ltd., 1951), especially pp. 266-272.

In the nature of its commercial activities, Kuwait developed close relationships with Basrah and Arabic speaking Persia, particularly the shaykhdom of Muhammarah on the Shatt-ul-'Arab. When the Ottomans' control was firmly reestablished over southern Iraq in the late nineteenth century, they tried to assume control of Kuwait. Mubârak's initial problems, therefore, were how to safeguard his autonomy. He found his strongest ally in Britain, whom he courted beginning in 1897. At his insistence, the British arranged a formal agreement, signed January 23, 1899. It led in 1903-04 to Kuwait becoming fully a protectorate of Great Britain. This forestalled Ottoman ambitions with respect to Kuwait and, not incidentally, also blocked German ambitions to use Kuwait as a railhead in the Gulf for the ambitious project known as the Berlin to Baghdad Railroad. On the strength of his 1899 agreement with Britain, Mubârak announced Kuwait's autonomy from the Ottoman Empire, and his descendants continue to dominate the house of Âl Sabâh in the modern politics of the State of Kuwait.

Stanley Mylrea, the main architect of the Arabian Mission's work in Kuwait, says of Mubârak: "He was the maker of modern Kuwait, a man of long vision and great ability. Under him there was good government. Order and tranquillity were the order of the day and of the night. Mubârak's influence extended far out into the desert. He was the real tribal shaikh." Writing his memoirs in the late 1940s, Mylrea adds, "My memory still lingers over Mubârak with the greatest admiration."[90]

These adulatory comments are somewhat tempered by those of Paul Harrison. From his uncompromised hero-worship of 'Abd-ul-'Azîz Âl Sa'ûd, Harrison (who knew both men well) was of the opinion that, while Mubârak was an able administrator and governor, he lacked the charisma of his younger protégé and would not have made as strong a mark on history were it not for his cleverness in making an alliance with the British.[91]

[90]C. Stanley G. Mylrea, *Kuwait Before Oil: Memoirs of Dr. C. Stanley G. Mylrea, Pioneer Medical Missionary of the Arabian Mission, Reformed Church in America* (mimeographed typescript of the original manuscript owned by Elizabeth Zwemer Pickens and edited by Samuel M. Zwemer; originally written between 1945 and 1951 and circulated in limited edition by Dorothy Van Ess), p. 37.

[91]Paul W. Harrison, *The Arab at Home* (New York: Thomas Y. Crowell Co., 1924), pp. 140-141. Robert Lacey gives what is perhaps a rounded portrait of Mubârak when he speaks of him as a shrewd Machiavellian political personality with a fine sense of strategy, balancing off powers (the Âl Sa'ûd and the Âl Rashîd, the Turks and the British) against each other in order to assure for himself a greater measure of autonomy, security, and influence in central Arabia [Robert Lacey, *The Kingdom: Arabia & the house of Sa'ud* (New York: Avon Books, 1980), pp. 36-37].

The Arabian Mission, almost from the first days of its establishment, had considered Kuwait to be a very promising site for its work.[92] It had two principal virtues. First, it was a relatively clean place. Compared to Basrah, Bahrain, and Muscat, it was a healthy place. It was true that flies were everywhere and carried endemic eye diseases especially afflicting children, but in Kuwait there were few mosquitoes and, therefore, no malaria except in the oasis settlement of Jahrâ', some twenty miles west at the end of Kuwait Bay. Tuberculosis, syphilis, and scurvy (among pearl divers) were endemic, and smallpox epidemics broke out from time to time. Its low humidity was matched by some breathtakingly high day-time temperatures – sometimes as high as 160° Fahrenheit in the shade – during the summer, but its nights were almost always pleasant. You could sleep on the roof at night without a mosquito net, and all that annoyed was the persistently pesky fly in the morning heralding the rising of the sun. By and large it was a town that one could easily come to enjoy.

Kuwait's second and more significant virtue lay in the fact that it was a commercial hub with many routes of access into the interior deserts. Its influence reached far inland and was strengthened by the close relationship which evolved between Mubârak the Great and 'Abd-ul-'Azîz Âl Sa'ûd, Sultân of Najd. Even though the mission established itself in Kuwait after 'Abd-ul-'Azîz embarked upon his political career, on more than one occasion members of the Sa'ûdî royal family availed themselves of the medical services provided by the mission in Kuwait, and both Drs. Bennett and Mylrea could justly claim to have been friends of the founder of the modern Sa'ûdî state.

[92]Robert Lacey describes Kuwait in those days as "this unpromising driblet of sand in the armpit of the Persian Gulf…" (Lacey, *The Kingdom*, p. 34). It is not a fair description, but it's cute.

From 1896 Mubârak was the mentor of the exiled scion of the house of Âl Sa'ûd, 'Abd-ul'Azîz, and protector of his father, 'Abd-ur-Rahmân. 'Abd-ur-Rahmân bin-Faysal had taken refuge in Bahrain under the terms of his surrender in 1891 to the house of Âl Rashîd. In 1893 he applied to Muhammad bin-Sabâh Âl Sabâh for refuge in Kuwait and moved there with his family. Muhammad was a client of the Ottomans and, being weak, was fast letting the power slip out of his hands. Mubârak, the younger half-brother of Muhammad, assassinated the ruler in the spring of 1896 and assumed the amîrate. He was pleased to continue giving sanctuary to 'Abd-ur-Rahmân Âl Sa'ûd, who had proven himself no friend of the Ottomans. Mubârak was also ambitious for a larger slice of influence in Arabia. That brought him into conflict with the Âl Rashîd and their Shammar tribal confederation. To strengthen his position, he pleaded for stronger relations with Great Britain.

Through all these maneuvers, the young 'Abd-ul-'Azîz was Mubârak's observant student, and it was Mubârak who gave his blessing to the undertaking which resulted in 'Abd-ul- 'Azîz's dramatic coup against the Âl Rashîd in Riyadh in January, 1902. Mylrea commented:

> It is to Mubarak that the great king, Ibn Saud, owes his early training, for Ibn Saud spent his boyhood in Kuwait. Mubarak took a great fancy to the young lad and undoubtedly molded his character in the impressionable days of boyhood. It is not too much to say that had it not been for Mubarak, Ibn Saud would never have become the historic commanding figure that everyone acknowledges today to be perhaps the greatest Arab since the days of the early Caliphs.[93]

Indeed, in the years to follow it was 'Abd-ul-'Azîz Âl Sa'ûd who grew to become the unchallenged Great One of Arabia and to dominate all developments there for over half a century.

---

[93]Mylrea, *Kuwait...*, p. 37.

From early 1902, therefore, the militant Wahhâbî state of 'Abd-al-'Azîz Âl Sa'ûd was the major force reshaping the Gulf region. It was the enduring power in Arabia to be reckoned with into the early 1930s, when it was itself overwhelmed and displaced by the rise of the politics of oil.

The Wahhâbî movement, to the leadership of which 'Abd-ul-'Azîz fell heir, had a great impact upon the Arabian Mission. Stanley Mylrea, who served in Kuwait from 1914 to 1941, was witness to several events which shaped the history of Kuwait-Sa'ûdî relations and, hence, the evolution of the political configuration of the peninsula.

The year was 1914; the season was spring. 'Abd-ul-'Azîz had but recently (1912) expelled the Ottomans from the eastern province of al-Hasâ' and established his position as Imâm of the Ikhwân. A special conference was to be held in Kuwait between him, Mubârak, the British, and representatives of the Ottoman government. The agenda of the meeting was to be the Ottoman demand to establish a consulate in Kuwait, and behind that was the question of whether Kuwait could be pressured into becoming the terminal for the southern extension of the Berlin to Baghdad railway. Toward neither project was Mubârak particularly sympathetic, but it was a time for delicate diplomacy. The winds of war were rising, but people still talked of peace.

'Abd-ul-'Azîz approached Kuwait city with a considerable host but chose not to enter it, fearing (Mylrea speculated) Ottoman treachery. It is also likely that he understood how difficult it would be to restrain his Ikhwân,[94] so newly enlisted in his cause, within the freewheeling atmosphere of Kuwait town. In any case, a fever had struck the Sa'ûdî camp, and 'Abd-ul-'Azîz sent a request to Mubârak that Mylrea come and treat his sick. Mylrea was duly sent. Arriving at the camp he set straightaway to work. Only after he had done what he could do medically did he report to the amîr.

They fell into a long discussion on medicine in which 'Abd-ul-'Azîz showed himself well versed in classical Arab medical theory, particularly that of Avicenna (Ibn-Sînâ).

> ...As the discussion proceeded I ventured to suggest that the spiritual side of the doctor's work was even more important than the physical side. The doctor must love his patients. Ibn Saud

[94]We have noted the evolution of the Ikhwân in part 1, pp. 64, 65, and 69-70, especially footnote 32.

agreed with me. Then he went on to say that medicine was a prime requirement for humanity. It was then that I said to him,

"Why don't you let us come to Riadh and build you a hospital?"

"Doctor," he said, "let me tell you a story. The Angel Gabriel was once standing at the Gates of Paradise when a believer arrived and asked to be admitted. Gabriel questioned the man awhile and then said to him, 'You may enter, but before you do, you must first sacrifice a sheep to the big golden statue you see to one side of the gates.' 'I asked pardon of Allah,' came back the answer. 'I am no idolater. I do not sacrifice to idols.' 'Well, well,' allowed Gabriel, 'a sheep is a big thing to insist on. What about a fowl?' 'It makes no difference,' vociferated the applicant for admission. 'I do not sacrifice to idols.' 'Not even a fly?' queried Gabriel. 'If you offer a fly, you will satisfy the letter of the law and can go in.' 'Never, never, never!' shouted the poor man. 'There is no God but Allah and Muhammad is his prophet.' As he said these words, a booming voice rang out from the distance. 'Admit him, he is a true believer.' Not long afterwards another believer presented himself for admission and was faced with the same test. He successfully withstood Gabriel's command to sacrifice either a sheep or a fowl, but when it came to a fly he lost his courage. The possibility of being shut out from Paradise was too much for him. He sacrificed the fly. Once more the booming voice rang out. 'Away with him to Gehennum! He is no true believer.'

"Do you see what I mean?" went on Ibn Saud. "In Central Arabia we are not only men of one religion, we are all members of the same sect of that religion. I know perfectly well that if you missionaries come into my territory and settle there you will come with your special message and your books. Men's minds will become unsettled and I shall have trouble. No. Not even a fly will I offer to any other religion. When I need you I will send for you, but I cannot invite you to live permanently in my country."[95]

That is as fair and clear a statement of 'Abd-ul-'Azîz's policy with respect to the mission as can be read anywhere. Even after repressing the fanaticism of the Ikhwân, he personally departed from it only toward the end of his life.

[95]Mylrea, *Kuwait...*, pp. 71-73.

The First World War broke out in the Gulf, and Britain was anxious to court 'Abd-ul'Azîz's support to keep peace in Arabia. In 1915 a significant development took place that, in the outcome, weakened Kuwait as a Gulf power and poisoned Kuwait-Sa'ûdî relations for years to come. In January 'Abd-ul-'Azîz suffered a defeat at the hands of the Âl Rashîd Shammar forces supported by the Ottomans. In the engagement, the talented British political agent in Kuwait, Captain William Shakespear, who was manning a field gun for the Sa'ûdîs, was killed. As a result of the defeat, 'Abd-ul-'Azîz's prestige was damaged, and the powerful 'Ajmân tribe saw it as an opportunity to assert their independence. Toward the close of the year 'Abd-ul-'Azîz was beleaguered in the city of Hufûf by the 'Ajmân. He called for help from his mentor, Mubârak of Kuwait, and the latter sent an army which was successful in defeating the 'Ajmân besiegers.

'Abd-ul-'Azîz wanted to punish the leaders of the offending tribe, but the leader of the Kuwaiti army, Shaykh Sâlim bin-Mubârak, for reasons not altogether clear,[96] granted them sanctuary in Kuwait. 'Abd-ul-'Azîz was furious; he never forgave Sâlim. It is one of the quirks of history that on November 28, 1915, Mubârak, who might have managed to defuse the situation, died, while the victorious Kuwaiti army was still several marches from home. Jâbir, Mubârak's eldest son, was elected to succeed him, but Jâbir was not to reign for very long.

Before Kuwaiti-Sa'ûdî relations deteriorated further, a second memorable encounter between Mylrea and 'Abd-ul-'Azîz took place in November, 1916. Shaykh Khaz'al of Muhammarah (who frequently vacationed in Kuwait and maintained a rather grand residence there), Shaykh Jâbir bin-Mubârak of Kuwait, and 'Abd-ul-'Azîz Âl Sa'ûd had been called to meet in Kuwait for a *durbar*[97] convened by Sir Percy Cox, then British political

---

[96]Perhaps Sâlim's motive was to appear as the magnanimous prince granting sanctuary to one who appeals for it. In bedouin culture, even a sworn enemy may take refuge in your home if he can first gain entrance.
[97]A British-India term describing a high-level consultation of chiefs customarily accompanied by much ritual and pomp.

resident in the Gulf, but already a "ruler" in his own right. The three Arab rulers, after the affairs of state had been concluded with all the trappings of British oriental pomp and ceremony, paid a courtesy call on Stanley Mylrea in his fine new house on the hill. The animated discussion in the Mylrea sitting room had to do with "the efficacy of charms in illness."[98] Over against the Shî'ah Shaykh Khaz'al, who was in 'Abd-ul-'Azîz Âl Sa'ûd's eyes nothing but a rank *kâfir* (an unbeliever), 'Abd-ul-'Azîz argued that it was faith in God that made any medical therapy effective. It was a statement that much impressed Mylrea.

This was probably the last contact the mission had with 'Abd-ul-'Azîz through Kuwait. The fault for this was by no means Mylrea's. It had to do with the sudden deterioration of relations between Kuwait and Sa'ûdî Arabia that shortly followed. In any case, it significantly changed the role Kuwait station was expected to play as a doorway into the Arabian interior.

A little more than two months after Mylrea had played host to the three rulers, in February, 1917, Shaykh Jâbir Âl Sabâh took ill. He refused to see Mylrea – much to the latter's disgust – and instead insisted upon being treated by a bedouin healer with his amulets, and then he died February 5. Jâbir, who obviously got along well with 'Abd-ul-'Azîz Âl Sa'ûd, was succeeded as ruler by his brother, Sâlim, who did not. And Sâlim's reign was neither peaceful nor prosperous.

In 1918 the British instituted a sea blockade of Kuwait because they believed that supplies were reaching Ottoman forces through that port. Sâlim was certain that this was the result of 'Abd-ul-'Azîz's machinations against him. The British blockade hurt Kuwait's economy seriously, and invective began to fly back and forth between Kuwait and Riyadh. The breaking point was reached in September, 1920, when 'Abd-ul-'Azîz imposed his own embargo on trade between his desert tribes and Kuwait.[99] At the same time he sent his then-loyal lieutenant, Faysal ad-Duwwîsh, a brilliant desert general and hardline Ikhwân leader, against Kuwait with a large army.

Kuwait had had some advance warning. Sporadic incidents in the desert had concluded with a defeat of Kuwaiti forces in April, 1920. The town had

---

[98]From the original hand-written account by Stanley Mylrea in a report entitled "Kuwait Medical Report, 1916-1917," in the author's document collection.
[99]This embargo was not officially lifted until 1940.

long since outgrown its two sets of old city walls. Mubârak's boast that *he* was the city's walls no longer applied. So Sâlim, on May 22, 1920, ordered a new wall built in the midst of the summer's worst heat. It was completed in September, four months later,[100] and stretched from the slaughterhouse on the city's west side three miles to encompass Dasmân Palace on the eastern end. It was a remarkable achievement withal, and was completed just in time to meet the threat.

In spite of British warnings that they must leave Kuwait alone – Kuwait, after all, had been fully a British protectorate since 1903 – the army of Ikhwân moved in, and on October 10, 1920, they attacked the oasis town of Jahrâ', where Sâlim and Kuwait's forces had concentrated. Kuwait was bested in the initial engagements, and Shaykh Sâlim was trapped in the Jahrâ' fort. Were it not for British naval and air support and the entirely unexpected but timely intervention of 600 Shammar cavalry, Kuwait would have lost everything. As it turned out, the Ikhwân had to withdraw with heavy losses on October 11. The Battle of Jahrâ' was won. The new Kuwait city walls never had to be tested.[101]

Shaykh Sâlim died quite suddenly February 27, 1921, five months after his historic victory over the Ikhwân. He was succeeded by his nephew,

---

[100]It is interesting to note that the date of 1920 and the building of the city wall were used in the 1950s as the marker for establishing whether a resident of Kuwait qualified for citizenship as a "native."

[101]The walls, built of coral rock and mud and dotted at regular intervals with turrets and five main gates – clockwise: Dasmân, Bra'sî (meaning "desert gecko" and now renamed more elegantly, "Sha'ab," or "people's gate"), Shâmiyyah, Jahrâ', and Maqsab – were difficult to maintain. Finally, after those for whom those walls were a nostalgic reminder of heroic times had died, the walls were quickly dismantled. They were gone by December, 1954. Only one piece, that which "guards" Dasmân Palace, was spared. The gates were left standing and now are surrounded by landscaped parkland. Of these, the Slaughterhouse Gate (*Bâb-ul-Maqsab*) on the west side of the city, the most modest of the five structures, was the only gate to be blown up by the Iraqi forces of occupation during their retreat in 1992. A poor replica of it has since been erected on the same site, like a bookmark holding a place.

Shaykh Ahmad bin-Jâbir Âl Sabâh, March 28. Ahmad had been in Riyadh pursuing peace negotiations with the Sa'ûdîs when Sâlim died. He was the people's choice for ruler. Many of the townsfolk resented Sâlim's policies, feeling that he had precipitated the war with 'Abd-ul-'Azîz Âl Sa'ûd and the hardship of the desert embargo. Ahmad took over on the condition that he accept a council of advisors and not follow the autocratic style of his predecessors.102 The townsfolk had no desire to be caught up in another unpopular war such as Shaykh Sâlim had forced upon them. Ahmad was a man more like his father, a man of peace. During the Battle of Jahrâ', Ahmad had been the commander of the defenders of Kuwait city. He had been watching the work of the mission, and throughout his long reign he was steady in his high respect for it.

Forty-one years old when he assumed the amîrate, Shaykh Ahmad had an uphill climb ahead of him. The small country was still recovering from the Battle of Jahrâ', but complications mounted up. Between an assertive Sir Percy Cox managing British interests in Iraq and the Gulf, and the sultan of Najd who had still not satisfied his political ambitions, it was Ahmad's main task simply to survive. Remarkably, he did.

At the 'Uqayr Conference (concluded December 4, 1922), Ahmad was represented by his British political agent, Major More. At the end of a frustrating five days of fruitless debate between 'Abd-ul-'Azîz Âl Sa'ûd and the representative of King Faysal of Iraq, Cox took a blue pencil to a map and carved out the boundaries, taking two-thirds of Ahmad's territory to placate the other two.

This was not the end of it. The borders defined by the 'Uqayr Conference did not stop the movement of bedouin tribes. Some Najdî tribes took refuge in Kuwait from 'Abd-ul-'Azîz's taxations. When Ahmad refused to be his tax collector, 'Abd-ul-'Azîz slapped Kuwait under a trade embargo. It was kept in force from 1923 to 1937.

Kuwait was still struggling back from the economic impact of the war-time embargoes imposed by the Sa'ûdî and British authorities together. Then the

---

102A twelve-member "Consultative Council" of Kuwait's most prominent personalities was formed and began regular meetings in April, 1921. Within two months, however, it had fallen into a cycle of internal bickering and ceased to function. Ahmad, therefore, returned to the pattern of autocratic rule [Husayn Khalaf al-Shaykh Khaz'al, *Tarîkh-ul-Kuwayt ulSiyâsî* [*A Political History of Kuwait*] (Beirut: Matba'atu-Dâr-il-Kutub, 1970)].

Japanese began flooding the world market with cultured pearls. A third blow! Kuwait depended heavily upon its pearling industry, and now the bottom fell out of an already erratic market.

As the desperately bleak period of the mid-1930s drew to an end, oil exploration began. Soon, some small relief was in sight. The first concession was negotiated by an AngloAmerican consortium in 1934. The first productive well was drilled in 1938. The popular excitement and anticipation were quickly dampened, however. With the advent of the Second World War, wells were plugged, and the Kuwait Oil Company (KOC) kept only a skeleton staff in the country while the war raged.

Unrest grew in Kuwait as people became aware of the potential for wealth, and subversive activities out of Iraq inflamed the revolt of a significant portion of Kuwait's merchant class in 1939. The "Merchants' Revolt" was quickly suppressed. Kuwait was a small community, and the high cost of the suppression left scars in Kuwaiti society that are still detectable. While the missionaries were not involved, many of their friends were.[103] The missionaries were grieved by the division of Kuwaiti society. Kuwait was emerging out of an innocent age, and the first signs of a more complex future were becoming evident. Two efforts were made to establish representative government (a revival of the Consultative Council, with which Ahmad began his reign) but were quickly abandoned.

The war years in Kuwait were grim. The cost of staple goods skyrocketed. Trade was restricted and controlled by the British for the war effort. As Japan threatened to overrun India, even missionaries in the Gulf were enlisted into militias and given basic weapons training. There were a series of extraordinarily hot summers. People seeking relief from the heat lay down on wet beach sand and fell asleep and died in the rising tides. Malnutrition was endemic and heat prostration was common. The winters were, by contrast, bitterly cold, and people died of carbon monoxide poisoning, huddled over charcoal brassieres, their windows closed. The days held abject misery, and Arabian Mission personnel – both medical and evangelistic – found themselves worked to the bone.

---

[103]Not a few were still in prison in 1942. In a letter to Garry and Ev DeJong, dated "Acadia," Kodaikanal, S. India, 13th May, 1942, (Bessie had died April 16) Stanley Mylrea wrote, "If Lew [Scudder] would visit my friends in prison some time & give them my salaams, I should be much obliged:- Yusuf Marzuk, Suleiman Adasani, Masalaam Khuthair, & the rest of them. I know they will be sorry to know that Bess has gone" (original hand script in the author's collection).

Development of the oil fields, delayed by the war, was resumed in earnest in 1946. A major contract was given to the large construction company of Bechtel to build KOC's gathering, storage, refining, and delivery systems. As oil company staff increased, the workload on the mission hospitals also increased, but the oil company was generous in its support, even after opening its own hospital facilities in Maqwaʻ a few years later.[104]

Oil exports were modest at first, but they opened up in a major way in 1951. The AngloPersian Oil Company was nationalized by the Iranian prime minister, Muhammad Mosaddeq, in 1951, and the ʻAbbadân oil terminal was shut down.[105] Kuwait was poised to take up the slack and *did*. Even after ʻAbbadân was reopened and oil began to come out of Iran again in 1954, Kuwait's new position as a major exporter was firmly established. By the time its second field, developed by the American Independent Oil Company (AMINOIL, in partnership with Getty Oil) began producing in 1953, wealth was pouring in like a tidal wave.

From 1946 onward, therefore, Shaykh Ahmad's and Kuwait's prospects brightened. But on January 29, 1950, at the age of sixty-nine, Ahmad died. The attending physician was Lewis Scudder, Sr. Ahmad's two sons, Jâbir and Sabâh, both then young men, collapsed in grief.[106] The Scudders took them into their home and for several days tended them personally until they had recovered the public poise expected of them.[107]

---

[104]John Buckley, chief engineer for the oil port of Minâʼ-ul-Ahmadî in the 1950s and 1960s, who married the missionary nurse, Joan Oltoff, in 1949, became virtually an adjunct missionary. Joan, John, and their children were included in all mission family celebrations, and if Dorothy Scudder ever ran up against a sticky engineering or construction problem, the first person she called was John Buckley. His ebullient sense of humor and his resourcefulness made him a much-appreciated individual. The Buckleys retired from KOC in 1968 and lived in Cornwall, England, where Joan continues to live. John died in 1984.

[105]The oil port of ʻAbbadân, downstream from the city of Basrah, began exporting oil in 1909. The Anglo-Iranian Oil Company, owned by British Petroleum (BP), was nationalized by Mosaddeq in March of 1951, and the company closed down. Mosaddeq was ousted by an American-led campaign to restore Shah Mohammed Reza Pahlavi in the summer of 1953. In 1954 BP, along with several other western oil companies, formed a management consortium which reopened the Iranian fields and managed the new National Iranian Oil Company. This did not affect Kuwait's oil production.

[106]Violet Dickson, *Forty Years in Kuwait* (London: George Allen & Unwin Ltd., 1971), p. 190.

[107]Shaykhs Jâbir and Sabâh presented to the Scudders a state-of-the art wire recorder as a token of their gratitude. This continued to survive in the Scudder household for at least two decades.

Ahmad was succeeded by his cousin, Shaykh ʻAbd-Allâh as-Sâlim. Shaykh ʻAbd-Allâh, from early years active in government, had shown both an awareness of his historical moment and a deep, measured wisdom—a man who in many ways justly deserves his reputation as a visionary who shaped the path of modern Kuwait. The fifteen years of his reign were marked by an explosion in Kuwait's oil income and standard of living.

As he came into power, ʻAbd-Allâh was sharply aware of the broader situation in the Middle East. The war over Palestine was at a standstill, but the problem of Palestinian refugees was massive. Kuwait, anticipating radical modernization, was in need of able hands. Among ʻAbd-Allâh's first acts as amîr, therefore, was to issue an invitation to the Palestinian people to come to Kuwait, there to earn a living for themselves and help build up the modern state. ʻAbd-Allâh was quite sensitive to the injustice which the Palestinians had suffered, and, as an Arab nationalist, felt a family obligation toward them as well.

The Palestinians came in large numbers. (Among the first of them was a young electrical engineer trained in Egypt, Yâsir ʻArafât, who found a job with the new Ministry of Public Works.) And Kuwait became for them a true haven, not just for those who physically came, but also for those who remained in the sprawling refugee camps in Lebanon, Jordan, the West Bank, and Gaza, beneficiaries of the substantial cash sent by their relatives in Kuwait. It was not long before the Palestinians came to make up almost half of the population (in the 1970s, some 750,000). They provided Kuwait with productive workers in all sectors and at all levels of the booming economy. [108]

From the point of view of the mission, this sudden influx, which included Christian Palestinians as well as Muslim, meant an abrupt rise in the number of Arabic-speaking Christians. The worshiping community swelled and became at once more complex and more interesting. [109]

[108] Eventually it became a Kuwaiti joke that the government could not afford to hire more Kuwaitis to work in government because, having hired the Kuwaiti, it would have to hire two Palestinians to do his work for him. It indicates that, as the 1960s wore on, the relationship with the Palestinians began to stale. Kuwaitis came to resent the Palestinians' dependence, and yet they were unwilling to take up the tasks non-Kuwaitis came to do. It was a serious moral quandary.

[109] The author, then a teenager, recalls the Saturday evening Arabic worship services bursting at the seams with young Palestinian and other Arab bachelors. Gradually the transition was made to families. But the music in worship, when these new people came, was fantastic.

Shaykh 'Abd-Allâh became amîr at a time when the oil industry in Kuwait was idling in low gear. Perhaps he owed a special debt of gratitude to Muhammad Mosaddeq for closing down the operations of the Anglo-Persian Oil Company in Iran and for increasing Kuwait's production to top speed. But to use this new and unexpectedly abundant revenue responsibly was Shaykh 'Abd-Allâh's greatest challenge. He designed a welfare system which first concentrated on providing essential services – education at all levels and for both boys and girls, health services, cheap power, abundant sweet water, good roads, industrial infrastructure, and public works of all kinds. He then contrived various means for spreading the wealth as broadly as possible.

There can be no doubt that 'Abd-Allâh, a just man, had no choice but to see that every citizen had a share in the new wealth. Its qualitative impact, however, was something he could neither predict nor control. On the heels of years of extreme hardship and suffering, oil wealth came as something of a "rear-end collision" and had what can only be described as a "whiplash" effect upon the moral, spiritual, and cultural dimensions of society not only in Kuwait but in the Gulf as a whole.

Aware that Kuwait had more money than it could responsibly spend on itself, in 1961 'Abd-Allâh initiated the Kuwait Fund for Arab Economic Development, a fund which he explicitly modeled upon his perception of the Arabian Mission. Its purpose was to initiate and fund projects in less advantaged Arab states in education, health care, and public works. Aside from the then-impoverished amîrates down-Gulf, assistance was also given to the Sudan, Jordan, Yemen, Egypt, Tunisia, Algeria, and virtually all Arab countries. By 1968 it had disposed of billions of dollars in low- interest loans and outright grants.

Kuwait's new role as a growing economic giant brought it, somewhat bewildered at times, onto an international stage. The Suez Crisis of 1956 was received with mixed emotions. The growing popularity of Gamâl 'Abd-un-Nâsir of Egypt was backed in Kuwait by a legion of newly installed Egyptian teachers as well as by the youths whom they influenced. The burgeoning Arab expatriate population was also, in large measure, enthralled by the young Egyptian leader. The Suez Crisis, therefore, inspired demonstrations against British interests in Kuwait. They were repressed rather easily, much credit going at the time to Shaykh 'Abd-Allâh al-Mubârak, minister of interior and defense.[110] On the other hand, the more traditional Kuwaiti population reacted ambiguously and seemed to resent the impingement of these remote complications upon their newly prosperous existence. But it was a trend that could not be resisted.

On June 19, 1961, the British, dismantling their empire, gave up their sixty-year role as protectors of Kuwait, declaring, "The Agreement of the 23rd of January, 1899, shall be terminated as being inconsistent with the sovereignty and independence of Kuwait."[111] With independence, Kuwait quickly announced its intention to become a full member of the community of nations.[112] Shaykh 'Abd-Allâh also declared his intention to promulgate a constitution and hold elections for a National Assembly.[113] No sooner had this happened, however, than on June 25, 1961, republican Iraq, under Colonel 'Abd-ul-Karîm Qâsim, announced its intention to annex Kuwait to

[110]Among the more colorful of Kuwait's modern Shaykhs, 'Abd-Allâh was the last son of Mubârak the Great (born after the latter had died and always suspected of having been otherwise conceived). At the time of the Suez Crisis he is said to have heard of a demonstration headed for the British Embassy. Jumping into his automobile and before any of his body guard could react, he rushed down to take up a position across the mob's line of march. Parking his car across the road, he waited for the marchers to arrive. When they came, he casually asked them where they were going. "To the British Embassy to burn it down," they replied. "No," he answered, "you are going home." He drew a line across the road. "The first man who crosses this line will die." The mob dispersed.

'Abd-Allâh got a great deal of mileage out of that rather remarkable story (whether true or not). And, evidently, a good deal of his popularity went to his head. When Sa'ûd bin 'Abd-ul-'Azîz, the new king of Sa'ûdî Arabia, visited Kuwait in the mid-1950s to heal old wounds, it was 'Abd-Allâh al-Mubârak who was in charge of the radio and television coverage. He placed himself prominently in all the events and eclipsed the ruler in the public eye. This did not sit well with Shaykh 'Abd-Allah as-Sâlim and his advisors, and in the time that followed, 'Abd-Allâh al-Mubârak had his wings clipped. He was finally encouraged to seek rest and relaxation outside Kuwait and did so until just a few years before his death. 'Abd-Allâh alMubârak was a great favorite and good friend of Lew Scudder, Sr., and of the mission.

[111]Albaharna, *The Arab Gulf States*, p. 40.

[112]Kuwait joined the Arab League in 1962, in the midst of the Iraq crisis, and, after having its application at first vetoed by the Soviet Union, was admitted as the 111th member of the United Nations on May 14, 1963.

[113]The author, then a student at Hope College, recalls receiving a letter from his father, rejoicing in Kuwait's giant steps toward becoming a true democracy. It was the fulfillment of a missionary dream and one in which the whole mission took pleasure. A constitutional assembly began meeting in 1962. Having drafted a constitution, it was dissolved, and open elections for Kuwait's first National Assembly were held in January, 1963.

the governorate of Basrah to which, Qâsim proclaimed, it historically belonged.

Upon the appeal of the Kuwait government, the British came back in force on July 1. They and the Sa'ûdîs deployed strong military detachments on the Kuwait-Iraq frontier and defied Iraq to act upon its words. Qâsim, who seemed to think that Kuwait would welcome the announcement, had taken no military measures of his own. But his failure in this affair did much to undermine his credibility as a major Arab leader and led to his downfall and death on February 9, 1963, at the hands of a coup mounted by the Ba'ath Party.[114]

Shaykh 'Abd-Allâh died November 24, 1965, a man full of years and honor. He was recognized as the builder of modern Kuwait, whose steady wisdom had guided the people into a new era. He was succeeded by his less resolute half-brother, Shaykh Sabâh as-Sâlim, whose experience in government had begun in 1938. His thirteen-year reign was marked by increasing complexity but no dramatic internal crises or changes in policy. In his days, however, the Egyptian-based movement of the "Muslim Brotherhood"[115] gained strong influence in Kuwait's internal affairs and, when the mission's hospitals were closed in March, 1967, the government moved quickly to expropriate the property and close down the church as well. What would have been forbidden under his predecessor and might even have been disallowed by his successor, Shaykh Sabâh allowed to happen. Popular Kuwaiti revulsion at these sudden developments, however, restrained the move against the church, and the situation of the worshiping community eventually stabilized. Perhaps the timing of these things is otherwise managed. The hospitals, once closed, fell into the hands of the Kuwaiti people and, interestingly enough, they have been cherished for what they symbolized.

---

[114]Iraq remained a serious problem for Kuwait, however. Whenever the various Iraqi regimes which succeeded each other in Baghdad (1963, 1966, 1968, and 1979) needed money, there was no more productive method than finding a pretext to revive tensions with Kuwait.

[115]The Egyptian Muslim Brothers are not to be confused with the Wahhâbî Ikhwân. In Kuwait, they went under the name *Jam'iyyat-ul-Islâhil-Ijtimâ'î* (the Society for Social Reform), led by Yûsuf ar-Rifâ'î. He became, for a time, Kuwait's minister of state and promoted partisan interests in crucial sectors of the government, among them the Ministry of Health. He was removed from under a cloud of disgrace, suspected of malfeasance in office.

Shaykh Sabâh, in his turn, died in 1978, and the succession passed to his cousin (once removed), Shaykh Jâbir al-Ahmad al-Jâbir, a great grandson of Mubârak the Great. Jâbir is a quiet man, soft-spoken, and carefully dignified in public posture. His rule has been cautious, protecting the economic viability of the country against the vagaries of the oil market and carefully guiding Kuwait through the ever more tangled business of international relations. The most dramatic moment of his reign, however, was marked by the Iraqi invasion of August 1990 and its aftermath.[116] To his credit, Kuwait continues to be a viable political entity and has struggled to maintain an open economic cultural posture.

Bahrain: A Pivotal Place

Bahrain is a collection of islands about thirty miles off the Arabian coast, northwest of the thumb of Qatar. Geology has blessed it. The water from the eastward tilting Arabian plate drains toward the Gulf, and around and within

---

[116]Saddâm Husayn at-Takrîtî – the power behind the Iraqi presidency since 1968 and president himself since 1979 – pushed the customary Iraqi ploy with Kuwait beyond its usual bounds. After having fought an inconclusive war with Iran from 1980 to 1988, with a war debt of over 80 billion dollars, Saddâm Husayn went to the well one more time. He demanded that the Arab Gulf states forgive his debts (60 percent of the total) and claimed 2.5 billion dollars from Kuwait as compensation for having "stolen" oil from under Iraqi sovereign territory. Rebuffed by Kuwait, he invaded August 2, 1990, an action that had been planned some two years before. Kuwait was liberated by an allied undertaking – "Desert Storm" – led by the United States (with Britain, France, Sa'ûdî Arabia, Syria, and Egypt), which brought American and Sa'ûdî troops into Kuwait City on February 27, 1991. By Friday, February 28, Desert Storm had concluded.

Among the ambiguities in the whole affair was the position taken by the PLO and Yâsir 'Arafât in particular. The justifications for Palestinian support for Iraq against Kuwait just do not add up against reality. (Similar stands taken by the Sudan, Yemen, and Libya are less difficult to explain.) When the Kuwaiti government was reinstalled, therefore, the mass and official reactions against the resident Palestinian population came as no surprise. They were tragic, but understandable. By 1993, only a handful of Kuwait's more than 700,000 Palestinians remained. The ones that did were those who were able to document their partisanship for Kuwait or were well attested as having been active in the resistance against the Iraqi occupation. The same applied to citizens of Yemen, Sudan, and Libya. But with respect to the Palestinians, the loss of the Kuwait link and relationship has proven a true disaster.

Bahrain it springs up in natural artesian wells.[117] That feature is held to account for its rather curious name: "The land of two seas" – the salt and the sweet.

Bahrain is a land of ancient habitation, perhaps *the* most ancient in the Middle East, the original home of the people later known as the Phoenicians, although that is still debated. Certainly, the archeological remains on the main island indicate a maritime civilization that is at least as old (although with monuments not so grand) as Sumer, the early dynasties of Egypt and the civilization of Mohenjedaro in the Indus valley. With each of these civilizations Dilmun, as the ancient civilization of Bahrain is known, had commercial and cultural links. Situated off the shore of the Arabian mainland, it has always attracted the eye of strategists, and so it has had a stormy history, passing through the hands of many empire builders.

While in some senses Bahrain was a lovely place – given its abundant fresh water, the beauty of its palm groves, and the sultry soft blue sea in which it nestled – it was also a difficult place. Only a few meters above sea level at its highest point, Bahrain marinated in the tepid backwaters of the Arabian Gulf, was massaged by sluggish summer breezes, and was oppressed by a cloying humidity. Stagnant water abounded and provided breeding places for all sorts of pestilence. Malaria, rare elsewhere in Arabia, was rampant. Cholera and dysentery were constant problems. It was indeed, as Cantine had first observed, among the most unhealthy places in the Gulf. Between its benefits and its drawbacks, therefore, Bahrain drew more than its fair share of attention.

The islands, which had once boasted a Christian bishopric, fell early to the Muslims during the Wars of Secession in the mid-seventh century. They had a checkered history, mainly attached to the mainland oasis province now

---

[117]Recent drilling for water in Sa'ûdî Arabia's "Empty Quarter" and massive depletion of the Arabian aquifer has caused many of Bahrain's artesian wells to cease to flow, and there are indications that salt water has begun to leach into the large underground reservoir.

known as al-Hasâ' (or al-'Ahsâ'). At one point Bahrain (which then shared its name with the whole oasis region of eastern Arabia) was a part of the radical heterodox Shî'ah Qarmathian state which terrorized the Muslim world during the tenth and eleventh centuries, impeding trade and pilgrimage and even, at one time, removing the sacred Black Stone from the sanctuary of Mecca. When that state was finally suppressd by a curious alliance of Fâtimid and 'Abbâsid interests, Bahrain fell into obscurity. By the dawn of the sixteenth century, however, it was again involved in the changing patterns of power.

The Portuguese, under the ruthless Alfonso de Albuquerque, occupied Bahrain in 1521 and ended a brief interlude when the sharîf of Mecca ruled the islands. They built a massive fortress whose ruins still stand above the archeological remains of ancient Dilmun on the northern coast. In their turn, the Portuguese were expelled in 1602 by a local revolt which invited in the Safavid Persians. The rising power of Oman, nemesis of the Portuguese, then became a factor in Bahrain's history. The al-Ya'rubî sultan, Sultân bin-Sayf II, expelled the Persians from Bahrain in 1717 even though, by 1720, the Omanis had to sell rights to Bahrain back to the Persians, and Persia even moved into Oman to intervene in the wars of succession which destroyed the al-Ya'rubî dynasty.

The modern history of Bahrain, however, was determined by a force which rose up as if in secret and, quite abruptly, made Bahrain its own center and not just a pawn of other powers. The rise of the 'Utûb in eastern Arabia has already been introduced in our discussion of Kuwait. When the leading families of the 'Utûb in Kuwait – the Âl Sabâh, the Âl Khalîfah, and the Âl Jalâhimah – agreed to part company in 1766, the Âl Khalîfah took for their base the port Zubârah on the peninsula of Qatar.

From Zubârah, the Âl Khalîfah developed a strong commercial presence in the Gulf, dominating the local tribes. Their success was such as to kindle the jealousy of the Persians who, in 1782, attacked Zubârah from Bahrain. They were repulsed, and in their counterattack the Âl Khalîfah found themselves, surprisingly, in possession of the islands. Shaykh Ahmad Âl

Khalîfah, known as "Al-Fâtih" (the Conqueror), governed both Zubârah and Bahrain until his death in 1796. He was succeeded by his son, Salmân.

The year before Ahmad's death, the Âl Sa'ûd of Dar'iyyah had defeated the Banî Khâlid decisively and established Wahhâbî control of eastern Arabia. In the meantime the Âl Bû-Sa'îdî dynasty had emerged in Oman under its powerful Ibâdî Imâm, Ahmad, and had driven the Persians out of Oman (1744). Under Ahmad's son, Sultân, the Omanis retook Bahrain, and Shaykh Salmân retired to his stronghold in Zubârah. But Salmân's troubles were not over. The Âl Sa'ûd were in the business of fervently bringing Arabia under God's rule. The Âl Bû-Sa'îdî, Ibâdî heretics as they were, could not be allowed to hold a strategic position so close to the Âl Sa'ûd's newly won provinces. In 1809 Wahhâbî forces conquered Bahrain, driving out the Omanis and taking the added precaution of conquering Zubârah as well. The hapless Shaykh Salmân Âl Khalîfah and his family were marched off to exile in the Wahhâbî capital of Dar'iyyah.

The next year Salmân won his freedom. Leading his own forces and assisted by both Oman and Persia (a strange conglomeration of bedfellows), the Âl Khalîfah retook Bahrain. Salmân abandoned the old stronghold of Zubârah. It was too vulnerable to Sa'ûdî harassment and too easily assailed by his Âl Jalâhimah cousins, now established in Ra'-sul-Khaymah as the maritime arm of Wahhâbî policy.

That was not the end of the business, however. Twice more the Omanis tried to take the islands but failed. The picture was stabilized with Great Britain's entry into the region. In 1890 the British entered into an "Exclusive Agreement" with the ruler of Bahrain to provide protection. That agreement was reaffirmed in 1892. And Bahrain began referring all its foreign affairs to the British Agency in Busheir. This relationship – characterized by consistent loyalty between the British and the Âl Khalîfah family – proved a critical factor in the establishment and development of the Arabian Mission's work in Bahrain.

Given this swirl of movement through history, by the turn of the century when the Arabian Mission began probing the possibility of establishing a station on the islands, Bahrain was home to a very ethnically diverse society. Arab and Indian seafarers rubbed shoulders with Persian traders and Levantine Jewish pearl merchants. But in the villages there had developed a stolid and hard-working community who knew themselves simply as the Bahârnah (the "quintessential Bahrainis"). In contrast to the ruling group, whose roots lay in Najd and whose religious conditioning was Sunnî, the Bahârnah were Shî'ah Arabs. Their roots lay in the small but pestilential land of Bahrain from of old. The division between the Najdî rulers and the Bahârnah population provided for an internal tension that has continued to bedevil the Island, not least of all in recent times.

Bahrain, however, developed as a moderately open and prosperous society. The occasional dynastic struggles had no great impact upon its overall development. Its wealth lay in its active merchant fleet, and its people made their living on modest agriculture, date production, fishing, and pearl diving – all of which made Bahrain an exporter of staples and a regular stop on the trade routes between Mesopotamia, the Indian subcontinent, and East Africa.

In 1861 Shaykh Muhammad, feeling the pressure of Wahhâbî ambitions, signed a "Perpetual Treaty of Peace and Friendship" with Great Britain, in which the shaykh committed himself against the slave trade and promised to promote British trading ventures in the region. For their part, the British curbed the son of Muhammad's old rival, 'Abd-Allâh, also named Muhammad, and the Wahhâbî interests that he represented.

In the late 1860s tensions broke out between Qatar and Bahrain. In the course of his successful campaign, Muhammad bin-Khalîfah fell afoul of the British. A complicated series of incidents followed in which 'Ali bin-Khalîfah, Muhammad's brother, was killed, and the British finally intervened directly in 1869. Both contenders in the political instability were exiled to India, and the British political resident in Bushier convened the local notables to express their preference of ruler. Their choice fell upon 'Îsâ bin-'Alî bin-Khalîfah. Then residing in Qatar, the young shaykh returned to Bahrain to take up his fifty-four year rule, and came to be known in local legend as 'Îsâ the Great. On the basis of two treaties (signed in 1880 and 1892), Shaykh 'Îsâ bound himself even more closely to the British.

During the reign of Shaykh Hamad bin-'Îsâ (1924-1942), as James Belgrave puts it, "Bahrain was transformed into a modern state."[118] Oil was

---

[118]James H. D. Belgrave, *Welcome to Bahrain* (Bahrain: The Augustan Press, 1975), pp. 134-135.

discovered, and the first concession agreement was signed inaugurating the Bahrain Petroleum Company in 1930. As we have noted in the discussion of Kuwait's history, the Japanese had been introducing cultured pearls onto world markets, and Gulf pearling fleets had suffered. The revenues from oil, therefore, came at an opportune moment for Bahrain. Bahrain became an important resource for fueling the British war effort during World War II. Shaykh Hamad's son, Salmân, took up the reigns of government when his father died early in 1942. He carried on the progressive development of Bahrain, establishing in 1958 normal relations with Sa'ûdî Arabia, a notable and necessary achievement.

In December, 1961, Shaykh Salmân died and was succeeded by his son, 'Îsâ. It fell to Shaykh 'Îsâ to regain Bahrain's independence from Britain in August of 1971, the groundwork for which had been laid by his father. In 1973 Bahrain joined the United Nations and the League of Arab States, and in December of that year Shaykh 'Îsâ promulgated a constitution and a National Assembly was elected. But the mission remembers Shaykh 'Îsâ particularly for his breadth of vision and his appreciation of the work which the mission had done, both in the field of medicine and in education. The tradition Shaykh Salmân had established of opening the doors to constructive progress gave Bahrain society a strong foundation. In spite of its relatively modest revenue from oil, that foundation has made Bahrain an influential presence in the Gulf.

In its work within and out of Bahrain, the cosmopolitan and liberal character of the island proved a main factor in the fortunes of the Arabian Mission. The mission has continued to find a welcome in Bahraini society to the present day.

Oman: From Empire to Dependence

Oman was the third area in which the Arabian Mission established its presence in Arabia.

Oman is another a land of antiquity. Archeological finds trace a history at least as ancient as that of Palestine, and it is part of what the Bible knew as the lands of incense. In the book of Esther it is known as "India" and linked to Ethiopia. This is consistent with the history of the whole of southern Arabia, contested as it was between the Ethiopians and the Persians. But Oman also had a long history of its own, having developed as a major maritime power in the dim days of recorded history.

Arabian mythology claims that Arabia as a whole was settled by the descendants of two individuals, 'Adnân and Qahtân. Historians have exercised themselves to determine whence these names came, but it is clear that there is at least a cultural distinction to be drawn between the Arabs of the peninsula's central deserts and northern towns,[119] and the Arabs of the mountains, wilderness, and seaports of the south.[120] Wendell Phillips argues well that, whatever the case, the cultural profile of South Arabia shows an ancient link with the Mesopotamian valley and with Canaan.[121] Oman, as such, was probably first settled by migrations from the west, where the culture of Shebah (present day Yemen) was well rooted. A second and much later migration of northern Arabs seems to have been of approximately the same magnitude as the first. For at least the last 2,000 years, therefore, there has existed a structure of inter-ethnic tension still very much a part of the Omani consciousness. Predating these Arab colonizations of Oman, there were also prolonged periods of Persian rule, the marks of which remain in the intricate and still operating underground water conduits known locally as *aflâj* (the singular is *falaj*), some of which may date from as early as the ninth century BC.

In the seventh century, Oman easily converted to Islam in the first waves of conquest. But by the latter part of the century, it moved away from the two elitist forms of mainline Islam and the majority of Omanis adopted what came to be known as Ibâdî doctrine.[122] The country was never very stable

119These are noted as descendants of 'Adnân and known as *Arabized* Arabs (*al-'arab al-musta'ribah* or *al-muta'arribah*) and who claim an Abrahamic root through Ishmael.

120These claim descent from Qahtân and know themselves as *Arab* Arabs ('arab-ul-'urûbah or simply al-'âribah) and who claim an Abrahamic root through his son by Keturah.

121Phillips, *Oman*, pp. 1-3.

122The "Ibâdîs are a sect of Islam represented now only in Oman and in North Africa. It is a moderate branching off from the Khârijite movement which dates from 656. Essentially, as with other Muslim sectarians, they parted ways with other Muslims over the question of political succession. For the Khawârij the Imâm of Islam was chosen on the basis of his talent and merit—in short, on the basis of charisma. He had to be, in short, the best man of his time. The Sunnî thesis was that the Imâm had to be descended from the clan of the Prophet (at least from his tribe, the Quraysh) and have the sanction of the Muslim elite (*ahl-us-sunnah wa al-jama'ah*); for the Shî'ah in their various branches, except for the 5ers of Yemen, the Imâm had to be a blood descendant of the Prophet through the line of Fâtimah (the Prophet's daughter) and 'Alî (the Prophet's cousin and son-inlaw, the fourth of the "Rightly Guided" caliphs). The radical views of the Khawârij on

but occasionally knew periods of high prosperity and culture. The enterprise of importing black slaves into Arabia is said to have been begun by Omani rulers in the eighth century, and thereafter slavery was an important component of the local economy and enterprise. By the thirteenth century, Omanis had established strongholds in East Africa and controlled the trade between there and Arabia proper. Adventurous seafarers from before the days of Islam, Omani initiatives expanded under the Muslim dispensation and Omani ships ventured as far as China. The Islamization of Malaysia and of the islands of the Malay Archipelago was primarily the work of Omani missionary merchants.[123] The almost total Omani monopoly of trade in the Indian Ocean was virtually unchallenged until the Portuguese rounded the Cape of Good Hope in the last years of the fifteenth century and became the spearhead of the western imperial transformation of the region. "Within

this subject made them a contentious and rebellious element as the Muslim state struggled to establish itself. The breakaway movement also had a difficult time producing leaders who were unquestionably the "best men of their times." The radical elements of this movement were severely defeated in 658, while the more moderate of them, under the leadership of the scholarly 'Abd-Allâh bin-Ibâd (whence the movement's name), prospered quietly for a time in and around the town of Basrah. It was characterized by high standard of religious scholarship and strict pietistic ethics. The Ibâdîs, true to the Khârijite root, continued to practice a political meritocracy. It was the Achilles' heel of the movement, because it meant that the leadership was discontinuous and given to in-fighting. Ibn-Ibâd was succeeded in leadership of this growing group by another scholar, his contemporary and protégé from the Omani town of Nizwah named Ja'far bin-Zayd al-Azdî. It is this Ja'far al-Azdî who brought Ibâdî teaching home with him when he was exiled from Basrah in the early years of the eighth century. Sunnî persecution pushed the Ibâdîs increasingly into a revolutionary stance and, after the ground had been prepared through zealous missionary work, the Ibâdîs of Oman rose in revolt in 750. Although defeated by 'Abbâsid armies in 752, the Ibâdî movement continued to grow. By 793, and with the immigration of the remnant of the leadership of Basrah between 795 and 808, Oman had become the spiritual center of the movement. The Omanî saying has it that "[true Ibâdî] knowledge was laid as an egg in Mecca; it grew as a chick in Basrah; then it flew to Oman." From the ninth century into modern times, a somewhat discontinuous series of Ibâdî imâms ruled Oman with greater or lesser fortune, alternating with the rise and fall of secular tribal leaders, and the occasional incursion of outside powers, among them the Qarmathians of Bahrain. But by and large it was Ibâdîsm which stamped Oman with its unique cultural and national character. (See T. Lewicki, "Al-Ibâdiyya," in B. Lewis, *et al*, eds., *The Encyclopaedia of Islam, New Edition*, vol. III (Leiden: Brill, 1979), pp. 658-660.

[123]The adventurousness and enterprise of Omani seafarers is reflected in the stories of Sindbad the Sailor, said to have been a native of the Omani town of Sohar.

eight years of their arrival, the 'civilizing' Portuguese were in virtual possession of strategic parts of the East African coast south of the Equator and held the rest in fear; Portugal had reached the bloody zenith of the short-lived golden age."

In August, 1507, Albuquerque, the Portuguese admiral, raided and occupied the key port city of Musqat (Muscat). There, and in the twin city of Matrah, the Portuguese built fortresses and extended their control deep into the interior. The Ottomans, under their great admiral Piri Ra'îs, for a brief time asserted themselves in the Indian Ocean. They sacked and occupied Muscat and Matrah in 1551, expelling the Portuguese, but within two years the Portuguese were back. Under the Ibâdî Imâm, Nâsir bin Murshid al-Ya'rubî, the Omanis expelled the Portuguese from the interior in 1620. Their fortresses in Muscat and Matrah fell, in 1650, to Nâsir's successor, Sultân bin Sayf al-Ya'rubî I. The Portuguese occupation of Oman was a grim phase, and the Christian cross became a hated symbol – with ample justification.

With the expulsion of the Portuguese, the power of Oman was able to recollect itself and, by 1698, consolidate the traditional Omani holdings in East Africa into a loose-knit empire, particularly the island of Zanzibar. During the years of conflict with the Portuguese, the strong navy which Oman had developed got into the habit of raiding whatever shipping passed through their zone of influence. This eventually attracted the attention of the English East India Company, which began to work toward eliminating Arab piracy in the Indian Ocean and the Gulf.

Sultân bin Sayf II, who succeeded his grandfather to the Omani throne in 1711, continued to expand Oman's empire-building efforts. He briefly captured Bahrain, expelling the Persians. But with his death in 1719 there followed a protracted civil war, followed by the destruction of the Omani navy in a storm in 1723. Oman was severely weakened.

In 1737 the Persians, under Nâdir Shâh, occupied Oman, ostensibly to settle the civil strife. But the Persians were unwelcome. A leading merchant and governor of the ancient port city of Sohâr, Ahmad bin Sa'îd Âl Bû-Sa'îdî, rallied the Omani factions and eventually expelled the Persians. This occurred while the Âl Sa'ûd were emerging as the power to be reckoned with in eastern Arabia, and the 'Utûb were shaping their destiny out of Kuwait. In 1749 Ahmad bin Sa'îd was elected imâm of the Ibâdî tribes of Oman, and the Ya'rubî dynasty was officially brought to an end.

The modern state of Oman was born in 1749 with the rise of the Imâm Ahmad bin-Sa'îd. He proceeded to reestablish Oman as the major power of the Arab Gulf. His descendants, the Sayyids (later the Sultans) of Oman continued to be vigorous rulers but did not have the religious sanction within the Ibâdî Muslim tradition.[124] The Âl Bû-Sa'îdîs controlled a maritime empire which included the island of Zanzibar, the port of Mombassa, and large parts of the hinterland of East Africa now split between Kenya and Tanzania. It was a mercantile empire supported by a well-disciplined and active navy. Oman, under the Âl BûSa'îdîs, also controlled the Arab Gulf, with possessions even on the Persian mainland – especially the ports of Bandar 'Abbâs and Gwadar. And Omani merchants dominated trade as far afield as Malacca (in modern Malaysia), Calcutta, and Jakarta in Indonesia.

By the late 1700s, however, with growing British intervention against Arab piracy and the slave trade (the backbone of the Omanî empire's economy), and with the flood of cheap European manufactured goods in the market, Omani influence and power declined rapidly. In 1798 Oman came under treaty restraint by the British. In 1822 and 1845 the sultan signed treaties which effectively ended Oman's official participation in the slave trade. In 1892, hedging against French interference in the Indian Ocean, the British obliged the sultan to pledge that he would not sell property to any foreigner other than the British, a matter which caused the Arabian Mission some inconvenience. Other agreements followed which gave the British first call on mineral rights, rendering Oman a protectorate of the British in all but name. Britain became increasingly involved in the Âl Bû-Sa'îdîs' dynastic struggles, supporting one claimant against another and inconsistently addressing itself to problems arising out of a chronically rebellious interior.

The last Âl Bû-Sa'îdî sultan to rule also as an elected imâm of the Ibâdîs was 'Azzân bin-Qays from 1868 to 1871. For forty-two years, from 1871 to 1913, there was no imâm in Oman. As Wendell Phillips explains, "The office of Imam was never...continuous....The Imam...is elected, to make good

---

[124]Ahmad bin-Sa'îd could not pass on his mantle as Imâm to his descendants. That was none of his affair. The choice of the appropriate leader rested with the tribes of the mountains and the consultative council of Ibâdî shaykhs, and the traditional contest for power between the sultan on the coast and the imâm in the mountains sputtered along down through the 1960s. In fact, the rulers of this dynasty have seen in the office of imâm a burden rather than a privilege. For the most part, they have not sought it.

the shortcomings of the people in the knowledge of the *shar'* [the Islamic code of law]. The man elected must be a mature male free from physical blemish; the election is accomplished in a solemn conclave of Ibadhi elders according to a set pattern; the supposition is that the person chosen has certain qualifications – personal piety, humility, theological learning."[125]

Unlike the classical Sunnî and Shî'î doctrines of the imâmate, the Ibâdî imâm did not have to have a family link to the Prophet Muhammad. The Khârijî movement from which the Ibâdîs descend was criticized by its opponents for insisting that the imâm must be "the best man of his time." In theory, the elected imâm was not limited in jurisdiction: He was elected to hold office as the *Imâm-ul-Muslimîn* (the imâm of all Muslims whatso- and wheresoever). The Ibâdî provision that there can be long times when the office is left vacant, however, did provide the possibility that, even during a time when the office was occupied, the Âl Bû-Sa'îdî *sayyids* or sultans might still exercise their worldly authority. The difficulty arose when the elected imâm chose to challenge them.[126]

The Arabian Mission entered Oman late in 1893 during the reign of Sultan Faysal bin-Turkî. Faysal was not a strong ruler, although he was characterized by personal courage, and his reign was turbulent. The now separate jurisdiction of Zanzibar, long a vital part of the Omani maritime empire, and the British frequently and inconsistently interfered with internal affairs. Surviving as a ruler in Oman took some finesse. In the end, surviving one extremely serious coup attempt in 1895 when Muscat itself was looted, Faysal managed it.[127] Already having shut off the importing of slaves through Omani ports, and endeavoring to control the arms trade which annoyed the British in India, Faysal imposed strict control over the importation and export of weapons, an important part of the Omani economy since the second Afghan War of 1880. In 1913, incensed by the interference, the Ibâdî tribes of inner Oman elected the first imâm of the

---

[125]Phillips, *Oman: A History*, p. 154.
[126]Phillips, *Oman: A History*, pp. 154-156.
[127]During the mid-point of his reign (1901-1904), the British political resident in Oman was Percy Cox, the same that was to make his mark as the manager of British affairs in the Gulf and Iraq. He observed that Oman might have coal reserves and negotiated a special British concession in 1902. The British later (1923) also negotiated for priority in prospecting for oil.

twentieth century, a person named Sâlim bin-Râshid al-Kharûsî. Under him, open rebellion broke out. As the rebellion gained momentum and seized control of the Jabal Akhdar heartland, Sultan Faysal died of cancer.[128]

Fortunately for the next sultan, Sultan Taymûr, he took the throne with no contest from his brothers and was strongly supported by British India forces. These had taken positions in the Rûwî valley outside of Matrah to guard against any incursions from the mountains. In 1915, the imâm's forces endeavored a frontal assault upon the British positions and were soundly defeated. The capital area was never directly threatened again.

By the second decade of the twentieth century, however, the sultans of Oman, ruling from their capital city of Muscat, had lost control of the interior. Britain's treaties with the sultan were what kept the Âl Bû-Saʿîdî dynasty alive. In 1920 the Imâm Sâlim was murdered in his sleep, and his elected successor, Muhammad al-Khalîlî, was constrained to open communications with Sultan Taymûr. They ratified an agreement in September, 1920, in which the rebels, in return for amnesty, gave up their demands with respect to arms and slaves. This agreement had the salutary effect for the mission of opening up the interior of Oman again for their touring doctors and evangelists. The Ibâdî Imâm Muhammad bin ʿAbd-Allâh became a friend of Wells Thoms and Dirk Dykstra,[129] and the missionaries found themselves, after many years of restriction, able to move around freely in Oman's interior.[130]

Taymûr also established the first Omani government budgetary process and ruled with a four-man council of ministers. In 1929 Taymûr's son, Saʿîd, became president of this council. Early in 1932, having served as sultan for twenty-seven years from the age of sixteen, Taymûr abdicated quite voluntarily in favor of his son, Saʿîd, who had just turned twenty-one.

---

[128]Phillips, *Oman: A History*, pp. 155-157.

[129]Wendell Phillips records the account of Wells Thoms's and Dirk Dykstra's first meeting with the imâm in the city of Nizwah, in which the imâm told them, "We believe you are mistaken in some of your doctrines but we respect you because you fear God, the Praised and Exalted one; therefore you may proceed in safety in our land. May God give you skill and wisdom to heal the sick man" (Phillips, *Oman: A History*, p. 187).

[130]The Imâm Muhammad died in 1954. A claim to the imâmate was raised by Ghâlib bin-ʿAlî, and he reignited the rebellion of the interior. Sultan Saʿîd responded with a strong drive to assert his sovereignty over the interior, and Ghâlib resigned his claim at the end of 1955. The revolt flared up again in 1957.

The Omanis, for the most part, came to value the presence of the missionaries. But the British encouraged the sultans to treat the Americans with caution. As will be recounted elsewhere, the mission developed a modest educational program and (especially from 1929) a fairly ambitious medical service. The impact of the latter, the only modern medical facility Oman knew for four decades, was felt far into Oman's interior. But especially during the reign of Sultan Saʿîd bin-Taymûr, whose later years were typified by a suspicion of all things that might bring about change, the mission experienced a great deal of interference.

When Sultan Saʿîd bin-Taymûr Âl Bû-Saʿîdî succeeded his father, many hoped that his father's obstructive policies would be lifted. The Arabian Mission in particular thought that with Wells Thoms's return to Oman in 1939[131] relations with the sultan would improve to the benefit of the mission's program in general and its medical work in particular. Thoms and Saʿîd had known each other as boys, and Saʿîd respected the memory of Well's father, Sharon Thoms. In fact, Thoms did have remarkably free access to the sultan, and the period until the early 1950s proved peaceful. In 1948 the sultan even donated land to the mission to build a contagious diseases hospital in memory of Sharon Thoms. There was a great deal of building and developing in that ten-year period, and the mission's medical effort in Oman grew dramatically, supplying that whole large country with its only modern medical facilities.

Beginning in 1949, however, the sultan became embroiled in a drawn-out struggle with Saʿûdî Arabia over the Buraymî Oasis, a water-rich region on the edge of the Empty Quarter thought also to contain large oil reserves. This crisis was precipitated by ARAMCO's greed for more oil concessions and came at a time when diplomatic relations between Oman and the

---

[131]Wells Thoms, son of Sharon Thoms, who first began medical work for the Arabian Mission in Oman in 1909, had returned to the Arabia field in 1930. After language study in Jerusalem, along with his wife, Beth Scudder Thoms, he had served with distinction in Bahrain and Kuwait before being posted to Oman in 1939. We will have occasion to speak more of this remarkable missionary couple later. Suffice it to note here that the mission hoped the legacy which he brought with him to Oman would prove an asset.

United States were at a low ebb.[132] As the Buraymî dispute dragged on, the sultan, because of his British alliances, also became the object of a persistent and annoying attack by the radio propaganda of Nâsir's newly republican and Arab nationalist Egypt.[133] The unrest in the Jabal Akhdar interior which

[132]Oman was unique among the Gulf states in having cultivated cordial commercial and diplomatic relations with the United States since the presidency of Andrew Jackson, in the mid-1800s. Now, Robert Lacey observes, "The dispute [over Buraymî] was not about history; it was about oil….It was a measure of the success of America's oil men in Arabia that within a decade of their oil strike of March 1938 they were helping to shape the foreign policy of the Al Sa'ud" (Lacey, *Kingdom*, pp. 290-291). The Sa'ûdî coffers were now always short of cash because of 'Abd-ul-'Azîz's extravagances, and his financial managers found that squeezing ARAMCO was always a way of getting more. In a kind of quid pro quo, the company (which saw black gold in the sands behind the ill-defined frontiers of "Trucial Oman," of which Buraymî was a major part) deemed that to enlist "…Abdul Aziz's help in the claim for Buaymi was a good way for Aramco to increase the king's sense of partnership in their affairs…" (Lacey, *Kingdom*, p. 292). The seventy-year-old king, however, was probably not aware of what the company was doing. It is unlikely that he very much cared. It is likely that the sovereign approved of the plan for the traditional Sa'ûdî desire to control Buraymî's still thriving slave market. On September 1, 1952, Sa'ûdî tribal warriors led by Turki bin-'Abd-Allâh bin-'Utayshân and transported on ARAMCO trucks occupied the Buraymî town of Hamâsah and celebrated the "liberation" of Buraymî as well as the Muslim Feast of Sacrifice with a lavish feast. In alliance, Oman and Abû Dhabî, the two offended parties, planned a military response but were restrained by the British who sought a diplomatic solution. Phillips suggests that this intervention by the British was requested by "certain Americans" since for the Sa'ûdîs to be forcibly expelled would have entailed an unacceptable loss of face for both the king and for the ARAMCO instigators of the plan (Phillips, *Oman: A History*, p. 169). The "Standstill Agreement" that followed permitted the Sa'ûdîs to consolidate their position. The matter was referred to the International Court of Justice in the Hague, but when that body failed to function, in October, 1955, Omani and Abû Dhabî forces joined to expel the Sa'ûdîs from the Buraymî Oasis. The legal wrangle over the oasis continued into the 1970s, but the "facts on the ground" excluded any Sa'ûdî presence. Of the nine Buraymî towns, six are governed by Abû Dhabî and three by Oman. In 1971, as the federation of the United Arab Emirates came into being and the British finally withdrew, King Fahad bin-'Abd-ul-'Azîz, the third son to succeed his august father, negotiated a settlement of the Buraymî dispute in which Sa'ûdî Arabia abandoned its claims to a piece of the oasis for another slice of Abû Dhabî's desert. For an exhaustive and disciplined treatment of this tangled matter, see Husain M. Albaharna, *The Arabian Gulf States: Their Legal and Political Status and Their International Problems* (Beirut: Librairie du Liban, 1975), pp. 196-238.

[133]There is a link between the Buraymî dispute and Egyptian propaganda. Upon the death of King 'Abd-ul-'Azîz in 1953 and the ascension of Sa'ûd, his son, a strange chapter in Sa'ûdî Arabia's international relations began, which saw the flirtation of Sa'ûd with the Egyptians. Egyptian propaganda had as one of its main themes

began in 1954 was linked to these. The Imâm Muhammad died in 1954, and the pretender to the imâmate, Ghâlib bin-'Alî, received Sa'ûdî and Egyptian assistance in raising a revolt. Sultan Sa'îd responded with a strong drive to reassert his sovereignty over the interior, and Ghâlib resigned his claim to the imâmate at the end of 1955. The revolt, however, broke out again in 1957 and dragged on intermittently until the 1970s.[134]

Adding to the sultan's troubles, Britain's position in the Hadramaut and Aden became untenable in the mid-1960s. Britain had held Aden as a colony since 1839 and had extended its control over the whole Hadramaut through a series of protectorates. From 1951 onward, there evolved a growing movement for independence which yielded, in the early 1960s, to open and violent revolution. In November, 1967, Britain surrendered Aden to its fate, withdrawing to permit the emergence of the Democratic Republic of South Yemen.[135] The new Marxist regime which came to power immediately set about igniting a guerrilla war on the Oman-South Yemen frontier, taking advantage of susceptible and fractious tribes in the southwestern Dhofâr region of the sultanate. The guerrilla war Oman had to fight on its western border became a fullblown Cold War brush fire. It linked to the endemic unrest in the mountains, was expressed in incidents even in the capital area, and spilled over outside its borders and affected others. Apart from a major British commitment of support (employing many highly motivated Aden veterans), Jordan and Iran also contributed troops and materiel to Oman's anti-insurgency efforts in Dhofâr.[136] Oman then took on the aspect of an

---

the expulsion of the British from the Middle East, and any country friendly to Britain was automatically a target. Oman was a target.

[134] See Robert Geran Landen, *Oman Since 1856* (Princeton, N.J.: Princeton Univ. Press, 1967), pp. 58-70 and 388-414. See also comments of Mason and Barny, *History*, pp. 141-42.

[135] For a full treatment of the British experience in Aden and the Hadramaut, see Julian Paget, *Last Post: Aden 1964-1967* (London: Faber and Faber, 1969).

[136] Expanding its interest to encompass other regions of the Gulf, the Patriotic Front for the Liberation of Dhofâr (or of the Arab Gulf) on April 10, 1964, exploded a bomb board the *Dara*, a liner of the British India Line, shortly after it had left port in Bahrain. The ship burned for two days. Aboard were Arabia missionaries Rose and Jerry Nykerk, as well as Pushpa, an Indian nurse working for the mission hospital on her way home from Bahrain for vacation. The Nykerks managed to get off safely and were rescued. Pushpa, in a lifeboat that capsized, was lost. For years thereafter, Rose Nykerk could tell the most spell-binding story of the incident, explaining how to scale down a ship's hull on a flailing rope ladder while the ship burned.

armed fortress. It was a nasty little war whose front was not always clearly defined.[137]

The tension increased and spread to other parts of Oman as, during 1964, oil operations got underway, and Oman became yet another player in the politics of oil. The sultan's frustrations led him to monitor more closely developments within his country; to view innovation with suspicion; and, as far as the mission was concerned, to constrict medical development by taxing the mission's imports of drugs, controling the movement of its members, and restricting visas for medical personnel.

Anomalously, this coincided with growth in motor car sales. The Land Rover jeep became ubiquitous. It facilitated more ready access to Matrah and Muscat cities from the interior, and the square across from Al-Rahmah Hospital would often be stiff with vehicles. The case load at the hospitals, both in Muscat and in Matrah, became extremely heavy. The more casual days of medical touring on donkey back into the interior were at an end. Even missionaries took to Land Rovers.

As in the other Gulf states, it was oil (Oman's concession going to the Dutch) that opened up Oman's future. Shell Oil discovered oil in 1964 and Oman began to ship it out in 1967. But its production was and will remain modest in volume compared to the other producers in the region. The reserves that Oman may count upon are also relatively small. Nonetheless, the mere discovery of oil created rising expectations, and, while Sultan Saʿîd attempted to suppress those expectations, discontent in the country became far more generalized in the latter years of his reign.

---

[137]Jeanette Boersma gives a good impression of the sense of instability, noting the convergence of the Dhofâr insurgency, the Arab-Israeli war of 1967, and the discovery of oil in Oman. In addition to recording the incident which destroyed the *Dara*, she relates another bombing on board the *Dawarka*, another British India liner, just as it was about to leave Muscat harbor. But her tying in of the assassination of Maurice Heusinkveld on September 12, 1967, has proven to be inaccurate, even though it did contribute to the overall sense of living in a cauldron of unrest and danger. Her observation that all of this eventually led to Sultan Saʿîd's overthrow on July 23, 1970, however, is accurate (Boersma, *Grace...*, pp. 173-77). It was at this time also that the *barastî* slums (a sprawling huddle of palm frond and reed dwellings in which lived people who had migrated to the capital from the interior) near the mission hospital in Matrah was set afire on several occasions, an effort on the part of the revolutionaries to unsettle the Omani poor.

The political situation in Oman changed dramatically when, with clear British backing, Qâbûs, the son of Sultan Saʿîd bin-Taymûr Âl bû-Saʿîdî, deposed his father on July 26, 1970.[138] During the coup, which took place in the summer palace in the Dhofârî center of Salâlah, Sultan Saʿîd wounded himself while jerking at a pistol. Otherwise, the coup was bloodless, and Saʿîd was put aboard a Royal Air Force transport jet and flown to London.

Sultan Qâbûs pledged to throw open the doors for rapid modernization of the country. He was backed by oil money, support from Saʿûdî Arabia and other Gulf states, and the presence of the British. After a somewhat shaky beginning, during which he was tempted to self-indulgence, he has been able to win a long guerrilla war on his southwestern borders with Southern Yemen and to overcome peacefully the reticence of the parochial Ibâdîs of the interior. He has united the country with an ambitious program of road building and economic infrastructure.

The Arabian Mission, without hesitation, greeted the coup and the new regime of Sultan Qâbûs with joy. The local missionaries immediately sent Sultan Qâbûs a telegram stating, "May God bless you in your new responsibility STOP We pledge our continued endeavor toward the welfare of this country SIGNED The American Mission."[139] In 1971 the Arabian Mission, with its medical program, offered to continue to function under the oversight of the new Ministry of Health and asked for assistance to meet the suddenly exploding demand. In 1973 the hospitals and key personnel were transferred to serve as a nucleus for the government health service.

[138] Jay Kapenga wrote to Ken Warren, then Middle East secretary for the Reformed church, July 27, 1970: "There was an attachment [sic.] of U. K. Marines in Salalah and their officers probably under Foreign Office direction managed directly while keeping the Sultan's Officers and Army informed. This is conjecture...but I have often wondered to whom an English Officer serving in the Sultan's Army is ultimately loyal. The answer is obvious now" [document in author's correspondence file].
[139] Kapenga to Warren, July 27, 1970.

Part Three

Foundations

Arabia Calling

The Arabian Mission had a curious birth within the Reformed Church in America.[1] As early as 1643, not long after the first Dutch migration to the New World and while the fledgling denomination was still under the oversight of the Classis of Amsterdam, the Reformed church supported independent mission efforts among Native Americans.[2] When it came to

[1]The Reformed Church in America, from 1624 until 1772, was a client communion of the Consistory or Classis of Amsterdam under the administration of the Dutch West India Company. With the British conquest of New Amsterdam in 1664, freedom of worship was guaranteed to the Dutch settlers of that colony, but Anglican pressure to unify religious practices counseled that stronger guarantees be applied for. British Royal Charters began to be granted to Dutch congregations in and around the colony now known as New York in 1696. From 1772 until 1794 (the Revolutionary War period), the RCA was in a transitional phase, but in 1794 autonomy was formally established from the Classis of Amsterdam, and the General Synod of the Dutch Reformed Church in North America was constituted. By the turn of the century its name had been changed to the Reformed Dutch Church in America. It is not to be confused with the "Reformed Church in the United States of America" (commonly known as the German Reformed), which eventually joined the merger process that resulted in the United Church of Christ.

[2]Charles E. Corwin, *A Manual of the Reformed Church in America* (New York: Board of Publication and Bible-School Work of the Reformed Church in

"foreign mission," however, the church initially participated in the American Board of Commissioners for Foreign Missions (the ABCFM).3 The first Reformed church missionaries appointed under this arrangement in 1819 were Harriet and John Scudder. They left in June for Jaffna in Ceylon and finally arrived there via Calcutta in December. They finally settled in Madras in 1836 and, with the return to the field of their sons, Henry and William,4 the Classis of Arcot was organized in 1853 under the Synod of Albany in the United States.5

David Abeel, a young pastor in New York State who had come under the influence of the powerful John Henry Livingstone of Marble Collegiate

America, 1922), p. 148. See also Marvin D. Hoff, *The Reformed Church in America: Structures for Mission*, No. 14 in *The Historical Series of the Reformed Church in America* (Grand Rapids, Michigan: Wm. B. Eerdmans Publishing Co., 1985), pp. 11-35.

3Corwin, *Manual*, p. 186. After a variety of experiments, the most deliberate of which was to assign the Synod of Albany as the missionary agent of the denomination, the Reformed church formed its Board of Domestic Missions in 1831 and its Board of Foreign Missions in 1832. These boards were directly responsible to the General Synod, and the latter had a kind of liaison and watchdog function with respect to the ABCFM.

4All seven surviving sons returned to India as missionaries. Their names (and periods of service) are: Henry Martyn (1843-1864), William Waterbury (1846-1872 and 1884-1894), Joseph (1853-1860), Ezekiel Carman (1855-1876), Jared Waterbury (1855-1910), Silas Downer (1861-1872), John (junior, father of Ida Sophie Scudder) (1861-1900). All seven were ordained clergymen, and five were also physicians like their father. Two surviving daughters, Harriet and Louisa, also returned to India as missionaries but fairly shortly thereafter were married to British citizens and went their own way. An eighth son, Samuel, drowned while a student at the theological seminary in New Brunswick. He too was preparing to return to India.

5Mrs. William I Chamberlain, "The Church in Foreign Lands," *Tercentenary Studies, 1928, Reformed Church in America* (New York: Reformed Church in America, 1928), pp. 494-495; and Dorothy Jealous Scudder, *A Thousand Years in Thy Sight: The Story of the Scudder Missionaries of India* (New York: Vantage Press, 1984), the definitive narrative of the Scudder missionary family's service in India. By 20th century wisdom, the organization of the Classis of Arcot was a violation of the basic principle that mission-planted churches be permitted to evolve their own indigenous identity and polity. Comically distorting the statistics of the Synod of Albany, the Classis of Arcot persisted from 1854 until 1902, when it participated in a merger with Presbyterian and Church of Scotland mission churches in the formation of the Synod of South India. The South India United Church, which represented a further merger with Congregationalist communions, came into existence in 1908. The long discussions with Anglicans and Methodists finally bore fruit in the formation of the Church of South India in 1947.

Church in New York City, resigned from his parish in 1829 to seek opportunities for mission work in the Far East. Initially working under the Seaman's Friend Society, he eventually transferred to the ABCFM. Riding the coattails of the British who had humiliated the Chinese in the Opium Wars (1839) and who had, thereby, won concessions for free commercial activity in China's ports, Abeel founded a mission in the port city of Amoy in 1842. The General Synod of 1857 tried to insist that the Amoy Mission follow the example of the Arcot Mission in India and form a classis under the Synod of Albany. Since the church in Amoy was composed of congregations related both to the Reformed Church in America and to the Presbyterian Church in England, the missionaries in China defied the order and established the principle that the Chinese church should develop independently of either the United States or Great Britain.[6]

In 1838 Abeel published a passionate little book entitled, *The Missionary Convention at Jerusalem.*[7] It is a fictional setting (which had a real successor) for the gathering of Christians from around the world, debating the issues of whether the church had an obligation to evangelize the heathen. Since Abeel was one of the early strong advocates of foreign missions speaking with a Reformed voice, there is little question that this book was read by those who, in later years, sat down together to consider founding the Arabian Mission. Chapter eleven[8] is particularly interesting in this respect (each chapter is devoted to a different voice). In that chapter the voice is that of a convert from Islam, and the argument he raised for the urgency and imperative of mission is almost identical to that put forward some fifty years later by John Lansing in the document declaring the founding of the Arabian Mission. There has always been a curious correspondence between the China field and Arabia; this is but the first instance.

---

[6]Hoff, *Structures*, pp. 37-38. Led by their main spokesman, John Van Nest Talmadge, the Amoy Mission continued to defy the General Synod of the Reformed church until, in 1864, the synod decided to let the matter rest for the time being (although it never did formally rescind the policy of bringing foreign churches planted by Reformed church mission activity under "proper" ecclesiastical order). Amoy, then, established Reformed Church in America (RCA) mission policy by default because, of the churches which were planted by RCA mission work, only Arcot ever conformed to the official policy of the denomination.

[7]David Abeel, *The Missionary Convention at Jerusalem; or an Exhibition of the Claims of the World to the Gospel* (New York: John S. Taylor, 1938).

[8]Abeel, *Convention*, pp. 58-62.

In the second half of the nineteenth century, the Reformed church experienced a heightening of enthusiasm for foreign missions. Marvin Hoff has argued that this was a spirit breathed into the denomination by the fresh Dutch immigration into the United States in 1846, which saw the establishment of settlements in Michigan, Illinois, Wisconsin, and Iowa.9 One of the early enthusiasts for foreign missions was Philip Phelps, founder and first president of Hope College in Holland, Michigan, and a man of some color and creative imagination. He was the father of Philip Tertius Phelps, one of the first three students who conspired in the forming of the Arabian Mission. Philip Phelps (Sr.) proposed the building of a "missionary ship" on the model of the London Missionary Society's *Morning Star*. This ship was to be based on Black Lake near Holland, Michigan, and its purpose, using the Welland Canal to carry missionaries and supplies to and from the field, was to be "a potent auxiliary for the publication of the Gospel in foreign lands." It was a ship that never sailed. Only its keel was laid with great fanfare June 24, 1864. In later years the keel was left to rot away, but the interest aroused by the aborted project gave new impetus to mission activity within the Reformed church.10 In 1931, Samuel Zwemer published a curious little pamphlet for the Board of Domestic Missions mostly dealing with the missionary seeds in the Dutch migration to Holland, Michigan, in 1846. It ends with a little vignette, "The Keel that Never Kissed the Sea," which gave impetus to many graduates of Hope College to volunteer for foreign missions.11

9Hoff, *Structures*, pp. 9-10. Hoff may be overstating the case. Through most of the experience of the Reformed church in foreign missions, the congregations in the east were extremely active and predominated in supporting mission work until the 1940s.

10Wynand Wichers, *A Century of Hope 1866-1966* (Grand Rapids, Mich.: William B. Eerdmans Publishing Company, 1968), pp. 60-61.

11Samuel M. Zwemer, *The Ship that Sailed and the Keel that Never Kissed the Sea* (New York: Board of Domestic Missions, Reformed Church in America, 1931). Commenting on this event in the booklet, "A Century of Missions in the Reformed Church in America: 1796-1896" (New York: Board of Foreign Missions, 1896), Henry Cobb said, "Nothing material appeared permanently to result from this movement, though considerable contributions found their way into the treasury of the Board. But there can be no doubt–there is none in the minds of those conversant with the facts–that a mighty spiritual and missionary influence was exerted among our Holland brethren, the effects of which are still visible to this day" (p. 14).

In 1857 the Reformed Church in America, responding to appeals from its missionaries in India and China, felt the time had come to organize its own autonomous Board of Foreign Missions. In that year it took the Arcot Mission in South India and the Amoy Mission in China under its independent control, although relations with the ABCFM remained cordial.[12] This cordiality was to be significant for the Arabian Mission. It drew heavily upon the advice, encouragement, and logistical support of ABCFM personnel in Syria and Turkey during its early years. Although institutions and mission policies have evolved greatly, those links still persist.

Having taken on the administration of these two foreign mission fields, the Reformed church almost surprised itself by successfully underwriting the ventures.[13] By 1859 it had even extended its work when Guido Verbeck and two medical companions, Brown and Simmons, opened Reformed church participation in Japan. Times had changed quickly. Interest in missions did not keep pace with the rising cost of commitments as mission fields elaborated their institutions. By 1889 the Board of Foreign Missions had developed what was for those times a substantial debt of $35,000.[14] When the proposal for an Arabian Mission was put to it in that year, therefore, the board deemed itself unable to accept the challenge. By 1894, however, the Arabian Mission had proved its ability to attract wide support from the denomination's congregations. In that year the Board of Foreign Missions did indeed become the principal administrative authority for the Arabian Mission, under an arrangement that had some novel wrinkles.[15]

---

[12]*Acts and Proceedings of the General Synod of the Reformed Church in North America,* vols. I-IX inclusive (New York: Board of Publication of the Reformed Protestant Dutch Church, 1738-1860), the *Minutes* of 1856, p. 114; and of 1857, pp. 227-229.

[13]RCA, *Acts,* the Minutes of 1858, p. 353.

[14]Mason and Barny, *History,* pp. 59-60; Zwemer, *Arabia,* pp. 354, 356. This debt bedeviled the mission effort of the Reformed church into the 1940s.

[15]As will be noted in more detail later, the Arabian Mission was first organized on an "undenominational" basis supported by a network of Arabian Mission Syndicates, a loose association of individuals, mission-minded societies, and single congregations, which worked through a Committee of Advice and a Board of Trustees incorporated in New Jersey. From 1894 when the Reformed church assumed responsibility for the administration of the mission, members of the syndicate's Board of Trustees were appointed from members of the RCA Board of Foreign Missions, and the distinction between the "undenominational" mission and the administering denomination became less and less clear. But the syndicate structure continued in legal existence until June, 1924, at which time

The Listeners

The inspiring genius of the Arabian Mission was Professor John G. Lansing, the Gardner Sage Professor of Old Testament Language and Exegesis at the Seminary of the Reformed Church in New Brunswick, New Jersey.

Lansing's history is given but scant treatment in our sources. He was born in 1851, the son of a Presbyterian missionary family in Damascus. His father was transferred to Cairo while John was still quite young, and it was in that city he grew up. Returning to the United States for his higher education, Lansing studied for two years in Monmouth College in Illinois before transferring to Union College in Schenectady, New York, from which he graduated in 1875.[16] In Schenectady he became a member of the Reformed church, and he demonstrated a strong loyalty to the denomination for the rest of his life. He married directly out of college and went for one year to teach in Cairo. In 1876 he returned to the United States and entered New Brunswick Seminary. Because of his native competence in Semitic languages, and no doubt for other attainments as well, he was permitted to complete his seminary degree in one year.[17]

Already at this time he was experiencing health problems. That, added to the fact that the Reformed church did not have missionary work in Arabia, constrained Lansing to remain in the United States. From 1877 he served as pastor to two churches in New York State. At the age of thirty-three, in 1884, he joined the faculty of New Brunswick Seminary as its first full-time professor of Old Testament. He was the only faculty member then under

it was fully "amalgamated" with the Board of Foreign Missions of the Reformed Church in America, and the Arabian Mission legally ceased to exist as a distinct entity. It became known simply as one of the fields of the Reformed church's foreign missionary effort along with China, Japan, and India. The appeal of the mission to people from many different denominations continued well after that date.

[16]Beside Lansing, Union College (at one time a Reformed church-sponsored institution) supplied two other missionaries to Arabia: James Cantine and John Badeau, both of whom concluded their missionary careers in the United Mission in Iraq.

[17]Howard G. Hageman, "The Golden Age of New Brunswick," *New Brunswick Theological Seminary Newsletter*, vol. 8, no. 3., March 1979 (New Brunswick, N. J.), pp. 8, 20.

sixty years of age, and he remains one of the youngest ever to have served in such a capacity at New Brunswick Seminary.[18]

As his career indicates, Lansing must have been a rather remarkable individual. He is described as having a striking personality, "accompanied by a rich voice and innate dramatic power."[19] He also seems to have been uniquely gifted in capturing the imagination of his students. His passion for the land of his birth continued strong, and when he accepted the fact that he could never himself return there as a missionary, Howard Hageman says, "He deliberately designed the Arabian Mission ...and sought students to volunteer for it ..."[20]

In 1888, partly due to the rise of John R. Mott's Student Volunteer Movement for Foreign Missions (organized in 1886), partly due to visiting missionary lectureships, and certainly due to John Lansing's own enthusiasm, there rose a strong ferment within the seminary community for foreign missions in general.[21] Three men—James Cantine, Philip Phelps, and Samuel Zwemer—felt moved by the idea of serving in some foreign field,[22] and these three went together to Lansing, whose "burning zeal for the evangelization of Moslems"[23] had drawn them under his particular angel.[24]

All the witnesses agree that without Lansing there would have been no Arabian Mission. It was *his* dream, *his* spiritual child. *He* it was who planted the seed; *he* it was who defended its organization as an autonomous mission project against those who would have let it languish for lack of official adoption; and *he* it was who, using all his considerable powers of eloquence, all his contacts, and all his personal charm, marshaled its support.[25] His friend J. Preston Searle, who himself later joined the faculty of New Brunswick Seminary, remarked, "Dr. Lansing in a sense died of his devotion to the Arabian Mission, for his strenuous efforts and his anxiety for it certainly helped to bring on the cerebral disease from which he shortly afterwards died."[26]

[18]Hageman, *Golden*, p. 8.
[19]Hageman, *Golden*, p. 20.
[20]Hageman, *Golden*, p. 20.
[21]Zwemer, *Milestone*, pp. 29-30.
[22]Zwemer, *Arabia*, pp. 353-354.
[23]Cantine, *Milestone*, p. 18.
[24]Zwemer, *Arabia*, p. 354, says this took place around the end of November, 1888.
[25]Cantine, *Milestone*, p. 19.
[26]Mason and Barny, *History*, p. 65. The "cerebral disease" to which reference is made here was described by the attending physicians as "cerebral disintegration"

That Lansing's own missionary passion was a deep expression of love for the folk of his birthland cannot be doubted. Set to several tunes over the years, the hymn which he composed and which others have misnamed the "Marseillaise" of the Arabian Mission,[27] is not a battle hymn at all but a love song:

I
There's a land long since neglected,
  There's a people still rejected,
But of truth and grace elected,
  In His love for them.

II
Softer than their night wind's fleeting,
  Richer than their starry tenting,
Stronger than their sands protecting,
  Is His love for them.

which completely destroyed his nervous system. (Hageman, *Golden*, p. 20). It is an event very cautiously spoken of. Following his resignation from the seminary in 1898 for reasons of failing health, Lansing moved to Denver, Colorado (Hageman, *Golden*, p. 20). But sometime after December, 1893, and before March, 1894, Lansing's name disappears without comment from the list of the trustees of the Arabian Mission as published in the *Quarterly Field Reports* of the Arabian Mission. At that point the histories cease to mention him until after his death. He simply disappears. Considering his importance in the founding of the Arabian Mission, this is peculiar. Lacking detailed documentation, at this point we can only indicate that during his retirement in Denver, Lansing continued to write scholarly material and attempted to support himself as a journalist. He surfaced briefly again as the subject of a denominational scandal, when he petitioned General Synod for a dispensation from monogamy in order to marry a second wife, using the example of David and Abishag as precedent (1 Kings 1:3-4). There is even a suggestion, attributed to a Rev. H. Studley, that he became a drug addict. (This is in a marginal note in P. T. Phelps's personal copy of the *Golden Milestone*, p. 27, probably inserted by a nephew, George Scholten: Box. No. H88-122a in the Joint Archives of Holland.) In any case, all mention of him was repressed in hopes of preserving his earlier efforts and accomplishments unblemished. John Gulian Lansing died at the age of fifty-five in Denver, September 3, 1906 (Hageman, *Golden*, p. 20). In Arabia, his contributions were recognized in the building (1910) of the Lansing Memorial Hospital, which was first located in Basrah and later (1925) moved up river to Amarah on the Tigris.
[27]Mason and Barny, *History*, p. 62.

III

To the host of Islam's leading,
   For the slave in bondage bleeding,
To the desert dweller pleading,
   Bring His love to them.

IV

Through the promise on God's pages,
   Through His work in history's stages,
Through the Cross that crowns the ages,
   Show His love to them.

V

With the prayer that still availeth,
   With the power that prevaileth,
With the love that never faileth,
   Tell His love to them.

VI

Till the desert's sons now aliens,
   Till its tribes and their dominions,
Till Arabia's raptured millions,
   Praise His love of them.

J. G. Lansing, 1889[28]

   The scriptural text Lansing chose as the motto of the Arabian Mission—"O that Ishmael might live before Thee!"[29] – is "the prayer which still availeth." He interpreted it as the prayer of a loving father for his firstborn son. That Lansing's interpretation does not quite fit the actual context and significance of Abraham's prayer did not matter a great deal to him nor to later generations of Arabia missionaries. Zwemer, in his first book, spent a great deal of effort analyzing this and other biblical passages to demonstrate (at least to his own satisfaction) that the Bible contains promises for the

[28]Mason and Barny, *History*, p. 7.
[29]Genesis 17:18.

redemption of the Arabs.[30] The prayer of Abraham for his elder son became the Arabian Mission's own petition from the outset and it "still availeth."

Obey, Not Object

Of the three students who approached Professor Lansing, the eldest was James Cantine, who was then entering his final year at the seminary. He was already a mature man of twenty-nine years who had left a career as a civil engineer with Westinghouse to enter the ministry. By later reputation and as is reflected in his correspondence and a few articles in the Arabian Mission's magazine, he was a man with a soft sense of humor. He perceived the tender parts of the human spirit and had a deep capacity for loving people. He had a knack for understanding how relationships worked between diverse personalities. But he remained to the end a kind of missiological engineer. He did not have a great flair for lateral thinking. That he left to his colleague, Zwemer, and later to people like John Van Ess and Paul Harrison, and when they went too "far out" he saw it as his duty to call them back into line. He had broad principles to which he was committed, and he knew how pieces fit together. The overriding passion of his career was to see the work of Mission (with a capital "M") borne by the whole Christian Church. To that end, he worked hard at building bridges between the Arabian Mission and other mission bodies in the region. His other major concern was that the Arabian mission survive. To achieve that goal he was willing to make compromises with political pressures which, it must be believed, annoyed his colleagues. Belying his accomplishments, he was not by nature a great adventurer; caution often marked his actions. He had his vision and his commitments and he stuck by them.[31]

[30]Zwemer, *Arabia*, pp. 393-408.
[31]The eulogies given at his funeral in July 1940 (printed in a memorial brochure, a copy of which is in the author's document collection) portray a man with few pretentions. He knew himself to have been an ordinary man caught up in extraordinary circumstances. As has happened from time to time in the Reformed church, a "Laymen's Commission" once complained mightily about the mediocre quality of most missionaries. Speaking to Duke Potter, he observed, "Well, Potter, I suppose they are right. Most missionaries are just ordinary people like me. But–I wonder if they realize that there are many tasks which only the ordinary missionary can do. The genius might not be ready to do

Samuel Zwemer was a contrast.[32] The son of a Reformed church minister in Holland, Michigan, in 1888-1889 he was a second-year student. As a youth he thought himself destined to become a medical missionary and, to that end, he aspired to become a physician. Financial choices, however, blocked that option, and he directed his path toward the Christian ministry. His thwarted desire to become a doctor of medicine remained unquenched, however. He had a voracious scholarly appetite, was strong minded, and could express himself eloquently in Dutch, German, and French as well as English. A gifted linguist, he was much admired by junior missionaries in later years for his eloquence in Arabic. His diaries, kept faithfully during his early years, reflect his strong idealism, and his taste for romantic adventure makes him a most winsome young man. Given these gifts, it is not surprising that, almost from the outset, he more than any other became the public voice of the Arabian Mission. Prolific writer, eloquent orator, he has left behind him literary and folkloric relics that are touched with reverence by many. He had an irrepressible and aggressive personality, earnest where Cantine was tender, driving where his colleague was contemplative. As he grew older, and as sorrows and rebuffs on the field left their scars, he became more conscious of his own personal image and, in the end, disdained to think of himself as a missionary foot soldier. He aspired, instead, to the status of missionary statesman. To him mission to Islam was, in every sense, a grand crusade. The important images in his writing are military, and his bright mind devoted itself to questions of tactic and strategy at every turn of the road.[33]

them." Apart from Cantine's zeal for mission and his devotion to task, his gift for making friends and his role as the mission's "Uncle Jim," Potter picked out one feature of Cantine's personality which differentiated him from his younger colleagues and which was infectious: He learned from his Muslim environment. Potter put it this way: "Long years of association with the Arab served also to bring to Dr. Cantine something of that spirit of submission which is a keynote of Islam, that overwhelming sense of the omnipotence and omniscience of God, though with him it was graced by an abounding faith in the love of God. Therein is found the secret of his imperturbable calm, his unwavering faith, which enabled him to face disappointment, suffering, and apparent failure with that sweet, philosophical smile of utter confidence in the fundamental rightness of things, which none of us who knew him can ever forget" (Potter in the memorial brochure, July 1940).

[32]For a review of the career of Samuel Zwemer in the mission, see note number 152 below.

[33]To read Zwemer is to look at Islam through very filtered lenses, and the admission that there are certain very striking Muslim graces to which the Christian must pay

The third man, Philip T. Phelps, another senior in 1889, is a shadowy figure. While he seems to have been the first of the three to move toward Lansing, he retired into the wings during the first act and fades almost entirely out of the picture by 1889 "for family and health considerations."34

In the early stages, these three and Lansing organized themselves into a society they called "The Wheel." Lansing was the hub and Cantine, Phelps, and Zwemer were the spokes. On May 23, 1889, The Wheel composed the first "Plan of the Arabian Mission." It was presented to the Board of Foreign Missions of the Reformed church, which referred it in June to the denomination's General Synod. Because the board was already severely in

heed comes hard off his pen. Zwemer became a master in the art of "Muslim controversy," and many of the stories about him show him in this light. But to win an argument, to silence an opponent, is not to win a heart.

34Cantine, *Milestone*, p. 19. Philip Tertius Phelps was the son of Philip Phelps, Jr., the founding president (1866-1878) of Hope College in Holland, Michigan. Philip Tertius was born in 1862 and, upon graduating from New Brunswick Seminary in 1889, embarked upon a career as a journeyman pastor for the Reformed church in the East, serving six parishes in New York State before his retirement in 1922. He died in East Northfield, Massachusetts, on October 22, 1944, one month short of his eighty-second birthday [Peter N. Vandenberge, *Historical Directory of the Reformed Church in America*, No. 6 in *The Historical Series of the Reformed Church in America* (Grand Rapids, Mich.: Wm. B. Eerdmans Publishing Co., 1978.), p. 136].

His memorialist, Milton J. Hoffman, wrote in 1944 in the *Church Herald* of December 1, "He had every intention of becoming a missionary in Arabia, but for reasons of health that ambition could not be realized. In subsequent years he always liked to talk about the great dreams which as theological students they cherished together." In a letter to James Cantine in 1939, when the latter was gathering material for inclusion in his chapters of the *Golden Milestone*, Phelps suggested the following summary of his contribution to the Arabian Mission: "Phelps, while disappointed that the new venture of missions could not be made a part of the R.C.A. activities, yet, because of health considerations had finally concluded that his place in the Lord's field was at home; that it was his to 'tarry by the stuff' which he did faithfully and efficiently for many years by praying and preaching and paying for missions, cheered by the old ordinance, 'As his part is that goeth down to battle so shall his part be that tarrieth by the stuff. They shall both share alike' I Sam. 30:22." In the same letter he made some point of the fact that he was at least at the boat to bid farewell to Cantine and even offered a prayer on the occasion, a prayer of which, for his part, Cantine had no recollection. An anonymous relative (probably his nephew, George B. Scholten of Wayne, New Jersey), commenting in margins of papers now in the Joint Archives of Holland (Box No. H88-122a) notes that, life long, "Unk" boasted of having been one of the founders of the Arabian Mission. But he also suggests that his reasons for not going were personal rather than pressing, and that he simply "backed off."

debt with heavy commitments in India, China, and Japan, the synod could only recommend that the board give the project its favorable consideration and act prudently. The board communicated its formal decision to Lansing June 26, to "decline to assume responsibility in the matter."[35]

There the dream might well have died. But as Lansing put it in an article announcing the organization of a mission effort independent of the Reformed church, "A responsibility Divinely imposed is not discharged by any admission of existing human difficulty....When God calls we must obey, not object."[36] On this principle the fraternity proceeded to devise an "undenominational" plan for the Arabian Mission. It was drafted August 1, 1889, and published by Lansing in the *Christian Intelligencer* August 28.[37]

The plan itself is disappointingly short on explaining "why" and long on outlining "how" the mission was to be organized. It assumed (without evident need to demonstrate) that there is "great need of and encouragement for... pioneer mission work in some Arabic-speaking country, and especially in behalf of Muslims and slaves."[38] In terms of location, it had in view "...Arabia and the adjacent coast of Africa," showing thereby the influence of the field reports of Major General F. T. Haig[39] of the Anglican Church Mission Society (CMS) and the Scots Presbyterian Aden mission of Ion Keith-Falconer. Both had focused upon the Red Sea coasts of Arabia and Yemen.[40] It was not until some time later (probably beginning in 1892 but

[35]Mason and Barny, *History*, pp. 58-60.
[36]Lansing, *Milestone* (Appendix), p. 150.
[37]Lansing, *Milestone* (Appendix), pp. 151-152; and Zwemer, *Arabia*, pp. 356-357.
[38]Lansing, *Milestone* (Appendix), p. 151.
[39]General Haig, an old raj India Britisher, was a chief inspiration particularly for Zwemer. A peripatetic soul, he found his Christian vocation as an explorer and advisor on missions. It was at his urging that Ion Keith-Falconer established his mission work in Aden. Haig began his trip around Arabia in October 1886 at the behest of the Church Missionary Society. It concluded with the publication of two articles in May and June of 1887 in the CMS's journal, the *Church Missionary Intelligencer* (Zwemer, *Arabia*, pp. 322-323).
[40]Lansing, *Milestone* (Appendix), pp. 151-153. See also Zwemer, *Arabia*, pp. 322-325, 331-343. The Aden mission was founded by the eccentric Scots nobleman, Ion Keith-Falconer, third son of the Earl of Kintore, who, having been moved by Dwight L. Moody and later guided by General F. T. Haig, chose Aden as a place for a mission which emphasized medicine as a tool for evangelism. The Scottish choice of medicine as their missionary vehicle strongly influenced the later evolution of the Arabian Mission. Already a Semitic scholar of some accomplishment, Ion Keith-Falconer met with General Haig in February of 1885 with an eye to responding to Haig's call for opening evangelistic work in Aden and

maturing into formal policy with the mission's final adoption by the Reformed church's Board of Foreign Missions in 1894) that the mission's tactics and strategy were more fully articulated:

> The object of the Mission, in accordance of its original plan, is the evangelization of Arabia. Our effort should be exerted directly among and for Moslems, including the slave population; our main methods are preaching, Bible distribution, itinerating, medical work and school work. Our aim is to occupy the interior of Arabia from the coast as a base.[41]

Within Christian circles in the West at the end of the nineteenth century, there was never a serious question whether Islam as a religion was the proper object of a major Christian evangelistic offensive. In Christian and western scholarly circles, it was accepted as a matter of course that Islam was a corrupt and demeaning religion which diverted its followers from the path of true salvation and stood in the path of human progress generally. Under its sway, it was held, the indigenous Christian population had been corrupted and subverted from its true evangelical calling. What was raised as an

Arabia generally. With the blessing of the Free Church of Scotland's Foreign Mission Committee, he and his wife arrived in Aden in October of the same year. He decided to locate his work there in the Aden suburb of Shaykh 'Othmân. By the spring of 1886 he had completed his survey of the land and returned to Great Britain, where he addressed the General Assembly of the Free Church of Scotland. Funding the effort out of his own resources, by the end of the year he, his wife Gwendolen, and a Dr. Stewart Cowen were hard at work. But on May 11, 1887, at the age of 30, he suddenly died of a fever. The romance of his story, however, was effective in inspiring others to take his place. Gwendolen and Dr. Cowen returned to Great Britain, but others came in their stead. The mission continued until 1965, when Britain granted independence to a turbulent Aden (which came to be called the Peoples' Republic of South Yemen), and most missionaries were obliged to leave.

[41] Mason and Barny, *History*, p. 196. Since the publication of this statement as Article 2 of the Rules of the Arabian Mission, it has been debated whether the Arabian Mission had any business serving non-Muslims in the area. It is clear in the sources, though, that among the first major activities of the mission in Basrah was the provision of spiritual nurture and opportunities for worship for English-speaking expatriates and sailors. It is interesting to note that the heirs of the mission have today seen matters come full circle in this regard. Among the main avenues through which the Reformed church continues to be involved in the Arabian Gulf is the supply of pastors for congregations of English-speaking expatriates in the states of Kuwait, Bahrain, and Oman.

objection to such a campaign was the matter of the obstinacy of Muslims in rejecting the Christian message. This obstinacy, and the fact that Muslim law and society were far from tolerant toward a Muslim who chose to become a Christian, caused some to advise that Islam as a whole should be left to wend its own way to perdition unhindered by Christian missionary efforts.[42]

In his article of August 28, 1889, Professor Lansing set himself to refute this position, showing that while conversions from Islam to Christianity were by no means a mass phenomenon, they nonetheless did take place, that converts were not necessarily subjected to persecution and could indeed live full and useful lives, and that, as he felt it, the door to religious freedom and spiritual awakening in the Arab world was in the process of opening.[43] For Lansing there was no doubt that "...the greatest marvels of missionary work ever witnessed are yet to be witnessed in Arabian territory and in the ranks of Islam."[44]

His enthusiasm and confidence fired the imaginations of many. Not only did he kindle a flame for work among Muslims, he also sparked a revival of interest in foreign mission work generally, particularly within the Reformed church.

As we have already noted, another judgment which dominated early western mission perspectives with regard to Arabia was a strong antagonism to what missionaries felt to be the once glorious, but now corrupted, Oriental Orthodox and Catholic churches. These, in the eyes of western observers, had reverted to nothing less than paganism. In certain instances, missionaries rated Oriental Christianity as lower and more deplorable than Islam itself. Except for a notable few, the Arabic-speaking associates whom the Arabian Mission recruited were individuals from historically Christian families of Assyrian or Suryânî background who had "converted" to Protestantism.[45] Many of these in the early years came from the city of

---

[42]Cantine, *Milestone*, p. 80; and Lansing, *Milestone* (Appendix), p. 155.

[43]Lansing, *Milestone* (Appendix), pp. 155-157.

[44]Lansing, *Milestone* (Appendix), p. 157.

[45]The designation, Suryânî, will be unfamiliar to anyone not conversant with contemporary middle eastern subcultures. It refers to those whose mother tongue is Syriac (*siryânî*), a contemporary language evolved from Aramaic which, as the *lingua franca* of the Middle East, replaced Babylonian and its Akkadian precursors in the seventh and sixth centuries BC. The Suryânîs are to be distinguished from the Âshûrîs (Assyrians). The former constituted a Christian

Mardin in what is now southeastern Turkey.[46]

All western Protestant missionary efforts in the Arabic-speaking world, except the Ion Keith-Falkoner Mission in Aden, focused upon the ancient Christian populations of Asia Minor, Mesopotamia, Persia, Syria, Palestine, and Egypt. This was understood to be "indirect evangelism" of Muslims through reviving an indigenous Christian witness. The Arabian Mission very deliberately turned aside from that focus. From the outset the mission was dedicated to "direct Muslim evangelism," an enterprise viewed as audacious if not foolhardy by the more experienced missionaries the two young men later met in Lebanon and Egypt.

tradition that, following Cyril of Alexandria (d. 444) and Jacob Baradaeus (d. 578), evolved distinctly from their cultural kin, the Assyrians. Surviving within the Byzantine Empire, their intellectual tradition remained in lively contact with the mainstream of Orthodox Christianity.

The latter, the Assyrians, developed outside the bounds of Byzantium. Separating from the mainstream in 424, they were labeled "Nestorians" by their detractors, a label they do not accept for themselves. Their main centers of activity lay within the Sassanian Persian Empire, where they thrived, sending missionaries as far afield as China as late as the fourteenth century. Their high reputation for learning stood them in good stead under later Muslim rulers, and they hit their high water mark under the 'Abbâsid Caliphs. They survived the first Mongol invasions in the thirteenth century handily, but in the second wave under Tamurlaine (Timûr Leng) in the fifteenth century they were almost wiped out. Much diminished, they survived in pockets in northern Iraq, southern Turkey, and northwestern Iran. They openly allied themselves with the British during the First World War and again were almost extinguished by the Turks. The British used them as an effective military force against the Kurds and other malcontents in the north during their mandate over Iraq from the end of the war until 1932. At that time they again found themselves on the brink of extinction.

Following the defeat and dissolution of the Ottoman Empire at the end of the First World War, many members of these two communities migrated southward. When the Arabian Mission began to seek 'native helpers' Suryânî and Assyrian Protestants were available. Several interrelated families settled in Kuwait and Bahrain and were closely related to the work of the mission in both.

[46]Mason and Barny, *History*, p. 113. It should be noted that, apart from their native facility in Arabic, native colporteurs who came from a Christian family background were no more well equipped to understand Muslim spirituality than were their western employers. Since the 1200s Arab Christians, responding to strong Muslim suspicion that they were subversive, had set about intentionally to separate themselves from intercourse with Muslims. In all but rare cases, Arab Christian ignorance of Islam was looked upon as a virtue. Recent Muslim converts, like Kâmil 'Abd-ul-Masîh and Ya'qûb Yuhann (among the first native colporteurs of the Arabian Mission), were far and away the most effective Christian witnesses. In the cases of both Kâmil and Ya'qûb, as noted further on, the Ottoman Muslim authorities were quick to take action to neutralize them.

Having designed their project, the members of The Wheel now had to launch it with an intense organizational and fundraising drive. By October 1, 1889, the day on which Cantine was ordained in Kingston, New York, a Committee of Advice had been chosen, and the first contributing members of the Arabian Mission Syndicate recruited. Sufficient funds came to hand so that Cantine could be set on his way to Beirut October 16. Zwemer and Lansing, meanwhile, continued to develop the financial base of the mission, with Zwemer concentrating his efforts in the Midwest and Lansing (as his now deteriorating health allowed) continuing to work on his contacts in the East.[47]

Cantine arrived in Beirut in early November after having stopped over briefly for talks with Free Church of Scotland mission officials in Edinburgh. Eight months after Cantine left New York, on June 28, 1890, Zwemer also set out for Beirut. In company with his father and older brother, he passed through Britain to talk with CMS officials and visited the Netherlands. Parting company with his father and brother in Europe, he arrived in Beirut on August 7.[48]

Occupy ... Arabia

Both Cantine and Zwemer were concerned to cultivate as wide a base of support and cooperation as possible with mission work already established in the Middle East. They wished to capitalize on the advantage they felt given them by their mandate as an "undenominational" mission. Both men had held consultations on their way to the field with mission agencies in

---

[47]In a marginal note on p. 31 of Philip T. Phelps's copy of the *Golden Milestone*, George Scholten remarks that among the active fundraisers for the Arabian Mission was Philip Phelps himself (Box No. H88-122a in the Holland Archives).

[48]Establishing accurate chronologies of the movements of the two pioneers can be, at times, quite a challenge. The sources do not always agree, and sometimes judgments have to be made as to which one to accept. The principal references used here have been *Milestone*; Mason and Barny, *History*; and Zwemer, *Arabia*, and the Zwemer diaries. These have been augmented where possible by other sources.

Great Britain–the Board of Missions of the Free Church of Scotland having oversight of work in Aden, and the Church Missionary Society having an out-station of their Persian mission in Baghdad. Good relations with the CMS proved in the end to be particularly important, and Major General F. T. Haig, the CMS explorer whom Zwemer considered the 'Father of Missions in Arabia,' was from the outset until his death in July, 1901, one of the Honorary Trustees of the Arabian Mission.[49]

When they arrived in Syria (Lebanon then being part of Syria), a third strong relationship was confirmed. The two young men were taken in hand by American Presbyterian missionaries working under the American Board (ABCFM). They studied Arabic in Sûq-al-Gharb and were instructed in the vicissitudes of mission work among Muslims by this well established missionary community. Those who most influenced Zwemer and Cantine were Henry Jessup[50] and the major editor of the Protestant translation of the Arabic Bible, Cornelius Van Dyke, whom Cantine described as "the Nestor[51] of the missionary force."[52] In Sûq-al-Gharb they also met and recruited a young Syrian convert from Islam, Kâmil 'Abd-ul-Masîh al-Aytânî, who became the third pioneer of the Arabian Mission and its first (perhaps its only genuine) martyr.[53]

In late November, 1890, Zwemer and Cantine set out together for Cairo. Professor Lansing had gone there seeking to renew his failing health "in the environment of his old home city" and had called for Zwemer and Cantine to come for consultations.[54] In Cairo Zwemer and Cantine came in contact

[49]*AMFR* #39, July-Sept. 1901, pp. 8-10.
[50]Jessup arrived in Beirut in 1856. Tibawi, *American*, p. 130. Jessup was among the mainsprings of the Presbyterian effort in the Levant. Rabidly anti-Turk, he was active in political causes as well as religious. He was among the founders of Protestant theological education in Syria and an important advocate in the founding of what is now known as the American University of Beirut (then the Syrian Protestant College). At the time Cantine and Zwemer encountered him, he was still serving as corresponding secretary for the mission in Syria (Tibawi, *American*, at several points).
[51]Van Dyke arrived in Beirut in 1840. Tibawi, *American*, p. 84. Nestor was the ancient counselor to the Greek armies before Troy whose wisdom held in check the hotheads, Achilles and Agememnon. Cantine's allusion suggests that Van Dyke was a sage and foresightful guide in matters of missionary strategy and policy, as well as something of a "presence."
[52]Cantine, *Milestone*, p. 26. Cantine also discovered, much to his delight, that he and Van Dyke were distantly related.
[53]Cantine, *Milestone*, pp. 25-27.
[54]Cantine, *Milestone*, p. 27.

with another convert from Islam, a fairly erudite Egyptian, a pastor named Habîb. He toyed with the idea of joining the expedition[55] but evidently, like Phelps, thought better of it. Lansing, meanwhile, insisted that Cantine go on ahead to Aden and that Zwemer stay on with him for a while in Cairo. Zwemer notes in his diary, "Though I much regret it I suppose I shall have to do it."[56] Holding the hope of working with the Scots there, Cantine sailed directly for Aden December 16, 1890.

The young Sam Zwemer was not equipped to handle the ordeal of watching the professor he idolized fall into irrationality. The entry in his diary for Thursday, December 4, notes, "Was with Dr. L.[ansing] last night. Very nervous and anxious 'to get well and go out to the deserts of Arabia.' 'Why must I stay here, O God! Let me go to Arabia and die there.' 'Sam, the Mission must not die.' 'God has promised it and Arabia must be redeemed.' — Such was the character of his talk. A never-to-be-forgotten night."[57] In the days which followed, Zwemer noted that Lansing was increasingly losing control. Pain and frustration are evident in his diary entries. On Monday, 22, he noted, "Very little improvement from day to day."[58] Two days after Christmas he wrote, "A dispatch from Mrs. L.[ansing]: 'Impossible. Patience. Better Return.' made Dr. L.[ansing]'s financial prospects look far from bright. He owes me £62.—nearly all my salary for two months."[59]

But not all the time Zwemer spent in Cairo was a burden. He enjoyed the fellowship of the Presbyterian missionaries in Egypt, and on Christmas day he joined all of them for Christmas dinner. There he met a Miss Work, a young single missionary from Pennsylvania, come to be a governess and teacher for the children of other missionaries. Five days later he met her again and notes, "She is a very pleasant person."[60] His entry for January 5 is a long description of Miss Work beginning, "She is a young lady of the Mission true to her name and a *good* [emphasis in original] work at that. I

---

[55]Personal letter from Samuel Zwemer to Peter Zwemer from Cairo dated December 10, 1890, in a file of Zwemer's personal letters in the Archives of the Reformed Church in America, New Brunswick Theological Seminary, New Brunswick, New Jersey.

[56]The Zwemer Diaries, entry for Monday, December 8, 1890, in the Archives of the Reformed Church in America in New Brunswick, New Jersey.

[57]Zwemer Diaries, entry for Thursday, December 4, 1890.

[58]Zwemer Diaries, entry for Monday, December 22, 1890.

[59]Zwemer Diaries, entry for Saturday, December 27, 1890.

[60]Zwemer Diaries, entry for Tuesday, December 30, 1890.

enjoyed her society very much." He ended the entry by saying that she seemed to him "daily to be more and more worthy of acquaintance and friendship."[61] On the eve of his departure from Egypt, Zwemer spent one last night in Cairo. "The gem of Egyptian cities lay stretched out before us. But near me was one who is beginning (or has already?) become dearer to me than sight seeing or citadel splendors. In walking down and up the well of Joseph I wondered whether God would give me the blessing of such an one to walk the ups and downs of life with. 'Two are better than one.'"[62] He was, in short, a very smitten, idealistic twenty-five-year-old man on his way to set the world ablaze, and the sap was running high.

As the time for his departure drew near, Zwemer went to see John Lansing one more time Tuesday, January 6. Lansing was disoriented and used his money irrationally. Deeply distressed by this, Zwemer nonetheless felt he could do nothing more for him. The £62 Zwemer wrote off in his own mind as a bad debt, and, with £15 borrowed from a sympathetic missionary, he arrived at Suez. There he bought second-class passage for £7 and sailed Friday, January 9, 1891, on a coastal steamer which stopped at various ports along the way—Jiddah in Arabia, Suakin in the Sudan, Mussawah in Eritrea, Hudaydah in Yemen, and, finally, Aden. A good deal of the voyage was in rough weather, and Samuel spent a good deal of time seasick in his bunk.

Traveling with him was Bishop Thomas Valpy French, missionary Bishop of Lahore, and his chaplain, a Rev. Maitland. They were seeking a place in Arabia in which to establish a new mission and had decided upon the port city of Muscat. Beginning January 9, Zwemer's diary indicates that, while he was attracted to Bishop French and Rev. Maitland, he held against them their high church ways. They did, however, provide him the Christian fellowship he cherished and there was no denying the spunk of the lean, crusty old man.

When the ship stopped in Jiddah, Zwemer availed himself of the opportunity to see the city and visit Eve's tomb there (110 paces long!). "Surely," Zwemer quipped, "she was the mother of all living. From the Moslem grave and tradition as to her immense size the apple tree must have been a poplar!"[63] Talking the idea over with the bishop, Zwemer felt that

---

[61]Zwemer Diaries, entry for Monday, January 5, 1891.
[62]Zwemer Diaries, entry for Thursday, January 8, 1891.
[63]Zwemer Diaries, entry for Monday, January 12, 1891.

Jiddah was a possible mission site, and it certainly was a strategic one.[64] In Suakin, the steamer's next stop, Zwemer consulted with General Haig, who was there on a relief mission, trying to rescue drought orphans from the jaws of death.[65] Haig, Zwemer noted, sympathized with his attitude concerning the bishop's high church liturgical preferences and, he added, Haig "...was more in sympathy with our Mission" than that of the bishop.[66] In Musawwah Zwemer visited a well-established Swedish mission and was favorably impressed by their medical and evangelistic work. After a brief stop at the Yemeni port city of Hudaydah (where Zwemer first began to consider a trip to San'â' in the interior), they made Aden port on January 23.[67] Zwemer found Cantine hard at work, having already made trips to Lahij and Shaykh 'Uthmân.[68]

[64]It must be remembered that in 1891 Jiddah was under the tolerant government of an Ottoman-appointed sharîf. The Wahhâbî era in *western* Arabia was not to make itself felt until after the First World War, and even in eastern Arabia it still lacked an inspired leader. Zwemer did, in fact, follow up on this early visit. After he had left Arabia and settled in Cairo in 1913, he and a Mr. Hooper of the British and Foreign Bible Society visited Jiddah and proposed that, working out of Port Sa'îd, the Bible Society "undertake active colportage work both on Pilgrim ships and at the ports mentioned during the pilgrim season which begins about October 1st and lasts for five months." He also proposed that a Bible depot be opened in the city under the joint oversight of the Bible Society and the Arabian Mission, and that a medical missionary–he nominated Paul Harrison–be sent to explore the possibilities of establishing a permanent medical mission. This, he thought, could all be accomplished at the reasonable expense of $300 a year. Zwemer had thoughtfully encouraged the establishment of a "Jiddah Fund" which, by action of the Arabian Mission and the Arabian Mission Trustees, had been transferred to Zwemer, so as far as anyone knew funds were available (in a letter from W. I. Chamberlain to Fred Barny, dated May 27, 1913, a copy of which is in the author's collection). The Jiddah project did not catch on.
[65]Zwemer, *Milestone*, pp. 48-49.
[66]Zwemer Diaries, entry for Thursday, January 15, 1891.
[67]Aden was a key link in the British imperial chain of communications and coaling stations. The British captured it in 1838. It was annexed to Bombay Presidency and became a Crown Colony in 1937. After three years of vicious fighting against a variety of nationalist groups, the British finally withdrew from Aden November 29, 1967. [See: Julian Paget, *Last Post: Aden 1964-1967* (London: Faber and Faber, 1969).]
[68]Zwemer Diaries, entry for Friday, January 23, 1891. Also see Zwemer, *Arabia*, p. 360. In later years (see *Milestone*, p. 50), Zwemer seemed to think that he made this tour to Lahij himself and recalls even some anecdotes about the visit, but his diaries do not mention it, and his earlier published work is more to be depended upon, in this instance, than the later, even though Cantine himself makes no mention of the visit. On a later occasion, Zwemer too did visit this small sultanate situated inland from Aden in the foothills of the mountains.

Kâmil 'Abd-ul-Masîh, a few days after his baptism in Beirut January 15, 1891, set out after the other two. He caught up with the two Americans in Aden February 7. Zwemer's traveling companions, Bishop French and his chaplain, did not tarry in Aden but sailed on to Muscat via Bombay on Tuesday, January 27,[69] anticipating that the two young Americans would follow. Though they knew him only briefly, because of his devotion to the cause of evangelizing Arabia Bishop French had a powerful impact upon both Zwemer and Cantine.[70]

Cantine had been talking and touring with the Scots in Aden. After mulling things over with Zwemer, it was decided that cooperation with the Scots "would not do for us." Aden was isolated geographically from the rest of Arabia by daunting mountains, its population was overwhelmingly non-Arab (largely Somali), its environment pestilential, the British military presence heavy, and the red tape involved in moving inland through Ottoman-controlled frontiers maddening. All of this, Cantine notes, "did not appeal to us."[71] On March 12, 1891, in a letter to John R. Karsten, a pastor in Alto, Wisconsin, Zwemer wrote, "Aden is a large city and only one of the many open doors to this immense country." But, he continued, "we are still looking for a best place. All the land is before us. Aden has many points in its favor but the great draw-back is fever. The city lies in a circle of grave yards."[72]

While they waited for salary checks to catch up to them, the men explored the region for other promising alternatives. Cantine continued to hobnob with the Scots, while Zwemer and Kâmil took an adventurous sea journey

---

[69]Zwemer Diaries, entry for Monday, January 26, 1891.

[70]See Zwemer's tribute to Bishop French in *Arabia*, pp. 344-352. Cantine recalled the following words of the bishop to him at the time the bishop left them in Aden: "I understand that you also are intending to visit Muscat and the Persian Gulf coast of Arabia. Do not let the fact that I am preceding you change your plans. I am an old man, and it may be God's will that I can only visit the promised land, while it is for you to enter it" (Cantine, *Milestone*, p. 40). His name has been revered by the Arabian Mission—especially by those who have served in Muscat—ever since. His grave in "Cemetery Cove," along with those of several Arabia missionaries, is still carefully tended and frequently visited.

[71]Cantine, *Milestone*, p. 39. Aden, since October 1885, had been a mission station of the Foreign Mission Committee of the Free Church of Scotland. When Cantine and Zwemer arrived the station was manned by the Rev. W. R. W. Gardener and Dr. Alexander Patterson.

[72]Among the Karsten Papers (W88-060, box 1) in The Joint Archives of Holland (Michigan).

up the Hadramaut coast to Makallah and back. In light of Zwemer's overall favorable impression of Makallah and the warmth of their reception by the local sultan, it is not altogether clear why Makallah did not figure more prominently in the choices later made.[73] Both Lahij and Makallah had been suggested to Zwemer by General Haig on the basis of his detailed analysis of the region. They were now scratched off the list as unpromising.

Cantine set sail for Muscat (via Bombay) May 26. The six-day leg from Bombay to Muscat occurred during the southwest monsoon season. He recalls:

> …as the second-class cabins in rough weather were rather trying, I spent most of the time between ports, both day and night, in my steamer chair, lashed to a midship stanchion. These coast steamers [of the British India (BI) Steam Navigation Company] were generally small and very old, with all that this implies, but they were our only connection with the outside world, and, indeed, with each other in our several stations, so that the names "Kilwa," "Pemba," and half a dozen others were certainly fragrant in our memories.[74]

During this leg of his trip, Cantine heard that Bishop French had died of heat stroke in Muscat May 14. Arriving in Muscat, Cantine contacted the American consul there and arranged to stay in the bishop's now vacant lodgings. He spent some time investigating the last days of that idealistic, stubborn, and rather glorious old man[75] and familiarizing himself with the town. Something of Bishop French's character and example (not to say his foolhardiness) must have rubbed off on all who followed him to Muscat, for it was a station that over the years has had more than its fair share of missionary "characters."

Zwemer, meanwhile, set out June 27 on a journey to San'â' in the Yemen by way of the port city of Hudaydah. His assessment of San'â' was guardedly favorable. He enjoyed the dry mountain climate but heartily detested the

---

[73]Zwemer, *Milestone*, pp. 50-55. Makallah did resurface as a possible mission site in the mid-1940s, but by then the Arabian Mission was settled in the Gulf, and it was the Southern Baptists who were encouraged to pioneer in the Hadramaut. It was a proposal that never bore fruit. The Baptists, for their part, found a more congenial base for their work in Trans-Jordan.

[74]Cantine, *Milestone*, p. 40.

[75]Cantine, *Milestone*, pp. 40-41.

Turkish authorities by whom he was harassed.[76] He returned from San'â' to Aden via Hudaydah. J. Christy Wilson, Zwemer's devoted biographer, relates that on the ship from Hudaydah to Aden were two British officers who, upon hearing Zwemer's exploits in Yemen, immediately proposed that he become a Fellow of the Royal Geographic Society. The notion pleased him. When in due time his nomination was accepted, the honor came with the obligation to pay the then rather significant joining fee of twenty pounds sterling for the privilege of putting the letters "F.R.G.S." after his name. This was an investment he thought more to the point than Cantine's expenditures on his hobby, photography.[77] Zwemer finally arrived back in Aden on July 29, having been held in quarantine for some days. He carried with him the firm conviction that the mission should establish its base in the mountains of Yemen at San'â'.

For his part, after a two-week stay in Muscat (the interval between visits of BI steamships), Cantine concluded that "from a missionary standpoint, I did not think Muscat sufficiently inviting to cancel further exploration."[78] On his way up the Arabian Gulf, he set foot for "an hour or two" on Bahrain and continued on to Busheir on the Persian side of the Gulf. There the British political agent showed him medical files which indicated that Bahrain was "the most unhealthy place in all the areas coming under the purview of the writer" of the medical reports. He adds with light humor, "This did not seem a very promising place for pitching our tent, and my thoughts turned approvingly to Zwemer's report on the mountain valleys and streams of Yemen."[79]

For two or three weeks Cantine stayed on in Busheir, at that time the port in Iran where the British political agent in the Gulf resided. He used the time to nurse an American miner back to health and was on the point of turning back to Aden. He wrote Zwemer a letter (which Zwemer received August 7) saying that he was in good health and would probably be returning to Aden shortly.[80] Then he received a letter from Dr. Marcus Eustace, a onetime CMS missionary then serving as the physician for the British

---

[76]Zwemer, *Arabia*, p. 360; and *Milestone*, pp. 68-69.

[77]J. Christy Wilson, *Flaming Prophet: The Story of Samuel Zwemer* (New York: Friendship Press, 1970), pp. 27-28.

[78]Cantine, *Milestone*, p. 42.

[79]Cantine, *Milestone*, p. 43. Zwemer's report on his trip to the Yemen seems not to have survived.

[80]Zwemer Diaries, entry for Thursday, August 7, 1891.

community in Basrah.[81] In the letter, Eustace invited Cantine to stay with him while Cantine examined the feasibility of Basrah as a base of operations for the new mission. Cantine accepted the invitation, and he arrived in Basrah in early August, 1891.[82] The possibilities of that city immediately impressed him as favorable, and he wrote to Zwemer to come and see. "Zwemer," Cantine continues, "at once agreed with me. The trustees at home took our word for it, and the Arabian Mission had at last taken root."[83]

"At once" is a bit of hyperbole. Zwemer received the letter September 27, while Kâmil was away on tour in East Africa. In his diary entry for that day, Zwemer notes, "The letter was a surprise. But after prayer I decided to go as nothing in Aden prevented and the importance of seeing that part of the field was not to be despised." He set sail October 1, after leaving two months'

[81]Marcus Eustace seems to have held a contract position arranged by a consortium of British companies doing business in Basrah. The limitation on this doctor was that, without a license to practice issued in Istanbul (Constantinople), he was not permitted to treat Ottoman citizens. Legally, he had to limit his practice to foreign nationals. It would seem, however, that Eustace stretched the rules whenever he could and, indeed, treated the poor and needy no matter what their nationality. His practice became a precedent which the mission tried later to emulate, much to their discomfort and embarrassment.

[82]Cantine, *Milestone*, p. 43; also *AMFR* #1, p. 3. The Arabian Mission was not the first Christian missionary effort to establish itself in Basrah. In the early seventeenth century, Carmelite monks had been asked by Pope Clement VIII to be his legates to Shah 'Abbâs of Persia, explaining Clement's policy of protecting Christendom from the Ottomans. As a missionary order they were also expected to "employ themselves in the Service of the Souls as their priesthood demanded and as conditions permitted in the Muslim land." The first Carmelite, Fr. Basil of St. Francis, came to reside in Basrah July 9, 1623, and by 1625 the Carmelite House in Basrah was founded. From there tours of Carmelite priests touched points throughout the Gulf but established no stations on the Arab side [Mgr. V.[ictor] Sanmiguel, *Christians in Kuwait* (Beirut, Lebanon: Beirut Printing Press, [1970]), pp. 53-54]. The early impact of the Carmelites (especially Fr. Basil himself) in the region of Basrah upon indigenous Christians as well as in the number of Sabaean and Muslim converts was reported to have been significant [J. G. Lorimer, *Gazetteer of the Persian Gulf, 'Omân, and Central Arabia*, vol. I, part II, appendix I (Calcutta: Superintendent Government Printing, India, 1915), note on p. 2387]. Carmelites have continued to be the most important Catholic participants in Christian ministry in the Arab Gulf to the present day. Especially since the Second World War, relations between Carmelites and members of the Arabian Mission have been cordial and cooperative. Under the leadership of Bishop Francis Micalef of Kuwait, the Carmelites are presently in the vanguard of ecumenical endeavors in the region as well.

[83]Cantine, *Milestone*, p. 44.

salary for Kâmil and retaining the house they were renting in Aden. Zwemer fully expected to return.

He changed ships in Karachi. On board the new vessel he met a man who had charge of "…a beautiful Turkish woman, formerly the wife of an English officer but now on return to Baghdad, her home. She is not at all jealous of her good appearance but parades in cabin and on deck even unveiled." He adds in Arabic, *najjinî min ash-shirrîr* [deliver me from the Evil One]![84] The steamer stopped in Muscat on the way, and Zwemer had a day's tour of the town. He visited Bishop French's tomb in "Cemetery Cove" where, he says, "I engaged in prayer at this grave. Asked God that the Bishop's Red Sea blessing might rest upon me and that as he said I might finish what he has begun. — Yes, I am ready to follow after for Jesus' sake even to the same end."[85]

The steamer stopped again at Bahrain where, in one day, Zwemer managed to see a great deal but regretted that he could not meet the ruler who bore the name 'Îsâ bin-'Alî (Jesus son of 'Alî).[86] Finally he arrived in Basrah Monday, October 26. That evening he wrote in his diary, "Now for our tour tales. Then for the problem as to the field of work. — The question is *Sanaâ* or *Bosrah* or *both* [emphasis in the original]. Tomorrow we will see this gate to the land of promise. Certainly Bosrah is a live town and occupies an important centre."[87] Zwemer was introduced to Dr. and Mrs. Eustace, toured the town with Cantine, and in his diary entry for Thursday, October 29, says, "Planned and decided after much prayer that Sanaâ must wait for the Gospel and that Bosrah is the place to be occupied. Cantine and I have also discussed the matter of my departure to America to increase our funds if possible."[88]

[84]Zwemer Diaries, entry for Thursday, October 15, 1891.
[85]Zwemer Diaries, entry for Sunday, October 18, 1891.
[86]Zwemer Diaries, entry for Thursday, October, 22, 1891.
[87]Zwemer Diaries, entry for Monday, October 26, 1891.
[88]Zwemer Diaries, entry for Thursday, October 29, 1891. Just why Zwemer felt he ought to return to America to raise funds is not unconnected with his intense personal interest in Cairo. He had maintained a serious correspondence with Miss Work, to whom he referred by the initials M. E. W. He frequently mentioned that his thoughts turned to Cairo, and M. E. W. was the lodestone drawing his thoughts thither. The fact that the road to America passed through Cairo was not insignificant to Zwemer.

The First Base: Basrah

When Zwemer and Cantine toured Basrah they examined the piece of ground Marcus Eustace had marked out as the site for the prospective hospital, and their talk turned to grand dreams. They cabled J. Preston Searle in New Jersey, informing him of their plans and suggesting that Zwemer return to the United States to raise the funds for establishing Basrah station – $25,000.[89]

On Sunday, November 15, 1891, Zwemer set sail for Aden, arriving November 28. Kâmil had returned from his tour in Djibouti with Stephanos, a colporteur of the Scots Mission, and he was in their rented house when Zwemer returned. Zwemer persuaded Kâmil (who seems to have settled in with the Scots rather better than had the two Americans) to join them in Basrah. Nothing daunted, Kâmil picked up and sailed for Basrah with the mission's baggage December 10, arriving in Basrah in early January, 1892.[90] Zwemer, for his part, settled in to await a reply from Searle concerning the proposal that he return to the United States on a recruiting and fundraising tour.

Zwemer's diary entry for Tuesday, December 15, reads, "Telegram at 3 p.m. from Searle and the Committee to *stay* [emphasis in original]. Dark day! – Where will reinforcements come from? Who will plead Arabia's needs? Where the $25,000? Had grace given me to bear the sore disappointment. Prayer proved a relief to my feelings. Wrote to the Committee etc."[91]

[89]Zwemer Diaries, entries for Saturday, October 30 through Saturday, November 14, 1891.

[90]Henry Harris Jessup, *The Setting of the Crescent and the Rising of the Cross, or Kamil Abdul Messiah: A Syrian Convert from Islam to Christianity* (Philadelphia, Pennsylvania: The Westminster Press, 1898), pp. 115-118. There is some evidence of disagreement between the two Americans. Zwemer could never quite surrender the dream of working in Yemen, even while the actual development of work focused increasingly upon the Gulf. Early issues of the *AMFR* indicate that Zwemer continued to keep alive the hope of establishing a mission station in San'â' even after Bahrain and Muscat had been opened, a project which would have hopelessly extended the mission's already over-extended lines of communication.

[91]Zwemer Diaries, entry for Tuesday, December 15, 1891. As he waited for the committee's answer, Zwemer was also awaiting word from M. E. W. When the negative response came from Searle, there remained the matter of Cairo. M. E. W. wrote Zwemer in Aden asking him to wait.

"Better than yes!" he wrote like a young boy whistling into the wind, "To wait

Intruding upon his complicated state of mind was a visit from Dr. Henry Cobb, secretary of the Board of Foreign Missions of the Reformed Church in America.[92] Cobb landed with a party of five in Aden January 25 in the course of an around-the-world tour. At the end of his day as host, Zwemer commented, "A happy day but no prayer or word of encouragement from the Doctor and the entertainment of the party cost me 20 odd R[upee]s."[93] The next day brought a second blow to his flagging spirits: The young lady in Cairo whose favor he sought asked him not to come to visit. He was obliged to return to Basrah, and in the course of the journey learned that the young lady had lost interest.[94] He landed in Basrah with a bruised heart but ready to begin work on February 22, 1892.

During Zwemer's absence and at Marcus Eustace's urging, in October, 1891, Cantine had headed up the Tigris River for Baghdad to pay his respects to the CMS missionaries there.[95] They encouraged him in his plan

is to hope and to have" [Zwemer Diaries, entry for Thursday, January 21, 1892]. Just what he meant by the twisted aphorism only he himself knew. Clearly, Zwemer was in a state of high excitement, and he burned off nervous energy on a tour inland with the Scots to see their medical work in action. On January 5 he wrote, "Mail day. Recd. letters from M. E. W. and also from Searle. He writes resolutions of the Com[mittee of Advice]. A medical man is under appointment and Peter [Zwemer, Samuel's younger brother] also is coming — Good news" [Zwemer Diaries, entry for Tuesday, January 5, 1892]. The entry has no comment on the burden of M.E.W.'s letter.

[92]Cobb was the secretary for the Board of Foreign Missions of the Reformed church from 1883 to 1910. He was a man of considerable scholarship and influence.

[93]Zwemer Diaries, entry for Monday, January 25, 1892.

[94]"I received telegram from M. E. W. Don't come. Ergo, I go to Busrah. Found earliest and cheapest steamer. Leaves tomorrow" [Zwemer Diaries, entry for Tuesday, January 26, 1892]. And then came the conclusion: While on the journey to Basrah his mail from Aden caught up to him in Karachi. "A letter from M. E. W. of wonderful and sad import," he reports to himself soulfully, adding, "Are all women false? Or are all men fools? *Allâhu ya'rif* [God knows]. Answered as I felt. —" [Zwemer Diaries, entry for Tuesday, February 9, 1892]. So ended his first fascination with Cairo. His later fascination was more vocational than romantic. It was what Cairo represented as a springboard to his becoming a "missionary statesman" that later drew him away from Arabia proper.

[95]Cantine, *Milestone*, pp. 43-47; also *AMFR* #1, p. 3. Baghdad in 1882 had been established as an "outstation" of the Church Missionary Society's mission in Persia. There the CMS had established a hospital and a school as well as a Bible dépôt in cooperation with the British and Foreign Bible Society (Lorimer, *Gazetteer*, vol. I, part II, appendix I, pp.2395, 2398-2399). Unlike their work in Persia proper and more in line with policies being followed in the Levant, in Baghdad the CMS worked primarily with the native Christian population with a relatively light stress upon evangelization among Muslims.

to establish the mission in Basrah, and he returned there. Shortly thereafter he met the agent for the British and Foreign Bible Society for the region, a Rev. Hodgson. Cantine and Hodgson negotiated an arrangement whereby the Arabian Mission would handle Bible distribution in the Basrah area and the Bible society would assist by covering some of the expenses for shop rental and colporteur salary.[96]

Shortly after his arrival in Basrah early in 1892, Zwemer too made his "pilgrimage" to Baghdad and the CMS mission there. Returning March 18, he brought with him Salome Antoon and Elias Gergis, two colporteurs trained by the CMS. Shortly thereafter a third colporteur, Ya'qûb Johann, an Iraqi convert from Islam, also joined the Basrah force.

Marcus Eustace left Basrah during the spring of 1892 to rejoin the CMS work in Persia and was posted to the Afghan frontier. His departure came as a blow. Not only had Cantine and Zwemer benefited from his counsel and enjoyed the hospitality of his home, but their association with his semi-illegal medical work among the indigenous poor had reflected well upon the two newcomers. Their relationship with Marcus Eustace had shown them in graphic terms that medical work could be a very effective opener of doors. It became, for them, something like an article of faith.

Their appeals for the appointment of a medical doctor, which they had been expressing ever since landing in Basrah, grew more importunate. In response the Committee of Advice rather hastily recruited a native of New Orleans, Clarence E. Riggs. Riggs arrived in Basrah March 20 and began medical work (without a proper Ottoman license to practice medicine) on the 28th.[97] This brought the missionary complement up to full strength–three western missionaries and four native colporteurs–and with them the station of Basrah may be considered fully operational. The first of the mission's Bible shops was opened in Basrah June 20. This milestone was

---

[96]Cantine, *Milestone...*, p. 46-47. This relationship with the Bible society was later extended to include Bahrain and other stations which the Arabian Mission established. It persisted for a long time and, under a different format, has been revived in recent years through close relations between the Family Bookshop Group and the Bible society.

[97]*AMFR* #1, p. 5, and #2, p. 10. The second reference puts the date for starting medical work as March 28, 1892. What is interesting to note is that, because Riggs began practicing without a proper Ottoman license, the clinic was forced to close between April 28 and June 30 while Riggs went to Istanbul to seek an Ottoman license. This taught the missionaries a lesson in compliance with the law, even when they considered the law unenlightened.

marked at the end of the first quarter of 1892, when the Arabian Mission Field Reports began to be published.

Two steps forward—one step back is not an unusual way to make progress. The full complement did not remain full for very long. The inclement summers of fever-ridden Basrah were the terror of the European community there. Kâmil 'Abd-ul-Masîh, accustomed to the milder climate of Lebanon, was taken ill and died June 24, 1892. The circumstances surrounding his death, its abrupt nature, and the way in which the Ottoman authorities handled the matter of his funeral led to suspicions that Kâmil had, in fact, been poisoned.[98]

Problems came in batches. The mission lost two of its three remaining colporteurs. After only four months of service, Elias Gergis left in July to seek his fortune in America. And Ya'qûb Johann, who had returned to Baghdad to visit his family, was put under police surveillance beginning in late June. Ya'qûb Johann, a convert from Islam, never did return to Basrah, and, after long persecution, may have recanted his Christianity—the record is not clear.[99]

As if those blows were not crisis enough, Zwemer and Cantine then found themselves seriously at odds with Clarence Riggs, their new doctor. A lovable red-bearded eccentric, Riggs marched to quite a different drummer from the other two.[100] Riggs's readiness to enter into confrontational situations with the Muslim authorities of Basrah sent chills of apprehension

---

[98]The Ottoman governor of Basrah at the time was the conservative Sultan 'Abd-ul-Hamîd appointment, Hidâyat Pasha. It was this same governor who, in November, tried to expel the missionaries but failed when, upon their own request, the British consul intervened.

[99]*AMFR* #3, p. 3.

[100]Quite seriously he proposed that the mission finance his renting a house under an assumed identity in Mecca. There he would tunnel under the sacred mosque, steal and destroy the precious Black Stone, and thereby undo Islam and allow them all to go home. The proposal did not strike the other two as clever.

Writing to J. Preston Searle May 20, 1892, Cantine described Riggs as too honest, too indiscreet, too sensitive, too quick to take offense, too short-tempered, too colorful in the use of language, too tactless and blunt, too

up their spines. Most stressful of all for Cantine and Zwemer, Riggs turned out to be something of a Unitarian who did not believe in the divinity of Christ. After an intense personal confrontation between the three men and a complicated correspondence with the Committee of Advice, upon the insistence of Cantine and Zwemer, Riggs was dismissed August 14, 1892.[101]

uncooperative and disruptive (the C. E. Riggs file in the Arabian Mission collection, the Archives of the Reformed Church in America, New Brunswick, New Jersey).

[101] Cantine later expressed the thought that Lansing had been somewhat remiss in his investigation of Riggs, but that is not entirely fair to Lansing. Riggs presented documents to the Committee of Advice which attested him to be a member in good standing of the Methodist Episcopal church. His personal letters used all the right language for one who saw mission as a daring and romantic adventure for Christ; his professional credentials were in order. When Lansing brought Riggs's name before the committee along with the documentation, and after they had all met him face to face, they voted on January 11, 1892, to appoint him. By the end of the month he had set sail for England.

From England he wrote a curious letter to J. Preston Searle (February 7). He reported that he had met a Rev. Brooke on board ship, a minister of the Unitarian Church in England. (The very word, "Unitarian," of course, would have caused Searle some alarm.) He said that Mr. Brooke would probably be willing to help support the Arabian Mission if Searle would but contact him (C. E. Riggs file). It is only speculation, but, given Riggs's innocence and impressionability, his romantic and volatile nature, it is likely (in spite of his later claims to the contrary) that his Christological views were changed during his crossing of the Atlantic. Certainly he arrived in Basrah speaking like a Unitarian.

In his letter to the Trustees of the Arabian Mission dated May 11, 1892, Riggs said, "Last night (May 4th, 92) we (Mess. Cantine and Zwemer and myself) were speaking on the subject of Jesus Christ. During the discussion I asked Mr. Zwemer if he believed that 'Christ was God.' He answered 'Yes,' and asked if I did not. I answered 'No.' My answer appeared to surprise both." The letter is altogether remarkable for its ingenuous candor. He stated that, both in personal interviews and before the committee, he had never been asked whether he believed Christ was God. All that had been asked of him was that he practice his profession as a physician and that, in religious encounters, he defer to Cantine and Zwemer as the specialists in that field. His personal religious views, he said, he would happily keep to himself and proceed with the business at hand. His colleagues, he continued, thought otherwise. They found it impossible to identify themselves as his brothers in the faith and in the work of the mission. Riggs concluded, if the committee felt that he must resign because of his religious convictions, then he would do so. He would, however, continue in his profession which was to relieve his fellow human beings of their suffering (C. E. Riggs file).

Cantine and Zwemer both signed as witnesses that Riggs's letter had stated the issues aright. Their letter (which Clarence Riggs, in turn, witnessed as correct) highlighted other issues, and it remains on record as a clear statement of policy.

Through this whole affair, the two novice missionaries believed they had kept faith with their mandate. But there was an awareness that something

The two began with a glowing report on Riggs's medical work but added that they shared no kinship of religious feeling with him, a matter they deemed "essential to the best interests of a spiritual work." The letter then describes the conversation of May 4 in terms that match with those of Riggs, and then concluded:

"Since that evening we had several long conversations on the matter and altho [*sic.*] we understood the better what each of us held to be true, Dr. Riggs did not change his views but on the contrary reaffirmed them and denied the possibility of his ever changing his belief.

"Therefore we submit the following to the Board as the reasons why we deem it our duty to inform them of this matter.

"1. The sending out and employment of any missionary, medical or otherwise, holding such a view would practically do away with the evangelical character of our Mission.

"2. Every missionary who labors in Moslem lands ought to have correct views not only as to the Person of Christ but be able to express them to others.

"3. It is impossible for us who hold evangelical views to work in spiritual harmony for the conversion of Moslems with one who holds an opinion so widely variant on a subject so vital.

"4. A medical missionary, no matter how closely confined to his special branch of work can not, while in daily close contact with Moslems, Moslem converts and inquirers, avoid a decisive attitude towards a question so universal and important.

"In conclusion, it is needless to add that the whole matter has been to us a cause of deep sorrow for our work's sake and of earnest prayer even as we can not help believe it will also be to the Board (C. E. Riggs file).

Following the Trustees' vote to support Cantine and Zwemer and dismiss Riggs, Lansing wrote hurriedly to Searle as follows:

"Dear Pres,

"The more I think of it the more I think that perhaps we were a little too quick in our action yesterday to cancel Riggs' appointment. We could easily have waited a week to consider. If you have not transmitted the action had you better not wait till Saturday's steamer to transmit it and in the meantime let me come over and have a talk with you? I enclose 3 letters. Read them. They certainly are clear. I think Riggs is not as bad as he is painted or as he paints himself" (C. E. Riggs file; to which three letters Lansing is referring is unknown).

But the communication had already gone out. The committee claimed that Riggs had joined the mission under false pretenses and, therefore, his passage back to the United States would not be paid. He was officially dismissed August 14. He then tried to set up private practice in Basrah in order to raise his fare, but, turning to alcohol, his personal life deteriorated so badly that Cantine and Zwemer finally paid his way out of their own pockets. He left Basrah September 17, wandered around the Orient for a while, tried to set up practice in San Francisco, was converted at a revival conducted by Dwight L. Moody in Chicago, and then went home to New Orleans to die a year or two after leaving Basrah (the references are vague) (*AMFR* #1, pp. 11-14, and #3, p. 6; and Cantine, *Milestone*, pp. 61-65).

had gone wrong. The Board of Trustees and the Committee of Advice were also aware that they were amateurs in the business of running a mission. It is likely that, at this time, thoughts began to turn toward availing the mission of more seasoned administration at home.

On the field, literature and scripture portions continued to be distributed through a small Bible shop and mainly through the efforts of the one remaining colporteur, the durable Salome Antoon. The two missionaries were young and inexperienced, desperately trying to learn the language, beset and frustrated by a cynical and even dangerous Ottoman bureaucracy which viewed their presence as undesirable, and trying as best they could to get a grasp on their situation. As we have pointed out, they were heirs to the ingrained western bias concerning Islam and the church in the Orient, which was not helpful. It was a conditioning that they shed only slowly and then not completely. By trial and error they were quickly learning how to manage their "business," but in the meantime their priority was keeping the mission alive.

Preaching in the streets of Basrah was soon determined to be "…unwise and detrimental to future work," and Cantine and Zwemer both reluctantly realized that evangelism could only be done through personal conversations with individuals and other private contacts.[102] They developed the conviction that, by whatever means, they had to gain the approval of the people—for the sake of the mission's survival, they needed to be needed—and they thought they knew how that could best be done.

Their calls for qualified medical personnel became almost strident. J. Talmage Wyckoff, the son of a Reformed church pastor and a most promising candidate, arrived to take over the medical work in March of 1893. There is some suggestion that he toured with Zwemer in Bahrain, bolstering up his medical practice. But in July he fell victim to a virulent case of dysentery and was shipped off to India to try to shake it off. He was not successful and elected to return from there to the United States. He did not

[102]*AMFR* #4, Oct. 1-December 31, 1892, p. 5.

fully recover for several years.[103] A tinge of desperation is evident in the expressions of disappointment after his departure.

Zwemer in particular expressed his desire to expand activities beyond the limits of Basrah as quickly as possible. At this time the phrase, "occupy the interior of Arabia," made its prominent appearance in reports of the missionaries.[104] Although Yemen was kept in mind until Zwemer's last abortive trip there in 1894,[105] attention began to center upon the island of Bahrain and other towns along the Gulf coast.

Dorothy Van Ess, although describing an incident of later years, has caught the humor that often attended the mission's early efforts to reach out beyond Basrah:

> Touring was the backbone of the work. At the beginning when no doctors had joined the mission permanently, the intrepid young clergymen would set off with a bag full of Arabic Bibles and Christian literature, a set of dental tools, and a supply of what they called "harmless but effective remedies." They doctored everything from colic to cholera, but fortunately never killed anyone that I have heard of. My husband [John Van Ess] when a very young man was conducting one of his "clinics" on the Pirate Coast, while he was touring there, and had to extract the tooth of a burly negress. He said he almost had to put his knee on her chest to get it out, and

[103]Mason and Barny, *History*, pp. 81-82. Wyckoff, having tried a rest cure in India, found that his illness persisted. Taking a job as ship's surgeon, he obtained passage to the United States for $68.00. He settled in Leonia, New Jersey, and by December, 1894, had fairly well made up his mind that he would not be returning to the Arabia field. His loss was much regretted (J. Talmage Wyckoff correspondence file among the Arabian Mission papers in the Archives of the Reformed Church in America in New Brunswick, N. J.).

[104]*AMFR* #2 & #3.

[105]*AMFR* #'s 10 & 11, p. 7, notes Zwemer as having departed from Bahrain June 14. He was on tour in Yemen through early August (p. 9). Dates from one source to another do not agree and, again, we have favored the source written at the time closest to the actual event. For a narrative of this rather arduous trip to distribute literature among the Jews of Yemen recalled some years later (1937) see: Zwemer, *Milestone*, pp. 71-77. This did not cure Zwemer of his yearning for Yemen, but it does seem that it was his last attempt to do something about it. It is interesting that the frontispiece for his first major (and perhaps still his best) book, *Arabia: The Cradle of Islam*, published in 1900, five years before he withdrew from the mission, is a picture of "a typical Arab of Yemen," the likes of whom few Arabia missionaries ever had opportunity to see outside of, perhaps, Dhofâr in Oman.

was sure he must have broken her jaw, but she wiped her face with her veil, pointed to the other side of her mouth, and said, "Here's another!"106

It therefore appears that at the very time when their field resources were cut in less than half, the resolve of the two missionaries to achieve their goals redoubled. Samuel Zwemer, having toured around Basrah and up the Euphrates, spent most of December, 1892, in Bahrain. After meeting his brother Peter there, he followed him back to Basrah for a mission consultation with Cantine. But by January 28, 1893, he was back in Bahrain to stay, opening the first Bible shop there February 4.107

By the end of 1893, Peter Zwemer, who had only arrived on the field in December, 1892, had stationed himself in the port city of Muscat.108 It was

---

106Typescript of a speech delivered by Dorothy Firman Van Ess, "75th Anniversary of the Arabian Mission," February 12, 1965, Bahrain, Persian Gulf.

107During Zwemer's first visit to the island, by dint of his amateur skills as a "medicine man," he was able to drive in a few stakes. He returned to Basrah with a strongly favorable report. Bahrain, as he had cause to know, was under firm British influence. It was an excellent jumping off point for touring inland into the "Pirate Coast" and Najd. It was Arab. And, best of all, "there are no Turks" [*AMFR* #4, October-December, 1892, p. 7].

On January 28, 1893, almost exactly a month from the date of his departure from the islands, Zwemer was back on Bahrain. He established a Bible depot and when, on March 1, the colporteur Da'ûd Yûsuf, arrived, after a short vacation in India, Zwemer was able to tour the island and begin regular though rudimentary clinic work (*AMFR* #5, January-March, 1893, p. 7; and #6, April-June, 1893, pp. 5-6). There was an incident with a local mullah over the sale of Bibles during Zwemer's first visit. Shaykh 'Îsâ bin-'Alî Âl Khalîfah, then ruler and great grandfather of the present ruler, Shaykh 'Îsâ bin-Salmân Âl Khalîfah, requested Zwemer to depart. The young American appealed to the British political resident in Busheir, and however the matter was handled with the Shaykh, the trouble passed [AMFR #5, January-March, 1893, p. 6. J. G. Lorimer, whose *Gazetteer of the Persian Gulf, 'Omân, and Central Arabia*, is a gold mine of information on the region at the turn of the century, laconically comments on this incident: "At one time the affairs of the (American) Arabian Mission in Bahrain gave some trouble to British authorities, who were responsible for the safety of the missionaries, and the Government of India would gladly have seen the latter withdrawn; but ultimately the dangers due to the presence of the Mission, such as they were, passed away" (p. 348).]. From then until his departure in 1905, Bahrain became Zwemer's main base of operation, Cantine holding down the work in Basrah and, later, also Oman.

108Peter Zwemer, Samuel's younger brother, had arrived on the field in December of 1892. After spending some eventful time in Basrah and Bahrain, he went to Muscat for a five-month stay beginning in early December, 1893 (*AMFR* #30,

Cantine's task to hold Basrah while the Zwemer brothers worked to gain footholds along the Arabian littoral. Both Bahrain and Muscat quickly came to be considered permanent stations staffed by peripatetic missionaries and their equally adventurous Assyrian colporteurs.[109]

In our discussions of the mission's work in evangelism, education, and medicine, we will return to the story of the development of Basrah station and of 'Imârah. In the early years it continued to be devoted primarily to noninstitutional evangelism (unless, of course, one considers the Bible shop to be an institution). Beginning in 1910, with the opening of the Lansing Memorial Hospital, however, Basrah flourished for a brief seven-year period as a medical center for the mission. Efforts to maintain a foothold in 'Imârah were persistent but under-staffed. In 1910, John Van Ess finally got permission to develop schools for boys and girls, a project which was implemented two years later. But at this point we may note that, following 1918, it was John Van Ess and his passion for education that dominated the character of Basrah station.

Van Ess was among the most powerful and creative minds in the Arabian Mission. He was a blotter for information, a voracious reader, a natural and brilliant linguist, and a man with encyclopedic interests. As a student at Princeton Theological Seminary, he had been at the top of his class and was shaping his goals to enter into the professorship when, in 1901, he heard of the death in Basrah of the young and promising Harry Wiersum. The appeal for someone to come out and fill the void had a powerful impact upon the idealist in Van Ess, and he responded. He never afterward regretted his decision.[110]

April-June, 1899, pp. 3-4). A shop was rented in the market almost immediately and, though Peter Zwemer moved back and forth for a time between Basrah and Bahrain, he finally took up permanent residence in Muscat in 1896. He established his home and school for freed slaves in the spring of that same year and devoted his primary effort to nourishing his charges until his departure in September and premature death October 18, 1898, in New York (Mason and Barny, *History*, pp. 94-95; *AMFR* #28, October-December, 1898, pp. 5-7).
[109]Some autobiographical recollections of missionaries mistakenly refer to "Armenian" colporteurs. Armenians in the Arabian Mission were very rare. Actually, the main source of colporteurs in the early days for both the CMS in Baghdad and for the Arabian Mission was the town of Mardin in southwestern Turkey. These were Arabic speaking Suryânî and Assyrian (or Chaldean) Christians–more the former than the latter–related to the missionary efforts of the ABCFM in that region.
[110]Van Ess, *Pioneers*, p. 20.

His first years on the field were exploratory–he explored both himself and the land. He arrived on the field early in 1902 and, as a language student, was posted in Bahrain. But from 1903 onward his base was Basrah, and his assignment was as touring evangelist. It was an assignment tailor made for him. Language tutor in tow, he traveled throughout the southern region of the Two Rivers, crossing the dangerous marshes and acquainting himself with the tribal leaders. He also accompanied the expedition given the task of redesigning the ancient drainage and irrigation works of the region. Other travels took him to the region then known as the Pirate Coast (now the United Arab Emirates) and up to Istanbul, traveling on the return journey by raft down the Euphrates. When, in 1912, he was able to start the Basrah School of High Hope for Boys, he brought all of the experience and insight gained during his youth's adventurous exploits to bear upon a landmark career that spanned forty-seven years.

The shape of that career indicates his profound grappling with the issues and realities of the day. As he showed in his relationships with the British at the outset of World War I, Van Ess was almost (but not quite) unique among the Arabia missionaries in his strong engagement in political events. Above all, he was a moral man who lived his own definition of morality: "It is simply a sense of oughtness, a sense of obligation, not of living down to our rights but up to our duties and privileges."[111] And his sense of duty and of privilege was summed up in his deep Christian commitment.

Dorothy Firman married John Van Ess in 1911. The two of them combined to become an institution. During a career in which one shoulder rubbed against the hovel and the other the palace, Dorothy Van Ess maintained an innate sense of personal integrity and a gifted intuition for context. Where John Van Ess was bred on an Illinois farm, Dorothy came out of New England aristocracy. They made an interesting "One Flesh" blend and complemented each other with marvelous completion.[112]

Dorothy, as her autobiography displays, had a persistent eye for humor with a strong shot of the wry. A woman of strong feelings, she rarely showed

---

[111]John Van Ess, *Meet the Arab* (New York: The John Day Company, 1943), p. 216.
[112]The Arabic language–which both Van Esses used with delightful facility–has a powerful emphatic construction which I here borrow. To "complement with completion" means, more prosaically, perfectly.

them. That made her a powerhouse of energy and dedication, always careful (in Arabia's male-dominated society) to show her husband honor.[113] Beginning in the 1930s she followed in the footsteps of Fred Barny and became the mission's historian. For years she wrote down the story of the comings and goings of that community which she deemed to be closer to her than family itself.[114]

The Van Esses founded their schools in 1912 and lived through the challenges and trials of the First World War, having a foot in both camps at one time or another. And while the tragedy of the closure of medical work in Basrah in 1917 was not something in which they rejoiced, it was that tragedy which opened up the horizons for them and let their gifts fully flourish. It was through education that Basrah finally established its identity as a station unique among the other stations of the mission. 'Imârah, after 1926, became a medical site.

Bahrain Station's Founding

Samuel Zwemer, as we have noted, took Bahrain as his base in 1892. For several years, until his marriage in 1896, he remained very much the "tourist," but he foresaw that Bahrain would have to be developed in a stable manner. When in Bahrain, the principal activities in which he was engaged were literature distribution and personal evangelism. He also dabbled in simple medical treatments. But it was Lankford Worrall who, following the precedent of Wyckoff, really set in motion the medical work on the island, touring out of Basrah. He backed up the amateur work that Zwemer had begun.

The doctors Thoms, Sharon and Marion, were assigned to Bahrain in 1900, and they brought to an end the era of makeshift medicine. It did not

---

[113]Edwin Luidens, addressing those gathered at "A Service of Remembrance and Thanksgiving for the Life of Dorothy Firman Van Ess (1885-1975)" on September 13, 1975, spoke of Dorothy's deep sense of calling, her enterprising ways, her commitment to truth, and her sense of loyalty. (A copy of the text of this address is in the author's document collection; the original remains with the Luidens family.)

[114]John Van Ess died in Basrah in 1949, on the very eve of his retirement, but Dorothy continued to fulfill the role of the Grand Dame of the mission for another decade and a half—the quintessential hostess and the soul of dignity. When she died in September, 1975, the end of an era was marked.

take them long to develop their practice to the point where they needed to move out of their ill-suited rented quarters into purposefully designed hospital facilities. Before any other buildings were built by the mission in Bahrain, therefore, land was purchased for a hospital. As the hospital building went up, the people of Bahrain were sure that it would be used as a fine residence for the missionaries themselves. They were quite surprised when the missionaries actually did what they said they were going to do. The Mason Memorial Hospital began to operate in 1903.

The years 1904 to 1906 were traumatic years for the mission in Bahrain. The deaths in 1904 of the two Zwemer daughters, Katarina and Ruth, along with the deaths of two children of the colporteur, Amîn, and the daughter of the Afghani convert and dispenser, Jahan Khan, stunned the mission with the high cost of devotion. That awareness was made all the more heavy with the death on April 25, 1905, of Marion Wells Thoms and, nine months later, of Jessie Vail Bennett, who had but recently arrived on the field. The old but well-cared-for cemetery within walking distance of the main mission compounds still bears eloquent testimony to the toll Bahrain exacted upon those who came to minister there. But it seemed worth the effort, and there were rewards for those who persevered.

The first mission residences in Bahrain were not built until 1908, and then only after a combination chapel-school building had been erected in 1905. This chapel/school was a unique building with a small but distinctive tower in which, in 1915, was placed the first public clock in Bahrain, a local marvel.[115] As it was committed to nurturing a Christian community in Bahrain, so too was the mission concerned to provide educational resources to all the people. The process of development in Bahrain, therefore, emphasized not only medical work, but education as well.

---

[115]In later years, when the second-floor chapel became too small for the expanding congregations that used it and the school had outgrown the ground floor, the ruler, Shaykh 'Îsâ, insisted that the designers of the new church building put a clock in the new tower. However, it has never been as reliable as the old one, which was of meticulous German manufacture.

In the same year that the Mason Memorial opened for business, Amy Zwemer, working out of her home, brought together a group of children and started what she called the "Acorn School." The Acorn School was first intended mainly for children of Arab Christians and helpers in the mission. It began to attract a few others. Even after the Zwemers left the Gulf for the last time in 1912, it continued in fits and starts as an attempt to offer education to the daughters of the wider Bahraini community. But it did not prosper. The educational work of the mission in Bahrain did not get a firm start until the 1920s. Until then it was essentially a medical station with a heavy program of medical touring. The Bible shop in the old market was also an active place, and Bahrain was a place to which the mission posted many of its new recruits for language training.

Oman Founded

Peter Zwemer established himself in Muscat city in 1893 and, like his older brother, was active in touring. Within days of his arrival, following the same pattern, a Bible shop was rented in Muscat's market on December 10, and a colporteur was retained. Oman was, for many years, primarily an evangelistic station.

In 1896, following the example of the Keith-Falconer Mission of Aden,[116] the mission became active in ministering to the homeless, although at the time the missionaries no doubt felt they were fulfilling the mandate concerning the mission's ministry to slaves. On May 27, 1896, Peter Zwemer, then in Muscat, assumed guardianship for eighteen[117] boys aged seven to thirteen. These were boys rescued from an Arab slave ship by a British frigate, the *H.M.S. Lapwing*. The younger Zwemer pledged to the British political agent and consul in Muscat, Captain F. W. Beville, that he would feed, clothe, house, educate, and prepare the boys for adult life. The

---

[116]*AMFR* #68, January-March, 1909, p. 9.

[117]The documents are unclear as to the exact number of boys originally turned over to Peter Zwemer. There is some suggestion that it was only sixteen boys, but a photograph published in 1898 (Jessup, *Kamil*, p.125) shows eighteen young individuals. The records of the names and ages of the boys, though, count only sixteen. What happened to the missing two is unclear. Two may have died early, and the records show another two of the sixteen as having died. That would leave fourteen as finally being sent out into the world after the mission's obligations had been discharged.

agreement stated that the boys would, upon attaining the age of eighteen, be sent off on their own.

In September a second capture of two dhows (both flying French colors) brought a second draft of 183 slaves into Muscat. Writing to Henry Cobb September 30, 1896, Peter Zwemer noted, "Among the slaves perhaps fifty are boys of an age suitable to enter the Mission School and my offer to take them would certainly be favorably received by the French Consul." He had proposed this in an earlier inquiry and had received a negative response. In his September 30 letter, he continued:

> But my hands are tied by the resolution that the number of slaves be *not increased* [sic.] for the present.
>
> This is to my very great regret. Opportunity offers now and may not offer another year of beginning a work of some importance among such freed slaves.
>
> Eighteen pupils makes but a very small school and humanly speaking scarcely worth while. As far as I have been able to learn such schools in other mission centers have been a success altho [sic.] there have been exceptional cases where pupils became a disgrace to their school who on account of their knowledge of English became the more pronounced and this justified a doubt as to the wisdom of educating them.
>
> I can not but believe, however, that the reception and education of such freed slaves is one of our legitimate lines of work, and that because we are a Christian Mission in a place where our work is largely under [here "British" is crossed out] European protection we should open our doors to all such freed slaves as we are in a position to train and support.
>
> I greatly regret that I shall be compelled to allow these freed slaves to be taken to Bombay where at present on account of the few slave dhows captured the last few years, there is no organized effort in their behalf.[118]

[118]In the box entitled, "Arabian Mission: Correspondence from the Muscat Station 1895-1908, letters written to Peter J. Zwemer, 1893-1895" in the Joint Archives of Holland, Michigan.

But the decision of the board stuck. From its founding, the home and school for rescued slaves was not to be a long-term institution. Zwemer, in youthful innocence, had assumed charge of the boys personally. That occasioned the legal problem of just who was custodian of the boys when he left the field in 1898. These matters, however, were cleared up by an accommodating new political agent and consul, Major C. G. F. Fagan, who drafted a new agreement for custody of the boys by the representative of the "American Arabian Mission" in Muscat. It was well he did this, for Peter Zwemer, a very sick man, departed from Muscat in May, 1898, and by October he was dead.

For a time following Peter Zwemer's death, the work in Muscat was borne by Cantine alone. He, in turn, was spelled by Fred Barny[119] and George Stone. The latter arrived in February of 1898 with only four months of language study under his belt. Barny had fallen ill with malaria and had to take a convalescent leave in India (where he met his future wife, Margaret), so Stone was obliged to take on the responsibilities in Oman alone.

---

[119]Frederick J. Barny was the sixth pioneer of the mission and among the most durable, joining in 1897 straight out of seminary. (His bride, Margaret Rice, joined him a year later, after their marriage October 19.) A slender if not quite dapper man, he was the mission's "utility infielder," serving in all the Arabian Mission's stations, and serving two stints "outside"–with the Arcot Mission in India from 1919 to 1920, and with the United Mission in Mesopotamia from 1925 to 1932. Dorothy Van Ess notes: "From pioneer days he has been almost continuously on the language committee, and he has also rendered conspicuous service in translation. His 'scholar's lamp,' burning late in his study window, is a familiar sight to his colleagues. Like all evangelistic missionaries, he has probably devoted most of his time to the uncounted service of personal work, with individuals or small groups. The dignity and beauty of his Sunday services, both Arabic and English, have been a notable contribution to every station in which he has served." [Mrs. John (Dorothy F.) Van Ess, *Who's Who in the Arabian Mission* (New York: Woman's Board of Foreign Missions, [1937]), p. 4.] Among his accomplishments in the mission, Barny was also a builder of note, having seen the Olcott Memorial Hospital in Kuwait through to completion and adding his own touches to the design of Dirk Dykstra. He was also the first historian of the mission, publishing with Alfred Mason the still much-refered-to *History of the Arabian Mission* in 1926.

Margaret R. Barny, the second woman in the Arabian Mission after Amy Zwemer, was a woman of fine features and an accomplished pianist, noted among the mission's "homemakers," and a sensitive evangelist in her own right.

The Barnys retired in 1940. Fred died in March 1951 and Margaret a decade later. Their daughter, Esther Barny (Ames), the first of the mission's children to return to the field, served as a physician in the mission from 1927 to 1945.

Cantine, returning in June during the extreme and unrelenting heat of the Muscat summer, found Stone distressed by persistent boils. Stone was given a few days off to travel with his language teacher up the coast to the town of Birka, a healthier location. While there and seemingly getting better, he contracted a sudden fever and quickly died on June 28, 1899, only nine months after his arrival on the field. His language teacher brought the body back to Muscat, and George Stone was buried beside Bishop French.

Thereafter the "Freed Slave School of the American Arabian Mission" was run primarily by James Cantine. As an active program, the Freed Slave School was closed by the spring of 1901.[120] The four youngest boys were placed in various homes and the older ones employed with reputable firms or with the British navy.

From 1899 to 1908, when Fred and Margaret Barny relieved them, James and Elizabeth Cantine held the station alone with occasional assistance from Jim Moerdyk[121] out of Bahrain. The main work in Muscat focused on the work of the Bible shop and itinerating evangelistic tours by Cantine and his colporteurs. Elizabeth DePree was the first single woman recruited by the Arabian Mission, beginning her work in 1902. After studying and working in Bahrain, she married James Cantine in 1904 and joined him in Oman. She inaugurated work among Omani women, and the two Cantines, building on the now vacant home for freed slaves, organized a day school for boys which was attended even by members of the royal family. It continued to operate until 1931 when, like the school in Kuwait, it was forced to close for lack of funds.[122] An outstation was also established in the village of Nakhl, part way

---

[120]Cantine reporting in *AMFR,* #38, April to June, 1901, p. 18.

[121]James Enoch Moerdyk, from Drenthe, Michigan, was a bachelor all his life. He joined the mission in 1900 and died "in harness" in July of 1941, in the midst of World War II. He is described as a meticulous man, gifted in keeping records, serving the mission as treasurer and secretary for many years, and pinch hitting for his colleagues in all the stations at one time or another (Van Ess, *Who's Who,* p. 21). Another of the Arabian Mission's "Uncle Jims," he was a builder too, helping to construct and dedicate both Lansing Memorial Hospitals, the first in Basrah and the other in 'Imârah. His touring record is also remarkable, and his valiant effort to establish a base in Nâsiriyyah will always stand to his credit. But his last years in 'Imârah and his beginning pastoral work among the lepers there is his personal "star" and, when he died, the testimony of his leper friends was extremely moving (Dalenberg, *Sharifa,* p. 147).

[122]Its closure has been deemed by the Omanis who benefited from the school a real tragedy and, by the mission, a real lost opportunity.

up the mountain, which not incidentally afforded missionaries a place of relief from the oppressive heat of the coast.

The Barnys took over responsibilities in Oman when the Cantines left for a well-deserved furlough late in 1907, but Barny continued to hold responsibility for Bahrain as well, as supervisor of the young Dirk Dykstra and a bevy of other very junior missionaries there. The Barnys were eventually reinforced. In 1909, Sharon Thoms and his family were assigned to open medical work in Oman. From 1910 to 1911 the evangelistic effort was also redoubled with the transfer of Jim Moerdyk to do tours in the mountains. Fanny Lutton was assigned to Oman to work with women in 1911. The site chosen for the new medical work was the marginally more healthy town of Matrah, separated from Muscat by a ridge of black basalt rock. Access into the interior of the country was also easier from Matrah.

Fred Barny continued to manage the Muscat endeavors of school and Bible shop. Fanny Lutton was assigned to women's evangelistic work in Muscat. Although hampered by the rebellion of the interior against the sultans of Muscat, an important part of the work in Oman was evangelistic touring. Then the outstation of Nakhl proved its worth. Barny and Moerdyk used it as the staging point for tours into the Green Mountain (Jabal Akhdar) region, a stronghold of Ibâdî conservatism. The rather fabulous topography and scenery of Oman, along with its colorful villagers and bedouin (usually very hospitable and friendly), always fascinated missionaries. The mountains also offered an often much needed break from the unrelenting heat of the coastal cities.

Oman had been primarily an evangelistic effort until, in 1909, Sharon and May Thoms were assigned to begin the main medical work.[123] In Oman,

---

[123] Mason and Barny commented, "Thus at the end of the decade the three stations of the Mission are all organized on an equal basis.... The force of missionaries was also being added to...bringing the number of workers up to twenty-seven. The force of native helpers, men and women, numbered twenty-five at the same time" (Mason and Barny, *History*, p. 135). The establishment of medical work in Matrah, Oman, gave the mission a sense that it was rounding out its profile, a real sense of accomplishment.

medical work never eclipsed the other missionary efforts as it tended to do at other stations of the mission. But it did become important. The medical work was begun in a rented house in the town of Muscat, and efforts to purchase land were launched.

As Sharon Thoms was negotiating for land on which to build the hospital in Matrah, he ran into obstacles from the sultan, from the British resident, and (much to his annoyance) from the honorary United States consul, a British citizen and Muslim by confession. To overcome the obstacle which this consul posed, James Cantine (then in the United States on extended furlough for the sake of his wife's health) paid a call on the State Department and argued vigorously that a new and more sympathetic consul be appointed. Correspondence with Henry Cobb throughout 1909 documents the eventual success of this lobbying venture, and John A. Ray was appointed United States consul in Muscat in September, 1909. Mr. Ray's initial reception by the sultan and the British in Oman was cool, but his intercession on behalf of the mission bore fruit. Land in the city of Matrah was procured.

Sharon Thoms and his family returned to the United States for furlough in 1910-1911, campaigning hard for funds to build the new hospital. The neophyte, Paul Harrison,[124] was charged to carry on the work in his absence.

---

[124]Paul Wilberforce Harrison came to the mission fresh from Johns Hopkins Medical School and from having refused a faculty position at Harvard Medical School in 1909. His Congregational conditioning on the "home mission" field in Nebraska had directed him toward a medical missionary's career, and Samuel Zwemer directed him toward Arabia. A more joyful Christian the mission never had. Tall, lanky, and unquenchably energetic, his slim figure and sun-squinted eyes became a kind of symbol of what an Arabia missionary should be. Quick of wit and inquisitive to a fault, Harrison was a born pioneer. His innovative medical techniques are legendary. (In Kuwait, when patient load was light, he was accustomed to going to the slaughter house and buy a sheep's head. Taking it to his clinic, he would patiently dissect it just to "keep his hand in." This earned for him the sobriquet of "the Butcher Doctor" in Kuwait.) Having opened medical work in Kuwait, Harrison then settled down in Bahrain, establishing himself as a medical tourist of some repute. In 1929 he was posted to Oman to refound the major medical effort there. Surrendering that to Wells Thoms in 1939, Harrison moved back to Bahrain, where he was the anchor doctor of the mission while Louis Dame and Harold Storm did most of the touring. He retired in 1948 but was back in Bahrain again from 1952 to 1954. Still full of vigor, he retired a second time in 1954 [Ann M. Harrison, *A Tool in His Hand: The Story of Dr. Paul W. Harrison of Arabia* (New York: Friendship Press, 1958), and other recollections]. He died in 1962 at nearly eighty of complications resulting from medical experiments he had been administering on himself. He was a prolific writer, a biblical scholar and teacher of great devotion, and an extremely effective public speaker. The mission never saw his like again.

Thoms, meanwhile, succeeded in raising the substantial amount of $6,000 for the hospital in Matrah.

The mission's work in the urban centers of Muscat and Matrah was dealt another blow in 1913. On January 13, Sharon Thoms wrote a post card to his mother in Three Rivers, Michigan: "We are all well and happy. I am putting our telephone up and May is giving the children lessons, etc. Will write a letter next week. Affectionately, Sharon ."[125] The promised letter was never written. On January 15 Sharon Thoms, while stringing phone wire to establish communications between his colleagues in Muscat and himself, fell from a ladder, struck his head, and died almost instantly.

James Cantine, who had to compose yet another obituary, wrote at the time:

> In some ways the last hours of Dr. Thoms were typical of the man. He always had a keen interest in mechanics and scientific research, and outside the regular routine of his work was often busy at something that would help in the general comfort and utility. The need of a telephone between the two mission houses, about two miles apart and separated by difficult mountain paths and an often dangerous sea, appealed to him strongly. He was able to interest a friend at home in the project, and the mission approving, no sooner had the materials arrived than he started on its erection. The Sultan had kindly given him permission to use his poles for most of the way but there was a short connection to be made at each end. The Waly of Matrah, his staunch friend, told me that he could have had the loan of a number of men if he had asked. But Dr. Thoms loved to do things himself, and knowing that he could do it better than anyone else at hand and having a just pride in mission work well done, he began with his assistants to do a little each day as opportunity offered. Just about sundown on January fifteenth, after the day's medical work was done, he attempted to tighten the wire at the top of a pole, but a little way from his house on the seashore. Somehow he lost his balance, and falling from the ladder, struck his head upon the rocky ground, and never regained full consciousness. The next day the Sultan with messages of condolence

[125]Among documents and pictures loaned to the author by Ethel Scudder Thoms Dickason and returned to her keeping.

and deep respect sent his son with his launch, and under the American flag he was taken to his earthly resting place in a rocky cove not far from where are the graves of his fellow missionaries, George E. Stone and Bishop French.[126]

Wells Thoms, Sharon Thoms's son, when he returned to Muscat in 1939 to carry on his father's work, was early on greeted by two smiling Omanîs who had sought him out. They informed him with some pride that they had been the ones holding the ladder from which his father had fallen to his death. Seeing the humor of it, Wells Thoms remarked to the effect that he didn't know whether they wanted a tip or his congratulations or what.[127]

With the loss of Sharon Thoms, the mission pressed Harrison, then in Kuwait, to spend several months in Oman. He was followed by the Worralls in 1914. Although the Worralls did not endure at that post (in fact they shortly resigned from the mission),[128] the medical work was maintained at a reduced level by a rotation of doctors from other stations. But the pressures of war, the difficulties of communications and travel, and the sudden loss to the mission of altogether too many of its medical personnel dictated that a choice be made in 1917. Kuwait and Bahrain would continue to have mission hospitals. The effort in Matrah, with land purchased but the hospital not yet built, was abandoned...or, rather, postponed.

Kuwait Station Founded

The Arabian Mission had cast interested eyes at Kuwait almost from the outset. Kuwait was viewed as a strategic point because of its extensive trade

---

[126]*AMFR* #85, April-June, 1913, p. 4. The name of the place is Shaykh Jabar, an almost inaccessible cove between Muscat City and the fishing village of Sidâb [noted in Wendell Phillips, *Oman: A History* (Beirut: Librairie du Liban, 1971), p. 229].

[127]This version of the incident is recalled by the author from Wells Thoms's "table talk" to which it was always a joy to listen.

[128]The cause for their resignation probably grew out of a personality conflict between the Worralls and Sarah Hosmon, which the mission tried to play down. Hosmon also began her work in Oman in 1914, and the likelihood is that the effort at reconciliation made at the previous year's annual meeting in Bahrain did not "take." In any case, the Worralls returned to the United States on furlough in 1915 and, before returning to the field, they resigned in 1917, ostensibly for health reasons. In fact they returned to the work of mission in Africa. Lankford Worrall died "in harness" June 8, 1930.

with the Arabs of the interior.[129] Early in 1895 Samuel Zwemer visited Kuwait for three days en route from Bahrain to Basrah and noted, "The place is the cleanest Arab town on the Gulf and has a fine harbor."[130] In May of the same year two colporteurs out of Basrah, Salome Antoon and Razouki Naaman, paid a five-day visit to Kuwait. Zwemer, in his report of their trip, claimed that "The door is now ajar; one more visit and that by our medical missionary will push it wide open, perhaps bear it off its hinges."[131]

Early in 1896, however, when another colporteur named Yûsuf Mîkhâ passed through, the door still seemed quite firmly closed–Shaykh Mubârak, newly come to power, forbade the sale of books.[132] The next attempt was not made until June of 1903, and it is the first record of a medical visit. Sharon Thoms, touring out of Bahrain with Salome and another colporteur, was given a cool reception by Shaykh Mubârak who, on the same day as they arrived, had Thoms and his companions transferred to a small boat and sent on to Fao whence they wended their way to Basrah, arriving much disgruntled.[133]

Under the circumstances, it is surprising to read in the very next quarterly report that "...our mission has by God's blessing been enabled to open definite work there, and at our last annual meeting it was decided that

[129]Eleanor T. Calverley, *My Arabian Days and Nights* (New York: Thomas Y. Crowell Company, 1958), p. 15. One of the items of the transit trade in which the mission doctors had a hand was not altogether anticipated. An interesting document which survived from files maintained in Kuwait is a certificate issued by Stanley Mylrea and Eleanor Calverley at the request of the British political agent. It documents the examination by the two physicians of the contents of fifteen coffins containing eighteen bodies bound for interment in the Iraqi shrine city of Najaf, sacred to the Shî`ah. The certificate testifies that the remains in the coffins were well over three years dead and could safely be shipped to their final resting place (document, dated May 12, 1919, in the author's collection). In his medical report of that same year, Mylrea noted that both he and Eleanor Calverley had to undertake the examination since a male doctor was not permitted to examine female skeletons. In the case where both a male and a female skeleton resided in the same container, he stood at the male end and Eleanor Calverley at the female end, both barely restraining their mirth, struggling to maintain the sober visage required by the occasion. He noted wryly that the skeletons did, indeed, make the trip safely.

[130]*AMFR* #13, January-March 1895, p. 5.

[131]*AMFR* #14, April-June 1895, p. 4.

[132]*AMFR* #17, January - March 1896, p. 3.

[133]*AMFR* #48, October-December 1903, pp. 14-16. Thoms was sure that Wahhâbî agents had followed them from Bahrain and had poisoned the atmosphere of the visit..

Kuweit be an out-station of Bahrein.[134] Evidently following Thoms's abortive visit, some time in July or August, the intrepid Salome Antoon returned to Kuwait and, with his wife and bevy of five children in tow, rented a house and opened a Bible shop. In any case, by the time Zwemer visited him in February of 1904, Salome seemed to be well situated and maintaining a good reputation in the town.[135] But the effort failed of its promise. Salome held Kuwait alone for one year[136] but then had to leave. Mubârak "unceremoniously closed the shop and sent the colporteur away in an open boat."[137]

Although references are made to subsequent visits by James Moerdyk and others by Samuel Zwemer, Kuwait seemed impenetrable. And the work in Kuwait almost never began. Stanley Mylrea recalled that the mission was on the verge of giving up on Kuwait. A motion was seriously entertained at the annual meeting of 1907 that the special fund of $1,200 being held to buy land for a hospital in Kuwait, donated by Frank Chambers of the Bronxville Church, be diverted to develop possible options in Dubay. He added, "The motion, I am glad to say, was lost."[138]

As it turned out, late in 1908 Arthur K. Bennett was serving as the mission's touring doctor out of Basrah. Shaykh Khaz'al, ruler of Muhammarah—a diabetic and Bennett's admiring patient—invited the doctor to meet Shaykh Mubârak aboard the latter's yacht anchored in the Shatt-ul-'Arab. Mubârak then invited Bennett to go to Kuwait[139] and there examine Mubârak's sister who had bad eyes. Bennett made haste to accept the invitation, knowing how dearly the mission desired a foothold in Kuwait.

---

[134]*AMFR* #49, January-March 1904, p. 5
[135]*AMFR* #49, January-March 1904, pp. 5-8.
[136]*AMFR* #63, October-December 1907, p. 11.
[137]Mason and Barny, *History*, p. 144.
[138]Mylrea, *Kuwait*, p. 40. Mason and Barny, *History*, p. 144.
[139]Stanley Mylrea, writing in 1922, relates an interesting tale: "In 1910, one of the leading men of Kuweit had successfully undergone a surgical operation in the Basrah mission hospital, and on his return home to Kuweit, he brought such a favorable report with him, and exercised such an influence on Sheikh Mubarek, that the latter gentleman invited the Arabian Mission to come to his capital and build a hospital there" [C. Stanley G. Mylrea, "Arabia – A Retrospect, 1912-1922," pp. 269-276 in *The Church Missionary Review*, vol. LXXII, 1922 (London: CMS), p. 273]. The date, 1910, we may question, but it is highly likely that this sort of prelude to Bennett's primary contact with Shaykh Mubârak did take place. This story has the feeling of an incident related to Mylrea informally in the course of his social contacts in Kuwait in later years.

In Kuwait, after receiving Mubârak's "license," he operated on the young woman successfully for cararacts.[140] This cemented a relationship of trust and friendship between the two men.

In the months which followed, another of Bennett's friends and patients, Sayyid Rajab Âl Naqîb of Basrah,[141] joined Shaykh Khaz'al in urging Mubârak to issue the mission an invitation. Rajab, chief religious figure of Basrah, was held by Kuwait's ruler in high esteem. Early in 1909, therefore, Mubârak issued his invitation to the mission to open medical work in Kuwait.[142]

In 1909, therefore, Arthur Bennett, John Van Ess, and Gerrit Pennings were assigned by the mission to maintain Kuwait as an outstation from Basrah, along with Stanley Mylrea and Paul Harrison, who were visiting from Bahrain. Bennett's visits to Kuwait included the first encounter of a missionary doctor with 'Abd-ul-'Azîz Âl Sa'ûd, then only seven years established as the Amîr of Najd.[143] Bennett also recalled that his relations with Mubârak were very cordial.[144] Nonetheless, although they eventually

---

[140]Bennett to Gerrit DeJong, December 31, 1963 (copy of a typescript transcription in the author's document collection). Bennett was eighty-two years old when he wrote the letter. Some aspects of his narrative seem to be at odds with those of Mylrea and Mason and Barny, but the sequence does seem to sustain Bennett's account.

[141]Mylrea, *Kuwait*, p. 41, records: "Still another piece of work at the hands of Arthur Bennett won us fame. A son of Seyyid Rejib suffered from a tumor of the neck, and the boy had been sent to India where he was seen by a number of specialists, all of whom refused to operate. Bennett was eventually asked to see him and advised an operation. Permission was granted and the tumor was successfully removed. (The patient, by then an old man, was living in 1949.)"\
Naqîb is a relatively little-used Arabic title for a leader. In the case of the hereditary Naqîbs of Basrah, the title denoted not only the city's chief native dignitary but also its religious guiding light. The Naqîbs of Basrah and Kuwait claim descent from the Prophet Muhammad's family.

[142]Mylrea, *Kuwait*, pp. 40-41. Bennett's name, in later years, came to fade away. It took Shaykh 'Abd-Allâh al-Sâlim Âl Sabâh, at the ceremony dedicating the Mylrea Memorial Hospital in 1956, to chide the mission to remember that it was Arthur Bennett who had first begun medical work in Kuwait, and he pledged that the Kuwaitis for their part would not forget.

[143]Bennett to DeJong, December 31, 1963: "He [Mubârak] took me with him out to the desert to a feast with Abdul Aziz As Saoud."

[144]Bennett recalls that he went on furlough in 1910, where he was asked by William Chamberlain to contact a Mr. Chambers of Rogers Peet and Company. Bennett goes on, "We had dinner together and he promised me enough money to build a hospital there. This he later did. Mr. Chamberlain wanted to give Shaikh

planned for something more permanent, and even purchased land for the construction of the mission's hospital in Kuwait,[145] Bennett, Van Ess, and the others continued to be transients, having their primary duties elsewhere. This arrangement of being something of a "side show" of the mission did not please Shaykh Mubârak, and he pressed the mission to settle someone permanently in Kuwait.[146]

In 1911 the mission purchased land out beyond the city limits on a small hill that would catch the breezes.[147] At its annual meeting, the mission appointed Paul Harrison, still a bachelor, to head up the medical work, Edwin Calverley to be the evangelist, and Eleanor Calverley to be in charge of medical work and other contacts among women.[148]

> Mobarrek Es Sabah some presents and when I told him he wanted binoculars and a Colt revolver, we got both of them and later I presented the Shaikh with them during a mejlis. The Shaikh used his binoculars daily, watching the boats in the harbor and was always my trusted friend....Later he gave me a beautiful stallion, a Hamdan full blood, which I regretfully had to leave behind me when I left Arabia" (Bennett to DeJong, December 31, 1963). (The funding through Mr. Chambers to which Bennett here refers must have been a commitment on Chambers's part to top up the money he had already donated to the amount needed to complete the hospital.)

[145]Bennett recalls, "Van Ess was my companion and a great fellow who spoke perfect Arabic. I remained in Kuwait for some time after buying the land for the mission. Capt. Shakespeare [sic.] was the Political Agent for the British. He was a charming gentleman and helped me train my full blood Arab horse which I had been given. For months we dined together almost daily. I always had to dress. In spite of the fact we two men were the only Europeans in the City" (Arthur K. Bennett to Garrett E. DeJong, January 14, 1964, photocopy of typescript transcript in the author's document collection).

[146]Mylrea, *Kuwait*, p. 41, notes that Bennett "had a good assistant–a Christian Iraqi– whom he left in Kuwait to run a dispensary and administer first aid." Here, perhaps, is the bridge between the transient visits of the physicians.

[147]Bennett notes that he "chose the west side of the city where there was an elevation and he [Mubârak] measured off the number of 'therats' [*dhrâ'*] cubits himself. This is interesting because he gave me the deed and years later here in America the Mission had to ask me to transfer the property from my name to that of the Mission" (Bennet to DeJong, December 31, 1963). The property chosen, evidently by Bennett and Van Ess together (Van Ess told his children that it was *he* who chose the parcel of land and the truth lies some where in between), was at that time outside the city and some distance from the main activities of the town. The popular prediction was that nobody would come such a distance for treatment. In later years (1920) a city wall was built which included the hospital within its embrace as an integral part of the city, and later still, in the early 1960s, the mission's property, now prestigiously situated, was evaluated as being worth several million dollars.

[148]Mylrea, *Kuwait*, p. 44; and Mason and Barny, *History*, pp. 144-145.

When the Calverleys, fresh from successfully passing their language examinations, arrived in December of 1911, the mission held lease on two houses in the center of the town. One, known as Bayt-ar-Rabbân,[149] was occupied by the colporteur, Jerjis, and his mother and sister, and by Gaylânî, Paul Harrison's Afghani medical assistant. It was in that house that the mission held its services of worship. The other, actually an annex to Shaykh Mubârak's rambling palace, served as both missionary residence and hospital, a customary kind of arrangement which served the mission in all its stations until proper hospitals could be built. Stanley and Bessie Mylrea replaced Paul Harrison in the winter of 1913.[150] In that same year Mylrea initiated work on the rather modest hospital building.[151]

For most of the next three decades, the history of this station is dominated by this fascinating American-educated Britisher.[152] Mylrea, as a senior

[149]The name was descriptive of the erstwhile owner of the house. He had been a ship's captain (a *rabbân*) who had murdered a woman in the house and stuffed her body down the well in the center of the courtyard. Having been found guilty, he was banished from Kuwait and the house was taken over by the ruler, Shaykh Mubârak. No Kuwaiti would live in it because a murder had been committed in it, and so, for a very reasonable rent, the mission was glad to take it over (Mylrea, *Kuwait*, pp. 45-46). But the name had a fortunate breadth of meaning. It might also be taken to mean, "the house of the learned one devoted to the Lord." As the principal place for Christian worship in the town until the building of the mission chapel in 1931, that connotation was prominent in Christian minds, and into the late 1940s the house (still only rented) continued to be the residence of the colporteur and the place where the mission gathered for its weekly Wednesday night prayer meeting.

[150]Mylrea, *Kuwait*, pp. 45-54. Mylrea notes in his "Annual Report - Men's Medical Department - 1913-1914," "It was on the fifth of December that I reached Kuweit from Busrah Annual Meeting. My first duty was to find a house which would make it possible for Mrs. Mylrea to live in Kuweit, for on that condition depended my assignment to Kuweit....The only residence that seemed in the least desirable was the one in which the Colporteur, Jurgius, was living and it was finally arranged to take over his house as soon as he should find another. He had little difficulty in doing this and on December 17th I left for Bahrein to get my furniture. By the day after Christmas I was back again in Kuweit and putting my house in order. On December 31st Mrs. Mylrea arrived from Busrah where she had been waiting until there should be a place for her to come to. On January 2nd I began to hold regular clinics..." (from original report in the author's collection).

[151]Funds for the building, $6,000, were provided by Frank R. Chambers of Bronxville, New York, who had earlier provided the seed money for the purchase of the property. The doctor's residence on the hill above the hospital was built in 1914, and the evangelist's home was completed two years later.

[152]The deepest impact, after the Mylreas and the Calverleys, was made by Lew and Dorothy Scudder from 1939 to 1990. Others who served with distinction were

medical student in Philadelphia, had been recruited for the Arabian Mission in 1905 by the timely intervention of Samuel Zwemer.[153] Of medium height, Mylrea had an oval face across which his mouth cut a straight line. He never lost his slightly wavy hair, and below it his heavy eyebrows overhung penetrating eyes that slanted downward at the corners. His most glaring self-confessed weakness was his hot temper, a weakness which was converted to an effective instrument for good on several occasions. His humor was of the understated, dry variety and very penetrating...cutting, when he took a notion.

He knew his King James Bible by heart as well as the ancient Anglican liturgy. People used to drive miles simply to hear him read the scripture at Sunday evening English services.[154] He was also a master storyteller, and another book he knew by heart was Lewis Carroll's *Alice in Wonderland.* In later years the children of the mission used to crowd around his knees before the fire in "Acadia," his retirement cottage in Kodaikanal, high in the Palni Hills of South India, just to listen to him tell the tale of Alice. He never turned a page of the great book on his lap.

Mylrea's public demeanor was customarily grave and formal, and that suited the Arab, whose ideal of a religious man and a man of wisdom Mylrea fit to a "T." He was the epitome of the *hakîm*, the sober man of deep spiritual learning. Precise in his dealings (and in the British twist with which he spoke

---

Mary Van Pelt, nursing supervisor and hospital manager from 1920 to 1941; Mary Bruins Allison, who followed an offbeat and colorful medical career from 1934 to 1963; Rose and Gerald "Jerry" Nykerk, who served there significantly from 1942 to 1949 and from 1963 until Jerry's death in 1964; Gerrit and Everdine DeJong, who, between 1926 and 1964, served several extended terms in Kuwait; Jeannette Veldman, who served there as instructor in nursing from 1955 through 1958; and Don and Ev Mac Neill, who served there from 1955 to 1961.

[153] Mylrea had actually applied to go out to Turkey with the American Board of Commissioners for Foreign Missions of the Congregational church. That board had been slow to take action on his application. When Mylrea expressed his frustration at a Student Volunteer conference, he was tapped on the shoulder by Samuel Zwemer and invited to consider Arabia as an alternative. This he did (Mylrea, *Kuwait*, pp. 8-10).

[154] H. R. P. Dickson, *Kuwait and Her Neighbours* (London: George Allen & Unwin Ltd., 1956), p. 439. Dickson writes in memory of his old friend, "A scholar in Arabic, as was also his wife Bessie, he knew his Bible by heart in both English and Arabic, and of a Sunday evening in the Mission Church it was like listening to some new story, not an oft-repeated tale, when he read the lessons almost without a glance at the Book."

his excellent Arabic), he was dogged in pursuit of the goals he set for himself. Even when galloping through the streets of the town on his horse with his dog, Khalaf, pelting along in their train, racing to meet an emergency at some home where illness threatened, he never lost his dignity. Overshadowing his gifted colleagues, Edwin and Eleanor Calverley, he outlasted them and placed his mark on a whole society no less surely than the great Shaykh Mubârak under whose rule he began his work.[155]

Bessie Augusta London Mylrea, Stanley Mylrea's wife from July, 1906, was a graceful woman, frail of constitution but nonetheless endowed with a durable beauty and a deep spiritual gentleness. The Arabs chose for her the name, Khâtûn Sa'îdah (the happy lady), an appropriate sobriquet. As Eleanor Calverley wrote, the name fit her, "…for she had a merry smile and an animated manner."[156] A pianist of some accomplishment, it was she who bore the burden of pumping the baby organ at the worship services, an athletic as well as artistic exercise. Bessie was one of those individuals who exceeded her limitations as a matter of course. She became, of necessity, a competent medical assistant, and, among the senior missionaries, she was renowned for her competence in Arabic.[157]

---

[155]In 1952 he had been retired (for the second time) for five years. It had become his custom to visit the Gulf during the cool winter. That year, almost as though he had a homing instinct, he was visiting Kuwait when he had a heart attack and died on January 3. Mylrea was buried in Kuwait.

[156]E. Calverley, *Days and Nights*, pp. 64-65.

[157]*AMFR* #196, April-June, 1942, pp. 3-5. The tributes to her by Dorothy Van Ess and Gerrit Pennings are quite unequivocal in their admiration and affection. It was Bessie who had the most to lose from the practice of Arab generosity. And that comment deserves an explanation:

There was an occasion on which Mylrea was invited by the Shaykh Mubârak for a celebration, during which the ruler showed off some of his horses in a race. Mylrea expressed great admiration for the winner and, on the next day, found the beautiful Arabian stallion tethered beside his house, a gift from the ruler.

In the course of time, the Mylreas invited the shaykh to dinner, not an uncommon courtesy in those days and one which, even as late as the mid-1950s, the rulers of Kuwait were accustomed to accept. After a fine meal, the men were entertained by Bessie Mylrea on their piano. The shaykh was greatly entertained and remarked with some emphasis upon the admirable qualities of the instrument.

The Mylreas were pleased with their success and had no premonitions of impending loss. But on the next day there was a knock at the door. Several rather burly retainers of the shaykh were standing there and said that the shaykh recognized that to move a piano might be beyond Mylrea's capability. So, to ease things, His Highness had sent them to move it for him. The piano, of course, found a new home that very day. Its fate thereafter is unknown.

As Stanley Mylrea's and Eleanor Calverley's medical reputations grew, the popularity of the Arabian Mission increased one step at a time. The more hard-line members of the community felt that it demeaned Kuwait to be so beholden to Christians. The "Muslim Benevolent Society of Kuwait" was formed; rented a house on the sea front; proceeded to furnish it as a hospital with apparatus, drugs, and instruments; and finally hired a Turkish doctor to take charge. Mylrea called it the "opposition hospital." And he commented, "The venture was never really a success."[158] The Turkish doctor turned out to be incompetent and unduly fond of alcohol; the organization behind the undertaking was incapable of supervising him; and Shaykh Mubârak sympathized not at all with the whole undertaking. In the end, the Turkish doctor, accused of serious malpractice, was deported, and in the summer of 1916 the remaining furniture and instruments of the defunct enterprise were turned over to the Arabian Mission.[159] It was an affirmation of sorts.

The initial reception of the Arabian Mission in Kuwait was less than encouraging. In contrast to the more casual acceptance of foreigners in places like Basrah, Bahrain, and Muscat, the common people of Kuwait viewed the missionaries with grave suspicion. Mylrea wrote:

> ...While it was true that Shaikh Mubarak wanted us, the great majority of the population including all the leading families were solidly opposed to the policy of allowing Christian missionaries to settle in their city. It was all very well to send for a doctor to come down from Basrah to attend an important member of the community who might be ill, but to have a colony of Christian missionaries living in their city? No, they did not want that!

[158] Mylrea, *Kuwait*, p. 101.
[159] Mylrea, *Kuwait*, pp. 101-102. Aside from one microscope, the rest of the salvaged equipment was of little use. The gesture, however, was significant.

...It used to hurt my pride to realize that in Kuwait I was looked upon as an unbeliever and an infidel. It should be noted that this curiosity and rudeness was a manifestation on the part of the man (and the boy) on the street only. The upper classes were aloof and supercilious but they never stooped to the cheap vulgarity of the common people. They kept their good manners and were courteous and civil even when they were probably suppressing inward prejudices. Only a very few were really rude to me.[160]

As late as the early 1950s, the western missionaries (and their children) still occasionally heard Kuwaiti children chant as they followed the westerners down the street, "*Yâ engrayzî bû taylah, inshallâh tamût hallaylah!*" ('Hey! be-hatted English guy, God grant this night that you might die!') The western pith helmet (*topee* in the idiom of Brjitish India, *taylah* in Kuwait) and the strange way western women dressed were things which were not easily absorbed. It was a chant that Stanley Mylrea heard thrown behind him (along with an occasional rock or clot of mud) all the days of his service in Kuwait. Eleanor Calverley, who was greeted with these words as she walked through Kuwait's narrow streets toward her new home, observed with remarkable charity (and some truth), "We could remember urchins in our own country jeering at foreigners in unusual garb."[161] Resistance to the presence of missionaries sustained in them a feeling of precariousness until greater events intervened.

Shaykh Sâlim al-Mubârak, who became amîr of Kuwait in 1917, unlike his self-confident father and affable and diplomatic brother, Jâbir, was a dour and straight-laced man, conservative in his ways, a man of blunt truthfulness and honest to his own lights. He was a man who prided himself on his strict Islam.[162] He resented the Sa'ûdî Ikhwân's arrogance in claiming to be the

[160]Mylrea, *Kuwait*, p. 42.
[161]E. Calverley, *Days and Nights*, p. 19.
[162]Of the rulers of Kuwait, the only one of whom no photograph exists is Shaykh Sâlim. He forbade any *'aks* (likeness) of himself to be made as a matter of religious principle.

exemplars of true Islam. True, he was tolerant of his Persian-speaking Shî'ah minority, some of his most productive citizens, and for this the Ikhwân held him in disdain. But while liberal in this regard, in other matters he was not. For a long time he bore the mission no goodwill.[163] He resented the presence of the increasingly popular Christian missionaries. It was the war with 'Abd-ul-'Azîz and his Ikhwân that changed the picture.

During the Battle of Jahrâ' and for two days thereafter, it was the mission hospital which singlehandedly kept many of Kuwait's combatants alive. Mylrea's efforts at relieving suffering (of 135 seriously wounded men brought to the hospital, only four died) won Sâlim's unrestrained admiration and gratitude and that of the whole town.[164] So changed was the ruler's attitude that a month before his death he granted the mission an additional piece of property to enlarge its compound, and encouraged his talented son,

---

[163]Mylrea, *Kuwait*, p. 76.

[164]Mylrea, in his edited memoirs, recounts how, on October 12, two days after the Battle of Jahrâ', he had to visit an incoming steamship in his capacity as Kuwait's quarantine medical officer. His boat had not yet made ready at dockside, so he went to wait in a coffee shop nearby, where many prominent men of Kuwait had gathered as well. In a state of fatigue and having a weaker than usual hold on his short temper, Mylrea responded to the ritual greetings in a petulant manner: "This is all very fine," he boiled over, "but talk is the cheapest thing in the world. You people pile all this work on me, but it never occurs to one of you to *do* anything or to help either financially or in kind. In my country the rulers would be the first to visit the wounded, and to do all in their power to ensure that those who had risked everything for the sake of their native land should have the best possible care and attention. Here the Shaikh's slaves dump helpless men on the hospital verandah and depart. That is all there is to it. No thought of how my small staff is to cope with all this extra work." He continued, "I said a good deal more in the same strain. All at once I noticed to my horror that among the important men listening to me, there was one of the senior Shaikhs of the ruling family. Slowly he rose from his seat, drew himself up with the traditional Arab dignity, wrapped his cloak about him and walked out without a word, or even a look in my direction. When the Shaikh left the rest of the assembly followed suit. All of them imitated the Shaikh precisely. In utter silence they filed out and I was left alone with the proprietor. Finally *I* left" (Mylrea, *Kuwait*, p. 94). Expecting disaster to strike as retribution for his outburst of pique, he was much relieved that evening when two of those who had been present in the coffee shop stopped by. They began by confessing the justice of his diatribe, presented Mylrea with a list of donors, and placed upon his desk in pledge of more support a bag with 1,000 rupees in it. The incident was followed by others much like it. The moment was pivotal in breaking the ice between Kuwaitis and the mission. Mylrea was correct in observing, "For the American mission it marked the beginning of a new epoch" (Mylrea, *Kuwait*, p. 100).

Fahad, to enroll in Edwin Calverley's school.[165] The mission's station in Kuwait was firmly founded as Shaykh Ahmad al-Jâbir came to the throne in 1921, a part of and not just a curiosity within the social fabric of the community.[166]

[165]Fahad was later to become minister of health and public works under his brother, 'Abd-Allâh. His experience at the mission school prepared him to pursue further education in Lebanon. He was among the more cosmopolitan and talented of the Sabâh family and was not averse to experimentation and innovation.

[166]The initial reserve and parochialism of Kuwait society was something that gave way quickly in the years to come and was more than compensated for by the gracious—indeed, the *proverbial*—hospitality of the people, their generous friendship, and their effort to integrate the mission as fully as possible into their social structure. This integration of the mission into Kuwait's social structure was something which the missionaries themselves took as a matter of course, at the same time knowing it to be a very special honor. It was expressed in various ways and on a variety of occasions, but the most striking example of how it worked was the practice of *tazâwur* (inter-visitation) for the purpose of expressing felicitations on festive occasions.

It was probably the missionaries themselves who first broke the ice by joining the moving crowds on the early morning of 'Îd-ul-Fitr, the Muslim festival of breaking the fast of Ramadân. The town was divided into three parts: Qiblah, Sharq, and Murqâb. On the first day of the feast, folk from Qiblah (the western district dominated by seafarers in which the mission was located as well) visited those of Sharq (in which most of the shaykhly families resided). On the second day the folk of Sharq visited the folk of Qiblah in the morning, and in the afternoon everyone visited the residents of Murqâb (populated mainly by lesser merchant families and situated directly behind the old market area). It made for a whirling two-day snake dance throughout the city of dignified Arabs all dressed to the nines.

The participation of the mission in this event probably led to the question, "But when do you sit? When may we visit you?" The answer was, "On Christmas." The choice was deliberate. Muslims, too, recognize and respect the birth of the Messiah. (The British political agent and other diplomatic missions, when they were finally established, sat for callers on New Year's Day.)

Quickly the Kuwaitis responded and it became a happy tradition. On Christmas morning we children would be roused at five o'clock, get dressed in all our finery, and wait at the door to the living room until Father lit the lights on the tree. (The tree was a wire and wood affair with fuzzy green cellophane branches that knew no imitator in nature. It was purchased in 1937 from Marshall Fields in Chicago and survived many a long year in the Scudder household.) Then there was a short reading of the Christmas story and a prayer, followed by a special but hurriedly wolfed-down breakfast. The ritual of gift unwrapping followed as soon as we could get our father to finish a last, leisurely sipped cup of coffee, and no sooner done than all evidence had to be cleared out of the way. The first callers began to arrive at 6:30 a.m.

The first visitor to come was always the ruler. The others would wait patiently

A Summation of the Pioneers

The year 1893 saw the Arabian Mission stretched out in a long thin line. The goal of the mission–to "occupy the interior" from the coast–demanded it. Seeing themselves as part of an overall strategy which included the Scots in Aden, the Arabia missionaries saw themselves as encircling the heartland of Islam with the intention to probe inward. Gradually the workers began to arrive, first in a slow trickle, and then in a regular stream: Dr. Lankford Worrall in 1895, Amy Wilkes Zwemer in 1896, Fred Barny in 1897, George Stone and the doctors Sharon and Marion Thoms in 1898, Harry Wiersum in 1899, James Moerdyk in 1900, John Van Ess in 1902, Jane Scardefield in 1903, Arthur and Jessie Bennett in 1904 along with Fanny Lutton ...one, two, three a year.

By 1898 the missionary work force had jumped from four to ten. By 1906, in spite of deaths and other departures, it was up to a stable fifteen. In 1910, the year after Kuwait station was opened, it was up to twenty-nine. In 1914, on the eve of the First World War, it had reached a high-water mark of thirty-one. By then the task no longer appeared so ludicrous. Three hospitals had

---

until he and his party had paid their respects. Then the others–eight, ten, twenty at a time–would stop first at *Bayt-ul-Qiss* (the mission padre's home), for it was recognized that, on this religious occasion, he had precedence. Then they would walk up the hill to *Bayt-ul-Hakîm* (the mission doctor's home) and enact the ritual again.

The same greetings were used as on 'Îd-ul-Fitr: "'*Îdu-kum mubârak!*" (Blessed be your festival!), to which the response was, "*Wa ayyâmu-kum sa'îdah!*" (Happy may your days be!). The bitter bedouin coffee spiced with cardamom was served in *finjâns* (small cups without handles). It was a high honor to be given the post of the server of coffee. One poured just a taste's worth into the *finjân* with the left hand and presented the cup with the right. It was ill mannered for any guest to accept more than three cups. Sweets were passed as polite conversation proceeded, but visits were short in order to make space for other guests arriving. With a mumbled "*Mu'âyidîn in-shâ' Allâh!*" (We have greeted your festival, God willing!) the guests rose and received a billow of incense at the door as they departed, on their way to the home of Yaqûb 'Abû-Habîb' Shammâs, the mission's colporteur since 1920 and known in the market as Yaqûb an-Nasrâni (Jacob the Christian), and that of his nephew, Sulaymân Sim'ân, the hospital's pharmacist.

On a Christmas morning, 200 to 300 well-wishers were not unusual, including members of the royal household. (When the Syrian pundits of protocol came into their own, they insisted with the ruler, Shaykh 'Abd-Allâh, that such visits were below his dignity.) The same practice was to be witnessed in other stations with minor variations, but nowhere quite so earnestly or fully as in Kuwait.

been built and a fourth seemed about to be built. The medical contingent, the hoped-for spearhead of the mission, had come to dominate in the complexion of the missionary work force.

Between 1892 and 1915, to augment the efforts of the two pioneers, forty-five new missionaries were appointed. Of these, twenty were medical professionals–fifteen doctors and five nurses. Seven of the doctors were women, as were all of the nurses. Eleven of the new recruits were ordained clergymen. Two were civil engineers. Seventeen were teachers or engaged in work with women. Of the forty-five, twenty-six were women, most of whom had strong professional credentials. From the outset, since they bore a full share of the load, women had equal voice in the mission's deliberations and decision-making process. And the missionary impact of the mission's children was early on apparent. The witness of the Christian home was understood and nurtured by the mission.

Not all of the forty-five remained active on the field for their full careers. A few were obliged to leave. We have already noted the abrupt departure of the colorful Clarence Riggs, as well as that of his promising replacement, J. Talmage Wyckoff, who left because of a case of dysentery he could not shake off. A second person, a nurse, Martha Vogel, was dismissed by the board of trustees at the request of the mission in 1914.[167] Some chose to leave. Samuel Zwemer, one of the two founders, with his wife, Amy, effectively left the field in 1905, he after only fifteen years of service.[168] Five

---

[167]Martha C. Vogel, by action of the Arabian Mission's annual meeting and confirmation by the board of trustees on November 26, 1913, was dismissed for reasons referred to as "very delicate," and all written records of the rationale were removed. She returned to the Gulf on her own recognizances in the Fall of 1914 and took up residence in the suburb of Basrah known as Zubayr. W. I. Chamberlain had to send Sir Percy Cox, the chief British political officer in the Gulf, a letter distancing the Arabian Mission from Mrs. Vogel in April, 1916 (Chamberlain correspondence is part of the author's document collection). British authorities subsequently expelled Mrs. Vogel from the region with no adverse repercussions to the mission by reason of their previous association with her.

[168]Somewhat reluctantly (reading between the lines of Henry Cobb's letter to Dirk Dykstra dated Sept. 27, 1909), he returned to Arabia for a two-year term in Bahrain from 1910 to 1912. After that he went to Cairo to spend the next seventeen years there, publishing under the Nile Mission Press his journal, *The Moslem World*, and training missionaries and pastors.

In a revealing letter he wrote to Mr. E. E. Olcott of New York June 21, 1911, explaining his move to Cairo, Zwemer said that, although he would like to remain

people–a doctor and two engineers and their wives–came to the field in 1911 on a special experiment in "applied Christianity" called the "University of Michigan Scheme." The two engineers in the scheme, Charles Shaw and Philip Haynes, built the Gulf's first reinforced concrete structure in 1913–

in touch with the Reformed church and the Arabian Mission, nonetheless he was not satisfied in Arabia. "When one has wholesale ideas," he wrote, "it is very hard to come back to retail methods, and I confess to you personally that the most attractive part of the work even in Arabia is the larger one of influencing hearts and lives to help with the Moslem world problem." Increasingly, from 1905 onward, he saw himself as a public figure and had a difficult time fitting in with the "retail" hands-on missionary work of the field. He thoroughly agreed with the statement written by Presbyterian missionaries in Cairo in July, 1911: "The Christian Church and those acquainted with the problems of the evangelization of Islam recognize in the Rev. S. M. Zwemer, D. D., a leader of thought and activity, whose talents and power qualify him eminently for literary and missionary enterprise and statesmanship, while it is our conviction that the most efficient use of those talents is necessarily somewhat handicapped by his present location upon the mission field [Bahrain] by its very geographical position..." [in the Zwemer file (labeled by him "For the Biography") in the Archives of the Reformed Church in America, New Brunswick, New Jersey]. The upshot of the matter was that he left Bahrain early in 1912 for the greater exposure he received working with the Nile Press in Cairo, and he left Cairo for Princeton Seminary for much the same reason in 1929.

From the point of view of the church in the United States Zwemer was, of course, the most visible of the Arabia missionaries. Early on, he sought and received honor. In 1904, while he was still in his thirties, Hope College in Holland, Michigan, conferred upon Zwemer a Doctorate of Divinity which, in 1918 and 1919, was followed by honorary degrees respectively from Muskingham College (L.L.D.) and Rutgers University (D.D.). From 1905 to 1910 he was in the United States as traveling secretary for the Student Volunteer Movement for Foreign Missions and enjoyed the public exposure and acclaim. In that same period he also campaigned effectively for the financial support of the mission and occasionally did so even thereafter. It was he who personally recruited some of the most capable and productive of the Arabian Mission's medical personnel, the doctors Sharon and Marion Thoms, Stanley Mylrea, and Paul Harrison among them. As an author, though (and he published *many* books), he was primarily an ideologue. It is well argued that his thoughts did not develop a great deal after his departure from Arabia; his intellectual impact upon the mission on the field was, thereafter, marginal at best.

In a negative sense, he contributed as much as anyone to the Arabian Mission's chronic sense of guilt over the small number of converts that had come forward in the Gulf. He made occasional (well publicized) forays into the Gulf and would deliver himself of pep-talks and harangues, as the mood took him. There was something almost fatuous in his glowing reports of mass conversions witnessed by other mission groups among less entrenched and more vulnerable Muslim communities in other parts of the world. The fact that, through the 1950s and even into the 1960s, he continued to be reverently held up as the icon of the

the mission hospital in Kuwait.[169] Shaw and Haynes left in 1914, deeming that there really was not enough happening in their line of work to keep them busy.[170] The doctor and his wife, Hall and Mercy Van Vlack, resigned

Arabian Mission by those who promoted it in the United States is testimony to the power of the myth with which he had cloaked himself.

If the impression he made on missionaries and westerners was positive, the impression he made upon Arabs was another matter. Nabîh Amîn Fâris, one of the most articulate Christian Arab advocates of Arab nationalism, studied under Zwemer at Princeton Seminary in the 1930s. Fâris was then aspiring toward a vocation as a Christian minister. In later years, while professor of history at the American University of Beirut, Fâris commented to one of his students (Dr. Dudley Woodbury) that Zwemer knew much about *Islam* but he did not love the *Muslim*. We might explain this rather damning statement as that of a man embittered against Zwemer for some unspecified past injury, but it has a certain ring of authenticity to it. Zwemer witnessed the death of one brother, two daughters, and several personal friends in Arabia. Whether this experience coupled with a lack of conversions contributed to coloring his attitudes in later life (when Fâris was his student) it is not possible to say with any assurance. Support for Fâris's observation was given by a leading Muslim *mullah* in Bahrain, who commented to Dr. 'Abd-ul-Mâlik at-Tamîmî during the latter's doctoral researches, that Zwemer was the most brilliant man in the mission and exclaimed, "Thank God he did not love us more!" The nickname Zwemer picked up during his trips through Yemen was one he cherished and publicized: Dhayf-Allâh (the guest of God). More popularly, in Bahrain, he was known as 'Iblîs' (Beelzebub), and the bicycle, which he introduced into Bahrain, is not uncommonly still called 'Khayl-Iblîs' (the devil's steed). It is clear that in one-on-one relationships with Muslims, he was not entirely at ease; he preferred a more remote platform from which to preach. With very little to show for his personal losses and with anger and frustration building, the prospect of raising and educating his remaining children there was something neither he nor his wife could accept. In any case, the Zwemer record in the Gulf is not untarnished.

He worked with the Nile Press and taught in Egypt from 1912 to 1929, and from 1929 to 1938 was professor of history of religion and Christian missions at Princeton Seminary in the United States. From 1911 to 1947 he was the founder and editor of the influential journal, *The Moslem World*—a task he eventually relinquished to the journeyman Islamicist, Edwin Calverley (who retired from the mission in Kuwait during the Depression in 1931). He was carried on the rolls of the mission and his name appears on its published list of missionaries until his death April 2, 1952.

[169]When the actual work of demolition began in early 1954, it was apparent with what skill the old had been built. The new hospital which took its place should have been built so sturdily!

[170]Part of the scheme was an early form of what now would be called tent-making ministry. The two engineers, with backing from the Students' Christian Association at the University of Michigan, were to support themselves as much as possible on revenues they were able to earn in the construction business. Had they held out for a few more years they would have found the situation changing in their favor,

in 1917, he to join the U. S. Army. Two women nurses came out on short-term appointment under this scheme and left early.

Others laid down their lives. Their number includes Peter Zwemer and George Stone, who died in Oman within a year of each other in 1898 and 1899 respectively. Harry J. Wiersum, another minister, died of smallpox in 1901 after less than two years on the field.[171] The two young Zwemer girls, Katarina and Ruth, died in Bahrain from an undiagnosed fever during the Summer of 1904, after having survived a typhoid epidemic. A physician, Marion Thoms, wife of Sharon Thoms, died in Bahrain in 1905 from typhoid. Arthur Bennett lost two wives on the field: Jessie Vail Bennett, a teacher, died of typhoid in Bahrain in 1906; Christine Ivorsen Bennett, a doctor of considerable attainments and dedication, died during a typhus epidemic brought into the mission hospital in Basrah by Turkish prisoners of war in 1916. Finally, Sharon Thoms died in Matrah in 1913, after his fall from a ladder.

Sixteen out of the forty-five, then, made brief but sometimes memorable contributions to the work of the mission. For his initiative in taking eighteen boys rescued from Arab slave traders by the British Navy and setting up a boarding school to educate and nurture them in Muscat until they were equipped to fend for themselves, Peter Zwemer will always be remembered. Others, like George Stone, left behind them the memory of their ardent youth and optimism. And all who died or departed left behind some token of their service. The remaining twenty-nine formed the backbone of the developing work well into the 1950s.

As the pioneer years drew to a close and others began to enter into the stream, preparing themselves to assume leadership, it is appropriate to try to summarize the vision as it had come to mature. Paul Harrison published a book in 1924, *The Arab at Home*. It was a wide-ranging meditation, displaying competent scholarship and profoundly compassionate firsthand experience, reflecting both insight and persistent prejudice, briming over

---

but they did not foresee that. Nobody did. Although the Students' Association found it difficult to sustain its commitment, the project fielded a sixth missionary in 1913 for a short term of three years. Mason & Barny, *History*, pp. 148-149.

[171] Harry Wiersum's death was sharply felt in the United States as well as on the field. It was upon hearing of it that the young John Van Ess, then a student at Princeton Seminary, turned his course away from pursuing a promising academic career and volunteered for Arabia [Dorothy F. Van Ess, *Pioneers in the Arab World* (Grand Rapids, Michigan: Wm. B. Eerdmans Publishing Co., 1974). p. 20].

with optimism, and powered by Harrison's unpretentious self-confidence. The fifteenth chapter, bearing the title, "The Arab and Christianity," is remarkable as a study in the missionary vocation and the Arabian Mission's dream now fleshed out by experience. Pieced together out of a much longer passage, the following fairly reflects a common Arabian Mission perspective that retained currency for years:

> The missionary is not simply certain that the Arab needs Christ; he also feels confident that Christ is adequate for the needs of Arabia. ...There is something in the simplicity and sincerity of the Arab character, especially that of the desert Bedouin, which corresponds most beautifully with the utter simplicity and contempt of subterfuge which marked Christ's character and teachings (p. 277). The missionary's contribution is thus a very simple contribution.... The missionary carries the teaching and the example of Christ. He believes that this simple contribution is sufficient to redeem the individual Arab from powerful appetites and from impenetrable conceit and to place the Arab race on the road toward a modern indigenous civilization that will be one of the finest in the world's history (pp. 278-279).

> ...It is not adequately realized how futile and childish is the notion that we can go out to an oriental country and usefully direct any task of social reconstruction....The only men who can be trusted to do it for Arabia are the Arabs. The less help those men get from the West, the better off they will be (p. 278). It is by means of genuine contact of one friend with another that the Arab is brought into contact with Christ (p. 290). A little Bohemianism of the soul is almost a necessity for a missionary in Arabia (p. 288). The method of the missionary is simple, unaffected, democratic equality; his message is the example and the teachings of Christ with no adulterations from the West mixed into it (p. 294).

> The...ultimate task of the missionary in Arabia is to guide those earnest men and women who desire to follow Christ into a real fellowship with him (p. 298)....The missionary to Arabia works for the redemption of the individual Arab and of the entire Arab race,

but his hope and vision go beyond even that....The Christian missionary dreams of the day when that same Arab mind shall study and interpret Christ's message so profoundly and simplify it so completely that we shall see it commanding the acquiesence of the primitive mind and the devotion of the primitive heart to a degree greater than Mohammedanism has ever done (pp. 300-301).[172]

[172]Paul W. Harrison, *The Arab at Home* (New York: Thomas Y. Crowell Company, 1924), pp. 275-304.

Part Four

Evangelists, Pastors, and Teachers

Evangelize First

Evangelism and literature distribution was the Arabian Mission's first priority. In a sense, everything else served that purpose. The ABCFM mission publishing house in Beirut supplied the fledgling mission with Christian literature; the British and Foreign Bible Society kept them stocked with scripture portions and Bibles; and the CMS station in Baghdad (up until the First World War) supplied them with trained colporteurs who knew their trade. These tools determined that there should be Bible shops and that, out of the Bible shops, there should be itinerant distribution of literature. The structure this provided obviously did not satisfy, especially when it became abundantly clear that conventional means for open evangelism were disallowed—on legal as well as practical grounds. Apart from distributing tracts and selling Bibles (or portions thereof), evangelistic work was primarily a matter of personal contact, visits in private homes, and conversations carried on in the environment of the Bible shop or the dispensary.

Eventually the mission defined evangelism under two headings: Men's Evangelism and Women's Evangelism. We will return to the work among

195

women shortly, but in general it should be noted that evangelistic work among men and women did not differ greatly.

Sunday services, with the sounds of music and singing, were considered an evangelistic tool. Even as late as the 1970s, the Rev. Wayne Antworth would urge his congregation in Kuwait to sing louder so that it might be heard outside as clearly as was the voice of the *mu'azzin* (mosque prayer caller) across the street. In Mylrea's day and up until the mission's chapel in Kuwait was built in 1931, services in Kuwait were held in the open courtyard of a traditional Kuwaiti house. Curious passers by would come in, lured by the strange sounds of the baby organ pumped by Bessie Mylrea and by the singing. At times they swelled the small Christian nucleus into a "congregation" of from sixty to 100 persons. Services were led by missionaries and the colporteur staff, and the sermons delivered were evangelistic homilies.

Muslims find sermons a good source of entertainment and enjoy a spirited religious discussion as much as anything. But there was little sensitivity on the part of the mission to the fact that Muslim sensibilities eschew the use of music and singing in the worship of God. What the Christians understood as an act of praise was, in Muslim eyes, quite otherwise perceived. "Different strokes for different folks," was one way they shrugged it off.

Men's evangelism was also conducted in the hospitals. After morning rounds and before the clinic was begun for outpatients, the missionary evangelist, the colporteur, the doctor, and the hospital staff would gather with others—both regular visitors and patients—and listen to the reading of scripture, a talk, and a prayer. The author remembers clearly such events in Kuwait. After reading a portion of scripture, Yaqûb Shammâs, the durable and much loved colporteur and Bible shop manager, would harangue his audience for twenty minutes or more. The Muslims attending would listen closely and politely, and then animated but friendly debate over the differences between Muslim and Christian beliefs would follow. Everyone would then go their way much satisfied with an hour well spent, and the work of the day would get under way.[1]

1Professor 'Abd-ul-Mâlik al-Tamîmî of Kuwait University, the only Gulf scholar to have made a detailed study of the Arabian Mission, suggests that people attended these clinic prayers for fear that, if they did not, they would not receive medical treatment ['Abd-ul-Mâlik al-Tamîmî, *al-tabshîr fî mintaqat-il-khalîj il-'arabî (Evangelism in the Arab Gulf Region)* (Kuwait: Sharikat-Kâzimah li-il-Nashr, 1986), p. 220]. Missionaries were quite aware that this kind of propaganda was

Every morning the doctors did rounds through the inpatient wards. It was a time not only for medical observation and the exercise of "bedside manners," but also for personal ministry to the sick. The mission clergy augmented this by regularly visiting the patients as well. They would sit with them without the pressure of having other things to do. They inquired after the patients' wellbeing, asked about their practical needs and desires, and opened conversational doors to their daily lives and their families. In this sort of conversation, there was always an opening for a Christian evangelist to quote scripture or tell a gospel story, of course. And to speak to Muslims about "the Lord Jesus" was not (and *is* not) in itself offensive. This kind of personal attention was something Muslim clergy did not provide, and the Muslim patients found it quite remarkable and memorable.[2] When invited to do so, the missionary padres[3] often followed up these contacts with visits

---

abroad, and the fact of the matter is that by the mid-1950s several mission evangelists, foremost among them Jay Kapenga, found this form of evangelism both depersonalizing and offensive. And actually, compared to the crowd which customarily waited to see the physicians at morning clinic, the group attending prayers was always modest in size (ten, twenty, or thirty out of a total morning clinic that could number as many as 300 or 400). People attended who were not even patients. They came because it was an entertaining and refreshing break in the day's routine or because (for the old men who were the regulars) it was an escape from boredom. Besides, it gave them an opportunity to talk religion in a manner which stimulated them and stretched their otherwise narrow perspective. Had the terminology been current then, one would have spoken of these events as dialogue encounters, because, after the formal ending, there would often follow an animated exchange of views and ideas. It is quite certain that attending prayers was never a precondition for medical treatment and everyone knew it.

[2]Professor al-Tamîmî quotes a Kuwaiti patient named 'Alî Husayn:

"Some twenty years ago I became sick and decided to go to the American Mission Hospital in Kuwait. I needed an operation. The doctors did that for me. In the hospital I was given every care, and I spent three weeks there. Every day one of the clergymen would come and sit with each patient. He would talk with him for a while. One of them talked with me. He began by asking me about my social situation and about my family. The conversation then turned to religion. His mastery of Arabic was excellent. He did not attack Islam, but rather most of what he had to say concentrated upon the Lord Christ. Sometimes he would read to me from the Gospel. On the day I was discharged he gave me a copy of it" (Al-Tamîmî, *al-tabshîr*, p. 219).

It is interesting to note that these rather vivid memories, generous in their assessment of the event, are drawn from twenty years in the past.

[3]How the title "padre" came to be conferred upon the mission's ordained members is not altogether clear. It probably had some connection with the British habit of calling their military chaplains "padres," and the mission easily came to accept the designation.

in patients' homes, getting to know their families, friends, and communities, and frequently developing significant friendships.[4]

Another main area of work was the Bible shop. It was invariably in an older part of the city. This was a place, like all Arab shops, where men (not women) might gather not just to do business and buy, but also to pass the time of day with the proprietor and talk about matters of current interest. Muslims were happy to buy scripture portions, respecting Christian texts as containing at least an approximation of the Torah and the Injîl (Gospel) as these had been revealed to Moses and Jesus. And to find Bibles in a Muslim home was not at all unusual.[5]

Singing in worship was one cultural anomaly for Muslims. Another was the Christian habit of closing one's eyes when praying. They thought it was some kind of magical practice. People in Kuwait speculated that Christians did this for fear that, should they not close their eyes, they might see Jesus pass before them and be blinded by the sight. From the outset tales of this nature circulated as Muslims observed Christians at prayer.

In his report, "Kuweit Evangelistic and Educational Work, 1915-1916," Stanley Mylrea complained that "the keeping of order is still a great difficulty and there have been Sundays when we have been much disturbed by rowdies who come in with no idea but to make trouble, and stones and

---

[4]Haydar Muhammad al-Khalîfah came into the employ of the mission through the efforts of Gerrit Pennings, whom he still holds up as the finest of the mission's clergy. Pennings followed the case of Muhammad, Haydar's father, during a long inpatient recuperation from major surgery. He followed that up with visits to the needy family's home. Without being pressed but simply by keeping in touch with the family during those days of the Depression, he would sometimes casually drop off a bag of rice or other staple needed from time to time. Observing the two elder sons, Jâsim and Haydar, he suggested that they might become supporters of the family. He recruited Jâsim and trained him as a cook. He served for a while as cook for the author's family, and none other has ever made bread to match that which Jâsim could produce! Haydar was put into the Gerrit De Jong household as a houseboy, where Everdine De Jong taught him English and other skills. He stayed with the mission for the rest of his professional career, training first as a medical assistant, then as an x-ray technician, and finally as a hospital administrator. He concluded his career as Administrator of the American Mission Hospital until it closed in 1967. He is and remains a sincere and observant Shî'ah Muslim with a serious sense of "mission" in Christ's footsteps.

[5]It was known to the mission, for instance, that Shaykh 'Abd-Allâh al-Sâlim Âl Sabâh, the ruler of Kuwait, kept a copy of the Bible and read from it regularly. He was a man of broad and deep insight and deeply affected by his excellent contacts with the mission, both its doctors and clergy.

dirt have been pitched over the wall from the street into the middle of the congregation. Then, too, as the time of the service corresponds with the dismissal hour of the neighbouring schools we get large numbers of small boys who are like small boys all over the world only more so." With his wry humor, Mylrea added, "However, the congregations are steadily getting quieter and less irreverent and we look forward to perfection later on. Meanwhile the poor have the gospel preached to them."[6]

Formal evangelistic preaching, therefore, took place primarily on the mission's own turf and in controlled environments.[7] Itinerating through the villages of Bahrain by 'Abbûd Haydar with Jim Dunham or Ed Luidens provided some colorful stories, but these excursions were rather exceptional. The doctors on tour in Sa'ûdî Arabia also frequently took an evangelist with them or served in that capacity themselves.[8] Wells Thoms and Harold Storm were enthusiastic evangelists and never set their hands to surgical tools without first intoning a formal prayer; Sarah Hosmon in Oman was also an avid tourist and evangelist. But the main work of preaching the gospel was done "on the compound" or in the Bible shops. In all the other areas of activity—schools and hospitals—the agenda of evangelism was always kept in mind and implemented in whatever manner seemed to fit.

But on the personal level, day-to-day, the evangelist had to struggle with the content and meaning of his or her calling. Jim Dunham has written an evocative description of the challenge, which we can do no better than to quote at some length:

> First, I hold strongly to the belief that the evangelist is in a unique and precarious position as a member of the Mission team. Yet, it is this very uniqueness and the very precariousness of his position

[6] Hand script in the author's collection now in the Archives of the Reformed Church in America, New Brunswick, New Jersey.

[7] Al-Tamîmî is somewhat correct when he observes that apart from the medical and educational institutions of the mission, evangelistic activities would not have been tolerated. (The caveat is the example of the Bible shops, which were quite independently situated in the marketplaces of the Gulf cities.) The mission had its priorities; Muslim society had its own as well. Al-Tamîmî argues that because of the region's abject need for medical service Muslims were prepared to be tolerant of but not susceptible to the evangelistic baggage that came with it (Al-Tamîmî, *al-tabshîr*, p. 221). This, of course, is a bit simplistic, but it is not without some verisimilitude.

[8] The first of these mission clergymen to accompany Paul Harrison was Gerrit Van Peursem in 1919.

that offers him his best opportunity to render his greatest service to the emerging Church and the Mission. I say unique position, because the evangelist alone of the entire Mission family is able to meet the Muslim as a Christian; nothing more nor less than a Christian. Doctors, teachers, builders, agriculturists, and other professionally and technically qualified people are constantly confronted with the frustration of being "used" by the Muslim community. On the other hand, the Muslim community has "no use" for the Christian evangelist. Hence,...it remains true that the evangelist of all missionaries will experience the greatest difficulty in making the acquaintance of the Muslim. The reason for this is obvious: the ordained Christian is the manifestation of Christianity's direct threat to the Islamic community.

The evangelist is in a precarious position, because the lack of perspective, or the loss of it, will render him vulnerable to all sorts and degrees of emotional and psychological problems as he experiences the loneliness thrust upon him by his Islamic environment. He should be aware of the fact that he will be tempted time and time again to retreat from this very trying environment with a call to "greater service" as an English language instructor, an audio-visual expert, a Mission maintenance man, a builder or you name it. That there can be a certain validity in such calls there can be no doubt. However, for myself, I find it necessary to resist and reject them continually.

For me, at least, it is necessary to stand in that unique and precarious position I have described. I say necessary, for I do not believe that I could honestly ask any Muslim to leave the Islamic community and stand as a Christian – an act that would immediately thrust him into that unique and precarious position, subject to greater pressures, strains and stresses that I as a relatively sheltered, white, foreign *sahib*, can imagine – unless I find the faith and Christian grace to stand as near to the Muslim convert as circumstances will permit. If such faith and grace is to be denied me, then there is a real question in my mind as to the validity of my call as an evangelist or my right to serve as a pastor in the Church of Christ in Arabia....

Dunham's understanding required that he differentiate two functions, the pastorate and evangelism, and decide which was his primary function. "This decision determines the whole character of the evangelist's relationship with the local Church." And he notes that, as far as the mission is concerned, his is primarily the role of the evangelist. Dunham then turns to describe the nature and work of the Omani Christian community and his role within it. He describes the leadership of the Omani Church, and then proceeds:

> To say that we are a working team would not be the truth. To say that all of them are equally committed to the work of the Church would not be true. It is true, however, to say that they have taught me more than I have taught them.
>
> A few weeks ago Rubaiya arranged a visit with an acquaintance of his in the village of Sidaab. On the way we offered four teen-age boys a ride. We reached the home of our intended host only to discover that he had gone elsewhere. Let's just say I was disgruntled, but Rubaiya, who is illiterate, took a New Testament from his handbag, handed it to one of the boys we had picked up and motioned for us to sit down in the garden in the shade of a bush. There we sat for close to a half-hour while this Muslim teen-ager, one of those "vigorous, disturbing, difficult people" read to us from the Gospel of John. We didn't baptize anyone, but four young men met us and sat with us as a Christian layman and a missionary, because of the initiative and tact of Rubaiya.
>
> People can criticize us here in Oman for not thinking in terms of a big program or tremendous projects, but they cannot deny us our great moments. Those great moments that are given to us as we meet our Muslim neighbor face to face, talk with him man to man, and walk with him side by side. Mass man we do not know, we know only people, and it is these people we seek to serve in Christ's name.[9]

---

[9]James Dunham, in an essay entitled, "Evangelism in Oman," probably dating from the late 1960s. Incomplete carbon copy of the original typescript in the author's document collection.

Women's Work

At a fairly early stage the young missionaries became aware of the needs of women in Arab society. But they could do little to meet those needs. The missionaries were single men in a strictly segregated society. Before leaving the United States, Zwemer and Cantine both signed a pledge drafted by Lansing to the effect that they would not marry for a specific term (one, two, or three years). As Cantine recollects, Zwemer signed on the line pledging himself to only one year of celibacy. As for himself, Cantine signed boldly across all the options. As it was, Zwemer remained a bachelor for five years after arriving on the field, and Cantine for fourteen years.[10] The mission began as a bachelor effort.

It was Peter Zwemer who, perhaps inadvertently, first stumbled upon the idea that work among Arab women was part of the fulfillment of the mission's mandate to work among slaves. Cantine recalls that, as a new recruit, Peter was...

> ... somewhat impatient with our caution in meeting social questions.
>
> "This matter of the equality of the sexes," he said, "is one of the glories of Christianity, and why should we not treat the women of Islam as we treat our own?"
>
> A few days afterwards in a solitary walk he passed a Moslem graveyard bordering a small village. A lone woman was mourning over a grave.
>
> "Here," he said, "is the opportunity to put my theory into practice," and he made what he thought was a sympathetic approach.
>
> The woman was aghast, insulted! Never before had a strange man spoken to her, and now this English dog of an unbeliever! Her screams were loud and continuous. The villagers with sticks and stones charged to the rescue. Peter was always willing to learn, and never again had occasion to prove how good a runner he was.[11]

In any case, when on May 18, 1896, Samuel Zwemer had the good sense to marry Amy Elizabeth Wilkes, an Australian missionary with the CMS in Baghdad, the Arabian Mission's bachelor days were over. Women's work,

---

[10]Cantine, *Milestone...*, pp. 106-107.
[11]Cantine, *Milestone...*, pp. 65-66.

when it began, was understood as a path of access into the inner circles of Arab families. The term "child evangelism" had yet to be coined, but those engaged in women's work were clearly also involved with children.

After 1896, as Amy Zwemer set about proving her worth in Bahrain, the mission's recruiting efforts began to emphasize not only medical personnel but families[12] and single women too. The first single woman appointed to the Arabian Mission in 1902 was a nurse, Elizabeth DePree (who married James Cantine in 1904).[13] Her appointment was quickly followed by that of Jane Scardefield (1903), Fanny Lutton (1904), Lucy Patterson (1904),[14] Martha Vogel (1905), Minnie Wilterdink (1907), Dorothy Firman (1909), Christine Iverson (1909), Josephene Spaeth (1910), Sarah Hosmon (1911), Gertrud Shafheitlin (1912), and a whole train of remarkable individuals, most of whom remained with the mission for their whole careers. In the home station of Basrah up until World War I, work among Arab women was developed by Margaret Barny, Emma Worrall, Dorothy Van Ess, Martha Vogel, Christine Bennett, Elizabeth Calverley, and Jane Scardefield, who also put in hours at the dispensary.

The mission's hospitals for women played an important role in reaching out to women. Each had a regular discipline of conducting gatherings during clinic hours. These sessions included scripture readings, short talks by either a missionary or a gospel woman, and the singing of simple hymns. Occasionally more than one person was involved in presenting the programs. The women attending enjoyed the presentations and participated enthusiastically, the regulars memorizing the words to hymns and even

---

[12]The Christian witness of the mission's children was quickly appreciated for the unique thing it was.

[13]Elizabeth DePree, a pioneer in her own right, by marrying James Cantine heads a remarkable list of single women missionaries who married, so to speak, "within the family": Minnie Wilterdink (Dykstra), Gertrude Shafheitlin (Pennings), Mae DePree (Thoms), Josephine Spaeth (Van Peursem), Dorothy Firman (Van Ess), Christine Iverson (Bennett), and Louise Essenberg (Holler). Anna Monteith "Monty" Bilkert, whose husband, Henry, was assassinated in 1929, married Paul Harrison, whose wife Regina also died in 1930. All but one of these served full careers in the mission. There is a shorter list of women who, while missionaries in other fields, married into the Arabian Mission: Amy Wilkes (Zwemer), Emma Hodges (Worrall), and Marjory Underwood (Kapenga).

[14]First of the short-term appointments, Lucy Patterson, a physician, came out to cover medical work among women during the absence on furlough of Marian Thoms.

some passages of oft-repeated scripture. But, much as with the men, these events were viewed more as entertainment by those attending than as any serious challenge to their own religious outlook. Gulf women, in any case, did not think of themselves as competent to enter into religious debate. What fit smoothly into the ordained scheme of things they might take with them. The rest ran off like water down a desert *wâdî*.

To take things deeper, the mission encouraged each of its women to cultivate personal relationships in Arab society. Mission homes were designed with a separate *majlis* or *diwâniyyah* (sitting room) for women with entrances isolated from those used by men. Individuals like Everdine De Jong and Bessie Mylrea, Fanny Lutton, Gertrude Pennings, Josephine Van Peursem, Minnie Dykstra, Beth Thoms, and Jeanette Boersma devoted much of their time to what the mission called "Women's Evangelistic Work." It was a main activity of the mission and remained much the same over the years it was carried on.

The individual responsible for the activity made herself and her home available to local women, usually on a set schedule. This was common Gulf Arab practice known as *majlis*, or the time when the person of the house sat (*yajlis*) to receive callers. In an Arab *majlis* it was a time to exchange news, spin yarns, and trade other items of local interest and gossip. It all transpired to the convivial accompaniment of refreshments and ritually presented bitter coffee. Men on their *majlis* circuit moved fairly briskly between a variety of venues. Women, however, took their time. The refreshments were more substantial, and callers stayed for considerably longer periods.

Adopting this local practice, the personnel of the mission assigned to women's evangelism used the occasion of their *majlis* to read scripture passages, tell Bible stories, teach a few hymns and songs, and engage women in discussions of these things. But it was also an occasion for broader educational opportunities. In the environment of the *majlis*, the life circumstances of callers were frequently discussed and friendships forged. Infant care and home hygiene became topics of discussion and demonstration. Not infrequently, assistance to women was given in a more direct fashion— clothing and food might be distributed. And depending upon the skills of the missionary, training in sewing and teaching elementary literacy could also have been among the activities.

In each station there developed a cadre of women who came regularly. They thought of themselves as "regulars" of the missionary's *majlis*. It became (as the missionaries came to call it in Basrah) a kind of a club.

The missionary would follow up on these *majâlis* (plural of *majlis*) by visiting her "club members" in their homes if possible and becoming acquainted with their families. It was, all in all, an activity which gave back deep personal rewards and was one that created a great deal of good will. When missionary women moved on (as they did from time to time), the "club" automatically transferred its loyalties and affections to their successors in the respective stations and so, with the cooperation of the local women, the activity had some cumulative effect and continuity.

Over the years the mission's ministry to women in the Gulf—through the *majlis* "clubs" and pastoral ministries in homes, through girls' schools, and through clinics and hospitals specifically for women—has had a profound and positive impact upon Gulf society, although that impact is difficult to quantify. Certainly a large number of women were affected over the years. They found the Bible stories entrancing, and many fell in love with the simple hymns that missionary hosts taught them. The education they received filtered back into the way they ran their households and raised their children. Basic values were communicated and came to infiltrate families, becoming a part of the nurturing process. There is no record of overt conversion among these women, but certainly a strong basis for "friends of Jesus" was laid. In the balance, one must suspect that the mission's ministry among women was very significant indeed.

After a time, language discipline by the mission was relaxed and fewer women were appointed to this nebulously structured activity. Then, in the 1960s, mission women insisted more strongly upon their homemaker's role and the privacy of their homes.[15] With these changes, women's evangelism gradually faded into the past. As mission women found less time or became less willing to make themselves available, much regret was expressed by the Arab women who had in some cases grown up under the pastoral care of the mission. But the seeds of many fundamental changes in Gulf Arab society, preparing Gulf society to cope with the onset of modernity, had been planted and nurtured.[16]

[15]The discussion of the role of missionary wives became a "hot" one in the 1960s. "There was a good resolution [at the mission meeting of November, 1962] that each couple 'conscientiously decide what and how much the wife should do.'" (In a letter from Joyce Dunham to her parents, November 5, 1962, in correspondence loaned to the author by Jim and Joyce Dunham.)
[16]Writing to the author on September 6, 1995, Ms. Sandra Shinn, archivist for the UNESCO project to renovate the mission hospital buildings in Kuwait, made the

Converts

The goal of the Arabian Mission was to invite Muslims, in the useful phrase of Kenneth Cragg, to "consider Jesus." In its first enthusiastic phase, predictions abounded that this or that breakthrough presaged a coming wave of conversions. It never materialized. The largest phenomenon within the mission's experience was that of Muscat/Matrah station, where a small Omani Christian community came into being particularly in the mid-1930s and continued to exist until the early 1970s. In 'Imârah a small Arab Protestant community came together, some of them proselytes from the ancient churches, and others converts from either Islam or from the Sabaean community. In Kuwait, 'Îsâ 'Abd-ul-Masîh was baptized in the 1930s and had to spend the remainder of his life on the mission property. The saintly Madînah[17] was a personality in the mission in Bahrain until her death on December 22, 1958.[18]

following comment: "I think that the members of the Arabian Mission would be delighted to know that the hospital buildings are being restored for use by the Dar al-Athar al-Islamiyyah [literally: The House of Islamic Antiquities] museum....Dr. Eleanor Calverley would be particularly gratified to find that its director is a woman. Dr. Mylrea would be vindicated in his trust in the progressive policies of Mubarak the Great in that that woman is a descendant of Sheikh Mubarak, and the Rev. Dr. Edwin Calverley would delight in knowing that she is a granddaughter of his dear friend, Sheikh Ahmad al-Jaber....Kuwait has, as you know, a high percentage of women in managerial positions, and the Mission can be given credit for setting the example for the avant garde. Most Kuwaitis can "only" remember the popular Scudder family, but the interaction between the Mission and Kuwait for the last century has been a productive one." What Ms. Shinn wrote of Kuwait could be repeated for Bahrain and Oman as well.

[17]Madînah was a slave, taken as a five-year-old from her home in Africa and shuttled on through Sa'ûdî Arabia to a household in Bahrain, where she was eventually mated with a fellow slave and bore him children, only one of whom survived. In the late 1920s she encountered Minnie Dykstra in Bahrain's market and pursued an intriguing contact to develop a strong bond with Minnie and then with Gertrude Pennings. She was baptized along with the infant Donald Luidens in 1946. As she got older, she came to live on Bahrain's East Compound and became a true mission institution, a person who embodied what Paul Harrison meant when he said to the Tambaram Missionary Conference of 1938, "The Church in Arabia salutes you." Still with the marks of slavery on her face, she gracefully declined into old age and then infirmity, but she remained the (if the expression will be pardoned) "Mecca" of each missionary's pilgrimage to Bahrain.

[18]Writing on December 28, 1958, to her parents in India, Joyce Dunham relates it as follows: "You needn't worry about a Christmas gift for Medina. She had the best Christmas she's had in many years. She passed away Tuesday afternoon and we had a lovely simple service at the cemetery Wednesday morning. I was in the

And then there was the courageous example of Khayriyyah 'Umm Miryam' Haydar in Bahrain. She successfully defied her Shî'ah family in open court and established herself as a force and personality within the mission to be reckoned with. For many years she served as the "mother" of its orphanage, and the principal women's evangelist. In the process she nurtured her own two sons to work in the mission and lead Bahrain's Arab congregation.[19]

kitchen when she rang her bell, heard her gasping for breath. I went to her and found her lying on the floor. She moved a bit for a few minutes then went quietly to rest. I had talked to her in the morning and she was as good as usual. Apparently she'd had one of her spells at noon, but when Cornelia [Dalenberg] and Ruth [Jackson] left her she said, 'I'm all right now, but even if death comes, I am grateful.' So are we all, although we shall miss her cheerful self....

"A bi-lingual Communion was held Saturday night with a good mixed congregation. Sunday morning Jim [Dunham] and Jay [Kapenga] went to Medina's room and served her communion, so in that respect too she was ready. She'd picked out her hymns and had told Nellie and Abood [Haydar] that she didn't expect to live for Christmas. She and we couldn't have been more prepared."

In an appended note, Joyce added: "A couple weeks ago she bawled me out for not going to see her, so I was glad I'd made it a point since to stop in every morning." (Correspondence loaned to the author by Jim and Joyce Dunham.)

Madinah was baptized with a missionary baby, and she was buried beside several missionary babies, including those from the Zwemer, Pennings, and De Jong households [Cornelia Dalenberg, *Sharifa* (Grand Rapids, Michigan: Wm. B. Eerdmans, 1983), pp. 92-96].

[19]Umm Miryam's daughter followed her children to the United States. Her two sons, 'Abbûd and Yûsuf, both established themselves openly as local Christian leaders in Bahrain's tolerant society. 'Abbûd, blind from an early age, died in 1984. He had a great reputation as an outspoken evangelist and was a much sought after counselor by both Muslims and Christians. Yûsuf, more sophisticated in training and outlook and for a time administrator of the American Mission Hospital, has continued to serve in the hospital as advisor and public relations consultant.

A young Bahraini of Sunnî Muslim background, Râshid Tâhir, was a counselee of several missionaries (among them the author in the 1980s). During a visit to the United States, he was baptized. Possessing a bright and inquiring mind, he went again to the United States for study, married an American girl, and settled down in Grand Rapids, Michigan. He has not returned to the island except for occasional visits. Another Bahraini convert (of Shî'ah background), Jamîl Mushayma', came to his convictions, not through contact with the mission, but during a student's sojourn in Britain. Upon his return to Bahrain in the 1980s, he was enthusiastically welcomed by missionaries and by the English Language Congregation of the National Evangelical Church but was somewhat more cautiously treated by the Arabic Language Congregation. He continued to live in Bahrain for fourteen years, marrying a young Danish missionary and beginning

In Oman there was the witness of Miryam Mas'ûd. The wife of Oman's first convert, Marash, she was led to Christ by her husband and baptized by Gerrit Van Peursem in 1923. When her husband died in 1930, she defied local custom and refused to go into mourning, declaring in the face of a crowd of angry Arab men that she was a Christian and believed in the security and peace of her husband's soul. Her idiosyncratic way of life made her a person who sustained relationships throughout the society of Muscat, taking in orphan children and raising them. She became the powerful center of the Omani Christian community that later developed. She died in 1972.[20]

Despite these examples, however, by and large the experience of the mission was that converts were not to be expected and that, when they came forward, they were both treasured and known to be seriously at risk. The example of Hannâ 'Abd-ul-Fâdî is one that is worth summarizing:

Hannâ, a twenty-two-year-old Kuwaiti of Iraqi descent, was baptized in 1962. He had been nurtured in his faith by Donald MacNeill and was like an elder brother to the author. The process of teaching through which he passed took over three years, and his decision was tested as well as that can be done. In addition to the MacNeills, he attached himself to Lew and Dorothy Scudder as parent figures and was well looked after by Mary Allison and other members of the mission. But he was largely shunned by the Arab congregation.

Writing the "Men's Evangelistic Report" in 1964, after having only recently arrived on station, Harvey Staal noted that Hannâ had been making "good progress in most areas of his life." He went on to observe, "However, we have been disappointed to hear that he has again left Kuwait without telling any of us here. Here is a young man who is much in need of our

a family. Eventually, during the unrest among Bahrain's Shî'ah majority in the mid 1990s, for the sake of his young family, he felt forced to leave for Denmark in 1995.

[20]The author is indebted to Marjory Kapenga for this information on Miryam Mas'ûd who, in answer to one part of a questionnaire circulated by the author, has composed a powerful profile of this interesting woman.

prayers, love, and attention. He had actually left the employ of the hospital saying that he had work elsewhere in the city. We pray that he may soon find a real purpose and direction to his life in service to his Lord."21

In his brief flare through the mission's experience, Hannâ22 highlighted several basic problems. First among these is the caution with which converts from Islam are treated by traditional Arab Christians. Hannâ, a young man of marriageable age, found a cool reception among the Arab congregation and, on the question of his eligibility for one of the daughters of the church, was categorically rebuffed.23

Second, the delicate psychology of the convert is obvious in his case. A convert establishes intimate relationships with individuals by whom he or she has been significantly influenced. In Hannâ's case, he had been ejected

---

21In the author's document collection now in the Archives of the Reformed Church of America, New Brunswick, New Jersey.

22Born in Baghdad in 1936, Hannâ's full name before his baptism was Jamîl 'Abd-Allâh al-'Ubaydî.

23It is essential to understand that Arab Protestants of traditionally Christian families, while in theory ascribing to the theory that Muslims might choose to become Christian, in practice participate in what might be called the *"millet mentality"* of their traditional culture. Under Islamic governments from as early as the eighth and ninth centuries, Christians were separately organized under the political guidance of their own religious leaders, their "ethnarchs." The net effect of this was to freeze their religious development and inhibit their social, intellectual, and cultural intercourse with both other Christian communities and their Muslim compatriots. It was understood by the Muslim majority that religious mobility existed in only one direction—toward Islam. For an individual to swim against the current and become a Christian could result in summary execution by family members, the shedding of his or her blood having been declared vengeance-proof or religiously approved (*halâl*). Although examples of even prominent Muslims becoming Christian are not unknown to history, conversions soon became very rare. More common in the experience of the Christian communities were the incidents of *agents provocateurs* probing whether a given community was, in fact, encouraging conversions. It became a deeply ingrained protective social reflex, then, that any Muslim who chose to "Nazarite" himself or herself (the verb, in Christian Arabic parlance for such a person's act is *tansîr*, and the noun describing that person is *mutanassir*, pointedly using the root of the Islamic term for Christian, *nasrânî* more commonly used in the plural, *nasârâ*), was not to be trusted. For a Muslim to truly become a Christian, in this view, was certainly improbable and virtually impossible. The author has had many discussions on this topic with Protestant Arab Christians and, while they might intellectually understand the contradictory effect of their instinctive reflexes, they shrug their shoulders and let it go at that. For Hannâ to be seeking a daughter of the Kuwait Arabic speaking congregation, therefore, was seen like a fox seeking entry into the chicken coop.

from his family when he declared his intention to become a Christian in 1957. From affluence, he fell into poverty. This was followed by frequent and often threatening visits from his uncle. Cut off and pressured like this, it is no wonder that converts like Hannâ develop strong dependencies during the formative stages. In Hannâ's case, the MacNeills left the station in 1962, reposted to Lebanon, and the Scudders had to leave on a medical emergency for a period of two years (1964-1966). Mary Allison was posted to Bahrain at about the same time, and the Vander Werffs, who had filled in the post of English Language Congregation pastor, left the field in 1964. Nobody filled the gap. The remoteness of Staal, who had been posted to Kuwait in June of 1964, is evident in the wording of his report. He did not even know Hannâ's full name. These pressures were added to the fact that among the other (especially Muslim) staff of the hospital he was viewed with disdain and in the wider community he was treated with open antagonism. He had nowhere to turn. His idealistic and sensitive nature bespoke some vulnerability, and it is little wonder that he became unstable.

Employed in the hospital's accounts department, Hannâ stole some money in 1963 and disappeared for a while. He returned, repaid his debt, and was reinstated. Staal's report noted above describes his second disappearance in 1964, but he did return to the hospital again. All the friends he had wrote encouraging letters to him, but in September, 1965, he disappeared from Kuwait for a third time, having stolen nearly 200 dinars from the till. He was never traced nor heard from again. In the scraps of paper he left behind, a person in despair is portrayed. He had given up on the associations which once he confessed to hold dear, feeling that they had given up on him.[24]

The experience of conversion, with all its promise of joy and significant fellowship, ushered Hannâ instead into a nightmare sequence of mind- and

---

[24]The quandary and ambiguous position of "foreign" missionaries is here revealed. For all that they may find ready access to local Muslim and Arab society, they constantly bear the mark of the alien. Even in *Sharî'ah* law, they occupy a different category: The local Christian is a *dhimmî* (a pledgebound one), while the foreign Christian is a *musta'min* (a person whose safety is guaranteed). The two categories are subject to quite different rules. The foreigner's homeland is elsewhere, and the day will come when he or she will leave and go back to it. In a crisis, that individual, being expelled from a country or society, has somewhere in which to seek refuge. The case for the indigenous Christian is quite different. The convert's situation is a seriously exposed one. It is the martyr's choice from which the expatriate Christian is excluded.

life-threatening challenges the likes of which all but the most stable and mature mind cannot hope to withstand. And the stable and mature Muslim is not likely to make an open break with his religious heritage.

The category of "secret believer" became important to the mission's sense of fulfillment. It crops up again and again, especially with respect to persons intimately engaged with missionaries as colleagues. As an early example, Stanley Mylrea said in his "Report on Men's Medical, 1918-1919,"

> I cannot close my report without a reference to our loss of Fakir Muhammad who died on April 21st as the result of injuries from a shotgun blowing up in his hands. He had been in the service of the Mission for some nine years & had made himself almost indispensable. He had become an excellent pharmacist, besides being unusually handy & resourceful in any necessity. His character so far as I know was beyond reproach—he was loved and trusted by all & though he never saw his way to confess Christianity, he lived a life that showed he was more a Christian than he was willing to admit.[25]

Similar sentiments have been expressed by many others in the mission and frequently in even stronger terms.[26] From the notion of "secret believer" to the idea that such believers are a "redemptive leaven" fermenting

[25]Hand script in the author's document collection, now in the Archives of the Reformed Church in America, New Brunswick, New Jersey.

[26]Ann De Young, speaking of a close Omani colleague, put it this way: "I consider him a true Christian. Even though he has left the mission and apparently has gone back to Islam, I don't know. But I consider him a true Christian. He was my closest Arab friend...of course, his background was Persian and not pure Arab, but nonetheless he was a local. He was a very fine man. He used to take my place when I went away on vacation as nursing supervisor. And he had no education to speak of but he took responsibility. He was a very sincere man. It's hard to understand. I'm sure we were sincere and they were sincere and then suddenly when the new day dawned and oil came, everything was gone. You don't know...I don't know God's plan in all this, but I'm not worrying too much about it." Interview with the author, January 25, 1990.

within Islam is not a giant step. In either case, the sense is that Christian witness in the midst of Islam is a process which more formally inducted and affiliated Christians may not be able to see clearly.[27]

The 'Launching' of Evangelism

Finding fitting instruments for evangelism sometimes provided a moment of humor. One such moment was the mission's endeavor to take to the water:

In 1908 the mission sent out an appeal to purchase a diesel-driven launch, and in 1910 a small launch was purchased. This did not make the Arabian Mission a regional sea power by any means. On the contrary, it soon became evident that, as the adage has it, "a boat is a hole in the water into which I pour my money." Among the first actions facing William Chamberlain when he came into his own as corresponding secretary for the board in 1912 was to approve the mission's strong recommendation that the launch be sold.[28] Public or rented transportation had, evidently, proved of superior value and convenience. The story of this first attempt to own the rivers for the gospel was to have a sequel some ten years later.

The sequel was played out a little further north, the vessel somewhat larger: 'Imârah had been an outstation of Basrah almost from the beginning of the mission. It had been difficult to staff in any permanent way until the 1920s. Rotating out of Basrah from 1912 onward, the task to sustain 'Imârah as a station was split between Jim Moerdyk, James Cantine, Dirk Dykstra,

---

[27] In the winter of 1996-1997 the author was contacted by a pastor in Canada asking for help in dealing with problems being faced by a member of his flock. It developed that the individual was an Omani convert, a man in his mid-40s, who confessed that he had come to his Christian conviction gradually over many years on the basis of the witness of Wells Thoms. He was baptized in Great Britain in 1990, twenty years after Wells and Beth Thoms had retuned to the United States and Wells had died. This was certainly an instance of the residual effect of a witness borne many years before a decision was actually made by the person affected by that witness.

[28] Secretarial letter from W.I. Chamberlain to F.J. Barny (mission secretary) dated June 18, 1912. Chamberlain commented with a little edge of humor that this action "interested me as I was one among the members of the congregations at New Brunswick invited to contribute toward the fund for securing a motor for the launch. I presume you have considered the questions that might arise in the minds of contributors should there come to you requests for information about the working of the launch!" He conceded, "However, these are matters which of course are best disposed of on the field."

and Gerrit Pennings. In 1920, with the assignment there of Henry Bilkert and his wife, Monty, that began to change. A deliberate effort was then made to intensify the work in the Marshes. To further that cause, at the annual meeting of 1921, a decision was taken to purchase a British-built war-surplus launch and to assign Dirk and Minnie Dykstra to 'Imârah to use it.

The forty-foot launch was purchased with funds made available by the Milton Stewart Evangelistic Fund of Pasadena, California, through its trustee, Rev. W.E. Blackstone. The boat was promptly dubbed the *Milton Stewart* in honor of the donor. It was operated by the only person in the mission with the skills and the inclination to use it.[29] In 1922 the Dykstras began a five year extended honeymoon on the *Milton Stewart*.[30] From the reports of their exploits it is evident that Dirk and Minnie never had a better time in their lives.

The Dykstras, in the course of time, were scheduled to go on furlough in 1927, and they did. In May the mission took a polled vote and decided to rent out the *Milton Stewart* until the Dykstras returned. Rent would provide for the maintenance of the boat. But in November at the annual meeting, the mission was already inclining toward reassigning the Dykstras when they returned from furlough. Dirk's gifts were more needed in Basrah and other stations—he, an Iowa farm boy and jack of all trades, was the mission's mechanic-engineer-builder *par excellence*.[31] The new post-war circumstances logically implied that the *Milton Stewart* be sold. Nobody else would or could use it. Given the improved roads the British administration in Iraq had been building, a boat was not as useful as it once may have been. The mission proposed that an automobile for the evangelistic work in 'Imârah be bought to replace it.[32]

---

[29]Mason and Barny, *History...*, pp.203-204. As an investment, it was far too specifically tied to the Dykstras. The whole experience of the *Milton Stewart* taught the mission a valuable lesson in the use of resources.

[30]Cornelia Dalenberg records the saga as well as hints at the romance (Dalenberg, *Sharifa*, pp. 100-101).

[31]By 1929 the Dykstras were building schools in Basrah. He also advised Gerrit De Jong on the building of the new chapel in Kuwait in 1931 and drew up the plans which Gerrit Pennings then executed for the building of the Olcott Memorial Hospital for Women in Kuwait in 1939. He advised on several projects in Bahrain. In 1930 he and Minnie found their final niche in Oman where a hospital and several residences needed to be built.

[32]Chamberlain to Bilkert (mission secretary), August 18, 1927 and January 31, 1928.

Chamberlain, still sensitive on the subject of the earlier launch sold in 1912, found himself in something of a quandary. Grace Strang, who had left the Arabian Mission in 1925 to join the United Mission in Mesopotamia (UMM), was on furlough in 1927. Chamberlain asked her to approach the Rev. Blackstone (a friend of her father) to gain support from the Milton Stewart Foundation for evangelistic work in Hillah, a UMM station on the Euphrates River. Since topics have a way of intersecting, Mr. Blackstone asked Strang whether the *Milton Stewart* could be of use in Hillah. The upshot was that the launch was sent (with a $500 check from Mr. Blackstone to cover costs of relocation and maintenance) to Hillah for the use of the Rev. A. G. Edwards of the UMM. It took Edwards and the UMM a little less than one year to return the unwanted launch to the Arabian Mission. No one there was willing to love it as a gadget as Dykstra had done, and it was too expensive to maintain and could not fruitfully be used. Finally, in December 1928 the mission was authorized to sell it and invest in an automobile for the evangelist at 'Imârah station.[33] It was a decision almost three years in the making which involved an agonizing amount of diplomatic finesse.

Mass Media

When mass media—particularly radio—began to catch the attention of promoters of religious causes in the late 1940s, the Arabian Mission too had its advocates. The most energetic promoters of this new instrumentality were Ed Luidens, Don MacNeill, Jeff Garden, and Len Lee, cheered on by the mission's new gadget man, Bill Dekker.[34] Intrigued by the potential he saw for developing media while teaching in Basrah, in 1957 Ed Luidens moved with his family to Beirut, where he helped begin the development of

[33]Chamberlain to Bilkert, December 23, 1928.
[34]Bill Dekker was a layman from Chicago, somewhat in the cut of Dirk Dykstra. A technician, he had been appointed in Bahrain to maintain hospital lab and x-ray equipment. He was a tall, always somewhat disheveled man, with a homely midwest American sense of humor. The author recalls visiting him and his wife, May, in their home in Bahrain while Bill tried to tune in the signal of the "Radio Voice of the Gospel" beamed from Addis Ababa. The main message being received at that time was a vast amount of static and other short-wave noise— squeaks and warbles. But, nothing deterring, Bill loved the idea of the radio and was a staunch supporter of the radio project. He was also frequently a resource to other mission stations, particularly in creative endeavors to patch together working solutions to technical problems with equipment.

the Near East Christian Council's radio program—the "Radio Voice of the Gospel" broadcast from Addis Ababa in Ethiopia. In 1958 he moved on to work with RAVEMCO in the United States, but was back in Beirut from 1961 to 1962.

In the Gulf itself, tape production centers were set up in Kuwait and Bahrain, the former by Don MacNeill and the latter by Jeff Garden. These centers employed and encouraged local talent, the most exceptional of whom was Alice Sim'ân, a daughter of the Bahrain church, who later moved on to a career in Bahrain Television. Don and Ev MacNeill went on to Beirut in 1962 to succeed the Luidens; they were succeeded there by Leonard and Aleen Lee.

The fortunes of the NECC's program were uneven, and the feeder programs in the Gulf depended upon that outlet. Shortly after Don MacNeill was reassigned to Beirut to develop the NECC's literature work, the recording studio in Kuwait was closed. When in the late 1970s Jeff Garden decided to devote his main efforts to agricultural extension in Bahrain, the studio in Bahrain also failed. It was a short-lived and expensive experiment, not least of all because radio was quickly supplanted by television, and the mission did not have the resources nor the inclination to enter into that high-stakes business. The "Radio Voice of the Gospel" in Adis Ababa, when the Ethiopian Emperor Haile Selassie was overthrown in 1974, became the "Radio Voice of the Revolution," and the NECC was put out of the radio business altogether.[35] The consensus of the missionaries was that the remote witness of radio had little or no impact in the Gulf area; what continued to have an impact was the witness of lives lived out in service.

Bible Shop to 'Family Bookshop'

The evolution of the Bible shops into the Family Bookshop Group (FBG) deserves to be told in this context: The origins of the FBG lie with a creative infusion of enterprise from the Danish Mission Society (DMS). When the DMS was finally forced out of Aden in 1967, its personnel had to relocate. An agreement between the DMS and the RCA was worked out which gave

---

[35]The Near East Council of Churches in 1974 was being reincarnated into the Middle East Council of Churches, and the crisis of the loss of the radio station was absorbed into the overall stresses of readjustment that especially affected the Protestant communions involved in the reorganization.

DMS personnel a positive option, and individuals found positions in virtually all of the Arabian Mission's major institutions. The principal contributions the Danes made, however, were in the area of book selling. Jørgen "Jan" Pedersen, a trained bookseller of considerable drive and ambition, had run a DMS book shop in Aden. In 1968 he opened a general service book shop in Bahrain called The General Bookshop which quickly demonstrated its appeal to the Bahrain reading public, both expatriate and Bahraini.

The Danish-inspired effort represented a departure from the mission's traditional Bible shops, most of which had a venerable history. The novel principle introduced in 1968 was that a general book shop which made good books for general reading available as well as Bibles and Christian literature would have a much broader and more significant ministry. The idea was enthusiastically taken up in Kuwait by Harvey Staal when he and his wife, Hilda, returned from furlough in 1968. Thinking the name used in Bahrain, "General Bookshop," lacked something, Harvey and his colleague, Ya'qûb Shammâs, coined the name, "Family Bookshop,"[36] a name which appealed to and would not daunt a Muslim who had a mind to enter and browse.

The Kuwait Family Bookshop opened in a space carved out of the old Olcott Memorial Hospital for women in Kuwait which, in March 1967, had been closed. A large plate glass window was mounted in an enlarged opening overlooking the heavily traveled new seafront boulevard, and an ample shop was designed with a large neon sign advertising its presence where once a quite different kind of medicine had been dispensed. Within the first month of operation, Staal remarked, the new book shop sold more Bibles than the Bible shop in the old market place had sold the whole previous year.[37]

In its seafront location, the shop soon ran into problems, however. Nine months after its encouraging beginning, the government informed the mission that the shop could not be maintained where it was. The area was not zoned for commercial enterprises. With the help of Haydar Muhammad al-Khalîfah, a small shop was soon found in the commercially active suburb of Salmiyyah. Yaqûb Shammâs, now aging rapidly and relieved of work in

---

[36]There are two ways of saying "family" in Arabic: *'usrah* and *'â'ilah*. The first is more polite and the other more folksy. The first term had already been taken by a local book shop in Kuwait, so the new Family Bookshop came to be known in Arabic as *Maktabat-ul-'Â'ilah*. It was so registered with the Ministry of Commerce with Yaq'ûb Shammâs as the requisite Kuwaiti partner in the enterprise.

[37]Interview of Harvey Staal with the author on February 7, 1994.

the Bible Shop, became the nominal controlling Kuwaiti partner for the new enterprise. When Leif Munksgaard of the Danish Mission came to manage it, that small Family Bookshop was quickly outgrown, and another larger shop had to be rented across the street in the same commercial district, which has been the shop's location ever since.

A similar undertaking was launched in Oman, perhaps initially with more sense of ambiguity. In 1966 Jay Kapenga was given permission to rebuild the old bazaar Bible shop in Muscat. The Omani Christian community financed the first flashy glass front ever seen in Muscat's old bazaar, and the intent was that there would be a place for the two Omani church elders, Wadî' and Rubayyi', to participate in the day-to-day routine of the new book shop and have a place to carry on relaxed conversations with friends and browsers.

The first manager of the remodeled shop in 1967 was Jeff Garden, who had tried his hand at almost every innovative undertaking the mission had assayed, from audiovisual programming to agricultural extension. In the next year when the new "Danish doctrine" for operating book shops was introduced, the Omani congregation was disappointed. Confused and overwhelmed by the flood of paperbacks and glitzy displays, Wadî' and Rubayyi', who for years had staffed the old Bible Shop, extended the hospitality of the house, and engaged the occasional visitor in conversation, now found themselves crowded out by phalanxes of book shelves and interrupted by the clattering cash register.

Kapenga, who took over from Garden when he moved on to his next serendipitous undertaking in 1969, found himself inundated "with sacks and sacks of English Books, Birthday, Xmas, Sympathy, and Anniversary Cards, Christmas Wrapping Paper, Stationery of all sizes and colors" all for an English speaking expatriate clientele, "...a veritable Hallmark Store."[38]

There had been a trade-off, and the merits of the choice were controversial. Kapenga characterized the old Bible shops as "DIALOGUE SHOPS...and that is a VERY important aspect of Mission"...where local Christians could and did sit with local Muslims and make their confession without the prestige trappings of hospital or school protecting them. The new modern

---

[38]From a paper prepared for a Muscat station meeting in 1975 (to which date there is added a question mark) by Jay Kapenga entitled "Muscat Book Shop." (Document in the author's document collection now in the Archives of the Reformed Church in America, New Brunswick, New Jersey.)

shop had no place where that sort of thing could happen.[39] Harvey Staal, who later came in to administer the book shop work in Oman, remarked, "It's a matter of the number of people that you can meet, and how effective you can be. Is one person sitting in a reading room with two or three people coming in a day…is that a viable ministry? Perhaps it is. The other viable ministry is to sell as much Christian literature and as many Bibles as you can, and let the Word do the work. And we chose that alternative."[40]

As the possibilities of the ventures in Bahrain, Kuwait, and Oman demonstrated themselves, the Reformed Church in America and the DMS searched for a regional partner organization which might become involved in the newly retailored literature enterprise of the mission. The Middle East Council of Churches, which in 1974 was just coming into being, was approached but found itself too preoccupied with internal concerns. Establishing that link had to be postponed. In the meantime, John Buteyn, then heading up the RCA Division of World Ministries, pressed the project forward. Hugh Thomas, a British CMS appointee, took over as managing director. The Family Bookshop Group (FBG) was formed as a limited liability company in Lebanon in June, 1974. Of the 104 shares, the Reformed Church in America and the Danish Mission Society each owned forty-nine; in order to qualify as a Lebanese company, two shares each were held by two Lebanese Christian businessmen, and two by the newly appointed Lebanese managing director of the FBG, Rafîq Habîb.

In 1977, when Gabriel Habîb established his position as general secretary of the Middle East Council of Churches, the council began to take an interest in the Family Bookshop Group. The Reformed church and the Danish Missionary Society each surrendered seventeen shares, giving the MECC the status of controlling shareholder with thirty-four shares. Subsequently they gave a further eleven shares each, increasing the MECC's holdings to fifty-four shares and reducing their own to twenty-one. In December, 1982, the remaining stock held by the DMS and the RCA was turned over to the council "in keeping with the established mission policies of both churches."[41]

---

[39]Kapenga, "Muscat Book Shop." When the government of Oman changed in 1970, and new freedoms were declared, Kapenga hoped to be able to build a second storey to the book shop with the hope, presumably, of giving space for more casual activities (Kapenga to Warren, August 5, 1970).
[40]Staal, February 7, 1994, interview.
[41]John E. Buteyn's report of the process included in Warren J. Henseler's "Middle

The Reformed church and the Danish mission both contributed personnel to the FBG effort over the years. While not participating as shareholders in the company, the Anglican Church Missionary Society, the Swedish Mission Society, and the Finish Mission Society also cooperated by contributing personnel.[42]

Thus the Family Bookshop Group grew out of a retooling of the old Bible shops of the Arabian Mission into full-service bookstores catering as much (or more) to the English-reading expatriate community as to the Arabic.[43] Through partnership arrangements in each locale, the FBG operated independently of the mission in each of the old stations as well as in other locations such as the United Arab Emirates, Qatar, the Sudan, Lebanon, Syria, and Egypt.

Led by Rafîq Habîb and ʿAbd-Allâh Ghusaynî and managed by a Lebanese board of directors, the policy guidelines of the FBG since 1982 have drifted ever farther away from evangelism and providing resources to local Christian groups and toward operating as a secular business. This, too, has disappointed some who have seen the legacy of the Bible shops thus allowed to be lost. On the other hand, the Family Bookshops in the Gulf did indeed become popular among the wider reading public (both Arab and expatriate) in a manner and to an extent never enjoyed by the seed structures, opening up avenues for broader education and cross-cultural engagement. But, responding to the constant criticism of the Christian communities, the Middle East Council has launched efforts to draw the company's policies back toward its original mandate.

East Trip Report, November 14-December 7, 1982," the document cited as GPC/WM 4/6-8/83 (in the author's collection).

[42]The most prominent of the CMS personnel were Hugh Thomas, the group's first managing director, and Hugh Cade, who served as shop manager in Bahrain. The Swedish Mission Society contributed personnel like Gunar Rask (in Oman). And the Danes, aside from Jan Pedersen in Bahrain, contributed Leif Munksgaard (in Kuwait and Bahrain) and Knud Banks (in Kuwait). The Reformed church personnel who served with the group included Harvey Staal, Jeff Garden, Paul Bosch, John Rottenberg, Gary Brown, and Robert Luidens.

[43]The loss of the old Bible shops has been mourned by those who saw them in a different light. They were not so much places which marketed literature. They were places where people came together. The old Bible shop was the kind of environment that the Arab Christian of the Gulf could understand and help manage. The sophisticated Family Bookshop, on the other hand, represented a real discontinuity, an abrupt change of the guard. And the reduced interest in the Arabic market was a sign of the times. It smacked of a kind of surrender.

Pastors to All

The ideological commitment of Protestant missionary activity, according to Roland Allen, is the planting of a self-sustaining, self-propagating indigenous church. In this effort there are two interesting cases, the first in Basrah and the other in Oman.

Basrah: The Traditional Christian Protestant Congregation

Following World War I, the Republic of Turkey under Mustafâ Kamâl Atatürk fought its way into existence. Non-Turkish minorities in that new nation were encouraged to affirm a Turkish identity or seek other options. It was at this time that a substantial migration of Suryânî (Syriac and Arabic speaking) and Assyrian Christians from the region around Mardin in southeastern Turkey, whose background lay in the Ancient Assyrian Church of the East or the Syrian Orthodox Church, moved into Basrah, then clearly under British administration. A substantial number of these were Christians who had become Protestants through the efforts of American missionaries. The Arabian Mission had already developed strong links with that community through the colporteurs it had hired. In a flash of insight, when the mission was approached to recommission its chapel for the Arab congregation, John Van Ess insisted that the Arab church seek its own place.

Until the time of this new influx, the small group of Arabic-speaking Protestants worshiping in Basrah had worshiped on the grounds of the mission in its small chapel (built in 1913).[44] The new migration introduced a dramatic change. The Evangelical church that came to be established in Basrah was led by the legendary pastor, "Usquf"[45] Gharabet 'Abd-al-Ahad, a powerful personality of almost Moses-like stature among his people.[46] The community he led maintained a strict autonomy from the mission from the

---

[44]It was built from local subscriptions amounting to $2,000. Until this time, missionaries and their indigenous colleagues worshiped in house churches. The Basrah chapel was the first building dedicated solely to worship built by the mission. It is a bit ironic that it never developed into a permanent center for Christian worship.

[45]Meaning "bishop" which, of course, in the case of Gharabet was merely honorific.

[46]He was an outspokenly honest man and was respected for it. When, after his bloody coup of 1958, 'Abd-ul-Karîm Qâsim came to Basrah for a visit, a gathering of dignitaries included Usquf Gharabet. When he went to shake hands with him, 'Abd-ul-Karîm asked Gharabet to pray for him. The pastor answered, "We prayed for the King but you killed him."

outset. While it welcomed missionaries as fellow worshipers, they were not accepted as voting or office-holding members of the congregation; there were no links which fostered dependence or threatened political compromise. The Arabic-speaking Protestant community in Basrah, then, grew strong and self-reliant and still continues.

Oman: The Convert Congregation

The case of Oman is quite different. Beginning in the early 1930s and pivoting around the personalities of Dirk and Minnie Dykstra, there developed in Oman a purely Omani church. It had two foci. One was the school for small boys and girls which the Dykstras had begun in 1939, the Muscat chapel, and the small but intensely busy maternity hospital. The other focus was the general hospital in Matrah. Although Peter Zwemer, the Cantines, Jim Moerdyk, the Barnys, the Van Peursems, Fanny Lutton, and Sarah Hosmon … not least of all Sarah Hosmon![47]…had labored ardently to stimulate the growth of a church in Oman, and although Paul and Monty Harrison had preceded them on station by two years, it is the common refrain by all who have observed this Omani church close-up that it was the witness and devotion of the Dykstras which pulled it together and out into the open.[48]

---

[47]Marjory Kapenga, in her answers (March 12, 1990) to a questionnaire circulated by the author, recounted the story of Wadî' Sulaymân, for many years the mission's colporteur in Muscat until he died early in 1969. She wrote, "He came to work as Dr. Sara Hosmon's cook. By that time he was married and soon had three sons. During his years with Dr. Hosmon, he got to know about Christianity and, by 1930, claimed to be a believer. But he hesitated about baptism until, according to Mission legend, Dr. Hosmon locked him in a room and told him to make up his mind. When he came out of that imprisonment, he had decided to be a Christian and he never deviated from his new faith. Immediately his wife divorced him and took the boys."

When Hosmon, after her resignation from the Arabian Mission in 1939, established a hospital in the amîrate of Sharjah, she instituted strong evangelistic discipline. One of the measures she employed was to wrap dispensary drugs in gospel tracts.

[48]Marjory Kapenga, "The Arabian Mission Dream" (an unpublished manuscript in the author's document collection), p. 6, wrote: "I truly believe that if they had spent most of their years in another station, the Church would have developed there. They demanded a lot of those who became Christians. They didn't spoil people by giving them too much, and they were constantly educating every single member from the oldest to the youngest. Their theology was as uncompromising as that of the Quran, their idea of the inspiration of Scripture much the same as

For forty years it seemed to be the "proof of the pudding" for the argument that education and medical work were effective evangelistic tools (interestingly, as much the former as the latter). And the Oman community was often seen to stand as an implicit indictment against the work done at other stations of the mission. There was that glow about the "Oman crowd" that other Arabia missionaries did not share…except vicariously…and it had to do with the Omani church.

There is a myth and a reality about the Arab church in Oman. Outsiders were persuaded that here, alone among the stations of the Arabian Mission, there existed a purely convert community—an authentically Christian and caring community. The insiders' view was somewhat different. The Omani church was made up of two congregations, which missionaries identified by township: the Muscat group and the Matrah group. The first related to the school, the church, and the maternity hospital in Muscat; the second related primarily to the main general hospital in Matrah. As Marjory "Midge" Kapenga, in an unpublished article, pointed out, the division was more than geographical.

> …All but one of the Muttrah Christians were Persian or Beluch with a Shia' background. They were emotional, volatile, superstitious, more or less amoral, and they understood us, the missionaries, better than we understood them. They had inexhaustible resources for getting what they wanted and they could easily pull the wool over the eyes of inexperienced missionaries or even of those older missionaries who always wanted to believe the best of everyone.
>
> In Muscat, on the contrary, most of the Christians were older Arab of 'Ibadhi Islam. Those few who were of Persian background had toned down their emotionalism and adjusted to a more Arab way of life. All of them worked for the Mission School, the Church or the Women's Hospital.…Muscat Christians were quieter, more dignified, more polite, stricter as to morals, and much more apt to do what they thought right without consulting the missionaries. They were independent. If they didn't want to come to church,

that held by Muslims. The discipline of the Church they founded was as strict as the discipline of Islam. But they truly loved the Arab people, individually as persons. That was the most important thing we learned from them as there was no way that we, who followed them, could be like them."

they didn't care what the missionaries thought, and they looked down on the Muttrah folk who always did what was expected of them, while at the same time resenting the fact that Muttrah people earned bigger salaries.

These two groups never really united and got along. We tried to make them one community, but we never succeeded. On the surface, things looked good, but underneath we always had two communities each of which considered itself superior.[49]

Not all of the members of these two groups formally went through the waters of baptism (that number was small, vaguely given as twenty-five or so). Those who had not been baptized, however, were no less part of their respective groups (numbering around 150 in the 1940s). *All* of the Omani Christians were associated with one or another of the mission's institutions. As on other stations, so too the discipline in Oman required that all mission employees (be they Muslim or Christian) attend daily morning prayers and church services on Sunday. And on Sunday the missionary group first gathered in Muscat for Sunday morning services and then trooped over the pass to Matrah for Majlis worship and a variety of educational and social activities. Even for those who were not baptized, in a society which knew little about "recreation," the community-building activities that were part of the Oman church's routine were refreshing and engaging.

The style was set by Minnie Dykstra[50] who, on every Sunday, insisted that all the children of the community come forward and climb up on a scale. She

---

[49]Kapenga,...Dream, p. 7.

[50]Marjory Kapenga, in answers (March 12, 1990) to a questionnaire circulated by the author, included a rather complete profile of Minnie Dykstra as seen in the few years prior to her retirement in 1952. "Before Jay and I moved to Oman [1948], Mrs. Van Ess said to me, 'Midge, if you can get along with Mrs. Dykstra, you can learn more about Arab women from her than from anyone in the mission.'" Midge went on, "[Minnie Dykstra] was built on the square, had her gray hair firmly skewered in a bun on top of her head, and always, whatever the weather, wore heavy cotton stockings. Her clothes had been made over numberless times and did not have much shape about them. She generally was going somewhere and carried a Bible and a low folding chair as her arthritis made sitting on the floor difficult for her. She even, sometimes, wore a topi! [the unflattering British-designed pith helmet]. She was always serious and had little or no sense of humor. I rather dreaded going to live in the same station with her.

"But live with her we did, right in the same house, for six months that seemed like six years. She was old enough to be my grandmother and was, in actual fact,

would then make comments to the parents about child nutrition. It was not a health exercise so much as a bonding ritual. Minnie maintained a prayer list for the small group,[51] and she and Dirk would visit the members in their homes in company of one or two men who had achieved the functional level of community elder. Commenting to Harvey Staal years later, several of the community elders said to him that the reason they were Christians was because they were loved into the Church by Dirk Dykstra.[52]

a lot like my German grandmother. She had a schedule that tired me out just watching from the sidelines. I was a language student in those days and while I sat on the wide verandah studying my verbs, I observed her rushing from one activity to another."

After describing her inexhaustible energy and activities, Midge continued: "I did learn to admire her and I learned a great deal about Arab women from her. She knew each one's history in detail and she went to all the weddings, funerals, henna parties, and teas to which she was invited and usually read from the Gospels and prayed on these calls. She really loved the women and Zone, one of our teachers, told me that in all her life no one had ever really loved her but Khatoon Ameena [Minnie's Arab-given name, meaning the "Faithful Lady"]....She was a strong woman and a remarkable missionary and she persisted in her purpose like no other missionary I've ever met. Just knowing her was a real education for me."

[51]Beth Scudder Thoms Dickason showed the author a small Arabic New Testament which Minnie Dykstra had given her just before their first furlough. In it all the names of the community were carefully recorded. The inscription reads: "We give what has become dear to us to him who is dear to us. Presented to Dr. and Mrs. W.W.Thoms 1948." After reading through the list of members of both the Muscat and the Matrah group, Beth Dickason commented: "Well, that's Mrs. Dykstra's own hand writing, and that's the sort of thing she would do. Each of these individuals was important to her, personally, a personal friend. She knew how to make friends with the Arabs, and because of her frugality and simple ways she meshed in with them." [From an interview with Ethel "Beth" Scudder Thoms Dickason, January 28, 1990.]

[52]To the sobriety of Minnie Dykstra, Dirk Dykstra was the foil. "The Rev. Mr. Dykstra was a genial, outgoing fellow, fond of engaging in conversation with just about anyone" (Dalenberg, *Sharifa*, p. 101). His sense of humor was legendary in the mission, but it was most frequently expressed in his ingenuity at escaping into another atmosphere. Dorothy Scudder remembered that when she and her husband were on their first vacation in Kodaikanal in 1939 Dirk Dykstra determined that their language studies should continue. He therefore designed a routine which, the Scudders soon discovered, was actually his means of ventilation. Little Arabic was actually studied. What he enjoyed was the opportunity to regale the Scudders with stories, the smell of Lew Scudder's tobacco, and the lavish cups of tea and trays of sweets (for Dorothy Scudder was always a generous hostess). "He was a dear," Dorothy Scudder would add with only the slightest undertone of pity.

Midge Kapenga, among her answers (March 12, 1990) to the author's

As the medical work developed in the neighboring city of Matrah, the Sunday routine came to include an afternoon trek over the pass from Muscat and afternoon worship and fellowship events on the hospital grounds. The doctors, Harrison and Thoms, then came to bear an influence as well. Several of those who were baptized came to the faith through Paul Harrison. As Beth Thoms Dickason remembers, Wells Thoms and Qambar Al-Mâs, his medical assistant...

> ...were coming back from a medical tour to the interior. They had been in Shaykh Issa's country to the east...east of Muscat...called Sharqiyyah. And the way back was off a plateau down a very narrow gorge that was walled by pure rock formations. They called it...Wâdî Dhayyiqah. They were coming down this gorge, and there was always some water in it. There was Qambar and Wells and the donkey boys.
>
> They had two or three donkeys. One for Wells to ride. One for Qambar to ride. And another couple with their equipment on them. And the boys that owned the donkeys would come along to manage them. And they were going down along this *wâdî*. It was just a very narrow stream at that point.
>
> Passing the sheer mountain cliffs, Wells noticed a date palm log about, oh, eighty feet up there on a ledge. He asked the donkey boy, "How in the world did that get up there?" "Oh," he said, "when it rains on the plateau all the water—this is the only outlet for the water—it all comes down this *dhayyqah* [this constriction, hence the name of the *wâdî*]. And the water rises very fast. It all comes...from the whole plateau comes down here."
>
> So Wells looked back and saw it was very cloudy. It looked like rain back there. He said, "That looks like rain. Maybe we had better

---

questionnaire, included the following anecdote: "After breakfast at the Dykstras, Mrs. Dykstra poured the remaining coffee into four cups and set them on the sideboard in the dining room. We could come and have them during the break from school if we wanted morning coffee. If Jay happened to open her refrigerator to get a bit of milk for his coffee, she'd ask about it and then exclaim, 'Oh, that's where that bit of milk went!' You can see she kept track of every crumb of food. So Mr. Dykstra had his own way of having morning drinks that were hot. Down in the garage yard where the maintenance men worked, they all gathered mid-morning, lit a primus [stove], and made tea. Mr. Dykstra was usually there. If Mrs. D. knew about it, she never mentioned it. A lot of tea was made in that garage."

get up on a ledge." Oh, the little boy looked back and said, "Yah, I guess we'd better." So they went on looking for a ledge, and they found one.

By that time the water had already begun to rise. From being by their ankles, it was now up to their knees. So they made for this ledge which had a path up to it. They got on the ledge. The water was just behind them. They spent the whole night on that ledge.

Wells had his Bible with him. He got it out of his pocket to read that evening. And Qambar said, "Read aloud to me." So Wells read from the Psalms about…I forget what psalm it was now, but it had to do with the 'Rock that is higher than I and you are my salvation.' And Qambar thought about that. He was very moved by it. And soon after they got back he said that he wanted to be baptized.[53]

Jay Kapenga and Jim Dunham, who inherited the mantle from Dirk Dykstra, worked intensively with the Omani Christian community. Its discipline and order were given into the hands of ruling elders, and a good deal of the preaching as well. Jay Kapenga argued fiercely that one or two of these elders, particularly Khodâ Rasûn, ought to be ordained. The mission as a whole, however, held back, arguing that he did not have the educational qualifications for the duties of Minister of the Word and Sacrament. Both Kapenga and Dunham have observed to the author that the mission's reticence on this point may be held to account greatly for what followed.

The change of regime from Sultan Saʿîd bin-Taymûr to his son, Qâbûs, in the summer of 1970 is Oman's great historical watershed. It was no less so for the Omani church. As the Reformed church negotiated with the Oman government to turn over the medical work, little thought was given to the impact upon the church. In fact, few seemed to be anxious for it. When the mission gave up its control of the medical institutions to the Ministry of Health of the Sultanate of Oman in 1973, the community continued to worship, now augmented by migrant workers from Syria, Lebanon, and Egypt. Jim Dunham, in a letter to his father-in-law, Cornelius De Bruin, dated April 7-20, 1974, said,

So far I have been fortunate, very fortunate, in my work as pastor for the Mediterranean Arabs here. Church attendance, on their

[53]Beth Dickason, *Interview*, January 29, 1990.

part, continues to increase—2-3 more each week. Now I must begin to think in terms of a broader and more varied Church program for these people. The happiest part is the progress that has been made in integrating these people with the Omani congregation. There is, in general, a very good spirit of community. My analysis of this happy situation leads me to the opinion that the presence of the Mission community is a key factor. Either group of Arabs could turn away from the other, but both want the fellowship of the Mission personnel.[54]

By 1977, however, the Omani Christian fellowship had begun to quietly fade out of view. Several of its leading members formally returned to the Muslim fold. And, in the end (by 1984), there was almost nothing left of it.

Then the agonizing question remained; why did the congregation disappear? The first answer—that the Omani church must have been all "rice Christians"—was rejected out of hand, because nobody was admitted into full communion without having had first to face the full glare of social reprobation. The Omanis who were baptized paid the price for their decisions; they had all shown the courage of their convictions. Some may have become "rice Muslims" (to coin a phrase) when their paymaster changed, but that would not have been decisive for most.

After the dispersal of medical missionaries throughout Oman, Don and Eloise Bosch noted, the Omani church dissolved because, as Rod Koopmans observed to them, their support group had vanished.[55] Furthermore, to some extent Jim Dunham's above observation may have been proved correct: When Alfred Samuel came from Egypt to take over the Arabic language ministry in September, 1984, the cultural gap between the simple Omani Christians and the strangely alien and more sophisticated Egyptian

[54]James Dunham to C. A. De Bruin, April 7-20, 1974, in correspondence loaned to the author by Jim and Joyce Dunham.

[55]These observations were made in a recorded interview between Edwin Luidens and Don and Eloise Bosch, June 13, 1988, in the author's collection.

Prior to the 1970 Revolution, by joining the government's health service, the missionaries may have appeared to have "sold out" to money and prestige. Lew Scudder, Sr., was offered Kuwaiti citizenship on several occasions. His Kuwaiti friends were rather surprised when he politely refused it. His answer, invariably, was that to have accepted it would have made it appear that he was trading upon his years of ministry as a missionary. He would not throw away the gold for silver. It is to be suspected that the missionaries in Oman may have been perceived as having done precisely this by the Omani Christians.

became too much to bridge. There was no "Dutch Uncle" with stumbling Arabic but sophisticated ideas to mediate between the two.[56]

The shift of the main worship center from the homely Muscat chapel to the modern and unfamiliar Ruwî complex was surely alienating for anyone who had taken pleasure in the simplicity of Oman's first place of worship. Another factor not to be discounted was that the children, now attending government schools, came to put pressure on parents to draw away. Also, new opportunities for recreation and social activity provided by a government-sponsored community and cultural program for all Omanis replaced that which the mission alone used to supply. The weekend, under government employment, shifted from Sunday to Friday, and even when worship was scheduled for Friday, people did not come. The reasons are legion.

"Our last years in Oman," Midge Kapenga wrote, "we would have Arab church with only two or three Omani Christians present. They were joined by expatriate Christian workers from Egypt, Palestine, or Lebanon. Things were never the same again." She added, "Most of us in the mission suffered a deep sense of failure. We examined ourselves and what we had done, looking for mistakes. But I wonder if we could have done differently."[57]

Still, there remain indications that the community continues to have some internal coherence, and that the practice of caring for each other is still alive. It is just a more private affair and quite beyond the sight of any intruders.

Ministry to the World: The Expatriate Chaplaincy

In Bahrain and Kuwait, the story of the church is still different. In both places there have been isolated instances of individuals who chose to become Christians and were, to a greater or lesser degree, oppressed for their choice by the Muslim community. But a strong core of indigenous Christians never coalesced. What eventually occupied the mission as a whole in all its stations was ministry to the expatriate community. It grew out

---

[56]But the dispersal of the Omani Christians cannot be laid at Alfred Samuel's door. When he arrived late in 1984, the dispersal had already largely taken place. His effort to meet the old Omani Christians was not well supported. Indeed, a very few Omanis continued to attend Arabic worship for several years after his arrival, and they seemed well content. It was the change in the communal complexion of the congregation more than its leadership that occasioned their finally wandering off.

[57]Kapenga,...Dream, p. 8.

of Cantine's involvement, almost from the first day of his landing in Basrah, in providing leadership in worship for expatriate English-speaking Christians—merchants, diplomats, and sailors—in that port city. Inadvertently, perhaps, this became a significant activity where the elements for it existed. From time to time the missionaries had to defend this activity to their colleagues, since it seemed to fall outside the mandate of the mission to deal primarily with "Muslims and slaves." The need for this ministry, however, was so clear, and the missionaries' own need for a fellowship in which they could pray in their native language so obvious, that it was and remained a component of mission activities from then on.

Given their focus on task, missionaries had sometimes to be reminded that this ministry was also important. The following excerpt from a letter written in March, 1909, from Henry Cobb, corresponding secretary for the RCA's Board of Foreign Missions, to the Arabian Mission's field secretary, Dirk Dykstra, is insightful:

> With reference to the [Arabian Mission] proposed conference by Mr. Barny with the Bishop of Lahore's Chaplain as to the need of a special chaplain for Busrah, it was resolved "that we recommend to the Mission the maintenance of services for the European community in all stations where we are carrying on work, in harmony with the resolution of the Boards 'Secretaries' Conference of 1909." It seems to the Trustees very desirable that the Mission should so far as possible cultivate proper friendly relations with the foreign community and that it would be in the interest of the Mission work in general if the means of grace were supplied by missionaries to such communities in order that the impression that the religion of the Gospel is one thing for missionaries and another thing for other foreigners and nominal Christians resident at the same port may be obviated as far as possible.[58]

Indeed, the Protestant expatriate community in Basrah was eventually mainly served by Anglican pastors, but the missionaries of that station often filled in and assisted as needed. In the other stations, Dr. Cobb's advice was more directly applied, and the mission's chapels developed into the nuclei

---

[58]Letter dated March 26, 1909, copy of letter in author's document collection.

of what are now major worship centers in Kuwait, Bahrain, and Oman. Kuwait is a good example of this ministry:

Kuwait: A Case Study of the Multinational Ecumenical Church

We have already noted the early beginnings of the worshiping community in Kuwait in *Bayt-ar-Rabbân*. Until November 15, 1931, the Christians in Kuwait worshiped in the old sea captain's house in the old part of the town. The intention to build a formal worship center, however, continued to occupy the missionaries, and Edwin Calverley developed a full set of plans for its building before he was obliged to retire in 1929. His design was left for his successor to execute. Calverley was succeeded by Gerrit DeJong who, in more than an engineering sense, was the builder of the foundations of the church in Kuwait. His account of the building of the original "chapel" is worth presenting in detail:

> After two years of Arabic study I was assigned by the Mission in fall of '28 to take over from Rev. Calverley in the spring of '29 when he went to Amarah for a few months, then on to the States for furlough. A heart attack in Cairo invalided him home and he was not permitted to return. So the building project was passed along to me. Dr. Mylrea gave what advice that he could. But my main help was from two Scottish young men in Basrah—one with the licorice company that exported licorice root to the U.S., and the other with Andrew Weir Shipping Co. They counseled me carefully and fully and regularly. They helped me order British cement from U.K. Also the steel beams. The cement came in barrels. We had no custom duty, so the lighter was brought right out front of our compound, where the barrels were off loaded. The coolies could not get the idea of rolling the drums but persisted in carrying the near 400 lb. weight even though it almost killed them. The big beams were a big problem but the Bros. Colin and Kenneth Munro counseled me as to how to go about it. The magnificent teak doors and frames, and windows and frames, also the 4 long teak tables— 1 for each [side] room—were made in Katpadi [South India] under the direction of Rev. Ben Rottschaefer. None of the above—that is, good cement or steel beams or real good teak—were available

in Kuwait. The 60 chairs were done in Karachi patterned after those that [Bernard] Hakken had gotten for Bahrain. These orders with proper sizes, etc. from U.K. were done by Ken Munro. Items from Katpadi and Karachi I had to take care of by letter. The red *kashee* (tiles) came from Basrah, and the yellow brick or tile in the ceiling of the main nave of the church came from Amarah via Basrah by sailing boat. The original Estey organ came from friends in the U.S. of Dr. Mylrea. The first communion table came from a church at home—I've forgotten which one.

The building. That was a job and thru-out [sic.] a blazing hot summer. We had no ice nor frig, and electricity only for 4 hrs. in the P.M. to save gas bills, etc. Our Kohler engines were used to help out. The stone was from the bay in front of the Mission—taken at low tide. Donkeys loaded up the stone and brought it to the building site. Also the cleanest sand we could find. The foundation was by digging down to hard sand—2 1/2 ft. wide—pouring in concrete—all by hand work—and when above ground level it was narrowed to 2 ft. for the height of the plinth so as to overcome termite damage. Above that the walls went up of coral rock with mud puddled clay for mortar to near to the ceiling then more cement to allay termite problems. The half pillars inside church were put in to help support the heavy steel beams plus the weight of the brick ceiling also smaller beams.

The clay used for the puddling into mortar was just from the desert wherever the donkey man was allowed to get it. But the clay that went into the mud roof was "sulbee" strong or tough clay that came from a place pretty well across town not too far from Desman. And for the roof we added "tibbin"—straw—that too was puddled, mixing the straw into it good and well, and doing so for at least three weeks, so the mixture came to smell pretty strong. Parts of the mud roof were 12" thick to allow for drainage via those protruding water vents. Such a layer of thick clay was helpful vs. the heat and also withstood winter rains so as not to leak. The wooden poles were all tarred vs. termites and inserted into the walls with cement. Then bamboo strips crisscrossed the top of the roof poles and such were laid with the straw mats. The poles were teak, all such purchased locally.

I mentioned the sulbee clay. For the concrete work we had to get "sulboukh"—hard, strong, almost granite or flint-like stone—small stones of course—from the desert and that was a job; and cost quite a bit but it was essential.

The lovely ceiling was the work of our head mason, Oosta Ahmed—an excellent workman of Persian descent, but far and away the best mason in Kuwait in those days. The Arab mason could not build a staight wall. Ahmed could and did. He took pains to do so and came up with excellent work. His assistant mason was Oosta Rada, father-in-law of Haidar.[59] ... Ahmed assured me that I need not bring down a mason from Basrah to put in the brick ceiling. Said he could do it. And he did! A beautiful job which has always commanded attention and admiration. He likewise also built the arch over the chancel or sanctuary or the pulpit area and built his own design into all of it. A remarkable man and excellent mason and such a clean worker. After Colin Munro instructed me in how to go about putting together a "koleb" (a form) for putting up the round pillars at the front porch and the half ones inside the church, young Yaqoub Najaar (carpenter) caught on right away and made the forms—in two halves, which we set in place with my level and fastened them together with iron rods screwed tight and made in the *sug* [market]. Ahmed learned quickly how to raise the 3 ft. form till he reached the height we needed, with a big stick pushing the air out of the concrete poured in by pans full that the coolies carried. Heavy work! Those round pillars were the first ever in Kuwait and occasioned much Arab delightful comment and all such was supplemented with the cement stucko on the outside of the building. Again Colin Munro gave the info as to how to do it and Oosta Ahmed did it. That was a first for that type of wall in Kuwait; and many took a strong fancy to it.

It was a busy summer and a hard one but the Lord did supply strength day by day. Though I was completely green at it, we did get it accomplished with such a splendid able and clean mason with a good assisting crew; and with the quick-learning and bright young

[59]Corrective note by Dorothy Scudder on the typescript: "Father-in-law of Jasim, Haider's brother. Oosta Radha was Jasim's wife, Miriam's father."

carpenter who caught on so rapidly and from then on Yaqoub was our Mission carpenter. He always had a better idea. He was good, and served us for many a year.

I thought too that we'd have to bring a mason from Basrah to lay the red floor tiles; but Ahmed said that he could do it, and HE DID. My hat remains off to him and his workers and to the carpenter; and to the Munro Bros.

I recall that Dr. Potter sent us $5000 for the job.[60] Indian currency was then the money in the Gulf and also Iraq. The exchange netted us a sum between 13 and 14,000 rupees. Even with all the imported items, I don't recall that we had to ask the Mission for anything more to avoid a deficit.

Yaqoub Shammas may recall when we dedicated the church.[61] I don't remember any more. Then the addition of the parish hall in '57/'58 will be available to you via that good friend and wonderful man Wm. Gearhardt who with his wife is in Kuwait now, I understand. Hope you can garner what is useful.

Sincerely,

G. E. DeJong[62]

The Kuwait Chapel, with the extension dedicated in 1958, remains the oldest still-standing and still-in-use Christian sanctuary in the Arab Gulf.[63]

---

[60]Marginal gloss by Dorothy Scudder on the typescript: "$5,000.00: Erection of the Kuwait Chapel was made possible from the Sumner Legacy."

[61]Marginal gloss by Dorothy Scudder on the typescript: "The first church service was held in the new chapel November 15, 1931."

[62]Carbon copy of transcription of two original air-form letters sent to Rev. Julius Brandt by Gerrit E. De Jong, dated September 14, 1978, glossed by Dorothy Scudder, in the author's document collection. What is more important than the detail of the construction is the attention paid by both Garry De Jong and Dorothy Scudder to the names of the local people involved. These were important relationships that were being cultivated and maintained.

[63]The first of the mission's formal worship centers, the unique Bahrain chapel, was built in 1905. It was demolished and a new church building (with far less character) replaced it in 1971. The chapel in Basrah was built in 1913 but eventually fell out of use as a building for worship and was turned over to the school.

When the mission entered the Gulf, Arab society knew nothing of the concept of "week-end." Upon first encountering it, they thought it rather a strange idea. There was a special time on Friday noon, during which mosques conducted special prayers and significant sermons were preached. But Friday remained a work day like any other. Westerners introduced the novel idea of a weekend with a religiously significant day of worship at its center. For this reason, there was no conflict at first with the idea that Christians worshiped on Sunday, and it applied to all Christians, most of whom either were westerners or nonwesterners who worked for western institutions or for the mission.

The Arabic language worship was on Sunday morning. Missionaries were integral to the community that gathered, and it was considered to be the primary worship event of the day. At some point—the early evolution in Kuwait is not clear— missionaries and their western friends began to gather together on Sunday evenings as well for a worship service in English.[64] That service had the flavor of an optional event, but everyone came.

For mission padres, the English service was not a primary occupation. For them it had all the virtues of being a "labor of love." Their primary attention was focused on preaching in the main Arabic language service and, during the week, in the hospitals. Otherwise they were engaged in administrative duties for the mission, in visiting the sick in the hospital, and in supervising work in the Bible shop and (up until 1928) the school. But quite aside from the release value it had for them, as the oil industry developed and the English-speaking community grew substantially larger, the padres found more and more of their time taken up in this "incidental" ministry. The English language congregation grew and developed, and significant things happened there.[65]

[64]In the course of a rather bizarre incident in which he had to deal with a barrage of accusations leveled against the mission by a disgruntled missionary who had been dismissed, the board secretary, Barney Luben, wrote to the Arabian Mission's secretary, George Gosselink, asking: "May we have some indication of what the history of the Sunday afternoon English service has been and also an evaluation of its worth to the nonmissionary community?" (Luben to Gosselink, January 19, 1955, copy of correspondence in the author's document collection.) The fact that the question was raised seriously indicates that it was, in fact, an issue.

[65]Oil became the major factor affecting radically the development of everything in Kuwait, the mission included. Some of the early drama of Kuwait's oil development was played out or at least symbolized within the mission. Two men came to Kuwait to do battle: Frank Holmes (a feisty New Zealander, who came to be

After 1948/49, the mission's church found itself in a strategic location at a crucial time. One of the more exciting developments was the influx of Palestinian and other Arab Christians in the early 1950s. The Arabic language congregation, which had numbered a mere handful (half missionaries and the rest Arab Christian hospital staff and evangelistic assistants), suddenly grew to the point of overflow. Without special privileges in their places of employment, the newly arrived Christian Arabs could not attend the regular Sunday morning services. A special Saturday evening[66] Arabic worship service was joyfully begun. Garry DeJong, Don MacNeill, and other mission clergy were stretched to keep up with the exploding demand. In October 1958 the capacity of the sanctuary was doubled by the addition of a "parish hall" extension.

Indian Christians, especially from Kerela, came in large numbers to fill medical, clerical, and commercial positions in the country's exploding economy. Their worship needs had to be met. A "Kuwait Town Malayalee Christian Congregation" was organized, and a small Tamil fellowship was begun as well. The English congregation, worshiping on Sunday nights, grew by leaps and bounds, swelled by Asian Christians whose own languages

called the "Father of Oil" in Arabia, speaking for Gulf Oil) and Archibald H.T. Chisholm (a tall, lanky, and urbane negotiator for the Anglo-Persian Oil Company). Heavy political and economic pressure had been exerted upon the Kuwait government by the British to preserve a place for British enterprise in the oil industry. Week after week, as the awkward negotiations proceeded, Holmes and Chisholm would attend Sunday evening worship with the missionaries and other expatriates in the newly built mission chapel. They would pointedly sit on opposite sides of the sanctuary. But on Sunday, December 22, 1934, with every show of casual ease, Archie Chisholm and Frank Holmes sat together as old friends might, and Fred Barny led the people in worship. The agreement between the Anglo-Persian Oil Company (later, British Petroleum) and Gulf Oil was signed the next day, and the Kuwait Oil Company was formed. The first producing well was brought in by KOC in its Burqân field in 1938.

The author was privileged to meet Archie Chisholm in Kuwait during the 1970s. A man with an irrepressible British turn to his humor, he was the guest of Dame Violet Dickson, who was also present along with Dorothy Scudder. In the living room of the Scudder house, the above anecdote was particularly fitting and gave Chisholm some pleasure in the telling. The bond established between him and Holmes matured into a deep and abiding friendship. His summary of the latter's colorful and distinguished career is a unique testimony to that friendship and a gem in the record of the history of the Arab Gulf (see part 2, p. 66n.).

[66]By Arabic time-keeping this was known and appreciated as "the evening of Sunday" and, therefore, deemed quite appropriate and in keeping with Protestant notions about "keeping the Sabbath."

were not being catered to but who were encouraged to organize small prayer groups in their mother tongues (primarily Telegu and Urdu).

Denominationally specific groups emerged and asked for worship and program facilities. These requests were invariably granted.[67] A truly ecumenical worship center was growing up like Topsey. As the ministry became increasingly demanding and complex, the missionary pastors in charge improvised and trimmed out a truly inclusive "attire" for the Church of Christ in Kuwait, often out of whole cloth. There were few precedents for that with which they were dealing. The need was becoming evident, therefore, for a more deliberate approach to this ministry.

In 1959 Yûsuf 'Abd-un-Nûr, from the Coptic Evangelical Church in Egypt, accepted an internship under Don MacNeill to serve the Arabic Language Congregation in Kuwait. He was enabled by the mission to study for a few years in the United States and then returned to Kuwait in the early 1960s. Yûsuf, a remarkable Egyptian, was a short man, tall in moral stature, and feisty enough to hold his own against patronizing missionaries. It amused him that he was finally granted full "missionary status" in 1964, permitting him to attend and vote in mission meetings, and it disgusted him that his new status should be challenged by the missionaries in Oman.

---

[67]The Catholics, following the major influx of Indians from Goa and Kerala, were an important early entry. From the mid-1940s they held worship services in the mission chapel [see Victor Sanmiguel, *Christians in Kuwait* (Beirut: Beirut Printing Press, 1970), p. 67]. Their first priests in Kuwait were Fr. (later Mgr.) Theophano Stella (1948), Fr. Augustine Clavenna (1951), and Fr. Herman Mizzi (1953). The latter was based in Kuwait City, while the other two worked out of the oil camp of Ahmadi. Mizzi, an athletically built Maltese Carmelite priest from Basrah, was a good friend of the mission and initially used the mission chapel for worship. The crowds of Catholics that began to come, however, soon made the small facility quite inadequate. The Catholics then rented a house immediately to the west of the mission compound, a few doors up from the first American Consulate. In 1955 Stella was ordained bishop of the new Apostolic Vicariate of Kuwait, and the first Catholic sanctuary, "Our Lady of Arabia," was dedicated in Ahmadi in 1956. As the concentration of Catholics shifted from the oil fields to Kuwait City itself, work toward building a cathedral in Kuwait was begun, and "Holy Family Cathedral" was dedicated in 1961. Stella retired in 1966 and was replaced by Msgr. Victor Sanmiguel, a Basque Carmelite whose main experience had been in India. Sanmiguel witnessed the first large-scale build up of the Catholic community and, upon his retirement in 1978, was replaced by Bishop Francis Micalef, another Carmelite [see Sanmiguel, *Christians ...*, pp. 6676; and Victor Sanmiguel, *Pastor in Kuwait* (Kuwait: Bishop's House, 1978), pp. 109-139].

Through the growth years, using remarkable pastoral skills, Yûsuf welded together a single congregation from Arab Christians of extremely diverse ethnic and denominational backgrounds.68 His ecumenical vision was far sighted, his pastor's heart profound, and his plan for the new shape of the church's future in Kuwait passionately advocated. He was one of the moving spirits in the formation of the Kuwait Council of Churches in 1967,69 and was a reliable resource to other Christian groups—primarily the Roman Catholics, the Greek Orthodox, and the Armenian Orthodox—as they sought to establish their own ministries to their people in Kuwait. The English Language Congregation pastors who served with him sometimes grated upon him, not infrequently contended with him, but they always learned a great deal from him. While still in his mid-fifties, he died quite suddenly in 1980 of a heart attack and was succeeded by his brother-in-law, Hilmî Hunayn, a man of quite dissimilar attributes.

The ever-growing English Language Congregation passed through the custodial tenures of several mission pastors, the most significant of whom for the current shape of the community were Donald MacNeill, Garry De Jong, Harvey Staal, and Jacob Holler, each in his own way firmly committed to an ecumenical ideal. With Don MacNeill's shift of assignment to Beirut and work with the NECC, the first full-time pastor to the English Language

68Yûsuf 'Abd-un-Nûr negotiated a special agreement with the Episcopal Arab Bishop of Jerusalem, Bishop Qub'ayn, in which the bishop recognized that the National Evangelical Church in Kuwait was to be the church home for the Arab Episcopalians in Kuwait. This meant that the large and active Palestinian Episcopalian community participated fully in building up the Arab congregation and were extremely significant in its leadership right up until the Iraqi invasion of 1990. When the Episcopal church in Jerusalem and the Middle East was being formed in 1973-1974 out of the Anglican Archdiocese of Jerusalem, a special diocese for expatriates comprised of Anglican churches in Cyprus and the Arab Gulf was thought to provide a good solution to a strange problem. The planned Diocese of Cyprus and the Gulf, which eventually came into existence in 1974 under the leadership of Bishop Leonard Ashton, was asked to take into account the presence in the Gulf of many Arab Episcopalians in the Gulf and the special relationship which pertained between the Bishop of Jerusalem and the National Evangelical Church in Kuwait. It proved to be a bit too wide a concept for the leadership in charge at the time, and the matter was simply ignored, the ecclesiastical status of Arab Episcopalians in the Gulf (but most especially in Kuwait) remaining murky.

69The first efforts at organizing an ecumenical fellowship was launched in January of 1960. Among those active was Bob Vander Aarde for the Arabian Mission. Yûsuf served as the perpetual secretary for the council, and most commonly the Catholic prelate was president (see Sanmiguel, *Pastor...*, pp. 148-151).

Congregation was appointed, Lyle Vander Werff.[70] Vander Werff's appointment represented a concession by the mission that the task was now larger than could be handled part time by a missionary trained for an evangelistic ministry among the indigenous community and burdened with other responsibilities. It also represented the beginnings in missionary language of distinguishing "church" from "mission." Lyle Vander Werff was followed by Leonard Kalkwarf (1964-1965),[71] Jacob Holler (1965-1970), Wayne Antworth (1970-1973), Lewis Scudder (Jr.) (1973-1976), Vernon Dethmers (1976-1977), Julius Brandt (1977-1981), Gordon Robinson (1981-1985), and Jerry Zandstra (1985 to the present).

In 1947 Kuwait Oil Company agreed to support an Anglican chaplaincy for its personnel under the authority of the Archbishop of Jerusalem and financially linked to the Jerusalem and East Mission.[72] In contrast to the Arabian Mission, this chaplaincy (like the Catholic presence) was explicitly nonevangelistic. It was dedicated primarily and in the first instance to the worship and pastoral needs of the expatriate personnel of the Kuwait Oil Company. In spite of this rather crucial difference in orientation, a close relationship developed from the first between St. Paul's Church in the oil camp town of Ahmadi and the mission.[73] After 1953, mission padres also

[70]Vander Werff went on, after three years, to earn his Ph.D. from Edinburgh, Scotland, writing as his dissertation under Montgomery Watt his *Christian Mission to Muslims: The Record: Anglican and Reformed Approaches in India and the Near East, 1800-1938* (South Pasadena, California: William Carey Library: 1977). He has since taught at Hope College in Holland, Michigan, and is now professor at Northwestern College in Orange City, Iowa.

[71]Len Kalkwarf's short tenure was due to his belief that the task—limited to the pastorate of the English-speaking Protestant community in Kuwait—could not justify a full-time appointment. Appointed in November, 1964, his resignation was effective in early November, 1965. Jake Holler, a veteran mission padre, succeeded him in the task.

[72]Since 1973, as the archbishopric in Jerusalem was ended in favor of the Anglican Province of the Episcopal Church in Jerusalem and the Middle East, St. Paul's Church has been part of the Diocese of Cyprus and the Gulf.

[73]The actual sanctuary with its padre's house was built in 1956. The pastors who have served there over the years have been: R.T.G. Pearson, T.R. "Dick" Ashton, H.R. Phillips, J.A. David Legg, Keith Johnson, John Pragnell, Patrick Kingston (who died in harness in 1977), and Michael Jones (taken as a hostage by Iraq in 1990). Since the Gulf War, the pastoral supply for St. Paul's Church has been irregular. After peace was established in Kuwait, Ralph Martin came for a few months beginning in March 1992; since then part-time ministry has been provided by the Rev. Dr. Adetola Roberts (Sanmiguel, *Christians...*, p. 81; and *Pastor* , pp. 145-146, augmented by the author's personal acquaintance with the parish going back to the 1950s).

began serving a small American fellowship in the AMINOIL camp of Mînâ'-ul-'Abd-Allâh. With Kuwait's nationalization of the oil companies in the 1970s, the number of expatriates working in their "camps" dramatically declined, and the Mînâ'-ul-'Abd-Allâh fellowship was urged to unite with St. Paul's Church in 1975, the respective pastors, Lew Scudder, Jr., and John Pragnell, advocating it persistently. Relationships between the National Evangelical Church and St. Paul's continued mutually supportive until the mid-1980s, when Michael Jones and Jerry Zandstra, men who marched to very different drummers, drew their congregations in different directions. The dream of developing a coordinated Protestant ministry to the whole of Kuwait, using the two parishes as mutually complementary centers, has been suspended for the time being.

Eventually…perhaps, inevitably…the season of constitution writing set in. Almost everyone had a hand in it from Don MacNeill to Garry DeJong to Lyle Vander Werff to Leonard Kalkwarf and Lew Scudder, Jr. But in the end, it was Yûsuf 'Abd-un-Nûr who was the pivotal figure. The first controversy that had to be settled was the matter of the name. From the mid-1940s the usage had become "The Church of Christ in Kuwait." Beginning in the mid-1960s, Yûsuf, supported by his elders, insisted that in the name must indicate the core community's indigenous credentials and show a link to the Protestant communities in Syria, Lebanon, Iraq, and elsewhere in the Arab world. This implied a second assertion, more important than the first: the Arabic Language Congregation was to be considered the "mother" congregation of this community, its official representative and voice. In the end (1966), the somewhat anomalous name, "The National Evangelical Church in Kuwait," was accepted and duly registered with the Kuwait government as legal heir to "The Church of Christ in Kuwait."[74] Yûsuf had won his point, but at the cost of an abiding and troublesome ambiguity.

---

[74]The Mission Executive Committee, meeting in Kuwait in October, 1966, took the following rather curious action: "Resolved that we commend the Church of Christ in Kuwait for obtaining a legally acceptable name from the Government of Kuwait as the first step in the process of transferring property to the Church. That name in Arabic is El Keneesa El Ingelia El Watania Fil Kuwait and shall be known in English by the nonliteral translation 'The Church of Christ in Kuwait'" (action number 66-57A). There was strong resistance among missionaries to this change of name, and this action reflects it. By 1968, however, the resistance had broken down and the proper translation of the Arabic was accepted in common usage.

The ambiguity lay in the fact that the whole of the Arabic Language Congregation, even those of its members who had been granted Kuwaiti citizenship (the Shammâs,[75] Sim'ân, and Gharîb[76] families), hailed originally from outside Kuwait and even from outside the Arabian Peninsula. They have never been recognized as truly indigenous by Kuwaiti society. Efforts to register the church as an indigenous institution qualified to hold property in its own name were consistently rejected by the government. However, the government did recognize the church's competence to adjudicate in matters of personal status—birth, marriage, divorce, and inheritance— among Protestant Christians. As a recognized religious body it was also granted the right to apply for residence visas for its pastors. The ambiguity of the Arabic Language Congregation's status always posed a point of tension, particularly between the pastors of the Arabic and the English Language congregations. Furthermore, given Yûsuf 'Abd-un-Nûr's vigorous leadership, the Arabic Language Congregation was not entirely trusted by the missionaries nor by John Buteyn, the Reformed church's area secretary. The respective mandates of the church, as an organized and self-administering community, and of the mission, as a goal-directed institution, were diverging.

The principle was established that the National Evangelical Church community, united legally, was apportioned out into congregations by language. These, initially, were three—Arabic, English, and Malayalee (the language of Kerala in South India). Each was denominationally blind, so to

---

[75]Yaqûb and Estîr Shammâs came from Mardîn, in southern Anatolia, to Kuwait before 1920. Making himself known to the mission, Yaqûb, a cobbler by trade, was soon hired by Edwin Calverley to work as a colporteur. They were the mainstays of the Arab congregation from the time of their arrival. When, in the 1950s, Kuwait's constitution was being drafted and the law of citizenship written, they qualified for full Kuwaiti citizenship because they had arrived before the city wall had been built. They had five children: Habîb, Aylî, Sa'îd, Farîdah, and Sâmî. Of these, the two daughters, Aylî and Farîdah, both worked for a time in the women's hospital before getting married. The three sons took up employment with the government. Habîb worked in the Ministry of Public Works, and both Sa'îd and Sâmî joined Kuwait's foreign service. Insofar as the church was concerned, it was Habîb who gave time and effort as part of the Arabic Language Congregation's board of elders ('umdah). His death somewhat before that of Yûsuf 'Abd-un-Nûr left a serious vacuum.

[76]The Sim'ân and Gharîb families are related closely to the Shammâs and arrived in Kuwait at a later date, their patriarchs, Sulaymân and Benyamîn respectively, being employed in the mission hospital.

speak. Any Christian confessing broad adherence to the basic ecumenical creeds of the Church could belong. To merit full membership on the Common Council, a congregation had to demonstrate self-sufficiency. Those that otherwise qualified but were not self-sufficient became clients of one or another of the member congregations. The Kuwait Town Malayalee Christian Congregation (KTMCC), however, was an anomaly.

The KTMCC revised its constitution in January 1964 to accommodate the fact that the Indian Syrian Orthodox community had withdrawn and established its own congregation with a resident priest. It was the beginning of a trend. But the constitution was at once so rigid and so full of loopholes of terminology that it was inoperable. The document defined the "congregation" as made up of five constituent communities. By "founder traditions," each of these had a designated number of seats on the KTMCC committee: Mar Thoma, five; Church of South India, two (these replacing the Syrian Orthodox); and one each for Pentecostal, Brethren, and St. Thomas Evangelical churches. A sort of "wild card" eleventh seat went to one of the last three. The president of the committee was traditionally the mission padre, making for a canonical twelve members. Inevitably the KTMCC, because of its membership within the National Evangelical church's Common Council, itself became the bone over which its five constituent communities fought.

The KTMCC's constitution, furthermore, specified that the congregation "shall" celebrate Holy Communion once a month (by implication, according to the Mar Thoma rite) but it shall do so only "if possible." It passed no one's attention that the KTMCC *never* celebrated Holy Communion and did not because it was perpetually *impossible* to do so. For instance, for a Pentecostal to break bread with a Mar Thoma was inconceivable to both. For either one to do so would result in excommunication from their parent communions in India. The Mar Thoma "missionary bishop" in charge of overseeing that community's flock in Kuwait, in fact, made this quite explicit.

Yielding to realities, therefore, at the same meeting which approved the 1964 constitution, the KTMCC "transferred" three of its weekly worship services as well as its obligation to celebrate Holy Communion to the Mar Thoma parish. This agreement was extraconstitutional and the constitution took no cognizance of it. The fact was ignored that, by this agreement, the KTMCC effectively ceased to function as a congregation of the National Evangelical church. It had yielded its central symbol (Holy Communion) to a body which refused communion with the National Evangelical church.

The Mar Thoma Syrian Church eventually organized its own distinct ministry with a resident pastor. In the mid-1970s its example was followed by the St. Peter's Church of South India Congregation. These two larger parishes, as well as the other three internally fractious groups, were guaranteed a voice within the National Evangelical church's Common Council through the members they designated to continue active in the KTMCC. So tenacious was the Malayalee community about maintaining this tortured arrangement that the other two member congregations of the National Evangelical church eventually had to wink at the abiding anomaly of the KTMCC's inability to function fully as a congregation, and matters were allowed to proceed as best they might.

The Common Council—presided over by the Arab pastor (who was both president and treasurer) with the English-speaking pastor as vice-president and the KTMCC chairman as secretary—was responsible for overall church maintenance, scheduling of activities in common facilities, organizing common events of celebration and worship, and setting official policy on matters that affected the church in general. Congregations not qualifying for membership on the Common Council were charged fees based upon their proportional usage of the church's facilities adjusted according to their ability to pay. The number of discrete groups involved in this rather cumbersome yet somehow functional arrangement in 1975 was fifteen. Recently that number has grown to thirty-six—sixteen major players, and the rest fairly small. The total number of Christians served under the National Evangelical Church in Kuwait in 1992 was estimated as well over 4,000.

The basic pattern cobbled together in Kuwait was cut and trimmed to fit the circumstances of Bahrain. The church's environment in Oman, however, required another approach, integrating the "Protestant Church in Oman" into the Diocese of Cyprus and the Gulf of the Episcopal Church in Jerusalem and the Middle East through the instrument of a joint chaplaincy between the Reformed church and the Diocese.[77] But the Kuwait precedent

---

[77]The mission clergy had preferred to refer to the worshiping congregations in whatever station as "Christ's Church in...." However, as each local autonomous church council came into being, one of its first orders of business was selecting a new name. The councils in Kuwait and Bahrain eventually both chose "The National Evangelical Church in...." Jim Dunham, writing to his in-laws June 6, 1969, about the process in Oman, noted that a new English-language church

has continued to be instructive. Through the 1980s, with foundations well set, the National Evangelical Church in Kuwait continued to offer a significant ministry to the burgeoning expatriate population, both Arab and non-Arab. Its role as a center for relief and assistance following the withdrawal of invading Iraqi forces was much appreciated.

Chaplaincy work among expatriate residents and itinerants, therefore, although down-played until the early 1960s, was clearly appropriate from the outset where conditions demanded it. This ministry is the only one which sustains the Arabian Mission's legacy in Kuwait, and it is a main component of Reformed church participation in the ongoing Christian witness in both Bahrain and Oman.

A Side Venture: ARAMCO

In the 1950s there was a rather unique development in this area of ministry. The needs of Christian expatriates living in the various oil camps established by ARAMCO in Sa'ûdî Arabia were recognized. The first personnel to minister to the small, not quite clandestine worshiping groups there were Edwin Luidens and Harvey Staal, working out of Bahrain. Allen Tichenor with his wife, Ella, and their family, were stationed in Bahrain in the early 1950s to take up the work full time. In mid-1950 Allan B. Cook was brought in to explore for a year the possibilities of a more developed ministry. In 1955 Cook returned and was permitted to live in Dhahran, within the ARAMCO camp, where he continued until 1960. The network of Protestant fellowships (or morale groups) evolved in several locations

committee had been elected with a layman in the chair and himself as co-chair: "three Indians…, two British, one Dutch, and one American other than myself. They are committed to the concept of a Church for all Christians. There remains a lot of work to be done, but I am most thankful that they have at least made that much of a start" (from correspondence loaned to the author by Jim and Joyce Dunham). Breaking the pattern set in Kuwait and Bahrain, the new church council chose the name, "The Protestant Church in Oman" (PCO).

Harvey Staal, who had served in every station of the mission at one time or another, was assigned to Oman to take over as pastor to the PCO in 1972. The Diocese of Cyprus and the Gulf, then forming, was encouraged to consider the PCO as part of its network of congregations, and Bishop Leonard Ashton "licensed" Harvey Staal to minister to Anglicans in that country. With Jim Dunham (who bore primary responsibility for the Arabic language congregation until he retired and Alfred Samuel, a young Egyptian pastor from the Coptic Evangelical Church, was appointed in September, 1984), Harvey attempted to

during this time and proceeded to govern themselves independently.[78] The degree to which the now self-sustaining "morale groups" within the ARAMCO system could be thought of as out-stations of the Arabian Mission is moot. If only for laying the foundations, certainly they owe a debt to the mission.

To Teach is Christ-Like

The mind is the most delicate of human instruments...it is the human being in essence. That was not something of which the Arabian Mission, in its first days, was ignorant; it was not something of which its host society was ignorant either. Islam has always placed a considerable emphasis upon *'ilm*, upon knowledge. An old Muslim adage has it, "Seek learning, even if you have to go to China for it." When the mission first entered the Gulf, Arab society (particularly in Basrah) was anxious to move beyond the rather rudimentary Qur'ân schools which were attached to the local mosques. The missionaries were immediately aware that they were responding to an

---

cover the whole vast country, making visits to construction and oil company camps in the interior and periodic visits to Salâlah in the Dhofâr region. They were given aid and comfort by the Anglican military chaplains. The worshiping groups used the Muscat "Peter Zwemer" Chapel until the new facilities were built in the Matrah suburb of Ruwî in 1975. Harvey Staal, who moved on to develop the new "Salâlah Ecumenical Church" complex in Salâlah at the end of 1977, was replaced by Rodney Koopmans, and it is at this point that the diocese was able to fund a part-time priest, Alan Gates, to share the parish responsibilities. The first full-time Anglican/Episcopalian priest appointed to the PCO was John Hall, who came at the end of 1979, and Rod Koopmans was replaced by Richard Westra in 1981.

The harnessing of British Anglicans with American Reformed has not been an easy task, but sustaining the principle has at least kept the church together. The role of the Arabic language congregation pastor in all this has been somewhat marginal and was seriously challenged during 1989 by the interference of late-coming personnel of the Finnish Evangelical Lutheran Mission (principally, the Rev. Pavo Norkko and Mr. Gunnar Righ). Working with a geographically larger entity than was known in either Kuwait or Bahrain, the church in Oman has had to stretch further. The effort in Salâlah drew off a lot of energy, but it has been established on its own resources since 1979. A second chapel, near the airport in Seeb, has been opened and is served by the PCO team. Recently, to keep track of the various groups and activities, a church administrator has been appointed. Pastoral visits to the interior are still a regular feature of the ministry.

[78]These broadly Protestant fellowships are matched by similar facilities for Episcopalians and Catholics within the ARAMCO structure. In the now nationalized company, however, their continued existence is always precarious.

existing demand. And what people most avidly sought was competence in English and basic science. Whatever else the missionaries might add to that was received as part of the price.

Education in Basrah

Early discovered by the Cantine and Zwemer, the virtually insatiable appetite among young Arabs for education dovetailed with conventional mission strategy. Both men saw the opportunities for education, especially the teaching of English. Soon after their arrival they tried to establish an informal school in Basrah. In this they were harassed by the Turkish government, and the dream of founding a school in that town remained only a dream for some years. In 1906 Fred Barny attempted to open a school for young men in his home. He even recruited thirty-five students. But Ottoman authorities in Basrah closed the effort down, stating that he had not applied for the proper permit. He duly applied but did not discover until after the British had occupied Basrah in 1914 that the papers had never been forwarded to Constantinople.

Emma Worrall, as though she did not have enough to do as a full-time physician, tried to open a school for girls under the umbrella of her clinic work. She managed for about a year but was then forced to cease and desist. An inveterate educator and a stubborn woman, she managed to conduct several smaller "Sunday schools" for several years without official interference.[79] But these small undertakings, always somewhat clandestine, were not satisfying and exposed the mission not only to official harrassment, but public disapproval as well.

Finally, in 1908, a new and more liberal regime took control in Constantinople. Arthur Bennett (the medical tourist in Basrah) started softening up the Turkish government in 1908, when by dint of great effort he gained permission to buy land. In 1909 he gained the official *irâdah* (expressed will of the government) to build a full hospital. Seeing opportunity, John Van Ess then went to Constantinople to acquire the much more delicate permission to operate schools for boys and girls.[80] In 1910 the

[79]Mason and Barny, *History...*, p. 132.
[80]It is at this time that Henry Morganthau, the American ambassador in Constantinople, became acquainted with the American missionaries in Basrah. He formed his assessment of John Van Ess at this time.

irâdah for the schools was issued and, remarkably, included the permission to teach the Christian religion as part of the curriculum.

The *irâdah* was only the first step. John Van Ess took a break to marry Dorothy Firman early in 1911. For the school there remained a mound of paper work to be completed for the Ottoman authorities, a good deal of which was processed by Jim Moerdyk. Upon his return, Van Ess plunged into the task of starting the school. He recruited two of the Basrah governor's staff to be part-time members of his new faculty and so assured himself of the favorable attention of the local government. His first students were from the cream of society—five sons and several grandsons of Shaykh Khaz'al of Muhammarah, the sons of Sayyid Tâlib Âl Naqîb, and several children of other prominent local families.[81]

In the autumn of 1912, having completed her language examinations, Dorothy Firman Van Ess set about opening her girls' school. First a few and then a rush of children from across the spectrum of Basrah society began to attend, and by the end of the second school year the enterprise was deemed a success. In her laconic manner, Dorothy Van Ess recalls, "We were ready for whatever the future might hold."[82]

The tragic typhus epidemic which closed the mission's hospital in Basrah in 1917 worked out, in a perverse way, to the station's advantage. From 1918 onward Basrah became the mission's educational center, and its only major effort in that field for at least a decade. With the closure of the Lansing Memorial Hospital, the School of High Hope for Boys acquired a ready-made campus on six acres of spacious grounds in the prestigious suburb of 'Ashshâr. From then on it developed rapidly.[83] Van Ess was quite proud that he was shaping Iraq's elite. The girls' school was shifted out of rented quarters into new premises of its own in 1921, and by 1924 boasted an enrollment of 100 girls. The schools were going concerns, and the mission was quite proud of them both.

In 1931, the British mandate for Iraq was ended and Iraq became an independent nation. Government employment preference shifted to favor graduates of the public schools. Van Ess then concentrated upon the children of the more disadvantaged Iraqi villagers and farmers. The results

[81]Van Ess, *Pioneers...*, pp. 67-73.
[82]Van Ess, *Pioneers...*, p. 79.
[83]The overshadowing of education by medical work was judged by several mission strategists to have been a mistake.

satisfied him greatly; he was (like others of the mission) a democrat at heart. The school continued to develop through the years, using the talents of short-term missionaries to augment its offerings.[84]

Van Ess died in 1949 as he was preparing for retirement. He and Dorothy were succeeded by George and Christine Gosselink. Apart from the impressive list of men who served short terms in Basrah, the schools also engaged an impressive list of the mission's third generation leaders: Edwin Luidens, Jay Kapenga, Donald MacNeill, Jacob Holler (again), Harvey Staal, and Robert Block (again). The ministry of the School of High Hope for Boys continued to be valued even after the Iraqi Revolution of 1958.

After a period of caution, the mission in 1960 voted to put into effect the improvements recommended by the board's survey of educational institutions in 1957. In 1962 the school was brought under the administration of the United Mission in Iraq, but then became trapped in the politics of the 1967 Arab-Israeli War. The Basrah School of High Hope for Boys was ordered closed in 1968, the property given over to the government. All missionary personnel were expelled.

---

[84]Among the innovations which enriched the School of High Hope for Boys in Basrah was the introduction, in 1922, of the position of short-term teacher. John Van Ess first proposed it to William Chamberlain in a letter written July 15, 1918, and it took a few years for the idea to bear fruit. The list of those who held this position is rather fascinating and shows how the spirit of John Van Ess returned in other guises both to the Arabia field, to the home church, and to other undertakings of the Church of Christ.

Those who served the short-term "internship" at the School of High Hope for Boys in Basrah were: George Gosselink (1922-1925, who later returned in 1929 for a full career in the mission), Theodore Essebaggers (1926-1929, who later served a full career with the Congregational church in India), John Coert Rylaarsdam (1930-1934, who became a professor of religion at the University of Chicago), John W. Beardslee III (1935-1938, who found his niche as a professor of church history at Central College, Pella, Iowa, and New Brunswick Theological Seminary), John Van Ess, Jr. (1938-1941, who died shortly after his term of service), Harry J. Almond (1943-1946, who returned to the mission for a second short period from 1948 to 1952 before devoting his time to the work of Moral Rearmament), and George Jacob Holler (1946-1949, who returned to the mission for a full career in 1950). Those who served under George Gosselink were John De Vries (1949-1952, who later entered the parish ministry), Robert J. Block (1952-1955, who returned to the mission in 1959 and served in the Gulf and with the United Mission in Iraq until 1969), Donald A. Maxam (1955-1958, who subsequently served briefly in the parish ministry before turning to an academic career at Central College in Pella, Iowa), and Donald D. Jiskoot (1963-1966, the last of the line, who found his career in prison chaplaincy).

The School of Girls' Hope in Basrah City, begun by Dorothy Van Ess in 1910, limited to the primary level of education, was always a more modest undertaking than the boys' school, but it was directed toward creating outlets for women in Arab society. May De Pree Thoms arrived in 1918 to take over and further develop the work. In 1922 she was relieved by Charlotte Kelein, and that marked a changing of the guard. Thoms moved on, after her return from furlough, to the United Mission in Mesopotamia's work in Baghdad. Ruth and Rachel Jackson arrived to augment the effort in 1923, and thereafter it was Rachel Jackson that led the effort. Ruth Jackson was transferred to Bahrain in 1936, Charlotte Kelein retired in 1954, and at the end of 1955 Rachel Jackson went on furlough to be reposted to Oman in 1956. Their work was taken up by Nancy Nienhuis (Garden), Daisy Hoogeveen, and Ruth Luidens until 1958, when the school closed.[85]

Education in Bahrain

Under Bernard Hakken, from 1924 to 1936, the mission operated a school in Bahrain for boys. It was an extremely popular venture, and it is still well spoken of, but the mission found itself severely pinched for funds at precisely the time that the Bahrain government was becoming affluent on oil revenues. Schools for boys were being opened in many places, and the mission was forced into an unpleasant choice. In the spring of 1936, Bern Hakken bid farewell to his last class of boys and went to the United States on furlough. In 1937 he and Elda were transferred to Baghdad to work with the United Mission in Iraq and fulfilled a distinguished career. The mission had decided that educating girls was to be its main contribution to Bahraini society.

Skepticism in Gulf Arab society concerning the merits of offering education to females was strong. Ruth Jackson, who may be credited with firmly establishing the girls' school in Bahrain, in a light vein characterized this reticence:

> When we were just starting my girls' school, we went to Mrs. Van Ess, and she'd talk about [the Arabs' attitude toward] sending girls

[85]The school was augmented by a network of clubs that gave the teachers, Dorothy Van Ess, and other women of the mission opportunity to follow up class work with visits to individual homes, and it availed also as a mutual support environment for their students.

to school. They said, "Girls! Girls can't learn anything!" And she said, "Well, you know, in other places the girls learn. Aren't the Arab girls as bright?" "Oh, yes, we're just as bright. But, goodness sake! who wants to send a girl to school? She doesn't need to know anything. She's got the Qur'ân. She can read the Qur'ân." "Oh, but when she comes to our school she'll read everything. And she'll write." Then they threw their hands up: "She might write to a man and disgrace the whole family! We'll have nothing to do with it."[86]

Elizabeth Dame, wife of the peripatetic touring doctor, Louis Dame, was assigned to Bahrain in 1919, and the serious effort that resulted in establishing Al-Rajâ' School for Girls was launched in 1922. Elizabeth began with only a few girls and provided a basic education through an early elementary level. Graduates of the school were then recruited as teachers and, under careful oversight, produced good results. Elizabeth Dame and her husband resigned from the mission in 1936 (she more reluctantly than he). To pick up the slack, Ruth Jackson was called down from Basrah as the new school year began. In her last report to the mission in October 1959, she wrote:

> As I present this my last report of the Bahrain school, my heart turns to God in praise and gratitude for having given me the privilege of serving Him in this work so close to my heart. It is a work full of opportunities to witness to our Savior and to impart a knowledge of His life and teaching and His surpassing love. It has been a service rich in reward as I have watched girls grow and develop and continue in loyalty and friendship, bringing now their daughters to follow in their steps. My mind turns back to my language study days when Mrs. Dame with great difficulty persuaded the first few parents to allow their daughters to attend the first school in Bahrain. Under her care the school grew and exerted a great influence, and through the years her interest and gifts have afforded much encouragement and help.
>
> When I was given charge of the school in 1936 there were sixty-odd pupils occupying the two rooms under the Church and a big hut in the playground. Although it had developed to six grades, there were only two teachers available. As girls graduated we

[86]Interview with Ruth Jackson by the author, July 6, 1990, Amesbury, Massachusetts.

gained more teachers, the curriculum was enlarged and standards gradually raised. All our teachers, except for the two upper classes, are still our own graduates but we have to get secondary graduates for those, and that is our most difficult problem. Now we usually have about 140 pupils and graduate between 7 and 10 each year. These must take the Government examinations if they wish to enter secondary school. Five of our seven graduates entered this Autumn, one is working in our hospital and one is married. Our pupils who have entered the Bahrain Government Secondary School have done well, and the girl who graduated at the head of the class this year was one of our graduates and a niece of our Ruler. Others have gone to Cairo, Beirut and England. This year we have opened with 140 pupils, including 5 boys. There are 9 Christians, 20 Jews and 111 Muslims.[87]

Gradually the prejudices against education for women broke down. Bahraini mothers came to take pride in their daughters being educated. Bahraini society in the 1930s, experiencing the first blush of oil wealth in the Gulf and the increasing sophistication that went with it, came to value education for all, their daughters included.

Al-Rajâ' School (as it came to be known) prospered under Ruth Jackson's leadership and developed a strong position in Bahrain, its graduates always taking the top honors in the country's national examinations at the presecondary level. It developed from the primary level into offering a course through the seventh (and then the eighth) grades with a strong curriculum in English. The faculty was made up of the school's own graduates and a few more highly trained (mainly Palestinian) teachers who could be attracted into service to teach demanding subjects like Arabic language and Qur'ân studies. In 1960, when Ruth Jackson retired, Al-Rajâ' School, still primarily a girls' school, was a striking example of what human devotion could achieve in the face of stunning shortages of material resources.

The impact of the school upon Bahrain society is difficult to gauge. It took in students from all levels of society. Its student body was Shî'ah, Sunnî, Jewish, and Christian. The friendships that evolved over seven years of

---

[87]"Bahrain School Report," dated October 1959, by Ruth Jackson (photocopy in author's document collection).

studying and playing together under thoughtful and purposeful tutelage broke down barriers of class, race, and religion. A frequent comment of graduates is that they appreciated most the life values they learned in the course of their education. And as young girls learned how to take initiative and express themselves, they discovered their own resources and began to see how they could be applied in Bahraini society. There can be little doubt that Al-Rajâ' School has had a profound impact not only on women in Bahrain but, through its graduates in the context of their families, upon generations of young men, their sons. The progressive reputation of Bahraini society—the saying in the Gulf is *"ahl-ul-bahrayn mâ khallû shay',"* which is, being interpreted, "The people of Bahrain have done it all"—owes not a little to the direct and indirect impact of this rather remarkable ministry.

In the years following Ruth Jackson's retirement, the school passed through the hands of several of the mission's more talented women, among them La Donna Teumer, Eunice Post Begg, and Nancy Neinhuis Garden. In the mid-1960s a talented Palestinian, Yvonne Bandak, became its first nonmissionary principal. After a brief interim with an Egyptian successor to Bandak, Laylâ Rummân, the Palestinian wife of one of the few Bahraini Christians, Yûsuf Haydar, was promoted out of the ranks and became the principal. She carried on the work devotedly into the early 1990s. The main developments in this period were the location of the school in new expanded facilities (1968) on the East Compound, and its step-wise evolution into Bahrain's first coeducational school through the eighth grade, which began to be phased in during Yvonne Bandak's tenure.

Laylâ occupied a transitional time and, with an aggressive Egyptian vice-principal, she found herself torn between a school board that demanded change and a clique of established interest which resisted it. The efforts of the board to implement programs for in-service training and faculty development, along with plans for upgrading physical facilities, ran up against administrative inertia. The sparring between Laylâ Rummân Haydar and the board extended from the late 1970s until June, 1991, when she was obliged to resign.

Laylâ Rummân Haydar was succeeded by a Scotsman, James Mulholland. He was a veteran of the British Council educational program in five countries, and he came to Al-Rajâ' School at the end of his career. From September, 1991, until June, 1994, he (along with the very active school board chairman, Rod Taylor)[88] put into effect ambitious plans for upgrading the school that had been developed over years of effort. The old East Compound, the mission's first residential compound in Bahrain, had already been housing the modest school plant, but the new plans commandeered the whole property, and residences were relocated elsewhere. Mulholland's task was to bring the school onto a competitive footing in the expanding private education sector of Bahrain.

Mulholland retired in June of 1994. Within eight months of returning to England he had succumbed to cancer. His place was taken by two interim superintendents until the principal designate, Gary Brown, completed studies in educational administration in the United States and returned to take up his post in 1995. [89] Since then the school's program has developed, taking full advantage of its new facilities. From an enrollment of 250 in 1970, the student body in the mid-1990s has grown to over 1,000 from kindergarten through the ninth grade. The school has a self-generated budget of $2.2 million. In an expanding private education sector, Al-Rajâ' competes with some twenty other schools in its category and sends over 80 percent of its

[88]Rod Taylor and his wife, Stella, are further fine examples of participants in the mission's program drawn from the resident community. Rod was a captain in the fleet of Gulf Air, and both of the Taylors were extremely active in the National Evangelical Church in Bahrain, leading the congregation's ministry of music and serving on committees. Rod served several terms on the board of the American Mission Hospital. In the late 1980s, he was persuaded to take on the challenge of chairing the board of Al-Rajâ' School. With some deep spiritual distress, he took on the task of moving the school into a new era. But once the new administration was in place, he supported Mulholland in launching the plans for a thorough upgrade of the school, and between the two of them they saw the matter well begun. Rod Taylor continues to minister in Bahrain.

[89]Gary Brown came to the field as a short-term missionary in 1970 from a Peace Corps background. He taught English, physical education, and carpentry for the first decade of his service. He also taught himself Arabic, becoming one of the mission's more competent Arabic speakers. In the course of seeking a deeper understanding for his own ministry, he began a youth club of young male graduates who gathered once a week for an energetic game of basketball followed by refreshments and conversation in his apartment. He resisted pressure to take up more formal administrative responsibilities but, following a four-year absence in which to mull it over, he returned to Al-Rajâ' in 1992 as head of its critical English Department. When Mulholland retired in 1994, Brown was appointed principal-designate. After a year of training at Columbia University, he took up his responsibilities as principal in 1995.

graduates into the government's secondary school system, where they perform with distinction.[90]

Brown notes:

> The major issues we are struggling with at present are:
> - The ongoing need to make limited resources cover a lengthy list of needs (or wants)
> - Parental pressure to add a secondary section to the school's program
> - Parental pressure to increase the amount of English offered
> - Bahrainization of school staff (currently at 40 percent)
> - Methods to ensure effective teaching and learning
>
> The Board of Managers today has a good balance of Christians and Muslims. Four of the ten members are parents and three members are alumni. So there is a deep concern by members for the well-being of the institution and its students....There is currently a good understanding of the difference between administrative issues and governing issues. In other words the board is performing its role in steering the ship and not attempting to row it, something that some previous boards have attempted to do (and cannot really be done except in short-term emergencies).[91]

Like the prospects for the American Mission Hospital in Bahrain, those of Al-Rajâ' School are good. But as with all the institutions that were previously managed by the mission and were directly accountable to the Reformed church, these institutions now are autonomous and largely self-guided.

Education in Kuwait

The mission's work in Kuwait, especially from early 1921 onward, was well supported both by the ruler and by the townspeople. Edwin Calverley opened a school for boys not long after he and his wife arrived in Kuwait in 1913. That school, which included such notables as Shaykh Fahad bin-Sâlim

[90]A great deal of the current information on Al-Rajâ' School was supplied by Gary Brown in a note to the author dated May 23, 1997.
[91]Brown correspondence, May 23, 1997.

Âl Sabâh (Kuwait's first minister of health and public works), Khâlid al-Ghunaym (the first speaker of Kuwait's Parliament), and several members of the larger, Bahbahânî, clan, was forced to close during the Depression and never did reopen. Nonetheless, the impact that Calverley thus indirectly had upon the development of modern Kuwait was great, and the gratitude of his students for both his ministry and that of his long-time assistant, Mu'allim Isrâ'îl,[92] was sincere and deep.

Stanley Mylrea noted a kind of "flattery by imitation" in the beginnings of Kuwait's modern educational system. Not long after Edwin Calverley had begun his school for boys, a similar effort was mounted to open a modern school run by Muslims. The Egyptian headmaster—who in the 1950s went on to became Sa'ûdî Arabia's first modern ambassador to Britain—turned out to be too free thinking. He was dismissed and replaced by a more pedantic Turk. But unlike the abortive first attempt to open a Muslim hospital, the school—called the "Mubârakiyyah" and located not too far from the mission compound—continued to operate into and through the 1950s, when its property was taken over for commercial enterprises. Nonetheless, Mylrea made some point of his judgment that the closure of Calverley's school (for whatever reason) was a serious mistake.[93] He was right.

Education in Oman

The Peter Zwemer School (later renamed the Al-Amânah School) in Muscat was a far more modest undertaking than the efforts in Basrah and Bahrain. After the home for rescued slave boys was closed in 1901, the mission ran a boys' school until, in 1931, like Kuwait, it had to be closed for

---

[92]The title, *Mu'allim*, means "teacher" and carries with it a sense of high honor. Isrâ'îl originally came from Mardîn in southeastern Anatolia, as had many of the mission's coworkers. Unlike many others, he had remained loyal to his Assyrian Orthodox roots. He was a man of broad bewiskered smiles below a crown of wavy hair which, by the time the author came to know him, had turned snow white. Isrâ'îl later changed his name to Ismâ'îl for reasons politic, but the Kuwaitis never let him forget his baptized name, and it was always a cause for good-humored jesting. He remained in Kuwait for the rest of his life, a close friend of Sultân 'Ajîl, also a strong supporter of the mission and a close friend to many missionaries, especially Mary Allison. Mu'allim Isrâ'îl died in the early 1980s, a man full of years and highly respected.
[93]Mylrea, *Kuwait...*, pp. 103-105.

lack of funds. The priority of medicine seemed to dictate the choice, but Omanis who benefited from that first school are quite frank in saying that they believe the mission made a mistake in this choice. And it is true that this school as well as the school in Kuwait, briefly though they endured, had long-term impact, and both were deeply appreciated by those who benefited.

When the Dykstras were appointed to Muscat in 1931, they devoted effort to running a shoe-string educational effort in their home for young children, both boys and girls. In 1939, as modest funds became available, the Dykstras redesigned what had been the residence of Fanny Lutton and Sarah Hosmon, the 'Zanânah' House, contriving a facility which served as the modest school for almost fifty years.

Since maintaining qualified Arab teachers proved to be extremely difficult, the Muscat school was largely staffed by the women of the mission and given real shape by Minnie Dykstra. Great effort was put into it by Midge Kapenga, Joyce Dunham, Eloise Bosch, and Margaret Doornbos over the years. Rachel Jackson, at the end of her career in 1959 and 1960, came to give the school some professional guidance. Nancy Garden, from 1963 to 1969, provided a competent educator's administrative base. Mary Markley, a Presbyterian "refugee" from Egypt, followed, and was, in her turn, succeeded by Nancy Rouwhorst in the early 1980s. Although it continued to be a modest undertaking, it was around the Muscat school that a significant part of the Omani Christian community gathered and, from it, fed talent into the hospitals.

The curriculum was limited to the very early years of primary education. Nancy Rouwhorst was appointed principal in the early 1980s as Oman was beginning to develop its own public school system. Assisted by Finnish missionaries, the Tuhkanens, she found the task increasingly daunting as she struggled with a growing government bureaucracy. The school was finally closed in 1987 when government interference made its continuation as a Christian school impossible.

Part Five

Gifts of Healing

A Medical Mission

Cantine's and Zwemer's early experiences with Dr. Marcus Eustace and the precedents set by the Anglican Church Mission Society (CMS) through its work in Baghdad and by the Scottish Mission in Aden provided a key to the evolution of mission work: If it could, the Arabian Mission was to become heavily committed to providing medical services.[1] Knowing that

[1]The Arabian Mission came quickly to realize what Stanley Mylrea observed some years later in an article entitled, "Some of the Rewards of the Doctor": "It is a subtle thing and not easily defined or described but it is a reality nevertheless. The profession of medicine carries with it in Arabia, as in most countries, a certain distinction. There is an Arab proverb which places medicine above religion. The very word, doctor, becomes in the Arab's mouth, Hakeem, the Wise Man. And so it is that in Arabia, the medical man is one whose advice is asked for and listened to, whose influence counts in the community and in whose hands lie many opportunities to mold public opinion and to lay the foundations for Christian progress in a quiet unobtrusive way, disarming alike to religious fanaticism and racial prejudice. Given the right personality, the Christian doctor's potentiality for good in a country like Arabia is almost limitless. It is surely a matter for surprise that it is so difficult to get recruits for medical work in the mission field.

the physician's vocation was held in particular honor in Muslim society, Zwemer fervently believed that medicine was the battering ram of Christian mission. He himself never traveled without his "handy Burrroughs and Wellcome medicine chest."[2] In a modest way, he as well as other itinerant evangelists were the first pioneer *medical* practitioners of the mission. But in medical matters Zwemer and the others frequently found themselves in over their heads.

Zwemer's impassioned calls for medical missionaries, expressed out of the depths of his sense of lost vocation, were also a matter of conviction. But they were slow in bringing the results he hoped for. The promising J. Talmage Wyckoff did not last long on the field. It was not until April of 1895, with the arrival of H.R. Lankford Worrall, that the mission's medical work really got under way. For a good portion of his career, Lankford Worrall was a touring doctor, filling in behind (and, wherever possible it must be assumed, correcting) the amateur medical efforts of Samuel Zwemer and others in Bahrain and elsewhere. But the beginning he represented for the medical effort soon ran into snags.

After ambitious starts in Bahrain, Oman, and Kuwait, by 1918 the number of medical personnel had been seriously reduced, although the overall number of missionaries had increased. The mission lost physicians: Sharon and Marion Thoms both died; the two Worralls resigned; Christine Bennett died and Arthur Bennett had to resign, a victim of typhus; and Hall Van Vlack joined the military. Minnie Holzhauser, a short-term nurse, also had to retire for health reasons. That left Stanley Mylrea, Paul Harrison, Eleanor Calverley, and Sarah Hosmon as trained physicians on the field in 1918. There were four nurses: Josephine Van Peursem, Mary Van Pelt, Regina Harrison, and Elizabeth Cantine, only one of whom was single and could be assigned according to professional priorities. "Native" medical helpers also declined drastically from a high in 1914 of around forty to only twelve in 1919. Trimming the sails in medical work, at least through the period of World War I, was definitely called for, painful though it was.

By 1929, however, the situation had rectified itself. A second phase of growth was experienced with Oman fully activated with medical work in

---

If only the youngsters at home could realize the rewards of the doctor on the mission field we should have no need to hold out appealing hands. The supply would far exceed the demand" (reprint from *AMFR*, #142, in the author's document collection).

[2]Cantine, *Milestone...*, p. 58.

Matrah as well as Muscat. Steady expansion of services continued through the Second World War, in spite of the war-time austerities that had to be accommodated. The introduction of sulfa drugs and antibiotics were a boon to the work, and reports of that period are invariably optimistic.

A quantum increase in the burden on the mission's medical work throughout the Gulf took place as the 1950s fed into the 1960s. On the one hand, the reason is obvious: medical technology's own pace of development—both in equipment and therapeutic drugs—accelerated to a blinding pace. But it is on the other hand that the real change came.

For most of the seventy-odd years during which the mission provided medical service virtually single-handedly to the whole Arab Gulf region, the mission institutions were modest affairs by western standards. People who came to them were, by and large, people of the local community. The numbers were manageable. The reputations of the hospitals, of course, extended far beyond the local population, but transportation for critical cases over long distances was usually fatal in and of itself. There were relatively few who came from really remote places. The mission hospital staff was hard worked, but it was still possible for doctors like Paul Harrison, Louis Dame, Harold Storm, and Wells Thoms to leave their hospitals in the hands of maintenance staff and go on extended medical tours into Sa'ûdî Arabia or the mountains of Oman and beyond into the so-called "Trucial Coast." It was also possible for them, when at the mission, to take time with patients and be to them persons as well as professionals.

The 1950s, however, saw a massive influx of migrant workers, a mechanization of trans-desert travel, and a mental breakthrough as well. People who only a decade earlier would never have considered abandoning village or tribal medical practices and who considered foreigners and Christians to be unclean, now began to attend the mission's clinics in droves. The number of cases treated jumped fantastically, and people who once were merely overworked were now inundated by the demands placed upon them. There was the old Christian physician's habit of not being able to say no to a person in need, and there seemed no way to slow the voracious demand that had suddenly developed. Physical facilities were taxed to the breaking point, and medical professionals were strained beyond levels of normal endurance.

Personnel became the big issue for the mission. From early on, some trained nurses from India and a few physicians had been a feature of the mission medical staff. Most of these were highly motivated, deeply Christian individuals whose missionary vocation was every bit as sincerely held as was the case with their western colleagues. They have never been granted the recognition and credit they deserve. As the pressures built, the number of these Indian recruits increased. The dream of developing a staff from the Arab or Persian communities native to the Gulf never quite materialized. The Gulf's prosperity came a decade too early for that to happen. In the 1950s, therefore, more Asian staff were recruited, and the demand for quantity compromised qualitative discretion. By the mid-1950s it could be correctly observed that many of the contract staff did not have the service motive of the missionaries, and that there were problems in the quality of patient care.

Prosperity brought an influx of foreigners; it also brought more lucrative and less taxing opportunities in government service or private enterprise for indigenous people. The old core of indigenous helpers and technicians, for the most part, remained loyal to the mission, but as they retired they were not replaced. Arabia was becoming increasingly dependent upon foreigners. That also applied to the mission. Strong ties were established between mission hospitals in the Gulf and their sister institutions in Vellore and Ranipet in South India. The closing of mission work in China in the early 1950s perversely afforded Arabia a shot in the arm with the transfer of Anne De Young and Jeanette Veldman, both highly capable nursing directors and instructors. But it was still always a game of catch-up ball. Demand always outstripped resources.

The early 1950s witnessed an expansion of the mission's hospitals. It was an ambiguous experience. It seemed that no sooner did more beds became available than they were filled, and modern equipment placed in service was rendered quickly obsolete. Modest expansion projects were undertaken in Bahrain and Oman. Kuwait station launched a new building program financed mostly by local subscription. It was a remarkable experience, still treasured by the Kuwaitis themselves. It brought together in one intent the aspirations of the mission and the hope and good will of the Kuwaiti Muslim community. A genuine sense of shared values was involved, and the Kuwaitis again adopted the mission as their own.

Medical Work in Iraq

The person responsible for beginning medical work in Basrah, Lankford Worrall, was also responsible for keeping a weather eye on the health of missionaries in the other two stations of Bahrain and Oman and was frequently on the road. But, in 1898, with the arrival of Sharon and Marion Thoms, both of whom were physicians, and with a missionary force swelled to ten (from the previous year's four), the medical work in Basrah took on more deliberate shape. In 1901 Worrall, while on furlough, had the wisdom to marry another doctor, Emma Hodge, also of Methodist Episcopal background and a missionary in India, so when the Doctors Thoms moved to Bahrain in 1900, with the hiatus of a year, the modest work of the Basrah dispensary continued to be well staffed.

After the recently widowed Arthur Bennett was reposted from Bahrain to Basrah in the spring of 1907, a year after John Lansing died in the United States, plans advanced toward building a full-scale hospital as Lansing's memorial in that city. Bahrain, enjoying less governmental interference, had already preceded Basrah in that respect, having built the Mason Memorial Hospital in 1902. With the persistence of Arthur Bennett and John Van Ess, and with the fortuitous coming to power of the liberal-minded Young Turks (The Committee of Union and Progress) in Istanbul in 1908, the official *irâdah* was finally granted by the Ottoman government allowing the mission both to erect a hospital in Basrah[3] and to open separate schools for boys and girls (as described in part 4). Land for the hospital and a residence was immediately purchased, and on March 3, 1910, the cornerstone was laid for the Lansing Memorial Hospital. Early in the following year the hospital opened for business. But it was all too little too late.

Despite all the effort of its launching, medical work in Basrah was short lived. During the early days of the British military occupation of southern Iraq, the Lansing Memorial was the only staffed and operating hospital. Early in 1916 it was swept by a typhus epidemic, its medical staff either killed or invalided—among them Dr. Arthur Bennett and his second wife, Christine Ivorson Bennett, also a physician.[4] After attempts to patch together a skeleton crew proved unsatisfactory, the mission reluctantly decided to close the hospital in 1917.

[3]Personal letter from A.K. Bennett to Gerrit DeJong dated Dec. 31, 1963.
[4]Now twice a widower, in mid-summer of that same year Arthur Bennett, with his three-year-old son, Matthew, was sent to convalesce in the United States. He eventually recovered his health and lived to a ripe old age, but he never did return to Arabia.

The resources of the Lansing Memorial Hospital lay unused in Basrah for almost ten years after its closure in 1917. In 1925, Bill and Cora Moerdyk[5] were assigned to open 'Imârah as a medical station. The name and resources of the Lansing Memorial were transferred there. At that point 'Imârah came into its own. A strategically located city, it drew into itself the productivity of the Great Marshes, and was linked by the river to the main centers of Iraqi life. It stood close to the frontier with Iran and was the center of much diverse traffic. The mission understood its potential.

With the strong support of Jim Moerdyk, Bill and Cora Moerdyk and the young Cornelia Dalenberg built up 'Imârah station brick by brick until the Moerdyks had to return to the United States on furlough in 1938.[6] By 1939 they were back on station, but in 1946 Bill was diagnosed with tuberculosis and was given emergency leave to return to the United States, where he and Cora reluctantly resigned from the mission.[7]

In their later years Jim Moerdyk (who died in 1941) and Gerrit and Gertrude Pennings served as the station's patriarchs. Their era lasted into the early 1950s. They were strongly supported by Cornelia Dalenberg (who was to make her main mark in Bahrain). Others also served in the station with distinction—Lewis (Sr.) and Dorothy Scudder, Donald and Eloise Bosch, Maurice and Eleanor Heusinkveld, Jerry and Rose Nykerk, Ed and Ruth Luidens, Harvey and Hilda Staal—and the children of the mission who sojourned there with their parents recall it with nostalgic affection. The last of the mission's physicians to direct the activities of the hospital was Gerald

[5]Bill was Jim Moerdyk's brother and had but recently completed language study. A short, wiry, and lean man of some energy and gifted with patience, he had a quiet sense of humor and a true physician's touch with his patients. Cora, for her part, was a capable medical assistant and a strong support for her husband.

[6]Lew and Dorothy Scudder, studying language at the Newman School of Missions in Jerusalem, were obliged to interrupt their studies and take up assignment in 'Imârah.

[7]Again, because they were already legally qualified to work in Iraq, their replacements in 'Imârah were the Scudders who had, from 1939 to 1946, been in Kuwait. The Scudders remained in 'Imârah until 1949, when they returned to Kuwait permanently.

Nykerk, a man of deep religious conviction, an irrepressible sense of humor, and boundless energy. He had also served in Kuwait and as a touring doctor out of Bahrain, but 'Imârah was to be the main test for himself and his wife, Rose.

In 1958, as a rather bizarre repercussion of the Iraqi Revolution, the 'Imârah hospital was expropriated and closed down by the Iraq government. There is much to suggest that the targeting of the mission's work in 'Imârah was a matter of local intrigue rather than Iraqi national policy. The new Republican governor (*mutasarrif*) of 'Imârah, 'Abdul-Hâdî Sâlih, had some axes to grind. He had been imprisoned by the Hâshemites on several occasions, and when he took over 'Imârah he was in a vindictive mood. On August 11 he had an interview with the American consul in Basrah who was visiting the town. It seems he was reassured that the American government had no vested political interest in the hospital.

In any case, the next day a letter was delivered to Jerry Nykerk in which the Sâlih requested the mission to give the hospital to the Iraqi government as a gift. The pretext for this request was that an American institution compromised security in the region, and only Iraqi doctors were to be allowed to practice there. There is some indication that the chief provincial medical officer also had his eye on the hospital and considered his own government facilities an inadequate representation of his true prestige. The "gift" was to be presented at 9:00 a.m. September 1, 1958. The only other western personnel in the station at the time were a young nurse, Christine Voss, and Dr. Burwell "Pat" Kennedy and his wife, Marion, of the Evangelical and Alliance Mission (TEAM).

By the August 19 most of the mission personnel (except for Rose and Jerry Nykerk) had left, and most household possessions had been packed and shipped to Basrah. Christine Voss left from Basrah for Baghdad on the 23rd or 24th of August on her own initiative and would not be put off by government officials until she stood, knees knocking together, before the desk of the minister of the interior, 'Abd-us-Salâm 'Ârif (himself later to rule the country). There she was informed that the central government would not interfere in the policies of Governor Sâlih. But, if with no other effect, the courage of Christine Voss gave pride to her colleagues in the mission.

By September 5, when Park Johnson (the Arabian Mission's area secretary) and Jacob Holler went from Basrah to intercede with the governor, it was evident that he was not in a mood to change his position, and that he was personally at odds with Gerald Nykerk. The conclusion was to leave the hospital closed until the situation clarified.[8] The Nykerks continued in residence.[9] Hopes were still maintained that the mission would recover the right to operate in 'Imârah.

By November 11, however, it was clear that the governor was determined to expropriate the property and that no monetary compensation to the mission from the Iraqi government was to be expected. By the end of the month, the mission was officially informed that Jerry Nykerk had been refused re-entry into Iraq after having left for a short vacation. When Harvey Staal, then senior member in the station, went to see Sâlih December 6, the governor, playing a cat-and-mouse game, expressed surprise that work in the hospital had not been resumed; he claimed that all he wanted was that the location of the hospital be changed.[10] The governor claimed that, because of its location, the grounds of the American Mission would be needed for a municipal garden.[11] The mission nonetheless continued the process of packing up equipment preparatory to final evacuation or relocation.[12]

By February 25, 1959, what ephemeral hope there was evaporated when the ministry of interior granted the local government permission to proceed with the expropriation of the mission property. Staal, then responsible for the station, grudgingly agreed to sign his receipt of the order to evacuate. He noted that, under the law of protection for minorities, the chapel on the compound would continue to be used by the small Arabic congregation under the protection of the chief of police.[13] On March 10 Hilda Staal and Marion Kennedy with the Kennedy children had moved into rented lodgings. Pat Kennedy and Harvey Staal remained on the mission property

[8]Letter from R. Park Johnson, field representative in the Near East for the Presbyterian Church in the U.S.A. and the Reformed Church in America, to Dr. B. M. Luben, dated September 10, 1958. Original carbon copy in the files of the author.

[9]Johnson to Luben, October 23, 1958.

[10]Harvey Staal circular letter to "American Christian Mission" colleagues, December 6, 1958.

[11]In March, 1967, when the author passed through 'Imârah, he noted that the shape of the old mission property looked unchanged, and that the hospital was in use.

[12]Staal to "colleagues," February 11, 1959. Staal notes that his wife, Hilda, was more pessimistic than he, and that, "Should we get our 'walking papers' from Iraq, we shall be heading for Bahrain."

[13]Staal to B. M. Luben, February 25, 1959.

until Thursday, March 18, when, in obedience to a court order, they also left the property.[14] The Staals left 'Imârah Monday, March 22, preceded by the Kennedys.

The lawyer that was to represent the mission at the court hearing, a member of the strong 'Ashû family of Basrah, was stopped at a military checkpoint on the road between Basrah and 'Imârah and delayed there until after the appointed time for the hearing. He arrived late at the court only to be informed that the mission had lost its right to the property by default. 'Imârah was closed. Little comfort there was in the fact that 'Abd-ul-Hâdî Sâlih, the governor, along with his chief medical officer, shortly thereafter disappeared into obscurity. The mission could do nothing but recognize at its annual meeting of October 16-24, 1959, in Bahrain that 'Imârah no longer existed as a station. There were no delegates from Iraq attending the meeting that year. The unstable circumstances forbade it.

Medical Work in Kuwait

As has already been recounted (in part 2), the work in Kuwait began at the invitation of Shaykh Mubârak the Great in 1909. The first proper hospital building was erected in 1913, to be followed by the erection of a hospital specifically for women in 1919. In the wake of the mission's remarkable service during the Battle of Jahrâ' in 1920, the service of the foreign doctors became deeply appreciated, and the work developed with wide popular support.

Kuwait, unlike the other stations, began specifically as a medical mission. The clergymen who accompanied the doctors were adjuncts to the effort in a professional sense and, to a certain extent, in a vocational sense as well. That is *not* to say that there was no attention paid to the evangelistic effort— Mylrea himself would not have tolerated such an interpretation. It was simply a matter of priority in the public eye—the mission *was* the hospital; it came first. On its shoulders all the other activities rested. The same cannot be said unequivocally about the work in the other stations of the mission.

Physically, the mission in Kuwait was blessed. Its compound, unlike other stations, was compact and efficient. Dominating its eastern aspect was a mound or small hillock, a feature which Mylrea deemed of great importance. Upon it he built his own residence in 1914 and lovingly cultivated the few

[14]Staal to B.M. Luben, March 15, 1959.

struggling salt pines that symbolized his English revolt against aridity. On their branches he hung clay water jugs to refresh passing birds.[15] Below the site for the doctor's house there was built in 1913 the string of rooms with its deep encircling verandah which was the first hospital building.[16]

[15]This was remarked upon by Haydar Muhammad al-Khalîfah in a taped interview with Edwin Luidens, November 12, 1988.

[16]To this core was added a separate operating theater in early 1930 when the old hospital building was thoroughly remodeled. In 1941 a laboratory building was added, and in 1945 an X-ray unit.

On the eastern side of the compound, two additional buildings were rented. One served as a residence for missionaries, a rather atypical two-storied affair with breezeways separating two blocks of rooms and courtyards on either side. When this building was demolished to make way for a new roadway, it was replaced in 1957 by a building situated at the northeast corner of the chapel. The other, a more traditional Arab dwelling with two large courtyards, served as the in-patient facility.

To the west on the seafront a women's hospital was built in 1919, along much the same lines as the 1913 structure. In 1939 there rose in its place the Olcott Memorial Hospital for women, an architecturally striking two-storied structure designed by Dirk Dykstra (to which Fred Barny added the refinement of making the arches peak) and built by Gerrit Pennings.

Behind the women's hospital and west of the doctor's house there was erected in 1916 the padre's house. A line of rooms was built beside it which initially housed the school but, over time, became storage rooms and an outside kitchen for the residence. In 1975 they were again restored to educational use for the church's growing program.

Toward the south end of the compound and on a north-south line bisecting the property, Garry DeJong built in 1931 the mission chapel, using an unusual and striking blend of techniques with concrete, steel beams, brickwork, a traditional mud roof, and heavy stucco. In 1958 the capacity of the chapel was doubled by an attached activities hall and beautified with rosewood pews and chancel furniture imported from Kadpadi in South India, where the Arcot Mission operated an industrial school. Ben DeVries himself came to supervise its assembly and installation.

On the east side of the chapel was laid out the obligatory tennis court, provided with lights in the 1950s. A small traditionally designed house of coral rock and lime plaster was built directly below and behind the doctor's house. This small house was used for many purposes throughout the years—a colporteur's residence, a residence for the Sulaymân family, an Indian nurses' residence, and finally an activities building for the church.

Just on the edge of the covered market, about a mile and a half from the compound, the mission was able to rent (then purchased outright in 1952) a shop for the sale of Bibles and which served also as a reading room and a place from which the colporteurs primarily cultivated their contacts with the people of the town.

A last interesting set of dates: Electric generators for the hospitals were installed in 1921. The mission imported the first Ford Model-T automobile into

Into this environment stepped Lew and Dorothy Scudder in 1939. Over
the half century of their service there, they were to become the embodiments
of the Arabian Mission in that city for the contemporary generation of
Kuwaitis.

Lew Scudder was a tall, graceful, physically strong and athletic man. He
had been a college football star before a cartilage had been torn in his right
knee. He was a life-long avid tennis player and used his vacations in
Kodaikanal to play golf and hike the hills of his boyhood. But he was also a
connoisseur of natural beauty and loved the smell of a rose. His passion for
hot curry was renowned. He possessed a gentle heart, soft and slow speech,
and expressive hands. The blue of his eyes was mild, and his manner warm
and affectionate. A child of India missionaries, he worshiped his father,
whose career both as physician and pastor is still spoken of with awe in
Ranipet, South India. Lew spoke Arabic virtually without accent, an
achievement no doubt eased by his having spoken Tamil as a boy. A gifted
surgeon, he was loved for his pastoral manner with patients. To accompany
him on morning rounds was a profound experience.

He left few literary memorials, but those which survive show how deeply
thoughtful he was. His command of English was extremely sensitive.[17] Over

Kuwait in 1921. The first x-ray unit was installed in 1943. The Kuwait mission's
first air conditioner was installed in the operating room in 1952.

[17]By way of an example and because it is a text worth preserving, here is how he
described his first impressions of Kuwait in 1938:

...in 1938...Mrs. Scudder and I paid our fist visit to Kuwait. We were met in
Basrah by one of the Kuwait missionaries whom many of you [in Kuwait] will
recognize as Khatoon Miriam, or Miss Van Pelt, driving a powerful new eight
cylinder Ford—and she whisked us across 150 miles of sandy desert track past
Zubeir and Jahrah—the only centers of life we saw on the way—to present us
before a great closed gate (we learned later called Jahrah Gate) in a high mud wall
that extended to the sea on the left and curved around to the right out of sight.
It being high noon on a Friday and all good people soundly asleep we had perforce
to knock long and loud at the gate to rouse Mohammed, the gate keeper, from
his siesta. He at long last came out of the guard room and, having satisfied himself
of the good intentions of the travelers, opened the left hand gate for us. Kuwait
vehicular traffic then traveled on the left side of the road, sign of the ubiquitous
English influence in the East. We entered the walled town of Kuwait.

against his parent's prototype, he judged himself lacking, but in this his judgment was not true. Jeanette Veldman, whose knowledge and experience in such things was extensive, spoke of him as the finest missionary physician she had ever worked with. He had, she said, a special knack about him—his touch with patients and the affection he was able to show.[18] That was the sentiment of many both within the mission and outside it. And while Stanley Mylrea projected a stern and sometimes tempestuous figure and was warmly admired for his adroitness and commitment, Lew Scudder—the

Inside we found ourselves upon a broad sandy open space between walled courtyards on either side along the middle of which meandered the sandy road that led to the Safat which was at that time the sheep and camel market. We were not a little surprised to see just in front of us as we entered a pile of camel thorn used as fuel for making coffee and tea, ten or more feet high moving along the road with no apparent means of locomotion. As we passed it we saw under it only the bobbing head and ears of a small donkey attached by a rope to the owner walking along in front. Because of the time of day we saw no other signs of life.

In complete absence then of any other kind of traffic, we turned down a narrow road between mud houses towards the sea and arrived a few minutes later at the American Mission on the shore. The building complex of the Mission then included two missionary homes, another for the hospital pharmacist, another the mission chapel, and on the shore a two storey stone and cement women's hospital not yet completed and finally a sprawling one storey eight-room little hospital for men that had served the medical and surgical needs of the entire population of Kuwait for more than thirty years.

The Kuwait of that time was a quaint, quiet, sandy little desert town whose main livelihood was the sea. It was often, therefore, that we heard the characteristic rhythmical sea chants of the sailors as they rowed boats on the bay or labored at raising the sail of a boom as she sailed majestically off on her voyage to India, Zanzibar, or off to the pearl fishing grounds. Herein lay Kuwait's source of income—trading or pearling. Kuwait was consequently not a wealthy town, but it managed a living very well by these simple means.

However, a great blessing had only just befallen Kuwait and there was much rejoicing because oil had been discovered in the territory of Kuwait. No one knew how much, but the company that had found it was convinced that there was a great deal. Not much money had yet flowed into Kuwait coffers as a result of this discovery and the pace of living in Kuwait was very leisurely.

We had a small circle of good friends that were much together in simple amusements and recreation such as tennis and bridge. For us of the Mission medical personnel, however, the hospital created more than a full-time job, so we never lacked for entertainment. There was little outside of the walls of Kuwait except a few drillers' houses and work shops at Magwa. The whole of Ahmadi was bare hillside right away to the sea. There were only the tiny oases of Fantas, Abu Halaifa, Fahaheel, and Fanaitees scattered along the coast." (From a copy of the draft of the "Commencement Address Delivered to the Class of 1971 of the American School of Kuwait, June 8, 1971.)

[18]Author's interview with Jeanette Veldman, January 26, 1990.

man with gentle, strong hands, soft smile, and reassuring bass voice who could be touched and deeply moved—came to be loved among the Kuwaitis.

Dorothy Scudder was different...*very* different. In a sense, she was the balance weight for her husband. She certainly was the backbone of the Scudder team in Kuwait. And they *were* a team. From 1939 through 1941 Dorothy was Stanley Mylrea's diligent pupil. From him she learned bookkeeping, and, while she was a competent nurse, she found her professional fulfillment in medical administration. A character of sharp, clear angles, Dorothy Scudder was a doggedly determined woman; working in a man's world, she accepted challenge as a matter of course to become the organizer of what was eventually acknowledged to be the most efficiently run of the mission's hospitals. She was emotionally highly controlled, but when she permitted herself a show of temper it was more often than not with an eye to breaking a frustrating log-jam or correcting a persistent mistake. As quickly as it blew in, it was over.

She was fastidious, a perfectionist, meticulous and tidy. A Kuwaiti friend, once asked his impression of Mrs. Scudder, thought for a moment then said, "She is *very* clean!"[19] She was also a style setter and had a remarkable eye

---

[19]Dorothy Lucile Bridger, born and brought up on an Illinois farm, vowed with her older sister, Marjorie, that she would get away from the farm. She did. Her fiancé, whom she called "Scud" until ten days before their marriage, was toying with the idea of working at the Mayo Clinic in Rochester, Minnesota, but really wanted to be a missionary doctor. It bemused her. He was taking her into a new world. The Board of Foreign Missions accepted their application and, on May 2, 1937, they appeared before the august body. When asked why he wanted to be a missionary, Lew Scudder's answer was, "What else is a Scudder to do?" After Duke Potter announced their appointment to Arabia, the chairman rose to congratulate them and wished for them many children. "Why!" Dorothy exclaimed many years later, "we weren't even married yet!" They were married July 10. On September 8 they boarded the Queen Mary and sailed away from everything that was familiar to her. "Cried a little," she wrote in her diary, "but became brave." On September 30 they landed in Palestine and were met by John Van Ess's agent, a helpful fellow named Jamîl Imâm or "Jimmy" for short. On October 1 they arrived in Jerusalem, to be installed in the St. George Hospice, a "terrible place." But Dorothy was learning how to be a missionary. Resourcefulness was essential. In five days they managed a transfer to the new YMCA hostel (room 221, "all finishings in green"), a lovely venue for a newlywed couple. With the Newman School of Missions, Mr. Bahûth was their language instructor and loved garlic. Dorothy learned Arabic through her delicate sense of smell (and, frankly, did not ever learn it very well). In 1938, after they had been transferred to 'Imârah in Iraq, they visited Lew's sister and brother-in-law in Kuwait. For the return journey, Beth Thoms packed for them chicken sandwiches, and they were put into a

for proportion and beauty. Until the very end of her life, she held onto the responsibility for arranging flowers in the church in Kuwait. Her garden on the hill, which supplied the wherewithal, was lovingly tended with a persistence that eventually won out green against Kuwait's harsh climate. Generous to a fault but cautioned by having been reared on an Illinois farm in the midst of the Depression, she was a person who counted every penny, paisa, and fils, which small coins seemed magically to multiply into dollars, rupees, and dinars.[20] As staff in the hospital developed with Indians and other nationalities, it was to the "can-do" Dorothy Scudder that her Kuwaiti and Indian medical staff turned for counsel and guidance, and while they worshiped Lew Scudder, they were devoted to her.[21]

Between the two of them, the Scudders welded an organization together out of people of many backgrounds and varied motivations. The Kuwaiti staff are the most memorable in the sense that they brought the local

crowded desert taxi, sharing the front seat with the garrulous Iraqi driver. At the mid-point, somewhere in the desert, they stopped for lunch. With his wonted generosity, Lew offered the driver a chicken sandwich. Not to be outdone, the driver shared what he had brought—a lump of goat cheese. Eyeing it with suspicion, Dorothy declined. "Oh, but you must eat it!" Lew insisted, "you're a *missionary.*" The lump came apart reluctantly, bound together as it was with long goat's hair and sundry additives. Lew consumed his with seeming relish, pleasing the driver. Dorothy, with a strained smile, managed to disappear her piece surreptitiously into a handkerchief in her purse. "Lew disgusted with me," is a frequent refrain in her diary. Later that evening, she buried the offering in the Van Ess garden in Basrah without ceremony.

[20]Describing the events celebrating the opening of the Mylrea Memorial Hospital in October, 1955, Joyce Dunham comments, "Our efficiency expert, Dot Scudder, is about worn out I guess, but everything well under control. We marvel at Lew's continued easy-goingness" (Joyce Dunham to her parents, letter dated October 10, 1955, correspondence on loan to the author from Jim and Joyce Dunham).

[21]The author spent an evening on June 20, 1990, with Simeon Thilagam, John Balasundaram, and Isaac Wilson, Indian nurses formerly on the staff of the Kuwait American Mission Hospital. In notes made after the event, the following was recorded: "While the Vellore/Ranipet [i.e., the Arcot Mission] connection was important in establishing a link to Kuwait, the Indian nurses (even on Mission pay) could make five times more in Kuwait than in India. The job opportunity, therefore, brought them in the first instance. But after being incorporated into the staff, their perspective changed. Their loyalty to the institution became passionate. They were strongly bonded by the Scudder team. Lew Scudder was a person who gave professional trust and treated them as real people. Dorothy Scudder went to great lengths to make them comfortable and treated them like family."

community and the mission together in joint ministry.[22] The Kuwait hospital was characterized by high morale and it built character. That was something which contributed to making Kuwait the happiest place in which Jeanette Veldman served.[23] The two most successful of the Indian physicians who served under Lew Scudder, Surendra Nawgiri and Jacob Oomen, considered themselves his disciples, and they both proved worthy of that claim.

[22]Dorothy Scudder recalled: "Apart from missionaries, there was no really trained technical staff until sisters Jamila and Labiba came in the mid-1930s. Trained practical nursing staff for the men's and women's hospital of Kuwaiti nationality were not developed until 1948. In the 1950s the mission began bringing in trained nurses and technicians from India, and sending Kuwaiti staff away for training. Mr. Haider Al-Khalifa was the first fully trained Kuwaiti staff member, and the first x-ray technician in Kuwait.

The oldest staff members who worked as dressers and who had received training in elementary procedures from Dr. Mylrea were Qambar, Hajji Abbas Abdallah, and Abd-al-Karim Faraj. They were later joined by Benyamin Yaqoub. The first pharmacist in Kuwait was Suleiman Sim'an Shammas. The practical nurses trained in the mission in the 1940s were: Alie Yaqoub Shammas, Farida Yaqoub Shammas, Haider Al-Khalifa, Abbas Rada, Ibrahim Hasan, Abdallah Abbas, Ali Abbas, Ramadan Al-Khalifa and Ali Shatti. The contribution these Kuwaitis made in the pioneer days of Kuwait medicine was extremely significant." (From a speech delivered by Dorothy B. Scudder before Kuwait's Family Development Society April 4, 1976, entitled, "The Beginnings of Medical Work in Kuwait," an original typescript in the author's document collection.)

[23]"The men who served the American Mission Hospital in Kuwait as permanent chief medical officers were: Dr. Paul Harrison (1912-1913), Dr. Stanley G. Mylrea (1913-1942), and Dr. Lewis R. Scudder (1939-1967). Others who served in relief or supplementary staff positions for longer or shorter periods were Dr. Wells Thoms, Dr. Harold Storm, Dr. Gerald Nykerk, Dr. Maurice Heusinkveld, Dr. Bernard Voss, Dr. Donald Bosch, Dr. Alfred Pennings, and Dr. Egbert Fell. Of these men, three died and were buried in Kuwait: Dr. Mylrea (1952), Dr. Nykerk (1964), and Dr. Scudder (1975).

No less important to the development of the work were the women doctors who served: Dr. Eleanor Calverley (1912-1929), Dr. Esther Barny (1930-1937), Dr. Mary Allison (1934-1940), Dr. Ruth Crouse (1940-1946), and, for a second time, Dr. Mary Allison (1946-1963). Amongst the capable women who made significant contributions were Miss Mary Van Pelt (Khatûn Miryam) (1916-1938) and Mrs. Eleanor Heusinkveld (1945-1949), under whom the training of our staff of Kuwaiti practical nurses was conducted" (D. Scudder, "Beginnings"). Omitted from the list was Jeanette Veldman (1956-1959), also in nurses training and administration.

A rather novel venture offered itself to the Arabian Mission and the Reformed church in 1948. With new oil revenues, Kuwait was considering how to develop its own government medical service and was contemplating building a large new hospital. Jerry Nykerk, then the mission's chief medical officer in Kuwait while Lew Scudder covered for Bill Moerdyk's abrupt departure from 'Imârah, was asked by Shaykh Ahmad al-Jâbir whether the Board of Foreign Missions would be willing to act as screening and recruiting agent on his behalf to find an appropriate person to lead the enterprise. The position was described as personal physician to the ruler and architect of the government's new health service.

The request was forwarded, with Kuwait Station's enthusiastic endorsement, to Duke Potter, the Reformed church's secretary for the Board of Foreign Missions. The mission saw in it a real opportunity to give strong moral guidance in the very early stages of Kuwait's development as a modern state. Potter, however, did not view it as an opportunity but an imposition.[24] Both Dorothy Scudder and Mary Allison, in later years, recalled that he did not really consider the undertaking as truly a missionary challenge. Potter's efforts at recruitment were not nearly as rigorous as he would have applied to a candidate for the mission itself. His examination of Dr. Levon A. Agopiantz, whose name he finally put forward as a candidate and introduced to the urbane 'Izzat Ja'far, the ruler's personal advisor, was cursory and did not include a rigorous examination of the man's moral character or sense of Christian vocation.

The appointment ended badly. Agopiantz proved an unpleasant man, entirely unsuited to the task.[25] The hospital he built in 1949 was woefully

[24]In a letter written to the mission secretary, Dorothy Van Ess, dated September 1, 1948, Duke Potter reported that he had introduced Dr. and Mrs. Levon A. Agopiantz to 'Izzat Ja'far, the ruler's personal aide. Commenting on the experience, he said, "This is a rather new and interesting venture and it has kept me pretty busy. It is not so easy to find the right sort of doctor for a job like this even when one has practically 'carte blanche' in the matter of salary" (document in author's collection). What Potter failed to take enough into account was that the "sort of doctor" Shaykh Ahmad had in mind had been shaped by the mission's physicians, whom he had come to trust and respect. Potter was looking for a different sort. That was Potter's mistake.

[25]Informed by Rose Nykerk, Potter was aware that Agopiantz was not working out well already in December of 1948 (letter to George Gosselink dated December 12, 1948, in the author's collection).

inadequate. He left hurriedly after a brief tenure under suspicion of malfeasance in office.[26] The mission was never again formally approached by the Kuwait government to assist in this sort of thing.[27] Agopiantz was replaced by a fine British physician, Eric Perry, who, along with Allen Mersh of the Kuwait Oil Company's new hospital facilities in Maqwa', developed very close relationships and cooperation with the mission's personnel and medical program.[28]

But the handwriting was on the wall. Kuwaiti society was coming to expect better medical facilities than the mission had previously been able to afford,

[26]Agopiantz was back in New York in September of 1949, breathing vengeance against the ruler of Kuwait for "breach of contract" and generally trying to justify himself. Potter's comment to Gosselink (September 15, 1949) was, "I am deeply pained over this result, after the careful investigation which I made prior to his going out. He had a very fine record of performance in China, and evidently made a very thorough study of the situation in Kuwait. Apparently, however, he did not succeed in developing the mutual understanding which was essential to make his service a success" (document in author's collection). In fact, Potter himself is to be held accountable for the sad experience. Although in later years Potter proclaimed himself a good friend of Shaykh Ahmad and was more than willing to recount all the favors he had done him, in this particular affair he had served him badly. The mission was not enriched.

[27]An exception to this was the appointment of Shirley Stephens, a young Presbyterian teacher, who came out in the early 1950s to act as governess and tutor for the children of the minister of health, Shaykh Fahad as-Sâlim. Her presence in that household and her intimate relationship with the mission strengthened a subtle bridge of trust that had been damaged in the Agopiantz experience.

[28]In a paper, "The Beginnings of Medical Work in Kuwait," delivered to the Kuwait Family Development Society April 4, 1976, Dorothy Scudder noted: "As for other medical endeavors in Kuwait, the Muslim Benevolent Society opened a clinic in 1916. It was staffed by a Turkish doctor, but was closed in the same year by Sheikh Mubarak because of malpractice. In 1939 the Government opened a clinic near the Seef Palace; it was staffed by a Syrian doctor, Dr. Yahya Al-Hadidi, still [1976] in Government service as director of the Contagious Diseases Hospital. It was not until the Government Health Service came under the leadership of Sheikh Fahed Al-Salem that the Amiri Hospital was opened in 1949. Also in the late 1940s, the Kuwait Oil Company opened its hospital in Magwa. The close cooperation between the American Mission, Amiri and KOC hospitals in the 1950s did much to advance the development of health care in Kuwait" (original typescript in the author's document collection).

and the new institutions being built both by the government and by the oil company gave testimony to that. The growing pressure on the mission hospitals in the early 1950s, therefore, had in it an element of competition— not so much ideological as professional and technological.

This local pressure coincided with application of pressure from a different direction. In Christian ecumenical circles it had recently become fashionable to question whether the missionary enterprise ought to depend so heavily on expensive, high profile institutions like hospitals and schools. The Arabian Mission was not immune from the questions being raised. The mission in the Gulf insisted that, for the sake of a Christian witness even in prosperous environments like Kuwait, the hospital was vital.[29] In the early 1950s plans were developed for building a new hospital in Kuwait. The funding for the new facility was met largely through enthusiastic donations from the people of Kuwait,[30] and the Mylrea Memorial Hospital, built on the site of the old hospital, was officially opened for business October 8,

[29]Haydar Muhammad al-Khalîfah, who, although a Shîʿah Muslim, devoted most of his professional life to the work of the mission hospital in Kuwait, observed to Ed Luidens (taped interview, November 12, 1988) that, even though the church might understand that the church came first and gave birth to the hospital, the local Muslims saw the relationship the other way around: the hospital came and then the church was given legitimacy. Don Hepburn, the chief executive of the Bahrain Petroleum Company (BAPCO), when he took the chair of the American Mission Hospital Board of Directors in Bahrain in 1979, came to the same conclusion. He had to face the same challenge. In his understanding, the hospital gave a legitimate and openly respected environment within which Christian witness could be carried out in a manner and to an extent not otherwise possible (taped interview by the author with Donald Hepburn, Bahrain, March 13, 1990).

[30]When the Kuwait station decided to approach the Kuwaiti public for help, there was at first a puzzled reaction. In Arab and Muslim society, large-scale philanthropy was traditionally either the work of government or of exorbitantly rich individual benefactors. The mission's appeal was to Kuwaiti society as a whole, selecting no one for special recognition. Once the idea had penetrated that small people working in concert could achieve large and worthwhile goals, it was enthusiastically adopted and the funds were raised. When, a few years later, the mission needed to extend the church sanctuary to accommodate the burgeoning Arabic and English Language Congregations, and the money was not forthcoming from Christian sources, again the mission turned to the Kuwaiti Muslims and found the same generous response. Why? As another of Kuwait's Muslim spiritual leaders, Shaykh ʿÎsâ al-Qanâʾî, put it to Don Mac Neil as he handed him a rather large check, "A house of prayer is a house of peace." Kuwaitis from across the social and economic spectrum came to appreciate the mission and its institutions as somehow uniquely theirs, a significant moral fact whose weight was not added to the scales by the Reformed church in the events that were to follow.

1955,[31] with the public presence and approval of the ruler, Shaykh 'Abd-Allâh as-Sâlim, and much celebration.[32]

The opening of the new hospital in Kuwait was among the last major celebrative events of the mission (with the exception, perhaps, of the dedication of the new church building in Bahrain in 1971). The hospital was instantly appreciated by the Kuwait public, many of whom had contributed personally to its construction, and several of whom endowed parts of its operation.[33] But hard times loomed ahead. The mission had had only nine years to develop their new facility when Gerald Nykerk, who (after a short period in Oman) had returned to Kuwait after the closure of 'Imârah to share the increasing load with an overworked Lew Scudder, suddenly died of a heart attack March 20, 1964. A short while later, in August, Lew Scudder himself collapsed and quickly had to be flown back to the United States for the removal of a life-threatening subdural hematoma.

The two main surgeons of the hospital were thus suddenly lost, and the load fell heavily upon the young Alfred Pennings (an internist by trade and

[31]The mission had hoped to design a hospital that was an enclosed building fully air conditioned throughout. Henry Bovenkerk, then in charge of the financial aspect of the board, insisted that air conditioning was not something which every Kuwaiti family had. He saw this as ostentation. Plans had to be revised. The main wards were not to be air conditioned. Central air conditioning was applied only to the central block—doctors' offices, waiting rooms, operating theaters, laboratories, xray, and two private care patient rooms. Within two years of its having been opened, the structure of the hospital began to take on a patched appearance, as unit air conditioners had to be installed almost everywhere. It stood as an excellent example of how micro-management from a remote position could not only be short sighted, but prejudicial to the mission's best interests.

[32]The Mylrea Memorial Hospital was dedicated at the time of the mission's full annual meeting. The author remembers the event as a whirlwind of activity. The full assembly of the mission (children included), along with all of Kuwait's notables, high brass from the local expatriate community, and Henry Bovenkerk from the Reformed Church in America's Board of Foreign Missions made for a massive affair. In spite of its design drawbacks (upon which Bovenkerk had insisted), opening the new hospital was deemed a worthy achievement. (A description of the event was written and circulated by Dorothy F. Van Ess to "Dear Friends" October 20, 1955, copy in the author's document collection.)

[33]Apart from the ruler, Shaykh 'Abd-Allâh, who gave the single largest donation, prominent among the benefactors was 'Abd-Allâh al-'Uthmân, a leading religious figure in Kuwait. He contributed heavily to the building itself, presented several expensive pieces of diagnostic equipment, and endowed a ward for the indigent. Apart from his help to the American Mission Hospital, he was well known for having built one of the more beautiful and most heavily frequented mosques in the city.

inclination) and a small staff of Indian doctors. Egbert Fell, a friend of Scudder's since his days as a student at Rush Medical School, had just retired from the University of Chicago Medical School and offered to come out in the winter of 1964 to cover during the crisis.[34]

The major surgery Lew Scudder underwent in Chicago was successful, and his recovery was dramatic.[35] During his year-and-a-half convalescence,

[34]In the conversation between the author and Simeon Thiligam, John Balasundaram, and Isaac Wilson in Chicago June 20, 1990 (to which we have already referred), the following observations are recorded in the author's notes: "When Pennings took over after Nykerk died and LRS was taken to the USA sick, there was a dramatic change. Pennings was a Cook County trained physician and very pedantic as a surgeon. What took the others fifteen minutes took him three hours. The hospital almost emptied out. Thiligam observed that it was almost as though he intended to close the hospital. Jacob Oomen returned and things picked up.

"Al Pennings had a hard time communicating and did not inspire confidence as a leader. Incident: Al explaining something to a bedouin in the hospital for fifteen minutes. Afterward the bedouin called Thiligam over: "Ya Rafîq, hadhâ shinû yagûl?" [Hey, buddy, what's this guy saying?] [Author's comment: In his defense, Pennings thought of himself not as a surgeon but primarily as an internist.]

"Egbert Fell, who then arrived, was not a missionary doctor. He was a Chicago specialist who did not know how to rely on simple operations and do quick diagnoses. Incident—hysterectomy on a young woman: The uterus was removed and when sliced open revealed a four-week-old foetus. Thiligam observed that that would never have happened with LRS.

"Fell, in his specialty of open-heart surgery, was very good. The little things baffled him and he was awkward. He too, almost from the day of his arrival, spoke of closing down the hospital."

[35]The story of this event deserves a cameo: After his collapse in Kuwait, Lew Scudder was first diagnosed as suffering from exhaustion. He had shouldered a double load of responsibilities after Jerry Nykerk's death. But as signs of paralysis became evident, it was clear to his attending physician, his friend, Peter Wilson, that he was suffering from a growing blood clot on the right side of his brain. Wells Thoms flew up from Oman to accompany Dorothy and Lew back to Chicago, Illinois. On the same PanAm flight from London to Chicago was a Mr. Maxwell, the managing editor of the *Chicago Tribune*. He asked Wells Thoms to explain who the man on the stretcher was. Thoms could spin a good tale when put to it, and he did so then. When they landed in Chicago, Lew was quickly admitted to Presbyterian-St. Luke's Hospital. His diagnostician was Dr. Bertram Nelson, his medical school friend. The surgery—one exploratory procedure and a second major operation—by Eric Olberg was quickly and competently done. The very day of his first surgery, on the front page of the *Chicago Tribune*, there appeared a full column article on Lew Scudder and his trial. Almost immediately the gathered family could feel a presence around them. And then the cards began pouring in from the Midwest and around the country. There was a palpable nexus

Lew and Dorothy Scudder were encouraged by John Buteyn, secretary for the Middle East for the Board of World Mission, to consider early retirement. With that possibility in mind, Dorothy returned to Kuwait to pack up personal effects. By the spring of 1966, however, they had made up their minds to return to Kuwait. The need of the hospital was urgent, and Lew Scudder's recovery was so satisfactory that they both felt they could resume their responsibilities.

John Buteyn, pursuing another agenda, insisted that they delay their return until a new administrator for the hospital could be found. Dorothy Scudder, he insisted, had to find other areas of activity. He noted that there were unacceptable tensions between mission staff which had their focus in Dorothy Scudder.[36] The condition for their return to Kuwait was that she not continue officially as hospital administrator. In the end, Haydar M. al-Khalīfah assumed the position of administrator, a task for which the Scudders had been grooming him in any case.[37]

---

of prayer focused upon Lew Scudder in those days, a good deal of it inspired in people by having read the newspaper. The *Tribune* continued to follow the story through Lew's hospitalization. Under the watchful eye of Bert and Helen Nelson, the quick and full recovery which he made in the months which followed was, in Christian terms, a testimony to the power of prayer—a true miracle.

[36] Dorothy Scudder formed strong opinions about people and could express them bluntly. She was not among the saints who "tolerate fools gladly." She had often crossed swords with Gerrit De Jong, and during his final term as pastor in Kuwait she did not get along well with Jake Holler. But it became clear that the main tension to which Buteyn referred was between Dorothy and Elaine Sluiter, the matron of the Olcott Memorial Hospital, who resented her elder colleague's administrative oversight and interference.

[37] The rather heavy discussion leading to the agreement between Buteyn and the Scudders took place July 18, 1966, in Chicago. In his report of that discussion, Buteyn reflects the tension building between himself and Dorothy Scudder, a tension which he was prepared to resolve by dictate if necessary. His principal concern was that the Scudders had built the hospital operation into a family business in which other missionaries did not participate. The sense of discontent on the part of those "others" was clearly part of the tension which he noted. In removing Dorothy Scudder from a pivotal role in the hospital, he anticipated that a greater sense of "team spirit" would evolve. When he accepted Haydar al-Khalīfah's appointment as hospital administrator, the way was cleared for the Scudders to return to Kuwait. (Confidential report: Summary of Interview with Dr. and Mrs. Lewis Scudder, July 18, 1966, is in the author's document collection.) Predictably, what actually evolved was that, as Dorothy had been accustomed to do in a car all her married life, she simply carried on administering the hospital "from the back seat."

Buteyn's conditions having been met, the Scudders arrived back in Kuwait in September, 1966.[38] In their absence the hospital had fallen on hard times. Alfred Pennings had tried valiantly to keep the system running assisted by Haydar al-Khalîfah.[39] Egbert Fell had filled a gap, but his case work-up and surgical methods were schooled in a different culture and setting, and the surgical load had fallen drastically in spite of the presence of Jacob Oomen, a brilliant Indian surgeon, on the staff. Income was down; hospital beds lay vacant; morale was low. This, with a tremendous outpouring of energy, was quickly rectified and the hospital soon returned to a healthy posture. Egbert Fell soon moved on to a short-term appointment in Iran whence he retired a year later.

At the same time John Buteyn was spearheading a determined drive to pare back the mission's medical program in the Gulf.[40] In 1964, with the retirement of Harold Storm, the mission hospital in Bahrain declared itself to be in serious fiscal and administrative crisis. In response, in September, the board recruited a consultant, James C. McGilvray,[41] to conduct with

---

[38]A small but highly symbolic gesture was made by an old neighbor as the Scudders returned to Kuwait. They were told by their good friend, Muhammad Sâyir, that he wanted to pay a formal call. He came with a lamb and performed a ritual sacrifice of thanksgiving on Lew Scudder's feet. It was a highly symbolic moment of return.

[39]Haydar al-Khalîfah had been recalled urgently from his studies in hospital administration in Tanta, Egypt, to take over the administrative load in Dorothy Scudder's absence.

[40]Since the mid-1950s the board had been engaged in close examination of the Arabian Mission's major institutions. This was inspired by the serious question, whether the mission of Christ's Church was actually prospered by its being locked into supporting increasingly expensive hospitals and schools. Spencer T. Snedecor, a physician from Long Island, New York, was appointed to head up a Medical Advisory Committee in October, 1962 (upgraded in 1966 to a Medical Consultants Council). Between 1962 and 1966 this committee regularly came forward with constructive recommendations for improving the overall medical program of the mission. The most important recommendation had to do with strengthening the local fiscal and administrative accountability and autonomy of each mission hospital's board of managers.

[41]McGilvray was a Presbyterian with a history of missionary service in Pakistan and India. In 1964, when he was asked to visit Bahrain, he was associate medical secretary for the Commission on Ecumenical Mission and Relations of the United Presbyterian church. In 1965 he had moved on to the Christian Medical Council of the Division of Overseas Ministries of the National Council of Churches. His presence in the process was ominous. He brought with him a reputation, earned in Iran, as a determined institution closer.

Snedecor an investigation into the situation of Bahrain. Given that Kuwait at the time was also limping, they visited Kuwait as well. McGilvray had visited Kuwait the previous spring in the course of a tour that also covered Presbyterian hospitals in Egypt, Syria, Lebanon, and Iran.[42] As of the Board of World Mission's meeting in April, 1965, at which Lew and Dorothy Scudder and Mary Allison were guests, there was still no formally recorded suggestion that any of the mission hospitals be closed.

Seemingly moving off on a new tack, at the end of 1965 the board appointed a group comprised of McGilvray, Snedecor, and Buteyn. They were to focus upon the impact which increasingly autonomous medical programs were having upon the life of the church in the Gulf. This mandate was interpreted rather more broadly than it was recorded. By the end of 1966, a full-scale Arabian Mission Medical Study Team had been appointed. McGilvray, Snedecor, and Buteyn were part of it, to be sure, but it also included Russel Paalman (of the board); a second consultant, John Y. James;[43] and Donald Bosch (then chief medical officer in Bahrain) for the mission. They worked intensively between October 20 and November 1, 1966.

No sooner had they gotten back in harness, therefore, than the Scudders had to deal with the ten-day tour of the Arabian Mission Medical Study Team, and before them loomed the serious prospect of impending closure of the institution they had spent their whole lives building up. The litmus test the study team applied to determine whether a hospital would close or remain open was whether it was deemed essential and openly acknowledged to be so by the local government.

---

[42]His first visit to Kuwait took place from May 18 to 23, 1963, and his report (in the author's document collection) was frank and truthful. Significantly, in a rather proscriptive tone, he highlighted the question of whether it was healthy that the hospital had come to dominate in the life of the church in Kuwait. He also noted two incipient personnel problems: Dorothy Scudder was a competent hospital administrator but lacked the ability to delegate responsibility; Elaine Sluiter insisted upon more administrative responsibilities and was experiencing a "failure of gratification in work accomplishments." As we have noted, between Dorothy Scudder and Elaine Sluiter there was little love lost. The general tension within the mission group was further exacerbated, however, when Jake Holler (who, as pastor, should have maintained a measure of neutrality) openly favored Sluiter's cause. Buteyn had chosen Holler as his principal local advisor. This, in essence, was a time-bomb waiting to explode.

[43] John James represented Hospital Planning Associates, a consultancy group based in San Francisco.

In 1966 it was obvious that the hospitals in Oman could not be closed. They were then the only institutions of their kind in the whole country. The hospital in Bahrain, on the other hand, was on rocky footing. After 1964 it had had to pare back its activities and trim down its expenses, but the Bahrain government quite emphatically insisted that it was still a needed institution. The ruler in particular, Shaykh 'Îsâ bin-Salmân Âl Khalîfah, was adamant on that score. When John Buteyn and John James approached the Kuwait minister of health, 'Abd-ul-'Azîz al-Fulayj, for a similar statement to the one they had received in Bahrain, he told them that while the people of Kuwait had deep respect for the American Mission Hospital, and while it was a valued institution in the country, he would *not* say that it was vital to the state's overall medical program.

Had the question been raised during the reign of Shaykh 'Abd-Allâh as-Sâlim, the answer would have been differently given. But the regime of Shaykh Sabâh as-Sâlim (ruler since 1965) was less friendly toward the mission, and the question was posed at a time when the government—the Ministry of State and the Ministry of Health in particular—was under the strong influence of the Muslim Brotherhood movement. The Kuwait government simply did not have the political will to make the kind of statement the study team demanded as a condition for keeping the hospitals open. And whatever else the study team may have thought they were saying, the requested statement was perceived as a *political* demand.[44]

In spite of this, in discussions with Buteyn and James during the team's visit, the Scudders believed they had received reassurance that the Kuwait hospital, of all the mission hospitals in the Gulf, was in the best state of health. In fact, except during the period of crisis between 1964 and 1966, reserves generated in Kuwait had been significant enough to subsidize the

---

[44]The demand of the study team was, in fact, a political demand. Apart from the social forces working in the Kuwait government which were unfriendly to the mission, Kuwait was also walking a tightrope with its powerful northern neighbor, Iraq. Iraq was militantly anti-American, and Kuwait was trying to establish a little political distance between itself and the United States on the assumption (mistaken, as it turned out) that it would make for better long-term relations with Iraq. To be seen as making any concession to Americans, at that time, was against policy. The second political dimension was Islamic: Kuwait, then attempting to project an Islamic image for the benefit of its other large neighbor, Sa'ûdî Arabia, could not be seen as confessing itself beholden to a Christian body, much less proclaim that its presence was vital. Both of these factors, but explicitly the latter, were made quite clear to the study team.

medical work in Bahrain and Oman. They were told that Bahrain's hospital, with its dilapidated facilities, financial crises, and shaky administration, was the most likely to close. While that did not cheer them, it did ease their local anxieties.

The Board of World Mission met in Warwick, New York, November 15-17, 1966, and received the report and recommendations of the Medical Study Team. It decided to close the Kuwait hospitals within a period not to exceed two years. How that decision related to the overall health and prospects of the church in Kuwait does not seem to have been a consideration.[45] As Christmas season approached, the utterly unexpected November decision of the board was brought personally by Buteyn. He presented the decision to a meeting of Kuwait Mission Station on the morning of November 19. The hospital's board of managers was informed on Tuesday, November 22.[46] The timing was not felicitous. There was no Thanksgiving.

That word of the Board of World Mission was not received without challenge. Buteyn proceeded to communicate the board's decision to Kuwait's minister of health, 'Abd-ul-'Azîz Ibrâhîm al-Fulayj, and to execute the mandate he had been given as quickly as possible. As soon as word got out to the wider Kuwaiti community, there was a last-ditch attempt to change the board's decision. A group of Kuwaiti merchants, led by Shaykhân al-Fârisî, offered a plan for endowing the hospital, and the Community Medical Corporation offered to run the hospital as a private concern, but

[45]Simeon Thiligam, interviewed with his colleagues John Balasundaram and Isaac Wilson June 20, 1990, noted that the closing of the hospital was universally deplored as unnecessary. McGilvary explained to him that the purpose of Jesus' raising Lazarus was not to bring him back to life but to demonstrate the Kingdom. Therefore, having done the demonstration in Kuwait, McGilvary noted, the mission was free to move out. The author's contemporary note: "Thiligam still does not quite understand the argument." Neither does the author, for that matter.

[46]John Buteyn's "Summary Report on J. Buteyn's Visit to Kuwait – November 18 to 24 – Schedule and Guidelines for the Phasing Out of the Medical Program at the American Mission Hospital in Kuwait," dated November 29, 1966, is in the author's document collection.

these offers were rejected out of hand.[47] Given the quick and energetic response from the Kuwait public, Buteyn did not see any reason to prolong the agony to the two year maximum time allowed.

The ensuing contest pitted two very strong-willed people against each other: John Buteyn and Dorothy Scudder. But in his hand lay the balance of power, and Buteyn pressed on to resolution. He set the closing date for the 31st of March, 1967.[48] The near coincidence of this action with the subsequent Arab-Israeli War of June, 1967, and the precipitous further plunge of American prestige in the Gulf was most unfortunate. More unfortunate still was the fact that it seriously compromised Buteyn's relations with the church in Kuwait for years to come and left a deep reserve of distrust and pain in his relations with the Scudders senior which never fully worked itself out.

Through the early months of 1967, the Scudders dealt with the agonies of shutting down the medical program. There were the many delicate personnel questions to be dealt with. A good number of the staff were placed with the government's health service.[49] Elaine Sluiter, matron of the Olcott Memorial Hospital for women, chose to go into government service.[50] Ruth Joldersma came out to assist Dorothy Scudder and Marj and Bob Vander Aarde (the hospital chaplain) through the painful transition, and her presence was a genuine comfort.[51] After the medical operations had been shut down but

---

[47]Letter from John Buteyn to Lew Scudder, Sr.; Bob Vander Aarde (hospital chaplain); and Mr. Hamilton (chairman of the hospital's board of managers) dated January 13, 1967, p. 2 (document in the author's collection).

[48]John E. Buteyn, area secretary, "Report on Hospital Closing and New Programs in Kuwait (Revision from Presentation to the Board on April 13, 1967)" (document in the author's collection).

[49]Among the most exceptional of these was Nurse Rukmani, who had been with the mission since the early 1950s. She went on to serve in the clinic of the small village on the Island of Faylaka, where her missionary motivation won her the love and respect of everyone whom she touched. Many of the others found places in various government hospitals and clinics and served well, keeping in close touch with the Scudders.

[50]Elaine Sluiter, who had joined the mission in 1962, had a somewhat prickly personality. She did not take to the experiment of a missionary serving in a government institution and resigned from the mission in the spring of 1970 and returned to the United States.

[51]Ruth Joldersma, for entirely different reasons, was not to continue long in the employ of the Reformed church. With the restructuring of the denomination's boards and agencies into the General Program Council, Ruth was structured out of a job. It was a serious loss of talent to the denomination.

before the formal closing ceremonies on March 30, Lew and Dorothy Scudder took a much-needed break, driving with their son and daughter-in-law overland to Beirut, where the younger Scudders were to begin language study.

In the aftermath, the elder Scudders were offered three options: they could go to another of the mission's hospitals; they could be seconded to the Kuwait government as Elaine Sluiter had elected to do; or they could retire. Feeling seriously isolated and carrying a burden of pain, disappointment, and resentment, the Scudders decided to remain in Kuwait. Their decision was conditioned by four factors: they were deeply committed to the people of Kuwait to the point of shared identity; there was some major public relations repair work to be done in Kuwait for the mission; they felt that they had many more good years left to give; and they felt a vocation toward sustaining the National Evangelical Church in Kuwait, which now lay exposed.[52]

Eventually they were asked by the then minister of defense, Shaykh Sa'ad al-'Abd-Allâh, to take over and develop the Kuwait Military Hospital. And this, for his sake and in memory of his father, their friend, Lew and Dorothy decided to do. They were seconded to the Kuwait government but remained active missionaries until the end. Lew Scudder, at sixty-nine years of age, died of a heart attack on the Kuwait Club tennis court April 3, 1975, and was buried in Kuwait as he had wished. Dorothy continued to serve in Kuwait until the early summer of 1990, when she was forced into extended leave by the Iraqi invasion of Kuwait. A few months short of eighty years old, ill in Chicago but still insisting she was going to return to Kuwait, Dorothy Scudder died of multiple strokes in the aftermath of cancer treatments July 10, 1991. It would have been her fifty-fourth wedding anniversary. She was the longest serving of Arabia's missionaries (fifty-four years).

[52]Their continued presence in Kuwait through the '60s and the '70s benefited the church. On several occasions Lew Scudder was asked to mediate with the Kuwaiti authorities as pressures to close or move the church were brought to bear upon it. The continued close relationship between the Scudders and the present prime minister, Shaykh Sa'ad al-'AbdAllâh, assured the church of a sympathetic hearing at an effective level.

Following the hospitals' closings, the mission at first tried to think what it might do with the vacant buildings. Harvey Staal ran a book shop for a while in a portion of the Olcott Memorial Hospital for Women, but he was obliged by zoning regulations to relocate in a commercial district. A leading suggestion was that the mission set up and operate some kind of youth and community program along the lines of the YM/YWCA. Another proposal was to develop an ecumenical center, possibly offering communities like the Greek Orthodox and others permanent places for worship. But this remained just talk. Public sentiment was against it. John Buteyn, warned that serious developments were in the offing, in April, 1967, tried to "sell" the portion of the property on which the church actually stood to the National Evangelical Church for one Kuwait dinar.[53] However, when the church tried to effect the transfer of ownership, it was rejected by the government for a number of reasons, the most ominous and serious of which was that the National Evangelical Church, in and of itself, could not be considered an indigenous entity in Kuwait entitled to own land.

There was popular disgruntlement with the mission for what the Reformed church had done. Mary Allison observed, "The Arabs considered the hospital to be the mission itself. They came to the conclusion that Christianity was inferior to the wealth and power of the world."[54] Since the Reformed church had freely chosen to close its hospitals, the special dispensation permitting the mission to own property was thereby abrogated. In March, 1969, the government announced its intention to begin expropriation proceedings against the mission. The whole property—hospitals, church, residences, all—was to be turned over to the Kuwait government, and the Reformed church was to accept compensation in the amount of KD 840,000 (roughly equivalent to $3,150,000). This was about ten percent of the value of the property and the buildings. It was a deliberately administered slap in

[53]The proposal that the mission deed over the church portion of the property had been under consideration by the board since at least June 1964. Action on the proposal continued to be postponed for a variety of reasons, none of which were very convincing to the Arabic Language Congregation.

[54]Mary Bruins Allison, *Doctor Mary in Arabia: Memoirs by Mary Bruins Allison, M. D.* (Austin, Texas: University of Texas Press, 1994), p. 252. If possible, even more intensely than the Scudders, Mary Allison continued embittered about the hospitals' closure until the day she died in 1995. Expressing this in her memoirs, she said, "The hospital was my child. I was witnessing its dying gasp. And it was my Church that was killing it" (p. 252).

the face, but, disappointing though it was, it did not come as a great surprise.[55] More serious was the threat it posed for the National Evangelical Church, which worshiped on the grounds of the mission.[56]

In 1974 the government bonds were sold at discount. John Buteyn told the National Evangelical Church that, in the eventuality that it had to relocate and rebuild, it could draw the equivalent of KD 84,000 ($250,000) from these funds.[57] The total expropriation funds were transferred to the New York account of the Reformed church, viewed as windfall, where they went a long way to keeping the denomination afloat through the bad years that followed.[58] 'Tis an ill wind truly that blows no one any good.

[55]As early as the beginning of 1967, the mission had warned the board that the Kuwait government would be entirely within its rights to expropriate the property. The response of John James and John Buteyn at the time was incredulity that such an ungracious attitude would be adopted.

[56]The upshot for the National Evangelical Church was, truly, serious. Minister of state, Yûsuf ar-Rifâ'î, contemplated offering the church building to a Muslim organization to be transformed into a mosque. But he fell from grace and out of power before he could do anything serious in that regard. The whole affair was one deeply regretted by a significant portion of Kuwaiti society. The church, represented by Lew Scudder and Harvey Staal and advised by Haydar al-Khalîfah, applied to the government for some arrangement whereby they might continue to worship on the grounds. They were finally granted a nominal annual lease of half the property for KD 75 a year, which amount Yûsuf 'Abd-un-Nûr, pastor of the Arabic Language Congregation and President of the National Evangelical Church's Common Council, religiously paid to the Ministry of Housing every year. In later years the government cast covetous eyes on the property for prestige development—first to erect prestige housing for Kuwaiti university graduates who had missed the land-grab of the 1960s (mid-1970s) and then to build the headquarters of the Kuwait National Petroleum Company (the late 1980s). But the Kuwait public, at both times, raised an outcry to forbid it, and the buildings were eventually registered as historical buildings, marked for preservation. In 1995 the two hospitals and their outbuildings were given over to Dâr-ul-Âthâr al-Islâmiyyah museum for restoration to their original design as part of a UNESCO-staffed project. These buildings will then serve the museum as temporary quarters. Their long-term fate is still an open question.

[57]This decision was taken by the General Program Council in April, 1969.

[58]That this is indeed what happened was pointed out to the author some years later by Arie Brouwer, then general secretary of the Reformed church. John Buteyn had gone on record as pledging that the funds received would go to assisting other places where there was need in the Gulf. And truly, to have invested the funds to bring Bahrain or Oman's medical work up to standard would have made a world of difference at the time. Eventually, after intense discussion, the $250,000 pledged to the National Evangelical Church in Kuwait were transferred to Kuwait in 1975 to be held in trust against major needs. Other than this amount,

Medical Work in Bahrain

From its beginnings in 1892 with Samuel Zwemer's medical bag, we have already had occasion to remark upon the beginnings of medical work in Bahrain. The Mason Memorial Hospital was built by the Drs. Thoms in 1901, and from then on the work developed steadily.

The Mason Memorial Hospital served both men and women. In 1924, in memory of Marion Wells Thoms who died in 1905, a hospital for women was built and did much to relieve the strain.[59] When the new women's hospital opened, Cornelia Dalenberg (a highly competent staff nurse) and Regina Harrison together covered the basic needs, calling in the male doctors from the Mason Memorial Hospital for serious cases. Mary Tiffany (from 1927 to 1933) and Esther Barny (from 1936 to 1945), physicians both, helped meet the needs of women in Bahrain as the new hospital attracted more patients. In 1950 an annex to the Marion Thoms Memorial Hospital provided delivery rooms and extra ward space. But the old Mason Memorial was condemned in the early 1950s. Bahrain's high humidity and rising damp had undermined its foundations and walls, and the old bedraggled building was the cause of much anguish (and some anxiety).[60] Funds to rebuild were not

none of the Kuwait funds were used in the Gulf, in spite of obvious major needs in the other stations. When asked why, Brouwer responded that, after all, it was the Reformed church's money, and it had to be used where the denomination most needed it. It also represented a breaking of publicly pledged word. To that observation Brouwer responded merely with a shrug of his shoulders.

[59]Interestingly, the land on which this new hospital was built was donated by ʿAbd-ul-ʿAzîz al-Qusaybî, the agent for ʿAbd-ul-ʿAzîz Âl Saʿûd in Bahrain. Of the 35,000 rupees it took to build the hospital, 25,000 was raised locally.

[60]Having just returned to Bahrain from celebrating the opening of the Mylrea Memorial Hospital in Kuwait, Joyce Dunham, in an encyclical written to "Dear Friends" in November 1955, made these observations: "The [mission] meetings began with the dedication of the new Mylrea Memorial Hospital, a beautiful, new, modern building which will no doubt render real Christian service to the people of Kuwait for many years to come. There was a day when the mission hospital here in Bahrain had the respect of the whole island, but lately we have been told that unless we improve our buildings and equipment we will lose that respect and the government may be rather hard on us. We realize that the building is not the whole matter, and so do many patients who could get the use of better equipment in the government hospital, but who still come to us because we offer something "special." However, we feel that a Christian hospital should at least come up to minimum standards and we are hoping that it will be possible in the not too distant future to have a new hospital in Bahrain" (from correspondence loaned to the author by Jim and Joyce Dunham).

raised until 1961, and the new Mason Memorial Hospital, built on a shoe-string budget by Casey De Jong, opened for business February 23, 1962.[61]

By 1964, however, the hospital found itself in serious financial crisis. In June of that year, Harold Storm retired. Donald Bosch took over, for three years, as chief medical officer, moving up from Oman.[62] Patient load dropped dramatically (blamed on the advent of free government health care). The aging Marion Thoms Memorial Hospital for women was gobbling up maintenance funds. The mission called for help, and the board sent James McGilvray and Spencer Snedecor to take a look. Their report recommended a severe paring back of the medical program, reducing the drug inventory severely, closing half the wards, and shutting down the women's hospital altogether. These measures had a palliative effect, and the prospects for recovery began to look better.[63] But by the time the Arabian Mission Medical Study Team began its work in October, 1966, Bahrain hospital was still only just managing to survive. The only factor which diverted the ax from falling on the Mason Memorial Hospital in Bahrain instead of the Mylrea and Olcott Memorial Hospitals in Kuwait was the strong intervention of the Bahrain government and the personal demand of Shaykh 'Îsâ that the hospital not be closed.[64]

[61]There was strong resistance in the mission to building an expensive new hospital in Bahrain. The cost of the new hospital in Kuwait seemed to some excessive. The pressure to downscale aspirations for Bahrain in the 1950s, in the long run, proved damaging.

[62]The assassination of Maurice Heusinkveld in Oman in 1967 made it necessary for Don Bosch to return there [Angela Clarke, *The American Mission Hospital, Bahrain: Through the Changing Scenes of Life: 1893-1993* (Bahrain: The American Mission Hospital Society, 1993), p. 199].

[63]Angela Clarke, the historian of the American Mission Hospital in Bahrain, observes, "By the early 1960s it was apparent that the Arabian Mission's hospitals in Bahrain had become a clinic operation with an expensive in-patient facility attached to it." The management procedures of the hospitals were eating away at its foundations, and she quotes James McGilvray to say, "If this trend continues it may become necessary to close the hospital. What are the alternatives?" (Clarke, ... *Changing Scenes*, pp. 197-198).

[64]Interview with Donald Hepburn, March 13, 1990. The ruler's open attitude toward Christians was epitomized in the words he spoke on the occasion of the dedication of the new National Evangelical Church in Bahrain on June 3, 1971. As Mary Allison has recorded them, they were as follows:

"Ladies and gentlemen. It gave us great pleasure to be invited to open this church this afternoon. The reason is simple. We, our government and our people, are aware that the American Mission has done much work in Bahrain for many years to the advantage of the people, irrespective of race or religion. This has

As an institution, the hospital was competing for attention with a quickly expanding school and a thriving church community, both of which required urgent investment to keep pace with their growth. Don Bosch's brief tenure as CMO of the hospital was bedeviled by the trauma of the closure of Kuwait Hospital in 1967. Bosch had to return to Oman in May, but he was not replaced until, in November, Alfred Pennings (still convalescing from a confrontation with tuberculosis) arrived to assume the hospital's leadership. In the meantime, the mechanism had been kept going by Yûsuf Haydar (as business manager) and Dr. Abraham Koshy, an Indian physician on local contract. "As Pennings later remarked, Dr. Koshy bridged many years with Drs. Harrison and Storm, saw this whole period of change and remained a thread of continuity throughout."[65]

always been appreciated, but it is not often that we have such a good chance to say so in public.

"The medical services which you provide, and all the additional services which you give, are fine examples of generosity and good works, qualities for which you are well known throughout our islands. The book shop which you run is also to the educational advantage of our people.

"In Bahrain today we try to foster the spirit of tolerance, education and progress, and this we hope, explains the reason why we are so pleased to be here to express our appreciation of what you have done in the past, what you are doing now and what we hope you will continue to do.

"It is therefore with great pleasure that we are able formally to open this beautiful new church. We hope that freedom of worship will always exist and different religious will continue to flourish side by side in Bahrain" (Allison, *Doctor Mary*, p. 272).

[65]Clarke, ...*Changing Scenes*, p. 202. Aside from the legendary service of Abraham Koshy (1952-1983), Bahrain was blessed by the service of several outstanding and devoted Indian medical professionals. There was Dr. Jacob Chandy who, as a young bachelor physician, served the mission hospital in Bahrain between 1938 and 1944, before going on to a distinguished career as a professor of medicine at the Christian Medical Center in Vellore, South India. Miss Ramba Singh, a nurse, came to the American Mission Hospital in 1945. She was an adventurous one, accompanying the mission doctors on tours into Sa'ûdî Arabia on several occasions. She retired in 1967 but continued as a definite presence and in residence in Bahrain with her nephew, Anand Singh, until he left Bahrain in 1992. Nurse Pushpa came to the Mission Hospital in Bahrain in 1948 and died upon the high seas when the BI liner *Dara*, was bombed by an Omani revolutionary group in 1964. James Simon was another Indian nurse who died in harness, serving from 1945 to 1965. C. Swamickan, a tall, even-tempered Tamil, came to the hospital in 1957 and worked himself up until he became director of the nurses' training program. He retired in 1983, a year after that program was closed down.

Having been recruited by Cornelia Dalenberg, in 1954 a twenty-one-year-old Indian nurse arrived in Bahrain. S. Rathinam John Peter (known by the last two

After several consecutive years of deficit budgets, under Pennings's leadership and with an active board of managers, the year 1969 ended in the black.[66] In 1971 the hospital was given a new constitution for its Board of Managers, and that coincided in August with the declaration of Bahrain's independence from British oversight. Independence ushered in a new Ministry of Health, which set about issuing new regulations for medical practice. The increasing government interference raised anxieties. In 1973 the hospital experienced the invasion of modernity in the form of an employee strike for higher wages. It brought the institution to the edge of a serious crisis. The staff responded to Pennings's appeal, they returned to work, and salaries and benefits were improved. But the hospital was still pulling heavily on a up-hill grade.

By 1974 the financial picture and performance statistics had shown a marked improvement, and a master plan for the hospital was adopted in 1975. Angela Clark observes, "The encouraging statistics for the early 1970s can only be interpreted as evidence of immense staff commitment and perseverance as they struggled to live and work under very trying conditions."[67] The 1975 master plan was reevaluated in 1976, and the whole

names only) was as much a child of the Arcot Mission as any missionary child. He came to Bahrain with a high missionary motive which was quickly appreciated. From 1959 to 1964 he was given leave of absence to study at the University of Pennsylvania, earning qualification as a nurse anesthetist and taking special courses in ophthalmic nursing at Wills Eye Hospital at Temple University. His return to Bahrain upgraded the staff significantly. He married a young dietitian, Rosalind, in 1966, and her arrival further strengthened the services the hospital offered (she retired in 1986). Beyond his duties in the operating room, John also shouldered duties as the manager of the hospital's stores, a position which came to dominate his work schedule. In 1978 he was given special training in purchasing and hospital materials management and continued as purchasing director until his retirement in 1994, a remarkable forty-year career. As any missionary, both John and Rosalind Peter were active in the local church, serving to build up both the English Language and Tamil Christian congregations. In 1965, John founded the local chapter and became the local contact person for Alcoholics Anonymous and ministered in a discreet manner to several members of the Bahraini community. (From notes written by John Peter and in conversation between him and the author, November 11, 1995.)

The story of the Peters is not unique, although it is outstanding. The Mission was blessed in Bahrain and other stations by Indian servants of Christ who were no less 'missionary' than their western colleagues.

[66]Suggestions that capital from the sale of the property in Kuwait might be well used in Bahrain were never seriously entertained.

[67]Clarke, ...*Changing Scenes*, p. 218.

process of physical improvement was put on hold pending the design of a financial program to support it.

It was at this point that a powerful influence was introduced into the hospital's board of managers in the person of Donald F. Hepburn, chief executive of the Bahrain Petroleum Company.[68] He came onto the board early in 1979 and, with the departure of Alan Moore from Bahrain, was elected to the chair in November 1979. As he came into his responsibilities, Alfred Pennings also announced his resignation to be effective in June, 1980. Reflecting upon the challenge before him at that time, Hepburn said,

> I was probably the least qualified to take the job, because I was probably the most recent member of the Board, and had no medical background. But what they were looking for was someone with managerial skills that they presumed I had.
>
> At the time the Hospital was in a very, very difficult condition. And, in effect I was being asked to manage its closure...manage its demise. I took a look at the situation and said, "Well, there are things that we can do to help overcome the problems."
>
> They had a very unbusinesslike way of running a hospital. I looked at the fee structure and discovered that the way they had structured the fees was that the hospital would recover the operating costs, but would not include in the fees structure the major maintenance and reconstruction program. There was no depreciation, in a technical accounting sense, being added. So the money being recovered in expenses did not provide for any reconstruction work nor any major maintenance work. And the hospital was gradually falling down.
>
> Now, apart from the obvious economic problems that represented, it had a very depressing impact on the hospital staff and on the people who were using it. And the people who were using the hospital—loyal to the institution—were gradually feeling that the institution itself was dying.
>
> About six months after I became the chairman Al Pennings decided that it was time for him to go back to the States. I had

[68]From 1979 Hepburn served on the American Mission Hospital Board of Managers, much of the time as its chair. If the ruler, Shaykh 'Îsâ, was the primary factor in the hospital's survival, Don Hepburn was certainly the person who made the Shaykh's resolve a practical one.

admired Al enormously, but in a sense Al and I had started from different points of view: I was a business man charged with the responsibility of looking at the business operation of the hospital. I had defined a considerable overstaffing problem of about thirty or forty people which I recommended that we release forthwith in order to cut down on our operating costs. As a missionary and a humanist—a human being—Al had great difficulty in coping with that. In the end, however, he recognized the inevitability: You either fire thirty or you release a hundred and thirty, because the hospital would shut down. There would be no jobs for anybody. So the practical aspect of this proposal became apparent and he accepted it. And he proceeded to release the people whom I had identified as being surplus to our needs.

From that we ended up with a new understanding...a new relationship. But I suspect that I made Al Pennings' last six months in the hospital very uncomfortable.[69]

There can be little doubt that, without Don Hepburn, the Reformed church would probably have closed down Bahrain Hospital, the objections of the ruler notwithstanding. But Don articulated a special vision for the hospital and its role:

During this period, as I said, for four years we had several visitors who recommended that we shut down, and the RCA representatives came out and at times we had rather intense debates. And what I told them consistently, uniformly and with some emotion was that to shut down the hospital would be a serious mistake in judgment, because the hospital represented something very special in terms of the Christian presence on the Island.

The hospital had its roots in the history of Bahrain not in a casual or superficial way, but in a deeply held respect for the institution by the Bahrainis, by the Muslims. They [the Bahrainis] saw the hospital as a manifestation of Christian charity, Christian service, Christian caring, and it was a contrast to many of their own institutions. It provided something of a model, something of a standard to be achieved.

[69]Hepburn, *Interview*, March 13, 1990.

... My argument was that the hospital also had a lot to do with the attitude of the ruler towards religious freedom—his very liberal attitude toward the presence of other faiths—and the open practice of Christians and others was because he had seen in the hospital and its service to the community. This was an admirable, commendable institution in his eyes, and these people represented no threat in his society...in his country. They were not subversive, they did not represent anything like a disturbance of the community that would cause problems socially. (I don't mean socially but in a community sense.)

We have about 150,000 expatriates in Bahrain, and many of them are Christians. We have something like twenty-six different churches. We are the only state in the Gulf that has complete freedom, and this despite the fact that we are right next door to Saudi Arabia where there is no freedom. And the contrast between the two states is tremendous. The hospital, therefore, to me, provided the basis of the special relationship which enabled Christians to practice Christianity and for Christians to demonstrate to the community what Christianity was about. And I was fearful that if we lost the hospital we would lose our freedom of religion, because in some way I suspected that the pressures that would ultimately come to bear on the whole question of freedom of religion might gather momentum if, in effect, we withdrew the RCA and along with it the hospital and even along with it the RCA presence in the church.

... I had been in India where I had seen the withdrawal of the Christian church in the context of Christian mission. I had seen what happened to the church as a result of the withdrawal. I felt very strongly that the Christian institutions led and managed and supported by the kind of leadership that the RCA provided would provide for the Christians that came and worked here—the migrant laborers, if you like, many of whom are very simple people with simple faith—an umbrella under which they all sheltered and continued to praise the Lord in a very alien and potentially hostile environment.

...The Christian church in the mission context in Bahrain has a witness of a very special kind. It's not measured in how many people were converted; it's measured in what kind of impact we have on society. I told you the other day about Yûsuf Shirâwî, minister of development and industry, acting minister of state for cabinet affairs, a spokesman for the Bahraini Government. I was sitting in the Diplomat Hotel with thirty people, among whom were represented the ten most important merchant families in Bahrain, together with the American ambassador, the admiral of the U. S. Joint Task Force and a whole lot of very influential people.

Unprompted by anybody Yûsuf got up and made a speech. In the context of that speech he chose to talk about the impact of the American Mission Hospital in Bahrain, speaking of it as having established a standard of ethical practice. He said it had made a very important contribution in society, and he called upon Hussayn Yateem and Ahmad Kanoo to bear witness: "Remember who was born there and the service of these doctors, the outstanding performance of people who selflessly served the community, for which there was no parallel?"

The hospital demonstrated something very special which came out of a Christian environment. The caring and the concern was what Yûsuf measured as the witness of Christians in this part of the world. To me, oddly enough, I think that the fact that there was a hospital, that there was a school that went with it, and that there was a church that provided a place in this area for Christians to worship in—the clear unequivocal stand of being Christians in a Muslim community—earned respect not just back in 1896 (or whenever it came to Bahrain) but over a succession of four consecutive rulers and has been sustained for a hundred years.

…Last year—in fact, the year before last—when His Highness agreed to be the patron of the hospital, he was making a public statement that, as a Muslim ruler in a country in which [Muslim] fundamentalism is an issue, and living next to Sa'ûdî Arabia in which the intensity of the Muslim expression is well known, he had the courage to say, "I am the patron of an American Mission Hospital."

…Now when I came onto the hospital board, I didn't know any of that. I didn't realize any of that. But in the time that I was on the board and before I became chairman I caught a glimpse of what this hospital meant. And when I saw it, when I saw its value and I recognized and understood it, I became committed to making sure it didn't disappear. I think the greatest ally I had in that campaign was Shaykh 'Îsâ.[70]

From then on, through the incumbency of two successor CMOs, Drs. Jack Hill (1980-1985) and Ted Herbelin (1985-1987)—spelled, occasionally, by the mission's veteran physician, Corine Overkamp[71]—the direction was in the firm hands of Don Hepburn and his chosen personnel, whether that direction was exercised directly from the chair of the board or from behind the scenes. The harder policies Hepburn insisted upon led to the resignation of Yûsuf Haydar as manager,[72] and in the spring of 1981 a new face appeared on the financial management staff, that of C. R. Panicker.[73] Gradually, the administrative patterns and fee structures were brought into line with goals, and serious investment in the physical plant was stepped up with the enlistment of Malcolm "Bud" Anderson as superintendent of the physical plant in 1985.[74]

[70]Hepburn, *Interview*, March 13, 1990.
[71]Dr. Corine Overkamp perhaps deserves a chapter by herself. Something of a character and with not the most charming of bedside manners, she has continued to serve as a missionary, celebrating her twenty-fifth year of service in Bahrain in 1990. At that celebration, officially hosted by the Bahrain Government and to which Dr. Alfred Pennings was also invited, many of Corine's detractors were amazed by the outpouring of affection and respect on the part of the Bahraini community for this devout and diligent physician.
[72]Another casualty of the Hepburn austerities was the mission hospital's popular and productive nurses' training program. For a variety of reasons, all of them accepted with some reluctance, the program was phased out in 1980.
[73]Officially Panicker, a Hindu, acted as assistant to Joanne Hill, who had been appointed acting business manager. While it was initially she who presented the hospital's business affairs to the Board of Managers, she soon came not to take an action without a strong briefing by Mr. Panicker. Subsequently, the fiction was laid aside, and Mr. Panicker became a regular feature of board meetings. In analyzing the performance of the hospital, Panicker brought pressure to bear upon the discipline of the physicians on the staff. As staff discipline improved, so did service, and the financial picture reflected the better performance of the hospital as a team.
[74]Angela Clarke quotes Bud Anderson: "You may laugh, but we actually decided to renovate the toilets first. We ripped them out completely and rebuilt them with brilliant white tiles, brilliant white fittings, and brilliant white walls, lots of lights and mirrors in order to give the impression of sparkling cleanliness and that we were moving forward. It worked. It actually worked. Almost immediately after we opened the toilets back up for use, the comments started flying as to how the hospital was really changing" (Clarke, ...*Changing Scenes*, p. 256). Anderson's

There was an ambiguity concerning the ultimate authority over the hospital. In 1971 John Buteyn had intimated in his sometimes too cautious and circuitous language that the hospital Board of Managers was the ultimate authority, but the circumlocution was too subtle. Until 1987 the board actually continued to think of itself as an agent for the Reformed Church in America, and of the Reformed church as actually making the final decisions on the board's recommendations. When that was clarified by Warren Henseler[75] in 1987, the board (and Don Hepburn) girded up their loins and began to move things in a decisive direction. All talk of closure ceased.

March 17, 1988, was a significant day in the history of the hospital. On that day Shaykh Khalîfah bin Salmân, the minister of labor and social affairs, issued Ministerial Order Number 5:

> We hereby charter the establishment of the "American Mission Hospital Society, Bahrain" in accordance with its Constitution which is attached to this order…[and which] shall be published in the Official Gazette and shall come into effect from the actual date of their issue."[76]

The registration of the American Mission Hospital Society, Bahrain, as a Bahraini philanthropic society took a full year to achieve once the terms of reference with the Reformed church's General Program Council had been sorted out.[77] The granting of the American Mission Hospital, Bahrain

---

approach to the overall problem of the hospital's physical plant, of course, was far more systematic and practical than this would suggest, but what he brought to his task was a lively sense of humor and a personal commitment that was infectious. Whatever he touched began to look better…healed, even. And a manifest sense of healing is a good one for a hospital to project.

[75]The Reformed church's Middle East and Africa secretary from 1980 to 1992.
[76]Clarke, …*Changing Scenes*, p. 268, quoting the *Official Gazette* of March 31, 1988.
[77]Hepburn remembers, "When I was working on the preparation of the registration of the hospital as a registered Bahraini institution—because that was what the law required in order for it to practice medicine—there was a big debate about what we should call the hospital. And he (the ruler) wouldn't hear of a change in the name.
   "When the constitution was written—which was a labor of love over about a period of a year and a half, tremendously frustrating, but it was accomplished—and we looked like having problems, I said to His Highness, 'It's going rather slowly.' And all of a sudden it went rather quickly, and one of the things he said was, 'The American Mission Hospital in Bahrain is its name.' He retained the

charter was accompanied by a second and no less important statement. It came in the form of a letter from Shaykh ʿÎsâ bin Salmân Âl Khalîfah, the Ruler of the State of Bahrain, to Mr. Donald F. Hepburn, Chairman of the Board of Directors. It was dated October 3, 1988, and read:

> It afforded me much pleasure to receive you and the other members of the Board of the American Mission Hospital Society in audience at Raffa'a Palace last Sunday. The enduring devotion of the doctors, nurses and staff of the American Mission Hospital in caring for the health and welfare of patients for almost ninety years has earned the profound admiration and gratitude of the government and all members of the community in Bahrain. In accepting your kind invitation to place the Society under my Patronage I extend to all at the Hospital my most heartfelt thanks for their constant and continuing dedication and my warmest good wishes for the future.[78]

A new leadership had taken over from Ted Herbelin as the end of 1987 approached. Dr. Paul Armerding became chief medical officer, and Ed Ryan took over as hospital administrator. They were in place to witness the last touches put upon the new charter of the hospital, and they have worked to keep the wheels of progress rolling.[79] The American Mission Hospital, Bahrain, continues to remain a viable institution.

Medical Work in Oman

Permanent medical work in Oman began as a service to women. Surprisingly, while the general medical ministry was caught short-handed, work with women in Oman was amplified by the building in Muscat of a

---

concept of its being 'mission.' He retained the concept of its being 'American.' Because they— both 'mission' and 'American'—were part of the heritage that it represented. Talk to almost any Bahraini over the age of forty, and his recollections of the hospital's role in this community is more than just an appendix operation or the curing of the flu and that sort of thing. It was much more. It represented something *of value* in the community" (Hepburn interview, March 13, 1990).

[78]Clarke, ...*Changing Scenes*, pp. 268-269.

[79]There are still those who, looking at the hospital's new direction and mandate, wonder whether the hospital continues to fulfill the qualifications of a mission institution. That debate will not end soon.

dispensary for women in 1913,[80] and, in 1914, with the posting there of a woman physician, Sarah Hosmon. With her peg leg, aggressive evangelical attitudes, straight-laced conservatism, and medical competence; with her love for touring in the villages when none other could even get beyond the capital area's defensive cordon; and with her sheer tirelessness, she provided the mission in Oman with one of its more colorful characters and fruitful workers until her controversial resignation May 12, 1939.[81] From 1916 until

[80]It consisted of a drug and treatment room, a ward with eight beds, and an operating room all surrounded by a wide verandah. It cost $1,300 to build.

[81]In a letter to the secretary of the mission, George Gosselink (dated May 15, 1939), Duke Potter recounted: "My recollections of Muscat are saddened by the thought of Dr. Hosmon's resignation. Only this morning I received a letter from her from Philadelphia, dated May 12th, in which she finally explains the reasons for her resignation. She traces these back to the winter of 1934, when in one of my official letters to the Arabian Mission I called attention to courses of study in the Union Theological Seminary of New York City and sent literature concerning what was being offered to missionaries. In the past year some similar reminder was sent. Dr. Hosmon has interpreted my action as 'definite official approval of modernism' and has decided that she must 'come out from among them and be separate.' The same letter conveyed to me the information that she had already applied to the Independent Board for Presbyterian Foreign Missions and had been accepted. I regret exceedingly the loss of a worker who has rendered such magnificent service down through the years. It is a real sorrow to me that an action of my own has so clearly brought this about. I do not accept all of Dr. Hosmon's accusations against Union Seminary nor do I feel that one who studies must isolate himself from those whose attitudes he may not entirely approve. At the same time, I only regret what has happened. I confess that I do not understand at all the procedure which Dr. Hosmon has followed. I tried very hard when in Muscat to get her to confide in me as to the reason for her prospective resignation. This she refused to do. Nor do I understand why she did not write to me in 1934 when the offense was first committed. I can quite understand disapproval but I cannot understand why this should not have been brought to my attention long ago for the frank interchange of opinion which I believe is called for under such circumstances.

"Under present circumstances it seems to me that Dr. Hosmon's withdrawal points pretty clearly to the closing of the hospital at Muscat. We have a large hospital now at Matrah and there is a general condition throughout the field of being understaffed in our medical work. There seems little prospect of remedying the condition radically in the near future. Our fiscal year just closed shows a budget out of balance by nearly $20,000. Under such circumstances it seems to me clear that concentration is called for " (document in author's collection).

In fact As-Sa'âdah Hospital, as the maternity facility in Muscat came to be named, was not closed. Nurse Mary (see the next note) was able to carry the routine clinic load with emergency assistance from Paul Harrison and Wells Thoms, the doctors in Matrah. The women's hospital continued to operate as part

1928, when the Harrisons were finally permanently posted in Matrah to resume the main medical effort, Hosmon, Fanny Lutton, Gerrit and Josephine Van Peursem, and the legendary "Nurse Mary"[82] held Oman virtually alone.

Beginning in 1929, Harrison built up the medical work in Oman for ten years, and made as lasting a mark there as in Bahrain. With the posting of

of the mission until 1973, and after that under the administration of the government of Oman.

As for Sarah Hosmon, she returned to the Gulf under her new mission sponsors, the Orthodox Presbyterians, to establish a hospital in the amîrate of Sharjah. She retired in 1962 and died July 25, 1964. By latest reports, the hospital she established in Sharjah is still operating.

[82]Recruited by Sarah Hosmon, Nurse Mary joined the mission in Oman in 1917. She had been trained in the Reformed church's Arcott Mission in Madnapale, India. She was a large woman with a gift for her main task of midwifery, and a strong and earnest sense of her missionary calling. When Jeanette Boersma first met her in 1949, she was fifty-five years old and very much a local institution. Jeanette recalls, "Technically, I was coming into the [Muscat] hospital as Nurse Mary's supervisor. But I knew I could never pull rank on this very special woman. I concentrated on learning from her and putting her skills to the best use" (Boersma, *Grace in the Gulf*, p. 96). Nurse Mary retired in 1952, a much and deservedly honored woman.

Midge Kapenga, in an anecdote among her answers (March 12, 1990) to a questionnaire circulated by the author, wrote: "Nothing we did in Muscat went unnoticed. One time we missionaries planned a progressive dinner that went to each of our homes and ended in Muttrah. The old mission house had an inside stair so one in another building could not see people going up and down. We all lived upstairs. Nurse Mary, our fine Indian nurse, watched some English people come to Jeanette's house, the mission house. They came up the front stairs but then left by the inner stair as Jeanette wanted to lock up her house. Jeanette locked her doors and closed her curtains and we all went on to Muttrah. But Nurse Mary had never seen us leave. She thought the worst. Next morning she came to Jeanette very angry and nearly in tears and began upbraiding us. She said all these men and women had come to Jeanette's house and then Jeanette had pulled the curtains and turned out the lights and what were we doing? Were we dancing? Or worse?? Jeanette explained to her that they had all gone on to the doctor's house in Muttrah for dessert and that she just hadn't seen them leave. She also had to admit that at the doctor's house we did Scottish dancing. Nurse Mary was not much mollified. Clearly we were not up to the standards of D. Hosmon, Dykstras, Pennings, and Van Peursems who would never have done such things. She had not slept all night contemplating our wickedness! What was the Mission coming to? Knowing Jeanette (Boersma), one of the most missionary-like of all of us, a truly good person, it was ironical that she had to face Nurse Mary's wrath."

Dirk Dykstra to Oman in 1930, the Knox Memorial Hospital[83] in Matrah was built and opened for business in 1933.[84] The Harrisons went on furlough in 1939 and were relieved by Beth and Wells Thoms. In Oman the

[83]First named after the donor of the funds, the hospital was later renamed more meaningfully *Ar-Rahmah* (Mercy) Hospital. The Women's Hospital in Muscat was given the name *As-Sa'âdah* Hospital (The Hospital of Happiness) at the same time.

[84]Dykstra introduced the use of concrete into Oman. Beth Thoms Dickason tells the following story:

"Mr. Dykstra was a very gifted man. He had lots of different skills. The mission appointed him to build the Knox Memorial Hospital. It was called that because the Knox family had been donors towards building it. And the mission...or the board gave him a certain sum of money...I forget how much it was now...and told him, 'That was it.' The doctor's bungalow and the Knox Memorial Hospital were to come out of that sum. So he began to study the situation. And he discovered that he could get sand almost free. Labor was very inexpensive. And he could get a whole shipment of Portland Cement out of England. And he figured he could do it within the $200,000 or so that they had given him. I think it was $80,000. I forget exactly, but that number...that figure is stuck in my mind: 80,000. So he gathered together masons and taught them how to mix cement, and he hired the local carpenter and worked with him.

"And they started building. The carpenter—his name was Khâbûrî, I remember...and we had some experience with Khâbûrî—he was a very gentle, kindly soul. Wells used him to make crutches for the patients that needed them. And Khâbûrî came proudly with crutches he had made and said, 'I got two crutches out of one strip of teak.' 'How did you do that?' 'Well I got one whole crutch and the other one I pieced.' Wells said, 'Let me see.' He put his weight on the crutches and the one that was pieced gave away. Wells said, 'This will never do.' That was the type of carpenter he was.

"When Mr. Dykstra built the hospital, the first thing they had to put up was the water tank. They built a cement water tank way up on stilts, on metal supports, and all the cement was poured. In order to pour the cement they had to build a wooden frame to hold the liquid cement in. So Khâbûrî was told to go and build the frame and build support for the frame. Well, after the cement had dried— they gave it a good long time to dry—Mr. Dykstra said to Khâbûrî, 'Well, you can knock out the supports now.' Khâbûrî didn't say anything, but he disappeared. He didn't come back for a long time. When he came back Mr. Dykstra said, 'Khâbûrî, where have you been?' 'Oh,' he said, 'Sahib, I've been to the mosque to pray. When I knock out those supports that'll come down on my head.'

"We had another experience with Khâbûrî. I wanted some shelves to put in the kitchen. We had just a plain cement square for the kitchen, nothing in it but a shelf of cement built up for a sink. So I asked Khâbûrî to put in shelves. He did. He came to me and said, "Khatûn, the shelves are ready. Do you want to come see them?" So I went into the kitchen and here the shelves were on wooden frames...the frame was in the corner of the kitchen. And I looked at them and they swayed over to the left. I said to Khâbûrî, 'That'll never do. They're leaning way over.' 'Oh,' he said, "*indî fikr*—I have a thought. I'll fix them.' So, in a little

Thoms found their niche. When the Harrisons returned from furlough, they returned to Bahrain and freed up Harold Storm for more active work in itinerating. From 1939 until their retirement in 1970, therefore, the Thoms were to be the dominant spirits in the Oman effort.

Wells Thoms was the second of the children of the Arabian Mission to return to the field as a professional and an adult. Beth Thoms was also a missionary child, daughter of L. R. Scudder of Ranipet, born and bred in India, a staunch member of the Scudder missionary clan. She had even served in India as a short-term teacher from 1927 until her marriage in 1930. After their appointment in 1930, the Thoms first studied Arabic in Jerusalem and then, under John Van Ess, in Basrah. In 1932 Wells was appointed to Bahrain to support Louis Dame as touring doctor and in the operating of the Mason Memorial Hospital until 1937. For two years, in relief of the furloughing Mylreas, they worked in Kuwait until their own time for furlough arrived. When it came time for the Harrisons to go on furlough in 1939, it seemed quite fitting that the Thoms should be assigned there. The Thoms's place in Kuwait was taken by Lew and Dorothy Scudder. (Missionary appointments often resembled a game of Chinese checkers.)

Wells Thoms brought with him a high evangelical and medical motive bequeathed to him by his early memories with his father, the most shocking and abiding of which had been the sight of lepers at the gate of Matrah city, unable to attend his father's clinic.[85] Thoms was another of Arabia's ever-energetic missionaries. At work or play, in his wake he left exhausted others wondering where on earth he came by his stamina.[86] He possessed a

while, he called me back. He'd fixed them. He'd put a nail in the wall and tied a string to them.

"So that was the type of workman that Mr. Dykstra had to deal with to build a solid cement hospital and a solid cement doctor's home." [From an interview with the author, January 28, 1990.]

[85] Wendell Phillips, *Unknown Oman* (Beirut: Librairie du Liban, 1971), pp. 27-28.

[86] The mission's commemorative statement after Wells's death in 1971 could not but mention this: "First, there was his boundless energy. No one in his right mind ever tried to follow Wells' physical footsteps through the course of a day" (Allison,

compact physique that always seemed to work well for him and was a person who felt deeply and gave of himself freely. Not unlike Mylrea in Kuwait, Wells had a passion for growing things. "The scrawny trees and bushes around his home attested. They survived under his care, even with scant and brackish water."[87] Gifted with a fine sense of the absurd, he was never at a loss for a rollicking story, and his love of laughter bound people to him with a light touch.[88] On vacations he was a tireless hiker and play-maker and had a gift for appreciating beauty which endowed his talent for sketching with insight. He was an impassioned Christian and was always ready to make his defense to anyone who demanded from him an account for the hope that was in him. And he did it with gentleness and reverence.[89]

Beth Thoms was different, cut from much the same cloth as her brother, Lew Scudder. To Wells's bubble and flamboyance she lent an alto voice of calm, and she enjoyed the role, her eyes flashing with amusement or deep set with compassion and understanding, as the situation dictated. Thoughtful and deliberate in speech, she mastered Arabic well. Hers was the sort of soft and deep-set sparkle that caused the Omanis to name her *Khâtûn Jawharah* (Gem Lady). A fine and diligent understudy for Minnie Dykstra, she picked up her missionary task with a distinctively different style. Yet her work among the women of Oman will continue to bear fruit in generations to come. When the Dykstras retired from Oman in 1949, Beth Thoms became the quiet keystone of the mission family, gently serving the young Kapengas,

---

Doctor Mary, p. 294). Ann De Young recalls, "I can remember in Muscat, come Saturday noon, we would be exhausted and ready for a siesta. Well, Wells Thoms was there always ready for a picnic. We went on a picnic every week. And after work it was out to the volley ball court with the hospital staff in Muscat or tennis. He had a lot of energy" (interview with the author, January 25, 1990).

[87] Allison, *Doctor Mary*, p. 293.

[88] At the author's graduation from Hope College in 1963, Wells and Beth Thoms attended *in loco parentis*. The author had won the Eerdmans Prize for Poetry that year, and Wells, over a sumptuous lunch, made much of the fact that, had the event occurred in Arabia, a recitation of a poem would have been demanded. He was quite aware that such a demand would have proven very discomfiting to the author, but he kept up his teasing with a deadpan face. Only Mary Allison, among the mission characters, rivaled Wells Thoms in his gift for deadpan humor.

[89] This paraphrase of 1 Peter 3:15-16 may also be applied to others of the mission, but none so epitomized adherence to Peter's counsel as Wells Thoms. Whether the company was Muslim or Christian, he was a person who, whenever undertaking a serious task, always began with prayer. It became a hallmark of his among the Omanis and they respected him for it and came to expect it of him.

Jay and Midge, and the new head of the Muscat women's clinic, Jeanette Boersma.[90]

Sultan Saʿîd bin-Taymûr Âl Bû-Saʿîdî succeeded his father in 1932 and began his reign with a promise that his father's obstructive policies—not least of all with reference to the mission—would be lifted. It was hoped that with Wells Thoms's return to Oman in 1939, relations with the sultan and the Oman government would improve. Thoms and Sultan Saʿîd began on the right footing. They had known each other as boys, and Saʿîd had high respect for *Sharon* Thoms, Wells's father. In 1948 he even donated land so that the mission might build a contagious diseases hospital as Sharon Thoms's memorial. But a series of serious political and international crises arose in the late 1940s to bedevil Sultan Saʿîd. These influenced him quickly and decisively to restore his father's policy of Omani isolationism. The Wells Thoms-Sultan Saʿîd ten-year "honeymoon" was over, and the mission was not exempt from the effects of the turnabout. Thoms's access to the sultan

[90]Jeanette Boersma, whose memoir, *Grace in the Gulf,* has been quoted in these pages, began her missionary career in ʿImârah, where the author and his sister, prying and impious children that they were, had opportunity to test her mettle and patience since, like it or not, she had to bunk in with the Scudder family. But Jeanette made her full mark in Oman. At the Full Annual Meeting held in Kuwait in October, 1955, Joyce Dunham, having described the festivities celebrating the opening of the Mylrea Memorial Hospital, went on to describe some of the program reports that had been delivered. Then she added, "Jeanette Boersma is our heroine, however, for she has seen more patients in the year than any of the doctors, in addition to doing the Muscat women's evangelistic work!" (letter from Joyce Dunham to her parents in Katpadi India, dated October 10, 1955, loaned to the author by Jim and Joyce Dunham). As her memoirs make clear, Jeanette was a person whose every breathing moment was devoted to her vocation in mission. There is an other worldly air about her still, and certainly a quite innocent disregard for the things of this world. On a visit to Oman at the celebration of the mission's centennial there in 1993, Margaret Kapenga Shurdom and her mother were guests in the apartment which Jeanette used to occupy, then the home of Roger and Lee Bruggink. On the wall Margaret spotted a watercolor painting of Oman which had been done by her grandmother. "Oh," Margaret jested, as she told the story to the author, "it was probably given to Jeanette, and she left it behind when she left. She just didn't remember things like that."

became abruptly less easy. With the sultan's growing paranoia, the mission was seen as potentially subversive, and repressive measures became the order of the new day. The hospitals' imports of drugs and equipment were taxed, medical development was deliberately obstructed, missionary movements were curtailed and closely monitored, and visas for much-needed new personnel became almost impossible to obtain. Frustratingly, these restrictions were imposed precisely at a time when donkeys and camels were yielding to motorized transportation for the people of Oman's interior, an innovation which increased the load on the mission's medical institutions manyfold.

Ann De Young joined the Al-Rahmah staff in 1958 after four years in Bahrain. She was a veteran missionary who had begun her career in China. Her arrival meant a marked rise in the quality of nursing care and a more disciplined approach to nurses' training and supervision.[91] In 1961 Dr. Alice Vander Zwaag, a Dutch Mennonite, was brought in finally to replace Sarah Hosmon, who had resigned in 1939. The level of service and the work load at *Al-Sa'âdah* (Happiness) Hospital in Muscat rose as rapidly as that of *Al-Rahmah*. The number of births increased as women came miles from small mountain villages simply to "have a live baby."

By the 1960s the load required that more doctors be assigned to Oman. Among the new arrivals, at different times and for short periods, were the two sons of Wells and Beth Thoms, Peter (1961-1962) and Norman (1964-1965), and their families. Norman was a surgeon. Elaine Fieldhouse was a short-term nurse who had volunteered to help Lew Scudder (Sr.) during his convalescence in Chicago in 1964 before diving straight into the appalling conditions in Oman. She related to Marilyn Scudder (the author's elder sister) how, when she was assisting Norman at surgery one day, the ubiquitous flies finally caused her to burst out:

"We have to do something about these flies!"

"We have," Norman replied laconically through his mask.

"What?" she asked frustratedly.

"We've adjusted." And he went on with the surgical procedure.

---

[91]Ann De Young recalls the weighty responsibilities that fell on her shoulders: "In Oman [in contrast to Bahrain] I was *the* matron, as we called it. And it took every ounce of experience and training that I had to try to run a hospital. I don't mean that I ran it, but, let's face it, we didn't have a hospital administrator. We didn't even have a secretary. So that was sort of pioneer work in Oman...in Matrah" (interview with the author, January 25, 1990).

At about the same time, Maurice and Eleanor Heusinkveld arrived (late in 1966). She was a gifted and highly efficient nurse and teacher; he a physician internist with a gift for administration (a gift much sought after in Oman). Don and Eloise Bosch also came for a time to give depth to the surgical capacity before being transferred to Bahrain. Also in 1966 Harvey and Margaret Doornbos, fresh from language training, were assigned to Oman. Assisting in the absence of Wells Thoms was Dr. Fred Richards, a colorful, knock-about character who had also served a well-remembered tenure in Kuwait with the American Independent Oil Company. But even with all the new talent, the strain on physical facilities was overwhelming. The call went out pleading for resources to upgrade and expand the hospitals. But neither funds nor board inclination were forthcoming.

Mary Allison, who returned to the field from her retirement in 1971,[92] was assigned for the first time to Oman. Her main experience before then had been in Kuwait and then (for a shorter period) Bahrain. She was to spell Harvey Doornbos when he and Margaret went on vacation, and then she stayed for four years. This is her description of the wards in *Al-Rahmah* Hospital:

> The day when I arrived, I stowed my belongings in the apartment above the storeroom, put on a white uniform, and walked over to the plain, gray, cement hospital building to the tune of "Onward Christian Soldiers."
>
> Dr. Doorenbos blithely turned over his inpatients to me before leaving on his vacation, saying, "You can find them easily. My charts have a red patch on the corner." I trusted that all his patients would be in the final stages of convalescence and entered the hospital through the milling crowds at the door.
>
> ... Hospitals at home were quiet, orderly, and immaculately clean. Here, everything was confusion, noise, and disorder, with callers, family members, babies, and children sitting on the floor talking, fanning, and eating. The bedding was messy, and piles of

[92]She retired for the last time in 1974, among the most durable, lovable, and eccentric of the mission's physicians. Her memoirs, published in 1994 only a few months before her death in August of that year, are perhaps the most honest and forthright of those published by Arabia missionaries, reflecting a life-long spiritual struggle with her own humanity and brimming over with her wry sense of humor.

blankets were shoved under the beds with an occasional bowl of leftover food. The toilets smelled. After the first couple of days, I knew I would get used to it and feel it was all quite human, sociable, and natural.

But for now I studied the rows of about a hundred inpatient charts, bewildered by the simple problem of finding the patients. Rooms one, two, three, etc., were quite clear, and BQ meant the Bedouin quarters. I asked one of the Indian nurses, who was a vision in her neat white sari, to help me make rounds. Most of the charts were classified under various capitals. H meant the patients put in beds lining the halls outside the rooms because the rooms were filled. K meant the small rooms that had been built for kitchens for the families before the hospital fed the patients. G meant the old garage which had room for two patients. DDO meant Dr. Doorenbos' office. Since he was on vacation, it could be used for a hospital room. NSA and NSB were two treatment rooms—Nurse's Stations A and B. NL was a little space near the laboratory. US was under the stairs, where a cot could be squeezed. "What is UT, then?" I asked, bewildered. Sister Indira showed me. It meant "under the tree" ward. There were two scrawny mesquite trees between the two wings of rooms. Cots had been set out under them, suiting some Bedouin families very well. They could hang blankets from the branches for privacy and drape any excess clothing there, too. The nurses hung bottles of fluids for intravenous medication—even blood if we had any—to run down from the branches.[93]

On the night of September 13, 1967, the mission was shocked to hear that Maurice Heusinkveld, while closing the gate to the driveway at his home, had been shot and killed by an unknown assailant. The ripple of sadness and puzzlement went through the whole Gulf among missionaries.[94]

[93]Allison, *Doctor Mary*, pp. 278-279.
[94]Joyce Dunham, in a letter written to her parents September 24, wrote: "More details on Maurie's death finally arrived yesterday. Someone must have shot him at very close range when he was closing the gate. Ellie had gone into the house. He was conscious for a few minutes, long enough to say, 'Father, forgive them, for they know not what they do.' So far they have not been able to find the man or a reason. Many people called on Ellie, and there were quite a few Muslims,

It was widely suspected that the assailant had been a disgruntled patient with high social status who had been forced to wait his turn like everyone else at morning clinic. This had been a discipline which Heusinkveld doggedly enforced in the teeth of all advice to be more flexible. But it emerged years after the event that, in fact, the assailant had been a hired hand, sent by a member of the ruling family. The high born individual had become outraged when Maurie insisted that he leave the consultation room while he examined the patient, the man's wife. Following the event, the British officers of the Omani Police advised the mission not to ask too many questions and not to press the matter. The whole affair was left to drift and die away. Ellie Heusinkveld and her sons, after the school year was finished, elected to retire from the mission and return to the United States.

Don and Eloise Bosch were called back from Bahrain, and, with their arrival October 30, 1968, the ranks were filled. In the middle of mounting pressure, the Thoms returned from their furlough for a last term which was completed in 1970.[95]

It was a transitional moment, although few in the mission could have anticipated it. When the Omani coup of July 26, 1970, took place, the mission rejoiced. The new sultan, Qâbûs, came into his own promising freedom and progress. Jay Kapenga remarked in a letter to Ken Warren dated July 27, "Today is a holiday, and since yesterday I have not read a sad countenance on anyone's face." Warren, then temporarily area secretary, wrote on August 6: "Praise be to God! For this is an exciting time to be alive and to be linked with the church in Muscat, Oman."[96] But they did not see only through rose-tinted glasses. Kapenga again: "Tarik [Sayyid Târiq bin-Taymûr, the new sultan's uncle] is here and is listed as Prime Minister. A cabinet is to be formed, and here is the problem. There is such a lack of personnel and such an ignorance as to personnel and, those who have had

including the Wali (mayor) of Mutrah in attendance at the funeral service, which Jay conducted in Arabic and English. Ann writes that some of the routines which Maurie was establishing in the hospital were just getting under way and how they would miss him" (in correspondence loaned to the author by Jim and Joyce Dunham).

[95]Within a year of his retirement, Wells Thoms was attacked by a virulent form of cancer and died. His ashes were returned to Oman and interred next to the grave of his father. Beth Thoms eventually married Fred Dickason, her daughter's father-in-law and an old family friend going back to college days, who had recently lost his wife.

[96]Memo from Ken Warren to RCA executive staff, August 6, 1970.

some sort of job, have really had no responsibility. Boy, it will be an interesting year of delights."[97]

After the government of Oman changed, it opened negotiations with the Reformed church concerning its medical work (beginning in December 1970). The negotiations concluded in 1973 with the decision to turn over the medical work of the mission to the new Omani Ministry of Health. Don Bosch, upon whom Wells Thoms's mantle had fallen,[98] transferred to direct Al-Khawlah, the new central receiving hospital which the government had built in 1975. Along with the Indian staff like Dr. Dass and others, Alice Vander Zwaag and the nurses, Jeanette Boersma and Ann De Young, also joined the government health service. They were posted, one by one, away from the capital area to locations where the government needed them to build up new staff in new facilities. The final transfer of the Matrah and Muscat hospitals to the government took place in 1975.[99] For years to come, Don Bosch insisted that the Ministry of Health would welcome any personnel the Reformed church might care to put forward.[100]

In a wide-ranging interview with Ed Luidens, conducted in Newark Airport in New Jersey June 13, 1988, Don Bosch made several insightful remarks. Among others, he related his oft-repeated metaphor of what the mission hospital used to do. Medically, he said, the mission's role was like that of a person standing at the foot of a cliff, picking up the people who fell off, repairing them only to watch them fall off again. The mission never had

---

[97]Kapenga to Ken Warren, August 5, 1970.

[98]The allusion to the Elijah-Elisha relationship in the case of the Thoms-to-Bosch succession is appropriate in more than merely the figurative sense in which it is casually used. The two men shared many characteristics: short stature, boundless energy, ebullient personalities, and an unabashed Christian deportment. For years after Thoms had left the field, Don Bosch was frequently mistaken for "Tomas," especially by Omanis from the interior who came to the hospital seeking a healer by that name. The author, visiting Oman in the early 1970s, had occasion to witness one such incident personally. It should be noted further that, like the Mylrea-Scudder succession in Kuwait and the Harrison-Storm succession in Bahrain, the Thoms-Bosch succession in Oman was a legitimate and fruitful one. Don Bosch proudly claims Wells Thoms as his mentor. And he is quite right.

[99]It was in 1975 that, for unclear reasons, the highly gifted Harvey and Margaret Doorenbos were refused reentry into Oman. After a time of assessment, they accepted reassignment to a frontier mission situation in Ethiopia, where they endured throughout the difficult times of the Communist regime. Their loss to Oman and to the mission's fellowship in Arabia, however, was significant.

[100]Don Bosch in a recorded conversation with the Oman mission group, March 20, 1990.

the time, symbolically, to climb the cliff and put up guard rails. When the Reformed church took the decision to offer the Oman government its medical resources—hospitals, staff, and all—there were many who misgave. But Don was one, he said, who saw it as a positive development. On the one hand, it gave the mission medical personnel the inestimable opportunity to participate in designing and building a whole national health system. And in that, Don insisted, they played a significant part. Furthermore, it let the mission out of its frustrating vocation at the foot of the cliff. The missionaries could now be part of the team that built the guard rail at the top, helping in the development of Oman's public health program and building up its new rural health centers.

Finally, Don pointed out, "Actually the really important thing we had a role in was this whole concept of integration into the government health services once the new ruler came into power. It was a very significant and historic thing for a Christian organization to voluntarily start working under a Muslim ruler's ministry of health. And of course a lot of people opposed it. They felt that we were surrendering our freedom to witness. But I personally believe that it did exactly the opposite. It opened the door so that we did have the freedom to talk to everybody, and we were no longer like salt grains in a salt shaker but rather shaken out into the society. We were no longer behind the walls of the compound—you know, 'These are the Christians in here.' There were no compound walls once we moved in with the government. For me that was the most significant point because it represented a real departure from traditional methods...a genuine willingness to work under the Health Ministry, knowing that they are Muslims and not Christians."[101] After noting that he had been assigned to Khawlah Hospital and Ann De Young went to Tanâm (then Sûr, then Sohâr) and Jeanette Boersma went to Sûr, Don went on to say, "You see, once we moved in under the government, then was accomplished what the mission had long since said was one of its objectives, and that is to get into the inland of Arabia. And our people did get into the inland of Arabia, but not under own power, but under the auspices of the government itself. From that standpoint, you would have to say that this was fantastic, it was the achievement of one of our goals."

---

[101] Recorded interview between Edwin Luidens and Donald and Eloise Bosch, Newark Airport, Newark, New Jersey, June 13, 1988, in the author's collection.

Medical Work in Summation

The Arabian Mission launched its medical work, responding to an obvious need for enlightened treatment of disease and the need for creating a consciousness in matters of personal hygiene and public health, with a clear eye toward eliciting a response of gratitude. Through touring medical teams from 1917 through 1956, it was believed that the goal of establishing work in the Arabian heartland could be accomplished. Whether institutional or mobile, medical work became the main activity of the mission. The period of expansion of medical institutions went on until the last new Mason Memorial Hospital building in Bahrain was opened in 1962. Plans were being made for the expansion of the mission's medical work in Oman as late as 1972.

But as ambitions and pressures increased, so too did the questions become more insistent. To what extent did medical work promote the primary goals of the mission? As governments in the Gulf took up more and more of the burden for providing health care for their people, ought not the mission rethink its medical strategy? Jay Kapenga, writing to Don Bosch in August 1955, recognizing that after sixty years, during which the Arabian Mission's medical work was "the only show in town" and had earned the gratitude and respect of many, asked: "...After 60 years is it not time to assume good-will and prestige and to discuss, in the light of the many other medical facilities present in most places, the size of our Mission Medical Work, the kind of Mission Medical Work, and lastly, how in the world we can really make our hospitals pay off more than before as real live evangelistic centers?" He continued, observing, "...We are too anxious in trying to recapture the glory of the old days when we were King-pins. That day is over and we've got to change, and have courage to think change and more positive, progressive (if not revolutionary) thinking in the Mission purpose and our particular projects related to that purpose."[102]

The gap between the medical and pastoral/evangelistic staff also began to grow at this time. Kapenga observed, "In my own experience I have not felt that in many cases the hospital, school and Church were in the least integrated. The majority of padres were doing little work in the hospital. They had no enthusiasm for evangelizing in hospitals other than a clinic talk

[102]Transcript of letter from Jay Kapenga to Donald Bosch, dated August 10, 1955 (in the author's document collection).

or some other weekly or daily meeting." He felt that mission evangelists were legitimately putting pressure on the doctors not simply to fulfill their increasingly demanding professional role but to implement their missionary calling as evangelists as well. He went on: "I sincerely believe that we must be willing to think, criticize, examine and even change direction and emphasis. We must see new and more distinctive possibilities which are more in keeping with what we really want for an evangelistic impact. I myself believe the answer lies in a new kind of medical institution. As Christian Mission people, I do not believe we can remain faithful to our call and job if we do not willingly think more progressively, and act progressively. It is stupid to remain bound to the past and the past way of working. What was real, necessary and required *then* does not mean that it is so *today*."[103]

The outspokenness of Jay Kapenga reflected thoughts that had been percolating through the mission for some time. The depersonalization of the institutions that set in during the 1950s was distressing to evangelists and physicians alike. The institutional inertia, demanding growth and expansion, however, seemed irresistible. The medical cadre was swept along with it; the evangelistic cadre, if not willing to be co-opted, was left in the dust. Frustration was the result.

While the mission was in a quandary, other forces came into play. Missiological discussions growing out of the experience of mission agencies in India and elsewhere during the early 1950s raised questions about the propriety of missions owning and operating large institutions like hospitals and schools. They came to be seen as creating dependents and clients out of potentially autonomous and self-propagating indigenous churches that ought to have lives of their own. Major mission institutions—particularly hospitals—were pictured as millstones around the indigenous churches' necks, the more so as the cost of running them rose geometrically and as mission agencies experienced increasing financial limitations. Small, local churches could not sustain these kinds of efforts out of their own resources.

As this discussion proceeded, it correlated with budget tightening by mission boards. Beginning the mid-1950s, the Reformed church conducted several surveys of the Arabian Mission's educational and medical institutions. And the question was posed: Apart from the medical professional's personal sense of vocation, what is the role of medicine in the missionary calling of

---

[103]Kapenga to Bosch, August 10, 1955.

the Church? Is it instrumental or integral, or must the question be answered on a case-by-case basis? In the end, the value judgment was made that support for the institutional base for medical work was the responsibility of government.

By the mid-1960s it was determined that hospitals in the Gulf would have to be closed or founded upon entirely different bases. The Kuwait medical program was terminated unilaterally in March of 1967. The medical work in Oman was turned over to the newly progressive regime which came to power there in 1971. In 1988 the American Mission Hospital in Bahrain was locally incorporated under the patronage of the ruler, with mission personnel being employed in top positions but with no responsibility taken by the Reformed church for the actual financial welfare of the institution.

Mission in Motion: The Tourists

One feature of the mission's early statement of purpose—the aim to "occupy the interior of Arabia"—was extremely influential in shaping the mission's physical shape and character.[104] No matter where the mission took root, it always wanted to be somewhere *else*. Basrah, in a sense, looked along the rivers to the north and across the great marshes into the Syrian desert, where the great tribes of the Ruwallah and Shammar wandered. Bahrain, as islands will, looked toward the mainland and was early used as

---

[104]In contrast to Cantine, who seemed content to find his niche and stay in it, Zwemer was an inveterate traveler. Touring, of course, was recognized as a principal missionary activity. Henry Martyn, the archetype of Protestant missionaries to Islam, had visited Muscat and Busheir in 1811 as part of his last missionary tour. His journal became an inspiration to those who followed (Lorimer, *op. cit.*, p. 2394. Also Zwemer, *Arabia...*, pp. 316-319). General F.T. Haig, whom the mission respected highly as one of its guiding lights, toured the Gulf for the CMS in 1886 (Lorimer, *Gazetteer...*, p. 2395). Touring, then, became a regular activity of Arabian Mission and contributed to the spread of its reputation throughout the region.

In later years those who toured were primarily medical personnel, but in each of the main areas where tours became a regular feature the ground was broken by ordained missionaries, most frequently Zwemer himself, and every one of the mission stations that was founded was first opened by a preacher (Zwemer, *Milestone...*, p. 68). The exception to this statement is probably Kuwait, even though Zwemer did visit there and attempt to establish a book shop there. The station itself was only permanently established by medical people backed up by evangelists.

the principal staging area for realizing the dream. Kuwait, on the edge of the desert, looked out across that desert after caravans of merchants, pilgrims, traders, and migrating bedouin, and in the early days it seemed that the longed-for invitation into the interior might be best fielded there. Matrah and Muscat moved people, like the proverbial bear, to climb mountains to see what they could see. Muscat and Matrah, of course, had their own "interior," the great Jabal with its fiercely independent Ibâdî tribal villagers, but it also served as a position from which to look toward Najd and the Pirate Coast from a southern perspective.

The mission's stations, as one by one they came into existence, strung out over that thousand-mile front, stretched the mission's resources always far thinner than wisdom would dictate. But that always seemed acceptable. There was the "somewhere else," the mirage-like promised land of The Interior, which beckoned. Even as late as November, 1944, Harold Storm, in a report circulated to the other mission stations overflowing with his typical enthusiastic optimism, could say:

> I believe we are standing on the threshold of an opportunity to open work in the interior. Just when or how it will come one can not predict for a surety; but that it may come very soon and certainly will come I am convinced....We should make more and more visits and stay longer each time until the public demand keeps us there. We must keep before us the challenge of the interior of Arabia and work and pray in faith believing that God will open the doors for permanent occupation in the very near future....I believe we are on the threshold of great things and it may not be long before the mission will realize the fifty-year-old-dream and have a station in the interior of Arabia.[105]

The mission remained always "on the threshold," and perhaps that is as it should be. Along with its wistfulness, there was always in the Arabian Mission a poignant spirit of expectancy. The poignancy lay in the fact that there was a price to pay.

[105]Document in the author's collection. Report dated Bahrain, Nov. 28, 1944. It is interesting to note the wording of the closing sentence. A "station" in the interior of Arabia could only have been another fixed position. One wonders, had Storm's hopes been fully realized, whether the experience would have fulfilled the dream.

The disruptive effect touring had upon the stability and continuity of work in the stations already occupied was recognized virtually from the beginning. Although an early tourist himself, Stanley Mylrea soon came to disapprove of touring. It hampered work in progress, and he believed it more effective for the mission to focus its efforts on doing quality work in already established centers.[106]

In later years, Jeanette Veldman, in a thoughtful comment, said that the Arabian Mission's primary interest lay in touring. There was great prestige attached to the activity, and it was justified as a means for penetrating into the heart of Arabia. In the 1950s that was still a priority in the mission's thinking. But Jeanette was unable to see anything tangible resulting from touring. Rather it seemed that injury was done to the medical operation at the station from which tours were launched. When the doctor and main nursing staff went on tour, at times the hospital itself had to close down. "You can't do tours and hospitals," she said.[107]

While recognizing this fact early on, for the sake of the grand obsession laid upon it from its natal crib, the mission accepted the trade-off...the anomaly. The anomaly expressed itself in this way: If permanent work was be established in Najd, then the mission must seriously consider closing operations in one or more of the other stations since these, from the beginning, were deemed to have been established only to serve as staging points for the main strategic goal. In fact, this strategy was never seriously considered. The permanent establishments became rooted, and the resources for new ventures became ever more scarce.

Nonetheless, it became a touring mission, working always toward those "unoccupied" places just over the horizon...over the sea...over the mountain. Itinerating was an activity which fulfilled the yearning of the missionaries to penetrate into that always beckoning Interior of Arabia, the ultimate goal of all the effort. Following early trips by the Zwemer brothers, Jim Moerdyk, Sharon Thoms, John Van Ess, and other pioneers, the more deliberate touring program was spearheaded by Paul Harrison, Louis Dame, Wells Thoms, Harold Storm, Gerald Nykerk, Esther Barny (Ames), Josephine

---

[106]Allison, *Memoirs...*, p. 52.

[107]In an interview by the author with Jeanette Veldman in Holland, Michigan, January 26, 1990, the notes of which are on record. Stanley Mylrea, after a few years in Kuwait and some exploratory work from that base, came to the same conclusion. Among the leaders of the mission, he was one voice advocating that touring be curbed.

Van Peursem, and Cornelia Dalenberg beginning in the second decade of the century and continuing into the mid-1950s.

In its founding stages, the mission station in Kuwait was seen as a likely jumping-off point for fulfilling the Arabian Mission's dream. When, during World War I, Kuwait was isolated by British and Sa'ûdî embargoes, however, the prospects seemed to dry up. But one possibility briefly teased the mission.

With the change in political atmosphere, the young missionaries in Kuwait began to examine other possibilities for fulfilling the mission's mandate to "occupy the Interior" from their position. In his medical report for 1918-1919, Stanley Mylrea noted, "Sheikh Salim, in opposition to Bin Saud is courting Bin Rashid & we are thus beginning to form what I trust are valuable connections with Hail. Nothing approaching an invitation to that Capitol is yet forthcoming however & one man who at first I thought might do something, eventually put me off by saying that I was doing such valuable work here that I surely would be unable to leave it."[108] In fact, Mylrea and Edwin Calverley received an invitation in 1921 to at least visit Hâ'il, the Rashîdî capitol, with the end in view of establishing a school and medical mission there. And they became quite keen on the project.

Wind of this got to C.C. Garbett, the British political agent in Kuwait, however, and was reported to the high commissioner. James Cantine, then residing in Baghdad and for many years mission secretary, received a letter from Garbett expressing the "opinion" of Sir. E. Bonham Carter, the British high commissioner in Baghdad, that "the proposed expedition was inopportune" and hoped that Cantine would "discourage it." Reporting this to Calverley, Cantine added that "the Commissioner is unable to approve of your proposed trip inland from Kuweit, and I am sure that you will, in deference to his wishes, postpone it for the time being."[109] The British, at that time, were assiduously courting 'Abd-ul-'Azîz Âl Sa'ûd. Sa'ûdî-Kuwaiti tensions were embarrassment enough, not to add to them a serendipitous scheme for encouraging the Rashîdîs hatched by a naive American and an impetuous British missionary. The project was dropped, and the hope of

[108]Mylrea's "Report of Men's Medical, 1918-1919" in the author's document collection now in the Archives of the Reformed Church in America, New Brunswick, New Jersey.

[109]Letter from Cantine to Calverley dated March 26, 1921, in the author's document collection now in the Archives of the Reformed Church in America, New Brunswick, New Jersey.

extending into the fabled interior from Kuwait along that particularly risky line was snuffed out. The mission thereafter placed its hopes in Bahrain as the principal base from which the interior would be penetrated, with Oman playing a secondary role.

In the mythology of the mission, the medical institution in Bahrain itself was frequently eclipsed by the fact that Bahrain was the mission's main jumping off point for tours, medical tours, into the interior. The exploits of the tourists made up some of the more colorful tales the Arabian Mission had to tell, but their actual achievements were harder to assess. And the fortunes of the touring enterprise were tightly locked together with the caveats and whims of 'Abd-ul-'Azîz Âl Sa'ûd, the ruler of Arabia, and other political variables. An example may suffice:

At the turn of the century Dubay was one of the more active ports of the Pirate Coast, now one of the United Arab Emirates. During the first decade of the century, the Arabian Mission took an interest in Dubay, especially for purposes of evangelistic and medical touring. At the end of 1910, the British established that consignments of contraband arms were being trans-shipped through Dubay to Iran and thence on to the rebellious northwest frontier of India. To punish the local shaykh, the British navy bombarded the city and sent a landing party ashore. The upshot was that the whole of the Pirate Coast was suddenly closed down to casual western touring by 1913, and "Bahrain station lost this part of its touring territory."[110] The same events had repercussions in Oman, which also limited the mission's activities. The doors into the Pirate Coast and other areas closed as the second decade of the century ended.

What is not well reported by the mission is the fact that, to travel unimpeded by British interference, missionaries were often obliged to report on their movements and contacts to the British political agents. On occasion, especially in the freewheeling ports of the Pirate Coast, missionaries observed active slave trading and other activities they considered repugnant. These they did not hesitate to report. On the positive side, they gained unique insights into tribal configurations and practices, and their information could pave the way for successful British diplomatic ventures. But there was always a certain unease of conscience which may be detected between the lines in writings by Paul Harrison.

---

[110]Mason and Barny, *History...*, p. 140-141.

Harrison was a man of strong and wiry constitution, robust American political views, a sensitive and insightful moral and theological conscience, and a pragmatist's audacity to navigate through treacherous water toward a desired goal. If, as a pragmatist, he could justify providing the British with intelligence on areas through which he toured, he could choose *what* intelligence he passed on. At the same time, he was working to promote an image of the Arab as the quintessential democrat, and he persistently needled his British hosts on matters political. Although he served them, the British knew he did so under duress. A complex person walking a delicate tightrope, it was far more important for Harrison that he won the respect and trust of the Arabs than that he held that of the British, and it was he who blazed the trail for others to follow.

Paul Harrison received the first invitation to go to Riyadh and attend to the needs of the royal family and the townspeople in July of 1917, and the mission heralded the event as the first step toward occupying the Arabian interior. As the first Christian to be admitted into that town, he had to face the prejudice of the local populace. But, over the subsequent years of frequent visits by mission doctors and their evangelist side-kicks, that parochialism and bigotry broke down. Harrison was invited back into the Pirate Coast in 1919. Until 1927 Harrison toured out of Bahrain quite regularly, often accompanied by Gerrit Van Peursem or one of the other ordained missionaries. He came to know the eastern province of Sa'ûdî Arabia intimately. From 1920 he toured in shifts with Louis Dame, even entering into Oman by the back door, as it were, when touring out of Muscat and Matrah was impossible. In 1929, when Harrison was assigned to develop the medical work in Oman, Dame came to bear the lion's share of the mission's touring program until he resigned from the mission in 1936. From 1936 until he was transferred to Oman in 1938, Wells Thoms toured out of Bahrain, and then his place was taken by Harold Storm.

Storm, a bundle of energy and bubbling humor, was ideally suited for touring and, spelled in the mid-1940s by Gerald Nykerk, was the backbone of the effort. Among Storm's major exploits was his trans-Arabian tour. For eighteen months in 1935 and 1936, with an Omani assistant, Qambar al-Mâs, he undertook an exploratory 8,000-mile trek across the forbidding Empty Quarter, down the coast of western Arabia, and finally back along the south Arabia coast, concluding the tour in Muscat. A remarkable explorer's achievement though it was, just what this tour accomplished apart from stirring the missiological conscience of the mission is difficult to say. Toward the end of the era, Storm himself perhaps best summarized the optimism of the tourist. It is given in a much-quoted parable he told entitled, "El-Khokha—The Little Door":[111]

> "Again I say unto you, it is easier for a camel to go through the eye of a needle, than for a rich man to enter the Kingdom of God" (Matthew 19:24).
>
> Most Arab houses have large doors. They are large in order to enable a donkey or a camel to enter the courtyard bringing wood or water, or bags of rice. Within the large door is a small door, only large enough for a person to enter. The Arabs call it El Khokha, the little door. It corresponds to the small door called the Eye of the Needle by Jesus.
>
> The great doors to Najd and the interior remain closed to this day, but there are little doors through which the messenger of Christ can enter with His message of life, peace, and hope.
>
> Many of these little doors which give entrance into the homes of the Arabs and into the hearts of the Arabs themselves are opened by the doctor making outcalls. Sometimes these small doors open into the houses of the rich and ruling class, and sometimes they open into the tents and date-stick huts of the poor.
>
> Light and hope can enter through the Little Door.[112]

It was with the Little Door in various shapes that the mission had to content itself.

There were three locations which, for a time, promised to bear fruit for missionary touring: Nâsiriyyah, northwest of Basrah on the Euphrates, was looked upon almost from the founding days of the mission as a most promising location.[113]

It was, in many ways, a key both to the great marshes and to the desert, an Ottoman (and, later British colonial) administrative center, located as it was near to the political hub of Sûq-ash-Shuyûkh. But, in the end, after

---

[111]The Arabic word, *khawkhah*, actually means "little green plum," and what that has to do with a little door is hard to fathom.

[112]Quoted in Van Ess, *History...*, pp. 54-55.

[113]In his interview with Edwin Luidens June 20, 1988, Barny Luben expressed the opinion that perhaps it was a mistake to favor 'Imârah over Nasirîyah.

James Moerdyk's last valiant effort to establish it in 1920, the mission acknowledged it could not hold Nâsriyyah and withdrew. The effort and resources were diverted further northward toward the emerging United Mission in Mesopotamia, James Cantine's final legacy.

Attendant upon Harold Storm's report that the city of Makallâh, in the Yemenî Hadramaut, was ready for a mission effort, there was a flurry of correspondence toward the end of 1944 and through 1945 on whether or not the mission could stretch far enough to do the task. The proposal that the Southern Baptists might be enticed into doing it was being mooted.[114] Harold Storm was also pointing out that al-Hasâ' was showing signs of being a possible location opening up and could become a mission station. To that end Paul Harrison, always ready to stretch further than his reach, was quite prepared to talk about giving up the work in Bahrain, since the municipal services were looking fair to filling the medical need. But, writing to Duke Potter from Kuwait, the sober voice of Stanley Mylrea observed, "If Storm is right, we may be able to occupy Hassa in the near future, but we certainly won't be if we dissipate our energies in Hadharamaut or Central Africa [strangely, another option being suggested quite seriously]. I don't want to labor the point, for you know just as much about this question of personnel as I do. I merely ask you not to forget that the Dykstras, Vanes', Harrisons, Van Peursems and the Pennings [he omitted the Mylreas] are very close to the end of their careers. If you took them out of the mission tomorrow, there wouldn't be much left, would there?" Apart from Harrison, who noted that "[i]t is altogether too easy for missionaries too to become preoccupied with the difficulties of our work, and lose our vision and almost our hope for immediate results. I think that a project like Hadhramaut would be very valuable indeed," the balance of wisdom seemed to come down on holding on to the gains already made.[115]

The city of Doha on the peninsula of Qatar, ruled by the Âl Thânî family, held promise of becoming a full-blown mission station in the late-1940s. Efforts by the mission to staff a clinic there with Cornelia Dalenberg, the Storms, and medical personnel from other stations were valiant. But they

[114]See in part 6 the discussion of the correspondence between Duke Potter and the officials of the Southern Baptist Convention, 1942 to 1951.
[115]The gleanings of this correspondence are in a small set of papers in the author's document collection, drawn from originals in the correspondence files of the Board of Foreign Missions at that time.

proved too burdensome.[116] Despite the shaykh's substantial participation, it seriously drained particularly Bahrain station. In the fall of 1951, Jerry and Rose Nykerk both fell victims to tuberculosis. They had contracted it in Sa'ûdî Arabia and had to return for extended treatment in the United States. Their sudden departure meant that there were just not enough medical personnel to sustain a regular rotation, and the project in Doha had to be abandoned early in 1952.[117]

Not to be daunted, in 1952, writing in the annual report number of *Arabia Calling*, Harold Storm reported that his customary tour to the Eastern Province oasis area of al-Hasâ' that year had been unique. By the merchants and the Amîr (Ibn-Juluwî), the mission had been asked to leave its medical equipment in place and return after the summer. "This interest on the part of the merchant class and the ready acquiescence of the Amîr to their request," Storm observed,

> … seem to be an indication that Hassa is just about ready for the
> Mission to consider taking up work there. It seems important for
> us to make the best of this opportunity because life has changed so
> completely in the Nejd that the official call for Mission doctors is
> not nearly so acute as it was even ten years ago, and will be even less

[116]Early in 1949 Ed Luidens accompanied Harold and Ida Storm as they returned to Doha, after a year's absence, to reopen the hospital built there by the shaykh for the mission. He wrote, "It had to be closed after its very successful 'premiere' because there were not enough doctors in the Arabian Mission to man the mission's hospitals. There were not enough doctors to allow the Arabian Mission to penetrate Arabia. After more than fifty years of prayer, sweat and blood, the Christian Church has been invited to serve in Arabia. But our Church is found wanting—in men!" Ed was using the Arabian Mission's litany: 'Penetrate the Interior!' Ed concluded the article as follows: "If ministers, teachers, doctors and nurses learn that thousands of people in the Arab East are dependent on them, they must certainly respond. One minister, if he comes to Arabia, will preach the Gospel to literally thousands of people who never would have heard the good news without him. One teacher will teach hundreds of boys or girls who would have no education at all without him. One doctor will operate on thousands of people who would receive absolutely no medical care whatsoever without him. One nurse will minister to a whole hospital filled with patients who would be unattended without her. The business of the Kingdom of Christ in Arabia is waiting on these 'ones.'" (Public relations flier entitled "Open for Business…If," by Edwin M. Luidens, published and circulated by the Board of Foreign Missions of the Reformed Church in America, March, 1949; document in the author's document collection.)

[117]*AMFR* #227, spring 1952, p. 14.

in the years to come. If the Mission doctors are not permitted to enter at this opportunity, it may be that the opportunity will not recur and certainly if medicine does not get in, there is very little hope that the evangelist will ever get in.[118]

In November, 1952, the Arabian Mission's Annual Meeting voted "...that the Mission fully approve the establishment of a permanent station in Hassa, that a long tour be made immediately with that purpose in view, and that this new station be given parity with others in its personnel requirements."[119] On December 3, 1953, the mission rented an imposing building in the town of Hufûf, which was called "Bayt Faraj," to use as a hospital, and the medical team set up residence in a building just behind it.

In spite of the action of the mission to designate al-Hasâ' a full station, the work there continued to be a touring function reported by the mission under the activities of Bahrain.[120] The great king, 'Abd-ul-'Azîz Âl Sa'ûd, died in the winter of 1953 just as the program in al-Hasâ' was starting to settle in. In his son and successor, Sa'ûd, the mission had no friend (even though Louis Dame had once mended his broken arm), and a sense of rivalry with the nascent government health service led to increasing government interference.[121] Royal permission for the mission's work in Hasâ' was finally withdrawn at the beginning of 1956, and Harold Storm went in to terminate

---

[118]*AMFR* #227, spring 1952, pp. 13-14.

[119]*AMFR* #232, summer 1953, pp. 5-6. The article by Cornelia Dalenberg, one of the participants in establishing the program in al-Hasâ', is entitled "Forward to Hassa," and is a review of the history of Hassa Station up to 1953.

[120]Reporting in the winter of 1953, Harold Storm wrote, "We are a bit more comfortable than on previous tours. We have one semi-European toilet which is rather a blessing to us three who have passed the fifty mark and who do not find ourselves overenthusiastic about native toilets. We also have been granted an electric extension line from the hotel and so we have one electric light in each room from sunset to around midnight. Despite these improvements it is still touring—ask Marianne [Walvoord, a single nurse who had gone in place of Cornelia Dalenberg]." (In a letter from Harold Storm to "Dear Colleagues" dated November 20, 1953, a copy in the author's document collection.)

[121]Storm noted, "The uproar was started by the group of Syrian doctors in Hassa who have always been jealous and this bunch a bit more than the rest. They sent wires flying here and there demanding our expulsion, etc. So far all the answers have been in our favor which of course has not eased the local medical wrath" (Storm to "Dear Colleagues," November 20, 1953).

the lease on the two rented buildings, sell off furniture, and bring out supplies and equipment.[122]

Withdrawal from Doha and al-Hasâ' was the end of the mission's dream to "occupy the interior from the coast as a base." The established stations were too firmly entrenched, the investments too preoccupying, and the personnel and material resources too thinly stretched[123] to do what had to be done to establish the foothold which Doha and al-Hasâ' promised to become.[124] In the case of al-Hasâ', the loss of royal patronage marked the end of an era and of a dream. To wrap the matter up, the annual meeting of 1961 approved the motion "That the Nejd Touring Account balance of Rs. 455.00 be transferred to the Bahrain Hospital Building Fund and that the Nejd Touring Account be closed."[125]

Did touring prosper the overall impact of the mission in the Gulf? Most likely it did, but it did not prosper its medical institutions. The two were never seen as precisely the same thing. From the point of view of the work in Bahrain, it was frequently detrimental. Until 1930, when the doctor was

[122]*AMFR* #242, Winter 1955-56, p. 17. In a letter to her parents dated February 26, 1956, Joyce (De Bruin) Dunham wrote, "Speaking of Hassa, that's the crisis of the moment. Since Harold came back this week with all the stuff from there, except for what he sold, it looks as though Hassa is definitely closed for the time being at least. That means that the Thoms won't need to come here after their furlough, and Muscat has already circulated a petition that they return to Muscat....This morning Harold read us an article about Saudi Arabia. Things are in a sad state there—the government is thoroughly corrupted, going farther and farther into debt, trying to shut out all western influence because they are afraid of being overthrown, which is a strong possibility." (In correspondence loaned to the author by Jim and Joyce Dunham.)

[123]In the 1950s personnel coming to the field were also less willing to tour. The primary reason given was "family." In a letter from Bahrain to his in-laws, the DeBruins of India (January 2, 1955), Jim Dunham observed: "It's beginning to look as if we won't be able to occupy Hassa or the interior if we don't do it soon. Right now there don't seem to be too many of the mission who are interested in touring. We think we might like it, but if we have a family that's one thing to consider. That's what seems to hold a lot of them back. The Bosches were approached and felt that they couldn't go in and leave their family behind or that it would be wise to take them in. Now that the Thoms' family will soon be gone, it was thought they might take over the job, but they would rather tour in Oman." (In correspondence loaned to the author by Jim and Joyce Dunham.)

[124]Qatar later established a fairly strict Wahhâbî policy with respect to non-Muslims resident there. Whether this had something to do with the failure of the mission to fulfill the dreams of its ruler for a mission hospital on his soil is difficult to say.

[125]Minutes of the Annual Meeting of the Arabian Mission, Bahrain, 1961, p. 16.

away work in the Mason Memorial Hospital virtually came to a halt. From 1930 onward, hiring doctors from India, the mission usually managed to enforce what came to be known as the "two doctor rule" in Bahrain station—one to tour, and one to keep an eye on the home base. The impact of touring, thereafter, was only a lesser inconvenience, since there were those who could put a finger in the dike during the sporadic absences of the senior medical personality.

What touring achieved was not its goal. But it did help prepare regions in which the mission was not established for the advent of modernity and the overwhelming influx of expatriate labor and enterprise. This influx, a trickle in the early 1930s, was running in full spate by the end of World War II and became a torrent in the 1950s.

Part Six

A Still More Excellent Way ...

All Together ... Different

It is not surprising, perhaps, that the Arabian Mission should have moved so quickly from the loose-jointed pioneer phase into that of established institutions and fixed "stations." Even as early as 1897, Peter Zwemer, contemplating things from the perspective of Muscat, was aware that the pioneer period was swiftly drawing to a close; he regretted that there would soon be no new frontiers to cross. The initial thought of the strategists was that the stations of the mission would be simply staging points from which to launch the mission's main campaign to "occupy the interior of Arabia." Eventually it became apparent, however, that each of these places generated its own center of gravity. With a somewhat schizophrenic effect, they all came to be viewed as permanent establishments existing in their own right and for their own ends. Certainly each new investment on the "periphery" made the goal of the "interior" less attainable. Even in November, 1914, the following paragraph from minutes adopted by the mission to celebrate twenty-five years of work sounds like whistling in the dark:

> The Mission, while it has not outgrown its pioneer character, as it hopes it never will, until every Arab tribe has received its message, has shown its intention of permanently occupying every position

gained, by gradually placing Christian homes and institutions in every center of population it has been possible to enter.[1]

Indeed, to "permanently occupy every position gained" increasingly forced the mission into a less mobile posture. They suspected that was true in 1914. They only acknowledged it in 1956.

Topography, geographical situation, political events, and climate all had their effects upon the manner in which each station evolved. The local ethos and culture, distinctive in each station, also shaped the outlook of missionaries—mission children were particularly sensitive to this, arguing heatedly among themselves about which place was best.[2] Mission stations were also imprinted by dominant personalities: John and Dorothy Van Ess, Fred and Margaret Barny, Rachel Jackson, and George and Chris Gosselink in Basrah; Gerrit and Gertrude Pennings, James Moerdyk, and Bill and Cora Moerdyk in 'Imârah; Stanley and Bessie Mylrea, Edwin and Eleanor Calverley, Gary and Everdine DeJong, Lew and Dorothy Scudder, and Don and Evelyn MacNeill in Kuwait; Paul and Monty Harrison, Harold and Pat (and later Ida) Storm, Gerrit and Josephine Van Peursem, Cornelia Dalenberg, and Ruth Jackson in Bahrain; and Paul and Monty Harrison, Wells and Beth Thoms, Dirk and Minnie Dykstra, Jay and Midge Kapenga, Jim and Joyce Dunham, and Don and Eloise Bosch in Matrah and Muscat.

These were individuals, men and women, who marched together. They were strong individuals with remarkable personal characteristics. The imprint they left upon the wider society is still felt. Others in the mission had wide impact because they moved from station to station. James and Elizabeth Cantine were two such, others were James Moerdyk, Gerrit and

---

[1]Mason and Barny, *History...*, p. 163. It is interesting to note in this statement the mission's awareness of the significance of the Christian home. The missionary family was known to be a strong witness.

[2]In the recollection of the author, Muscat usually won, both because of the eloquence and physical persuasiveness of the advocates, and because the beaches there were clearly superior.

Gertrude Pennings, Paul and Monty Harrison, Fred and Margaret Barny[3], Donald and Eloise Bosch, Harvey and Hilda Staal, and Maurice and Eleanor Heusinkveld. So, while each of the stations had distinctive characteristics, there was also a considerable degree of commonality which these peripatetic ones helped cultivate. The commonality was reinforced by the intense experience of the annual meetings and by the brisk station-to-station correspondence that missionaries maintained.

The mission concentrated upon the events that directly affected their environment. They understood with a fine-honed nicety the permutations of local politics. They were entertained by rulers and leading merchants. They were guests in leading families' homes, counselors for their families, ministers to their needs, and, indeed, friends. Both by obligation and inclination, missionaries were also aware of the presence of British and other foreign interests in the region. Many British colonial administrators, other western diplomats, oil explorers, and company executives are counted among the close friends of missionaries. Many of these dignitaries were also strong supporters of the missionaries' work and fellow members of the local bodies of Christian worshipers. But, in a manner quite unique, the missionaries also knew life in the hovels of the poor and daily dealt with the physical and emotional problems of the less advantaged. They were earnest interpreters of the virtues of Christian democracy—sometimes quite unaware of the seeds they were planting—and listened with excited sympathy to those bright and winsome Arabs who sought after wisdom, the better to engage responsibly in a shrinking and increasingly highly charged and challenging world.[4]

---

[3]Fred and Margaret Barny's daughter, Esther Barny Ames, now living in New Jersey, was the first of the mission's children to return to the field (1927). She was a physician and worked in Kuwait (1929-1932) and Bahrain (1936-1945). In 1943 she married an oil man (as several other single missionaries had done and were to do again) and finally resigned from the mission in 1945. She continued active in mission affairs as a staff physician with the Associated Mission Medical Office in New York for many years.

[4]Paul Harrison was an aggressive advocate of democratic values, and he believed the Arabian bedouin epitomized the essentially American virtues he admired. His table talk and casual conversations were memorable. The impact of Edwin Calverley upon a pre-Depression generation of Kuwaiti boys extended a significant influence into the crucial early days of Kuwait's nation building in the 1950s. Donald MacNeill, in Kuwait, took in occasional students to study English. One of these was a young Palestinian electrical engineer in government employ named Yâsir 'Arafât. Ed Luidens, teaching in Basrah, recalled several individuals who later participated in successive republican regimes with whom, during the later days of the monarchy, he had discussed the principles of democracy.

Although in 1889 they had a general organizational plan for the support of the Arabian Mission in the United States, on the field it was clear that the plan of attack was strictly "improvise!" It could hardly have been otherwise. Cantine and Zwemer were young men, typical of their own culture, with little experience of foreign societies. They were driven by great enthusiasm and a sense of purpose the realization of which might have seemed quite feasible when viewed from the western shores of the Atlantic. But on the fringes of the decrepit Ottoman Empire, there were realities that had to be faced and difficult lessons to learn.

There were tools in hand to provide some definition; using them, permanent institutions were built. But there were other occasional efforts that were either never quite established,[5] had a built-in term element, or were notions of individuals or projects that were person-specific.

One of these undertakings had a profound symbolic significance. It was the occasional care and shelter the mission gave to the homeless. From 1896 to 1901 the mission took in a boatload of slave boys in Oman and trained them until they were of an age to venture off on their own.[6] In the same key, the mission took into its care orphans in Bahrain. In the early 1940s, on the "East Compound," Josephine Van Peursem set aside a large room as a nursery, and the house and household that was eventually built to shelter the orphans came to be known as *Bayt Saʿīd* (The Happy Home or, more precisely, Home of the Happy One). The children who were taken in formally adopted the family name, Saʿīd. The last one, added to the family June 9, 1957, was a two-day-old baby boy who was named John.[7]

[5] By way of example, a consequence of the First World War was a feeling in the mission that there was work to do among soldiers and military-attached civilian bachelors in Iraq. Edwin Calverley out of Kuwait and Henry Bilkert and Gerrit Pennings out of Basrah became involved with the YMCA work among British India troops in Baghdad. The effort was sustained for a couple of years and then discontinued as other agencies took up the task.

[6] Wells Thoms, while a college student, recalled running into one of these individuals on a Lake Michigan ferry. He was serving as a cook.

[7] In Joyce Dunham's letter to her parents June 9, 1957, she wrote: "Guess what our newest problem is—a baby! Someone left a two-day old boy in the cemetery right across from our hospital, to where a woman who had found it brought it. Some

Although many missionaries, particularly the women, helped with the orphans over the years, the person who became most intensively involved in this work was Madeline Holmes. She picked up the task from Bill and May Decker in the spring of 1957 and continued until 1969. Initially she worked intimately with Khayriyyah "Umm-Miryam" Haydar (who doubled as the evangelist at the women's clinic at the hospital). When Umm-Miryam was retired and moved out and during Madeline Holmes's furlough year (1958-59), the Zabânas, a Palestinian family, served briefly as house parents. Several of the younger children in particular came to truly bond with Madeline as their mother. When she retired and returned to the United States, the shock these children experienced was significant. After the Bahrain government began to take up responsibilities for this kind of service in 1957, the mission, with a certain sense of relief, went out of the orphanage business in 1973, but relations with the 'Bayt Saʿîd Family' continued very much a concern of Bahrain-based missionaries well into the 1980s.

An unusual ministry undertaken by one missionary couple was that which marked the late career of Jay and Midge Kapenga. Called back from an indefinite leave of absence in 1973, they were specifically assigned under the Oman government's Ministry of National Heritage to work at encouraging and helping market the products of a variety of village and cottage crafts in rural areas. It was a tailor-made assignment, which the Kapengas very much enjoyed until their retirement in 1982. It took them into the breathtaking Omani hinterland which they had never had the leisure to explore before and gave them stimulating contact with the straightforward rural Omanis whom they loved. It also challenged Jay's gadgeteer mind as he tried to balance preserving traditional ways against down-to-earth technological improvements which would improve productivity and, therefore, increase

of us feel it should go to Beit Saeed, and some feel very strongly that it shouldn't. Madeline, who will have the care of it now, wants it. It seems that there is more future for the church in the orphanage than in the school or hospital right now. But these orphans can cause some mighty big problems. Some of the kids themselves think we ought to take the baby. As they say, 'Where would we be if the mission hadn't taken us?'" (correspondence loaned to the author by Jim and Joyce Dunham). Little Johnny was kept, and Madeline raised him up to be a tender-hearted and caring individual. After a rocky start being educated by the mission in an academic stream, he was finally given opportunity to pursue his chosen vocation in mechanics and engineering. He has prospered in adult life, marrying a young Danish missionary and raising two children.

income for those with whom he worked.[8] Upon their retirement, had there been an apprentice in training with the Kapengas, there is no reason why this work might not have continued.

Perhaps the most ambitiously conceived of these occasional efforts were the agricultural extension projects conducted by Jeff Garden in Oman and Bahrain. Garden and others were also involved in setting up expensive audiovisual production facilities in Bahrain and Kuwait which were linked to the Near East Council of Churches' Radio Voice of the Gospel project broadcasting out of Addis Ababa.

Family Patterns

Seen in its several parts, the impression of the mission is somewhat misleading. We are speaking about a small group of people (never numbering more than about fifty) who attempted to cover a thousand-mile front with the resources of a single small American denomination behind them. It was an exceptional achievement, and its success was due primarily to their awareness that the whole fragile spider-web structure was interdependent. It was "The Mission," a single thing, to which they were all committed. And they nurtured that sense of solidarity in different ways.

From its early stages, the mission was a field-directed operation. The limits were partially set by what happened at the home base—the offices of the board in New York and the Reformed Church in America in whose name that board functioned. What happened within those material limits was a matter which, for most of its life, was left largely to the mission's own ingenuity.

One example of that ingenuity occurred during the Second World War: Supplies were hard come by in Oman, but transportation was vital to the mission's ministry there. There came a day when the tires of one of the hospital Land Rovers finally gave out and had to be replaced. Wells Thoms,

---

[8]By way of example, among a community of weavers in a village otherwise famous for the making of Omani *halâwah* (similar to but far better than Turkish Delight), Jay introduced—not without difficulty—a metal comb on the looms which replaced the old rig made of bamboo and wood. Keeping the same techniques and skills, the innovation increased the efficiency with which they made a *wizâr*, the wraparound skirt-like cloth the Omani working men prefer to wear, similar to the Indian *dhoti*. Other crafts the Kapengas encouraged were mat and basket making and the making of Oman's unique bedouin and village kilim rugs.

then in charge of the Matrah hospital, sent out a call for help, and replacements were finally located on Kuwait's thriving black market. Lew Scudder, Kuwait hospital's CMO, was Wells Thoms's brother-in-law. Some judicious inquiry turned up the needed tires and they were purchased. Scudder then forwarded them to Oman along with the hefty bill. Thoms wrote back that there was no way that Muscat station could come up with the money. Lew Scudder responded a short while later to say that the Kuwaiti merchant who had sold him the tires at usurious rates had just had to undergo a rather expensive hernia operation. The bill had been settled to everyone's satisfaction.[9]

Nowhere was the mission's ingenuity better expressed than in the annual meetings. Customarily, in the fall of the year, the missionaries gathered at one of the stations.[10] There was nothing particularly unusual about what they would do once they came together. What was unusual was the fact that they—educators, evangelists, and medical personnel, all—rolled up their sleeves and dug into each other's business with a focused, deliberate determination that made an educator a specialist in medical policy, a doctor a leading authority on evangelistic outreach, and an evangelist a consultant architect/engineer.

In interviews with elder missionaries who worked under that system and in the questionnaires Arabia missionaries completed the sentiments of Ruth Jackson were echoed: "...[S]eparated though we were, we were yet one mission with one loyalty to everybody. I think that was a wonderful thing. You know, to belong to that mission, you belonged to a family." She continued, "We were all just as concerned about the hospital—if there was somebody there, or somebody else could sacrifice to help them—or a school—if somebody was sick, somebody else would go and help. It was a complete mission, in that sense, not stations. Stations were secondary. And I think that was good, and I think there was a spirit there that was very

---

[9]From the table talk of James Dunham, 1993.

[10]Forty-odd American missionaries descending upon Bahrain or Kuwait in the 1940s and the 1950s was a thing of which British-administered government bureaucracies took account. Right up through the 1970s, the landing cards given out by Kuwait immigration authorities listed all the customary reasons why a person might be traveling—business, pleasure, family visit, residence, etc. In the midst of these was the option, "mission meeting." It was an indicator of the mission's significance.

fine."[11] They worked at each other's problems and they designed each other's solutions. They fought for their causes and they disagreed with each other, sometimes vehemently; they bickered and they argued till they were hoarse. But always they worked for the good of the whole. The exercise forged a rapport and a common bond. And when it was all over, they were friends. They belonged. They were family.

It was a thing Dorothy Van Ess proclaimed to be "the climax of all the rewards." As she affirmed, "There is a bond that is closer than the ties of blood and family; an understanding so complete that it needs no words."[12]

Spanning the particular issues and environments and personalities of the various stations of the mission there was from the outset a human competence which defied the notion of the impossible. These men and women knew they had worked through some of the most ludicrously complex and difficult problems that had faced any organization, and they had done it well. They earned—by dint of open compassion, hard work, and honesty—the trust that the Gulf people had in them, and they would continue to keep faith with them. It was preposterous that in 1893 three young men should hold together three fledgling stations and do in them work which was to become a major factor in building human dignity, relieving suffering and despair, and preparing the ground for the invasion of modernity throughout the Arab Gulf. So when the mission gathered it was with an attitude that, although reality was more frequently than not a grim thing, nothing was out of reach, and everyone would be sustained so that the whole would manage with both grace and honor.

The mission was from the outset a pure democracy. The almost endless talk to which this "inefficient" system yielded could frequently frustrate the more practical and goal-directed mind. But it was important. Everyone who was qualified (who had passed their second language examination, that is) had a voice in virtually all mission decisions. Between gatherings, each station conducted regular meetings, and when there was a matter to be dealt with by the whole mission, it was handled through a circular letter, and the consensus gathered. The authority of the mission as a whole to assign people to stations and approve furloughs, to divide up budgeted resources, and to

[11]Author's interview with Ruth Jackson, July 6, 1990, Amesbury, Massachusetts.
[12]Transcript of a speech by Dorothy Firman Van Ess, "75th Anniversary of the Arabian Mission," February 12, 1965, Bahrain, Persian Gulf, p. 5. Document in the author's collection.

modify or initiate programs was reinforced by the board's corresponding secretaries. When, as occasionally happened, individual missionaries tried to approach the board directly, they were inevitably referred back to the field. From Cobb to Chamberlain to Potter (for over fifty years), the democratic and consultative mechanisms of the Arabian Mission were considered the proper channel for decision-making. The policy of the board strengthened the sense of interdependence among missionaries.

Another instrument that kept the mission together was the Round Robin letter. These letters were written periodically by each station and circulated to the others. In them were chatty news bits, requests for prayer, reports on significant developments of the moment, family news, and friendly gossip. The local mission issues were not ignored, but the purpose of the Round Robin was to share the taste and texture of life. The letters broke the sense of isolation within a strange culture that frequently resented the missionaries' offerings. They were family letters. Responsibilities for writing them were taken seriously. By this instrument, at any given time during the year, everyone knew what everyone else was doing and what they were facing. And understanding was simply assumed.

Among missionaries, there were always those who were fairly well fixed in their positions; there were also those who, from time to time, were shifted from one station to another to fill in for vacancies or to meet rising demands. Repostings were frequent, especially for certain families (the Heusinkveld family may hold something of a distinction in this regard). While this inevitably had its serious drawbacks, it also meant that people who moved from Kuwait to Bahrain, for example, took Kuwait with them to Bahrain. They carried the touch of the place with them and they shared that in their new home. It was a kind of sub-missionary movement which cross-fertilized the wisdom of the whole.

Then there was Kodaikanal: From the early days, missionaries had customarily taken their long vacations in South India in the Palni Hills. The hill station of Kodaikanal would often find more than half of the Arabian Mission on vacation there.[13] The hot season in Arabia came after that of the

[13]In one of his secretarial letters to the Arabian Mission's secretary (dated August 18, 1927), William Chamberlain remarked, "First and foremost, we were delighted to receive on July 14 a cablegram from Kodaikanal, *one of the summer outstations of the Arabian Mission*, announcing the advent of a little son, who is to be known as Timothy, in the temporary abiding place of Dr. and Mrs. Paul Harrison" (emphasis added—document in the author's document collection).

Arcot Mission, the Arabian Mission's sister mission in India. The cottages which were used in May by India missionaries, in June, July, and August would be taken over by those from Arabia. So complete was the complement at times that on a few occasions, as in 1920, official meetings of the mission could even be held there. When Lew and Dorothy Scudder took their first "vacation" in Kodaikanal in the summer of 1939, Dirk Dykstra made sure that they carried on their study of Arabic.[14]

Kodaikanal, aside from being the place where mission children attended boarding school, was then a kind of Chautauqua for the Arabian Mission. In a more relaxed and casual atmosphere than they could have in their places of work, missionaries found time to unlimber, simply enjoy each other's company, play hard at tennis or golf, hike together in the hills, participate in cultural activities, and in general ventilate. Again, from across the Arabian Mission, people would find time to renew acquaintances, deepen friendships, and in the course of easy dialogue anticipate problems and look toward solutions. It was not all fun and games, but the fun and the games helped soothe the soul, lighten the spirit, and relax the mind so that the work ahead looked not so daunting. And, again, the family commitment was reinforced.

In Search of the Wider Family

From the outset the mission had an ecumenical orientation. The fact that no other Protestant mission agency had taken the risk of working in the Gulf area had to do with the fact that it posed an almost impossible challenge.[15]

---

[14]In 1927 the mission took action to insist that new missionaries still studying Arabic be obliged to take their vacations in Arabic-speaking environments. The action, of course, had obvious logic on its side. But it clearly was not adhered to religiously. Kodaikanal had a powerful call.

[15]The late John Piet, a veteran of India and long-time professor of English Bible and missions at Western Theological Seminary, once told the author of an encounter he had had with a representative of the Lutheran Church in America. The Lutheran had told him that they had been watching the Arabian Mission for years with the secret prayer that it might fail. Why? John Piet asked. Because, came the reply, the longer it continues the more grows the pressure upon us to get involved too. It was not long after that, under the leadership of Fred Neudorfer, that the Lutherans and the Reformed church established strong programs of cooperation particularly in Egypt and geographical Palestine. The area of the Arabian Mission was not directly involved. In these programs the most prominent participants, from the Arabian Mission side, were Harold and Neva Vogelaar.

The mission recognized that it needed help and back-up not only materially but in a spiritual sense as well. It sought ecumenical contacts and, from the days of the first international missionary conference in Edinburgh to its successors in Jerusalem and Lucknow, there was always someone to speak in the voice of the Arabian Mission. In the early years in particular, such participation in international councils was seen as extremely important. Samuel Zwemer, early on, drew the mission's eyes out beyond its parochial concerns, serving as a key organizer of the first Conference on Behalf of the Mohammedan World in Cairo in 1906, and the second in Lucknow in 1911.

The mission's impact upon these gatherings was frequently powerful. Stephen Neill, the Anglican missionary bishop and scholar, recalls: "At the great Tambaram Missionary Conference of 1938, the most moving of all the speeches was that of the veteran Dr. Paul Harrison who, having told the story of the five converts that the mission had won in fifty years, sat down with the quiet words: 'The Church in Arabia salutes you.'"[16] What the Arabian Mission brought to these gatherings was the integrity of mission pursued, as John Lansing had put it, on the basis of faithfulness to "...a Responsibility divinely imposed," and without the rewards of numerical success which missionary effort experienced elsewhere in the world.[17]

Apart from having an influence upon the larger ecumenical movement, the mission sought to participate in the rationalization of missionary effort in the Middle East in particular. In a sense this was more difficult because, in a psychological sense, Egypt and Lebanon were farther off than India. The Gulf was oriented toward India in its politics, commerce, and world view. The British-India steamers on which missionaries traveled up and

---

[16]Stephen Neill, *A History of Christian Mission* (New York: Penguin Books, 1964), p. 368.

[17]Ending a staff circular to Reformed church missionaries dated June 30, 1961, the following quotation from Charles Forman's *A Faith for the Nations* was given: "The most that we can do is to hear and to heed a call. The rest is with God. If others accept that message of God's great love, this is cause for rejoicing. But it is not the cause for our mission. That lies in the call of God. If others do not accept the message, this is no reason for despondency. After all, the mission is taken out of love for people as they are, not love for them as they will be after they have accepted God's love. Therefore, their acceptance is not the basis of the mission, nor does their refusal frustrate the mission. 'It is not required of men that they be successful....It is required of them only that they be faithful'" (document in author's collection). [The quotation is from Charles Forman, *A Faith for the Nations* (Philadelphia: Westminster Press, 1957), p. 90.]

down the Gulf would pass through Bombay and Karachi on their way to or from Oman. Almost from the outset, there was also a strong link between the Arabian Mission and the Arcot Mission in India. The British colonial government of India which, by the advent of World War I, had become the *de facto* political administrator of the Gulf, strengthened this orientation.

But the mission strove to be involved in those concerns which moved its sister missions in Egypt, Palestine, Lebanon-Syria, and Iraq. James Cantine was among the first to work with tangible impact in this direction. Almost single-handedly he brought into being the United Mission in Mesopotamia (1924).[18]

The Anglican CMS missionaries in Baghdad had been a source of help and encouragement for the Arabian Mission from the outset. Following the British occupation of Baghdad in 1917, however, the CMS was in something of a quandary. With its main effort in Iran and fearing that its Christian vocation would be compromised by the presence of British occupying forces, the CMS decided to close its substantial out-station activities in Baghdad in 1920. This put new pressures on the Arabian Mission. James and Elizabeth Cantine moved to Baghdad at the end of 1920 to try to hold what gains the CMS had made.

The mission vacuum which threatened to develop in Baghdad in 1920 was not one which the Reformed church nor the Arabian Mission felt able to fill on its own. It would have been financially draining, and the mission as a whole felt that Baghdad drew it too far afield from its seminal commitment to Arabia proper. Pressed by Cantine, William I. Chamberlain, the secretary for the Board of Foreign Missions and at that time also president of the Alliance of Reformed Churches, was able to join forces with the Presbyterians' Robert E. Speer and put together a plan for a joint mission venture. The

---

[18]This is, admittedly, a bit of a hyperbole. The concern Cantine voiced (along with others) was a strong factor. The fact that he and his wife and then Henry and Monty Bilkert held Baghdad as a temporary station of the Arabian Mission from 1919 to 1924 is also a matter of record.

The "UMM," following the establishment of the modern state of Iraq, was later renamed the United Mission in Iraq (UMI). A primary reference for the United Mission in Iraq is a pair of papers prepared by the Rev. James W. Willoughby: "The United Mission in Iraq, 1924-1962, a Brief Historical Survey," and "Goals and Fields of Activity of the United Mission in Iraq, 1924-1962, Supplemental to The United Mission in Iraq, 1924-1962, a Brief Historical Survey," published in mimeographed format by the Joint Office for Upper Nile and Iraq, New York, N.Y., September 20, 1962 (documents in author's collection).

UMM (or UMI), established formally in 1924, eventually drew together resources and personnel from the Evangelical and Reformed Church, the Presbyterian Church in the U.S A. and the Reformed Church in America. In 1956 the Presbyterian Church in the U.S. also joined. While the Arabian Mission continued directly responsible for Basrah and 'Imârah through the 1950s and into the 1960s, the UMM (UMI) became a presence that could not be ignored. Iraq as a state was moving along its own political lines, and the developing program of the UMI became increasingly relevant to what was happening in Basrah. In 1962 Basrah Station was incorporated into the UMI structure.[19]

Aside from the Cantines (1924-1929), the Reformed church also contributed to the ecumenical effort in Iraq Mae DePree Thoms (1925-1943), Fred and Margaret Barny (1925-1931), John and Margaret Badeau (1928-1936), Barny and Elda Hakken (1937-1958), Elizabeth Calverley (1938-1940), Belle Bogard (1943-1947), Raymond and Dorothy Weis (19571958), George and Christene Gosselink (1962-1966), and Robert and Vi Block (1962-1968). The government of Iraq obliged the United Mission in Iraq to declare itself out of business on September 25, 1969.

Beginning in February, 1954, the mission made an effort to organize the various churches for which it had responsibility. The Basrah Conference of 1954 ...

> ...was one of the first attempts to draw together these churches into a spiritual fellowship. Here Christians, from non-Christian as well as Christian backgrounds, were brought together in study, discussion and worship. It became apparent, at this time, that we should consider the necessity of organization of what were heretofore called mission churches, and explore avenues that

[19]The stations of 'Imârah and Basrah, although in Iraq, were held to be an intrinsic part of the Arabian Mission, and not until January, 1962, was Basrah finally integrated into the UMI structure.

would ultimately lead to the organization and establishment of an Arab Evangelical Christian Church in our area.[20]

As conversations along this line proceeded into the 1960s, the organization envisioned to give proper ecclesiastical shape to the church was first called "The Conference of the Church of Christ in the Arabian Gulf" and then the "Presbytery of the Gulf." Draft constitutions and statements were produced as befits such an august body. But, while relations between the Arabic-speaking congregations in Kuwait and Bahrain were close, Oman was always the exception. As for the Arab Protestant congregation in Basrah, it had been isolated from the others by the Iraqi revolution of 1958. In any case, it had its own northward orientation and problems and showed no enthusiasm to identify itself more closely with an American-led initiative.[21] Conversations dribbled off inconclusively, and by 1965 it was clear that no larger ecclesiastical body would emerge. That left a series of local congregationally governed communities with more or less elaborate structures.[22] Under encouragement

[20]This appeared on page 7 of a "Memo to Missionaries" from the staff of the Board of Foreign Missions of the Reformed Church in America dated November, 1955 (document in author's collection). The memo also notes in preface, "In recent years there has been an increasingly larger number of people from various national and ancient Christian backgrounds, who for political and economic reasons are literally swarming into certain parts of the Mission area. The Mission has concerned itself with the stimulation of spiritually-alive fellowships, under the direct supervision of the Mission, and under its leadership and administration. It has been felt, however, that these fellowships should not become provincial in their outlook, but should share with one another in their common faith and witness..." (p. 6).

[21]While in each station, congregations worshiping in other languages were more or less formally organized and shared local responsibilities with the Arabic-speaking congregations, it was maintained that the Arabic congregations were the "mother" congregations of the church in each place. (The principal difference between Oman and the other stations was that the Arabic-speaking congregation there was almost exclusively a convert group, while the Arabic-speaking congregations elsewhere were made up mainly of Arabs from traditionally Christian families and who had migrated into the area either in association with the mission, as colporteurs or medical personnel, or on their own initiative.) The envisioned Presbytery of the Gulf was seen as the association of these Arabic-speaking congregations without much reference to those worshiping under the same roof in other languages.

[22]The most elaborate structures evolved in Kuwait and Bahrain. There the first name chosen by missionaries was The Church of Christ. Later, at the insistence of the Arabic language congregations, in order to identify themselves more closely with Protestant churches in Syria-Lebanon and Egypt, the name was changed to The

from the mission, these occasionally recognized a historical tie to each other but were, for the most part, largely self-absorbed and self-contained.

Especially in Kuwait and Bahrain, but to some extent also in Oman, the mission's churches served as the anchorage for growing and proliferating ethnic and denominational congregations that began to take shape in each locale as expatriate labor poured into the region, especially during the early 1950s. Muslim governments in the Gulf had come to tolerate the worship services held on mission premises and even recognized the churches as, in some sense, "their churches." But in a Muslim society, there was little tolerance for the Protestant penchant (which the Indian contingent typified with a certain depressing verve) for establishing a multitude of competitive congregations, often worshiping in private homes. It fell to the mission chapels, therefore, to provide not only the home for the congregations it had itself nurtured, but also for others that came into being among segments of the burgeoning expatriate population. Among the first of these were Roman Catholic congregations, initially served by itinerant Carmelite priests working out of Basrah.

When the Catholic church was able to do so, however, it acquired its own facilities and defined its communities as distinct and separate. Two Roman Catholic dioceses were established in the Gulf, one responsible only for Kuwait, and the other, with the bishop's seat in Abu Dhabi, covering the rest of Arabia. The Anglican church, which frequently cooperated with the Arabian Mission in providing pastoral services to expatriates, organized itself under the archbishopric of Jerusalem with financial backing from the

National Evangelical Church (NEC). To keep the congregations of various language groups together, the instrument of a "common council" was devised to deal with common issues, but each language-defined congregation was constituted to deal with its own internal business—including calling pastors and providing housing and salaries. Other groups who chose to define themselves in denominational fashion and remain distinct from the NEC became more or less clients and tenants. (Far and away the largest of these was the Marthoma Syrian Church of Malabar.)

Jerusalem and East Mission. When the archbishopric was dissolved to make way for the organization of the Episcopal Church in Jerusalem and the Middle East in 1973, the Gulf was made part of the somewhat ersatz expatriate Diocese of Cyprus and the Gulf, a pro-cathedral being established in Bahrain.

Emulating the Catholic and Anglican examples, Christians from the Indian subcontinent brought their church structures and community patterns with them, replete with itinerant supervising bishops and visiting evangelists to ensure the loyalty and material support of church members working in the Gulf for their home communions in India and to regularize the rotation of pastors. Syrian Orthodox, Marthoma, Church of South India, St. Thomas Evangelicals, the whole spectrum of Pentecostals, as well as other congregations defined by language (Telegu, Tamil, and Urdu) evolved to meet the demands and expectations of special groups. These were sometimes given facilities with the Anglicans, but in Kuwait, Bahrain, and Oman they were given shelter under the umbrella of the Arabian Mission's client churches which, by the 1960s, had already developed their own clearly distinct Arabic, Malayalee, and English congregations.[23]

The growth of the expatriate Christian community and the proliferation of these groups led to an increasingly complex local picture, the most tangled of which was and continues to be that in Kuwait. The absorbing local pressures to make increasingly complex accommodations, and the special local mix and entanglements, further isolated the congregations related to the Arabian Mission from each other. It also raised questions about the degree to which the Arabian Mission ought to concern itself with issues that tended to draw the mission further away from the indigenous Muslim population.[24]

---

[23]In Bahrain, for the Malayalee congregation, one must substitute Tamil, Telegu, and Urdu congregations.

[24]Clearly the mandate of the mission and those of the churches which entered into the region later differed. The notion that the new expatriate communities could form the base of a new dimension of Christian witness in the region was seductive and had a certain degree of theological legitimacy. But in practice these new congregations and communities tended to strictly disassociate themselves from any suggestion that they were ordained to bear witness to their faith in the Gulf's Muslim milieu. Their principal interests lay in their attachments to "home," wherever that might be. That tended to frustrate missionaries and reinforce the artificial distinction between "mission" and "church." This debate continues. We will touch on it again.

The mission endeavored to establish working relationships with other mission organizations interested in work in the Gulf and the Middle East as a whole. Other prospects beckoned from a distance too far away for the mission effectively to respond. Bearing mention are Jiddah on the Red Sea—occupied briefly in 1913 by missionaries from Egypt—and the area between Muhammarah in the north to the port of Linga in the south on the Iranian side of the Gulf.[25] For these undertakings, the mission encouraged other organizations to take up the slack.[26]

Since the days of Samuel Zwemer's first visit there, the mission had kept alive a dream of working in the Hadramaut in the coastal sultanate of Makallah, bathed by the vast expanse of the Indian Ocean. An effort to do this, inspired by an article written by Samuel Zwemer, was made in 1903 by the Danish Arabian Church Mission through its first missionary, Rev. Oluf Høyer, but that good gentleman, after a warm reception as a guest, was summarily packed aboard an Arab dhow and shipped back to Aden when he declared his intention to remain as a resident. On his fabled trek through Arabia's outback from June, 1935, to March, 1936, Harold Storm stopped off briefly there. He brought word that Makallah was now ripe for a medical mission.

In the 1940s a cooperative scheme was essayed between the Reformed church and the Southern Baptist Convention whereby the latter, using the Arabian Mission as a resource and support group, would open work in Makallah. The dream was pressed vigorously by Harold Storm and especially by his second wife, Ida. She was Southern Baptist by background and inclination and vigorously campaigned for the idea among Baptist women's groups in the United States. Correspondence between Duke Potter, then the Reformed church missions secretary, and officials of the Southern

[25]The mission hoped the burden for this latter region would be shouldered by the Reformed Church in the United States, more popularly known as the "German Reformed." This denomination, as part of the Evangelical and Reformed and then the United Church of Christ, later became involved in the United Mission in Iraq. As it turned out, the German Reformed church did not respond to the invitation.

[26]Mason and Barny, *History...*, pp. 162-163.

Baptist Convention began December 18, 1942, with Potter proposing that the Baptists start work in the Hadramaut and that the Reformed church provide Baptist missionaries with language and orientation training. The correspondence continued into 1949 and 1950, reporting the progress of two doctors (Brown and McRae) and a nurse, studying in Bahrain. By the end of 1950, however, the Southern Baptists felt that the initiative had stalled in Bahrain, and they began looking for other options. The CMS hospital in 'Ajlûn, Jordan, was being abandoned, and by December, 1950, there were already tensions between RCA and Southern Baptist personnel on the field regarding the building of one church in Arabia. The Baptists on the field refused even to visit Makallah and by July, 1951, had pulled out of the Gulf in favor of Jordan.[27]

Beginning in 1928, when medical work in Oman was reestablished and Oman's interior was again opened up for touring, Paul Harrison and Wells Thoms had cultivated particularly good relationships with the ruler of Abu Dhabi, Shaykh Shakhbût. The shaykh pressed first Harrison and then Thoms to open a mission hospital in his country, offering the town of al-'Ayn in the Buraymî Oasis as a promising site. Encouraged and directly assisted by Thoms, The Evangelical and Alliance Mission (TEAM) led by Burwell "Pat" and Marion Kennedy (who had trained with the Arabian Mission and played a supportive role during the traumatic closure of 'Imârah station in 1958) eventually exploited the relationship and the opportunity, opening a hospital in al-'Ayn toward the end of 1960.[28] Again, the Arabian Mission

---

[27]The file of this correspondence is in the Archives of the Reformed Church in America, New Brunswick, New Jersey, primarily between Potter and G.W. Sadler, secretary for Africa, Europe, and the Middle East for the Southern Baptist Convention.

[28]To establish the contact and make the introduction of Pat Kennedy to Shaykh Shakhbût, Wells Thoms had gone to al-'Ayn. When, finally, Kennedy arrived almost too late, the shaykh told him to pace off how much land he needed. Thoms, who knew how essential space was for medical work and having experienced the frustrations of too little land in both Bahrain and Oman, urged Kennedy, "Don't get tired of walking!"

offered itself as a resource and support group, supplying language-study facilities on Bahrain. But links between TEAM and the Arabian Mission quickly deteriorated, leaving a bitter aftertaste. Little mutual benefit was derived from the experience.

Of the cooperative ventures, one which did give much satisfaction was the work with the Danish Missionary Society (DMS). The Danes had taken up work in cooperation with the Scottish Mission in Aden in 1904. But when, between 1965 and 1967, missionaries were expelled from there, the Danes cast about for alternatives for their capable and well-trained personnel. A close and cooperative relationship with the Arabian Mission seemed a natural option. An agreement was worked out between the Reformed church and the Danish Mission Society in 1967 (formalized in 1969),[29] and an influx of some twenty highly qualified and well-motivated missionaries into the Gulf gave new life to the Arabian Mission. The DMS provided book sellers, nurses, doctors, chaplains, and one engineer to the work in Kuwait, Bahrain, and Oman.[30]

[29] RCA General Program Council Executive Committee action number EX-69-51.
[30] The work of the DMS in the Gulf traces its beginning to a growing awareness in small prayer groups for work in the Muslim world. The prayer groups knew themselves as "the Danish Arabian Church Mission" and developed a base strong enough to send out Rev. Oluf Høyer. Toward the end of 1903, Høyer was in Jerusalem and read an article written by Sam Zwemer appealing that work be taken up in the Hadramaut. He went to Aden in 1904 and explored possibilities in Makallah. After an initial warm reception there as a guest, the sultan quickly changed his mind when it became evident this man intended to stay and set up shop. Høyer was expelled from Makallah and reappeared in Aden, much worse for wear. He was taken in by Dr. Young, then heading up the Scottish mission work in Shaykh 'Uthmân and, having recovered his health, was offered a cooperative arrangement in medical and evangelistic work. In 1910 the DACM decided to take up its post rather in Aden city itself, operating a school and a book shop. It also posted missionaries in Hudaydah. The First World War disrupted work between 1914 and 1919, but it was resumed by Rev. C.J. Rasmussen, Høyer having become home secretary and returned to Copenhagen. The resources of this mission were expanded in 1946 when it merged with the Danish Mission Society. Their work in Aden included founding the "South Arabian Church," a medical clinic, a girls' school, and a book shop. Between 1965 and 1967, most

A second ecumenical venture was undertaken with the Lutheran Church in America (LCA) under the leadership of the flamboyant Fred Neudorfer. In the later 1960s, the Lutherans assigned Bruce Schein to investigate possibilities for ministry in the Middle East. Schein had a background in the Lutheran church's program of dialogue with the Jewish people. Based in Beirut, Schein traveled extensively in the region, even touring in the Gulf.[31] His strong recommendation was for building a diverse team of personnel, scattered in various places on the Mediterranean littoral from Lebanon to Egypt but brought together for periods of fellowship, who would press forward the enterprise of Muslim-Christian dialogue in a variety of environments.

Danish missionaries were obliged to leave Aden. A few remained until 1971. The willingness of the DMS to endorse the Arabian Mission policy not to establish denominationally dependent congregations in the Gulf led to a cordial and fruitful cooperative relationship which still continues. (The author is obliged to Leif Munksgaard of the DMS, a friend and missionary colleague, for the substance of this summary, especially the more modern information. A note on the Danish Church Mission of Aden is also to be found in Mason and Barny, *History...*, pp. 229-230.)

[31]Schein was a driven man, much aware of the cumulative effects of anyotrophic lateral sclerosis (Lou Gehrig's disease) from which he was slowly dying, and which undoubtedly contributed to his frequent impatience and occasional cantankerousness. His evaluation of the Arabian Mission's work, particularly in the area of Muslim-Christian dialogue, was extremely critical. The author and his wife, then working among university students in Beirut, spent many hours with Schein, allowing him to ruminate upon his findings in the relaxed atmosphere of their home. His annoyance with the Arabian Mission had to do with the absence of any initiative on the part of the mission's clergy to engage with local Muslim clergy in a regular discussions on matters of mutual concern. He felt that the mission, instead, had chosen to exploit its hospitals and schools to "get at" the more vulnerable and less sophisticated Muslim "laity." In his recommendations to the LCA, he strongly urged that they not become involved in the Gulf but limit their involvement to areas in which Muslim leadership was more sophisticated and more open to peer relationships with western Christians. He thought Muslims under Israeli occupation would be particularly susceptible to this kind of approach. Schein was also extremely skeptical about the Arab church's willingness to engage in these sorts of dialogue relationships. The project, until recently, has had no close links with the Middle East Council of Churches (see note 35 below).

Cooperative relations with the Reformed church were established, permitting the assignment of Harold and Neva Vogelaar to this venture. After an initial period of service in Oman followed by a stint in the United States, earning for Harold a doctorate, the Vogelaars served in theological education in Egypt. Later they returned to the United States and became involved in establishing programs of Muslim-Christian dialogue in the Chicago area. A second family with Arabian Mission roots who joined this venture, Peter and Kathy Kapenga (Peter, the son of Marjory and Jay Kapenga of Oman), served in the Friends' School in Ramallah on the Occupied West Bank. Lewis (Jr.) and Nancy Scudder were appointed to work with the Middle East Council of Churches under this same arrangement in 1994.

While ecumenical efforts within the mission's area of endeavor were a concern, it also maintained an active relationship to the emerging regional ecumenical body. What is now known as the Middle East Council of Churches organizationally had roots in an intermission consultative structure known eventually as the Near East Christian Council (NECC, inaugurated in 1932), with its headquarters in Beirut, Lebanon. The Arabian Mission soon became a member. The council's broader activities, such as radio work and literature production, occasionally lured away members of the Arabian Mission to the lights and glamour of Beirut. Prominent among these were Edwin Luidens, who left Iraq in 1957 to pursue his interest in radio (and then on into fields yet more distant); Donald MacNeill, who in 1961 followed his interest in literature development, adult education, and publications; and Leonard Lee, who succeeded Ed Luidens in radio work.

The Near East Christian Council was dissolved in 1964 so as to make way for the Near East Council of Churches (still NECC).[32] This body, in

[32]From April 14 to 17, 1964, at its meeting in Cairo, the Near East Christian Council, in the first vote taken during its plenary session, voted to disband itself and to constitute in its stead the Near East Council of Churches. "Those who represented missions, as I did," reported Raymond Weiss, "had only one opportunity to vote in the plenary sessions of the Council and that was to vote ourselves out of a vote

addition to the Protestant communions of the Middle East, involved one of the ancient Oriental churches as well—the Syrian Orthodox church—through its Patriarchate of Antioch. Mission agencies, then, stepped back a pace to allow ecclesiastical entities to take their true position as partners in cooperation and dialogue. Organizations such as the Arabian Mission continued to relate through the several service departments of the NECC. Of the churches in the Gulf which had links with the Arabian Mission, only the Arabic Congregation of the National Evangelical Church in Kuwait joined the NECC. The churches in Bahrain and Oman, for very different local reasons, held back. The Kuwait church continued to maintain its membership as the NECC dissolved itself to make way for the formation of the Middle East Council of Churches (MECC) in May of 1974.

Unlike its predecessor organizations, the MECC was and continues to be a truly ecumenical association of *all* the major Christian communities of the Middle East, with the exception of the Ancient Assyrian Church of the East[33] and (up until 1990) the oriental communions in union with the Roman Catholic church. The new organization was not greeted with unanimous approval within the Arabian Mission. For one thing, it represented, at least in part, a deliberate surrender of the old western Christian bias against the eastern churches. Not all missionaries felt that bias was unfounded. They predicted that an organization dominated by tradition-bound eastern ecclesiastical bodies would betray all that for which they had labored for over a century. The fact that the MECC has not only built upon

at any future plenary sessions." Those who carried on were representatives of churches, the Gulf being represented by one co-opted member, Sâmî Shammâs of Kuwait. The mission agencies were related to the new NECC under the newly formed Commission on Witness and Evangelism, presided over at its inaugural session by Harold Davenport of the United Mission in Iraq with R. Park Johnson as general secretary. Weiss further observed that "at present some agencies of the NECC are larger, better organized and better staffed than the NECC itself. In fact, most are aware of the NECC through its agencies and the programs for which they are responsible, i.e., Radio Voice of the Gospel, the Sunday School curriculum, the literature work, the refugee program and the study committee on Islam." (From a copy of "Report to the Arabian Mission on the Meeting of the Near East Christian Council, Cairo, Egypt, United Arab Republic, April 14-17, 1964," by Rev. Raymond E. Weiss. In the author's collection now in the Archives of the Reformed Church, New Brunswick, New Jersey.)

[33]The membership of the Ancient Assyrian Church of the East in the MECC was approved by the council's executive committee in June 1996. At the council's next general assembly in early 1999, it will be officially received into membership as a member of the Catholic family of churches.

the ministries that western mission organizations had begun, but has also amplified them and moved beyond them into areas they could not have touched is eloquent testimony to the gospel's ability to break down walls of division.

Leaving that old bias aside, the Arabian Mission assumed, with some justification, that as soon as the Middle East Council was formed, with its larger constituency oriented around the Mediterranean Basin, concern for work among Muslims in the Gulf would be diluted in the major pressing issues which challenged the larger communions of Egypt, Syria, Palestine, Lebanon, and Turkey.[34] As an exception, one important initiative bears mention here:

In 1980 the Middle East Council, in dialogue with the Reformed Church in America, recognized the virtues of a project first put forward in 1976 and then rejected by the National Council of Churches in the United States. The project addressed itself to a manifest and growing need to serve the expanding Christian populations of the Gulf and to enrich the resources of and communications between its increasing number of divergent communions. They assigned Lewis R. Scudder, Jr., to be the MECC's liaison officer for the Gulf, with his base in Bahrain. They chose him partly on the strength of the argument that he had been among the framers of the original proposal in 1976, and also because he had experience both with the MECC during his sojourn in Lebanon (1967-1973) and with the challenges of pastorate in the Gulf (1973-1976).

Funding for the position was provided by the Reformed Church in America and the program budget by the MECC; the residence requirements were met by the National Evangelical Church in Bahrain (not without some sense of irony, since it still refused formal association with the MECC). A surprising amount of the operating budget of the office was generated locally in the Gulf, mainly through the strong participation of the Roman Catholic church in Kuwait and scattered expatriate Christian fellowships which sometimes did not even call themselves churches. The promise the

---

[34]In a formal sense, the churches in Turkey do not relate to the Middle East Council; their official orientation is toward Europe. In a practical manner, however, their constituencies and those of the Middle East Council overlap to the extent that a high degree of cooperation is essential. Furthermore, the American Board in Turkey (heir to the work of the ABCFM and presently related to the United Church Board of World Mission) maintained relationships with much of the work of the Middle East Council.

MECC Liaison Office in Bahrain showed in organizing three major conferences of Gulf Christians and in building communications between the diverse Christian communions active in the Gulf has not yet been fully realized.

In 1986 Lewis Scudder resigned for personal and family reasons and withdrew.[35] His replacement was Ian Young, a young Anglican curate seconded part time to the work by the Diocese of Cyprus and the Gulf of the Episcopal Church in Jerusalem and the Middle East. But Ian Young had been burdened by his bishop with several other ongoing tasks. He was not able to devote enough time to the work of the MECC Liaison Office. When Young had to withdraw in 1990, the position was left vacant for a time. The Reformed church then took back the facilities it had provided. The ecumenical center that had been evolving was shut down. In 1992, however, the Swedish Evangelical Lutheran church (through the Church of Sweden Mission) assigned a couple to pick up the task—Hans and Åsa Degerman. The role of host at the base of Bahrain, the Reformed church having backed off, was taken over by the St. Christopher's Episcopal Church. The need for this ministry is still very much alive, and it is now being further developed.

The Language of the Angels: The Medium of Relevance

Finally, there was language study. It was not seen as a direct mission effort but rather as a tool for doing the work of mission in this context. It was the irreplaceable tool for communing with the people and for becoming part of the community. Without it crucial bridges could not have been built, leaving aside the whole matter of daily survival. Speaking the language is, to coin a phrase, the only way to speak.[36]

[35]The Scudders returned to active service as RCA World Mission Associates, taking a call to the Union Church of Istanbul, where they served from 1990 to 1993. After a sojourn in New Brunswick, New Jersey, devoted to the completion of this book, they were assigned to the staff of the Middle East Council of Churches, this time in Limassol, Cyprus. Lew Scudder, Jr., was assigned duties in the Communications Department of the council and, following the reorganization of the council in early 1995, was asked to serve as an assistant to the new general secretary, Riad Jarjour. In this assignment the Scudders were supported jointly both by the Reformed Church in America and by the Evangelical Lutheran Church in the United States. With their return to full missionary status and the developing interest of the MECC in the region, the Scudders were also encouraged to reestablished ties with the Gulf.

[36]Van Ess, *Meet the Arab*, pp. 42-53, a lighthearted chapter on the significance and joy of Arabic upon the tongue by the mission's acknowledged master of the medium.

For most missionaries it was a life-long fascination, obsession, or frustration. Cantine and Zwemer drove themselves hard in their study of Arabic during their early years, an enterprise in which Zwemer excelled.[37] The "Rules of the Arabian Mission," which the two men wrote in 1897 and which was updated periodically thereafter, laid heavy stress upon missionaries becoming competent in the Arabic language. Like the pioneering pair, the first recruits had to take their language training "on the hoof." Given major responsibilities virtually from the day they arrived, their talents were immediately pressed into service while they were tailed about by an Arab tutor/translator— usually one of the colporteurs, not always a competent teacher, who, in any case, also had other duties to perform.

Toward the end of the first decade of the twentieth century, however, as the total work force grew, missionaries were posted as full-time language students in stations where there were mentors. John Van Ess was the mission's Arabist *par excellence*, so a good many missionaries trained under him in Basrah. In the years before his preeminence was firmly established, it was customary for newcomers to take their first years in Bahrain under the tender ministrations of Mu'allim Nasîf and Sitt Sârah and one of the senior missionaries like Fred Barny or Gerrit Pennings. Occasionally language students were posted in Kuwait, where Bessie Mylrea and Mu'allim Isrâ'îl, and later Sitt Sârah, monitored their progress.

Arabic held a fascination. There were those in the mission who fell in love with it, and it infected their speaking in whatever language they spoke. Don MacNeill, like many another Arabic aficionado, fell in love with the word *ya'nî*. Now *ya'nî* has a simple lexical meaning, but it has so far transcended it as to make any dictionary definition trite. I can still see Don, rippling up his forever-ascending forehead, placing two fingers of his fabulously expressive hand over the bridge of his nose, flinging them then up in a gesture of eloquent emphasis, and declaiming, "*Ya'nî!*" as though it were gospel truth. It meant, "It means." But it could also mean, "Eh, maybe so, maybe not." It was also sort of a Victor Borge punctuation mark, to be inserted when other words failed (and so MacNeill). It always meant just

---

[37]Until the latter 1960s, the discipline of language study was strictly enforced by the Arabian Mission. The discipline was only relaxed in cases of dire emergency. Even then, until an individual had passed the rigorous language examination, full status in the mission was not given. Henry J. Wiersum's description of the process of learning Arabic is humorous but indicates as well how very seriously it was taken (*AMFR* #33, pp. 6-8). See also Mason and Barny, *History...*, pp. 108-109.

enough and never too much and shades in between wherever handy. Harvey Staal, another master of the language, with his fulsome deep voice, glinting eyes, and commanding stature, would smile his shy smile at an ambiguity and say, "*Allâhu 'a'lam*" (God is the more knowing). It was to him almost as good as *ya'nî*.

Arabic titillated and teased, tested and tangled and taught the mind to strain at new conceptions, and those who entered into it with gusto, like Maurie Heusinkveld or any of a dozen others, were like addicts. Others smote the language hip and thigh all their lives. None racked up more scholastic hours studying Arabic than Mary Allison, but she could never put together an Arabic sentence without making an Arab snicker. Gender, case, number, and tense all came out end-over-tea-cozy, making for linguistic exotica which would be joyfully repeated, sometimes for weeks. The Persian speakers in Kuwait, many of whom spoke Arabic with deliberate atrociousness, could not but envy her gift.

Lew Scudder, Sr., spoke Arabic with hardly an accent and loved the taste of the language on his tongue. He was not a proud man, nor did he find it easy to poke fun hurtfully at others. But among the stories he loved to tell was one about Mary Van Pelt during her early years in Kuwait. Called upon to go to a Kuwaiti home in the middle of the night to attend a woman in childbirth, she thought she had the directions right. When she stood before the house she had intended and found the door fast closed against her and no lamp of welcome lit in the courtyard, she became anxious for her patient. In the middle of the narrow canyon of an alley, her small lantern clutched in her hand, in a commanding voice she demanded, "*Manû yuhibbu-nî?*" And she would not relent to the silence that fell after each far-echoing repetition.

Now, in early Arabic lessons, a student is taught that "*yuhibbu*" means "he wants." The tickler is that it has that meaning *only* with reference to *things*— he wants this kind of food or that article of clothing. With reference to people, the verb takes upon itself a meaning quite different. In real terms, what the sedate Kuwaiti neighborhood was hearing this benighted foreign woman shout at the top of her lungs in a dark alley at midnight was, "Who is it that has set his desire upon me?" And finally, looking bleary-eyed out of his upper floor bedroom window, the lord of the house got the message and responded, "*Anâ, in-shâ'-Allâh*" (God willing, it is I).

The first task of a newly arrived missionary was Arabic and *only* Arabic. Passing the two language examinations became the final hurdle for anyone who wanted to serve in Arabia and a key element in mission discipline.[38] It might seem wasteful to take a fully trained doctor, for instance, and reserve most of his or her time for a task other than medical practice, but the wisdom of the founders was that the apparent waste in the short run meant significantly greater personal satisfaction and effectiveness over the long haul. They were right, of course. It did mean recruiting two years ahead of anticipated needs, and that required both fiscal courage and a vision of how the mission would develop. But those qualities were not lacking, neither in the leadership of the Reformed church's board nor on the field.

Over the years, however, it became clear that the study of Arabic was, in itself, a *missionary* expression. Arabs have an abiding love affair with their language unexcelled by any other culture. Learning it was an eloquent compliment paid by the missionaries to the people among whom they worked, an indication that they took them seriously. It demonstrated their respect for the culture and society and illustrated the missionary's desire to be a part of the lives of the Arabs that could be communicated in no other manner. It provided a unique opportunity for Christian witness, since an Arab Muslim could often be amazed that someone learning the difficult language would not automatically become a Muslim, especially since a significant part of language training involved readings in the *Qur'ân*. The idea that a non-Muslim could be conversant in Arabic and Islam and even sympathetic with Muslim spiritual strivings was a novel and winsome thought. Without a doubt it was a key component in the trust which the Muslims of the Gulf came to vest in the mission, particularly in its medical work. But it was also a reason why ordained evangelists in company with a mission physician often found a warm welcome even in Riyâdh, the Wahhâbî capital. While the mission stuck to this discipline, this aspect of direct mission may not have been as obvious as when the discipline was dropped at the close of the 1960s.

---

[38]It had its humorous side too. Lew and Dorothy Scudder, on their first visit to Kuwait after their appointment in 1937, fell in love with Mary Van Pelt's new Ford car. But Lew was strictly warned off by the proprietor of said vehicle. He had not passed his language examinations, she said, and until he had he was not to drive any mission-owned vehicle nor (which seemed less onerous at the time) exercise a vote in mission meetings.

The mission tried several different approaches to the discipline. The pioneers, as has been previously stated, learned Arabic as best they could on the job. Often on the road, they would move around with their colporteur/tutor, gathering in the language, and some did it very well. Zwemer always had a reputation as a virtuoso. John Van Ess was a master, both of classical Arabic and of the dialect of southern Iraq. Paul Harrison could chat comfortably in the heavy drawl of the bedouin, a signal achievement. Bessie Mylrea became known as one of the finest speakers of Arabic in the mission. And Everdine De Jong wrote a still valuable text on Gulf Arabic and could chat with the bedouin women with at least as much facility as Harrison could with the men.

Eventually, certain stations became language-learning centers. Basrah was one, and the name of Mu'allim Jalîl Amso, who tutored missionaries under the watchful oversight of John Van Ess, became a person dearly loved by novice missionaries. Bahrain, with Mu'allim Nasîf, was an important center as the 1920s phased into the 1930s. Kuwait, with Mu'allim Isrâ'îl and Sitt Sârah, also was a place where missionaries were tutored in Arabic. But in the 1930s the mission also experimented with having people who were heading to the field stop first in Jerusalem and attend the Kennedy School of Missions, where Mu'allim Barghûth breathed upon them his gentle benediction of garlic breakfasts. The younger Thoms, Mary Allison, and the Scudders senior were taken on this route. In the 1940s, Basrah was again the language learning station until the death of John Van Ess, when the activity shifted back to Bahrain.[39]

In the early 1960s, Maurice Heusinkveld became fascinated with the problem and, while serving in Bahrain, designed a language training program which was very effective. The mission invited the fledgling TEAM (The Evangelical Alliance Mission) missionaries to benefit from this facility. The TEAM group, however, proved to be much too aggressive and fractious. In 1966, the mission station in Bahrain requested the phasing out of the

---

[39]Beginning in the early 1940s, American mission boards set up a cooperative program for orienting missionaries. It was begun at Princeton Seminary in Princeton, New Jersey; was soon shifted to Meadville, Pennsylvania; and finally came to rest as a two-phase program beginning at Drew University and concluding in the Missionary Orientation Center (MOC) in Stoney Point, New York. This program had the distinct and added virtue of nurturing many practical ecumenical relationships and intermission friendships that sometimes spanned the globe. It was discontinued in the early 1970s.

study program, or at least restricting it to Reformed church missionaries. The last career appointed missionaries to Arabia, the Scudders junior and Henrietta Van Bruggen, were sent to Beirut for language study at the Synod Language Center in 1967.[40]

As the Board of World Mission was dissolved to be replaced by the General Program Council's Division of World Ministries, language study and intensive orientation were abandoned for a variety of reasons. The decision (if, indeed, it was ever really deliberate) was made at the time the Reformed church reorganized itself on the corporate model. Thereafter, a short-term view of efficiency came into vogue. This meant that missionaries were to come and go with greater frequency, many being appointed to tasks in which Arabic proficiency was not considered essential.[41] Another consideration was that language study and field orientation were thought to be too expensive. In a day when budgets had to be trimmed, it is not surprising that language study came to be seen as something of a luxury by those who had donned the newly designed close-up lenses. Furthermore, it was argued that English had became more common as a *lingua franca* among the more sophisticated classes of Arab Gulf society as the expatriate population of the Gulf's main centers grew to massive proportions.

Perhaps a more significant reason was that recruitment came to focus on specific tasks with short-term commitments. In the new administrative format, members of the General Program Council were quite unable to see the Arabia field (or any other overseas endeavor) as a unitary thing. It was a classic example of not being able to see the forest for the trees. All activities, wherever they might be going on, were divided up into types of program and pooled together—India, Arabia, Taiwan, and Japan—all together. The temptation was to focus on minutiae, and the study of language required a broad understanding based upon a farsighted, integrated vision of what was happening and what was intended. Farsightedness the new missiological spectacles did not permit.

---

[40]Peter and Patty Ford, appointed in 1982, were given the exceptional opportunity to study at the Kelsey School in Amman, Jordan, from January 1983 to February 1984, following an orientation program given at Selly Oak Colleges in Birmingham, England.

[41]A stop-gap measure was to use the four-month missionary orientation program offered by Selly Oak College of the University of Birmingham in England for preparing missionaries for the field, but this was not altogether satisfactory. What it offered in terms of a "taste of Arabic" was, in fact, often confusing.

The other casualty of the times reflects the same loss of focus. The practice of deliberately recruiting and formally commissioning career missionaries at what had always been an impressive ceremony during the Reformed church's General Synod was dropped. Coincidental as they were, these two changes were symbolic and extremely significant in their impact upon the mission's staffing, development, and morale. The last missionaries formally commissioned and given full and formal language training were appointed in 1966.[42]

The Mind of the Mission

Of course, to speak of one mind for the mission is preposterous. There were many. But there were certain common threads that linked its members intellectually and spiritually to one another, and all of them together to their context. While the annual meetings were times for some of these threads to show, the meetings tended to focus upon practical questions. Those who attended simply assumed a shared bedrock of consensus (which, in fact, did not always exist). And it is true that it was an extremely busy mission. The *doing* of things is what absorbed people when they came together. And, indeed, that perspective was missiologically sound.

The mission began with a common outlook upon its task. The few who were involved had similar training and had developed the plan together. The outlook on Islam was a given; it did not require long discussion. When an obvious dissonance arose, as in the case of Clarence Riggs, it proved distressing. But as the mission continued to labor and more people from wider backgrounds began to contribute their wisdom, there developed a fascination with the deeper aspects of what made Muslims tick. The few mission scholars—Gerrit Pennings, John Van Ess, Paul Harrison, Fred Barny, Edwin Calverley, Marjory Kapenga, and a few others—found in the study of the twelfth-century Muslim theologian, Abû Hâmid Muhammad al-Ghazzâlî, a window onto the Muslim soul that softened judgment. Centuries before, al-Ghazzâlî (known then in the West as Algezzel) had been among the key Muslim theologians who sharpened the disciplined mind of Thomas Aquinas and, through him, affected western Christian

---

[42]The exception to this statement, as already noted, is that of Peter and Patty Ford, appointed in 1982.

theological development. But what these missionaries found in this eloquent Muslim man of faith was his mysticism, his hearty awareness of the human dimensions of faith and the struggle for faithfulness. It became clear to them as to all the mission that when a Muslim spoke of God and a missionary spoke of God, it was to one God that they both referred. There was a basis upon which to carry on a discussion; there was something shared not merely on the intellectual level, but between hearts as well.[43]

The missiological perspective of the Arabian Mission is problematic. It was seemingly very hard to step away from the commitments of the past—the hard aggressive attitude toward Islam, with all the cultural imperial arrogance that was linked to it. The failure of Muslim religious institutions to provide leadership and to pastor their people, and their proclivity for shrill and frequently militant responses to crises did not give a great deal of basis for changing the missionaries' overall negative assessment of Islamic institutions. It was rare for Arabia missionaries to engage in deep discussions with Muslim religious leaders. It must be recalled as well that the patterns of the mission were established at a time when the educational level of Muslim religious scholarship in the Gulf was at a very low ebb. Muslim clergy avoided any but polite social encounters with missionaries. Reciprocating, the mission avoided the public religious debate. It was with willing individuals of whatever level that the missionaries carried on spiritual dialogue. Individually, many missionaries felt deeply touched and moved by their Muslim friends' faith. And that was bound to foster a growing lack of clarity about what the mission intended to see happen as a result of its efforts.

In the day-to-day labors of hospital, school, and Bible shop, in other tasks which took them into the fields and market places and streets of the city, the missionaries were in more or less constant touch with Muslims. They became aware that institutional Islam could be as oppressive and destructive of soul as any establishment the world over. While this disturbed and often affected them, they knew that they were not primarily where they were to challenge an institution. Their concern was for people. And making allowances for variety—the good, the bad, the beautiful, and the ugly—the simple

---

[43]An interesting series of essays composed by John Van Ess in Arabic and then translated into English express this confident awareness: John Van Ess, *Living Issues* (Beirut: The John Van Ess, Jr. Memorial Fund, no date).

experiences of ordinary life confirmed the contemplative conclusion: Muslims found fulfillment in their faith in a manner that could not be brushed aside.

Having said that, without exception the Christian missionaries knew they had a treasure to share as well. It needed sorting out, because their western culture was a factor of which they were aware, and some aspects of their "mission" were clearly cultural—their educational system, their preoccupation with theological talk (which Muslims did not share), their concepts of health and hygiene and the whole art of western medicine, their sense of social justice and liberation—these were things heavily conditioned by culture. But the missionaries were convinced that, informing these and, in a sense, transforming them, there was a powerful spiritual force that moved in their own persons as they worked. It was their bond in Christ; his bond to them. While Christ in them grew more "Arabized" with the years, he remained the essence of God's intent for humankind, the crystal in the heart, refracting back the light of God. And the missionaries remained aware of their unique offering. As they cherished with honor the offerings Muslim friends came to give them, they came more deeply to appreciate that the offering they bore was precious beyond price. They came to prove to themselves that Christians engaged in Muslim society became more profoundly spiritual. And it was part of their amazement at the grace showered upon them. It gave them confidence that the risk of building true friendship was worth it.

In 1913 James Cantine composed a small essay, "The Best Way to a Muslim's Heart," which served as the Arabian Mission's touchstone for years to come:

> Like attracts like. The nearest way to the Muslim Heart is to use that which appeals to the heart rather than the intellect. Our individual attainments or the attainments of the Christian Church and Christian nations in knowledge, in riches or in power are not in themselves persuasive. These things that are known as the fruits of Christianity, will not lead many Muslims to desire to be engrafted into the true vine. Neither, I think, has our superior theology been the means by which Christ has approached the hearts of most converts from Islam. The Muslim's heart is not different from yours or mine. What would appeal to us will appeal to him. It must be the heart that touches the heart. The things of the heart—love,

joy, peace, long-suffering, gentleness, goodness and the like—are what the heart esteems worthwhile the world over. The way, then, for him who would open the door, is to bring of these gifts which the heart always craves.

If it were enough to tell of them and the source from which they spring it would be simple, but the human heart demands more than this, else had the Gospel ended for us with the story of the disciples. There is only one way to prove to our Muslim friend that Christ can and will give to him these blessings and that is to show him that He has given them to us. To use an analogy which will be familiar to many, we are as commercial agents persuading merchants to trade with the firm we represent. We have an abundance of printed appeal at hand, clear and convincing, but in addition to this there is need of the living epistle. We must show our samples and these, for us missionaries, are nothing less than fruit of the Spirit in our lives. We say to him, "Believe in the Lord Jesus Christ and He will give you blessings of peace, joy and holiness." At once he replies, "You have believed, I will judge of the worth of your religion by comparing your samples with these samples of ours."

We are not introducing our goods where there are none like them but rather do we have to show that we have, that our Head can supply, a better article than has been known before. The Muslim has something of all those things that we would offer to him with Christianity and, unless he is convinced that we have in our characters and lives more of love and benevolence, more of brotherliness and piety, more of true prayer and true submission to God, our progress will be slow indeed. There are things in the Muslim faith of which he is proud and justly so. We must show him that, in these, we are better Muslims than he. There are things in which his faith is lacking. We must show him these, our riches, that he may recognize his poverty. It is in this very way the evidential value of Christian love and pity that our hospitals are such a help in reaching the heart. In the opportunity given for brotherly help lies the present value of our schools.

All this means that the nearest way is the hardest way for us. We have first to know the Muslim heart and the things he holds dear. We cannot know, understand, appreciate without first loving. We have to touch their hearts with our hearts, to come into intimate contact with his life. For this we want no flattering tongue nor imperfect means of communication. We want to enter into his life and forget the things in which we think our civilization is superior. In short we must approach him just as Christ approached the people in Judea and Galilee. It is only by such a way of self-denial and service that we can get near enough to show forth the things that commend our faith and will lead our Muslim brother, in God's providence, to accept it as his only comfort in life and death.[44]

This little homily is revolutionary because it sets aside "Muslim Controversy" as irrelevant. Argument is fruitless; polemics are only hurtful. The mind is not what the Spirit of God engages. Our theological sophistication in the West, not appreciated in the East, is of little worth in the enterprise of sharing the Bread of Life. In its time, it was also revolutionary because it urged the Christian to appreciate those things which are held dear by the Muslim heart, and because it recognized that the Muslim is religiously alive. And it is insightful in placing the challenge in its rightful place: It is not description but depiction that rivets the attention; it is not explanation but execution that confirms the integrity and authenticity of faith.

In the months before he died, Lew Scudder, Sr., used to visit his son, his pastor, and speak about his shortcomings as a missionary. He berated himself for never having mastered the art of theological fencing (of which, he held, Samuel Zwemer was the master), and he bewailed his inability to pursue religious discussions with fluency and Arabic eloquence. But the well over 1,000 people who crowded into Kuwait chapel for his funeral bore witness to something else. High and low-born, Kuwaiti and expatriate, Muslim and Christian, they all bore witness to the fact that the Christ within this man had touched and healed and spoken to them in a manner far more eloquent than the words he might have spoken. He was the sort of person whom Kenneth Cragg—the master of eloquence and at whose feet many of the Arabian Mission went to study—saw as making up the unique Christian event that was the Arabian Mission in the Gulf.

And it is fitting, at this point, to remark upon Kenneth Cragg. He was an Anglican clergyman who had done his journeyman's stint in Lebanon and fallen in love with Muslims. A scholar of profound achievements, he knew

[44]Found in a latter day transcription (in the author's collection).

Arabia's pioneers, Zwemer and Calverley, had studied with them, and, when they passed on the baton, it was to him they handed it. He was enlisted by the Near East Christian Council to lead retreats for people engaged in witness among Muslims. His influence on Arabia missionaries became powerful from the mid-1950s onward, filling in the vacuum left behind by the passing of their earlier mentors. Not seldom running in harness with Harry Dorman—the delicate Presbyterian with his smile-creased face, satchel full of yarns and lilting Lebanese fluency in Arabic—Cragg made several visits to the Gulf, and between the two of them they helped the rather isolated missionaries see that they were fulfilling the call of God. Cragg's irenic spirit persuaded them to await the moment when one shares personal faith with patience. And for most of the individuals that moment eventually came.

But it came often in a cross-fertilization of spirituality. That was one of the experiences of Arabia that could not be denied. It was uniquely for them a land filled with spirit. Duke Potter spoke of James Cantine as having been informed by his Muslim intimates to see God's time in things and be patient. Potter spoke of it as a fatalism but it was, in reality, an awareness of the divine dimension close about him to reassure and nurture a smile. John Van Ess came to picture Christ in Arab dress and Arab demeanor, and he constantly (but particularly toward the end of his career) was on the lookout for Christ in the society around him. Paul Harrison, who unabashedly projected his midwest American values of democracy and hardihood upon the bedouin found it resonating back upon him, and he came deeply to admire the simple sincerity of those to whom he ministered. And the experiences of these men were recapitulated in the generations that followed.

All of this is by way of saying that the mission belonged in the Gulf. In spite of all the cultural differences, there was a sense of fitting-in-ness and fittingness that both the missionaries and their Arab friends recognized. It took time to evolve, but evolve it did. And as they came to feel at home in the Gulf they grew to appreciate that what had been given them was a historical moment. It was a moment of peculiar equanimity—eventually shattered as other and alien forces entered into the Gulf—but it was theirs for a time. And in that moment they became aware that Christ's mission is faithfulness. Simply, faithfulness. It was enough.

Jim Dunham related an incident to his father-in-law in a letter. He had been playing host to a young man very much absorbed in his new and very private experience of salvation in Christ. In the course of a conversation,

... I mentioned my misgivings about what was happening in Islamic society as blood flows in Iran as Muslim turns on Muslim.

"Jim, that is not your concern," was the reply and the young man recited the Great Commission.

"True, my friend, but there is a commandment prior to that and more important."

Surprised, "What's that?"

"You shall love your neighbor as yourself, and love implies acceptance."

The young man laughed in embarrassment, and in that sense left me with the impression that he had never related the two. A Japanese friend put it more succinctly: "It makes a great difference whether we do evangelism with a crucified mind, or a crusader's mind."[45]

What redeemed the Arabian Mission was that, in most of its members, it had given up the crusader's mind with which the mission had begun. It had found the liberation of the crucified mind, the mind of Christ. It was the mind of the mission.

---

[45]James Dunham to Cornelius De Bruin, January 27, 1979, in correspondence loaned to the author by Jim and Joyce Dunham. The specific identity of the individuals has been deliberately obscured at the request of the author of the letter.

Part Seven

Home

'Home' is...Where?

Among the words missionary children learned almost from their cradles was the curious term, "home." It was, in fact, a British coinage developed in the empire environment. "Home," in this usage, referred to a place evoking a curious and ominous sense of potency, a place one rarely saw and only then when passing through as a special visitor. It was a place peopled by a list of rare and seldom seen "real" relatives and cluttered with crowded churches in such numbers and of such magnificence as boggled a young mind. Children observed their parents go from one of these churches to the next like bouncing balls down steep steps until, eventually, the confusing year called "furlough" passed and everyone could go...Home. And Home (with a capital H) was Arabia.

Frances Thoms, one of the first of the mission's children, wrote a poem after she had left Arabia for the United States as a teenager, never to return. It is evocative still of the experience.

To Arabia
by Frances M. Thoms

Arabia, thou art my land, my home;
I scarce can wish but what I long for thee.
First light of day, first moon and stars I saw
Were thine. First mother's smile and fatherly
Cares I sense in thee. My love of God
In part is love for thee, Arabia!
I knew the desert islands of Bahrein,
Where beauteous pearls are sought and found and sold
With souls of countless price, and rare. Barefoot
I ran the sandy beach to gather shells;
Of shifting sands built cities manned with bits
Of drift-wood bleached; and dipped with childish fear
Into the shallow edge of endless sea.
Gardens I saw in Muskat and Bahrein;
Saw graceful palms of Basrah stoop and bend
O'er dank canals. I loved the rugged crags
On Oman's coast; the thunderous howl and war
Of cruel waves that beat relentlessly
Upon those stalwart rocks that will not yield.
I love thee all in all and love thee still.
Beyond thy sand-driv'n coast and barren crags
I see a land of worth — my promised land,
My choice forevermore, I long, I long
For thee, my heart's desire — Arabia.

The experience of the missionary child was a paradigm. Although exaggerated and skewed by childhood's lack of other memories, it modeled the schizophrenia inherent in becoming a career missionary to foreign parts. Back beyond the horizon there was a culture and a society which felt it had a claim upon the missionary. On one level—a theological level, if you will—that claim was valid. In midwestern churches, when people stood to pray, they invoked God's blessing upon "our-missionaries-and-our-soldier-boys-across-the-seas" all in one breath and without any evident sense of ambivalence. After all, they were praying for a mission of the Reformed

Church *in America*, and congregations of the denomination had made commitments to support the mission's members in their work and livelihood, in their ministry and witness. "Home" held a claim...but possession was another matter. The old nine-tenths law still applied.

The Mission and the Home Church

Since 1894 the Arabian Mission was presented as an effort of the Reformed Church in America, along with China, India, and Japan.[1] In that understanding, the mission was a formal expression of the denomination's evangelical concern to reach those who had not heard of nor confessed the lordship of Christ. Mission "on behalf of" Muslims, then, was an appropriate expression of the common convictions and devotion of the people in Reformed church pews. That base of conviction and devotion was moved to send forth missionaries, and the rousing hymns of the missionary movement are still sung with enthusiasm.

But the environment into which those missionaries were sent was not easily communicated; the experience of being engaged in mission was not easily translated. From the outset there was a physical and psychological gap between the pew and the mission. What happens in a sendor/sendee relationship when "our missionaries" become *their* friends, neighbors, and spiritual advisors? Perhaps inevitably, the intricacies of the psychology of ownership come into play. The effect does not necessarily rebound upon the cause—or rather, it does, but not always in the desired manner.

The Moral Relationship:
Whether cast in terms of involvement in a Grand Cause or nurtured as an individual relationship with a person who has felt "the call" to be a missionary, the link between a mission and a person in a pew is a difficult thing to gauge. Of course, as in most missionary endeavors, the strength of this link had a financial impact upon the Arabian Mission. More importantly, it was a subtle factor in the morale of missionaries. In the early years, apart

---

[1] When China closed its doors to missionaries in 1949, the investments made there were shifted to Formosa and to the Philippines. Efforts in the Americas were reported under the Board of Domestic Missions (which included Mexico), and work in other parts of South America and Africa was not undertaken until much later.

from a few congregations that took on the full support for individual missionaries and thereby enjoyed a very personal bond, the mission presented itself to its supporters as a whole thing, a Cause, grand and romantic. The early period of pioneer exploration and institution founding lent itself to this, and it was heartening how the network of syndicates underwrote the general budget of the Arabian Mission. That network was kept intelligently and prayerfully engaged through an active program of publication, promotion, and an intentional use of direct missionary-congregation contacts.[2]

When the mission came under the supervision of the RCA in 1894, a few supporting syndicates and private individuals dropped out of the picture, but by and large (and this was a prerequisite for the new administrative arrangement) the syndicate structure held together. Anxious for its network of support to continue, the mission publication included the following notice on its back page:

> N.B. – The Arabian Mission depends for its support and the extension of its work, not on the treasury of the Board of Foreign Missions of the Reformed Church in America, though under its care and administration, but upon contributions specifically made for this purpose. The churches, societies and individuals subscribing are not confined to the Reformed Church. Members of other denominations are among its supporters and its missionaries. Regular gifts and special donations are invited from all who are interested in Mission work in Arabia. Regular contributors will receive quarterly letters and annual reports without application. All contributions, or applications for literature or information, should be sent to "THE ARABIAN MISSION," 25 East 22d St., New York.[3]

[2]William Chamberlain, writing to the mission's secretary, Henry Bilkert, September 29, 1928, noted that the Arabian Mission had more than its fair share of eloquent penmen: "Let me emphatically congratulate the Mission upon the admirable Special number of the Christian Intelligencer and Mission Field of July 18, 1928, made up so largely of articles prepared by members of the Arabian Mission. It was certainly well entitled, 'An Exposition and an Appeal'. I thought the articles were strikingly emphatic and feel sure they must have proved effective. The members of the Arabian Mission of the present generation have certainly learned well the lesson which the founders of the Mission taught themselves and their successors in making vivid and real and appealing the work of the Mission in 'Neglected Arabia' to a constituency which at that time was scattered and independent" (document in the author's collection).
[3]This notice began to appear in *AMFR* #29, January to March 1899, and appeared regularly until the format of the publication was changed in the 1920s.

Very gradually over the years following 1894, the syndicate structure atrophied. The ambiguity of the Arabian Mission's unique status over against missions in China, India, and Japan made itself felt within the Board of Foreign Missions structure. Participation by non-Reformed church individuals and congregations dropped off. The amalgamation of the mission into the general budget of the Board of Foreign Missions in 1924 and the dissolution of the separate corporation of the Arabian Mission reflected a fundamental change in the relationship between pew and mission.[4]

Mission interpretation on a sustained and practical level had always been largely left to the board itself and its agents. Furloughing missionaries received warm receptions in congregations and were avidly sought as speakers at mission festivals, but it was understood that their primary work was on the mission field and that the commitment to keep them there was the church's to sustain.[5] The policy of encouraging particular congregations to support specific missionaries was a fruitful and practical one at the outset.[6] The relationship between individual missionaries and individual congregations in the United States was, at times, extremely intimate and

[4]Duke Potter, writing in 1925, noted, "This step, marking the passing of the Arabian Mission into full partnership with the other fields of the Church, is a significant culmination of the thirty-six years of history of this pioneer Mission...." Further along, he wrote, "We are particularly desirous of assuring the faithful circle of syndicates and individuals who have made the work in Arabia possible, that the amalgamation with the Board brings no change in the work whatsoever, and we trust and believe that you will continue through the years to pray for and to support this hard and now more promising enterprise which has so challenged the faith of the Church" (Mason and Barny, *History...*, pp. 236-237).

[5]Samuel Zwemer was perhaps unique in the Arabian Mission as one who felt a real calling as a fundraiser, and he spent a good deal of time in that effort to the detriment of work on the field. Other effective publicists were Paul Harrison, John Van Ess, and Stanley Mylrea who, at one time or another, extended the length of furloughs in order to more thoroughly communicate with the churches. Legends concerning Harrison in particular could be delightful. On one occasion in Wisconsin, a teenaged boy was brought to him whose leg had been mangled in a farming accident. The leg had been set, but gangrene had set in. Harrison, on the spot, designed a hyperbaric device out of glass, fitted it to the boy's leg, filled the small chamber with oxygen, and the gangrene was arrested. The boy's leg was saved. The author met the subject of this experimental operation in Beirut in 1972 and heard the story.

[6]Samuel Zwemer's full support first came from a single Southern Presbyterian congregation. [Noted in C. Stanley G. Mylrea, *The Story of the Arabian Mission After Fifty Years, 1889-1939* (New York: The Board of Foreign Missions, the Reformed Church in America, [1939]), p. 7.]

mutually rewarding. Many of the women of the mission were supported by the Women's Board of Foreign Missions, a powerful institution which functioned in parallel to the Board of Foreign Missions from 1875 to 1946, dedicated to "aid the Board of Foreign Missions of the Reformed Church in America by promoting its work among women and children in heathen lands."[7] But if a person were not so supported, his or her salary was underwritten by the board from general subscriptions. The missionary's primary relationship was to the denomination as a whole. This relationship was underscored by the formal commissioning of newly appointed career missionaries during the proceedings of the General Synod.[8]

Having weathered the Great Depression from 1929 to 1935 in spite of a fifty percent loss in revenue for benevolence, the RCA struggled to regain its financial footing. In early 1944 the Board of Foreign Missions instituted a "new unit plan" for missionary support. These units quickly came to bear the unfortunate label of "shares," as though missionaries were a sort of commodity on an evangelistic stock market. The shares system seemed to be an appropriate method for stabilizing and expanding support for missionaries, and indeed the RCA's revenues for benevolence work recovered in 1945 to pre-1929 levels.

Through the 1940s the number of units or shares it took to support a missionary family was four, each of $700.[9] Missionaries could maintain good communications and nurture relationships with four congregations in the

---

[7]Hoff, *Structures...*, p. 46.

[8]The act of commissioning missionaries was discontinued after the synod of 1966. The symbolism of this omission was significant.

[9]Discussing the old policy and explaining the new in a letter to Garry DeJong in 1944, Duke Potter explained, "As you know, in the old days one church would support the husband and another church the wife, but support was only on the basis of regular salary which represents usually only about half the real cost of supporting the missionary family when you include heavy travel items, children's allowances, etc. We are now calculating that the full support of a family represents $2800., four units of $700. each, and we are working to assign these units to different churches and organizations. Each of them is credited with having a share in the support of the man and wife. I think you will see at once the advantages of this system. We are informing various missionaries when the change is made" (document in author's collection). The report of the Board of Foreign Missions to the General Synod of the Reformed church in 1941 contains a list of individual missionaries and their supporting churches or organizations (pp. 128-131). It is clear, in that listing, that not all missionaries were supported by individual subscription of particular congregations. The report on the new policy appears

United States. But missionaries, as if they were some kind of weakening commodity, saw the proportional value of shares in their support halved, then quartered, then subdivided again and again. In 1967 when the Scudders Jr. went out to the Arabia field, the number of their supporting churches was thirteen, spread in random fashion from the Atlantic to the Pacific, and the number only kept climbing, with churches dropping out and others joining in all the time. They hit a high water mark of twenty-five, and by comparison to some of the other missionaries that was a low figure.[10]

To put a good face on it, the managers argued that under the share system more congregations could participate in mission across a broader spectrum of social and economic groups. But this argument was convincing only up to a point and then it became, instead, a hollow rationalization for a system gone out of control. To keep track of all but a few special congregational relationships became virtually impossible for the missionary. And, for their part, people in the pews found it increasingly difficult to feel that they had really sacrificed and merged their concerns with those of "their" missionaries. A congregation's sense of being involved in mission, therefore, was pegged to a person or a list of persons (often sheer abstractions), each person being involved in a specific task on some mission field remote from the congregation's experience. Affluent congregations developed the pattern of parceling out their benevolence for mission over a large number of small shares in many missionaries in a variety of locations, developing a stable of missionaries that became a mark of prestige. The broad sense of participation in a coherent cause was badly blurred.[11]

in the board's report of 1945. Barny Luben, the Board's field secretary at the time, was charged with putting it into effect. It was noted that the figure of $700 per share was low. The figure ought to have been set at $850, the report indicates (p. 4). Further, it is interesting to note that lists of churches taking shares in missionaries' individual support cease to be published as of 1942.

[10]In 1993 the estimate of what it cost to maintain a missionary family in the Middle East was $83,000. (The national cost of the U.S.-based administrative structure for mission is pro-rated into this overall figure.) Each share was valued at $3,100. If only full shares were assigned, then a missionary family required twenty-seven shares to be fully supported.

[11]The author recalls a conversation with Harold Colenbrander in which Colenbrander (for many years active on the Board of World Mission and for a time its president) reminisced that in Wisconsin where he grew up, the impact of the Arabian Mission Syndicate was significant and how, with its dissolution, something precious was lost. Congregational awareness of Arabia atrophied. He expressed a real sense of bereavement.

By the mid-1950s the Arabian Mission had lost all of its great orators and public figures. James Cantine died in 1940, John Van Ess died in 1949, Samuel Zwemer and Stanley Mylrea died in 1952, and Paul Harrison died in 1957. There were none to replace them as interpreters of mission, none who were granted recognition such as they had had, and none who thereafter so moved their audiences. But it was also a time when America turned its back on orators. After the example of Hitler had so terrorized western culture, to be moved to adopt a cause by an impassioned speaker—be that cause good or bad—was to become the victim of demagoguery.[12]

The radio, with its mass audience broken into small groups or single individuals sitting isolated in kitchens or living rooms, made the great church gatherings of earlier decades less appealing. People became reluctant to submit themselves to the chemistry and contagion of a large and excited crowd. The atomization of America had set in, and its patterns of communication and response were changing.

In the new circumstances, missionaries agonized over how to nurture a true involvement of Stateside Christians in the mission, how to communicate their visions and dreams, how to move people to share their excitement and commitment. In 1968, on the heels of the Arab-Israeli War of 1967, a letter from Jim Dunham to the congregation of the Second Reformed Church in Kalamazoo through Jay Weener, its pastor, reflects this agony. The Dunhams had spent a furlough year working in Second Church and had developed many close personal relationships. And after thanking God "for your fellowship in the Gospel" through continuing shares in their support and personal gestures of concern, Jim continued:

> ... Please permit me to share some of my thoughts on the Church of Christ in the Middle East. I force myself upon you without apology, for I feel, personally, a desperate need to penetrate the fog that seemingly isolates the Church at home from life in the Middle

[12]The author came up against this personally. At the Reformed church's General Synod held in Hamilton, Ontario, in 1980, he spoke out with some passion on the issues of the Middle East, proposing that the Theological Commission be charged with developing a serious position paper on the mission of the Church among Muslims and the relationship of the Church to Islam. As he was walking away from the meeting hall, an individual came up beside him and, in the course of their chat, remarked that it was a terrible thing to be endowed with the eloquence to move a large group to adopt a personal cause.

East today. I pick on you because my experience with you assures me that here at least is one pastor and his congregation that has the courage (that's a synonym for faith) to look at a situation straight and open eyed.

He proposed to Second Church a process of self-education using the resources of Clarence Linder (then president of the Board of World Mission) and John Buteyn (its Middle East area secretary) to engage in discussion of a series of issues which Jim outlined for them. He continued, "Once these facts have been digested, imagine yourself as a member of the Board of World Missions trying to formulate a policy or a program for the Arabian Mission in Oman," and when you have a policy formulated, "explain it to the Reformed Church in America. Picture yourself presenting your policy to the classis of Kalamazoo, to the Committee of the Concerned." He concluded,

My furlough in Kalamazoo convinced me that we have much to learn from one another. But we shall never be of any help to one another unless we direct our thoughts and efforts to the real problems that confront us. ...Like you, personally I want to be faithful to my vocation; I frequently hunger for intimate Christian fellowship, a fellowship that is not afraid, of itself, of life, of the changes that life brings. I know that this is an unobtainable ideal in this life, for we are all afraid. So I try to remember that our faith is not in ourselves but in Him.13

What Dunham was reflecting was that, even where relationships were good and responsive, there was a growing gap between the concerns of the field and the preoccupations of the church at home.

The "isolating fog" breaking the church up into component parochial parts, some might think, could have one positive effect: it might shield missionaries from the negative attention of certain factions within the home church. But it did not. On two occasions, once on the initiative of South

13Letter from James W. Dunham in Muscat, Oman, to the Rev. Jay Weener "and Members of the Congregation," Second Reformed Church, Kalamazoo, Michigan, dated January 20, 1968. Found in the author's document collection.

Grand Rapids Classis[14] and once on that of Zeeland Classis,[15] Jay Kapenga of Oman was challenged to prove his orthodoxy. The author was also once

[14]Ruth Young, a highly strung young woman with a wide and worried smile and troubled eyes (a child's view), came from a very sheltered background. She was appointed to the Arabian Mission in 1949 to work in women's evangelism. From 1950 through 1951 she was assigned as a language student to Kuwait, where she also received the tutelage of veteran evangelist, Everdine DeJong. She was one of the very rare people whom Lew Scudder, Sr.'s, spontaneously affectionate nature could not move. Indeed, she attacked him for being overly familiar, especially with women. Following the completion of her language studies, she was assigned to evangelistic work in Bahrain (1952), but again she came in conflict with colleagues. In those days Oman often was seen as a place in which redemption could be found, because it sported a more primitive and raw missionary challenge. Besides, the steady Dykstras were there as well as Beth Thoms, a gifted mentor and role model. The young Kapengas and Jeanette Boersma (who came from a similar background to Young's) were willing to accept the challenge of befriending her. So, late in 1953, Ruth Young moved to Oman.
　　She found no rest there either. Again her relationships became tense, a situation which finally moved the mission to request that she take an early furlough, with the recommendation to the board that she not return to the field. Upon her return to the United States in the summer of 1954, drawing upon her unhappy experiences in all three stations of the mission where she had served, she launched an attack on the mission.
　　She leveled a barrage of accusations, not just against Jay Kapenga for allegedly denying Christ's divinity and virgin birth, but also against the moral laxity of the mission in general for dancing, movie-going, smoking, attending parties at which liquor was served, worshiping on Friday, and worshiping in English (an activity she deemed not properly missionary). Gary DeWitt, an aggressive young pastor in the Chicago area, chose to champion her cause, and the issue quickly became a hot one in Michigan's South Grand Rapids Classis. Settling the dust Young raised consumed a great deal of the attention of Barny Luben in New York and of missionaries on the field in the late months of 1954 and 1955.
　　Answering a well-intentioned letter from Peter J. Breen of Byron Center, Michigan, Harvey Staal opened with the wry observation: "We...are looking forward to our return to the States in the spring [of 1955], and do hope that we have the opportunity of seeing you personally. However, after your letter and what we have been hearing from Grand Rapids, I wonder a little whether it will be safe for us to be there!" Jesting aside, he carried on to reply to the accusations noted by Mr. Breen and then concludes, "I am personally most concerned about the matter and the adverse effect it might have on the whole mission work of the church in the Grand Rapids and Chicago areas. I feel with you that it is entirely the wrong approach and hope and pray that it may be arrested before it does too much damage. I see no chance of avoiding getting into the whole affair since we plan to come to Grand Rapids in May, so you might just as well go ahead and use any of this you can, in whatever way possible to try to bring it to a halt. We pray for your success in this matter. It would be very serious indeed to be cut back any more than we have been this year as far as finances are concerned, and we would certainly not want to lose the confidence nor the prayers of the people back home.

called on the theological carpet by a rural church in western Michigan, a matter which blew up as the result of casual and seemingly innocent remarks in personal correspondence between his wife and a Women's Guild member of the congregation. The growing impression of missionaries, then, was that the home church seemed progressively to lose trust in them as their missionary tasks grew more alien. If an expression of serious interest was heard it was more often leveled in criticism than in affirmation. The meaning of the positive challenge before both home and field seemed to be slipping through all their fingers.16

We pray that the church at home may understand what we are doing and may have full confidence in us. We ask for your prayers, too, that we may be the very best possible witnesses for Christ in order to win many souls for Him and to bring the Gospel into the very heart of interior Arabia." [Correspondence, Breen to Staal dated January 7, 1955, and Staal to Breen dated January 24, 1955, found in the author's document collection.]

The board asked Young to resign from the mission quietly "for health reasons," but she chose instead to press on with her campaign, cheered on by the South Grand Rapids heresy hunters. Eventually cooler heads prevailed; the storm passed over by the middle of 1955. But it poisoned the atmosphere for years to come.

15The other occasion, in the early 1970s, involved two young nurses on short-term assignment. The father of one of these was a powerful pastor in the Reformed church. The young women, having been asked to return to the United States early, accused Kapenga of preaching heresy. The indignant father chose to believe the accusation. After it became clear that the case involved aspects of personal deportment which might cause the young ladies embarrassment in their home societies and had little or nothing to do with theology, the father was persuaded to cease and desist.

16The author participated in three prominent examples of the denomination's positive response. (1) At the General Synod of 1976, pressed by other members of the Arabian Mission (prominently by Mary Allison and Donald Bosch), as a missionary delegate of the Classis of Holland, he placed upon the floor of synod a resolution calling for the Reformed church to reject the notion that the State of Israel was the fulfillment of biblical prophecy and urging it to view its role in that conflict as seeking for those things which made for genuine peace. This resolution was passed with strong affirmation. (2) As a result of this initiative, he was called upon by the denomination's Social Action Commission to present a critique of Zionism and an assessment of what the appropriate Christian response might be to the distressing conflict in the Middle East. The results of this initiative were far more ambiguous, but the point is that a genuine response was made. (3) At the General Synod of 1980 he was again privileged to be a delegate. At that synod a paper was approved giving the theological foundations of the relationship between the Church and the Jewish people. The author, then, proposed to synod that a similar and parallel study be made by the Theological Commission of the denomination of the relationship between the Church and

Furthermore, the Arabian Mission challenged the Reformed church in a manner which left some uneasy. Especially during the tenure of Duke Potter, it was characterized as the "toughest" field of mission. Its statistics, when compared with any other major field of mission endeavor, were disheartening, but the breakthrough was always just over the horizon ...around the next bend in the road ...beyond the next hurdle. Except perhaps for the hopeful experience of Oman, there was never even a suggestion that an indigenous movement for conversion from Islam would emerge in the Gulf. Individual converts there were, but nothing vaguely resembling the base for a self-propagating Christian community. Jay Kapenga speculated that, with respect to the convert Arabic congregation in Oman, the mission's hesitation to ordain the congregation's leading elder, Khudâ Rasûn, and several other church fathers had the effect of making it impossible for that congregation to become self-propagating. The mission's insistence upon Reformed standards regarding the question of autonomy and self-reliance and the proper educational credentials and procedures for ordination to the pastoral ministry inhibited the Omani church from evolving in a locally fitting manner. The dissolution of that congregation following the radical changes instituted in the relationship between the mission and the Omani government between 1970 and 1975 supports Kapenga's analysis. [17]

On several occasions in the 1960s, overtures were put before the General Synod that the Reformed church should withdraw from Arabia on the principle that, "if anyone will not welcome you or listen to your words, shake off the dust from your feet as you leave that house or town" (Matt. 10:14). As "church growth" became fashionable in the denomination in the 1970s, these same feelings were given the twist that ministry in unfruitful regions was simply bad allocation of resources. The Reformed church should shift

---

the Muslim community. Again, synod adopted the resolution and charged the Theological Commission with the task. In 1984 he was asked to frame a working paper on the subject for the commission, and during a furlough in 1985-1986 he served as consultant to the commission (along with others) in developing that first draft. The document that went before the synod of 1986 (at which he was again present) was returned to the commission for further work. But the point is that again, the denomination seriously engaged a vital issue with which the Arabian Mission had struggled for more than a century.

[17]Document attached to Jay Kapenga's questionnaire returned to the author in 1990.

its mission investment to communities more susceptible to the gospel by reason of economic or social vulnerability. This dampened enthusiasm for the mission where Arabia had to compete for attention with doctors who penetrated the rain forests of South America, the winsome romance and heroic struggle of ministries in places like Chiapas in Mexico, and frontier efforts among primitive tribes in Kenya. And as oil politics and the volatility of the Arab-Israeli conflict blew dust-devils of confusion concerning the Middle East into American minds, the whole venture of the Arabian Mission became politically suspect, or at least ambiguous. Missionaries were painted as being agents of Arab interests, having been forced into that service by those whom they were obliged to please on the field. This sort of slander was openly spoken, but the heart's pain was something of far more enduring significance.

The Reformed church continued to talk about mission in general. Individual congregations with active programs and healthy budgets took pride in posting the long lists of missionaries whom they supported—a spot here, another there across the faces of maps on church bulletin boards. Mission ceased to be objective-oriented. Statistics became a thing in vogue. The gross number was the thing; it was less important to examine a broad mission objective, work out a strategy for meeting it, and then determine what staffing and resources it required. Long-term investment in well-oriented, field-competent personnel all but ceased as the 1960s drew to a close. Mission became a kind of prestige game subject to the whim of individual pastors or changing consistories[18] and managed by an increasingly disheartened staff—a very poorly staged spectator sport in a society growing accustomed to ever more sophisticated mass media presentations.

---

[18]The author and his wife at one point found themselves in a very rewarding relationship with a congregation in California. A member of that congregation had taken it upon herself to keep in touch with them, and a brisk correspondence developed characterized (or so they felt) by increasing familiarity, friendship, and even trust. The day came, however, when a new pastor arrived and decreed that this congregation would now focus on local mission projects and suspend their shares in world mission relationships. The congregation's correspondent wrote one final letter reporting this development, announcing she would therefore not be writing again. The Scudders wrote back pleading that, whatever the new pastor's preferences and the change he had instituted in mission support patterns, that need not affect the correspondence and growing friendship which had so invigorated them. There was no response to this plea.

Worship and Mission:

These developments point up one of the fundamental anomalies in American Protestant spirituality. Worship and mission are not seen to be activities continuous with each other. Following 1946, as fundraising was detached from the offertory during worship, the distance between RCA pew and mission increased, and the average Reformed church member became vulnerable. Without being an extension of Communion and the community in worship, mission was detached from the focus of what made each congregation the Church. "Mission," a spiritual engagement, became "program," an object of promotion. Successful mission organizations in Protestant America in the '60s and thereafter were those which could afford a slick pitch, spending heavily on television spots and direct mail and consulting advertising gurus about how to seduce American Christians into loosening their grip on their money. And there was no shortage of pious pitchmen on "Christian" radio and television to satisfy the spiritual hedonism of American society.

On the one hand, as money from Reformed churches began to flow heavily toward smoothly advertised causes outside the denomination, the bureaucracy could only wring its collective hands in despair. This was so because, on the other hand, the Reformed church's watchdogs in classes and on consistories would not permit the denomination's agencies to spend the kind of money on publicity that the public demanded.[19] It was a classic catch-22.

In any case, the drift toward superficial self-gratification in matters spiritual afflicted the Reformed church no less seriously than it did the rest of American religion. Mission, being a matter for serious thought, became a more remote concern as pabulum came to predominate in the diet—both homiletically and liturgically. Mission became the business of the denomination's elite, and an ever more select elite at that. And it was upon structural matters that this elite focused—the "how" and not the "wherefore."

[19]The success of the United Advance program of 1946-1948 which doubled RCA benevolence giving convinced the denominational leadership that secular instruments for fundraising could legitimately be exploited to fund denominational benevolence programs (Hoff, *Structures...*, pp. 78-87). In the aftermath, however, a suspicion grew in the pew that church members were being manipulated, and a reaction set in which bedeviled the work of the Stewardship Council, an organization instituted by General Synod in 1952 to exploit the lessons learned during the United Advance effort.

Mission as An Imperative Responsibility:

The question is: Which is cart and which the horse in the business of mission? Initially, the community's sense of a God who calls and the response of individuals from within it to God's call defined the giving patterns. Funds were raised on the basis of needs declared by those who labored in the field. The congregation and the denomination attempted to keep the imperative in focus.

In the '40s something happened which turned the relationship of giving and employing funds askew. The budget became the object, and progress was measured by the extent to which the budget expanded. An expanding budget dictated expanded program. The effectiveness or imperative nature of the work was eclipsed as a standard of measurement. Missionaries found themselves in the somewhat weird position of having to dream up new ways to spend money. On the other hand, a contracting or static budget meant that the mission could not think about responding to new challenges.

Denominational staff, as a managerial entity, increasingly intervened between those who gave and those who got. There was a buffering effect between missionary and congregation, and the grassroots paranoia against the denominational hierarchy housed at "475 Riverside Drive" (the RCA address in New York City) was not altogether unjustified. The local pastor, protecting his (later his/her) turf, aided and abetted the trend. The denomination became increasingly "clergy ridden." As the pot shrank in the 1930s and early 1940s, the tendency to minimalist thinking about mission strengthened. The renewal of an upward trend in church giving in the latter '40s and the '50s does not necessarily weaken this observation.

One significant concurrent development: The office of elder lost its potency in the denomination. Qualifications for the office were watered down, and laity became increasingly less able to participate critically and constructively in the wider issues of the denomination's government—its policies and program. Minimalism, therefore, held a natural appeal. Ordinary local Christians could comprehend ordinary local issues but increasingly confessed themselves baffled by what happened in wider circles. Without a strong eldership, disciplined and feeling the weight of responsibility, the resources of the congregation to strive for a broad understanding were diminished.

The saying fondly and frequently repeated by fundraisers, "Interest follows money," might not be as true as we have been led to believe. Money is directed toward that which is understood to be a compelling need. Throwing money at an increasingly complex mission program whose goals grew more diffuse and ambiguous with each passing year did not work out. The interest did not follow. Congregations passively rebelled, and the budget took torpedoes in the side. In the latter '60s and early '70s what bailed the RCA out of serious financial crisis was the "windfall" sale of property in Kuwait. In the 1980s the same function was performed by funds "repatriated" from Japan.

Instead of examining and responding to moral imperatives, the post-World War II years found the Reformed church captive to the American fascination with the myth of success—a theoretically quantifiable pursuit in which bigger and more became measures of better and valid. There was a flash-in-the-pan effect. Post-war prosperity and optimism seemed to be adequate proof against sober judgment and reassessment. Marvin Hoff came close to revelation when he observed, "The more the denomination quantified the measures of success—a larger mission budget next year, greater giving for mission/education, more members this year than last, a larger number of children in Sunday school this year—the more the phenomena of 'adaptation,' 'relative deprivation,' and 'upward comparisons' shaped her self-perceptions as a church, both locally and denominationally."[20] Instead of the church being challenged to strive toward the High Calling of the Upward Way, it was appealed to on a lower level, a level of self-gratification.

There was no vision driving the church's will to self-expression. The church-growth weavers were busily warp-and-wefting biblical clothing out of the profit motive. In the small Reformed church, increasingly anxious about its own survival, people got excited about blending Americana and evangel so cleverly together. The fine new fabric tempted many to believe the Church *itself* to be the object of worth, the home-spun of the gospel notwithstanding. Prophets were out of fashion.

Thus the high expectations for the 1970s were not so much left unrealized as intuitively perceived as being vacuous. But the gospel does withstand, and self-gratification is no substitute in the end for moral vision and the majesty of the call, which demands of the Church that it keep its modest dress of humility that it may go out to press the harvest of its soul with an earthy joy and so give drink to a thirsty world.

[20]Hoff, *Structures...*, p. 56.

But weavers complained about communications (or rather the lack thereof), and the medium continued to be confused for the message. The sense of disillusionment deepened. The more the despondency, the more frantic the efforts to affirm the flickering chimera for the bread and wine of reality, its flesh and blood. Horse and cart had flipped positions, but the horse-and-buggy design had not been fundamentally modified to accommodate the new configuration.

Structure and Vision:

To be explicit, beginning in 1968 a new corporate approach was implemented as the Reformed church's mission pattern. The various boards and agencies were all brought within the "General Program Council" (GPC). In effect, this new and more sophisticated approach treated the world in abstract, focusing policy upon five *types* of activity: evangelism and church growth, Christian community, human welfare, personal growth and relationships, and social issues. The effect was scatter-shot; it reduced the attention paid the geographic and cultural regions in which the world mission effort had been carried on. It picked apart the collage of mission effort into discrete programs and lost the symphonic sense of how disparate activities harmonized with unique regional characteristics. It made mission far more difficult to picture and hear, and that too exacerbated the alienation of the congregations.[21]

As its support base and the Arabian Mission drifted farther apart, matters financial were increasingly the consuming business of denominational staff. As budgets grew tight, expenditures were more jealously monitored. This was further aggravated by the deliberate weakening of the deliberative and

---

[21]Over the years, Carol Hageman—insightful, patient, and long-suffering wife and partner of the colorful RCA personality, theologian, preacher, and seminary president Howard Hageman—served on many of the denomination's boards and agencies. In a lecture delivered at New Brunswick Theological Seminary April 14, 1994, she expressed the profound insight that when "mission" became "program" something serious was lost to the Reformed church. A comparison between the reports to the General Synod of the Board of World Mission with those of the General Program Council reveals the loss of published information concerning mission activities and the growing sense of alienation between missionaries and their supervising body. And a comparative review of the minutes of the respective bodies only underlines the fact that the average member of the GPC could not possibly be aware of the interplay of factors affected by the decisions he or she was called upon to make.

decision-making structures on the field, and that finally broke up the support groups to which missionaries could turn for help. It was inevitable, perhaps, that by the early 1980s the qualifications and functions of agency secretaries became less a matter of competence in dealing with issues on the field and having a vision of what the mission was doing there, and more a matter of abstract skills in public relations and fund-raising within the denomination on behalf of particular programs or individual missionaries. The spiritual engagement of the people in the pews in mission was a lost battle. Successful mission became a question of competent manipulation. The wise man's warning in the King James Bible, "Where there is no vision, the people perish," echoed lost in chancels and sanctuaries.[22]

The Administrative Agency

Through the permutations of the relationship between the Arabian Mission and the person in the pew, the administrative structure and personnel of the denomination's mission agencies played a crucial role.

What did the Board of Foreign Missions[23] represent? It might be argued that this agency, with its changeful name and shifting definition, was indistinguishable from the mission itself. That would be an error. On the other hand, it might be the contention of some that the agency was only the voice of the Reformed Church in America, the sending body of the mission. This, too, would be a misapprehension. The board was, truly, an agency. The question is, an agency of whom?

In his sweeping survey of the structures which the Reformed church put in place to execute its mission mandate from 1643 through 1980, there is a refrain that Marvin Hoff several times repeats: "Because there had not been significant theological reflection when the 'boards' were created, nor at the time of their incorporation into the church's official polity, the persons conducting the revisions in the structure in the mid-twentieth century did

---

[22]The more accepted translation of this passage, Proverbs 29:18, is, "Where there is no prophecy (or prophetic vision), the people cast off restraint" (RSV & NRSV among others). The words become perhaps *more* pointed.

[23]Its name was first changed to the Board of World Missions, then the Board of World Mission (remove the plural 's'), then for a brief time the Board of *Christian* World Mission, then the Division of World Mission of the General Program Council, and then, most recently, the Mission Services Unit of the General Synod Council.

not inherit a theological tradition for the place of 'boards' in the life of the church."[24] He argues throughout that pragmatic, *ad hoc* responses to mission challenges only served to complicate the picture further and to render the General Synod's agencies for mission ever less effective. By the end of the process, that observation certainly rings true.

In the wisdom of the ecclesiastical instinct (or, more likely, by the mercy of God), the board at its best and most appropriate functioned as a buffer, an interpreter, a facilitator, a "Dutch uncle" between mission and denomination. It gave grounding and credibility to the claim that the mission was, indeed, a mission *of* the Reformed Church in America. But it also gave space to the movement of creative initiative which, in many cases, produced a witness on the field which the ordinary member of the Reformed church would find strange and exotic,[25] often challenging and exciting,[26] and sometimes discomfiting and even offensive. That is, the board endeavored to give expression to the reality, for all the proprietary instincts of a denomination, that the mission (indeed, *any* Christian mission) was under the guidance of the Spirit of God, intended to give glory to God alone, and gave witness in any particular locale to the Universal Body of Christ, the Holy Catholic Church.

This stance made for a fundamental tension between discipline and freedom, between the poles of accountability in an increasingly complex net of relationships, between the energy (or finances) *for* and the actual product *of* mission, between the often theoretical agenda of management and the actual experience of labor, between the authority of the church and the conscience of the Christian. And while the tension often made for discomfort and even struggle, it was a tension that could only be dampened or denied to the detriment of the overall effort. Brokering the volatile potential of this tension was the task of the board and its responsible administrators. When

---

[24]Hoff, *Structures...*, p. 45.

[25]There is not a missionary who has not experienced the pregnant pause after explaining to an American church group what he or she has been doing. The psychological distance between audience and speaker can frequently be tremendous.

[26]Witness is borne here by physicians who came and worked for short periods of time as volunteers with the Arabian Mission in the early 1960s, like Spencer Snedecor of Long Island, New York; Russel and Kay Paalman of Grand Rapids, Michigan; and Alfred and Barbara Vande Waa of Zeeland, Michigan. In their reports and public presentations after they returned to their homes there is obvious excitement and a continued engagement in promoting mission causes for years to come.

it did its job well, there was health; when it did not function creatively or when the challenge of managing ambiguity exceeded the vision of those responsible, there was crisis and (more seriously) demoralization.

The Independent Mission (1889-1894)

The Arabian Mission was launched into a world that was shifting into new configurations. Imperial Britain was reaching its zenith as the nineteenth century drew to its close. In the Middle East, it had been the main prop for the tottering Ottoman Empire, but (since 1877, when Sultan 'Abd-ul-Hamîd abandoned reform) it increasingly faced the expanding imperial ambitions of Germany. To protect its investment in the Suez Canal, Britain chose to deal with Egypt (formally an Ottoman dependency) as an independent power. In 1880, 'Abd-ul-Hamîd interfered in the succession of the Egypt's ruling line, and in 1881 the British moved in on the pretext of quelling a local revolt and established themselves as *de facto* rulers of Egypt. An empire oriented heretofore toward India suddenly became deeply entrenched in the Middle East and North Africa.

A second movement was also afoot—the growth of particularistic nationalism, a groundswell of parochial pride that challenged the very foundations of any empire. In eastern Europe the Jewish community was beginning to take the first steps toward an organized Zionist movement. The first Jewish migration (Aliya) from eastern Europe to Palestine began in 1882 as the Ottomans lost control of their European provinces, although the Dryfus Affair in France and Theodore Herzl's publishing his Zionist manifesto, *Der Judenstadt*, didn't happen until 1894. Within the Arab provinces of the Ottoman Empire proto-Zionism had a counterpart. There was a strong mood developing for independence or at least autonomy. American missionaries were active in fostering that mood. And in the Gulf itself, since the early 1880s, Britain was actively linking together a chain of dependencies, becoming the Gulf's leading power and shifting Arabia's economic and political ties more surely eastward toward India. At the same time, the groundswell in Gulf society was toward greater self-awareness of the region as distinct. The winds of change were blowing. It was not a time which was tolerant of the naive.

From 1889 to 1894 the administrative agency of the Arabian Mission was its board of trustees, which was officially incorporated in the state of New

Jersey in January, 1891. The board, acting through a "committee of advice," was chaired by the scholarly J. Preston Searle but with John Lansing as dominant member. Lansing was in Egypt in 1890 but was back in New Brunswick, New Jersey, by May, 1892. And the crisis of the appointment and subsequent dismissal of Clarence Riggs revealed growing tensions in his relations with Preston Searle. With his proprietary attitude toward the whole venture, it is understandable that Lansing, though precipitously failing in mental and physical health, continued to try to assert himself in the mission's business.

In 1893 the committee hired the thirty-one-year-old Frank Scudder—a classmate of Samuel Zwemer at New Brunswick Theological Seminary—as its secretary/treasurer. Perhaps what commended him to the committee, in spite of his youth, was the fact that he was a child of the Arcot mission and, therefore, might be able to understand what foreign mission was all about. He was the first American-based staff person paid to administer the mission's business. Frank Scudder took office in the unsettled atmosphere which attended John Lansing's return to the United States from Egypt with rapidly deteriorating health. Scudder's tenure was short. In 1894, the Arabian Mission was taken under the wing of the Board of Foreign Missions of the Reformed church. Scudder moved on to other things.[27]

The official reason for this change was that the individuals engaged in the mission—the Zwemer brothers and James Cantine—believed that being part of a recognized and duly organized denomination gave a legitimate ecclesiastical base to their undertaking. Why this had not been an overriding

[27]Frank Seymour Scudder was born April 28, 1862, in Coonoor, South India, a son of Ezekiel Carmen Scudder, one of the founders of the Arcot Mission. After attending Rutgers University, Frank Scudder pursued theological studies at New Brunswick Theological Seminary, graduating in 1890, in the same class as Samuel Zwemer. Before taking on the job of secretary-treasurer for the Arabian Mission, he served a parish in Illinois for two years. Following his work for the Arabian Mission, he took a pastorate in Mt. Vernon, New York. Three years later, in 1897, he went under the ABCFM to Japan as a missionary, where he founded a mission station in the mountain temple center of Nagano. In 1906, broken in health and widowed with three young children, Frank Scudder accepted the suggestion of his cousin, Doremus Scudder, that he follow the trail of the Japanese labor migration to Hawaii. When the ABCFM concluded its work in the Hawaiian Islands, he became the superintendent of the Japanese Department of the Hawaiian Board—the regional successor to the ABCFM—and edited their newspaper, *The Friend*, until he retired in 1936. He died five days short of his 94th birthday in Honolulu on April 23, 1956.

consideration at the outset when the mission was first organized is a question with which we have already dealt. But the board of trustees of the "undenominational" undertaking known as the Arabian Mission, to put it quite frankly, was composed of inexperienced amateurs who had other primary duties to fulfill. The matter of money management, with the decline of John Lansing into irrationality, was an embarrassment. The youthful Frank Scudder, while indications are that he improved things, must not have produced the hoped-for results. Quite simply, the mission had to be put into professionally competent hands. Henry Cobb's indication that the Board of Foreign Missions was in a position to assume the administration of the mission, provided that its network of supporting syndicates could be kept active, came as pure relief. Not only would Cobb supply the experienced administrative genius, the administrative expense of running the mission could be sharply reduced as well, and the money contributed by the syndicates could mainly go toward the work on the field.

The Arabian Mission's Board of Trustees continued to be incorporated in New Jersey as a separate entity. Under the new arrangement, its members no longer were elected by the supporting syndicates but rather were appointed from the membership of the Board of Foreign Missions. In 1894, therefore, the corresponding secretary for the mission became Henry Nitchie Cobb, the erudite and peripatetic secretary for the Board of Foreign Missions since 1883.

Henry Nitchie Cobb (1894-1910)

Cobb, of medium stature and slender frame, but graced with a handlebar mustache of heroic proportions, was a commanding figure held much in awe within the denomination and by missionaries, too. His grasp of foreign affairs and the business of the denomination's missions in India, China, and, more recently, Japan was encyclopedic, and he was a person of considerable tact and insight. He had also maintained an interest in the work of the Arabian Mission from its inception and did not pick up the task in ignorance.

He oversaw the mission through the tumultuous days of the Ottoman Empire's final collapse. They were the days of the dangerous and erratic Sultan 'Abd-ul-Hamîd (labeled 'Abdul the Damned'), and the solid alliance of the Ottoman state with Germany preparatory to the First World War. The pogrom launched by the sultan against the Armenian people and its effect upon the whole Christian community in the empire was a matter which riveted the attention of the world.

In 1904, along with Maneius Hutton (the president of the board), Mrs. Eben E. Olcott (of the RCA's Women's Board and in memory of whom the women's hospital in Kuwait was eventually built), and her son, Cobb, visited Bahrain and Muscat. This was the first official visit by board personnel to the Gulf. They were unable to visit Basrah because of the strict and time-consuming quarantine procedures, but their visit was noted as "a distinct uplift for the missionaries," who recognized the value of these visitors as interpreters of their work and who found their encouraging words and sympathetic insights nourishing.[28] It was good that this was so because 1904 took a heavy toll in mission lives: two children of Jahan Khan, the convert Afghan dispenser in Bahrain; Katharine and Ruth Zwemer, Ann and Sam's two daughters; and Saʿîd Musqof, a fruitful colporteur in Oman. The testimony of the board delegation when it returned to the United States was fruitful in stimulating supporters of the mission to increase their efforts on behalf of Arabia, and in the next two years six new missionaries were appointed.

In 1894 Cobb had assumed responsibilities for five missionaries on the field in Arabia. Upon his retirement in 1910, in spite of deaths and debilitating disease, there were thirty-one on station and another six waiting in the wings. Kuwait was about to become a full station, and the development of Basrah and Bahrain stations had been significant. From 1889 to 1899 the total receipts of the mission had been $68,811.41; from 1900 to 1910 they were $218,155.17. The role Cobb played in executing the Forward Movement of the Church fund drive authorized by the 1906 General Synod, tapping into the Laymen's Missionary Movement, and his adroit use of the oratorical gifts of Samuel Zwemer within the denomination and in the wider circles of the Student Volunteer Movement was testament to his gifts as a visionary administrator.[29]

On the field, Cobb's style was to encourage field initiative within the constraints of the funds available. He monitored the work of the mission with close attention to detail and actively consulted his board of trustees. He was an able interpreter of the work of the mission, and only occasionally did he feel led to revise field decisions, and then only in matters of detail and not

[28]Mason and Barny, *History*..., p. 128.
[29]Mason and Barny, History..., p. 138.

substance. He continued in office until 1910, at which time he was replaced by the towering figure of William I. Chamberlain.

William I. Chamberlain (1910-1935)

As another child of the Arcot Mission in India and having served there himself, Chamberlain brought with him an innate instinct for foreign missions and an embracing awareness of the Church of Christ. He was a competent scholar, following in the footsteps of his educator father. In a day when movements for Christian reconciliation were gaining momentum, he had strong ecumenical commitments which earned for him an appointment as the president of the World Alliance of Reformed Churches in 1923.[30] He also understood the powerful missionary motive behind the developing ecumenical awareness of the time.

In the footsteps of Cobb, Chamberlain's quarterly secretarial letters were thorough discussions of the current issues facing the mission. His enlightened questions probed the decisions on the field, and his comments were carefully read because they were never frivolous. His administrative style, through some of the more delicate years of the mission's development, left the missionaries with the firm assurance that he was a person who respected their judgment and was one upon whom they could depend.

He carefully shepherded the Reformed church's far-flung missionary enterprise through a world war and the Great Depression. He did this by placing great trust in the leadership on the field. The complex realignment of the region, after 'Abd-al-'Azîz Âl Sa'ûd and his Wahhâbîs had overthrown the Ottoman puppet in Riyadh in early 1912 and embarked on his own program of conquest and Arabian unification, was a matter best left to the insights of those on the field. He related to the missionaries as a sort of senior counselor and resource when they needed it, and his secretarial letters show a man who, having all the relevant information well in hand, nonetheless returns the decision to those who, in the end, had to live with it.

Britain's efforts to contain the ambitions of the Âl Sa'ûd were largely successful, and British administrators and political officers made a friend of the ambitious Amîr of Najd. Having been frequently frustrated in their

---

[30]Between May and December of 1920, when Chamberlain led a deputation of churchmen on a tour of the mission fields, the Rev. A L. Warnshuis (a veteran of the China field) took over duties as corresponding secretary for the board.

efforts by Wahhâbî agitators, the missionaries on the field largely approved the British initiative. Nonetheless, as World War I began and the United States held back from the Allied cause, Chamberlain had to get involved in an unpleasant piece of business which may have had a long-term effect of repressing free expression among missionaries and between missionaries and their supporters in the United States.

It began early in 1917 with a letter sent to Chamberlain by James L. Barton, chairman of the Committee of Reference and Counsel of the Foreign Mission Conference of North America.[31] Barton had been called in by the British ambassador in Washington and informed that if any missionary in the region was found "to have acted in a manner hostile to the Government of India as by law established [in India, Mesopotamia, and the Arabian Gulf], the Government of India must be considered justified in ordering the expulsion of the entire mission involved."[32] Barton went on to explain to Chamberlain that this British policy of collective punishment specifically singled out "missionaries who are not British subjects, and especially...new applicants for appointment whose attitude toward the British Government cannot be authoritatively established." The British were particularly concerned about Americans of German or other national descent known to be hostile to Britain. Barton concluded:

> I am sure it is not necessary for me to add anything to emphasize the necessity, under the circumstances as they now exist, of each mission organization doing everything in its power to see that its mission body in British India, either as individuals or as a mission, does not countenance any utterance or act detrimental to the Government of India.[33]

In his covering letter to Cantine, Chamberlain stated:

> By direction of the Board of Foreign Missions a copy of the...[Barton] ...letter is sent to each member of the Missions in India and the Persian Gulf, as also to those under appointment to

[31]Letter dated Feb. 6, 1917, in the author's document collection.
[32]This policy of collective punishment was one which the British applied in many places, including the restless environment of Palestine in the period between the two world wars.
[33]*Ibid.*

these Missions. The Board calls the attention of all those receiving the letter to the grave consequences of any indiscretion in this very important matter.

Writing more informally to Cantine on April 5, 1917, Chamberlain elaborated:

> ... if there are in the Arabian Mission missionaries of this Board who cannot heartily and cheerfully abide by the conditions as therein [in the officially stated policy] set forth they should at once return to the United States.
>
> I am also directed to request you to take note of any doubtful cases in the Mission and see that all such, if any there are, either comply at once with the requirements of the Indian Government or withdraw from the country [in which they are serving].
>
> ...We do not anticipate that any members of your Mission will be affected by these instructions for the reason that we are assured that every member is thoroughly committed to both a personal and official attitude of entire loyalty to the Government of Mesopotamia as by law established.[34]

By May, 1917, however, the United States had entered the war on the Allied side. Writing to Cantine May 3, Chamberlain observed that many young people who might otherwise have volunteered for missionary service had instead entered the military. While expressing some regret on that score, he did indicate that perhaps now the British might feel more relaxed about American presence in British imperial domains since they were now to be considered allies and not suspect neutrals in the conflict. In any case, he was anxious to be the beneficiary once again of frank expressions of opinion and good political analysis from the field, something the previous situation had repressed.

James Cantine, however, was a more cautious and less imaginative person. He developed a survival mentality and, as the mission became more established, he threw his moral weight behind more conservative policies. As senior missionary and the secretary of the mission on the field, he knew

[34]Letter dated April 5, 1917, in the author's document collection. In fact, although they had points to criticize in British administrative policy, by and large Arabia missionaries were quite enthusiastically pro-British.

that the British were tolerant of the mission's presence only so long as it served their interests. He knew his mail was being censored, and he reminded Chamberlain several times that it was. He was well aware that the British were not above imposing collective punishment, and one missionary's misadventure could still become the whole mission's regret. The good will of the British authorities was essential, and Cantine instructed the members of the mission not to express themselves in public on matters political. This, no doubt, Chamberlain regretted, but he did nothing to undermine Cantine's moral authority in the mission. In 1921, Cantine returned to the United States for health reasons. Leadership on the field then fell to the second generation. But the atmosphere in this regard did not change.

Writing to Charlotte Kelein, the mission secretary, December 21, 1922, Chamberlain put forth an appeal:

> The Executive Committee [of the board] appreciated the force of the Resolution of the Mission noted in Item 5 regarding the undesirability of missionaries pronouncing upon or discussing in the public press the secular and political problems involving relations of a governmental character. We know something of recent circumstances that have given force to such a self-denying ordinance. Possibly with the settlement of political conditions and the gradual disappearance of War nervousness, such restraint will not need to be placed upon members of the Mission in the distant future, but for the immediate present its relevance and importance are obvious.[35]

The resolution in particular noted that missionaries ought not make public comment upon "secular and political problems involving relations between the British authorities and local potentates." It was stimulated by British reaction to a rather outspoken article which Paul Harrison had written for the *Atlantic Monthly* entitled "The Situation in Arabia." In it he discussed the British role in the Gulf with cool detachment, noting that their alliance with 'Abd-ul-'Azîz Âl Sa'ûd was a fragile affair, and expecting the Sa'ûdî wrath to turn against the Hijâz and the Sharîf of Mecca in spite of British opposition. He concluded that the end product toward which Sa'ûdî

---

[35]Chamberlain to Kelein, December 21, 1922, a carbon copy of which was seen in the document collection of D.B. Scudder in 1991.

policies were directed was the disestablishment of British influence in the region. It was, in short, a powerfully written and insightful article which embarrassed the British, and they wanted to make sure that voices like that of Paul Harrison were silenced. The mission complied. Necessary or no, this was a restriction with which Chamberlain (and no doubt some members of the mission too) was uncomfortable since it cut out a crucial area of discussion and, hence, was also repressive of thought. In any case, Harrison wrote no more articles in a similar vein.[36]

Two major changes took place under Chamberlain's management that had long-term effect upon the Arabian Mission. First, the syndicate structure that had sustained the Arabian Mission from its inception was dissolved. Although it worked a gradual transformation both in the make up of the mission and of its support base, the amalgamation of the Arabian Mission into the Board of Foreign Missions in 1924 and the dissolution of the separate Arabian Mission Corporation in 1925 had no immediate impact upon the way in which the board related to the field. The gradual dissolution of Arabia interest groups among the congregations of the Reformed church and of other denominations, however, did eventually decrease the intelligent awareness of the Middle East in Reformed church pews and elsewhere and cut a vital channel of communication that was not board-dependent.[37] The

[36]Harrison himself, intinerant doctor that he was, required the good will of British colonial administrators. In order to travel in Oman or the Emirates, he found himself obliged to submit reports on local tribal conditions to British political officers. Many of these have been dutifully kept in the Colonial Office Archives in London. But for all his distress at being put in this position, he was able to say very little in an open fashion.

[37]James Cantine, writing in 1925 as the years of his retirement neared, noted, "It is sometimes said that the first missionaries were men of vision, men of faith, but in the opinion of the writer, far greater was the faith of those mature minds, who by their support of this venture, assumed the responsibility for the activities of young and untried workers, in an unknown environment, attempting a task that many deemed hopeless" (Mason and Barny, *History...*, p. 239). He went on to highlight particularly the roles of John Lansing, Preston Searle, and Henry Cobb, but he noted that from the beginning the mission was able to tap into broad pools

syndicate structure was a unique institution which had served a very special kind of function. The atrophy of an informed base of mission intelligence at the grassroots level of the denomination was not a foreseen consequence of the dissolution of the syndicates, but it was a consequence nonetheless.

The second innovation was the launching at the end of 1923 of the United Mission in Mesopotamia (later known as the United Mission in Iraq) with the Presbyterian Church in the U.S.A. (led by the mission ideologue, Robert Speer) and the Evangelical and Reformed church. Iraq, in 1923 a British mandate under the League of Nations, had been a side interest of several mission efforts (the Presbyterians out of Syria, the Congregationalists out of Anatolia, the Anglicans and Presbyterians out of Iran). The most substantial of these "sideshows" was that of the Anglican Church Missionary Society (CMS, 1882-1919) in Baghdad.[38] With the British military presence large in Iraq after the First World War, the CMS judged that it could no longer operate freely in the country, compromised as it would be by the politics of colonialism.

As the CMS withdrawal in 1919 became imminent, James Cantine insisted that the Arabian Mission step in and take over Baghdad as a temporary station.[39] No mission board had resources at its disposal to take on the full load of an independent initiative in Iraq, and the Arabian Mission was reluctant to be drawn further northward. But Chamberlain came to sympathize with Cantine's sense of the imperative and, with Robert Speer and A.R. Barthalomew (of the Evangelical and Reformed church), put together a coalition that, on November 8, 1923, formally initiated the Joint

of talent and resources primarily because its base was "interdenominational." The non-Reformed personnel of the Arabian Mission, he continued, were pleased to go along with the amalgamation (pp. 239-240), but behind Cantine's words, in the turns of phrase and the caution with which he expressed himself, can be read a deep sense of unease. The loss of the broad base of income is not so much the thing to be regretted as the loss of appeal to the broader reaches of the Christian church when it came to attracting mission personnel. This proved a valid anxiety.

[38] At first the work in Baghdad was an outpost of the Persia Mission of the CMS. Then, for twenty years, they identified their effort there separately as the Turkish Arabia Mission. CMS work was interrupted by the First World War from 1914 to 1918.

[39] Henry and Monty Bilkert followed the Cantines in the holding operation there when in 1921 the latter had to return to the United States for reasons of Elizabeth Cantine's deteriorating health. The Barnys replaced the Bilkerts in Baghdad in 1925.

Committee for the United Mission in Mesopotamia (UMM).[40] As an experimental format for doing mission, the UMM bore the particular stamp of William Chamberlain's ideology. He served as chairman of the joint committee from 1923 until his retirement in 1935 when he was succeeded by Duke Potter.

The 'Duke' (1935 [1918]-1952)

The year 1935 marks the end of one era and the beginning of another. Upon Chamberlain's retirement,[41] his faithful understudy Francis Marmaduke "Duke" Potter became secretary of the Board of Foreign Missions. He had served four years as an educator with the Arcot Mission in India (1913-1917) before becoming the associate secretary and treasurer for the board in 1918. His main area of responsibility under Chamberlain was finance. He had been instrumental in the amalgamation of the Arabian Mission in 1924 with the rest of the Board of Foreign Mission's fields and had juggled hard-come-by funds during the Great Depression.

Duke Potter, no less than his illustrious predecessor, became something of a legend in the denomination and among missionaries. Potter was the first layman to hold so high and powerful a position in the Reformed church's clergy-ridden hierarchy, and he held it well through the recovery years following the Great Depression and through the Second World War— nearly twenty years. His knowledge of the business of mission was extensive. His skill with finances was legendary; in 1942 he managed finally to liquidate the deficit that had dogged the board since the mid-1880s. He ran a lean administrative structure and kept a great deal of the information concerning the mission fields of the Reformed church in his mind's cavernous and well organized file. So long as he was healthy and functioning, that method worked well. His death in office on August 17, 1952, provoked a crisis; his vast store of information was no longer accessible. The regime which followed his had to improvise a great deal from scratch.

Potter was a master in the business of keeping things in order.[42] He had his limitations and had not the breadth of vision which had so characterized

---

[40] The relationship of this new venture with the Arabian Mission was both close and ambiguous, since the mission withheld the stations of 'Imârah and Basrah from the UMM's jurisdiction.

[41] William I. Chamberlain died in the fall of 1937.

[42] He was also remembered for his affection for children. He had a trick which mission children remember of folding a table napkin into the shape of a mouse and then "bringing it alive" in his hand. Certain things stick in the memory.

his predecessor. His were years when the Arabian Mission's institutions settled in permanently and verged on expansion. Plans for building a new, much larger hospital in Kuwait were being developed.[43] Medical work under the leadership of Paul Harrison and Wells Thoms expanded in Oman. The hospitals and the school in Bahrain under Harold Storm and Ruth Jackson, respectively, grew, and their influence radiated broadly. The years were economically lean in the region. People suffered from rising prices on basic commodities and foodstuffs. There was also a succession of severe summers when, exacerbated by malnutrition, fatalities from heat stroke were almost at an epidemic level. As the Potter years ended, the tidal wave of oil prosperity was poised on the horizon, but it had yet to inundate the region. They were good years to be a missionary. The needs were everywhere poignant and apparent.

Potter's were the years of World War II and their aftermath. Adolph Hitler came to power in Germany in 1933. Japan invaded China, flexing its muscles, and when rebuked by the League of Nations, withdrew from that world body. Relations between Japan and the United States proceeded to deteriorate, seriously affecting mission work there. The United States, as European countries defaulted on debts they had incurred after the First World War, went into a new phase of isolationism. But these were also days when American oil companies—Standard Oil, Texaco, and Gulf—were exploring for oil and developing concessions in the Arab Gulf.

In Palestine in the early 1930s, systematic efforts by Zionists to consolidate their position by gaining control of land were arousing the violent reaction of the Palestinian population. It broke out in open rebellion in 1936. Britain,

---

[43]By 1947, plans for erecting a sixty-bed hospital in Kuwait had advanced to the point that Jerry Nykerk could write to Major Tandy, the British Agent in Kuwait, informing him that "three and one quarter lacs of rupees" were already in hand, and that construction would begin as soon as materials became available. (The letter is dated January 28, 1947 and is in the author's collection.) Actually, ground was not broken for the new hospital until early in 1954, and the hospital opened for business in October of 1955.

as the mandatory authority, responded inconsistently to both sides. While the repercussions of this were of interest to sensitive people in the Arabian Mission,[44] events in Iraq had more immediate impact. British manipulation of the Iraqi monarchy at a time of rising nationalist sentiments led to increased resentment among intellectuals. The prewar years seethed with unrest, and the war's outbreak led to the attempted coup of Rashîd ʿAlî al-Gaylânî.

In the years succeeding the war, the world became increasingly complex, not least of all for American missionary enterprises. During the postwar reconstruction in Europe, the burden America assumed for such programs as the Marshall Plan was immense. From the death of president Woodrow Wilson until December 7, 1941 and the attack on Pearl Harbor, the United States had adopted an isolationist frame of mind. The internationalist impulses of the American people had—except for the interruption of World War I—been expressed through a sustained interest in foreign missions funneled through Christian mission boards and societies. Not even the Depression had had a serious effect upon the amount of work which the churches were able to support overseas. World War II, however, was an event which ushered in a time of serious social and cultural disillusionment and, with America's commitments to foreign aid attaining massive proportions after the war, American Christians turned their attention inward. Their sense of urgency for foreign missions declined sharply.[45]

This was the mood of the Potter era in the Reformed church's Board of Foreign Missions. He took over responsibility for a far-flung mission effort which had achieved a certain degree of institutional stability. The Arabian

[44]John Van Ess took a personal interest, visited Palestine immediately after the war, and even had the temerity to put forward his suggestions for a resolution of the crisis.

[45]Roger Nemeth and Donald Luidens of Hope College note that, prior to World War II, the proportional distribution of an average Reformed church congregation's resources was two portions for internal use to one portion for external use (mainly missions). Following the war, a different picture emerged, and today the proportion is eight to internal and one to external causes.

Mission still spoke about penetrating the interior of Arabia. Touring was still very active. But even before Potter died, the reorientation of American sentiment was already clear, and within two years of his death, the Arabian Mission's dream of penetrating the interior had to be set aside. Personnel were scarce, funds were drying up, and people's attention was turned elsewhere.

The 'Triumvirate' (1952-1962)

The new regime which began to administer the mission efforts of the Reformed church in 1952 was a sort of triumvirate. Senior in the system was the powerful personality of Ruth Ransom. A lady of substantial presence in more respects than simply her indomitable spirit, Ruth Ransom had begun her career as a Methodist missionary in Peru. From there she had dabbled for a time in Christian education for the Methodist church before moving on to become the secretary for personnel for the Methodist Board of Foreign Missions. In 1943 she was hired by the Reformed church's Women's Board of Foreign Missions as its executive secretary. Duke Potter brought her onto his staff as personnel secretary in 1946 when the Women's Board of Foreign Missions merged with that of the denomination. For the next fourteen years she held the position as a fief.

The other two members of the triumvirate were the Rev. Henry "Heine" G. Bovenkerk and the Rev. Bernard "Barny" M. Luben. Both of these men had experience on the field in Japan as well as having worked in mission promotion in the United States—Bovenkerk in relief work among Japanese Americans during World War II, and Luben as Midwest field secretary for the Board of Foreign Missions. While Ransom managed to remain somewhat above the fray, the relationship between Bovenkerk and Luben was difficult almost from the start. The pattern of authority and accountability was not clearly defined, and they found themselves not infrequently at cross-purposes. Since Bovenkerk, as secretary-treasurer, controled the financial side of the administration and was a man of deliberate frugality, not infrequently the case was that he and Luben, the executive secretary, were found to be contending between the dollar and the demands of the field.

The period 1952-1962 began with the denomination in something of an affluent mood and ended with the onset of serious budget crises. It was also a time, on the field, of expensive modernization of hospitals and schools, particularly the Kuwait hospital, the School of High Hope for Boys in Basrah, and Al-Rajâ' School in Bahrain. These expansion projects of the mission's educational and medical programs occasioned deliberate reviews by the Board of Foreign Missions. Administratively, given Bovenkerk's outlook on matters financial, it was also a time when the mission was forced to consider budget first and need second. An inversion of administrative style had set in. Instead of looking at the need in the first column, this style viewed the income from church contributions as the principal conditioning factor. That is, the denomination no longer looked at the mission challenge in the first instance. The denomination's staff was obliged to look at the budget for mission as the primary consideration, and from that vantage point they looked for what that limited pool of material resources could be made to accomplish. This inversion was a critical turning point in mission, not just for the field in Arabia but worldwide.

As the 1950s matured, it became apparent that the unusually long honeymoon period of the mission was over; its time was running out. The politics of nationalism were in the air everywhere, and oil was becoming a major player. The Gulf was no longer a backwater. The close relationship the mission had had with the Hâshimite regime in Iraq during the days of John Van Ess did not stand the mission in good stead. The regime which came violently into power in 1958 was passionately anti-American, and, it will be recalled, the mission was known locally as the *American* Mission. For the Arabian Mission, through the months of August to October of 1959, this resulted in the expropriation of the Lansing Memorial Hospital in 'Imârah by an over-zealous local governor who played himself off over against a stubborn and high principled American doctor (Gerald Nykerk).

The expropriation of the 'Imârah property turned from a bitter taste in the mouth to serious gastric distress for the mission when the attitude of fiscal conservatism deepened on the board. Although the boy's School of High Hope in Basrah along with the United Mission in Iraq's operations in Baghdad (but not in Mosul) had survived the 1959 crisis and, paradoxically, seemed to be on a better footing than before; and although the states of

Kuwait, Bahrain, and the rest of Arabia viewed what had happened in Iraq with alarm and gave the mission assurances that such would not happen elsewhere, it was difficult from the perspective of United States to justify further capital investment in the Arabian Gulf. Pastors' meetings began to ask questions about whether, when, and how the mission could turn over property and church buildings to "indigenous" Christian congregations.[46] Financial screws were tightened, and the mission depended increasingly upon generating its operating budget on the field. The rising tide of oil money made this possible. The most successful of the mission's hospitals in these years was Kuwait, whose annual surpluses, devised as though by magic by a resourceful Dorothy Scudder, Kuwait's hospital administrator, served to keep the mission's medical program afloat not only in Kuwait but in Bahrain and Oman as well.

In the middle of this period (from 1956 to 1960), the Arabian Mission engaged in an experiment. Aware that matters were growing phenomenally complex, Barny Luben advocated and succeeded in appointing R. Park Johnson, the veteran Presbyterian missionary administrator, to the post of "Field Representative in the Near East" in July, 1956. Johnson wore this hat for both the Reformed Church in America and the Presbyterian Church in

---

46It escaped no one's attention that, apart from the congregation in Oman and one family in the church in Bahrain, the Arabic-speaking Christians in the Gulf were not indigenous, not even those who held a Gulf nationality. In the Protestant fellowships, a good many of the core group were, in fact, Suryânî or Assyrian in origin, and everyone knew it. Nonetheless, facing the real fears of the moment, the argument was that, unlike westerners and others of foreign sort, the Arabic-language congregations represented that portion of the Christian community in the Gulf which would most likely stay the longest and would, in any case, have the highest profile in any time of crisis. The experience of the Middle East, examined from today's vantage point of some thirty years and in the midst of the crisis caused by the outbreak of Islamic fundamentalism, does not substantiate this prognosis. The emigration of Christian Arabs from their homelands has become a major concern for the Middle East Council of Churches, which views it with such alarm that it speaks in terms of the extinction of Christianity in the lands of its birth.

the U.S.A. Operating out of his base in Beirut, he covered virtually the whole of the Middle East from Syria/Lebanon and Egypt to Iraq, Iran, and the Arabian Gulf. The fact that Johnson was able to cover this broad field and do it with sensitivity and wisdom during a period of extremely rapid change is the measure of an exceptional individual.

From the outset of Johnson's brief tenure, one can note an improved attitude on the part of missionaries. The hit-or-miss business practices of individual stations were brought into line. The Mission Executive Committee (MEC) was inaugurated (first meeting, January 22, 1957) to deal with ad-interim business between the annual meetings of the delegates of the stations (which were then eventually scheduled every three years), and the awkward method of circular letters generating mission consensus was rendered obsolete. At mission behest, in 1956 Johnson also advocated the appointment of a "Field Consultant to the Board," an office conceived as a way of giving a field presence at board deliberations. In this the mission was rebuffed,[47] but that did nothing to detract from Johnson's effectiveness with the feisty Arabian Mission group. And it was Johnson who shepherded the mission through the trauma of 1959 occasioned by the closure of 'Imârah station. In 1960 it was felt that, over-extended as Johnson had become, he should focus more of his attention on Presbyterian matters. He officially continued as field representative for the board, but at a reduced level of involvement, until November, 1967, when he was transferred by the Presbyterians to West Pakistan.[48]

[47]In a rather defensive and strongly worded secretarial letter from Barny Luben to George Gosselink, November 26, 1956, Luben questioned the grounds on which the mission asked for such a liaison officer. Clearly, the frustrations the missionaries felt in their endeavors to communicate with the rank and file membership of the board were serious, the more serious at a time when the mission's very existence was being questioned. The staff buffer between missionaries and the members of the board exacerbated a growing sense of alienation from the denomination.

[48]Minuted Action 67-100 of the Board of World Mission. In anticipation of Johnson's departure, the board approved the position of a "liaison to the Area Secretary" for the Arabian Mission in April of 1967. Ken Warren, commissioned as a missionary to be resource for administration for the medical institutions in the Gulf in 1966, was nominated by the mission to fulfill this liaison function in September of 1967. This represented something of a compromise with the mission's request of 1956 for a field consultant to the board.

The Ransom-Luben-Bovenkerk period concluded with a new direction being set for shaping mission policy. It was ushered in by a series of studies on the mission overall and in its several parts. Communications and travel had improved to a degree which allowed quick trips to the field by board secretaries and delegations. The mid-1950s witnessed a series of investigations of the mission and its programs—particularly the medical and educational.

The reigning philosophy was spurred on by two factors. First, the lack of statistical success in gaining converts (or "midwifing" the birth of an indigenous church) came home to roost. Arabia was notorious for its lack of "success," and the Roland Allen school of missiology demanded the planting of indigenous self-sufficient and self-propagating congregations.[49] Zwemer's conviction that medical work would be the wedge that would kick wide open the door to the vulnerable Muslim heart, after fifty years of the experiment, had proven more than optimistic. Both Bovenkerk and Luben were

[49] Roland Allen, once a missionary for the Anglican church's Society for the Propagation of the Gospel in China, became a prominent spokesperson against traditional missionary approaches. His principal thesis was that, by the power of the Holy Spirit, the Church *will* expand spontaneously if we do not stifle the Spirit. In any case, a mission effort which does not bear the fruit of self-sustaining, self-governing, and self-propagating churches is probably wrongly motivated and poorly founded. The arguments of Allen, from the date of the publication of his book, *Missionary Methods: St. Paul's or Ours* (New York: Fleming H. Revell Company, 1913), to the appearance of *The Spontaneous Expansion of the Church and the Causes Which Hinder It* (London: World Dominion Press, 1926), became the ideological testing ground for missions well into the 1970s. The Arabian Mission was not excepted. His argument against missions building institutions (see *Spontaneous Expansion*, p. 106ff) became particularly popular in the 1950s and lie at the root of some of the radical decisions taken with regard to the Arabian Mission's major institutions in the 1960s.

It is worth noting here that the circumstances of the Arabian Mission were always difficult to fit into normal ideological arguments. No indigenous church ever threatened to emerge except in the case of Oman. Jay Kapenga, echoing Allen, has noted that the reluctance of the mission to trust the Omani church enough to approve the ordination of its leading elders to the ministry probably stifled the emergence of a truly autonomous community. That error may be held to account for why that community dissipated when the mission structure was withdrawn in the early 1970s (document attached to Jay Kapenga's missionary questionnaire in the author's document collection).

convinced that the mission had spent altogether too little effort in touching the malleable souls of youth in the Gulf. Instead of hospitals, therefore, perhaps the mission should have invested more heavily in education, social programming directed toward youth, and the various communications possibilities of the printed page and radio.[50] In any case, the question of why the indigenous church had not emerged became a focal issue, bringing into question the whole reason for the mission's existence.[51]

The second factor was the rising cost of modernity. It inspired a review of major institutions (particularly medical institutions). Newly affluent Arabs were being sold western models for medical institutions, and the mission had been caught in a competitive spiral. Foresightfully phrased in a day of lesser affluence, the vision of Paul Harrison that the mission pioneer and continue to experiment with culturally fitting models for medical care[52]

---

[50]A prominent merchant of Oman, interviewed by the author in 1990 and preferring to remain anonymous, seemed to support this view. He noted that, in a hospital, an individual came to be treated, was touched briefly, and then returned to his or her own home environment. A school, on the other hand, gave opportunity for teachers to shape the outlook of a young and impressionable student over a long span of time, and the result would be that, returning to a home environment, that student would introduce values and perspectives that could be infectious. He pointedly said that, tactically, the mission had made a mistake in giving education short shrift. This, he said, was good for Islam, but unfortunate for the mission. In another interview, Jeannette Veldman echoed this sentiment. She felt that, as the mission gave up its opportunity to specialize in nursing education, it gave up one of its most effective instruments of witness. In 1957 in their "Deputation Report on Arabian Mission," John Buteyn and Barny Luben, citing the comment of a "missionary statesman" that "Our schools are the places where what is going to happen is getting ready," recommended "That the program of education receive increased attention on the field and the Board give its early endorsement to as many of the recommendations of the Educational Survey as may be possible" (p. 3; document in the author's collection).

[51]In several consecutive General Synods of the Reformed church, the Classis of South Grand Rapids, prominently represented by Ronald "Tiny" Brown, introduced overtures demanding that the mission to Arabia be abandoned for precisely this reason.

[52]Paul W. Harrison, "The Medical Missionary," pp. 3-8 in Jesse R. Wilson, ed., *Men and Women of Far Horizons* (New York, Friendship Press: 1935). Harrison wrote, "To duplicate for [the Arabs] the exceedingly expensive hospital equipment of the West is a dubious favor. In such a hospital the environment is so strange as to be frightening, and with this strangeness there goes an unheard-of insistence on cleanliness which takes all the joy out of their life and most of the gratitude out of their hearts. To give adequate and thorough medical attention to patients who remain in an environment where they feel at home is the essence of our task."

languished for lack of a visionary interpreter. Having to keep up with the pace of change in Kuwait and Bahrain, the mission's medical work was threatening to become a heavy drain on both capital and personnel. Although growing and remodeled facilities like those in Kuwait were heavily financed by local subscription, Bovenkerk (the long-term financial threat aside) questioned whether the mission could continue to justify the way in which medical institutions absorbed not only the medical but also all available personnel in a particular mission station.[53]

Noting that the mission hospital in Bahrain looked more like a "Bedouin encampment" than a western medical institution, he concluded, "We are able to maintain a psychological atmosphere more favorable to recovery than any we could easily find in the United States." He then asks, "But under such circumstances is it possible to do good work?" He answers himself, "It is. Good surgical technique and clean wounds do not depend on ponderous equipment and a multitude of assistants" (p. 5). Lew Scudder, Sr., toward the end of his career, used to laugh when asked about sterile technique in the primitive facilities he used to have. "The fact that we had hardly any cases of post-operative infection," he added gravely, "is one proof I have that miracles really happen. Of course, liberal doses of sulfadiazine before we shut the patient up helped too."

[53]In his "Deputation Report of Board Treasurer," submitted to the Board of Foreign Missions, Reformed Church in America, January 16, 1956, Bovenkerk cites as one of the "weaknesses of the Christian hospital program" the fact that (p. 6) "the medical work is requiring a constantly increasing proportion of the missionary personnel. Well over half of the present missionaries are related to hospitals. Many evangelistic missionaries give large segments of their time to hospital maintenance tasks. There is a demand for an increasingly large proportion of missionary personnel to meet growing hospital needs" (document in the author's collection). Advocating the appointment of a "builder-contractor" for the mission, Buteyn and Luben in their 1957 report noted the strengthening undercurrent of tension between ordained and medical personnel: "...ordained men must give considerable time to building supervision and maintenance—a task for which they have no adequate training. At times such tasks demand the major attention of missionaries for periods from six months to a year. It certainly does not seem to be an efficient use of personnel to have the ordained men thus engaged. Though some enjoy this activity and find wider contacts through such work, the direct evangelistic benefits are hard to find—except in rare cases. Most of the ordained men are quite unhappy in this situation and feel that it diverts them from their main mission and the deputation feels this is the case" (document cited above, p. 4). Dorothy Van Ess, in her history of the Arabian Mission, notes that, for better or worse, the mission had put its eggs by-and-large in the medical basket. Questions from outside and tensions within the mission in the mid-1950s and into the 1960s indicate a rather deep questioning of this traditional focus of the mission. As the 1950s broke into the '60s, the lack of consensus on the missiological role of medicine and disorientation on this question prepared the ground for the traumatic closure of medical work in Kuwait in 1967.

Reflected in these discussions is the growing undercurrent of questioning whether the Arabian Mission any longer had *any* role to play. The Gulf no longer appealed by reason of the misery of its population. The oil-fed spendthrift affluence of Gulf Arabs began to flood American media with images of extreme and sometimes comic conspicuous consumption. A missionary mystique based upon America's calling to lift up the poor and the downtrodden could no longer justify a call to Arabia. Quite the opposite, in fact.[54]

At the end of 1962, a consultation, "On the Unity and Mission of the Church," was held in the mountain resort of 'Alay in Lebanon under the aegis of the Near East Council of Churches, an institution then still heavily dominated by representatives of western mission agencies. John Buteyn attended for the Board of World Missions. The report of the consultation noted: "In the past decade, studies in the mission of the Church have increasingly called into question the continuing necessity and advisability of maintaining many of those [educational and medical] institutions as part of the Church's mission in the future."[55] The report continued, "In the face of these insistent questions it is evident that many of the churches in the Near East remain convinced that the traditional Christian institutions continue to fill an important place in the life and mission of the Church."

Keying on the question, "Is the present need for medical, educational or welfare services such as would impel the church at this time to *start* [emphasis in original] a given institution, if it were not already in existence?" (p. 5), the report then set the stage for considering the possibility of abandoning many of those services. The principle invoked to achieve this was: "In sharing the resources of the churches of the Near East and of the

---

[54]To what extent this may be correlated with the increased Zionist political activity in the United States is difficult to establish. By the mid-1970s, however, the argument that Arabia missionaries had allowed themselves to be "bought" by their Arab friends in order to argue against America's polarization on the Arab-Israeli conflict began to be easily spoken. Undermining the credibility of Arabian Mission spokespersons in the United States benefited the mission not at all. It went hand-in-glove with the tendency within the RCA to view with suspicion the qualification of missionaries to be given an influential voice in directing the denomination's mission policy in general. It underscored the fact that, with congregations turning inward, the era of denominational statespersons rising out of the ranks of the denomination's missionary endeavor was virtually at an end.

[55]"The Report on the Consultation on the Unity and Mission of the Church," Aleih, Lebanon, November 8-15, 1962, pp. 3-4 (document in author's collection).

churches of the world, it is considered important that resources of both personnel and material aid be utilized in such a way that both the indigenous development of the Church and the fullest expression of the missionary concern of the world-wide Church is strengthened" (p. 6).[56]

As applied to the Arabia field, the question became ecclesiastically hazy. In a sense, the issue of what was to be done in Iraq had been removed from the agenda. The Iraqi government had expropriated the Lansing Memorial Hospital in 'Imârah in 1958-59. The boys' School of High Hope in Basrah, in spite of the reluctance of George and Christine Gosselink (who retired in 1966), had been taken under the wing of the United Mission in Iraq in 1962 and was out of the Arabian Mission's jurisdiction.[57] The manifest lack of an "indigenous" church in the remaining stations of the Arabian Mission, but the presence of growing multicultural churches locally constituted, made for doubt as to whether the Reformed church, acting in the Gulf, really had any indigenous "partner" with whom to negotiate on the declared principle. In the end, the Reformed church determined that it could act unilaterally. The 'Alay Consultation laid the ideological groundwork. The failure of the churches in the Gulf to form into an ecclesiastically acceptable community of interest provided the pretext.

Ruth Ransom retired quietly in 1960, to be succeeded by Ruth Joldersma, a social worker from Long Island. With Ransom's retirement, in a flurry of disgruntlement, Bovenkerk resigned in December of the same year. He accepted a position with the Japan International Christian University Foundation. By March of 1961 Barny Luben had resigned to become the executive secretary for RAVEMCCO.[58] Remaining on station were Ruth E. Joldersma in personnel and J. Robert Harrison stepping up from controller to treasurer. As Luben stepped down, John E. Buteyn was appointed area

---

[56]The phrasing of the last part of this statement is indicative of the reigning mindset. As Roland Allen had warned nearly fifty years before, indigenous client churches of missionary organizations were not seen as having "missionary concerns" in the same sense as their western founders. They were primarily the object of mission. They were still developing. They remained dependents. The same phraseology could not have been used ten years later.

[57]In 1967, following the Arab-Israeli War in June, the School of High Hope in Basrah was also closed by governmental decree.

[58]Radio, Visual Education and Mass Communications Committee...of the Division of Foreign Missions of the National Council of the Churches of Christ in the United States of America

secretary for Africa, Arabia, India, and the United Mission in Iraq, and temporarily acted as staff coordinator.[59] James P. Ebbers was appointed secretary for Promotion (Interpretation and Church Relations) in July of 1962. And, finally, Max De Pree for the Board of World Mission announced the appointment of Edwin M. Luidens as general secretary, effective April, 1964.[60]

The Luidens Interlude (1962-1968)

The task facing Ed Luidens was to pick up the pieces of the Bovenkerk/ Luben decade and to weld into a working group several powerful personalities who were already in place by the time he arrived, somewhat reluctantly, on the scene. It was a thankless task conducted in a heady atmosphere of intense power struggles within the RCA during the first years that Marion de Velder was stated clerk of the denomination.[61] These were also the days

[59]While a pastor in Rochester, New York, John Buteyn began his relationship to the Board of World Missions in 1956 as field secretary for the three western synods of the Reformed church. He had traveled overseas with Barny Luben, visiting the Sudan, India, and the Middle East in 1957. From June, 1960, he had taken the position of secretary of Church Relations and Promotion (the position filled the next summer by Jams Ebbers).

[60]Edwin M. Luidens, graduate of Hope College and New Brunswick Theological Seminary, had been assigned to the Arabian Mission as an evangelist in 1944. His main service was in Bahrain and 'Imârah. In 1957 he went to Beirut to chair the Radio Committee of the Near East Christian Council. (Several of his colleagues in the Arabian Mission felt this was a real loss to the mission and squandrous misuse of Ed Luidens' talents.) In 1958 he returned to the United States, serving as executive secretary of RAVEMCCO. Replaced in that position by Barny Luben in 1961, he returned to Beirut to be general director of the Radio Project of the Near East Council. When asked to take up leadership of the staff of the Board of World Mission in that same year, Luidens resisted, and that accounts, as much as anything, for the delay in his appointment.

[61]Marion de Velder succeeded as stated clerk James F. Hoffman, who had served from 1942 to 1961. De Velder, then fifty-one, had achieved high standing in the Reformed church, having served as pastor to three of the denomination's more prestigious congregations. From 1946 to 1948 he had chaired the denomination's "United Advance" fund drive as well as (from 1948 to 1952) the Commission on a United Approach to the church. He had been a member of the denomination's Board of Education, and in 1958-1959 was president of the General Synod. He was, in short, a personage and a presence.

when Arie Brouwer was moving from the parish ministry into a denominational and ecumenical role.[62]

As he came onto the staff, it was perhaps inevitable that Ed Luidens should have experienced some tension with John Buteyn, who had already served for three years as *de facto* administrator of the world mission program. But both were grown men, and the style was quickly set for getting on with the business of mission to which both were devoted. Staff meetings were wide-open affairs, and individuals expressed their challenges to each other quite freely. In this, Ruth Joldersma was not infrequently a feisty combatant. It was a structure perhaps too heady with talent and, in terms of personalities, not as balanced as it might have been. But, at least for a time, through some of the more uncertain years of the denomination, these five—Luidens, Buteyn, Joldersma, Harrison, and Ebbers—worked together with remarkable smoothness and complementarity, at least as far as Arabia missionaries who worked with them could see. Their impact upon the mission was noticeable; their common mission outlook strengthened the trend toward centering control of mission program in the home office.

[62]Arie R. Brouwer, in his early thirties, with nine years of pastoral experience in Michigan and New Jersey, had served on the Board of World Missions, on the Board of New Brunswick Theological Seminary, and on the Board of Theological Education. Brouwer was on a pilgrimage out of a narrow theological perspective and into a broad awareness of the Church in the world. A gifted scholar, he had the capacity for absorbing and synthesizing ideas into structural models, and those gifts, along with an awareness that power could be used, took him quickly into areas of involvement which tested his talents to their limit. His involvement in world Christian issues took him eventually from a position as executive secretary of the General Program Council (1968-1977), to becoming Marion de Velder's successor as general secretary of the Reformed church (1977-1983), to the position of deputy general secretary of the World Council of Churches (1983-1984, at the end of which term he was a candidate for general secretary), to the position of general secretary for the National Council of the Churches of Christ in the United States of America (1985-1989). But what remains most remarkable for this study is the fact that, in his last years (1989-1993), he devoted himself to organizing and leading (and to providing a good deal of the funding for) "Middle East Peacemakers," an organization devoted to advocating bold initiatives for understanding and addressing the conflict in the Middle East. Arie Brouwer died at the end of 1993 at the early age of fifty-eight, a controversial figure to the end.

Structurally, the Reformed church had been going through a long agony of uncertainty and reorganization since 1946. In that year, the staff of its five boards and agencies met together for the first time in a joint staff conference, an event which continued annually thereafter.[63] The staff recommended to the General Synod a united approach to fundraising, giving strong impetus toward unifying these boards and agencies. Responding favorably to the staff conference's recommendations, the General Synod of 1946 appointed Marion de Velder, then pastor of Hope Church in Holland, Michigan, to chair a two-year fundraising effort called the "United Advance."[64] The United Advance succeeded in doubling the RCA's per member giving to benevolences, and its success was followed by the appointment of a "Commission on a United Approach," also chaired by de Velder. On the advice of the commission, in 1952 the General Synod formed a "Stewardship Council" to coordinate all fundraising for the synod's various activities. The Stewardship Council's fundraising efforts were augmented, in 1961, by General Synod's appointing a General Synod Executive Committee, whose task it was to exercise *administrative* control over the denomination's boards and agencies.

A corporate model for the denomination's structure was evolving piecemeal out of improvisation. That model was more explicitly developed from 1961 and produced a new structure at the end of 1967. The process was shepherded by Marion de Velder. The drive was supplied by two elders, both well-trained, successful, and canny corporate executives—Max De Pree (of Zeeland, Michigan, president of the Board of World Mission) and Ekdal Buys (of Holland, Michigan, president of the Board of Domestic Mission).

The major point at issue in the restructuring, aside from redefining the position of stated clerk into the role of a full-fledged chief executive for the denomination,[65] was the supervision and direction of the denomination's

---

[63]In 1945 these boards numbered seven: the Board of Foreign Missions, the *Women's* Board of Foreign Missions, the Board of Domestic Missions, the *Women's* Board of Domestic Missions, the Board of Education, the Minister's Fund, and the Board of Direction. In 1946 the Women's Boards of Foreign and Domestic Missions were dissolved, leaving five boards and agencies.

[64]De Velder designed the United Advance along the lines of secular fundraising efforts such as the Community Chest. This was a significant departure from the manner in which the denomination expected its resources to be generated.

[65]The office of stated clerk was eventually redefined as "general secretary" of the Reformed Church in America.

boards and agencies. The corporate model, unifying all of the General Synod's activities under a "General Program Council" (GPC), was launched June 17, 1968. J. Robert Harrison was co-opted from his position as treasurer of the Board of World Mission to serve as "Coordinator for the Implementation of Changes in Denominational Structure," a role he completed in 1970. The functions of the Board of World Mission were then assumed under the office of the secretary for program (later, executive secretary) of the GPC as the Division of World Ministries.[66]

As this tense process of change drew to its conclusion, it was Ed Luidens's task to keep the world mission efforts of the denomination on track. Ed, a gentle but persistent person of innate democratic instincts, trained in the rough-and-tumble, often confrontational, decision-making style of the Arabian Mission, was not well in tune with the far more subtle and dangerous workings of politics within the RCA. From the time he assumed office, it is evident that he was not always in the information loop. His political constituency was made up primarily of missionaries on the field. Nonetheless, after four years of leadership, he was mooted as being in line for a position of high responsibility when the new structure came into effect. It came as a shock, when the new structure was implemented, that he was passed over for the major administrative position of secretary for program as well as for the second position he could have accepted, that of secretary for world ministries. He was forced out of the denominational staff picture along with Ruth Joldersma in 1968.[67] Arie Brouwer, in an appointment

---

[66]Hoff, *Structures...*, is the most complete study now in print of this process from 1624 to 1980. What it understandably omits is the human side of the story, an aspect which is still tender. The General Program Council continued to serve the General Synod until it was dissolved by vote of the classes and the act of the General Synod in 1993, being replaced in its turn by a new structure, called the "General Synod Council." This new structure, which falls outside the historical scope of this study, places world mission concerns under the "Mission Services Unit."

[67]There is little doubt that personalities had something to do with appointments. Marion de Velder, although not officially a member of the selection committee (chaired by Max De Pree), served nonetheless as that committee's staff person. His disapproval of Ed Luidens's administrative style, especially his tolerance for the process of collegial challenge, made Ed, in de Velder's eyes, unfit for high administrative duties. Neither Luidens nor Joldersma, therefore, were recommended for significant new staff positions.

Ed Luidens was quickly hired as the secretary for the Far East for the National Council of Churches' Division of Overseas Ministries, a position which he held

which surprised even him, was assigned overall administrative responsibility for the General Program Council, and John Buteyn moved up to take over the new Division of World Ministries. Buteyn also continued to hold the portfolio for the Middle East.[68]

The Buteyn Era (1962-1982)

The General Program Council, as it began to function, made a certain degree of sense for the denomination as a whole. But even a cursory examination of its minutes, when compared to those of the Board of World Mission, reflects how the denomination was turning in on itself. Large and unwieldy, the GPC, when it met, had to spend a lion's share of its time on internal priorities. Those issues which had advocates closer to the seats of power received a more attentive hearing. Notes concerning overseas involvements become ever more sparse and less and less informative. And the new breakdown in the manner in which the council pictured its program—by activity type rather than in overview by field—made it ever more difficult to hold a unified understanding of the mission as a whole in any given region. The fact that regional deliberative bodies with real authority to oversee program, like the Arabian Mission, were being dismantled piecemeal at this time, placed increasing discretionary power in hands of denominational staff.

and executed with distinction until his retirement in 1984. Having taken this extended leave of absence from Middle East affairs, he then reentered, carrying out a landmark survey of the phenomenon of labor migration to the Middle East sponsored by the Middle East Council of Churches and the Christian Conference of Asia. In 1987 he was asked to write a history of the Arabian Mission to be produced to coincide with the mission's centenary. At about the same time he was diagnosed as having cancer of the prostate. His effort to control that disease was valiant, but it took him prematurely in May of 1989.

[68]John Buteyn, speculating on why he was preferred to Ed Luidens for the new position, thought his handling of the closure of Kuwait hospital in 1966-1967 had something to do with the selection committee's considering him the better administrator.

As far as the Arabian Mission was concerned, from 1961 John Buteyn was the board's person in charge, his role but amplified by the appointment of Kenneth Warren as Arabia secretary on the field (from 1968-1972).[69] Buteyn was perhaps the most exceptional of all the bureaucrats that have ever served the Reformed church. His qualities are difficult to define. The most prominent of these was that he was a consummate survivor. In a day when restructuring had turned into a kind of vicious parlor game for the denomination, he outlasted all his colleagues by proving himself both flexible[70] and well-nigh indispensable. He was a tireless administrator, meticulously attentive and responsive to everything that was brought to his attention.[71] He had the ability to keep working when all others had fallen into exhaustion. He was a highly committed individual, an instinctive diplomat,[72] a person of deliberate and even meticulous habits of mind, but

[69]Ken Warren, initially recruited to be field consultant in administration for the various mission hospitals, actually served as mission liaison to the area secretary from 1968 to 1969; thereafter he was transferred to New York where he continued as area secretary under Buteyn (then overall secretary for world ministries) until 1972, when he resigned for personal reasons and returned to private life in Kalamazoo, Michigan. Thoughts of replacing Warren were entertained, but eventually Buteyn simply resumed his direct handling of the Middle East portfolio.

[70]The term, "flexible," was a favorite expression of John Buteyn. The author and his wife used to joke with him about it when he, with some frequency, encouraged them to remain flexible. But Buteyn's flexibility was not of the spineless variety. Many times missionaries were made aware of how seriously he fought for their interests in the environment of GPC staff meetings and before the GPC itself. He had the grace and native instinct, however, to know when to make accommodations with reality and cut his best deal.

[71]The joke ran that he buried others under a mountain of paper. But he could not have done that without help. Here no missionary will forget the role that Betty Wallace played as his secretary and administrative assistant. The trust that Buteyn rested in her and her ability to fulfill that trust became something which missionaries simply counted upon. If Betty was on duty, none need despair. Nobody ever wrote John Buteyn a letter without getting a response whether he was in New York to receive it or not.

[72]His diplomatic talents failed him only once. That was with Dorothy Scudder over the issue of the closure of Kuwait hospital. She was fighting for survival and could be a formidable adversary. In that case, he felt he had to forego diplomacy and simply do what had been decided should be done. It seriously weakened a relationship which had been built on mutual admiration. It is that bruised relationship, Buteyn confessed to the author in 1994, which still brought him pain when he thought about the consequences of the difficult decision to close the Kuwait hospitals.

In the same context of Kuwait and for the same reason, Buteyn had alienated

one who was a pastor first and foremost. The fact that he handled (*mis*handled, others would insist) some of the most controversial and difficult decisions which affected the Arabian Mission deeply does not change this.

Buteyn had the misfortune (or was given the challenge) of living in "interesting times." As the fifties gave way to the sixties and the Kennedy era, government-sponsored philanthropy like the Peace Corps attracted many young idealists who in an earlier day would have volunteered for Christian mission.[73] This had a gradual and cumulative impact upon the Arabian Mission. The best and the brightest were no longer looking to church-sponsored programs for opportunities to serve. And new attitudes shaping policy had created an atmosphere of question with regard to the definition of the whole Christian missionary enterprise.

Taking up the reins in 1962, John Buteyn followed a consistent path. We might call it the Buteyn Doctrine. He had inherited a mission field structure that was accustomed to acting as a body of the whole, making decisions in annual meetings and through the Mission Executive Committee, for each station. This, Buteyn came to believe, was an anomaly. It was inefficient for Kuwait to tell Bahrain what to do and irrelevant for Oman to present its local solutions to problems as a model for others. The idea that the mission was a single entity spanning the Gulf he saw to be an anachronism, a romantic indulgence. He, therefore, worked steadily toward disentangling the stations from each other, and disenfranchising each station as a deliberative and administrative body.[74]

As he saw it, the time-consuming and inefficient democracy of the early mission no longer worked. Arriving at this conclusion, he displayed a certain

the pastor of the Arabic Language Congregation of the National Evangelical Church in Kuwait, Yûsuf 'Abd-un-Nûr. Only a bit less tenacious than Dorothy Scudder, Yûsuf made himself less accessible to Buteyn than the latter desired. Over the years, with quiet patience, he persisted with Yûsuf, and the author was witness to (and was, perhaps, somewhat instrumental in) his eventual success in restoring at least a positive working relationship with the strong-minded Egyptian.

[73]Not incidentally, they would have brought with them the support and enthusiasm of their local congregations, the flagging of whose zeal for denominationally supported mission correlates in terms of time.

[74]In retrospect, Buteyn may have underestimated the nature of the interstation and communal process of decision making in the Arabian Mission. That process was more one of generating perspective through collegial diversity than of this or that station imposing its will upon the others. It also kept the whole effort integrated in an awareness, shared by all involved, of the mission as a whole.

lack of judgment concerning the value of "inefficient" mission deliberations for the building of a broad community of personal and spiritual support of missionaries for each other. Whatever the case, Buteyn set himself the goal of strengthening the autonomy of individual programs from the mission as a whole and from the local station, routing their accountability to himself as area secretary. The managing boards of institutions—church councils and boards of hospitals and schools—created at the insistence of Bovenkerk in the mid-1950s, became increasingly independent of the local mission station. After 1968, this fell in line with the GPC's breakdown of program not according to geographical field but according to activity categories, focusing deliberative and executive authority in itself and its staff. It effectively disrupted the mission's sense of shared responsibility for a collage of activities making up one thing known as The Mission. And, in search of an ecclesiastical relationship in the region, the attempt to form a "Synod of the Gulf" having failed by 1965, John Buteyn emphasized a deepening relationship with the Near East (after 1974, *Middle* East) Council of Churches (MECC). The effect of this was to draw attention away from the traditional area of the Arabian Mission toward a more diffuse interest in the Middle East generally.

As with many departures of this kind, a strong personal relationship played a part in Buteyn's cultivating strong ties of cooperation with the MECC. He was not the only denominational bureaucrat to be so inclined in the late 1960s. Gabriel Habib was the rising star on the ecumenical scene in the Middle East. A close relationship between Habib and Lewis Scudder, Jr. (then involved in language study and student work in Beirut) had developed during the latter's sojourn in Lebanon between 1967 and 1973. On the recommendation of Scudder and Ken Warren, Habib (then Middle East secretary for the World Student Christian Federation) was invited to participate in a GPC-sponsored Consultation on World Mission, which led into the RCA's Mission Festival '71 in Milwaukee, Wisconsin. Habib proved to be a quieter, far more profound and constructive presence there than either of the festival's more highly profiled Third-World speakers, John Gatu of Kenya or Jose Miguez-Bonino of South America. Buteyn was well impressed and grateful. It was the beginning of a long friendship which still persists.

When Habib became general secretary for the Middle East Council in 1977, Buteyn was ready to move. From Buteyn's perspective, the MECC provided not only a legitimate ecclesiastical relationship but also a responsive partner which could involve the RCA in creative areas of ministry both within and beyond the Arab Gulf.[75] Within the Arab Gulf, the most significant fruits of this relationship were the participation of the MECC in the Family Bookshop Group beginning in 1977 and the appointment of Lewis Scudder, Jr., as the Middle East Council's liaison officer in the Gulf beginning in 1980, both of which were Buteyn initiatives.

The Buteyn Doctrine was difficult and sometimes painful to implement. In the history of the mission, Buteyn's were radical (and often unpopular) insights yielding sometimes drastic actions. The most painful of these was the closure of the hospitals in Kuwait in 1967; the most logical of these was the dissolution of the regional organization known as the Arabian Mission in 1973. The least intended by-product of his efforts was the traumatic loss to missionaries of a local and regional support structure and network of collegial relationships, a loss which had significant repercussions in the depression of missionary morale.

The Buteyn Doctrine had a certain logic on its side. When the mission had first begun, the notion of nation-state had not yet found rooting soil in Arabia. But with British administration of the region (they liked their world to conform to their notion of what was "tidy"), borders were defined and individual sovereignty of the various amîrates in the Gulf was asserted (first against the Ottoman Empire and later against the expansionist tendencies of Sa'ûdî Arabia). The long-term effect of British policy was to distinguish increasingly Basrah from Kuwait from Bahrain from Oman. The political, cultural, and social structures which continued to evolve in those different areas increasingly diverged, becoming more unique and distinctive. Unified mission structure, which obviously made sense in 1910, at the dawn of the 1960s appeared cumbersome and out of place.

John Buteyn, pursuing tendencies already evident during the Luben/ Bovenkerk era, set himself the goal of rationalizing the patterns, making them conform to what he perceived as emerging reality. Furthermore, his deliberate administrative style meant that he participated in every major

---

[75]The idea that mission personnel could serve elsewhere had precedent in the relationship between the Arabian Mission and the United Mission in Iraq and in the roles played by Ed Luidens, Don MacNeill, Leonard Lee, Lew Scudder, Jr., and Harold Vogelaar, who served in various capacities outside normal Arabian Mission boundaries.

field conference and directly influenced every important field decision. Since he took his role as administrator for the Reformed church seriously, his very presence in this process weakened the old autonomy of the mission, much to the distress of some of those who were accustomed to the old style of autonomous mission action. Given Buteyn's capacity for work and his outlook, he quickly became the focal point of field policy, as well as bearing responsibility for communicating with the home constituency.

Looking back over that achievement one cannot but be thunder-struck. Without a doubt John Buteyn became one of the most well-informed secretaries ever to have worked for the Board of World Missions, as well as one of the most powerful. The impact he had upon the evolution of the Arabian Mission was radical—thoroughly radical. As secretary for the Middle East he was replaced by Warren Henseler in 1980.[76] Buteyn was then given the overall portfolio for world mission and stepped back from direct involvement in Arabia except when it was absolutely necessary. Upon his retirement in 1982, a vacuum was left in the structure which has never been filled.[77]

[76]Warren J. Henseler at fifty-four years of age had had a distinguished thirty-year career in the pastoral ministry in New Jersey, holding the office of president of the Particular Synod of New Jersey from 1971 to 1972. He had also been elected to serve on the General Synod Executive Committee, and, with Edwin Mulder, was a member of a delegation that went to investigate the situation in South Africa for the Reformed church in 1979. His qualifications for the position were internal to the Reformed church and had little to do with any serious international or overseas experience. This was not a matter which went unobserved by those with whom he interacted. A pedantic administrator, he brought to satisfactory completion a number of policies that were in process when he assumed his duties. He retired as secretary for the Middle East and Africa in 1992.

[77]John Buteyn was replaced, upon his retirement, by Eugene P. Heideman. He brought into the position of secretary for world ministries qualifications as good as anyone could have dreamed up. After a short period of pastoral service in Canada (during which he earned his doctorate), he was appointed a missionary to India in 1960, where his main activities were in the area of literature development and theological education for the Church of South India. The tightening restrictions of the Indian government on missionaries dictated an early departure. In 1970, Gene Heideman became chaplain and professor of religion at Central College in Pella, Iowa. In that position he established a reputation as a missiologist and visionary for the Reformed church, composing the denomination's "Song of Hope" and publishing several small theological meditations on the denomination's mission history. In 1976 he became academic dean at Western Theological Seminary, his old alma mater, and continued to play a role as in the denomination as a missiologist. He was the chairperson of the

1973 and Thereafter

From March 21 to 24, 1973, a meeting of "Representatives of the Arabian Mission" was held in Oman whose task it was to dissolve the organization. In the spring of 1970, the mission's executive committee had adopted a new "Organizational Pattern of the Mission." That document was never accepted by either the General Program Council or the Danish Mission Society (which was, by then, part of the administrative picture, considered to be one of the "cooperating church organizations"). The most important change in the way of doing business had been the increasing autonomy from the mission of the boards of managers of institutions and councils or congregational committees of the various churches. As the chair of the meeting, Harvey Dornbos observed that the new reality of the Arabian Mission was that it had become nothing more than a sort of fellowship of interest. And John Buteyn logically insisted that the 1970 document should be updated to reflect the new reality. In the resolutions of the Oman meeting, the following wording appears:

> Resolved, that the following pattern replace all previous organizational structures:
>
> In the light of the purpose of the Arabian Mission to be a Christian witness and to assist in building the Kingdom of God in the Arabian Gulf,[78] and in the light of the differences of development of Church and Mission programs in Kuwait, Bahrain and Oman, be it resolved that
>
> A)-The Mission shall be reorganized as a regional fellowship with a Chairman and Secretary to assist in planning inter-area meetings. …The primary Organizational structure will be the Area Fellowship groups in Kuwait, Bahrain and Oman. These groups may take varied forms in the three areas. …

GPC's special task force on advance in mission, which published in 1980 a landmark study on directions for the denomination to follow in the 1980s. In 1982, at the insistence of the incoming general secretary, Edwin Mulder, Eugene Heideman was appointed secretary for program, a position which he held until 1992 when, in the latest restructuring, he was given the post of secretary for Africa. An evaluation of Heideman's actual performance in these roles falls outside the scope of this study.
[78]It is interesting to compare this wording of the mission's purpose with the original.

B)-Local responsibility for programs shall be within Program Boards and committees in accountability to the Area Secretary of the General Program Council on behalf of the Cooperating Church Organizations. ...

C)-Arrangements for personnel and programs shall be made directly between Program Boards, Committees, or Heads of Institutions and the Reformed Church in America Area Secretary. Missionaries are accountable in their missionary assignment and work to the local church, institutions, or program boards in which they serve. Relationship of missionaries to the Cooperating Church Organizations shall not supercede this local accountability....

D)-The Cooperating Church Organizations may arrange occasional meetings for inter-area fellowship meetings in cooperation with the greater Christian community in the region....

E)-The basic direction of these proposals was approved by the Arabian Mission in April, 1970. Following approval by the Cooperating Church Organizations this procedure will be implemented by or before January, 1974.[79]

The day had come. From 1973 onward one might speak of the Arabian Mission only as a metaphor that had less applicability with each passing year. What continued to exist was a series of programs, institutions, and church-to-church relationships, each locally autonomous and directly related to the General Program Council's Division of World Ministries and having less and less reference to each other. The gesture toward maintaining something of the old Arabian Mission ethos by authorizing the organization of "area fellowships" in each of the former stations was ambiguous. With no mandate

---

[79]Noted as Mission Meeting Action 73-10, pp. 12-13 of the "Minutes of the Meeting of Representatives of the Arabian Mission, March 21-24, 1973, Muscat, Oman." The proposed "chairman" and "secretary" for the new structure, proposed in article A of the resolution, were never appointed. This omission is implicit in article D. The "greater Christian community" noted in article D included the then Near East Council of Churches. The "primary organizational structure" of local area fellowships indeed took varied forms, and there was virtually no communication or coordination between them. It is interesting to note that at this meeting, while the participants were aware that the mission was being dissolved, no explicit recognition was given to the fact.

to deal with the *substance* of mission, these gatherings frequently turned into sessions where complaints and frustrations were voiced with no significant means available for addressing them. Many newly assigned missionaries felt themselves at sea with no mentor structure to help them get their bearings, particularly on the job. The discipline of the missionary vocation was noticeably weakened. The valuable cross-fertilization of ideas among a broad range of competent and well-oriented colleagues and their commitment to uphold each other in their daily tasks had gone by the board. Close monitoring of local program increasingly depended upon the experience and insight of the rather remote area secretary. With the retirement of Buteyn in 1982, this became a rather hit-or-miss affair. With an over-committed General Program Council less and less able to pay attention to the small details of human need and absorbed in the internal concerns of the home church, there was a sense among the missionaries of having been orphaned, and from once having been home, the mission field now came to feel more like exile.

Conclusion

Making Port is a Transition

The Event (A Summary)

The Arabian Mission has made port. It has taken some of us a while to realize that, and to say it may seem almost an impiety. But it does need saying and recognizing. As a ship makes port, there is an ending. There is a sector completed; something accomplished. The voyage is ended. But a ship in port is not at home. A ship belongs upon the high seas. Making port, therefore, is only a transition. The ship attends upon tide and season to make for the free and open sea again.

When the mission first began to work up and down the Gulf, the days of open Arab slave trading were virtually over. The terror of Arab sea raiders had been overcome by the British Navy after the advent of the steam ship. Pearl diving was still a significant industry, but the merchant sailing fleets of

412

the Gulf's port cities, which once dominated the maritime trade routes in the East, were swiftly losing ground to more modern means of transportation. At the turn of the century, apart from the British-protected shaykhdoms, Oman and the Hadramaut, the Ottomans were still nominal overlords of Arabia and Yemen.

The pioneer years of the mission were also the years preceding the First World War, the last quarter century of the Ottoman Empire, and the age when the last of the Victorians left their unforgettable memorials on the altar of history. It was also a period in which American optimism and idealism hit their high-water marks. There is irony in the fact that these were also the days when Theodore Hertzl was struggling to give articulate birth to political Zionism, a skeptic's movement which, as it gained momentum in the context of world disillusionment, was to overshadow and poison with cynicism Middle East politics and interfaith relations for the succeeding century.

In the history of modern mission, India was the first great point of focus; from it flared off interest in other parts of the world—China, Africa, the Pacific, Japan, South America, and, finally, the Middle East. Islam in India stimulated the German Lutherans in Peshawar to develop the literature and analytical base for the discipline of "Muslim Controversy" (required of every new missionary). It fired the passion of the forever-young Henry Martyn. In his steps, out of India, came Major General F.T. Haig, the CMS intelligence gatherer. On the basis of Haig's reports came the Scotsman, Ion Keith Falkoner, and the indefatigable bishop, Thomas Valpy French. In this train there followed the founders of the Arabian Mission—John Lansing, James Cantine, and Samuel Zwemer.

Reformed Church in America authorities, when given the dream of these three men to share, expressed amazement, then sympathy, then regret. Nothing daunted, the three turned, as a second choice, to an ecumenical audience. There they struck a vibrant chord of interest and found their dream quickly subscribed with substance. The mission, therefore, drew its enthusiasm, sense of commitment, dollars, and talent from a wide diversity of sources coordinated through an "undenominational" network of syndicates focused upon and dedicated to its work. This broad base was crucial in shaping the unique character of the mission, and it continued to be influential through the first three decades of its development, even after the mission had been fully adopted by the Reformed church and the founding syndicates were dissolved.

To use Ed Luidens's phrase, "The Reformed church adopted a born and weaned child" when, on September 14, 1925, the Arabian Mission Corporation was dissolved and the denominational agency took over. "It isn't the Reformed church's mission. It took it over."[1] Among the questions that will continue to be asked is whether or not this denominationalizing of the mission did either it or the broader cause of Protestant mission any good. Ed Luidens again: "What is the interplay between the institutionalizing of the mission and the whole mission? I can see in the Arabian Mission the steps: pioneering, institutional development of program, denominationalizing the program, a period of high visibility, and then disintegration. It is a very clear pattern. You could write a play about it. But the play ends. You might say, 'You can write another play.' But there is not another act to the play that was begun. That is what intrigues me. Is there something about institutionalizing/denominationalizing that almost automatically means a kind of termination is coming up? What is the interplay between institutionalizing for strength and the witness and work of the Holy Spirit?"[2]

The first station of mission was established in the port city of Basrah in August, 1891. In 1893 both Bahrain and Oman were "occupied," and 'Imârah was an outstation. The mission's first long-term doctor (a Methodist) was finally appointed in 1895 as the Reformed church began to take over the mission. By 1900 the first hospital was open and running in Bahrain, and the mission's total work force had swelled to ten westerners and about the same number of middle eastern assistants. The first schools were being founded at the time Kuwait station was being established in the century's second decade. The story of expansion and institution-building continued into the 1950s. But the dream of penetrating the interior of Arabia grew more tenuous the more structured the mission became.

---

[1]Taped interview by Edwin Luidens with John Buteyn, September 14, 1988. This tape, while frustratingly incomplete, is an extremely valuable source. It is a fragment of a private dialogue between the two most important Reformed church missiologists active from the late 1940s into the 1980s.
[2]The Luidens-Buteyn dialogue of September 14, 1988.

No sooner was the peak reached than the down-cycle began, especially for the medical program. One hospital ceased to exist ('Imârah, 1959); another was abandoned by the Reformed church (Kuwait, 1967); another was turned over and absorbed into government structures, its impact upon the community undergoing radical transformation (Oman, 1973); and the last underwent a purgatory of self-doubt only to be bailed out and encouraged by local authorities to continue as an independent quasicommercial initiative (Bahrain, 1989). It essentially denied the assertion—virtually an article of faith for the mission since its founding—that the ministry of healing was the vanguard element in the mission's life and witness.[3] In 1973 the Arabian Mission was dissolved as an entity. To speak of an "Arabian Mission" thereafter is not helpful.

The Reformed church's interest in Arabia thereafter became particulate, flickering, fading. The fading of Reformed church interest coincided with the new structure of the denomination's agencies, in which specific area focus was lost. It coincided also with the articulation and application worldwide of the missiological principle that the indigenous church was to guide the efforts of mission in its own environment. Westerners were to be only partners in the efforts of local Christians. But Arabia *had* no indigenous church to speak of or to speak to. If, in principle, the western "partner missionary" had lost qualifications as an interpreter of the situation on the ground, then Arabia had no advocates, no qualified interpreters.[4]

Without a clear picture of the mission and its needs, the appeal was much weakened. An overall involvement in Arabia (the Reformed church's "place" under the middle eastern sun) became more and more something sensed and seen only (if even then) from the perspective of the administrators

[3]John Buteyn: "Looking at the Middle East and the Arabian Mission, we finally developed programs that were centered around human need, and when those human needs began to be met in other ways, then you really honestly had to say, 'We're really not here to do that any more.'" Ed Luidens: "No question about it." Buteyn: "But then the question is: 'What then?' Does that mean the end of our being there?" (Luidens-Buteyn dialogue, September 14, 1988).

What neither Luidens nor Buteyn remarked upon here is that the Arabian Mission did not launch medical work primarily as a response to human need. The human need was there, but medical work was launched as a vehicle of access and authentication in a society to which access and within which authentication were proverbially difficult to achieve.

[4]The developing expatriate congregations, which have indeed endured, were seen not to fit the definition required of an "indigenous partner" church.

in the United States. The conclusion of this process was to break up the integrating field structure of the mission itself. A locally engaged authority qualified to closely test and correct the missiological orientation of institutions no longer existed. The support group vanished. Fellowship around a common vision became a thing of the past.

Each Protestant effort launched to deal with the challenge of Islam since the 1820s has begun with a dash of youthful idealism and freedom to improvise. Every effort has gradually evolved habits that became patterns that hardened into institutions. Sometimes, as in the case of the Arabian Mission, this evolution was extemely rapid. At each point along the line, the missiological motive has been differently stated, the cultural, economic, and political factors molding them rapidly transforming. For the old American Board of Commissioners as for the Basil Mission and the Anglicans (mainly Church Missionary Society), the motive was both cultural and evangelistic, with a sharp sense of the need to confront, overcome, and eventually destroy Islam as an institution and as a community. It was a neo-Crusade.

The Arabian Mission, while sharing these basic attitudes, added another critical ingredient to its own motivation: Among its clearly stated policies was the employment of means which would gain for the mission acceptance by the indigenous Muslims. That desire did not fit in easily with the neo-Crusader thrust. The ambiguity, however, was not readily apparent at first blush. One notes in the contrast between what missionaries *wrote* and what they actually *did* a fair degree of disparity. Perhaps it was not so much a disparity as an ambiguity that became less and less easy to resolve. The policy involved them in risking esteem for Muslims in order that Muslims might esteem them in return. It implicitly assumed a common ground of ethical and spiritual values, broadly conceived, to be sure. In the environment of the late nineteenth century, that was indeed a daring proposition, and the risk taken required either courage, wit, or naiveté (or a blend of the three).

The effort to gain the good will of the local population in the Arab Gulf led immediately to the building of major service institutions. Although schools were not insignificant, for better or worse they were given secondary status. The premiere institutions of the Arabian Mission were medical. Ed Luidens asked another question that penetrates at this point: "Suppose we say that that whole phase of mission rode on the current of the technological wave. The mission had some very simple technological advantages that became hospitals and schools and audiovisual equipment and radio and all that technological stuff. But then the gap between the western technology which enabled the missionary to have an advantage was closed. The missionary no longer has that advantage. What crest, surf, or wave does the missionary ride now? If that is the right way to put the question, then one has a whole new idea of mission, because the mission is riding on the wave of history. It is not creating history. Ah! We thought we were changing history."[5] But this wry observation must be tempered with the knowledge that the body that rides the crest of history's wave affects that wave—in a small way, more than likely, but perhaps that small effect can be crucial.

Over the years there were two things that puzzled the Arabian Mission. The first of these was that the preaching of the gospel, in any visible or conventional sense, was fruitless. No indigenous Christian community emerged. Into the Gulf there eventually migrated hundreds and then thousands and then hundreds of thousands of Christians from both the Middle East and elsewhere. Churches were organized and flourished. But, in a statistical sense, there was no ferment of conversion from Islam to Christianity among the Arabs of the Gulf themselves. And there was no good explanation for this.[6] The formulae predicting a return on faith's investment in loyal and devoted missionary service never seemed to work.

The other phenomenon that puzzled missionaries was their remarkable success in winning the acceptance of the local populations in Oman, in

---

[5] Luidens-Buteyn dialogue, September 14, 1988.
[6] The observation of 'Abd-ul-Mâlik at-Tamîmî: "The conversion from his religion of a Muslim of the Arabian Peninsula is not less difficult than converting a Catholic resident of the Vatican from his" (Tamîmî, *at-tabshîr*, p. 237). In all fairness, the mission was aware of this. It was still not a satisfying explanation.

southern Iraq, in Bahrain, and in Kuwait. They sought this, it is true. And to this end they built their service institutions. What was achieved in this field remains one of the most amazing displays of Christian philanthropy and devotion in missionary annals. They were heroic ventures ventured by heroes. They were life-intensive undertakings that utterly absorbed those who undertook them. And they radiated into the society with a powerful influence, reaching hundreds and thousands of miles beyond themselves with an effect that remains tangible years after their metamorphosis or demise.

The presence of Arabia missionaries was also welcomed in the interior of Sa'ûdî Arabia, where they were invited guests of the great king, 'Abd-ul-'Azîz Âl Sa'ûd himself.[7] (That too they had aspired to and achieved.) They could venture into the so-called "Green Mountains" of Oman when no other foreigners dared tread outside of the fortified cities of the coast without heavy guard. They were sought after in Qatar and in the area we now know as the United Arab Emirates, breaking ground there for the easy entry of other—and, one must add, less responsible—mission organizations.

John Van Ess relates an incident the likes of which other missionaries could also tell. When Faysal bin-Husayn Âl Hâshim, king in Iraq, died in 1933,

> ...a memorial service was held in Zobeir, a large fanatical town about twelve miles out in the desert from Basrah. A committee came in and asked me to make a speech. For reasons of expediency I declined to make a speech, but told them that I would be glad to come. When I asked how many foreigners or Christians had been invited, they said that I was the only foreigner and, in fact, the only non-Moslem. When I expressed surprise that I, a Christian missionary, should be so honored, they said quite frankly: "It is just because you are a missionary and are true to the tenets of your faith as you understand them that we trust you, for, as the Arab proverb has it: 'He who is true to Allah will not betray Abdullah [the servant

[7]Dorothy Van Ess, *History*, p. 44, relates an event reported by Josephine Van Peursem, in which 'Abd-ul-'Azîz Âl Sa'ûd commended to his household Arabia missionaries on tour in Riyâd in 1933 because of the authenticity of their Christian religious confession, the sincerity of their service, and, therefore, their trustworthiness.

of Allah, i.e. the Muslim].'" And for four hours I sat in the place of honor next to the Arab governor amid hundreds of fanatics while I listened to the glorious Arabic of the Hegira days.[8]

Not only were personnel of the Arabian Mission welcome and respected; they had a strong impact upon local policy, especially as the resources for development became more available to governments and societies in the region. The rulers in Kuwait, Oman, and Bahrain readily (although not always officially) acknowledged the debt they owed to the "American Mission" in developing their ministries of education and health and in influencing public attitudes toward service and professionalism. The models missionaries provided were not merely administrative but also moral, and it was as moral agents that they were most highly regarded.

One unnerving spin-off of this puzzling acceptance was that the entry of other western and nonwestern personnel into the Gulf was made easier. Businessmen and oil company representatives were welcomed not least of all when they demonstrated that they were Christians. The principle of the freedom of worship has been steadily sustained in Oman, Kuwait, and Bahrain, sometimes against strong opposition by Muslim purists, not the least reason being the continued positive assessment of the work of the Arabian Mission.[9] This has meant that, over the long haul, as migrant labor flooded into the Gulf, churches and sundry Christian worshiping groups multiplied and mushroomed in the region, creating ecclesiastical pandemonium quite unique in the history of the Church.

Administratively, many of the first congregations that emerged in the Gulf were mission-managed and staffed. As the congregations (and here we *include* the Arabic-speaking congregations) exploded with new expatriate members, it was quite natural to move toward giving these enthusiastic and dedicated Christians a stake in the guidance and management of what were quickly (not always willingly) recognized as having become *their* congregations. Releasing control, however, was difficult and happened slowly. Missionaries adjusted to the new circumstances by distinguishing

---

[8]Van Ess, *Meet the Arab*, p. 158.
[9]After a period of disillusionment with quality of life of "Christian" westerners, which at times threatened to undermine the credibility of the mission, Muslims in the region have learned to differentiate between the "Christian-in-name" and the "real Christian." It has become a distinction that is applied to others than formal missionaries.

between "mission" (which still maintained its separate structure) and "church."[10]

This distinction was disturbing. Does it not break up the great Pauline concert? Are not many gifts given to many members of what is, in the end, one Body, with Christ the Head comprehending and guiding the whole? How, then, can we distinguish between church and mission? Having made a distinction, can we still affirm the one Body?

On the other hand, the modern cliché which simply states that "church is mission" seems too facile. The Body is indeed one. But the members of that Body are diverse, and it belongs to that diversity that individuals are called to different tasks. The Church in worship is the reality's center. Where the Body and the Blood are assumed (consumed) in the Sacrament, there an awesome power is resident. But then there follows what the Orthodox call the "liturgy after the Liturgy," a dispersal (embodied in the members) of the gifts of the Spirit into the world, and the power goes out...as true power will do. And there are times, as in the experience of the Church in Antioch, when the Spirit chooses individuals to do particular tasks. Commissioned by the Church (and here we speak of the Church Universal even though the specific act of commissioning may be parochial), these individuals "go out" to do the thing for which the Spirit chose them. They become missionaries, and the cause in which missionaries coalesce as a community becomes a mission.

In the Arabian Mission's experience an ambiguity arose. It was probably inevitable that it should. To all intents and purposes, for over half a century the Arabian Mission as a community—missionaries and "native helpers"

---

[10]The author circulated a questionnaire in 1990 to as many Arabia missionaries as he could find still living, as well as to others still active on the field. In it, the following two questions were asked:

Do you draw a distinction between "mission" and "church"?

Explain. (That is, is it a useful administrative distinction, or is there something peculiar to the missionary role in which other Christians do not or cannot participate?)

On the practical level, day-to-day, was such a distinction made in the environment within which you served? If "yes," can you explain why? Should such a distinction continue to be made or should it eventually diappear?

The great majority of those who responded to these questions (most but not all) came down, sometimes only shakily, on the side of saying that there is a difference between "mission" and "church."

alike—formed the core of the Church in the Gulf. Apart from a few British civil servants, journeymen diplomats, tradesmen, shopkeepers, an explorer or two, and the odd semi-itinerant businessman, they were all there was of the Church. They met all together for worship, and more often than not it was with those civil servants, diplomats, and tradesmen that they built, operated, and developed institutions and served as mission-church. But it was commonly acknowledged that not only was the root identity of the church missionary, but the mission was also distinctly "American." It was known by all as the American Mission. In that commonly acknowledged identity were seeds of ambiguity.

From the late 1940s onwards[11] migrants moved into the Gulf in great numbers and from many places; proportions and the ethnocultural complexion of the resident church were upset. But what is the difference, after all, between a migrant and a missionary Christian? "The wind blows where it chooses....So is everyone who is born of the Spirit"[12] St. Paul, wherever he went, related to the migrant Jewish community, and migrants were principal instruments in the spreading witness of the early church. Amazed by the thing that was happening to them and around them, missionaries in the Gulf faced first in one direction and then in the other, dizzied by the event, while the local community went about blandly adjusting to the incredible as though it happened every day. 'Awad Dûkhî, a Kuwaiti singer of the late 1960s, sang the popular mood: "*allâh! allâh! zîd an-ni'am!*" ("God! O God! Rain down more blessings!")

In the new rather bizarre situation, Arabia missionaries tried to refocus their notions of sending and receiving and to evaluate again their vocation and circumstances. The matter came to a head during the closure of the Kuwait hospitals in 1966-1967. It was a decision concerning which the local Christian community felt they were not consulted. Torn between the Reformed church and the timid, uncertain, disoriented, largely expatriate and local church, missionaries' loyalties were confused. The Reformed church, expecting allegiance and exercising the rights of ownership, did not clarify matters.

In the end, the distinction drawn between mission and church was pragmatic and institutional, not theological. The fact that the Reformed

---

[11]With its delayed entry into the Gulf's development sweepstakes, in Oman we must speak of the early 1970s.
[12]John 3:8.

church felt quite entitled to "repatriate" (take to itself *for* itself) funds realized from sale of "mission" property in the Gulf only underlined the fact that this distinction was being made. And when the dust had finally settled almost ten years later,[13] people stood back appalled. Awareness grew that a solumn covenant had been violated somehow. And it is comforting to realize that what happened in Kuwait has not been repeated elsewhere, neither in Bahrain nor in Oman.

Time has taken care of the rest. The practical distinction between mission and church has been eroded gradually if only by the fact that the mission has itself lost coherence as an institution, and the church, for its part, has taken on stronger definition. Nonetheless, while on that level the old distinction has become somewhat academic, something of the ambiguity continues to linger.

For all its exuberance and frenetic activity, the new somewhat misanthropic church in the Gulf is not indigenous to the Gulf. The ghettoized structure of society in most Gulf countries effectively has ensured its isolation. New defensive social patterns have buffered indigenous society against all but the most tangential contact with the expatriate community which dwarfs it in sheer mass. And, while the rewards for love's labor in the building of these expatriate ecumenical congregations have often been generous, they are not the rewards for which the mission labored and prayed. It is almost as though the approval weighed upon the mission as a word of condemnation—a superficially sweet but inwardly bitter commentary on the mission's failure to plant the Church in the Gulf. Yes, the ambiguity remains.

It should be confessed that the cult of personality was rampant in the Arabian Mission.[14] Mission undertakings perhaps inevitably organize

---

[13]The Reformed church received the last payment from the Kuwait government in April, 1974.

[14]John Buteyn observed to Ed Luidens that a kind of hero worship is also what encouraged people in American pews to support mission. Their support "centered around people in whom they had confidence, whom they came to love, and whom

themselves into something like a guild structure, with its hierarchy of master craftsmen, journeymen, apprentices, and novices. In the case of the Arabian Mission one observes a parallel language: senior (or founder or pioneer) missionary, veteran missionary, first-term/junior missionary, language student (perhaps not quite a missionary), and short-termer (only a quasimissionary). It was unavoidable. Institutions in Arab society do not stand on their own abstract merits. Islamic legal and spiritual categories do not accommodate "corporate personalities." Institutions must bear the sharp stamp of dominant individuals, and those individuals made the impact (and won the recognition). When individuals with recognized long-term career commitments ceased to be appointed and trained in Arabic in the latter 1960s, the mission's "guild structure" was short-circuited, and the institutions themselves went into serious crisis. The loss of mentors was critical and damaging throughout the mission in all its endeavors. Not to provide for and nurture "heirs apparent" worked like a slow but deadly virus. The institutional crisis in the Gulf was linked to swiftly evolving modern technology and new management philosophies. It is ironic that a fatal distance developed between the mission and its supporters just as better means of communications developed by quantum leaps.

At first it seemed quite natural to use the new technology and its instruments (the airplane and the telephone) to facilitate the transfer of more of the management load from the field to the board offices in New York. This did not happen overnight, nor did it happen without misgivings about accountability on the local and regional levels. But as the new administrative pattern evolved, the mission grew nervous about losing control. Surrendering responsibility cost the missionaries in dignity and self-esteem, to be sure. But these aspects were less significant than the fear that policy and initiative formed and taken remote from the field (good communications notwithstanding) invited the real risk of being inappropriate. Furthermore, as missionary dignity and self-esteem were undermined, the

---

they felt were really carrying on a mission that they [the missionaries] believed in. ...They maybe romanticized to a degree what these people stood for. Not that they [the missionaries] told false stories. They simply had high regard for them. ...They were genuinely ready to throw in their chips with them. ...I think that there are not that many sophisticated people [in the pew] who are really ready to wrestle with the bigger issues" (Luidens-Buteyn dialogue, September 14, 1988).

mission began to fear the new administrative patterns would result in loss of trust in the local community. (Their anxiety has since been proved well founded.) As that anxiety grew it expressed itself, on the side of the missionaries, in a lessening of trust in the American-based administrative structure.

New management philosophy moved toward a more impersonal, corporate structure for the Reformed church. It began to evolve in the late 1940s and emerged in 1966 with the establishment the General Program Council. The process correlated with the postwar loss of innocence, the growth of mass media and the advertising trade, the breakdown of traditional patterns and values, the breakdown too of the extended and even nuclear family, the growth of hedonism as an ethical norm, and the particularization of western society. This all yielded a triple disjunction: American society grew cynical about and suspicious of centralized structures; the centralized structures became more jealous of their prerogatives, privileges, and power; and the ancillary activities (which overseas mission initiatives came to be) were less and less clearly perceived in their context and, therefore, less effectively promoted, administered, and supported. At precisely the time when America became the dominant world power politically, American society became spiritually isolationist and more self-absorbed.

The direct exposure of American congregations to missionaries was, in Ed Luidens's estimation, the single most important factor which nurtured mission awareness in Reformed church congregations. "I am convinced that the congregation of Brighton Reformed Church was impacted by the annual visits of two or three significant missionaries like Van Ess, Zwemer, and Cantine as they came through. These people, whose thinking might ordinarily have been limited to the local level, were expanded."[15] As communications improved, however, *communication* degenerated. Easier travel meant that the old discipline of six years on the field/one year at "home" fell apart. The term was shortened to two or three years, interspersed by quasivacations of short duration. Along with other conditioning factors, this reduced exposure, and informed awareness declined.

The gap between the mission and its supporters became a fissure, then a gulch, and then a chasm. The crisis had a lot to do with the shaking off by the sponsoring   mission   agency   of   entangling   commitments.

[15]Luidens-Buteyn dialogue, September 14, 1988.

Deinstitutionalization became the missiological watchword from the late 1950s into the mid-1960s, a watchword which often translated into demoralization on the field. The number of long-term appointments was drastically cut and then ceased altogether by 1967. Mission, as an intricate and fragile orchestration of media and persons, was broken up into program modules with short-term goals and commitments, its vision shattered.

At the same time, the charismatic missionary leaders of an earlier day died off and were not replaced. Missionary access to the denomination's grassroots was muffled by an elaborated and increasingly distracted bureaucracy, and by a general malaise in western Christianity over the whole purpose of what is now being called "intercultural mission." The "church growth movement" did much to dampen enthusiasm for undertakings that did not exemplify the American profit motive.

This coincided with sharply declining funds available for denomination-based mission at the same time as individual congregations were actually becoming significantly more affluent. (Independent missions date their hey-day from this period.) The focus of mission interpretation in the Reformed church, as in other denominations, shifted from explaining the imperative of the missionary effort to trying to justify budget requests against a shrinking pot for mission programs whose justification had become a matter of tradition...inertia. "If one were to look at all the times that missionaries had what they thought was an inspired vision that the board couldn't deal with, couldn't resource with personnel or money, one could come to the conclusion that the board and the Reformed church as a whole totally failed to enable the vision of the Arabian Mission. There were all kinds of opportunities that were not used, when the mission cried out for assistance to do certain things and the board either refused or approved but was unable to provide the money or personnel."[16]

Another correlation was the complex and volatile nature of regional and world politics as oil became a key factor in the international economic picture. Money and power masked and sometimes mutilated the simpler

---

[16]Edwin Luidens during a recorded interview with Jim and Joyce Dunham, Newark, New Jersey, September 13, 1988. In a similar vein, John Buteyn observed: "Sometimes you wanted to do new things, but you had a structure within the denomination and the board that would not be open to some of the new opportunities that you really felt were great challenges that we ought to have responded to. There was a certain structure of limitation which that put on mission" (Luidens-Buteyn dialogue, September 14, 1988).

and clearer motives of an earlier missionary generation, and, under the tutelage of more sophisticated Syrians and Egyptians, there were many among the Gulf's population who quickly pretended to have "forgotten Joseph." From the very beginning of the mission, strong political attitudes were part of the Arabian Mission's mindframe. For instance, they were, with few exceptions, anti-Turkish and all in favor of Arab nationalism in its first stirrings. Some expressed themselves quite frankly on the virtues of British imperialism. Others openly advocated republican ideals while the British and the local governments were unabashedly elitist and dynastarian. But since the 1917 British-imposed stricture on their public expressions of political opinion, it became something of a norm for Arabia missionaries to think of themselves as strictly apolitical. It was almost a creedal stance with some. Particularly after the Arab-Israeli War of 1967, some missionaries felt increasingly called upon to play a role as interpreters of politics. This was a distinct role shift—some would say a violation of the missionary code of conduct.17 And the political voice which some Arabia missionaries began to raise on the controversial issues of war and peace in the Middle East did not go down well in a Zionist-conditioned North America. This too contributed to the cycle of decay which led to the dissolution of the mission in the spring of 1973.

A Catalogue

The centennial of Arabian Mission was celebrated in 1989 with two gatherings of the clan, the second, appropriately enough, at New Brunswick Theological Seminary. Put the launch date on May 23, 1889, when the plan for the mission was first put forward only to be rejected by the Reformed church a month later, or set it on August 28, when the small group of conspirators declared that they would go it alone and formed the "undenominational" plan for the Arabian Mission Syndicates, it makes little

---

17In 1970, on their way to the United States and retirement, Beth and Wells Thoms stopped for a short visit in Lebanon. In the course of that visit, Nancy and I spent a pleasant afternoon with my aunt and uncle in the mountains. At that time we were much involved in an organization in Beirut called, "Americans for Justice in the Middle East." When we talked about it, Wells Thoms responded, waxing downright acerbic about missionaries who get involved in politics. For him this was not funny, and he soundly rebuked us, even pulling rank as a missionary elder statesman, for our violation of the code.

difference. It all happened rather quickly. By October 1889 the first missionary, James Cantine, was on the high seas headed for adventure. And what J. Preston Searle called "a new and glorious 'romance of missions'"[18] had begun. Since that time a hundred years of sand have flowed through the glass.

Another standard of judgment would call the Arabian Mission a foolish undertaking. Its stated goals were out of reach, the object of its attention deeply inoculated against it, and the resources it could count upon for this shaking of the earth's foundations minuscule. Even the mission's friends were skeptics. One conspirator, Philip Phelps, early misgave himself. Another, J. Preston Searle himself, who helped launch this "dubious endeavor," did so at first only to humor John Lansing, his friend.[19]

At this remove from its genesis, there are those—found even among the members of the mission itself—who quite seriously believe that the Arabian Mission failed, as it was bound to do. They make that judgment on the basis of the goals set and the results achieved. But there is another yardstick: This was a mission taken up in *God's* name. The Arbiter of its fate and of its purpose clearly had a wider and deeper understanding of what the mission was all about, and there is no one even among its gainsayers who will declare that the mission was historically insignificant. No act of devotion has thrived with fewer rewards for love's labors. No effort of Christian witness has had to hew more closely to the fundamental motive of mission—obedience under a commission divinely imposed. No mission enterprise has had to justify its very existence so often. It survived both visionaries and bunglers, autocrats and ditherers, dreamers and dullards. And few communities have felt so supremely confident, in the teeth of their critics, that what they were doing was absolutely appropriate. Few ventures are there to compare with the way it evoked the best from the most.

It was a mission marked by determination, vigor, professionalism, and an understated intellectual vitality all enlivened by an irrepressible sense of humor. In it the free spirit found breathing space, the misanthrope a place

---

[18]Quoted in Mason and Barny, *History...*, p.137.
[19]Searle once confessed, "The writer must confess that the history of the Arabian Mission has been to him a constant cause of wonder and a continuous rebuke to unfaith. He was not in the remotest touch with its origin. He went into the Committee of Advice, a doubting Thomas, to help a friend through, or perhaps out of a dubious endeavor" (Mason and Barny, *History...*, p. 137).

and a mark to make, the thoughtful a corner in which to contemplate, and the diligent scope and more than enough scope for hard work. It commanded respect in world Christian gatherings all out of proportion to its size. It made significant contributions to missionary thought and to the evolution of a new Christian world perspective. At least three of its pioneer members were ranking Arabists: Samuel Zwemer, Edwin Calverley, and John Van Ess could walk into any gathering of their peers and command both recognition and respect. At least one of its many remarkable physicians, Paul Harrison, had world stature in his profession and, among his renaissance accomplishments, could claim to be no mean theologian as well. Explorers like Samuel Zwemer, Gerrit Pennings, John Van Ess, Harold Storm, Fred Barny, and Paul Harrison put new marks upon the maps of the world. And women like Everdine DeJong, Mary Allison, Cornelia Dalenberg, Dorothy Van Ess, Minnie Dykstra, Josephine Van Peursem, Eleanor Calverley, Margaret Barny, Esther Barny Ames, Eleanor Heusinkveld, Mary Van Pelt, Ruth and Rachel Jackson, Jeanette Boersma, Jeanette Veldman, Beth Thoms, Ann De Young, and Dorothy Scudder flung open the door of dignity and self-realization to thousands of Arab women that they might dream new dreams and see new visions.

As an American adventure in intercultural relations, the Arabian Mission is something of a high-water mark which tried to mediate symbols of meaning and value between Arab/Muslim and American/Christian society. The fact that much of what was mediated—in both directions—is presently overshadowed by the brash economics, politics, and cultural and spiritual distortions of the oil era does not mean that those gains have been lost. As oil gives ground to other sources of energy and wealth, and as the boom in the Arabian Gulf subsides, it becomes clear that there continues to be a profound legacy of good will and understanding between East and West, between Christian and Muslim which the Arabian Mission helped nurture at its very root. That legacy will be there to draw upon when men and women of good sense and good will find they need it.

As the purveyor of mass literature and modern education, an advocate for feminine dignity and worth, an instructor in matters of public health and modern medicine, in view of its very limited resources, the Arabian Mission's record is truly remarkable and readily acknowledged to be so by Muslim and Christian alike. Particularly with regard to the public health and medical services in Kuwait, Bahrain, and Oman, its influence can be extensively itemized and documented. The monuments of its work still stand. Young Arab men and women entering the medical profession in those countries are not infrequently urged by their parents to take as role models the missionary doctors and nurses who served them in their day. Missionary educators like John Van Ess, Edwin Calverley, Dorothy Van Ess, Ruth and Rachel Jackson, George Gosselink, and others continue to be remembered for their devotion. And pastors and evangelists like Gerrit Pennings, Gerrit Van Peursem, Fred Barny, Dirk Dykstra, Jay Kapenga, Jim Dunham, Don MacNeill, Ed Luidens, and their successors are recalled for their human touch and the love and compassion which they showed in their bodies.

In evangelical terms, it is in fruit that we verify the nature and purpose of any individual or group. On the surface, the chief fruit (and the one for which the mission is most acclaimed) is the building of communicative symbols for human integrity, peace, and cross-cultural understanding. These Christocentric models for how life should be lived continue to be vital in Arab Gulf society, and the models carry within them the presuppositions of faith that shaped them. Certainly if you could re-project Gulf history without the presence of the Arabian Mission, qualitatively you would have a completely different narrative. The Arabian Mission's models are tenacious and positive. That is recognized, and not to be scoffed at.

The Arabian Mission has also been a participant in the lively debate on how the Church and the Muslim community relate to each other in God's plan. The debate still goes on—sometimes audaciously, sometimes diffidently—and the Arabian Mission has contributed at both ends of the discussion's theological spectrum. Its very record of service involving Muslims in its initiatives and programs is a kind of dialogue-in-life between Muslim and Christian.

The central interest on the part of western missionary efforts in the Middle East has always been to encounter Islam, directly or indirectly, in a decisive and fruitful manner. How we have pictured the decision we will approve, and what we anticipate the right fruit will taste like has differed. What tools we have brought to the effort and what other bodies we have involved in our work has also differed. But the encounter with Islam remains the object.

The challenge of framing a Christian theological understanding of Islam (beyond those statements framed in the early centuries of the confrontation) remains. The challenge is not a serious one for those whose domains of salvation and damnation are neatly divided. The problems of tactics, logistics, and finances which faced nineteenth-century mission still face them. But if the issue is not so clear cut for others, then there is a need to come to the problem with a thought-through understanding of the theological significance of the Muslim-Christian encounter itself.[20] If that is accomplished, then the missiological issues will sort themselves out more clearly, the urgency (or panic) will abate a bit, and we might be able to get on with the task of building some constructive approaches to the problem overall. It is enough to say that the Arabian Mission has participated in all the phases of missionary thought and action and has supplied at least grist for the mill—and sometimes more than that, both for good and ill.

In the experience of building churches out of a rag-tag accumulation of Christians from around the world, the Arabian Mission has been an improviser and innovator in the "ecclesiology of expatriatism," if you will, and has provided test cases for the construction of the "ecumenical congregation."[21] Certainly there have been aspects of the experience of the church in the Gulf that have created new forms of relationship within the larger Body of Christ, both internal and ecumenical. In that context, there

[20]The Reformed church's General Synod of 1981 accepted a paper written for the Commission on Theology by James I. Cook entitled, "A Study of the Biblical Perspective on the Evangelization of the Jews for the RCA Today." The author, attending that synod, asked it to charge the Commission on Theology to conduct a parallel study on the "The Muslim Community in Christian Theological Perspective." Subsequently, through several drafts, he prepared a paper with the above title which the commission (with minor revisions) placed before the synod of 1985. It was returned to the commission for further work, for it had aroused some theological anxiety, and Paul Fries, chairperson of the review committee, strongly resisted airing these anxieties on the floor of the synod. (It was an anxious synod in any case.) The author returned to the Gulf, and subsequent efforts to put a text before synod also met with small success. Finally, the basic text the commission had been struggling with was completely abandoned, and the commission turned to a new (more theologically "right-thinking") group of drafters. At the 189th General Synod of the Reformed church in 1995, the commission brought forward a text entitled, "Christian Witness to Muslims: An Introduction to the Issues." Without discussion, it was approved. The process had taken nearly a decade and a half and the product is disappointing. It has not responded to the original mandate, nor has it contributed to the discussion of the issue as stated above. The upshot, of course, is that the task is still to be completed.
[21]Arie Brouwer, in his valedictory, *Overcoming the Threat of Death* (Geneva: WCC Publications, [1993]), pp. 67-68, spoke of cultivating "ecumenical congregations" by drawing upon the pluralism residing within most Protestant American

has been a true ministry to migrant labor, an issue of growing world significance. And the Arabian Mission, there too, has made a difference.

But what will continue to be intriguing is the way in which the Arabian Mission grew up, not as an organization but as an organism, having distinct life characteristics. The children of the mission can bear witness to this as much or perhaps more than any others. It was characterized by a high degree of egalitarianism, by strong bonds of loyalty and collegial coherence, by strong leadership and accountability on the field, by a readiness to depart from traditional norms when the situation dictated, and by an ingenuous willingness to identify with the environment into which it had entered to serve as Christ had served.

This is all the more surprising in light of the fact that it was a community of highly educated and trained, strong-minded and strong-willed individuals who came as if picked from a hat out of about as wide a diversity of western religious and cultural backgrounds as one could hope to imagine. The names of many personalities of the Arabian Mission—western, indigenous, and Asian—continue in litanies of affectionate and delighted recollection long after having been gathered into Abraham's bosom. The leaven of the mission continues to work in a subtle but persistent way throughout the Arab Gulf. The romance of missions continues—and perhaps the foolishness as well.

But in the end, the achievement of the Arabian Mission was one and one alone: the demonstration of faithfulness in service to a call divinely given. That faithfulness was tested and *continues* to be tested, as though a hundred years is but the overture to a symphony of endurance and hardly a fair expression of authentic devotion. Even today the comment is common in Gulf society that the "American Mission" served not for money but out of

congregations and thereby, in a search for the "fullness of the gospel," give a "burst of new life" to, what he termed, the "denominational malaise" that threatens to undermine the church in the United States and its in-grown denominational structures. Brouwer had at least nodding acquaintance with the Arabian Mission-sponsored ecumenical congregations in the Gulf. He would have done a service had he made a specific reference to them. The Arabian Mission in the Gulf has experimented with this form of the congregation over the past four decades, drawing upon a cultural and denominational cross-section of vast wealth and creativity and experiencing both the joys and agonies of the effort to draw people out of their narrow parochial conditioning and into a wider experience of the Body of Christ. It is, indeed, an experiment worthy of note and, certainly, some further study.

love, not for converts but out of obedience, not for victory but in self-sacrifice. It is the Arabs—the Muslims themselves—who are most conscious of this accomplishment. They are the ones who most often mention it, are still bemused by it, and insist upon it. Therefore, the witness has been borne and authenticated.

But the missionary effort is itself a communicative experience, an experience within which there is something to be learned, a transforming event for those who participate in it. That draws the eye of the historian to another question: What was the manifest purpose of the event? That is not to ask what the *intended* purpose was. Purpose emerges in the process and is organic to the event. In the end it may be stated in God-language: What, then, did *God* intend by launching the Arabian Mission (the motives of those caught up in it notwithstanding)?

Some years ago there was a movie entitled, *The Loneliness of the Long Distance Runner*. The portrait, as I recall, was that of a young man who found his misanthropy fulfilled in the solitary experience of the run itself, in the excellency of it, in the freedom it released, and the exhilaration of the soul that came when fatigue was transcended. The idea of winning seemed to play no part. And it is, in some ways, a paradigm of the Arabian Mission, a paradigm which is fading and may already have ceased to be. But the mission did demonstrate the virtues of that sort of long-term commitment, and if some of its members stopped short of the finish line and laughed at the howling spectators, that too belonged to the experience. There was a peculiar loneliness to this mission's experience which bound the members together in a fellowship that is still spoken of with a sense of reverence and awe. They did, you see, they *did* the impossible.

Perhaps that is where we must let the matter rest: With all its ambiguities and moments of brilliant insight, the Arabian Mission stands like a parable to be teased apart and poked at by those of us who seek in it understanding of divine doings. And the parable might well bear the title, "The grace of the Taskmaster for the task that has no end." The Arabian Mission in an intense and not concluded manner participated in the mystery of the Muslim-Christian encounter, and the story of its participation forms one of the more positive chapters in that now nearly thirteen-centuries-long saga. The mystery still stands. The task, impossible as it is, is still there to do. A parable—the Arabian Mission's story—of faithfulness has been fleshed out in how it may be carried on.

The Denouement

The story's ending is not yet clear; perhaps it hasn't yet arrived. There are successor institutions: The multilingual and multicongregational churches in Oman, Bahrain, and Kuwait; al-Rajâ' School and the American Mission Hospital in Bahrain; and a social service center in Oman called the al-Amânah Center; the Family Bookshops in Kuwait, Bahrain, and Oman. Pastors have been supplied by the Reformed church to the expatriate English-speaking congregations of the three churches; personnel have been recruited for the Bahrain hospital and school, as well as for the Family Bookshop Group; individuals have been posted in other middle eastern environments. Consultants in various short-term capacities have also been appointed.[22]

The change is one of seasons. It may not be winter; spring time may be approaching. In each of the surviving institutions there is new growth. The Bahrain hospital, led by Paul Armerding and encouraged by Don Hepburn, is experiencing something of a rebirth, wrestling with the problem of its mission identity. Ar-Rajâ' School, under the experienced leadership of Gary Brown, has found breathing room and is growing into a new physical structure. Roger Bruggink, working to develop the new program of the Al-Amânah Center in Muscat, knows that the course of the future is untrod.

Those who grope through the shadowed present ought to take heart. They, no less than the Arabian Mission upon whose legacy they build, are the expression of the Lord in whom all love and meaning are given profound fulfillment.

As for the Reformed church and its engagement in the Middle East, that is not for a study like this to answer categorically. Our focus has been too narrow. In any case, there seem to be no answers at present. The denomination's current mission agency structure seems to have scattered its interests widely. There is no clear focus; there is no clear vision. The Middle East still seems to be a problem. The Arabian Mission was always something of an enigma, a spiritual puzzle, because Arabia and Islam have always been

---

[22]The most recent of these has been Timothy Harrison (son of Paul Harrison) to the Ministry of Health in Oman. And Don and Eloise Bosch keep going back to Oman, where Don is an advisor to the sultan and his Ministry of Health.

enigmatic, disturbing the soul of the Church. And Americans are not great puzzlers. The Arabian Mission was born outside the Reformed church, and it dragged the Reformed church into an encounter the denomination might have preferred not to have entered. It may be that those within the Reformed church who hear the call to minister in the Arab world will have to pull hard again and remind the people in the churches that there remains an unfinished task, a call to faithfulness that has not yet been silenced. As Lansing foresaw, so the vision remains tantalizing, "The greatest marvels of missionary work ever witnessed are yet to be witnessed in Arabian territory and in the ranks of Islam."

What is the church to do?

In the days of excitement when western world mission was first awakened, the vision seen was that of a world bound in fetters to that which was not-God. Into that world with the gospel of Christ a stream of crusaders sallied forth. They were going to evangelize the world in their generation. Enlightened, they would bring light; robust, they would bring healing and health; vital, they would call forth out of the dark heathen tomb new life. And their vision was right on the money, even though the verbiage smacks anachronistic today. What was right on the money was their deep concern for all others of the human race. They wanted to share the profound spiritual food which gave them life in abundance. And to this end they went out and spent their lives—some long, some short, but they spent their lives—in a magnificent outpouring of marvelously heady nourishment. And the whole world (not just the Middle East) has been changed for their having done so. And *that* was right on the money. The church *knew* it, was *persuaded* of it, and it met the needs and obligations which made an age of prophecy possible.

Where the idealists of an age gone by mistook the signs was in seeing their effort as finite, short term, *this*-generational. Their task would conclude when the Word was scattered upon the face of the whole earth. To this end, as a certain sense of desperation crept in and people grew anxious that not all fertile ground had been seeded, recourse was had to the remote vehicles of mass media. It was a true digression. And again medium and message came to be confused because, as Christ demonstrated in his own body, the Word is only Word in the syllable of flesh. Paul Harrison articulated his missionary vocation thus: "The missionary from within whom flow rivers of living water, who is a radiant centre of divine life, is the man the situation demands."23

Perhaps those of us who are Protestant need to loosen our theological joints and let the images of scripture flow into meaning. For what knits mission and church together is worship, and at worship's heart is the Eucharist, the Lord's Supper. The Church is called to worship and *not* mission. The focus of worship is the sacrament of the Body and Blood of the Lord Jesus Christ. The offertory (our substance, symbolized in the elements of ordinary bread and wine) is brought into the sanctuary and laid upon the table at which the Lord is host. In its blessing and breaking, in its sharing and eating, in the thanksgiving (*eucharistia*) for the banquet, let our eyes be opened. For when the sharing is done, and all have partaken, what walks out of the door of the sanctuary and into the harsh glare of this world's light (sometimes quite unself-consciously) is the Body of Christ.

It is trans-substantiation, not upon the Table; it is trans-substantiation within the community itself. Each one who shares the host *with* the Host is known to be an in-Christed person, the presence of the Presence of Christ, the Risen Lord. This is the "ordinary" vocation of the Christian. It is inescapable. And no heroics are required to confirm it. It is an act of grace through the means of grace. It is a given and needs no further confirmation.

Read the gospels through this lens, especially John's gospel: "To all who received him, who called upon his name, he gave power to become children of God, who were born, not of blood or of the will of the flesh or of human will, but of God." Within this worshipful company of in-Christed souls the Spirit moves at times to identify people: "Set apart for me... " Saul and Barnabas, for instance. And the church in Antioch—cobblers and bakers, merchants and mothers, stone masons and slaves, prophets and teachers— did that. And what, then, did they do? They continued steadfast in prayer and worship and the breaking of bread.

The invitation, at its heart, is "Come and worship!" We are not bludgeoned to obligation. We are invited to the feast. At the feast we give thanks and celebrate with the Bridegroom. Some who sit at table will be called to set forth on missions that the Bridegroom shall define, sometimes defining it only one step at a time. And they go because, having been fed, they have the

---

23Paul Harrison in John R. Mott (editor), *The Moslem World of To-Day* (New York: George H. Doran Company, 1925), p. 337.

substance in them which the Bridegroom wants to share with those on the highways and byways of this world.

Missionaries do not stay missionaries out of a sense of obligation. Missionaries endure because they enjoy what they are doing and feel filled to overflowing to continue doing it. Among the questions Arabia missionaries answered was, "Had you to do it all over again, would you do it?" The overwhelming answer was yes—without qualification.

What has been distressing in the overall patterns of mission development over the past several decades is the distancing of mission awareness from worship, and the degeneration of worship into entertainment. This is what cannot be permitted to continue. It is the offering plate—the raw materials which Christ transforms into flesh and blood and gives us in our worship and multiplies beyond belief to meet the need of all who hunger and thirst for God's *shalom*—it is the offering of worship and *in* worship that perceives and supports mission. Not "Ketchum Incorporated."[24]

In the Middle East there has been a mystery. It is the mystery of the church that has lived there since Pentecost and has sustained its worship through the last thirteen centuries in the midst of the Muslim community. In some circles there is deep anxiety that there may come a day when the church will vanish from the Middle East. But I am not in those circles. What has grown upon me with every year that has passed is that simple, ordinary Christians have been walking out of worship services for generations and generations, and in each one of them an offering of flesh and blood has been given to their neighbors. It is a simple thing, and it is real.

I gave the sermon at the funeral of my father, Lewis Scudder, Sr., a simple Christian whom the Reformed church sent out as a missionary to Kuwait. In the hearing of hundreds of Muslims who had come to honor him, I said in clear Arabic:

> All who accept the missionary's service, and all who come to benefit from him, come, in fact, to Christ himself and accept Christ and benefit from him and no one else. God's love has no hidden agenda.

[24]The firm of Ketchum, Inc. was engaged by the Reformed church's Stewardship Council, the terms of reference having been approved by the General Synod of 1964. It was the first professional fundraising organization to be hired by the denomination to conduct a denomination-wide capital funds campaign (see Hoff, *Structures*, p. 102-103). The name of the group chosen was, perhaps, unfortunate. Rhetorically, however, it does serve to make the point.

It is not extended to a man against payment of something. It continues—beyond acceptance or rejection—to be the effective love of God toward that man. If you have received the missionary, Dr. Scudder, you have received Christ whether you have named him by his name or not.

By giving themselves to their Muslim neighbors, Arabia missionaries discovered this truth within themselves and were humbled. The Muslim is in need of those in-Christed ones who, in the sacrament of their lives, can sustain in that spiritual neighbor a dimension of life he or she cannot otherwise know.

By living and giving of themselves alongside their Arab Christian brothers and sisters (and they were *always* in their company), the missionaries of the Arabian Mission sang with their lives: "In Christ there is no East or West, in Him no South or North; but one great fellowship of love throughout the whole wide earth." This is profound (although, usually, quite unremarkable). And it is this fellowship which still calls to the Reformed church: "Come over and help us. Live among us. Learn about us. Come to love us. Break our bread and share our salt. Worship here, give thanks with us, and if need be die in our embrace. And show, with us, how love transcends and makes a broken world whole. Come and let us be, together, worked into the walls of the New Jerusalem that this 'nation' might enter in and be healed."

"Let anyone who has an ear listen to what the Spirit is saying to the churches."

The sermon now is ended. The book, praise God! concluded. The work is not.

Arabian Mission Time Line

This time line is designed to be somewhat encyclopedic. Included in it are significant developments for shaping of the Christian and Muslim attitudes. Correlations, where they occur, are fortuitous and, hopefully, instructive. But, then, that is why time lines are constructed. As we come into the twentieth century, it will be noted that events are focused more tightly upon the Reformed Church and the Arabian Mission. This is, after all, the purpose of this study. It is not to indicate proportional importance in a broad historical sense. The distinction between "church" and "mission" is not to be taken in an ecclesiologically precise sense. The intention in separating the category, 'Mission,' is simply to isolate events which specifically aimed at developing the Muslim-Christian encounter on grounds other than political or military. That is sometimes a dicey kind of distinction as, for instance, in placing the evolution of the crusading orders under the category of Mission. The justification is that those orders - the Hospitallers and Templars - reflected church attitudes concerning the appropriate response to Islam, and, later, these orders were used as prototypes for non-military (that is not to say non-militant) missionary structure

Year	West	Middle East	Arabia	Other Regions	Church Developments	Mission
484					Pope Felix III excommunicates Acacius, the Ecumenical Patriatch of Constantinople. Split between East and West becomes definite and permanent.	
565	Justinian (527-565), Holy Roman Emperor, dies. His efforts to reunify the Empire were not successful. The East became more and more Greek, and the West, left largely to the control of migrating Franks, Visigoths and other 'barbarians,' was the principal concern of the Roman Catholic Church.					
614		Sassanian Persians sack Jerusalem and carry off the relic of the 'True Cross.'				

Year	West	Middle East	Arabia	Other Regions	Church	Mission
622			Muhammad bin 'Abd-Allâh Al Hâshim al-Qurayshî establishes his authority as prophet in Yathrib (later Madînah) in the Hijâz. The seeds of the Muslim state are planted.			
630		Heraclius, the Byzantine emperor, after defeating the Persians in 628, re-enters Jerusalem as a conqueror and returns the 'True Cross.' Byzantine ascendancy seems to be assured.				
632			Death of Muhammad in Madînah and the proclamation of Abu-Bakr as the first Caliph (successor in political authority) to the Prophet.			
634			Abu-Bakr, 2nd Caliph, dies. He consolidated Arabia for Islam during the 'Wars of Secession.' He was succeeded by 'Umar. The first of the Muslim conquests outside Arabia are undertaken.			
635		Damascus falls to				

636	Muslim armies defeat the Byzantine forces in the Battle of Yarmūk and Syria falls to Muslim control.				
637	Muslim armies defeat the Sassanian Persians at Qādisiyyah. Iraq falls.				
638	Jerusalem falls to Muslim forces under the second Caliph, 'Umar. Christian worship and access safeguarded.				
641	Heraclius, Byzantine emperor, dies. His ambitious military ventures left the Empire impoverished.				
644	'Umar, Second Caliph, is assassinated. Under him the major conquests of Syria and Iraq were completed, and policies set for Muslim-Christian interaction. He was succeeded by 'Uthmān.				
645	Alexandria finally falls to Muslim armies after the first attempt in 642 fails.				

Year	West	Middle East	Arabia	Other Regions	Church	Mission
656			'Uthmān, second Caliph, assassinated. Under him the Qur'ān was collected and all variant readings destroyed. Egypt and Persia were conquered. He was succeeded by 'Alī, the Prophet's nephew and son-in-law.			
661			'Alī, fourth Caliph, is assassinated. Under him the factional movements in Islam proliferated. He was the last of the 'Rightly-Guided Caliphs.' From him authority passed to the 'Umayyad dynasty of Damascus.			
679	First Muslim seige of Constantinople (begun in 674) fails.					
688		Dome of the Rock in Jerusalem is completed. Jerusalem becomes a point of Muslim pilgrimage.				
713	Muslims complete their conquest of Visigothic Spain and found the province of					

Year			
726	The Iconoclastic Wars begin that tear at the fabric of the Byzantine Empire. They continue until 743, and draw some of their fire from the challenge of Islam to the use of icons in Orthodox piety.		
732	Charles Martel stops Muslim conquest of southern Europe at Poitiers.		
749			John of Damascus (675-749), last of the Church Fathers, dies. Up to 730 he was an official at the 'Umayyad court and is reputed to have participated in Muslim-Christian debates before the Caliph. 730 to 743 he wrote The Source of Knowledge which included a section on heresies in which he discussed Islam. He set the tone for Christian apologetics and polemics for centuries to follow.
750	'Umayyad dynasty in Damascus overthrown. They are succeeded by the 'Abbāsids who ruled from Baghdād till 1225.		

Year	West	Middle East	Arabia	Other Regions	Church	Mission
756	'Umayyad dynasty established in Cordoba, Spain (Andalus) and endures till 1031.					
800	Charlemagne (768-814) is Holy Roman Emperor. European power waxes stronger against Muslim threats. Charlemagne was crowned emperor by Pope Gregory the Great in 800 - the break between East and West becomes permanent.	Charlemagne establishes ties with the court of Harûn ar-Rashîd, the 'Abbâsid Caliph, in Baghdad, and sets precedent for French (and Roman Catholic) interests in the Middle East. Translation movement (800-1000) takes Greek texts through Syriac into Arabic. The majority of translators were Christians. It made Islamic culture the vehicle for preserving and developing the heritage of Greece.				The tract known as "The Apology of Al Kindi" is composed as an exchange of letters between a symbolic Christian, 'Abd-ul-Masîh Ishâq al-Kindî, and a symbolic Muslim, 'Abd-Allâh Isma'îl al-Hâshimî. It is among the earliest Christian apologies for the faith against Muslim detractors.
813		The Mu'tazilah movement begins in Basrah. It was an effort to use the categories of Greek philosophy to restructure Muslim thought. It was opposed by those who argued for strict adherence to the Qur'ân and the authority of the tradition of				

Year			
820	Al-Shāfiʿī, benchmark Muslim jurist, dies.		
825	Abū Bakr al-Rāzī, Muslim philosopher and physician dies.		
830			Composition of the pseudonymous correspondence between ʿAbd-al-Masîh Ishâq al-Kindî and ʿAbd-Allâh Ismaʿîl al-Hâshimî. Known as The Apology of Al-Kindi, this tractate was used to shape Christian polemic and apologetic in a Muslim environment. It has been revived and republished in our day.
847	The Muʿtazilah are repressed. Theology becomes a suspect discipline. Muslim intellectual process comes to be dominated by legists.		
855	Ahmad Ibn Hanbal, most prominent of the opponents of the Muʿtazilah, and founder of the most conservative major school of Muslim jurisprudence, dies.		
890		Qarmatians established in 'Bahrain'	
922	Abû Mansûr al-Hallâj, the Muslim Sûfî saint, is executed in Baghdâd.		

Year	West	Middle East	Arabia	Other Regions	Church	Mission
928			Qarmatians sack Mecca and remove the 'Black Stone' from the Ka'bah.			
941		Al-Ash'arî, benchmark Muslim theologian, dies.				
950		Al-Farâbî, Muslim philosopher, dies.				
969		Fatimid Caliphs are established in Egypt and gain control of Palestine including Jerusalem. Christian pilgrim access to Holy Land made more insecure. Fatimids govern till 1010 when it fell to minor Turkik governors.				
970	Begin 120 years of increasing economic distress in Europe.				An environment of spiritual crisis in Europe leads to increased emphasis on pilgrimage as an act of spiritual renewal and piety.	
1036		Ibn Sînâ (Avicenna), the great Spanish Muslim philosopher/physician, dies.				
1054					Split between Roman Catholics and Greek Orthodox churches becomes formal.	
1066	Battle of Hastings - the founding of					

1064	Abū Muhammad 'Alī bin-Hazm (994-1064) dies in Spain. Among the more brilliant of the minds of Umayyad Spain, bin-Hazm developed the main terms and arguments for the Muslim critique of Christianity. His writings anticipate many of the major points later raised by the Protestant reformers.		
1070			St. John's Hospital founded in Jerusalem to house and care for pilgrims. The monks in the order of St. John (under Benedictines) became the seed which later developed into the crusading order of the Knights Hospitallers.
1071	Aug. - Seljuks under Alp Arslān defeat Byzantines at the Battle of Manzikert. Turks control Asia Minor. Seljuk Turks capture Jerusalem and close access to pilgrims.	A sense of outrage against Muslims generally grows in Europe because of the closure of pilgrim routes.	

Year	West	Middle East	Arabia	Other Regions	Church	Mission
1074	Michael VII, the Byzantine Emperor, appeals for help to Pope Hildebrand against the Seljuk Turks. Efforts to form a military alliance fail as Catholic-Greek Orthodox differences persist.					
1095	March - Pope Urban II receives appeal of Alexis I, the Byzantine Emperor, for help.				Nov. - At the Council of Clermont Urban II declares the Crusade.	
1096-10 99	THE FIRST CRUSADE					
1096	Aug. - First Crusade sets out.	Crusader forces gather in Constantinople through the winter.				
1097		June 19 - Crusaders take Nicea and …. July 1 - defeat the Seljuk Turks at Dorylaeum.				
1098		June 3 - Crusaders take Antioch. Aug. - Fatimids expell Seljukes from Palestine south of Beirut.				

1099	July 15 - Crusaders break the Fatimid defense of Jerusalem and put the inhabitants to the sword. Latin kingdom of Jerusalem established until 1187.			
1111	Al-Ghazzâlî (1058-1111), Muslim theologian, brings Muslim theological work to its highest point. He also composed a small apologetic work on Christianity.			

Year	West	Middle East	Arabia	Other Regions	Church	Mission
1118						Gerard, Master of the order of the Hospitallers, dies. He made the order independent of the Benedictines. His successor, Raymond Le Puy, reorganizes the order to provide not only shelter but also armed protection for pilgrims. The Knights Templar organized as a crusader order under the Benedictines. They quickly established themselves as an independent order and, with the Hospitallers, formed the bulwark of the ongoing crusader effort. They won Papal sanction in 1128.[1]
1147-1149	THE SECOND CRUSADE					
1148		Crusaders are defeated at Damascus. Normans conquer Tunis and Tripoli.				Paul, the Melkite bishop of Antioch, wrote a pastoral encyclical in which he proposed a more peaceful approach by Christians to Muslims, arguing that Islam was God's work among and for Arabs.

[1] The alliance of missionary efforts with crusading ventures became common. Contemporary mission theorists came to justify this alliance on the grounds that the military efforts insured an environment within which the individual could make a free religious choice. That heritage of the crusades, along with the positive use of the word, 'crusade,' to describe honorable Christian ventures,

1153	Abû-l-Fath Muhammad ash-Shahristânî (1086-1153) dies in Persia. A noted theologian and colleague of the more famous Al-Ghazzâlî, Shahristânî composed a critique of Christianity which, more tolerantly than that of Ibn Hazm, presents a basic Islamic apology which Muslims still find useful.			
1160	Normans expelled from North Africa.			
1169	Ayyûbids, under Salâh-ud-Dîn (Saladin), conquer Fâtimid Egypt. Shî'ite Islam disestablished (until the emergence of Shî'ite regimes in Iran).			
1176	Saladin conquers Syria.			
1187	July 4 - Saladin defeats Crusaders in the Battle of Hittîm. Oct. 2 - Jerusalem falls to the Muslims. The Kingdom of Jerusalem continues in name but is besieged in Acre.			
1189-1193	THE THIRD CRUSADE			

Year	West	Middle East	Arabia	Other Regions	Church	Mission
1191		April 20 - Philip II of France arrives in Acre to relieve the resident crusaders. June 8 - Richard of England arrives in Acre after first conquering Cyprus from the Byzantines.				
1192		Sept. 2 - Richard establishes truce with Saladin.				
1193		Saladin dies.				
1198	The order of Teutonic Knights founded, a third crusading order. They had little effect on Palestine, but were mainly used in the Christianizing of Prussia.	Ibn-Rushd (Averroes), the Muslim philosopher, dies.				
1202-1204	THE FOURTH CRUSADE	Constantinople sacked by the Crusaders. A Latin Emperor established in Constantinople until 1261.				
1207					The conversion of Giovanni Bernadone, nicknamed Francis. He became a wandering mendicant friar. Francis of	

Year				
1210				Francis of Assisi is granted permission to found a monastic order first named the Penitents of Assisi but later known as the Minor Brethren.
1212	THE CHILDREN'S CRUSADE - origin of the legend of the Pied Piper of Hamlin?			
1215	The Magna Carta granted to the English barons by King John.			
1216			Pope Honorius confirms the Dominican order.	
1218-12 21	THE FIFTH CRUSADE			
1219- 12 20				Francis of Assisi goes to Egypt to preach to the Ayyūbid Sultan, Al-Kāmil, at Damiyetta. Francis received as a madman but treated kindly. He set a irenic model for Muslim-Christian encounter.
1225	The 'Abbāsid Caliph, al-Nāsir (1180-1225), the last vigorous caliph in Baghdād, dies and is succeeded by weak rulers.			
1226			Oct. 3 - Francis of Assisi dies.	
1228-29	THE SIXTH CRUSADE	1228 - Frederick II lands in Acre		

Year	West	Middle East	Arabia	Other Regions	Church	Mission
1229		Frederick II crowns himself king of Jerusalem after recovering it by negotiated treaty. After his departure the local barons fell to bickering and they lost Jerusalem in 1244.			The Synod of Toulouse, held to condemn the heresies of the Cathari and Waldensians, establishes the Inquisition. From 1231 onward, the Inquisition was led by the Dominicans, the Catholic Church's great order of educators, and by the Franciscans.	The Inquisition became the first official instrument whereby the Church purged Europe of Muslim influence, especially Islam in Spain.
1247		Egypt and Palestine conquered by the Mamlūke (slave) sultans.				
1248-1254	THE SEVENTH CRUSADE					
1250		Feb. - Louis IX of France, is captured by the Mamlūkes in Egypt. May 6 - Louis IX released by ransom.				
1254		April - Louis IX returns to France.				

				Thomas Aquinas dies.	
1258	The Mongol, Hulaku, grandson of Jenghis Khan, sacks Baghdad, and ends the 'Abbâsid dynasty. Iraq is wracked by two and a half centuries of chaotic rule by Black and White Sheep Turkomans and Mongol successor princelings. A shadow 'Abbâsid Caliph, al-Mustansir bi-Illâh, was adopted by the Mamlûke sultan, Baybars, of Egypt in 1260. That fiction was dissolved when the Ottomans destroyed the Mamlûkes and assumed the title of Caliph themselves in 1517. Sept. 3 - Mamlûkes defeat Mongols at 'Ayn Jalut in Palestine. The Mongol tide recedes.				
1270	THE EIGHTH CRUSADE Louis IX dies.				
1274					
1291	The last Crusader stronghold in Palestine falls to the Mamlûkes. The Kingdom of Cyprus remains the last crusading outpost.				

Year	West	Middle East	Arabia	Other Regions	Church	Mission
1292						Roger Bacon dies. A Franciscan scholar, Bacon was an advocate of an irenic encounter with Muslims.
1300	Beginnings of the Renaissance in western Europe.	Turkish (Ottoman) power established in Asia Minor.				
1307	Knights Templar suppressed by Philip IV of France. They were abolished by Pope Clement V in 1312.					
1308		Knights Hospitallers take the island of Rhodes after abandoning Palestine.				
1315						Raimon Lull (1232-1315) dies. A Majorcan, Lull was converted in 1266 and joined the Franciscan order. Working in Tunis, his goal was to convert Muslims by peaceful means. In 1315, he was stoned to death. Toward the end of his life he became an advocate for the military crusade. He was the prototype missionary for Samuel Zwemer.
1337	Beginning of the Hundred Years' War in Europe.					
1348	The Black Death					

Year			Church	Mission
1384			Proto-reformer, John Wyclif (1328-1384), dies. He began his reformatory work in 1376, preaching against the affluence of the Church, and translating the Bible into English (1382-1384). His body was exhumed and burnt as that of a heritic in 1428.	
1389	Ottoman Turks defeat the Serbian army at the Battle of Kosovo and gain control of the Balkans.			
1401	Mongols under Timur the Lame conquer the Turkomans and devastate Baghdád a second time.			
1405		Timur the Lame dies.		
1415			Proto-reformer, Jan Huss of Bohemia (1373-1415) dies. He came under the influence of John Wyclif's writings, particularly concerning the headship of Christ and the authority of the Bible. He was judged and burned a heretic.	

Year	West	Middle East	Arabia	Other Regions	Church	Mission
1447	First record of a printed book in Europe.					
1453		Constantinople falls to Muhammad the Conqueror, the Ottoman Sultan/Caliph.			Gutenberg prints the Bible at Mainz.	
1464						Nicholas of Cusa (1401-1464) dies. He was a Latin Bishop who advocated the view that Islam could be a tutor to Christ.

Spain) surrenders to Ferdinand and Isabella of Castile and Aragon. The fall of Muslim Andalusia marks the beginning of the spiritual retrenchment of Islam even though, with the infusion of Turkish leadership in Asia, Islam continued a political and military force for some two centuries thereafter.

Oct. 12 - Christopher Columbus lands on an island in the Bahamas. He carried on to explore Cuba and Haiti (Hispanola). Aside from his achievement in crossing the Atlantic, spreading the rumor that the earth is round, and opening the New World for European colonization, the net product of his labors was the genocide of the Arawak people on Cuba and neighboring islands - some three to four million souls.

Year	West	Middle East	Arabia	Other Regions	Church	Mission
1497	Vasco da Gama and the Portuguese round the Cape of Good Hope and open sea lanes to India, bypassing the Middle East.			Ismā'īl bin-Haidu al-Safawi turns from being a man of simple Shi'ite piety to become the founder of the Safavid dynasty in Iran. In 1499 he ascended the throne in Tabrīz. Shi'ism becomes established for the first time as Persia's state religion.		
1502		Safavid dynasty is established in Iran. For the first time Shi'ism is the established Muslim ideology.				
1503				Afonso de Albuquerque builds a fortress in Cochin, on the west coast of India.		
1507			Portuguese conquer Socotra Island, off the coast of South Arabia, and block Arab trade to the Red Sea. Aug: Albuquerque raids Muscat and attacks Hormuz in the Arabian Gulf. Muscat occupied and fortified by the Portuguese. The kingdom of Hormuz made tributary to the			

Year				
1508	Shâh Ismâ'îl wrests Baghdâd from Turkoman control.			
1509	Portuguese defeat the Egyptian fleet off the coast of India.			
1510	Shâh Ismâ'îl visits Irâq on pilgrimage and massacres Sunnî leadership. This arouses Ottomans.		Goa established as the main Portuguese stronghold in India, interrupting Arab ship building by interdicting materials.	
1512				Michael Angelo completes painting the Sistine Chapel in Rome.
1513		Albuquerque fails in the attempt to occupy Aden.		
1515	Selim I succeeds to the Ottoman throne. Ottoman policy shifts eastward.	Portuguese occupy Hormuz whose dependencies were Bahrain and Qatif.		
1516	Selîm I defeats the Mamlûks at Marj Dabiq. The Ottomans become a Red Sea power against the Portuguese, and begin to claim the title of Caliph.	Bahrain and Qatif seized by the Sharîf of Mecca. Tribute from Hormuz to the Portuguese is reduced.		

Year	West	Middle East	Arabia	Other Regions	Church	Mission
1521	Hernando Cortés defeats the Aztecs in Mexico. Spain is the power of the Atlantic.		Portuguese occupy Bahrain and begin building their fort east of Manama. Their hold on Bahrain was always through governors ruling in the name of the king of Hormuz, and was tenuous at best.			
1523		The Knights Hospitallers' base on the island of Rhodes is destroyed by the Ottoman Turks.				
1524		Shâh Ismâ'îl dies. He is succeeded by his young son Tahmasp.				

1525	Anabaptist movement begun in Zürich by Conrad Grebel, Felix Manz and Balthasar Hubmaier. They divided from Zwingli (and the other reformers) on the question of infant baptism, which they came not to accept. By baptizing each other they instituted what they termed 'believers' baptism.' They rejected force in matters of faith, the principle of religious uniformity as a guarantee of public order, any link between church and state, & involvement in civil government. They advocated strict pacifism. For their beliefs, 'Anabaptists' in Zürich were publically drowned in 1526. The movement spread, especially in Moravia, southern Germany, Switzerland and the Netherlands. Roman Catholics and Protestants alike sanctioned the death penalty for 'Anabaptists.'			

Year	West	Middle East	Arabia	Other Regions	Church	Mission
1526				Babar establishes Mogul Empire in India.		
1531					Ulrich (or Huldreich) Zwingli (1484-1531) dies. He began his reform in 1522 in Zürich, contending that the Bible alone was binding on all Christians, and that Christ is the only head of his Church. In 1523 he broke with Luther over the question of Christ's presence in the Lord's Supper. In 1531 he died in battle against Swiss cantons loyal to Rome.	
1534		Under Sulaymân the Magnificent the Ottomans defeat Safavid Persia and occupy Iraq. Baghdâd fell without opposition. This is the peak of Ottoman power.			Nov. 3 - Henry VIII of England confirmed head of the Church of England by the Supremacy Act.	
1536					Erasmus of Amsterdam (1464-1536) dies. He printed the first Greek New Testament and, as a renaissance thinker, is deemed a sympathizer of the	

Year	West	Middle East	Arabia	Other Regions	Church	Mission
1543	Copernicus proves the Earth goes around the Sun and upsets the old cosmology.					
1545					The Council of Trent opens, and ushers in the Counter-Reformation.	
1546					Martin Luther (1483-1546) dies. The first of the open reformers, he published his '95 Theses' in 1517. He broke with Rome in 1521 (Diet of Worms) under the protection of the elector, Frederick of Saxony.	
1551			Piri Ra'is, Ottoman admiral, sacks Muscat and expells the Portuguese.			
1553	Mary assumes the throne in Britain and re-enstates the Catholic Church.		Portuguese reoccupy Muscat and strengthen its fortifications.		Thomas Cranmer, Archbishop of Canterbury, issues the 42 Articles. He was assisted in their writing by John Knox. Reaction to the 42 Articles led to the emergence of the Puritans, a party of more extreme reform. Queen Mary executes Cranmer and 78 other leaders of reform.	

Year	West	Middle East	Arabia	Other Regions	Church	Mission
1558	Elizabeth I becomes queen of Britain.				Elizabeth of England reestablishes Cranmer's reforms and assumes the title of 'Supreme Governor' of the Church of England.	
1564					John Calvin (1509-1564) dies. He came to a Protestant conviction between 1532 and 1534. Calvin was not an ordained priest but a lawyer and trained as a humanist. Forced to flee France, via Basel he found his way to Geneva. In 1536 he published his Institutes of the Christian Religion, which, as revised in 1559, continues to be his greatest legacy. He tried to devise a middle position between Zwingli and Luther on the question of the Sacrament, and held ranks with them on the question of baptism and the relationship of the Church to the state. From Geneva, he established the Reformed branch of Protestant churches	

Year	West	Middle East	Arabia	Other Regions	Church	Mission
1588	England defeats the Spanish Armada.					
1600	Charter of the English East India Company.					
1602	Charter of the Dutch East India Company.		Portuguese expelled from Bahrain by a local revolt which invited in the Persians.			
1603					Puritans in Britain openly begin to oppose the Church of England.	
1604					Carmelite embassy to Shah 'Abbás of Persia from Pope Clement VIII.	
1612						Carmelite convent founded on the island of Hormuz.
1616	William Shakespear dies.					
1619			Peace treaty between Ottomans and Persians.			
1620	British Puritans begin to emigrate to the American Colonies.		Ibadi Imam, Násir bin Murshid al-Ya'rubi, expells Portuguese from the interior of Oman.			
1622			Portuguese expelled from Hormuz; they establish a second base in Kung.			
1623			Persians, under Shah 'Abbás, conquer Baghdad. Safavids also in control of Basrah.			Carmelite convent founded at Basrah by Fr. Basil de St. Francois. Augustinians from Goa also active in Basrah.

Year	West	Middle East	Arabia	Other Regions	Church	Mission
1629					Cyril Lucan, reform-minded Ecumenical Patriarch in Constantinople publishes his Confessions, a heavily Calvinist work on Church doctrine. It was heatedly opposed by Latin influences in the Orthodox Church and condemned in the Council of Jerusalem (1673). Lucan was strangled by order of the Sultan in 1638.	
1638			Ottomans retake Baghdad.			
1643						Johannes Megapolensis of the Dutch Reformed Church begins missionary work among Native Americans in Albany, New York. The seed for the Reformed Church in America's missionary awareness was sown.
1648	Charles I is executed in Great Britain. Oliver Cromwell becomes Chairman of the Council of State and then (1653) Lord Protector.					

Year	West	Middle East	Arabia	Other Regions	Church	Mission
1650			Portuguese expelled from Muscat by local Omani forces under the Imâm Sultân bin Sayf al-Ya'rubî I.			
1652			Oman begins to regain control over East Africa from Portugal. Full control by 1698.			
1660	Charles II of England restores the British monarchy and the authority of the Church of England.					
1664	French Compagnie des Indes (Company of the East Indies) chartered					
1666						Carmelites evacuate Basrah along with Persian defenders as the city falls to the Ottomans.
1670						Carmelites back in Basrah. From then on their work was under French sponsorship. Basrah, having a church and a small school, continued to be the base for the Carmelite order in the Gulf thereafter.

Year	West	Middle East	Arabia	Other Regions	Church	Mission
1701	The War of Spanish Succession		As an outgrowth of their struggle against Portugal, Arab pirates (mainly Omani) have been operating in the Arabian Gulf and Arabian Sea for about ten years. Before that there is no record of Arab piracy in the region.			
1705			March: Arab sea raiders capture the English East India Company's ship, the Murwil, which is the first incident against the English of this kind.			
1711			Oct. 17: The death of the Omani Imâm, Sayf bin Sultân al-Ya'rubî I. He is succeeded by Sultân bin Sayf II. From then till his death in 1719, Sultân bin Sayf picks up the pace of empire building and nearly bankrupts the country.			

1716		The 'Utúb, a migratory group of the 'Anaza tribal confederation of central Najd, settle in Kuwait after a sojourn in Qatar and being scattered throughout the Gulf in port cities.
1717		Omani Imám Sultán bin Sayf II captures Bahrain from the Persians.
1719		April 20: Sultán bin Sayf al-Ya'rubí II dies. Oman is thrown into civil war as rival claimants for the Imámate contest the throne.
1720		Persia purchases Bahrain from Oman. Their rule over Bahrain, however, was very loose and there follows a period of chaos.
1722	Oct.: Afghans capture Isfahan and the Safavid Persian dynasty in disarray.	
1723		Oct.: A storm destroys the Omani fleet in Muscat harbor. Oman ceases to be a major maritime military factor in the Indian Ocean.

Year	West	Middle East	Arabia	Other Regions	Church	Mission
1736		Nâdir Qolī Beg, a bandit leader, disposes of the last of the Safavid pretenders and assumes the throne of Persia as Nâdir Shâh.	Nâdir Shâh deposes the last Safavid ruler in Iran and assumes power.			
1737			Persians under Nâdir Shâh intervene in the Oman civil war and occupy the country. Persian control over Oman very tenuous.			
1744			Ahmad bin Saʻîd Al Bû-Saʻîdî, then governor of Sohar, rallies Oman and expells the Persians from Oman.			
1745			Founding of the Saʻûdî state by the Shaykh Muhammad bin-ʻAbd-ul-Wahhâb — the Wahhâbî movement begins.			
1747		June 19: Nâdir Shâh of Persia assassinated. His empire falls apart.				
1749			Ahmad bin Saʻîd elected Imâm in Oman and founds the Âl Bû Saʻîdî dynasty. The al-Yaʻâriba dynasty ends.			
1750		The Zand dynasty emerges in Iran.	Âl Sabâh of the ʻUtûb establish themselves as rulers in Kuwait.			
1762	Rousseau publishes					

1756 to 17 65	Seven Years War in Europe – Britain emerges as undisputed leading colonial power.			
1766		Al Khalifah of the ʻUtūb leave Kuwait and settle in the port town of Zubārah on the penninsula of Qatar. Against opposition of local shaykhs they develop Zubārah into a thriving port city, sufficient to attract the adverse attentions of the Persians.		
1776	U.S. - American Declaration of Independence Adam Smith publishes his Inquiry	Basrah captured by the Persians under the Zand dynasty.		
1779		Qajar dynasty displaces the Zand in Iran.		
1782		Al Khalifah, under Shaykh Ahmad ʻAl-Fātih,ʼ having been attacked by the Persians from Bahrain, counterattack. The counterattack turns into an invasion. After Persian rout, the Al Khalifah assume power in Bahrain. Origins of the modern state of Bahrain.		

Year	West	Middle East	Arabia	Other Regions	Church	Mission
1789	The French Revolution					
1791						William Carey publishes his Enquiry. This is the bench mark for the beginning of the Modern Missionary Movement.
1794						London Missionary Society (LMS) founded in London.
1795			Wahhâbis defeat the Banî Khâlid of al-Hasâ and become the dominant power in central Arabia.			
1796			Death of Shaykh Ahmad 'Al-Fâtih' Al Khalîfah of Bahrain and Zubârah. He is succeeded by his son, Salmân.			The New York Missionary Society formed by a group of Presbyterian, Reformed and Baptist congregations for work among Native Americans.
1798	The last of the Crusading orders, the Knights Hospitallers, are overcome by the Ottoman Turks in the base on Malta.	Napoleon lands in Egypt and overcomes the Mamluk armies. His brief occupation of Egypt marks the beginning of steady incursion of western powers and ideas into the Middle East.				
1799			Oman, under Sultân bin Ahmad Al Bû-Sa'îdî, reconquer Bahrain. Shaykh Salmân Al Khalîfah retires to			CMS founded in London

1801	Napoleon is expelled from Egypt by British seapower. He returns to France and establishes himself as dictator.		
1806			The General Synod of the Reformed Church forms "The Standing Committee of Missions."
1809		Wahhâbîs conquer Bahrain and, from Zubârah, take Salmân Al Khalîfah and his family into exile to their capitol of Dar'îyah.	
1810		The Al Khâlifah retake Bahrain from the Wahhâbîs with Omani and Persian support. They abandon Zubârah and virtually the whole population of Zubârah moves to Bahrain away from the Wahhâbî menace. Salmân resumes his office.	June 27 - American Board of Commissioners for Foreign Missions (ABCFM) is founded; on Sept. 5 the Board is formed. Henry Martyn sets out from India for Arabia. He landed in Muscat on April 20,1811.
1815	Battle of Waterloo - Napoleon is defeated. Britain becomes the uncontested European superpower.		

Year	West	Middle East	Arabia	Other Regions	Church	Mission
1816			Sayyid Saʻîd Al Bû-Saʻîdî of Oman attacks Bahrain but is repulsed. Britain remains neutral.			The United Foreign Missionary Society formed by Presbyterian and Dutch and German Reformed churches for work among Native Americans. (Dissolved in 1826)
1819						Dr. John Scudder, the first foreign missionary of the Reformed Church, sent to Calcutta, India, under the ABCFM. ABCFM missionaries, Pliny Fisk and Levi Parsons, land in Syria
1820			Feb.: The co-rulers of Bahrain, ʻAbd-Allâh and Salmân, sign the 'General Treaty' with the British East India Company to refrain from raiding mercantile shipping.			
1822						The Missionary Society of the Reformed Dutch Church formed as an autonomous society whose Board of Managers served as 'The Standing Committee of Missions of General Synod,' a mirror image of the model later employed to adopt the Arabian Mission. The Syrian Mission Press established on Malta for publications in Arabic. (This was transferred to

1826			The United Foreign Missionary Society disbands, its assets are turned over to the ABCFM. The ties of the Reformed Church to the ABCFM are strengthened.
			John Schermerhorn appointed General Agent for Mission, the first full-time RCA staff person for mission work.
1828	Sayyid Sa'id's second attempt upon Bahrain fails.		
1831			General Synod of the Reformed Church appoints a 34-member "Board of Missions" to take direct control of domestic mission activities.
1832			The Reformed Church forms its own 15-member Board of Foreign Missions to oversee, under overall ABCFM oversight, those foreign fields primarily staffed by Reformed Church missionaries — primarily the Arcot Mission in India and the Amoy Mission in China. Schermerhorn resigns as Agent and A. Henry Dumont is appointed General Agent.

Year	West	Middle East	Arabia	Other Regions	Church	Mission
1833						The position of General Agent for mission is abolished by the RCA General Synod. Dumont, evidently in disgust, joins the Congregational Church.
1842						The RCA Synod appoints Ransford Wells Secretary of the Boards of Missions, both Foreign and Domestic. His functions are mainly those of a fund raiser. David Abeel arrives in Amoy, China and begins the Amoy Mission.
1844						Ransford Wells resigns as Secretary for Mission.
1847						The Arcot Mission was formed under ABCFM direction but staffed entirely by Reformed Church personnel.
1848		Muhammad ʻAlî dies in Egypt; he is succeeded by his son, ʻAbbâs Pasha.				
1852	The Crimean War begins on Oct. 4, 1852, and ends in March 1856 with the Treaty of Paris.	July, 1854: ʻAbbâs Pasha dies of poisoning in Egypt. He is succeeded by his brother, Saʻîd.				1854: The Classis of Arcot is formed in India under the Particular Synod of New York, the first and only such RCA classis outside the United States.
1856		Dec: Saʻîd Pasha grants Ferdinand de Lesseps the right to build a canal through the				

				Reformed Church re-forms its Board of Foreign Missions with 24 members and amicably separates from the ABCFM, taking full responsibility for Arcot and Amoy. The RCA General Synod instructs the Amoy Mission to form a Reformed Classis which conforms to the Reformed Church's polity.
1857				
1858	Great Britain takes over direct rule of India from the English East India Company after the Sepoy Rebellion.			
1860	May: Civil war between Druze and Maronites breaks out in Lebanon. France sends a force to protect Christians in Syria.			
1861	The American Civil War begins.	June 25: ʻAbd-ul-ʻAzîz becomes sultan of Ottoman Empire.	Bahrain officially becomes a protectorate of Great Britain.	
1863		Jan. 17: Saʻîd Pasha dies in Egypt. He is succeeded by Ismaʻîl. Ismâʻîl proceeds with plans to build the Suez Canal against British opposition.		

Year	West	Middle East	Arabia	Other Regions	Church	Mission
1864						The missionaries of the Amoy Mission defy Synod and refuse to form a Classis of Amoy, insisting that the Church in China be permitted to evolve its own polity independent of foreign structures. While General Synod did not agree, the missionaries won their case by default. The Classis of Amoy was never formed.
1865	The American Civil War ends.					The 'Van Dyck Version' of the Arabic Bible is printed.
1866		Ismâ'îl Pasha succeeds in establishing his as a hereditary dynasty in Egypt with the title of Khedive.				
1869		May 30: 'Abd-ul-'Azîz deposed as Ottoman Sultan. Murad V takes the throne under the influence of Midhat Pasha. Nov. 17: The Suez Canal is officially opened.				
1871	Germany united under Kaiser Wilhelm I. Germany becomes an imperial power.					

Year					
1875	Nov: Khedive Ismâ'îl sells the Suez Canal to Great Britain for £4,000,000.				The Women's Board of Foreign Mission organized by Reformed Church women to give support to the efforts of the Board of Foreign Missions with special emphasis upon work among women and children.
1876	Sept. 1: Murad V is deposed for mental incompetence. Sultan 'Abd-ul-Hamîd II begins his reign.				
1877	May 13: Rumania declares its independence from Turkey. June: Russia declares war on Turkey.	Feb. 5: 'Abd-ul-Hamîd II dismisses Midhat Pasha and Turkey turns from Britain to foster closer ties with Germany.			
1878	June 13: Congress of Berlin declares Rumania, Serbia and Montenegro independent from Turkey.				
1880	June 26: Ismâ'îl deposed by Sultan 'Abd-ul-Hamîd. Tawfîq, Ismâ'îl's son, succeeds as Khedive of Egypt.			"Exclusive Agreement" between Britain and Bahrain: no political relations with powers other than Britain. (reaffirmed in 1892)	

Year	West	Middle East	Arabia	Other Regions	Church	Mission
1881		July 11: Britain lands troops in Egypt in support of the Khedive against the rebel, Ahmad 'Arabi. Sept. 13: 'Arabi defeated by the British at Tel-al-Kabir. Britain assumes control of the administration of the Egyptian government. Egypt did not regain its independence again until after the First World War.				
1882		First Jewish 'Aliyah' from Europe to Palestine. This is made up primarily of eastern European Jews from provinces that were now breaking away from the Ottoman Empire. Legally, therefore, they were citizens moving to a new location.				
1883						Henry Nitchie Cobb appointed Secretary of the Board of Foreign Missions of the Reformed Church in America.
1884						Prof. J. G. Lansing appointed professor of Old Testament at New Brunswick Theological Seminary.

Year		
1885	'Abd-ul-'Azîz bin Faysal Al Sa'ûd given sanctuary in Kuwait under Shaykh Mubârak until the end of 1901.	
1886		John R. Mott organizes the Student Volunteer Movement for Foreign Missions.
1888		Lansing, Phelps, Cantine and Zwemer organize the fellowship of 'The Wheel.'
1889		May 23: Arabian Mission plan presented to RCA - declined. Aug 28: Arabian Mission undenominational 'Syndicate Plan' launched and a 'Committee of Advice' chosen. Oct. 1: Cantine sails for Beirut.
1890		Nov: Cantine & Zwemer meet Lansing in Cairo for consultations. Dec 16: Cantine sails from Suez for Aden

Year	West	Middle East	Arabia	Other Regions	Church	Mission
1891						Jan. 8: Zwemer sails with Bishop French on a coastal steamer bound for Aden. Jan. 31: Formal incorporation of the Arabian Mission in Newark, New Jersey. Mr. Thomas Russell elected president. Feb.: Bishop French sails for Muscat. Cantine & Zwemer tour Hadramaut separately. May 14: French dies in Muscat. May 26: Cantine sails for Muscat via Bombay. Aug: Cantine lands in Basrah
1892			"Exclusive Agreement" between Britain and 'Trucial Oman' - no political relations with powers other than Britain.			
1893						Rev. Frank Scudder, the first appointed salaried secretary and treasurer of the Arabian Mission. Arabian Mission Field Reports begin to be published.

Year				
1894	The 'Dreyfus Affair' in France stimulates Theodore Herzl to write Der Judenstaat.			The Arabian Mission brought under the oversight of the Board of Foreign Missions of the Reformed Church. Frank Scudder steps down. Henry N. Cobb, Secretary of the Board of Foreign Missions of the Reformed Church, takes over as corresponding secretary but the Arabian Mission Syndicate structure continues parallel to that of the Board of Foreign Missions.
1895				Sept. - Razouki Naaman sets out to occupy Amarah as an out-station for the Mission. Toward the end of the year Zwemer visited the station twice to settle troubles. A bookshop, however, is established.
1896	Herzl publishes his Judenstaat	Greco-Turkish war begins over the question of Crete. The war extends to Thessaly in the following year.		May 18 - S. Zwemer marries Amy Wilkes (1st woman in the Mission; beginning of work among women) 3rd Quarter - Salome Antoon resigns and returns to Baghdad.
1897	Aug. 27 - Herzl convenes the first Zionist Congress - the inaugeration of Political Zionism.			

Year	West	Middle East	Arabia	Other Regions	Church	Mission
1898						Oct. 1 - F. Barny marries Margaret Rice. John G. Lansing resigns from New Brunswick Theological Seminary and retires to Denver, Colorado, where he maintained himself as a journalist. He suffered from a serious degenerative illness of the brain.
1899			"Exclusive Agreement" between Britain and Kuwait: no political relations with powers other than Britain.			
1900						
1901		Tel Aviv founded in Palestine.				
1902		Permission granted to the Germans to complete the Berlin to Baghdad railway, an initiative strongly opposed by Britain.	Jan. 15 - ʿAbd-ul-ʿAzîz bin bin ʿAbd-ur-Rahmân Al Saʿûd captures Riyadh from the Ibn Rashîd governor. This dates the founding of the modern kingdom of Saʿûdî Arabia.			The Mason Memorial Hospital opens in Bahrain, the first of the Mission's hospitals.
1903						Amy Zwemer begins the Girls School in Bahrain.

1904	The second Jewish 'Aliyah' begins. This movement is driven by the evolving ideology of Political Zionism. Apprehensions begin to rise in the Palestinian community.			
1905	Henry Ford fosters the publication of the 'Protocols of the Elders of Zion', which stimulates political Zionism to greater efforts.	Kurds, in alliance with the Turks, carry out the Armenian massacres. International indignation runs high.		
1906	The 'Young Turk' movement begins among Turkish officers of the Ottoman army.			Sept. 3: John G. Lansing dies in Denver, Colorado.
1907				
1908	May 26: George Reynolds makes the first strike of oil in the Middle East at Masjid-i-Sulaiman in Ahwaz, Iran. July 24: Under the title of 'The Committee of Union and Progress,' the Young Turks take over Istanbul. Dec. 17: New Turkish parliament opened. A new era of liberal government is ushered in.	Sept.: Husayn bin-'Alî Al Hâshim appointed Sharîf of Mecca by the Committee of Union and Progress.		Land purchased by the Mission in Basrah for a hospital and residence. The Mission is a direct beneficiary of the more liberal policies of the reform minded government of the Young Turks in Istanbul.

Year	West	Middle East	Arabia	Other Regions	Church	Mission
1909		April: William D'Arcy launches the Anglo-Persian Oil Company (later renamed: British Petroleum - BP). April 26: 'Abd-ul-Hamīd II is deposed as Sultan; his brother, Muhammad V, succeeds him.				Arthur Bennett treats the daughter of Mubārak Al Sabāh on board his yacht in the Shatt-al-'Arab river and is invited to open medical work in Kuwait. The 'East House' missionary residence built in Bahrain.

				Church	Mission
1910				World Missionary Conference under the leadership of John R. Mott in Edinburgh organizes the International Missionary Council.	Henry N. Cobb retires as Secretary of the Board of Foreign Missions of the Reformed Church, and is succeeded by William I. Chamberlain, a child of the Arcot Mission who had served in India himself from 1887 to 1905. He too was a man of considerable experience and profound learning. Jan. - Bennett and Van Ess land in Kuwait. Work in Kuwait begins. Bennett makes the first Mission contact with the Sultan of Najd, ʿAbd-ul-ʿAzīz bin Faysal Al Saʿūd, and prepares the way for later tours into the Interior. March 3: Foundation laid for the Lansing Memorial Hospital in Basrah. Nov: At its annual meeting the Mission votes to establish Amarah as a permanent station, but no action is taken. Dec. 10: Deed granted for the Mission's property in Kuwait on the condition that it operate a medical facility.
1911					Lansing Memorial Hospital opens in Basrah.

Year	West	Middle East	Arabia	Other Regions	Church	Mission
1912		Oct: Balkan states declare war on the Ottoman Empire.				Samuel Zwemer founds the journal, *The Moslem World*, published under the auspices of the Nile Mission Press and advertised as 'the one magazine that will tell you all you want to know about Islam and the progress of Christianity's war upon it.' In the spring, John Van Ess establishes the School of High Hope for Boys in Basrah. Dorothy Van Ess establishes the School of Girls' Hope in the autumn of the same year.
1913		Abadan oil refinery opened.				Mission builds a chapel in Basrah. This is the first building erected by the Mission purely for worship.
1914		Nov. 1 - Turkey enters World War I on the side of Germany.	Oct. 31 - British India forces land at Basrah. Hostilities with Turkey begin.			Sir John Nixon, British commander in Basrah, asks John Van Ess to organize a school system for the occupied territories.

Year				Mission
1915	Husayn-McMahon correspondence in which Britain pledged to Arab self-determination.	Jan. 24: Capt. William Shakespeare, British Political Agent in Kuwait, dies in a Sa'ûdî action in the desert against the Al Rashîd. British beseiged at Kut-al-Amarah. Nov. 28 - Mubârak Al Sabâh dies in Kuwait. He is succeeded by Jâbir, his eldest son.		Typhus epedemic in Basrah. Christine Ivorson Bennett dies in January. Arthur Bennett invalided to U.S.
1916	May 5 - Sykes-Picot Agreement signed in which Britain, France and Russia agree to partition the Ottoman Empire's Asiatic provinces.	April 20: British garrison at Kût-al-'Amarah surrenders to the Turks. June 10: Husayn, the Sharîf of Mecca, declares the 'Arab Revolt' against Turkey. Nov. 2: Husayn bin-'Alî, the Sherîf of Mecca, declares himself King of the Arab Countries.		
1917	Nov. 2 - British government issues the 'Balfour Declaration' in which it 'views with favor' the establishment in Palestine of a 'Homeland for the Jewish People'	Jan. 3: Husayn recognized formally as King of the Hijâz by Britain and France. Feb.: British recapture Kût-al-'Amarah March: British capture Baghdad.		Early in the year Dr. Paul Harrison made the first tour by a missionary doctor into Najd at the invitation of 'Abd-ul-'Azîz Al Sa'ûd.

Year	West	Middle East	Arabia	Other Regions	Church	Mission
1918	Nov. 11: Germany signs the Armistice ending World War I.	Oct. 1: T. E. Lawrence and the Amīr Faysal bin-Husayn occupy Damascus. Oct. 30: The Truce of Murdos ends Turkey's participation in the First World War.				

				Other Regions	Church	Mission
1919	Jan. 18: The Paris Peace Conference convenes. The settlement of the 'Eastern Question' — the partition of the Ottoman Empire's Arab provinces — to be investigated by an inter-allied Commission to Syria. Zionist memorandum to the Versailles Peace Conference defines territorial desires which continue to represent the aspirations of the Israeli political institution. June 28: The Treaty of Versailles is signed by the Allied Powers, stating the League of Nations Covenant, outlining penalties and restrictions on Germany, and apportioning mandates to the allied powers for the administration of former German colonies and Ottoman provinces. July 9: Germany ratifies the Treaty of Versailles.	March 7: The Amir Faysal is elected by the General Syrian Congress to become the 'constitutional King over Syria.' May 15: Mustafá Kamâl Pasha assumes command of the Turkish nationalist movement. May 29: American members of the inter-allied Com-mission to Syria, Henry C. King and Charles R. Crane with a party of American specialists, leave Paris to investigate the situation in Greater Syria guided by Wilson's principle of self-determination. Britain and France withdraw from the Commission since France had no interest in the will of the Syrian people and Britain did not want an investigation of the situation in Iraq which the French demanded, quid pro quo. July 23: Mustafá Kamâl opens the first Turkish National Congress which, on Aug. 7, demands inviolability of Turkish Anatolia. Aug. 30: King-Crane Commission cables its report to President Wilson emphasizing that, without the force of an army, Zionist ambitions for Palestine cannot be imposed upon the Arabs. They also recommended that America assume the mandate for Greater Syria (including Palestine). The report was not published until after the U.S. Congress had approved its own version of the Balfour Declaration and the mandates for Palestine and for Syria had been awarded by the League of Nations to Britain and France respectively.		

Year	West	Middle East	Arabia	Other Regions	Church	Mission
1920	Jan. 10: Treaty of Versailles comes into force. The League of Nations formed. President Woodrow Wilson fails to persuade the United States to join it. Organized Palestinian opposition to Zionism begins as information concerning the Balfour Declaration becomes public.	March: Allies occupy Istanbul April 23: Mustafā Kamāl elected president of Turkey by the National Assembly meeting in Ankara. July 28: King Faysal expelled from Damascus by the French mandatory authority. Arnold Wilson proposes him as King of Iraq.			The Lambeth of the Anglican communions call for efforts toward Christian unity.	Dec.: James & Elizabeth Cantine move to Baghdad preparatory to the formation of the United Mission in Messopotamia (later the United Mission in Iraq). This followed hard upon the withdrawl of the CMS from Baghdad. Baghdad, for a while, functions as another station of the Arabian Mission before the establishment of the UMM.

Year	West	Middle East	Arabia	Other Regions	Church	Mission
1921		March 12: Winston Churchill, the British Colonial Secretary convenes the Cairo Conference to settle issues of British Middle East policy. Faysal emerges as the British choice as King of Iraq. March 16: Soviet Russia concludes peace with republican Turkey. Sept. 16: Turkish forces defeat the Greek army at Sakarya and Mustafā Kamāl is titled ghāzī (conqueror) by the National Assembly. Oct. 13: Soviet Armenia, Georgia and Adharbayjan conclude peace with Turkey. Oct. 20: France concludes peace with Turkey.	April: Sayyid Tālib Pasha, a son of Sayyid Rajab, the Naqīb of Basrah, was Interior Minister of Iraq and candidate for king. His open ambition and republican tendencies caused him to be exiled to Ceylon by the British High Commissioner, Sir Percy Cox. July: Iraqi referendum on the Hashimite monarchy. Aug 23: Faysal bin-Husayn Al Hāshim enthroned as constitutional king of Iraq. Nov. 2: Ibn Saʿūd takes Hā'il, the last stronghold of the Al Rashīd. Muhammad bin-Talāl Al Rashīd is taken to Riyadh. (He was murdered in Feb. 1954, the last of his dynasty.)			
1922		Aug. 18: Greeks with British backing resume hostilities against Turkey. Oct. 11: The truce of Mudania concluded and Greeks expelled from Anatolia. Fu'ad king of Egypt				

Year	West	Middle East	Arabia	Other Regions	Church	Mission
1923		July 24: Treaty of Lausanne concluded, awarding Turkey Asia Minor, Istanbul and eastern Thracia. The Greek population of Asia Minor was expelled. Oct. 23: The National Assembly declares Turkey a Republic. Muhammad V is deposed. His son, 'Abd-ul-Majid, assumes the title of Caliph but not of Sultan.	Major Frank Holmes negotiates first oil concession for eastern Sa'udi Arabia.			William I. Chamberlain appointed President of the Alliance of Reformed Churches. During the year of his service there he was replaced as Secretary of the Board of World Missions by A. Livingstone Warnshuis, a man with extensive experience in China and strong ecumenical commitments.

Year	West	Middle East	Arabia	Other Regions	Church	Mission
1924		March 3: Atatürk abolishes the Caliphate. The whole of the Muslim world deprived of a titular religious head. April 29: Turkey adopts a new constitution. Atatürk declines the title of Caliph. The Turkish revolution becomes an event studied closely by reformers and potential revolutionaries throughout the Middle East.	March: King Husayn of the Hijâz declares himself Caliph in 'Ammân. This presumption gave Ibn Sa'ûd the excuse to move against him directly. May 5: Sir Percy Cox steps down as British High Commissioner. He is replaced by Sir Henry Dobbs. Aug. 2: Rashîd 'Alî al-Gaylânî becomes Minister of Justice in new Iraqî cabinet. Thus begins a controversial political career. Shaykh Khaz'al attempts to defy Reza Khan Pahlavi, strongman in Tehran, is imprisoned, and his shaykhdom of Muhammarah is dissolved.			Spring: The United Mission in Mesopotamia (UMM) is established by the Presbyterian Church, the Reformed Church in the U.S., and the Reformed Church in America. Its field organization is also completed.

Year	West	Middle East	Arabia	Other Regions	Church	Mission
1925		Reza Khan deposes the last Qajar pretender and assumes full authority in Iran, founding the Pahlavi dynasty.	Aug.: Wahhâbî forces begin their advance into the Hijâz. Oct. 13: 'Abd-ul-'Azîz bin-Faysal Al Sa'ûd takes control of the holy cities of Mecca and Madinah in the Hejâz. Husayn of Mecca abdicates in favor of his elder son, 'Alî, but in Dec. 'Alî's forces surrender. 'Ali goes to Baghdad, and Husayn retires to Cyprus. Dec. 2: Maj. Frank Holmes negotiates an oil prospecting concession with Bahrain.			Elizabeth DePree Cantine falls ill and the Cantines retire from the field. Sept. 14: The 'Corporation of the Arabian Mission' is dissolved, and it becomes the Arabia Field of the Board of Foreign Missions of the Reformed Church in America.
1926			Jan. 8: Ibn Sa'ûd proclaimed king of the Hijâz at a ceremony in Mecca. Sa'ûdî Arabia becomes a kingdom.			The Marion Wells Thoms Memorial Hospital for Women opened in Bahrain.
1927			Oct. 14 - Iraq Petroleum Company strikes oil at Baba Gurgur in Iraq. Nov. 30: Eastern Gulf Company acquires Bahrain concession		The Jerusalem Missionary Conference begins to move mission organizations toward mission cooperation.	

Year	West	Middle East	Arabia	Other Regions	Church	Mission
1928						After the death of his wife, James Cantine returns to Baghdad and the UMM for one year of added service. New Lansing Memorial Hospital in Amarah put into service.
1929	Oct. 29: New York stock market crash sends the United States and the world into an economic depression — the Great Depression. Germany severely affected.					Jan. 21: Henry A. Bilkert, traveling to Kuwait with Mr. Charles R. Crane, is shot in the head by Wahhābī raiders in the open desert. In later years it was understood that the incident was not entirely accidental. July: James Cantine, for serious health problems, finally retires from the Mission, having served his last period as a member of the UMM in Iraq. Samuel Zwemer, in the Fall of the year, became Professor of History of Religion and Christian Mission at Princeton Theological Seminary.

Year	West	Middle East	Arabia	Other Regions	Church	Mission
1930			Karl Twitchell surveys Sa'ūdi Arabia for water and oil resources. Aug. 1: Standard Oil of California (SOCAL) acquires the Bahrain concession through its subsidiary, the Bahrain Petroleum Company (BAPCO).			After having occupied rented quarters since 1912, the School of Girls' Hope in Basrah builds and moves into a new campus on the outskirts of the city.
1931		June: Husayn bin-'Alî, father of Faysal of Iraq and Abd-Allah of Jordan, dies in 'Ammân.	The British Mandate for Iraq ends and Iraq, a kingdom, is admitted to the League of Nations.			The church in Kuwait is built using unique cement, brick and steel construction.
1932	Europe defaults on U.S. war loans and strengthens the mood of isolationism in the United States.		May 31: BAPCO strikes oil in Bahrain. SOCAL retains Twitchell to obtain Sa'ūdi concession.		Near East Christian Council (NECC), coordinating the activities of mission organizations in the Middle East is formed. The Arabian Mission participates.	

Year	West	Middle East	Arabia	Other Regions	Church	Mission
1933	Jan. 30: Adolph Hitler appointed chancellor of Germany. The Nazi Party comes to power. Germany accelerates its program of rearming itself. Feb. 24: League of Nations finds Japan guilty of aggression in China. Japan withdraws from the League. May: Japanese and Chinese sign a truce.		Feb.: SOCAL team of Twitchell, Hamilton and Philby begin negotiations for Sa'udi concessions. May 29: SOCAL signs concession agreement for eastern Sa'udi Arabia. 'Socal' organizes subsidiary: California Arabian Standard Oil Company (CASOC). Sept. 8: King Faysal I of Iraq dies in Switzerland. His son, Ghâzî I ascends the throne of Iraq. The loss of Faysal was deeply felt.			
1934			Dec.: Kuwait Oil Company (KOC) formed by British Petroleum and Gulf Oil Companies.			
1935	Oct. 3: Italy invades Ethiopia.		BAPCO begins refining oil on Bahrain. This refinery was eventually linked to the ARAMCO operations and a pipeline linked Sa'ûdî crude oil production to the Bahrain refinery.			William I. Chamberlain retires as Secretary of the Board of Foreign Missions. He as succeeded by a layman, F. M. "Duke" Potter, who had already been serving as Associate Secretary since 1918.

Year	West	Middle East	Arabia	Other Regions	Church	Mission
1936	May: Italy in control of Ethiopia.	April - Arab Rebellion breaks out in Palestine against the British Mandate.				March 28: Harold Storm begins a ten month 8,000 mile journey across Arabia in the company of Qambar al-Mâs, an Omani medical assistant.
1937						Sept. 28: William I. Chamberlain, a key figure in the development of the Arabian Mission, dies.
1938			March 3 - After 15 months of drilling, 'Casoc' opens Dammam #7, the first viable oil well in Sa'udi Arabia. April 3: King Ghâzi of Iraq dies in an auto accident. The 4-year old king Faysal II is brought up under the regency of his cousin, 'Abd al-Ilâh. April - KOC strikes oil at Burgan in Kuwait. Dec. 25: Nûrî Pasha al-Sa'îd becomes prime minister of Iraq			

1939	Sept. 1 - Nazi Germany invades Poland. World War II begins.	The Arab Revolt in Palestine is crushed by the British Mandatory Authority.	May 1 - 'Casoc' begins loading first tanker with Sa'udi oil. Development of Kuwait oil is suspended until after the war. Merchants' Revolt in Kuwait is suppressed. Ghâzi bin-Faysal, the king of Iraq, is killed in an automobile accident. His infant son, Faysal II, succeeds him under the regency of his maternal uncle, Prince 'Abd-ul-Ilâh.			The 'Kate V. S. Olcott Memorial Hospital' for women opens in Kuwait.

Year	West	Middle East	Arabia	Other Regions	Church	Mission
1940			Italian airforce bombs Dhahran by mistake. Their intended target was the BAPCO refinery on Bahrain. Oil production in Sa'udi Arabia is shut down. April 1: Rashîd 'Alî al-Gaylânî leads a rebellion in Iraq with strong pro-German sympathies. May: German and Italian aircraft and technicians begin arriving in Mosul in Iraq to uphold the Gaylânî government against the British. The British advance on Baghdad. May 28: Rashîd 'Alî al-Gaylânî flees and is granted refuge by 'Abd-ul-'Azîz al-Sa'ûd in Arabia.			
1941	Dec. 7: Japanese bomb Pearl Harbor. United States enters World War II.	Because of his Nazi sympathies, the British and Russians oblige Reza Shah Pahlavi to abdicate in favor of his				

Year				
1942	May 11 - Meeting at the Biltmore Hotel in New York City, an extraordinary conference of Zionists proposes articulates the intention to displace the Palestinian people. The United States becomes the power center for the Zionist Movement.		The Orthodox Youth Movement (Syndesmos) is founded. It emerges from the War years as a leaven for renewal and Christian unity within the Greek Orthodox Church in the Middle East.	Dec. 15: Harold Storm 'invested' in Bahrain with the 'Kaiser-i-Hind' decoration by the Government of India.
1943				Jan. 11: John Van Ess, Jr. dies in Basrah after a brief illness. Feb. 18: Stanley Mylrea 'invested' in Kuwait with the 'Kaiser-i-Hind' decoration by the Government of India.
1944		Jan. 31 - 'Casoc' renamed: Arabian American Oil Company (ARAMCO). Oil shipments resumed.		

Year	West	Middle East	Arabia	Other Regions	Church	Mission
1945	Sept. 2 - Japanese surrender.	Oct. 31 - Zionist violence on large scale begins in Palestine.	Feb. 14 - King 'Abd-ul-'Azîz Al Sa'ûd meets with President Franklin Roosevelt and, separately, with Winston Churchill in Egypt. He receives assurances from Roosevelt that the United States will defend Sa'ûdî Arabia against aggression and that no steps to settle the Palestine problem without first consulting him, an agreement which President Truman, of course, violated.			
1946	April - The League of Nations is formally dissolved and the United Nations is inaugurated.		Development of Kuwait oil fields resumes.			The Women's Board of Foreign Missions is dissolved. Ruth Ranson, its executive secretary, becomes personnel secretary under 'Duke' Potter for the Board of Foreign Missions.

| 1947 | Nov. 29 - United Nations General Assembly recommends the partition of Palestine into Arab and Jewish states with Jerusalem as a corpus separatum to be administered by the Trusteeship Council on behalf of the United Nations. The Security Council was charged with implementing the recommendation. | Large scale civil disturbances erupt in Palestine. | | The Church of South India is formed. | Nov. 20: Harold Storm and family move to Doha in Qatar to staff the clinic newly built there by the ruler for the Mission. |

Year	West	Middle East	Arabia	Other Regions	Church	Mission
1948	U. S. importing more oil than it exported. May 14 - British Mandate for Palestine ends; Ben Gurion announces the establishment of the State of Israel; United States recognizes the new State of Israel. May 17 - Soviet Union recognizes Israel. Sept. 17 - Count Folke Bernadotte, the UN Mediator in Palestine, was assassinated by the Stern Gang under Menachim Begin. Dr. Ralph Bunche appointed acting mediator.	March - Czechoslovakia ships arms to Zionists. Zionists take the offensive in Palestine. April 9 - Massacre at Deir Yasin by the Irgun leads to Arab panic. May 15 - Arab League armies enter Palestine. The civil war in Palestine becomes an international conflict.			The first General Assembly of the World Council of Churches is held in Amsterdam.	
1949	Jan. 13 – Arab-Israeli Armistice talks begin with the convening of Israeli and Egyp-					

Year		
1950	United Nations Relief and Works Agency (UNRWA) begins relief and resettlement efforts among Palestinian refugees in Jordan, Lebanon, Syria and Gaza.	
1951	Mohammad Mosaddeq comes to power in Iran as prime minister on a nationalist platform to nationalize the Anglo-Iranian Oil Company. Anglo-Iranian Oil Company closes down 'Abbadán port and all operations. The National Iranian Oil Co. is organized but cannot operate.	Kuwait Oil Company increases output dramatically to offset closure of Iranian oil operations.

Year	West	Middle East	Arabia	Other Regions	Church	Mission
1952		Free Officers coup deposes King Farûq of Egypt. Gamâl 'Abd-ul-Nâser emerges as new Egyptian strong man.	Shaykh 'Abd-Allâh al-Sâlim Al Sabâh of Kuwait invites Palestinians to come to Kuwait and assist in the development of the country. Large Palestinian influx into the Arab Gulf follows.			H. M. "Duke" Potter dies in office. He is succeeded by two people. (1) Henry G. "Heine" Bovenkerk was appointed Secretary-Treasurer of the Board of Foreign Missions. His experience had been as a missionary in Japan from 1930 to 1952. During the years of World War II he was much involved in relief work for Japanese Americans in the United States, and was instrumental in re-establishing mission involvement in Japan on an ecumenical footing after the War. (2) Bernard M. "Barny" Luben, who had already been serving since 1941 as a Field Secretary for the Board. He was now appointed Executive Secretary of the Board. His background was service as a missionary in Japan from 1929 to 1941, a field for which he continued to carry responsibility as Field Secretary from 1941

1953	Mohammed Reza Shah Pahlavi attempts to dismiss Mohammed Mosaddeq. He has to flee. With United States support, he is quickly returned and Mosaddeq is imprisoned.	Nov. 9: ʿAbd-ul-ʿAzîz bin ʿAbd-ur-Rahmân Al Saʿûd dies in Riyadh, having ruled Arabia since Jan. 2, 1902. He was succeeded by his son, Saʿûd. The American Independent Oil Company (AMINOIL) in Kuwait strikes oil in the Neutral Zone with Saʿûdî Arabia. A working agreement with Getty Oil is worked out dividing the proceeds between Saʿûdî Arabia and Kuwait.	
1954	Gamâl ʿAbd-ul-Nâser assumes premiership of Egypt, displacing the figurehead, General Nagîb. National Iranian Oil Co. resumes operations under management of British Petroleum and a consortium of other western companies.	Dec.: The old city wall around Kuwait city is dismantled.	Second General Assembly of the World Council of Churches in Evanston, Illinois.
1955			Oct. 8: Mylrea Memorial Hospital opens in Kuwait.

| 1956 | Oct. 30 - Israel, Britain and France attack Egypt along the Suez Canal. Nov. 2 - The UN led by the United States under President Eisenhower demands ceasefire and withdrawl. There's a brief warming in Arab-American relations. | Inaction of Iraq in the Suez War becomes a domestic issue held against the Hashimite regime. Baghdad's joining the American-inspired 'Baghdad Pact' with Iran and Turkey also held against the Iraqi monarchists. As Nasser emerges as a heroic figure after the 'Suez Affair', tensions deepen between Egypt and Baghdad. Undercurrents of unrest in Iraq, already evident, strengthen. | July: R. Park Johnson, a Presbyterian, appointed Field Representative in the Near East for the Reformed Church in America. A period of strong field leadership ensues. Annual Meeting of the Arabian Mission moves to create the Mission Executive Committee as a provision for conducting ad-interim business and as a replacement for Mission decision taken by vote through circular letter. They also voted to institute 'Hospital Boards of Trustees' in the several stations. The Meeting also proposed the creation of a 'New Missionary Committee' to be responsible for orienting new missionaries on the field. These actions were eventually approved by the Board of Foreign Missions and implemented. The Meeting also asked to be permitted to nominate a 'Field Consultant to the Board' so as to participate directly in Board discussion of field issues. This proposal seems to have been rejected (or ignored). Oct 30: Iraq-Persian Gulf educational survey partitially completed. Participating were Park Johnson (RCA Field Representative in the Near East), Walter Skellie (Assiut, Egypt) and John Karayusuf (Aleppo, Syria). The completion of the survey was delayed because of the |

1957	April - Jordan cracks down on Palestinian unrest; pro-Nasser sentiment among Palestinians intensifies.			
1958		July 14 - Iraqi Revolution under Colonel 'Abd-ul-Karīm Qāsim slaughters King Faysal and his Prime Minister, Nūrī as-Sa'īd. Anticipated good relations with Egypt do not materialize.		Kuwait chapel's capacity is doubled by addition of a new parish hall. Sept. 1: Lansing Memorial Hospital in Amarah expropriated without compensation. The fear that the same policy would be applied to the Basrah Boys' School was not realized. Nonetheless close association of the Mission in Iraq with the Hāshimit government and its identification as 'American' makes its position precarious.
1959			May 14: East Asia Christian Conference (now the Christian Conference of Asia) founded.	
1960				Ruth Ransom retires from the Board of World Mission. She is succeeded by Ruth E. Joldersma. Dec.: "Heine" Bovenkerk resigns from the Board of Foreign Missions. Robert Harrison becomes Treasurer.

Year	West	Middle East	Arabia	Other Regions	Church	Mission
1961			June 19: Kuwait gains its independence from Great Britain. Britain's protectorate over Kuwait ends. June 25: Iraq under Qâsim claims that Kuwait is properly a part of Iraq and threatens by massing troops on the ill-defined border. The British act to block the Iraqi initiative and are successful. July: Kuwait is admitted into the Arab League.		Dec.: Third General Assembly of the World Council of Churches held in New Delhi, India; the International Missionary Council joins the WCC; the Orthodox churches join the WCC	March: "Barney" Luben resigns from the Board of World Mission. John Buteyn, with previous experience within the U.S. on the Board and as Field Secretary (1956-1961), becomes staff coordinator and secretary for the Middle East.

1962		Kuwait, under 'Abd-Allāh as-Sālim, promulgates its new constitution. The first elected national assembly in the Gulf convenes. Yāsir 'Arafāt secretly organizes 'Fatah' in Kuwait while working as an electrician for Kuwait's Ministry of Public Works.	The Near East Christian Council gives way to the formation of the Near East Council of Churches in which the Syrian Orthodox Patriarchate of Antioch participates. The Ecumenical Office for Youth and Students in the Middle East is organized by Gabriel Habib in association with the World Student Christian Federation (WSCF), the heir to the Student Volunteer Movement of the late 1800s. Oct.: The Second Vatican Council begins, opening the door for wider Catholic participation in the Ecumenical Movement.
1963		'Abd-us-Salām 'Ārif takes power in Iraq. 'Abd-ul-Karīm Qāsim assassinated. May 14: Kuwait is admitted into the United Nations.	

Year	West	Middle East	Arabia	Other Regions	Church	Mission
1964		Jan.: Palestine Liberation Organization organized by the Arab League. The PLO's first meeting, chaired by Ahmad Shuqayrī, was held in Jerusalem under King Hussein's patronage. Shuqayrī effectively alienates King Hussein by trying to collect taxes from Palestinians in Jordan and declaring the East Bank to be part of Palestine. 'Fatah' joins with the PLO but as a distinct entity. It begins guerrilla operations with Syria as a base.	Oil is discovered in Oman.			March 20: Gerald Nykerk dies of a heart attack in Kuwait. April: Edwin M. Luidens accepts the position of the Executive Secretary for the Board of World Mission until the dissolution of the Board in 1968. Arabian Mission begins considering how it should reorganize. Lew Scudder (Sr.) collapses of a subdural haematoma in Kuwait. Kuwait hospital seriously crippled.
1965			Shaykh 'Abd-Allāh as-Sālim Āl Sabāh dies in Kuwait.			Sept.: New buildings for the School of High Hope for Boys in Basrah opened.
1966			The Ba'ath Party takes power in Iraq. 'Abd-us-Salām 'Ārif assassinated. Bakr Sidqī becomes president with Saddām Husayn ...			

1967				
	May - Egypt and Jordan sign a mutual defense pact which included also Syria, Saudi Arabia and Iraq. June 5-10 - Arab-Israeli war. Sinai, the Golan Heights, the West Bank and Gaza are conquered by Israel. 1,026,000 Palestinians fall under Israeli control along with 39,000 other Arabs. Of the 150,000 Palestinians who fled to the East Bank, only 20,000 were allowed to return. Nov. - The UN General Assembly passes Resolution 242 for the purpose of establishing 'a just and lasting peace in the Middle East.'	Oman begins exporting oil.	The meeting of the heads of the Oriental Orthodox churches in Addis Ababa prepares the way for the emergence of the Middle East Council of Churches in 1974.	March: Mission language school in Bahrain is closed. March 30: Kuwait Hospital officially closed by the RCA's Board of Foreign Missions. Serious demoralization of the Mission sets in. Sept. 13: Maurice Heusinkveld assassinated in Matrah, Oman. Sept. 28: Ken Warren is appointed field liaison between the Arabian Mission and the Area Secretary, John Buteyn. Danish Mission Society (DMS) comes into a cooperative relationship with the Arabian Mission, bringing needed personnel into all areas of program, but providing creative leadership particularly in the formation of new bookshops.

Year	West	Middle East	Arabia	Other Regions	Church	Mission
1968		Yâsir 'Arafât becomes chairman of the PLO.	The Iraq Ba'ath Party regains power in Baghdad. Col. Saddâm Husayn is the strong man of the coup de etat.		Fourth General Assembly of the World Council of Churches in Upsala, Sweden.	The Board of Foreign Missions was dissolved and reformed as the Division of World Ministries of the General Program Council (GPC) of the Reformed Church in America. John Buteyn continues as Secretary for World Ministries. Nov.: Question of reorganization or perhaps even closure of Bahrain Hospital reopened. Iraq government takes over the School of High Hope in Basrah and other Mission institutions in the country. Missionaries are expelled.
1969						May: The agreement between the RCA and the DMS for cooperation in Arabia is formalized. Expropriation proceedings against the RCA's holding property begun in Kuwait. Improved situation in Bahrain results in a stay-of-execution. The Hospital Board proposes the re-organization of the Hospital as an autonomous institution controlled by the Christian community

			Mission
1970	Sept. - King Hussein launches drive against PLO in Jordan - 'Black September'. PLO concentrates guerilla bases in Lebanon and Syria. Gamâl 'Abd-ul-Nâser dies; Anwar Sadât takes power in Egypt.	In Oman, Qâbûs, son of Sultân Sa'îd bin-Taymûr Âl Bû-Sa'îdî, deposes his father and estalishes a new, more progressive regime.	Nov.: Plans for development of the Mission hospitals in Oman are put on 'hold'. Dec.: Proposal for turning over the Mission hospitals to the Oman government health service is put forward.
1971		Dec.: Bahrain gains its independence from Britain.	Jan. 1: New arrangement with the Oman Ministry of Health initiated. Mission hospitals are turned over to government administration; Mission personnel are 'loaned' to the government. June 3: New building of the National Evangelical Church in Bahrain dedicated. Like the building which it replaced, it had a clock in its steeple. The Ruler, Shaykh 'Isâ bin-Salmân celebrated the occasion by giving a dinner for all the missionaries who attended.
1972			April: Al-Rajâ' School in Bahrain begins to build its new campus and institutes a process for phasing in co-educational student body. GPC moves to absorb the funds received from the expropriation of Kuwait property into its reserve funds.

Year	West	Middle East	Arabia	Other Regions	Church	Mission
1973		Oct. 6 - Egypt and Syria launch surprise attack on Israeli forces. The Yom Kippur War lasted three weeks. The mystique of Israeli military invulnerability damaged.	Shaykh 'Îsâ bin-Salmân Âl Khalîfah of Bahrain promulgates a constitution for the country. Dec.: Bahrain's first National Assembly is elected.			Feb.: GPC acts to guarantee the National Evangelical Church $250,000 for emergency use.
1974		PLO accepted as an official observer body at the United Nations.			May: The Middle East Council of Churches is formed in Nicosia, Cyprus. Beyond the Protestant members of the old NECC, it includes all Orthodox branches plus non-Arab communions – the Armenian Orthodox, the Church of Cyprus, and the Anglican and Evangelical churches of Iran. The member churches are organized by confessional families.	Jan.: GPC votes to turn over the property of Ar-Rahmah Hospital in Oman to the Oman government. Yâsir 'Arafât sends Don MacNeil (now resident in Canada and no longer connected with the Mission) a cable declaring the UN's recognition of the PLO the beginning of a dream's fulfillment. April: The Reformed Church receives balance of funds for the expropriation of the property in Kuwait. April: GPC votes to share in under-writing a 'Coordinated Bookshop Program for the Arabian Gulf.' June: DMS, RCA and the (then) Near East Council of Churches agree to joint development of their bookshops under the name, 'The Family Bookshop Group.' It is registered in Lebanon as a limited liability company, the two major shareholders being

Year				Church	Mission
1975		Aug.: Bahrain's National Assembly is dissolved.			April 3: Lewis R. Scudder (Sr.) dies in Kuwait. Nov. 25: Ruth Ransom dies.
1976					
1977					Marion DeVelder retires as General Secretary of the Reformed Church and is succeeded by Arie Brouwer. John 'Jack' Walchenback takes over from Brouwer as Executive Secretary for Program of the GPC.
1978	Camp David Peace accord signed by Anwar Sadat and Menachem Begin.				
1979	Feb.1 - The Ayatolla Khomeni lands in Tehran. Iran becomes an 'Islamic Republic'. The Pahlavi dynasty is ended. Nov.: American Embassy personnel in Iran held hostage.	Saddám Husayn establishes himself as sole authority in Iraq and is declared President.			
1980	July: Mohammed Reza Shah Pahlavi dies in Egypt.	Sept.: Iraq declares War on Iran, and invades 'Arabistán' (Khuzistan).			Warren Henseler appointed as Middle East secretary for GPC/DWM. John Buteyn continues as overall secretary for World Ministries.
1981	Jan. 20: American Embassy hostages in Iran freed.				

Year	West	Middle East	Arabia	Other Regions	Church	Mission
1982		June 6 - Israel launches its invasion of Lebanon. The 'Intifáda' (uprising) begins among Palestinians under Israeli occupation.				John Buteyn retires from the staff of the General Program Council. He is succeeded by Eugene Heideman as secretary for World Ministries.
1983						
1984						
1985						
1986						
1987		Dec. 8 - The 'Intifáda' breaks out in open civil resistance.				
1988		July 3: U.S. cruiser shoots down Iranian passenger airliner over the Gulf. July 18: Iran accepts UN mediated ceasefire with Iraq.				
1989			The Iraq-Iran War is concluded.			

1990			July 18 - President Saddám Husayn of Iraq accuses Kuwait of stealing Iraqi oil and deflating the world price of crude oil. The first steps are taken to prepare for the Iraqi invasion of Kuwait. Aug. 2 - Iraq invades Kuwait after talks over an oil and territorial dispute break down. Shaykh Jabir and Shaykh Sa'ad take refuge in Sa'údí Arabia.	The Catholic churches of the Middle East join the Middle East Council of Churches as full members.	Most of the clergy of the Kuwait churches either go into hiding or are absent at the time of the invasion. At the NECK, the property is ransacked, but small groups of worshipers continue to worship in the church building under the watchful eye of Iraqi soldiers.
1991			Jan. 15 - UN deadline for Iraq's withdrawl from Kuwait expires midnight New York time. Military action is sanctioned. Jan. 17 - US and allied forces begin bombardment of Iraq and Iraqi positions in Kuwait.		Dorothy Scudder dies in the United States on July 10. With the liberation of Kuwait, the NECK and other churches resume full operations with heavy emphasis on relief work. RCA sends $100,000 for reconstruction. Oct. - Strong pro-American and pro-British sentiment in the country leads NECK to the plan to recover the use of old hospital and other buildings formerly owned by the Mission.

Year	West	Middle East	Arabia	Other Regions	Church	Mission
1992						March - MECC sends L. R. Scudder, Jr. to investigate condition of churches in Kuwait and offer assistance. July - Warren Henseler retires as Middle East/Africa secretary. Eugene Heideman assumes responsibilities for the Middle East.
1993	Sept. 13: In Washington D.C. Yâsir 'Arafât and Yitsak Rabin sign mutual agreement leading toward Palestinian autonomy in Gaza and Jericho.					July - RCA reorganizes the structure of its denominational agencies. World Mission Services, under Richard Vande Voet financially cut loose from other agencies. 'Faith Mission' model adopted.
1994						March 24: Mission in Oman celebrates 100 years.

Missionary Appointments and Distribution by Station

Use of this Table:

This table is designed to incorporate all (or as much as possible) of the data on the placement and utility (not necessarily utilization!) of Arabian Mission personnel. For maximum coherence this table ought to be used in conjunction with Appendix A, the time line. One can see in this table the concentration of personnel in any given station in any given year as well as their overall area of responsibility. A person enters the lists on the first column at the left (Appointments) and leaves on the right (Absence). The "Absence" column is the most congested but perhaps the most significant since it carries a lot of information — absence due to posting outside the Arabian Mission's area of responsibility, furloughs, resignations, deaths, retirements, and any other cause for a person's absence from the field. To trace a person's career, reference should always be made to the Absence column. The time marker (eg. (3Q)) indicates when a person moved *into* a new situation. Unless one pays attention to the time markers, a person might appear to have served in two or more stations at one time. The Arabian Mission employed but few people with such exceptional talent.

Explanation of symbols:

Symbols used to designate profession or area of assignment:
+   clergyman (clergymen served as mission generalists, frequently
           serving as educators and/or as technicians/builders and even as
           medical assistants);
§   medical professional (either doctor or nurse, it being understood
           that many of these also served as evangelists and educators as
           well as builders and technicians);
°   educator/evangelist/mass media;
•   engineer/technician/builder;
¢   business/management.

<u>Note</u>: A combination of symbols indicates either a specialization or multiple
qualification — hence •§ would signify a medical technician.

Other Symbols:
°   indicates those individuals appointed under a special relationship.
           The Van Vlacks, Shaws, and Haynes, for instance, joined the
           mission under what was known as the "University of Michigan
           Scheme," and were separately supported.
4Q   is a time symbol: The number before the letter 'Q' indicates
           which quarter of the year a person moved to a new post.
(LS)   indicates a language student.
(ST)   indicates a person appointed on a short term of service in which
           language study was not required (the rest of the personnel not so
           designated may be assumed to be "career" appointments).
(UMM)   indicates a person assigned by the RCA after 1925 to the Arabia
           field generally but specifically attached, not to the Arabian
           Mission, but rather to the United Mission in Mesopotamia (later
           renamed the United Mission in Iraq). While they appear under
           the Appointments column, they do not otherwise show up in the
           actual work force of the Arabian Mission.
(LC)   indicates a person attached to the mission in "Local Connection,"
           meaning that the support for such a person was not the
           responsibility of the Reformed church but rather was generated
           and paid locally on the field. This became an increasingly
           common practice in the 1940s.
(V)   indicates a volunteer recruited either locally or through the
           Reformed church.

Year	Personnel / Work Force	Station 1 Staff	Station 1 Events	Station 2 Staff	Station 2 Events	Notes
1889	+J. Cantine Work Force: 1					
1890	+S.M. Zwemer Work Force: 2					
1891	+J.Cantine (Aug.) Work Force: 2					
1892	§C. Riggs +P.J. Zwemer §C.Riggs (Mar-Aug) +P.J. Zwemer (from Dec) Work Force: 4				Cantine proposes 'Imārah become an outstation of Basrah.	C.Riggs dismissed
1893	§J.T. Wyckoff +J. Cantine +S.M. Zwemer +P.J. Zwemer Work Force: 3	Outstation +S.M. Zwemer (8.5 mos.) +P.J. Zwemer (2 mos.) +J.Cantine (1.5 mcs.)		Outstation +P.J. Zwemer (in Dec)	Initial visit by colporteur, Na'ūm.	
1894	+J. Cantine §J.T. Wyckoff (March-July) Work Force: 4	Full Station +S.M. Zwemer (intermittently) §J. Wyckoff (part time)	First visit by colporteurs Dā'ūd and Salomi - they were ejected.	Full Station +P.J. Zwemer		J.Wyckoff retired for failing health
1895	§H.R.L. Worrall (from April 16) +S.M. Zwemer §H.Worrall (Q2) Work Force: 3	maintained by only a colporteur	S.M. Zwemer visits Kuwait. This is followed up by a colporteur visit. No permanent appointment.	+P.J. Zwemer	Out Station Occupied by Razūqi Na'mān, a colporteur, and occasionally visited by S. M. Zwemer from Basrah.	+J.Cantine on furlough from (Q1 to Q3, 1896)
1896	°A. Wilkes marries S. Zwemer May 18. +S.M. Zwemer °A.W. Zwemer (Q2) +J.Cantine (Q3) §H.R.L. Worrall Work Force: 5	+S.M. Zwemer (Q4) °A.W. Zwemer (Q4)	Another colporteur visit indicates door is closed.	+P.J. Zwemer		

Yr.	Appointments	Basrah	Bahrain	Oman	Kuwait	Amarah	Absence/Change
1897	+F.J. Barny Work Force: 4	§H.R.L. Worrall +J.Cantine (on tour) +F.J. Barny (Q4)	maintained only by a colporteur	+P.J. Zwemer			S. & A.W. Zwemer on furlough (Q1 to Q4, 1898).
1898	§S. Thoms §M. Thoms +G. F. Stone °M. R. Barny Work Force: 10	+J. Cantine (Q1 & 4) §H.R.L. Worrall +F.J. Barny §S.J. Thoms (Q4) §M.W. Thoms (Q4)	+F.J. Barny (Q2) °M.R. Barny (Q2) +S.M. Zwemer (Q4) °A.W. Zwemer (Q4) +G.F. Stone (Q4)	+P.J. Zwemer +J. Cantine (Q2) +F.J. Barny (Q4) °M.R. Barny (Q4)			P. Zwemer falls ill (2Q), arrives in New York on July 12, dies Oct 18. F.J.Barny marries M. Rice on Oct. 19.
1899	+H.J. Wiersum Work Force: 12	§H.R.L. Worrall (3Q) §S.J. Thoms §M.W. Thoms +F.J. Barny °M.R. Barny	+S.M. Zwemer °A.W. Zwemer §H.R.L. Worrall (Q1+2) §S.J Thoms (Q3) §M.W. Thoms (Q3)	+G.F. Stone (till Q3) +J. Cantine (Q3) +H. J. Wiersum (Q3)			G.F.Stone dies in Oman June 26.
1900	+J.E. Moerdyk Work Force: 10	§H.R.L. Worrall +F.J. Barny °M.R. Barny +J.E. Moerdyk +H.J Wiersum (Q4)	+S. Zwemer °A.W. Zwemer §S.J Thoms §M.W. Thoms	+H.J. Wiersum +J. Cantine +J.E. Moerdyk (Q4)			
1901	§E. H. Worrall Work Force: 11	§H.R.L. Worrall §E. H. Worrall +F.J. Barny °M.R. Barny +H.J Wiersum (till Q4)	+S. Zwemer °A.W. Zwemer §S.J Thoms §M.W. Thoms +J.E. Moerdyk (Q2)	+J. Cantine +J.E. Moerdyk (Q1)			H.J. Wiersum dies in Basrah Aug. 3 of small-pox.
1902	§E. DePree (Cantine) +J. Van Ess Work Force: 12	§H.R.L. Worrall §E. H. Worrall +F.J. Barny °M.R. Barny +J.E. Moerdyk (Q4)	+S. Zwemer °A.W. Zwemer §S.J Thoms §M.W. Thoms +J.E. Moerdyk §E. DePree (Cantine) +J. Van Ess	+J. Cantine			
1903	°J.A. Scardefield	§H.R.L. Worrall §E. H. Worrall +F.J. Barny (Q4) °M.R. Barny (Q4) +J. Van Ess	+S. Zwemer °A.W. Zwemer §S.J Thoms §M.W. Thoms §E. DePree (Cantine)	+J.E. Moerdyk (Q4)	June: Sharon Thoms ejected from Kuwait. (3Q) colporteur, Salome Antûn, establishes residence for only one		J. Cantine on furlough F.J. & M.R. Barny on furlough (Q1,2 +3). S.J. & M.W. Thoms on furlough (Q4)

Year						
1904	§A. K. Bennett °J. V. Bennett °F. Lutton §L.M. Patterson (ST) Work Force: 17	§H.R.L. Worrall §E. H. Worrall +F.J. Barny °J. Van Ess °J.A. Scardefield °F. Lutton	+S. Zwemer °A.W. Zwemer §S.J. Thoms (Q4) §M.W. Thoms (Q4) §E. DePree (Cantine) §A. K. Bennett °J. V. Bennett §L.M. Patterson	+J.E. Moerdyk +J. Cantine (Q2)	S. Zwemer visits Antûn in Kuwait. Antûn later obliged to leave.	L.M. Patterson (short term completed upon Thoms return) J. Cantine marries E. G. DePree. (Q4)
1905	§M.C. Vogel Work Force: 16	§H.R.L. Worrall §E. H. Worrall +F.J. Barny °M.R. Barny °J. Van Ess °J.A. Scardefield °F. Lutton	§S.J. Thoms §M.W. Thoms §A. K. Bennett °J. V. Bennett +J.E. Moerdyk °F. Lutton (Q3) §M.C. Vogel	+J. Cantine §E.DeP. Cantine		M.W. Thoms dies in Bahrain May 25. S. Zwemer & A.W. Zwemer withdraw.
1906	•D. Dykstra §C.S.G. Mylrea °B. L. Mylrea °M. DePree (Thoms) (to care for Thoms children) Work Force: 15	§H.R.L. Worrall §E. H. Worrall +F.J. Barny °M.R. Barny °J.A. Scardefield	§S.J. Thoms +J.E. Moerdyk °F. Lutton §M.C. Vogel §A. K. Bennett °J.A. Scardefield (Q3) °M. DePree (Thoms)	+J. Cantine §E.DeP. Cantine		J.V. Bennett dies in Bahrain Jan 21. J.G. Lansing dies in Denver CO, Sept. 3.
1907	°M. Wilterdink (Dykstra) Work Force: 19	§H.R.L. Worrall §E. H. Worrall +F.J. Barny °M.R. Barny +J. Van Ess °J.A. Scardefield (Q2) •D. Dykstra §A. K. Bennett (Q2)	§S.J. Thoms °M. DeP. Thoms +J.E. Moerdyk °F. Lutton §M.C. Vogel §A. K. Bennett °J.A. Scardefield §C.S.G. Mylrea °B. L. Mylrea	+J. Cantine §E.DeP. Cantine		J.E. Moerdyk on furlough (Q4)
1908	+G. J. Pennings §T. Josselyn Work Force: 19	§H.R.L. Worrall §E. H. Worrall +F.J. Barny °M.R. Barny +J. Van Ess °J.A. Scardefield §A. K. Bennett §M.C. Vogel (Q3) •D. Dykstra	§S.J. Thoms °M. DeP. Thoms +J.E. Moerdyk (4Q) °F. Lutton §M.C. Vogel §C.S.G. Mylrea °B. L. Mylrea •D. Dykstra (Q2) °M. Wilterdink (Dykstra)	+F.J. Barny (Q3) °M.R. Barny (Q3)		J. & E.DeP. Cantine on furlough (Q1) H.R.L. & E.H. Worrall on furlough (Q2)

Yr.	Appointments	Basrah	Bahrain	Oman	Kuwait	Amarah	Absence/Change
1 9 0 9	°D. Firman (Van Ess); §A. C. Iverson (Bennett); +E. Calverley; §E.T. Calverley; §P.W. Harrison; Work Force: 20	§H.R.L. Worrall; §E. H. Worrall; §M.C. Vogel; +J. Van Ess; °J.A. Scardefield; §A. K. Bennett; +G. J. Pennings	§H.R.L. Worrall (4Q); §E. H. Worrall (Q4); §S.J. Thoms; °M. DeP. Thoms; +J.E. Moerdyk; °F. Lutton; §C.S.G. Mylrea; °B. L. Mylrea; •D. Dykstra; °M. Wilterdink (Dykstra); §T. Josselyn	+F.J. Barny; °M.R. Barny; §S.J. Thoms (2Q); °M. DeP. Thoms (2Q); •D. Dykstra (Q2); +J. Cantine (Q4); §E.DeP. Cantine (Q4)	Late in the year A. K. Bennett meets Shaykh Mubârak of Kuwait and invited to open a permanent clinic.		F.J. & M.R. Barny on furlough (2Q); J.A. Scardefield on furlough (Q2); F. Lutton on furlough (Q2)
1 9 1 0	+G .D. Van Peursem; §J. Spaeth (Van Peursem); +S. Zwemer (returns); °A.W. Zwemer (returns)	§H.R.L. Worrall (Q2); §E. H. Worrall (Q2); +J. Van Ess; §A. K. Bennett; §M.C. Vogel; +G. J. Pennings; +J.E. Moerdyk (Q2); §P.W. Harrison; °J.A. Scardefield (Q4)	+S. Zwemer (4Q); °A.W. Zwemer (4Q); §H.R.L. Worrall; §E. H. Worrall; +J.E. Moerdyk; §C.S.G. Mylrea; °B. L. Mylrea; §T. Josselyn; +E. Calverley; §E.T. Calverley; °D. Firman (Van Ess); §A. C. Iverson (Bennett); •D. Dykstra (Q2); °M.W. Dykstra (Q2); °F. Lutton (Q3); §J. Spaeth (Van Peursem)	+J. Cantine; §E.DeP. Cantine; §S.J. Thoms; °M. DeP. Thoms; •D. Dykstra; °M.W. Dykstra; §A. K. Bennett (Q3); +F.J. Barny (Q4); °M.R. Barny (Q4)	Early in the year J. Van Ess and A.K. Bennett spend short time analyzing situation in Kuwait. Good prospects. March-July: G.J. Pennings and A.K. Bennett reside in Kuwait. Later A.K. Bennett purchased property for permanent settlement.	Nov: Mission decides to establish 'Imârah as a full station but no action is taken.	S.J. & M. DeP. Thoms on furlough (Q2); J. Van Ess on furlough (Q3); D. Dykstra marries M. Wilterdink.
1 9 1 1	§S. L.Hosmon; *§H. VanVlack; *°M. Van Vlack; *•C. Shaw; **A. B. Shaw; **P. Haynes	+J. Cantine; §E.DeP. Cantine; §H.R.L. Worrall; §E. H. Worrall; +J.E. Moerdyk; °J.A. Scardefield; §M.C. Vogel; +E. Calverley; §E.T. Calverley; §A.K. Bennett (Q4)	+S. Zwemer; °A.W. Zwemer; •D. Dykstra; °M.W. Dykstra; §C.S.G. Mylrea; °B. L. Mylrea; +G.J. Pennings; °D. Firman (Van Ess); §A. C. Iverson (Bennett); +G.D. Van Peursem	+F.J. Barny; °M.R. Barny; §S.J. Thoms (Q4); °M. DeP. Thoms (Q4); °F. Lutton; §P.W. Harrison	outstation of Basrah; +G.J. Pennings (supervisor); §A.K. Bennett and §P.W. Harrison visiting physicians.		D. Firman on leave to marry J. Van Ess (Q3)

	Appointments	Basran	Bahrain	Oman	Kuwait	Amarah	Absence/Change
1 9 1 2		+J. Cantine §E.DeP. Cantine +J. Van Ess °D.F. Van Ess §A.C.I. Bennett §M.C. Vogel *§H. VanVlack *°M. Van Vlack **C. Shaw **A. B. Shaw **P. Haynes	+S. Zwemer §H.R.L. Worrall §E. H. Worrall °J.A. Scardefield *+J.E. Moerdyk °M.W. Dykstra §C.S.G. Mylrea °B. L. Mylrea +G. J. Pennings +G.D. Van Peursem *J. Spaeth (Van Peursem) §S.L. Hosmon °G. Shafheitlin (Pennings)	+F.J. Barny °M.R. Barny §S.J. Thoms (died Jan 16, 1913) °M. DeP. Thoms +J.E. Moerdyk °F. Lutton	**Full Station** +E. Calverley §E.T. Calverley §P.W. Harrison		A.W. Zwemer withdraws (Q1) D. & M.W. Dykstra on furlough (Q2), he to study theology. S. & A.W. Zwemer reassigned to Egypt - Nile Mission Press (Q3). C.S.G. & B. L. Mylrea on furlough (Q3)
1 9 1 3	Work Force: 34 *§M. Holzhauser (ST)	+J. Cantine §E.DeP. Cantine +J. Van Ess °D.F. Van Ess §A.K. Bennett §A.C.I. Bennett +G. J. Pennings *§H. VanVlack *°M. Van Vlack **C. Shaw *°A. B. Shaw **P. Haynes	§H.R.L. Worrall §E. H. Worrall +J.E. Moerdyk °J.A. Scardefield +G.D. Van Peursem §J.S. Van Peursem §S.L. Hosmon °G. Shafheitlin (Pennings)	+F.J. Barny °M.R. Barny °M. DeP. Thoms °F. Lutton	+E. Calverley §E.T. Calverley §P.W. Harrison		S.J. Thoms dies in Oman, Jan. 16. M. DeP. Thoms resigns (Q2). M.C. Vogel on furlough (Q1)
1 9 1 4 W F 3 1	Work Force: 28 ++D. Dykstra (returns as an ordained missionary)	+J. Cantine §E.DeP. Cantine +J. Van Ess °D.F. Van Ess §A.K. Bennett §A.C.I. Bennett +G. J. Pennings *§H. VanVlack *°M. Van Vlack **C. Shaw *°A. B. Shaw **P. Haynes *§M. Holzhauser Work Force: 31	+J.E. Moerdyk °J.A. Scardefield §P.W. Harrison +G.D. Van Peursem §J.S. Van Peursem °G. Shafheitlin (Pennings) *§H. VanVlack (Q3) *°M. Van Vlack (Q3)	§H.R.L. Worrall §E. H. Worrall +F.J. Barny °M.R. Barny °F. Lutton §S.L. Hosmon ++D. Dykstra °M.W. Dykstra	§C.S.G. Mylrea °B. L. Mylrea +E. Calverley §E.T. Calverley		M.C. Vogel dismissed at field request (Q2) P. Haynes resigns (Q4) M.R. Barny on furlough (Q3) G. J. Pennings on furlough (Q3) E.T. Calverley on furlough (Q3) C. & A. B. Shaw resign (Q3).

Yr.	Appointments	Basrah	Bahrain	Oman	Kuwait	Amarah	Absence/Change
1 9 1 5	°C.B. Kellien	+J. Cantine §E.DeP. Cantine +J. Van Ess °D.F. Van Ess §A.K. Bennett §A.C.I. Bennett *§M. Holzhauser	+J.E. Moerdyk °J.A. Scardefield ++D. Dykstra °M.W. Dykstra §P.W. Harrison +G.D. Van Peursem §J.S. Van Peursem *§H. VanVlack *°M. Van Vlack	§H.R.L. Worrall §E. H. Worrall +F.J. Barny °M.R. Barny °F. Lutton §S.L. Hosmon	++D. Dykstra (part time) §C.S.G. Mylrea °B. L. Mylrea °G. Shafheitlin (Pennings)		E. Calverley on furlough (Q1) J. & E.DeP. Cantine on furlough (Q2) H.R.L. & E. H. Worrall on furlough (Q2) M.R. Barny on furlough (Q2) J.E. Moerdyk on furlough (Q2) P.W. Harrison on furlough (Q2)
1 9 1 6	Work Force: 25 §R. R. Harrison	+J.E. Moerdyk +J. Van Ess °D.F. Van Ess §A.K. Bennett §A.C.I. Bennett *§H. VanVlack *°M. Van Vlack *§M. Holzhauser	°J.A. Scardefield ++D. Dykstra °M.W. Dykstra +G.D. Van Peursem §J.S. Van Peursem °C.B. Kellien	+F.J. Barny °F. Lutton §S.L. Hosmon	++D. Dykstra (part time) §C.S.G. Mylrea °B. L. Mylrea °G. Shafheitlin (Pennings)		A.C. Ivorson Bennett dies in Basrah March 29. M. Holzhauser term ends (Q2) J.A. Scardefield on furlough (Q3) F. Lutton on furlough (Q3) A.K.Bennett invalided to U.S. (Q3) G.D. & J.S. Van Peursem on furlough (Q3) M. Van Vlack on furlough (Q3) P.W. Harrison and R. Rabbe marry
1 9 1 7	Work Force: 20 +H. Bilkert °A. M. Bilkert (Harrison) §M. VanPelt Work Force 22	+J. Cantine §E.DeP. Cantine +J.E. Moerdyk	++D. Dykstra °M.W. Dykstra §P.R. Harrison §R. R. Harrison °C.B. Kellien °J.A. Scardefield (3Q) +G.D. Van Peursem §J.S. Van Peursem +H. Bilkert (Q4) °A. M. Bilkert (Harrison) §M. VanPelt (Q4)	°F. Lutton §S.L. Hosmon	§C.S.G. Mylrea °B. L. Mylrea +E. Calverley §E.T. Calverley °G. Shafheitlin (Pennings)	**Full Station** +G.J. Pennings	J. & D.F. Van Ess on furlough (2Q) H. & M. VanVlack retire. H. Van Vlack enters the military. H.R.L. & E.H. Worrall retire for health reasons A.K. Bennett retires for health reasons. F.J. Barny on furlough (Q2)

Yr.	Appointments	Basrah	Bahrain	Oman	Kuwait	Amarah	Absence/Change
1918	°M.DeP. Thoms (returns)	+J. Cantine §E.DeP. Cantine +J.E. Moerdyk	°J.A. Scardefield ++D. Dykstra °M.W. Dykstra °P.W. Harrison §R. R. Harrison °C.B. Kellien +H. Bilkert °A. M. Bilkert (Harrison) §M. VanPelt +G.J. Pennings (Q2)	°F. Lutton §S.L. Hosmon +G.D. Van Peursem §J.S. Van Peursem	§C.S.G. Mylrea °B. L. Mylrea +E. Calverley §E.T. Calverley °G. Shafheitlin (Pennings)	+G.J. Pennings	
	Work Force: 22 §L. P. Dame °E. P. Dame						
1919		+J. Cantine §E.DeP. Cantine +J.E. Moerdyk +J. Van Ess °D.F. Van Ess +G.J. Pennings °M. DeP. Thoms	++D. Dykstra °M.W. Dykstra §P.W. Harrison §R. R. Harrison +H. Bilkert °A. M. Bilkert (Harrison) §M. VanPelt §L. P. Dame (Q4) °E. P. Dame (Q4)	°F. Lutton +G.D. Van Peursem §J.S. Van Peursem °C.B. Kellien §§S.L. Hosmon (Q4)	°J.A. Scardefield §C.S.G. Mylrea °B. L. Mylrea +E. Calverley §E.T. Calverley °G. Shafheitlin (Pennings) (Q4)	(manned only by a colporteur)	G. Shafheitlin on furlough; marries G. Pennings on return. S.L. Hosmon on furlough. F.J. & M.R. Barny - special assignment in India.
	Work Force: 27						
1920		+J. Cantine §E.DeP. Cantine +F.J. Barny °M.R. Barny +J.E. Moerdyk (in Nasriyyah out-station. Abandoned Q3) +J. Van Ess °D.F. Van Ess °M. DeP. Thoms	++D. Dykstra °M.W. Dykstra +G.J. Pennings °G.S. Pennings §P.W. Harrison §R. R. Harrison +H. Bilkert °A. M. Bilkert (Harrison) §M. VanPelt §L. P. Dame °E. P. Dame	°F. Lutton +G.D. Van Peursem §J.S. Van Peursem °C.B. Kellien §§S.L. Hosmon	°J.A. Scardefield §C.S.G. Mylrea °B. L. Mylrea +E. Calverley §E.T. Calverley §M. VanPelt (Q4)	+H. Bilkert (Q2) °A. M. Bilkert (Harrison) (Q2)	D. & M.W. Dykstra on furlough (Q2). C.B. Kellien on furlough (Q4). J. & E.DeP. Cantine move to Baghdad station from to lay the foundation for the UMM (Q4).
	Work Force: 30 °Ruth Jackson °Rachel Jackson §C. Dalenberg						
1921		+F.J. Barny °M.R. Barny +J. Van Ess °D.F. Van Ess °M. DeP. Thoms	+G.J. Pennings °G.S. Pennings §P.W. Harrison §R. R. Harrison §L. P. Dame °E. P. Dame °Ruth Jackson °Rachel Jackson §C. Dalenberg	+G.D. Van Peursem §J.S. Van Peursem §§S.L. Hosmon	°J.A. Scardefield +E. Calverley §E.T. Calverley §M. VanPelt	+H. Bilkert °A. M. Bilkert (Harrison)	J.E. Moerdyk on furlough. C.S.G. & B. L. Mylrea on furlough. F. Lutton on furlough.
	Work Force: 20						

Yr.	Appointments	Basrah	Bahrain	Oman	Kuwait	Amarah	Absence/Change
1 9 2 2	+B. Hakken °E. V. Hakken °G.O. Strang §W. Leak (ST) °G. Gosselink (ST)	+F.J. Barny °M.R. Barny +J.E. Moerdyk (4Q) +J. Van Ess °D.F. Van Ess °M. DeP. Thoms °C.B. Kellien (Q2) °G. Gosselink (Q4)	+G.J. Pennings °G.S. Pennings §P.W. Harrison §R. R. Harrison §L. P. Dame °E. P. Dame °Ruth Jackson °Rachel Jackson §C. Dalenberg +B. Hakken (Q4) °E. V. Hakken (Q4)	+G.D. Van Peursem §J.S. Van Peursem §S.L. Hosmon °F. Lutton (Q2)	+E. Calverley §E.T. Calverley §C.S.G. Mylrea (Q4) °B. L. Mylrea (Q4) §M. VanPelt §W. Leak (Q1) °G.O. Strang (Q2)	+H. Bilkert °A. M. Bilkert (Harrison) ++D. Dykstra (Q2) °M.W. Dykstra (Q2)	J. & E.DeP. Cantine on furlough (Q2) H. & A. M. Bilkert temporarily assigned to UMM (Q2) §E.T. Calverley on furlough (Q2) P.W. & R. R. Harrison on furlough (Q2) M.DeP. Thoms on furlough (Q2) E. & E.T. Calverley on furlough. G.D. & J.S. Van Peursem on furlough (Q4)
	Work Force: 34						
1 9 2 3	§W.J. Moerdyk §C. L. Moerdyk	+F.J. Barny °M.R. Barny +J.E. Moerdyk +J. Van Ess °D.F. Van Ess °C.B. Kellien °G. Gosselink °Ruth Jackson (Q4) °Rachel Jackson (Q4)	+G.J. Pennings °G.S. Pennings §L. P. Dame °E. P. Dame °Ruth Jackson (LS till 4Q) °Rachel Jackson (LS till Q4) §C. Dalenberg (LS till Q4) +B. Hakken (LS) °E. V. Hakken (LS) §W.J. Moerdyk (LS) §C.L. Moerdyk (LS)	°F. Lutton §S.L. Hosmon	+J.E. Moerdyk °J.A. Scardefield (3Q) §C.S.G. Mylrea °B. L. Mylrea +E. Calverley (Q4) §E.T. Calverley (4Q) §M. VanPelt §W. Leak (ST) °G.O. Strang (LS till Q4)	++D. Dykstra °M.W. Dykstra	W. Leak term ends H.R.L. Worrall joins a Lutheran mission in West Africa (Liberia). F.J. & M.R. Barny return to U.S. for health reasons (Q2). H. & A. M. Bilkert on furlough (Q2). M. VanPelt on furlough (Q2)
	Work Force: 31						
1 9 2 4		+F.J. Barny °M.R. Barny +J.E. Moerdyk +J. Van Ess °D.F. Van Ess °C.B. Kellien +H. Bilkert (Q3) °A. M. Bilkert (Harrison) (Q3) °G. Gosselink °Ruth Jackson °Rachel Jackson	§L. P. Dame °E. P. Dame §C. Dalenberg +B. Hakken (LS) °E. V. Hakken (LS) §W.J. Moerdyk (LS) §C. L. Moerdyk (LS)	°F. Lutton §S.L. Hosmon	°J.A. Scardefield §C.S.G. Mylrea °B. L. Mylrea +E. Calverley §E.T. Calverley §P.W. Harrison §R. R. Harrison °G.O. Strang §M. VanPelt (Q3)	++D. Dykstra °M.W. Dykstra	G.J. & G.S. Pennings on furlough (Q1). F.J. & M.R. Barny on furlough (Q2).
	Work Force: 31						

Year							
1925	°M.DeP. Thoms (returns with UMM) Work Force: 37	+J.E. Moerdyk °J. Van Ess °D.F. Van Ess +C.B. Kellien +H. Bilkert °A. M. Bilkert (Harrison) °G. Gosselink °Ruth Jackson °Rachel Jackson	+F.J. Barny °M.R. Barny +G.J. Pennings (3Q) °G.S. Pennings (3Q) §P.W. Harrison (4Q) §R. R. Harrison (4Q) §L. P. Dame °E. P. Dame §C. Dalenberg +B. Hakken °E. V. Hakken	°F. Lutton +G.D. Van Peursem §J.S. Van Peursem §S.L. Hosmon	°J.A. Scardefield §C.S.G. Mylrea °B. L. Mylrea +E. Calverley §E.T. Calverley §P.W. Harrison §R. R. Harrison §M. VanPelt °G.O. Strang	•+D. Dykstra °M.W. Dykstra §W.J. Moerdyk §C. L. Moerdyk	J. Scardefield leaves the field for health reasons (3Q). G. Strang resigns to establish an independent mission in Iraq (Hillah) in cooperation with the UMM. G. Gosselink term ends J. & D.F. Van Ess on furlough (2Q). S.L. Hosmon on furlough (2Q). F.J. & M.R. Barny transfer to UMM (4Q).
1926	+G. DeJong °E. K. DeJong °S. DeYoung °T. Essabaggers (ST) §W.H. Storm Work Force: 29	+J.E. Moerdyk +J. Van Ess (3Q) °D.F. Van Ess (3Q) °C.B. Kellien +H. Bilkert °A. M. Bilkert (Harrison) °Ruth Jackson °T. Essabaggers (3Q)	+G.J. Pennings °G.S. Pennings §P.W. Harrison §R. R. Harrison §C. Dalenberg +B. Hakken °E. V. Hakken	°F. Lutton +G.D. Van Peursem §J.S. Van Peursem §S.L. Hosmon (3Q)	§C.S.G. Mylrea °B. L. Mylrea +E. Calverley §E.T. Calverley §M. VanPelt	•+D. Dykstra °M.W. Dykstra §W.J. Moerdyk §C. L. Moerdyk	L. P. & E. P. Dame on furlough (1Q). J. Scardefield retires for health reasons.
1927	°V.F. Storm §E.I. Barny (LS with UMM) §M.N. Tiffany Work Force: 31	+J. Van Ess °D.F. Van Ess °C.B. Kellien +H. Bilkert °A. M. Bilkert (Harrison) °T. Essebaggers	+G.J. Pennings °G.S. Pennings §P.W. Harrison §R. R. Harrison §L. P. Dame (4Q) °E. P. Dame (4Q) +B. Hakken °E. V. Hakken	°F. Lutton +G.D. Van Peursem §J.S. Van Peursem §S.L. Hosmon	§C.S.G. Mylrea °B. L. Mylrea +E. Calverley §E.T. Calverley §M. VanPelt +G. DeJong (LS) (2Q) °E. K. DeJong (LS) (2Q) °S. DeYoung (LS) (2Q) §W.H. Storm (LS) (4Q) °V.F. Storm (LS) (4Q)	+J.E. Moerdyk §W.J. Moerdyk §C. L. Moerdyk	J. & E.DeP. Cantine retire Jan. 1. E.DeP. Cantine dies Aug. 30. D. & M.W. Dykstra on furlough (2Q). Ruth & Rachel Jackson on furlough (1Q). C. Dalenberg on furlough (1Q).

Yr.	Appointments	Basrah	Bahrain	Oman	Kuwait	Amarah	Absence/Change
1 9 2 8	+J. Cantine (returns with UMM) +J.S. & Mrs. Badeau (UMM) Work Force: 38	+J.E. Moerdyk (3Q) +J. Van Ess °D.F. Van Ess °C.B. Kellien +H. Bilkert °A. M. Bilkert (Harrison) °Ruth Jackson (3Q) °Rachel Jackson (3Q) °T. Essebaggers	+G.J. Pennings °G.S. Pennings §L. P. Dame °E. P. Dame +B. Hakken °E. V. Hakken §C. Dalenberg (3Q)	°F. Lutton §P.W. Harrison §R. R. Harrison +G.D. Van Peursem §J.S. Van Peursem §S.L. Hosmon	§C.S.G. Mylrea °B.L. Mylrea +E. Calverley §E. T. Calverley §M. VanPelt +G. DeJong (LS) °E. K. DeJong (LS) °S. DeYoung (LS) §W.H. Storm (LS) °V.F. Storm (LS) §M.N. Tiffany (LS)	+J.E. Moerdyk ++D. Dykstra (3Q) °M.W. Dykstra (3Q) §W.J. Moerdyk §C. L. Moerdyk	C.S.G. & B. L. Mylrea on furlough (3Q). C.B. Kellien on furlough (3Q). B. & E. V. Hakken on furlough (3Q)
1 9 2 9	+G. Gosselink (returns) °C.S. Gosselink °R. DeYoung (ST) Work Force: 45	+J. Van Ess °D.F. Van Ess ++D. Dykstra °M.W. Dykstra °C.B. Kellien (4Q) °A. M. Bilkert (Harrison) °Rachel Jackson °S. DeYoung °T. Essebaggers §C. Dalenberg (4Q) +G. Gosselink (LS) (4Q) °C.S. Gosselink (LS) (4Q) °R. DeYoung (3Q)	+G.J. Pennings °G.S. Pennings §L. P. Dame °E. P. Dame §C. Dalenberg +B. Hakken (3Q) °E. V. Hakken (3Q) §W.H. Storm (1Q) °V.F. Storm (1Q) §E.I. Barny (LS) (1Q) §M.N. Tiffany (LS - passed 4Q) +G. Gosselink (LS) (3Q) °C.S. Gosselink (LS) (3Q)	°F. Lutton §P.W. Harrison §R. R. Harrison +G.D. Van Peursem §J.S. Van Peursem §S.L. Hosmon	§C.S.G. Mylrea (3Q) °B.L. Mylrea (3Q) +E. Calverley §E. T. Calverley +G. DeJong °E. K. DeJong §M. VanPelt §E.I. Barny (4Q)	+J.E. Moerdyk +E. Calverley (3Q) °Ruth Jackson §W.J. Moerdyk §C. L. Moerdyk §W.H. Storm (4Q) °V.F. Storm (4Q)	H. Bilkert, shot; dies Jan. 21. J.E. Moerdyk on furlough (2Q). T. Essebaggers term ends (3Q) J. Cantine retires for health reasons in July. A. M. Bilkert (Harrison) withdraws (3Q) E.T. Calverley on Furlough (3Q). W.J. & C. L. Moerdyk on furlough (3Q). S.M. & A.W. Zwemer leave Cairo in Dec.

1930	§W.W. Thoms °§E.S. Thoms °J.C. Rylaarsdam (ST)	+J. Van Ess °D.F. Van Ess ++D. Dykstra °M.W. Dykstra °C.B. Kellien °Rachel Jackson §C. Dalenberg °S. DeYoung +G. Gosselink (LS) °C.S. Gosselink (LS) °R. DeYoung	+G.J. Pennings °G.S. Pennings §L. P. Dame °E. P. Dame °E. V. Hakken §M.N. Tiffany	°F. Lutton §P.W. Harrison §R. R. Harrison +G.D. Van Peursem §J.S. Van Peursem §S.L. Hosmon ++D. Dykstra (4Q) °M.W. Dykstra (4Q) °W.H. Storm (4Q) °V.F. Storm (4Q)	§C.S.G. Mylrea °B.L. Mylrea §M. VanPelt +G. DeJong °E. K. DeJong §E.I. Barny	+J.E. Moerdyk (3Q) +E. Calverley °Ruth Jackson §W.J. Moerdyk (3Q) §C. L. Moerdyk (3Q) §W.H. Storm °V.F. Storm
					+S.M. Zwemer becomes a professor at Princeton Theological Seminary. C.S.G. & B.L. Mylrea on sick leave (2Q) E. Calverley on furlough (2Q) P.W. & R. R. Harrison leave on furlough (2Q) R.R. Harrison dies at sea, an apparent suicide, May 4. H.R.L. Worrall dies June 8. F. Lutton on furlough (3Q) Ruth Jackson on furlough (3Q) C. Dalenberg on furlough (3Q) G.D. & J.S. Van Peursem on furlough (4Q) S. DeYoung marries Aug. 28 & resigns. R. DeYoung dies in Basrah (4Q)		
	Work Force: 39					
1931		+J. Van Ess °D.F. Van Ess °C.B. Kellien °Rachel Jackson °S. DeYoung +G. Gosselink (LS) °C.S. Gosselink (LS) °J.C. Rylaarsdam (3Q)	+G.J. Pennings °G.S. Pennings §L. P. Dame °E. P. Dame +B. Hakken °E. V. Hakken §M.N. Tiffany §W.W. Thoms (LS) °§E.S. Thoms (LS)	§S.L. Hosmon ++D. Dykstra (4Q) °M.W. Dykstra (4Q) §W.H. Storm °V.F. Storm	§C.S.G. Mylrea °B.L. Mylrea §M. VanPelt +G. DeJong °E. K. DeJong §E.I. Barny	+J.E. Moerdyk °F. Lutton §W.J. Moerdyk §C. L. Moerdyk §C. Dalenberg
					M. VanPelt on furlough (3Q) E. & E. T. Calverley resign. V.F. Storm dies after childbirth in Oman. P. Harrison and A.M.Bilkert marry.	
	Work Force: 33					

Yr.	Appointments	Basrah	Bahrain	Oman	Kuwait	Amarah	Absence/Change
1932	°A.M.Bilkert Harrison returns. Work Force: 31	+J. Van Ess °D.F. Van Ess °C.B. Kellien °Ruth Jackson °Rachel Jackson §W.W. Thoms (LS) °§E.S. Thoms (LS) °J.C. Rylaarsdam	§L. P. Dame °E. P. Dame +B. Hakken °E. V. Hakken §M.N. Tiffany	++D. Dykstra °M.W. Dykstra §P.W. Harrison °A.M.B. Harrison §W.H. Storm	+F.J. Barny °M.R. Barny §C.S.G. Mylrea °B.L. Mylrea §M. VanPelt §E.I. Barny +G. Gosselink °C.S. Gosselink	+J.E. Moerdyk °F. Lutton §C. Dalenberg §W.J. Moerdyk §C. L. Moerdyk	G.J. & G.S. Pennings on furlough. G. & E. K. DeJong on furlough
1933	Work Force: 31	+J. Van Ess °D.F. Van Ess °C.B. Kellien °Ruth Jackson °Rachel Jackson +G. Gosselink °C.S. Gosselink °J.C. Rylaarsdam	+G.D. Van Peursem §J.S. Van Peursem §L. P. Dame °E. P. Dame +B. Hakken °E. V. Hakken §W.W. Thoms	++D. Dykstra °M.W. Dykstra §P.W. Harrison °A.M.B. Harrison §S.L. Hosmon	+F.J. Barny °M.R. Barny §C.S.G. Mylrea °B.L. Mylrea §M. VanPelt	+J.E. Moerdyk °F. Lutton §C. Dalenberg §W.J. Moerdyk §C. L. Moerdyk	W.H. Storm on furlough. E.I. Barny on furlough. M.N. Tiffany marries in July and resigns.
1934	§M. Bruins (Allison) (ST) §H. Oudemool (ST) Work Force: 36	+J. Van Ess °D.F. Van Ess +G.J. Pennings (4Q) °G.S. Pennings (4Q) °C.B. Kellien °Ruth Jackson °Rachel Jackson +G. Gosselink °C.S. Gosselink °J.C. Rylaarsdam	+G.D. Van Peursem §J.S. Van Peursem §L. P. Dame °E. P. Dame +B. Hakken °E. V. Hakken §W.H. Storm (4Q) §W.W. Thoms °§E.S. Thoms §H. Oudemool (4Q)	++D. Dykstra °M.W. Dykstra §P.W. Harrison °A.M.B. Harrison §S.L. Hosmon	+F.J. Barny °M.R. Barny §C.S.G. Mylrea °B.L. Mylrea §M. Van Pelt §M. Bruins (Allison) (LS) (4Q)	+J.E. Moerdyk °F. Lutton §C. Dalenberg §W.J. Moerdyk §C. L. Moerdyk	J. & D.F. Van Ess on furlough (2Q).
1935	§J. Bast (ST) °J.W. Beerdslee III (ST)	+J. Van Ess (3Q) °D.F. Van Ess (3Q) +G.J. Pennings °G.S. Pennings °C.B. Kellien °Ruth Jackson °Rachel Jackson +G. Gosselink °C.S. Gosselink °J.C. Rylaarsdam	+G.D. Van Peursem §J.S. Van Peursem §L. P. Dame °E. P. Dame +B. Hakken °E. V. Hakken §W.H. Storm §W.W. Thoms °§E.S. Thoms §J. Bast	++D. Dykstra °M.W. Dykstra +G.J. Pennings (3Q) °G.S. Pennings (3Q) §P.W. Harrison °A.M.B. Harrison §S.L. Hosmon	+F.J. Barny °M.R. Barny §C.S.G. Mylrea °B.L. Mylrea §M. Van Pelt §M. Bruins (Allison) (LS)	+J.E. Moerdyk °F. Lutton §C. Dalenberg §W.J. Moerdyk §C. L. Moerdyk	D. & M.W. Dykstra on furlough (2Q) J.S. & Mrs. Badeau resign to Cairo. J.C. Rylaarsdam term ends (2Q) H. Oudemool term completed.

	Station 1	Station 2	Station 3	Station 4	Station 5	Events
1936 §I.P. Storm §E.I. Barny (returns) Work Force: 32	+J. Van Ess °D.F. Van Ess °G.J. Pennings °G.S. Pennings °C.B. Kellien °Ruth Jackson °J.W. Beerdslee	+G.D. Van Peursem §J.S. Van Peursem °Ruth Jackson (4Q) +B. Hakken °E. V. Hakken °W.H. Storm §I.P. Storm (4Q) §W.W. Thoms °•§E.S. Thoms §E.I. Barny (2Q) §J. Bast (2Q)	••D. Dykstra (4Q) °M.W. Dykstra (4Q) +G.J. Pennings °G.S. Pennings °P.W. Harrison §P.W. Harrison °A.M.B. Harrison §S.L. Hosmon	+F.J. Barny °M.R. Barny §C.S.G. Mylrea °B.L. Mylrea §M. Van Pelt §M. Bruins (Allison) (LS)	+J.E. Moerdyk §W.J. Moerdyk §C. L. Moerdyk	L. P. & E. P. Dame on furlough (2Q). Resign to work for ARAMCO Nov. 1. F. Lutton on furlough (2Q) then retires. Rachel Jackson on furlough (2Q) C. Dalenberg on furlough (2Q) B. & E. V. Hakken on furlough (2Q) J. Bast term ends.
1937 §L.R. Scudder II §D.B. Scudder in Jerusalem for language study. Work Force: 35	+J. Van Ess °D.F. Van Ess +G.J. Pennings °G.S. Pennings °C.B. Kellien °Rachel Jackson (2Q) +G. Gosselink °C.S. Gosselink °J.W. Beerdslee	+G.D. Van Peursem §J.S. Van Peursem °W.H. Storm §I.P. Storm §W.W. Thoms °•§E.S. Thoms °Ruth Jackson §E.I. Barny	••D. Dykstra °M.W. Dykstra °P.W. Harrison °A.M.B. Harrison §S.L. Hosmon	+F.J. Barny °M.R. Barny §C.S.G. Mylrea °B.L. Mylrea +G.J. Pennings (4Q) °G.S. Pennings (4Q) §M. Van Pelt §W.H. Storm (4Q) §W.W. Thoms (4Q) °•§E.S. Thoms (4Q) §M. Bruins Allison (LC) (Q3)	+J.E. Moerdyk §C. Dalenberg (2Q) §W.J. Moerdyk §C. L. Moerdyk	J. Bast marries Jan. 1 and resigns. A.W. Zwemer dies Jan 25. C.S.G. & B.L. Mylrea on furlough (4Q) C.B. Kellien on furlough (2Q) B. & E. V. Hakken transfer to UMM (4Q). W.I.Chamberlain dies Sept. 28. M. Bruins marries N. Allison in June; resigns; continues in local connection (LC)
1938 §M. Tull (ST) °J. Van Ess Jr. (ST) Work Force: 34	+J. Van Ess °D.F. Van Ess °Rachel Jackson +G. Gosselink °C.S. Gosselink °J.W. Beerdslee °J. Van Ess Jr. (3Q)	+G.D. Van Peursem §J.S. Van Peursem °Ruth Jackson +G. DeJong (3Q) °E. K. DeJong (3Q) §W.H. Storm §I.P. Storm §E.I. Barny	••D. Dykstra °M.W. Dykstra §P.W. Harrison °A.M.B. Harrison §S.L. Hosmon	+G.J. Pennings °G.S. Pennings §C.S.G. Mylrea (3Q) °B.L. Mylrea (3Q) §M. Van Pelt §W.W. Thoms °•§E.S. Thoms §M.B. Allison (LC)	+J.E. Moerdyk §C. Dalenberg §W.J. Moerdyk §C. L. Moerdyk §L.R. Scudder II (LS) (3Q) §D.B. Scudder (LS) (3Q)	W.J. & C.L. Moerdyk emergency medical furlough (2Q). W.W. & E.S. Thoms on furlough (2Q) F.J. & M.R. Barny on furlough (2Q) J.W. Beerdslee III term ends (2Q).

Yr.	Appointments	Basrah	Bahrain	Oman	Kuwait	Amarah	Absence/Change
1 9 3 9	§R.O. Crouse	+J. Van Ess °D.F. Van Ess °C.B. Kellien +G. Gosselink °C.S. Gosselink °J. Van Ess Jr.	°Rachel Jackson +G. DeJong °E. K. DeJong §W.H. Storm §I.P. Storm §E.I. Barny	•+D. Dykstra °M.W. Dykstra §W.W. Thoms (3Q) °•§E.S. Thoms (3Q)	§C.S.G. Mylrea °B.L. Mylrea +G.J. Pennings °G.S. Pennings §M.B. Allison (LC) §L.R. Scudder II (2Q) §D.B. Scudder (2Q) (LS)	+J.E. Moerdyk §C. Dalenberg §W.J. Moerdyk (3Q) §C. L. Moerdyk (3Q) §L.R. Scudder II (LS) §D.B. Scudder (LS)	P.W. & A.M.B. Harrison on furlough (1Q). G.D. & J.S. Van Peursem on furlough (1Q). S.L. Hosmon on furlough (2Q) - later resigns. M. Van Pelt on furlough (1Q) - later resigns. Ruth Jackson on furlough (1Q).
Work Force: 27 1 9 4 0	§M.A. Tull (ST) §G.H. Nykerk °R.W. Nykerk §R. Bakker (ST)	+J. Van Ess °D.F. Van Ess °C.B. Kellien °Rachel Jackson (3Q) +G. Gosselink °C.S. Gosselink °J. Van Ess Jr.	°Ruth Jackson (3Q) °Rachel Jackson §C. Dalenberg +G. DeJong °E. K. DeJong §W.H. Storm §I.P. Storm §E.I. Barny §R. Bakker (3Q)	•+D. Dykstra °M.W. Dykstra §W.W. Thoms °•§E.S. Thoms	§C.S.G. Mylrea °B.L. Mylrea +G.J. Pennings °G.S. Pennings §M. Van Pelt §M.B. Allison (LC) §L.R. Scudder II §D.B. Scudder §M.A. Tull §R.O. Crouse (1Q)	+J.E. Moerdyk §W.J. Moerdyk §C. L. Moerdyk	F.J. & M.R. Barny retire. J. Cantine dies July 1. M.B. Allison resigns (3Q)
Work Force: 33 1 9 4 1	°R.G. Sayres (ST)	+J. Van Ess °D.F. Van Ess °C.B. Kellien °Rachel Jackson +G. Gosselink °C.S. Gosselink °J. Van Ess Jr. °R.G. Sayres (3Q)	§P.W. Harrison (2Q) °A.M.B. Harrison (2Q) +G.D. Van Peursem (2Q) §J.S. Van Peursem (2Q) °Ruth Jackson §W.H. Storm §I.P. Storm §E.I. Barny §R. Bakker §G.H. Nykerk (LS) (2Q) °R.W. Nykerk (LS) (2Q)	•+D. Dykstra °M.W. Dykstra §W.W. Thoms °•§E.S. Thoms	§C.S.G. Mylrea °B.L. Mylrea +G.J. Pennings °G.S. Pennings +G. DeJong °E. K. DeJong §L.R. Scudder II §D.B. Scudder §M. Tull §R.O. Crouse (LS)	+J.E. Moerdyk §C. Dalenberg §W.J. Moerdyk §C. L. Moerdyk	J.E. Moerdyk dies of stroke in Amarah July 24. J. & D.F. Van Ess on furlough (3Q). G.J. & G.S. Pennings on furlough (2Q). W.H. & I.P. Storm on furlough (2Q). C.S.G. & B.L. Mylrea retire (4Q). M. Van Pelt resigns. J. Van Ess Jr. term

Year	Appointments	Kuwait	Basrah	Muscat	Bahrain	Amarah	Absence/Change
1942	Work Force: 30	°C.B. Kellien °Rachel Jackson +G. Gosselink °C.S. Gosselink °R.G. Sayres	§P.W. Harrison °A.M.B. Harrison +G.D. Van Peursem §J.S. Van Peursem °Ruth Jackson §W.H. Storm (3Q) §E.I. Barny §R. Bakker §G.H. Nykerk (LS) °R.W. Nykerk (LS)	°++D. Dykstra °M.W. Dykstra §W.W. Thoms °•§E.S. Thoms	+G. DeJong °E. K. DeJong §L.R. Scudder II §D.B. Scudder §M. Tull §R.O. Crouse (LS) §G.H. Nykerk (LS) (3Q) °R.W. Nykerk (LS) (3Q)	§C. Dalenberg §W.J. Moerdyk §C. L. Moerdyk	Bessie Mylrea dies in India April 16. M.B. Allison on furlough (2Q) then resigns. R. Bakker term ends. M. Tull term ends (3Q). R.G. Sayres term ends (3Q). G.O. Strang dies in Jerusalem Sept 24. M.B. Allison and N. Allison separate.
1943	+E.M. Luidens °R.S. Luidens °H.J. Almond (ST) °F.B. Bogard (UMM) - transfer from Japan. §E.I. Barny marries Ames (LC) (3Q) §R.B. Davies (LC) Work Force: 30	+J. Van Ess (3Q) °D.F. Van Ess (3Q) °C.B. Kellien °Rachel Jackson °G. Gosselink °C.S. Gosselink °H.J. Almond (3Q)	§P.W. Harrison °A.M.B. Harrison +G.D. Van Peursem §J.S. Van Peursem °Ruth Jackson §W.H. Storm §E.I. Barny Ames §R.B. Davies (4Q)	°++D. Dykstra °M.W. Dykstra §W.W. Thoms °•§E.S. Thoms	+G. DeJong °E. K. DeJong §L.R. Scudder II §D.B. Scudder §M. Tull §R.O. Crouse (LS) §G.H. Nykerk (LS) (3Q) °R.W. Nykerk (LS) (3Q)	§C. Dalenberg §W.J. Moerdyk §C. L. Moerdyk	J. Van Ess Jr. dies in Basrah, Jan. 11. M.DeP. Thoms retires from the UMM in Baghdad.
1944	§C.S.G. Mylrea (returns) +J.R. Kapenga §J. H. Boersma §H. Wanrooy (ST) Work Force: 31	+J. Van Ess °D.F. Van Ess °C.B. Kellien +G. Gosselink °C.S. Gosselink °H.J. Almond +E.M. Luidens (LS) (3Q) °R.S. Luidens (LS) (3Q) +J.R. Kapenga (LS) (3Q)	§C.S.G. Mylrea (3Q) §P.W. Harrison °A.M.B. Harrison +G.D. Van Peursem §J.S. Van Peursem °Ruth Jackson §W.H. Storm §E.I. Barny Ames §R.B. Davies §H. Wanrooy (3Q)	°++D. Dykstra °M.W. Dykstra §W.W. Thoms	+G. DeJong °E. K. DeJong §R.O. Crouse §G.H. Nykerk °R.W. Nykerk	§W.J. Moerdyk §C. L. Moerdyk §J.H. Boersma (LS) (3Q)	Rachel Jackson on furlough. C. Dalenberg on furlough. L.R. & D.B. Scudder on furlough
1945	§M.B. Allison (returns) (LC) Work Force: 36	+J. Van Ess °D.F. Van Ess °Rachel Jackson (3Q) °H.J. Almond +E.M. Luidens (LS) °R.S. Luidens (LS) +J.R. Kapenga (LS)	§C.S.G. Mylrea §P.W. Harrison °A.M.B. Harrison +G.D. Van Peursem §J.S. Van Peursem °Ruth Jackson §W.H. Storm §I.P. Storm (4Q) §R.B. Davies §H. Wanrooy	°++D. Dykstra °M.W. Dykstra §W.W. Thoms °•§E.S. Thoms	+G. DeJong °E. K. DeJong §M.B. Allison (3Q, LC) §L.R. Scudder II (3Q) §D.B. Scudder (3Q) §R.O. Crouse §G.H. Nykerk °R.W. Nykerk	+G.J. Pennings (3Q) °G.S. Pennings (3Q) §W.J. Moerdyk §C. L. Moerdyk §J.H. Boersma (LS) +J.R. Kapenga (LS) (2Q)	E.I. Barny Ames leaves the field (1Q). C.B. Kellien on furlough (1Q). G. & C.S. Gosselink on furlough (1Q). R.O. Crouse on furlough (3Q)

Yr.	Appointments	Basrah	Bahrain	Oman	Kuwait	Amarah	Absence/Change
1 9 4 6	§M.M. Heusinkveld §E.C. Heusinkveld °G.J. Holler (ST) Work Force: 37	+J. Van Ess °D.F. Van Ess °Rachel Jackson +E.M. Luidens (LS) °R.S. Luidens (LS) +J.R. Kapenga (LS) °H.J. Almond °G.J. Holler (2Q)	§C.S.G. Mylrea §P.W. Harrison °A.M.B. Harrison +G.D. Van Peursem §J.S. Van Peursem °Ruth Jackson §C. Dalenberg §W.H. Storm §I.P. Storm §H. Wanrooy	++D. Dykstra °M.W. Dykstra §W.W. Thoms °§E.S. Thoms	+G. DeJong °E.K. DeJong §L.R. Scudder II §D.B. Scudder +J.R. Kapenga (3Q) §M.B. Allison (LC) °G.H. Nykerk °R.W. Nykerk §M.M.Heusinkveld (LS) §E.C. Heusinkveld (LS)	+G.J. Pennings °G.S. Pennings §W.J. Moerdyk §C. L. Moerdyk §L.R. Scudder II (2Q) §D.B. Scudder (2Q) §J.H. Boersma (LS)	G.D. & J.S. Van Peursem on furlough (2Q) G. & E.K. DeJong on furlough (3Q). F. Lutton dies Dec. 8. R.O. Crouse resigns to go get married. H.J. Almond term ends (2Q)
1 9 4 7	°H.J.Almond °B.K.Almond §J. Oltoff (Buckley) §L. Essenberg (Holler) §N. Hekhuis (ST) °M.U. Kapenga	°J. Van Ess °D.F. Van Ess °C.B. Kellien +G. Gosselink °C.S. Gosselink °H.J. Almond (LS) °B.K. Almond (LS) °G.J. Holler +E.M. Luidens °R.S. Luidens §J.W. Oltoff (Buckley) (from Oct.) (LS) §L. Essenberg (Holler) (from Oct.) (LS)	§C.S.G. Mylrea §P.W. Harrison °A.M.B. Harrison §C. Dalenberg §H. Wanrooy §N. Hekhuis °Rachel Jackson §W.H. Storm & I.P. Storm in Hassa (Q1-3) and Qatar (Q4)	++D. Dykstra °M.W. Dykstra §W.W. Thoms °§E.S. Thoms	+J.R. Kapenga °M.U.Kapenga (Q4) §M. B. Allison §J.H. Boersma (3 months) §G.H. Nykerk °R. W. Nykerk §M.M. Heusinkveld §E.C. Heusinkveld	+G.J. Pennings °G.S. Pennings §L.R. Scudder II §D.B. Scudder §J.H. Boersma	H. Wanrooy term ends. Ruth Jackson on furlough W.J. Moerdyk & C. L. Moerdyk on furlough G.H. Nykerk & R.W. Nykerk on furlough (Q3) G.D. Van Peursem & J.S. Van Peursem retire C.S.G. Mylrea retires again.
1 9 4 8	°E. Post (3egg) §H.M. Wood (ST) Work Force: 39	+J. Van Ess °D.F. Van Ess °C.B. Kellien °Rachel Jackson (Q3) +G. Gosselink °C.S. Gosselink °H.J. Almond (LS) °B.K. Almond (LS) °G.J. Holler §J.W.Oltoff (till April) (LS) §L. Essenberg (till April)	§P.W. Harrison °A.M.B. Harrison §C. Dalenberg §W.H. Storm §I.P. Storm §N. Hekhuis §H. Wood °Ruth Jackson (Q3) +E.M. Luidens (Q1) °R.S. Luidens (Q1)	++D. Dykstra °M.W. Dykstra §W.W. Thoms °§E.S. Thoms +J.R. Kapenga °M.U. Kapenga §M.M. Heusinkveld (Q3) §E.C. Heusinkveld (Q3)	+G. DeJong °E.K. DeJong §M.B. Allison (LC) §J.W. Oltoff (Q2) §L. Essenberg (Q2+3) §G.H. Nykerk °R.W. Nykerk §M.M. Heusinkveld §E.C. Heusinkveld	+G.J. Pennings °G.S. Pennings §L.R. Scudder II §D.B. Scudder §L. Essenberg (Q4 - to care for G.S. Pennings) §J.H. Boersma	P.W. Harrison & A.M.B. Harrison on furlough then retire. W.W. Thoms & E.S. Thoms on furlough (Q2)

							Absence Change
1949	+H. Staal °H.V. Staal §C.A. Voss °R.G. Young °J. De Vries (ST) °E. Post §A VanKempen Work Force: 44	+J. Van Ess °D.F. Van Ess °C.B. Kellien °Rachel Jackson +G. Gosselink °C.S. Gosselink °H.J. Almond (LS) °B.K. Almond (LS) °G.J. Holler °J. De Vries (Q2)	§C. Dalenberg °Ruth Jackson §G.H. Nykerk (Q3) °R.W. Nykerk (Q3) +E.M. Luidens °R.S. Luidens +H. Staal (LS) °H.V. Staal (LS) §N. Hekhuis §J.H. Boersma (3 months of which stayed in Qatar for 1 month)	++D. Dykstra °M.W. Dykstra §W.W. Thoms (Q3) °•§E.S. Thoms (Q3) +J.R. Kapenga °M.U. Kapenga §M.B. Allison (LC) (Q3)	+G. DeJong °E. K. DeJong §L.R. Scudder II (Q3) °§D.B. Scudder (Q3) §M.B. Allison (LC) (thru Q2) §G.H. Nykerk °R.W. Nykerk §L. Essenberg §M.M. Heusinkveld §E.C. Heusinkveld §J.W. Oltoff (till June) §C.A. Voss (LS) °R.G. Young (LS) °E. Post (LS)	+G.J. Pennings °G.S. Pennings §L.R. Scudder II §D.B. Scudder §M.M. Heusinkveld (Q3) §E.C. Heusinkveld (Q3) §L. Essenberg (Q3) §J.H. Boersma	J. Van Ess dies in Basrah April 26. W. Moerdyk resigns for health reasons. C.L. Moerdyk resigns. J. Oltoff marries and resigns. G.J. Holler short term ends (Q2) J.R. Kapenga & M.U. Kapenga on furlough (Q3) P.W. Harrison & A.M.B. Harrison on furlough. W.H. Storm & I.P. Storm on furlough
1950	°A. Van Kempen •§W.G. Dekker °A.M. Dekker +D.R. MacNeill °E.M. MacNeill *+A.B. Cook **Mrs. Cook +G.J. Holler (returns) §D.T. Bosch °E.B. Bosch §M.B. Allison (reinstated as full missionary) Work Force: 46	°D.F. Van Ess °C.B. Kellien °Rachel Jackson +G. Gosselink °C.S. Gosselink °H.J. Almond °B.K. Almond °J. De Vries	§C. Dalenberg °Ruth Jackson §W.H. Storm (Q3) §I.P. Storm (Q3) §G.H. Nykerk (Q3) °R.W. Nykerk (Q3) +E.M. Luidens °R.S. Luidens +H. Staal (LS) °H.V. Staal (LS) °H.J. Almond (Q2) °B.K. Almond (Q2) §N. Hekhuis §H.M. Wood °Ruth Jackson *+A.B. Cook (Q4) **Mrs. Cook (Q4)	++D. Dykstra °M.W. Dykstra §W.W. Thoms °•§E.S. Thoms +J.R. Kapenga °M.U. Kapenga §M.B. Allison	+G. DeJong °E. K. DeJong §L.R. Scudder II §D.B. Scudder §M.B. Allison (Q2) §C.A. Voss (LS) °R.G. Young (LS) °E. Post (LS) °A. Van Kempen (LS) (Q4)	+G.J. Pennings °G.S. Pennings §M.M. Heusinkveld §E.C. Heusinkveld §L. Essenberg (till May) §J.H. Boersma §H.M. Wood (Q2) +G.J. Holler (Q4) §L. Essenberg Holler (Q4)	N. Hekhuis term ends. L. Essenberg marries G.J. Holler in May. M.B. Allison on furlough (Q2) J.H. Boersma on furlough (Q2) E.M. & R.S. Luidens on furlough (Q2) J.R. & M.U. Kapenga on furlough (Q1)

Yr.	Appointments	Basrah	Bahrain	Oman	Kuwait	Amarah	Absence/Change
1 9 5 1	§B.J. Voss °M.J. Voss	°D.F. Van Ess °C.B. Kellien °Rachel Jackson +G. Gosselink °C.S. Gosselink °J. De Vries	§C. Dalenberg °Ruth Jackson §W.H. Storm §I.P. Storm §G.H. Nykerk °R.W. Nykerk +E.M. Luidens °R.S. Luidens +G.J Holler (Q4) §L.E. Holler (Q4) +H. Staal (LS) °H.V. Staal (LS) °H.J. Almond °B.K.Almond °E. Post (Q3) •§W.G. Dekker (Q3) (LS) °A.M. Dekker (Q3) (LS) +D.R. MacNeill (Q3) (LS) °E.M. MacNeill (Q3) (LS) °R.G. Young (LS) (Q4) §H.M. Wood *+A.B. Cook *°Mrs. Cook	•+D. Dykstra °M.W. Dykstra §W.W. Thoms °•§E.S. Thoms §J.H. Boersma +J.R. Kapenga °M.U. Kapenga	+G. DeJong °E. K. DeJong §L.R. Scudder II §D.B. Scudder §M.B. Allison §B.J. Voss (LS) °M.J. Voss (LS) §C.A. Voss (LS) °R.G. Young (LS) °E. Post (LS) °A. Van Kempen (LS)	+°G.J. Pennings °G.S. Pennings §M.M. Heusinkveld §E.C. Heusinkveld +G.J. Holler §L.E. Holler §D.T. Bosch (Q3) °E.B. Bosch (Q3) §C.A. Voss (Q3) +E.M. Luidens (Q3) °R.S. Luidens (Q3) §H.M. Wood	G.J. Pennings & G.S. Pennings retire (Q2) F. Barny dies. H. Wood term ends. Rev. & Mrs. A.B. Cook's special assignment with ARAMCO fellowships ends (Q2). C. Dalenberg on furlough (Q1) G. & C.S. Gosselink on furlough (Q1) G. DeJong & E. K. DeJong on furlough (Q2) L.R. & D.B. Scudder on furlough (Q2) G.H. & R.W. Nykerk on health leave (Q3) Rachel Jackson on furlough (Q4) H.J. & B.K. Almond on health leave (Q4)
	Work Force: 54						

Year							Events
1 9 5 2	§°J. Veldman §°A.R. De Young §M. Walvoord °M. Holmes +J.W. Dunham °J.D. Dunham §M. Schuppe (Pennings) (ST) °R.J. Block (ST) §P.W. & A.M. B. Harrison return for special term.	°D.F. Van Ess °C.B. Kellien °Rachel Jackson (Q2) +G. Gosselink °C.S. Gosselink °J. De Vries °R.J. Block (Q4)	§P.W. Harrison (Q2) °A.M.B. Harrison (Q2) §C. Dalenberg (Q2) °Ruth Jackson §W.H. Storm §I.P. Storm §G.H. Nykerk °R.W. Nykerk +G.J. Holler §L.E. Holler +H. Staal °H.V. Staal °R.G. Young °E. Post (Q3) •§W.G. Dekker (LS) °A.M. Dekker (LS) +D.R. MacNeill (LS) °E.M. MacNeill (LS) §M. Walvoord (LS) §M. Schuppe (Pennings) §°A.R. De Young	§W.W. Thoms °§E.S. Thoms §J.H. Boersma +J.R. Kapenga °M.U. Kapenga	+G. DeJong °E. K. DeJong §L.R. Scudder II (Q3) §D.B. Scudder (Q3) §M.B. Allison §B.J. Voss (LS) °M.J. Voss (LS) °A. Van Kempen (LS) °M. Holmes (LS)	§M.M. Heusinkveld §E.C. Heusinkveld §D.T. Bosch °E.B. Bosch §C.A. Voss +E.M. Luidens °R.S. Luidens §J. Veldman (LS) §B.J. Voss (LS) (Q4) °M.J. Voss (LS) (Q4)	S. Zwemer dies. J. Scardefield dies. C.S.G. Mylrea dies, Jan. 3. A. Van Kempen marries and resigns. J. De Vries term ends (Q2) H.J. & B.K. Almond resign (Q3). M. DeP. Thoms dies. M.M. & E.C. Heusinkveld on furlough (Q2). B.J. & M.J. Voss on furlough (Q2). D. & M.W. Dykstra on furlough (Q1).
	Work Force: 50						
1 9 5 3	°L.C. Hoogeveen §B.L. Draper §J.B. Draper	°D.F. Van Ess °C.B. Kellien +G.J. Holler §L.E. Holler +D.R. MacNeill (Q2) °E.M. MacNeill (Q2) °R.J. Block	§P.W. Harrison °A.M.B. Harrison §C. Dalenberg °Ruth Jackson §W.H. Storm §I.P. Storm +H. Staal °H.V. Staal °R.G. Young °E. Post §B.J. Voss (Q2) °M.J. Voss (Q2) •§W.G. Dekker (LS) °A.M. Dekker (LS) +D.R. MacNeill (LS) °E.M. MacNeill (LS) §M. Walvoord (LS) §M. Schuppe (Pennings) (LS) §°A.R. De Young	§W.W. Thoms °§E.S. Thoms §J.H. Boersma +J.R. Kapenga °M.U. Kapenga °R.G. Young (Q4)	+G. DeJong °E. K. DeJong §L.R. Scudder II §D.B. Scudder §M.B. Allison °M. Holmes (LS)	§M.M. Heusinkveld (Q3) §E.C. Heusinkveld (Q3) §D.T. Bosch °E.B. Bosch §C.A. Voss +E.M. Luidens °R.S. Luidens §B.J. Voss °M.J. Voss §J. Veldman (LS)	L. Dame dies, July 2. G. & C.S. Gosselink on furlough (Q1)
	Work Force: 45						

Yr.	Appointments	Basrah	Bahrain	Oman	Kuwait	Amarah	Absence/Change
1 9 5 4	§A. Schmalzriedt +J.W. Dunham (LS - Cairo) °J.D. Dunham (LS - Cairo) ¢D. M. Begg (LC) §G.H. Nykerk & °R.W. Nykerk return (Q4)	°D.F. Van Ess °C.B. Kellien °Rachel Jackson +G. Gosselink (Q3) °C.S. Gosselink (Q3) +G.J. Holler §L.E. Holler +D.R. MacNeill °E.M. MacNeill °R.J. Block	§P.W. Harrison °A.M.B. Harrison §C. Dalenberg °Ruth Jackson §W.H. Storm §I.P. Storm +H. Staal °H.V. Staal •§W.G. Dekker °A.M. Dekker §D.T. Bosch (Q2) °E.B. Bosch (Q2) §B.J. Voss °M.J. Voss §M. Walvoord (LS) §M. Schuppe (Pennings) (LS) §°A.R. De Young ¢D. M. Begg (LC) (Q4) •E.Post Begg +J.W. Dunham (LS) (Q3) °J.D. Dunham (LS) (Q3) §°A.R. De Young °L.C. Hoogeveen (Q3) (LS)	§W.W. Thoms °§E.S. Thoms §J.H. Boersma +J.R. Kapenga °M.U. Kapenga §D.T. Bosch (Q4) °E.B. Bosch (Q4) °R.G. Young §M. Walvoord (Q4)	+G. DeJong °E. K. DeJong +D.R. MacNeill (Q2) °E.M. MacNeill (Q2) §L.R. Scudder II §D.B. Scudder §M.B. Allison °M. Holmes	§M.M. Heusinkveld §E.C. Heusinkveld §G.H. Nykerk (Q4) °R.W. Nykerk (Q4) §D.T. Bosch °E.B. Bosch §C.A. Voss +E.M. Luidens °R.S. Luidens §J. Veldman	G. S. Pennings dies. E. Post marries D. Begg just before Christmas. R. G. Young on 'early furlough' (Q3). P.W. & A.M.B. Harrison retire again (Q3). C.B. Kellien retires (Q2). G.E. & E. K. DeJong on furlough (Q2)
	Work Force:						

1 9 5 5						
§M. Tanis (Franken) (ST) °D.A. Maxam (ST) *+A.B. Cook and wife return to ARAMCO fellowships.	°Rachel Jackson +G. Gosselink °C.S. Gosselink +G.J. Holler §L.E. Holler °R.J. Block °D.A. Maxam (Q3) °L.C. Hoogeveen (Q4)	§C. Dalenberg °Ruth Jackson §W.H. Storm +I.P. Storm +G. DeJong (Q1) °E. K. DeJong (Q1) •§W.G. Dekker °A.M. Dekker §B.J. Voss °M.J. Voss §°A.R. De Young ¢D. Begg (LC) (Q4) •E.Post Begg +J.W. Dunham (LS) °J.D. Dunham (LS) °L.C. Hoogeveen (Q3) §M. Tanis (Franken) §A. Schmalzriedt (Lee)	§W.W. Thoms °•§E.S. Thoms §J.H. Boersma +J.R. Kapenga °M.U. Kapenga §J. Veldman (Q3) §D.T. Bosch °E.B. Bosch §M. Walvoord	+D.R. MacNeill °E.M. MacNeill +G. DeJong (Q4) °E. K. DeJong (Q4) §L.R. Scudder II §D.B. Scudder §M.B. Allison °M. Holmes	§M.M. Heusinkveld §E.C. Heusinkveld §G.H. Nykerk °R.W. Nykerk §C.A. Voss +E.M. Luidens °R.S. Luidens §J. Veldman §°A.R. De Young (Q3) §A. Schmalzriedt (Q4)	D.F. Van Ess retires (Q1). M.W. Dykstra dies. R.G. Young resigns. M. Walvoord marries and resigns (Q2) M. Schuppe (Pennings) term ends. R.J. Block term ends (Q2) D.F. Van Ess retires (Q2) H. & H.V. Staal on furlough (Q2) C.A. Voss on furlough (Q1) W.W. & E.S. Thoms on furlough (Q2) D.R. & E.M. MacNeill on furlough (Q4) G.J & L.E. Holler on furlough (Q4) W.H. & I.P. Storm on furlough (Q4) C. Dalenberg on furlough (Q4) Rachel Jackson on furlough (Q4) J. Veldman on furlough (Q4)
Work Force:						

Yr.	Appointments	Basrah	Bahrain	Oman	Kuwait	Amarah	Absence/Change
1956	°N.A. Nienhuis §A.G. Pennings §M.S. Pennings (returns) §B.L. Draper §J.B. Draper §T. Boomgaarden (ST) ¢R.P. Johnson (special appointment as Field Rep.)	+G. Gosselink °C.S. Gosselink +G.J. Holler §L.E. Holler +E.M. Luidens °R.S. Luidens °D.A. Maxam °L.C. Hoogeveen °N.A. Nienhuis (LS) §B.L. Draper (LS) §J.B. Draper (LS)	°Ruth Jackson §W.H. Storm (Q4) §I.P. Storm (Q4) •§W.G. Dekker °A.M. Dekker §B.J. Voss °M.J. Voss §J. Veldman (Q4) §°A.R. De Young ¢D. Begg (LC) •E.P. Begg +J.W. Dunham °J.D. Dunham §M. Tanis (Franken) °M. Holmes (LS) (Q4) §B.L. Draper (LS) (Q4) §J.B. Draper (LS) (Q4)	§W.W. Thoms °•§E.S. Thoms §J.H. Boersma +J.R. Kapenga °M.U. Kapenga §D.T. Bosch °E.B. Bosch §C. Dalenberg (Q3) +G. DeJong (Q4) °E. K. DeJong (Q4) §A. Schmalzriedt (Lee) (Q3) §M.M. Heusinkveld (Q4) §E.C. Heusinkveld (Q4) °Rachel Jackson (Q3)	+G.E. DeJong °E.K. DeJong +D.R. MacNeill (Q4) °E.M. MacNeill (Q4) §L.R. Scudder II §D.B. Scudder §M.B. Allison §T. Boomgaarden §J. Veldman °M. Holmes §A.G. Pennings (LS) (Q4) §M.S. Pennings (LS) (Q4)	§M.M. Heusinkveld §E.C. Heusinkveld §G.H. Nykerk °R.W. Nykerk +H. Staal °H.V. Staal §C.A. Voss §A. Schmalzriedt (Q4)	D. Dykstra dies. M.B. Allison on furlough (Q4) E.M. & R.S. Luidens on furlough (Q4) J.R. & M.U. Kapenga on furlough (Q4) J.H. Boersma (Q4) B.J. & M.J. Voss on furlough (Q4) W.G. & A.M. Dekker on furlough (Q4) D.T. & E.B. Bosch on furlough (Q4)
1957	•LaD.M. Teumer +R.E. Weiss (to UMI) °A.B. Weiss (to UMI)		§M. Tanis ¢D. Begg •E.P. Begg °Ruth Jackson +J.W. Dunham °J.D. Dunham §°A.R. De Young	§W.W. Thoms °•§E.S. Thoms §J.H. Boersma	§L.R. Scudder II §D.B. Scudder §M.B. Allison +J.R. Kapenga °M.U. Kapenga §J. Veldman		B.J. & M.J. Voss resign. E.M. & R.S. Luidens with NECC radio program in Beirut.
1958	§K.M. Diem °M.L. Nienhuis (to UMI)	+G. Gosselink °C.S. Gosselink +G.J. Holler §L.E. Holler °L.C. Hoogeveen	°Ruth Jackson §W.H. Storm •§W.G. Dekker °A.M. Dekker §M.M. Heusinkveld §E.C. Heusinkveld +J.R. Kapenga °M.U. Kapenga §M. Tanis ¢D. Begg •E.P. Begg +J.W. Dunham °J.D. Dunham	§W.W. Thoms °•§E.S. Thoms °Rachel Jackson §J.H. Boersma +G.E. DeJong °E.K. DeJong	§M.B. Allison §J. Veldman §C. Dalenberg §D.T. Bosch °E.B. Bosch §A.G. Pennings (LS) §M.S. Pennings (LS) §T. Boomgaarden	§G.H. Nykerk °R.W. Nykerk +H. Staal °H.V. Staal §C.A. Voss §A. Schmalzriedt §B.L. Draper (LS) §J.B. Draper (LS) •LaD.M. Teumer	M. Tannis (Franken) term ends. L.R. & D.B. Scudder on furlough. E.M. & R.S. Luidens in the US with RAVEMCO. A.R. De Young on furlough. M. Holmes on furlough.

Year							
1959	+R.J. Block •L. Block	+G. Gosselink °C.S. Gosselink +H. Staal °H.V. Staal	°Ruth Jackson §C. Dalenberg §W.H. Storm §I.P. Storm •§W.G. Dekker °A.M. Dekker §M.M. Heusinkveld §E.C. Heusinkveld §G.H. Nykerk °R.W. Nykerk +G.J. Holler §L.E. Holler +J.R. Kapenga °M.U. Kapenga +J.W. Dunham °J.D. Dunham §J. Veldman °N.A. Nienhuis •LaD.M. Teumer (LS) §K.M. Diem (LS)	§W.W. Thoms °•§E.S. Thoms §J.H. Boersma §°A.R. De Young °Rachel Jackson +G.E. DeJong °E.K. DeJong §A. Schmalzriedt §B.L. Draper (LS) §J.B. Draper (LS)	§D.T. Bosch °E.B. Bosch +D.R. MacNeill °E.M. MacNeill §J. Veldman §M.B. Allison °L.C. Hoogeveen §A.G. Pennings (LS) §M.S. Pennings (LS) §T. Boomgaarden	'Imârah Station Closed when hospital is taken by the Iraq Government.	D. & E.P. Begg resign.
1960		+G. Gosselink °C.S. Gosselink •§W.G. Dekker °A.M. Dekker	°Ruth Jackson §C. Dalenberg §W.H. Storm §I.P. Storm §G.H. Nykerk °R.W. Nykerk §J. Veldman °M.A. Holmes +H. Staal °H.V. Staal +G.J. Holler §L.E. Holler °N.A. Nienhuis •LaD.M. Teumer (LS) §K.M. Diem (LS)	§W.W. Thoms °•§E.S. Thoms °Rachel Jackson §J.H. Boersma §D.T. Bosch °E.B. Bosch +J.W. Dunham °J.D. Dunham +J.R. Kapenga °M.U. Kapenga §°A.R. De Young	§L.R. Scudder II §D.B. Scudder §M.B. Allison +D.R. MacNeill °E.M. MacNeill +G.E. DeJong °E.K. DeJong °L.C. Hoogeveen §A.G. Pennings §M.S. Pennings +R.J. Block (LS) •L. Block (LS)		Rachel & Ruth Jackson retire. A.B. Cook leaves ARAMCO. L.C. Hoogeveen resigns in April at field request. M.M. & E.C. Heusinkveld on furlough. A. Schmalzriedt on leave to marry W.L. Lee

Yr.	Appointments	Basrah	Bahrain	Oman	Kuwait	Amarah	Absence/Change
1961	§C.G. Anker +R.L. Vander Aarde °M. Vander Aarde	+G. Gosselink °C.S. Gosselink +H. Staal °H.V. Staal +R.J. Block •L. Block	§W.H. Storm §J.P. Storm §G.H. Nykerk °R.W. Nykerk §J. Veldman °M.A. Holmes +H. Staal °H.V. Staal +G.J. Holler §L.E. Holler °N.A. Nienhuis •LaD.M. Teumer (LS) §K.M. Diem (LS)	§W.W. Thoms °•§E.S. Thoms §J.H. Boersma §D.T. Bosch °E.B. Bosch +J.W. Dunham °J.D. Dunham +J.R. Kapenga °M.U. Kapenga §°A.R. De Young	§L.R. Scudder II §D.B. Scudder §M.B. Allison +D.R. MacNeill °E.M. MacNeill §A.G. Pennings §M.S. Pennings		K.M. Diem on furlough. M.R. Barny dies. C. Dalenberg on furlough then retires. G.E. & E.K. DeJong on furlough. E.M. & R.S. Luidens return to Beirut with NECC radio.
1962	°W.L. & A. Schmalzried: Lee (assigned to NECC radio work in Beirut) •C. DeJong (special assignment as builder) M. DeJong §E. Sluiter °J. Garden §N. Nienhuis Garden (returns)	+G. Gosselink °C.S. Gosselink +R.J. Block •L. Block Basrah comes under the administration of the United Mission in Iraq.	§W.H. Storm §J.P. Storm §J. Veldman °M.A. Holmes +H. Staal °H.V. Staal +G.J. Holler §L.E. Holler •LaD.M. Teumer •C. DeJong (Q1) M. DeJong (Q1)	§W.W. Thoms °•§E.S. Thoms §J.H. Boersma +J.W. Dunham °J.D. Dunham +J.R. Kapenga °M.U. Kapenga §D.T. Bosch °E.B. Bosch §°A.R. De Young •C. DeJong (Q3) M. DeJong (Q3)	§L.R. Scudder II §D.B. Scudder §M.B. Allison +D.R. MacNeill °E.M. MacNeill §A.G. Pennings §M.S. Pennings +G.E. DeJong (Q2) °E.K. DeJong (Q2) §C.G. Anker (LS) +R.L. Vander Aarde (LS) °M. Vander Aarde (LS)		D.R. & E.M. MacNeill appointed to the NECC's radio project and literature work in Beirut (Q2). G.H. & R.W. Nykerk on furlough. P.Q. Harrison dies in Nov.
1963	+D.V. Franken §M.T. Franken (returns) +H.S. Vogelaar §N. Vogelaar §A. Vander Zwag +L. Vander Werff °P.J. Vander Werff §E. Veldhuizen °C Veldhuizen		§W.H. Storm §J.P. Storm §M.A. Holmes +H. Staal °H.V. Staal •LaD.M. Teumer §M.M. Heusinkveld §E.C. Heusinkveld +R.E. Weiss °A.B. Weiss	§W.W. Thoms °•§E.S. Thoms §J.H. Boersma +J.W. Dunham °J.D. Dunham +J.R. Kapenga °M.U. Kapenga §D.T. Bosch °E.B. Bosch §°A.R. De Young §A. Vander Zwag •C. DeJong M. DeJong	+G.E. DeJong °E.K. DeJong §L.R. Scudder II §D.B. Scudder §M.B. Allison §G.H. Nykerk °R.W. Nykerk §C.G. Anker +R.L. Vander Aarde °M. Vander Aarde +L. Vander Werff °P.J. Vander Werff §E. Sluiter		G.J. & L.E. Holler on furlough. J.R. & M.U. Kapenga on furlough. A.G. & M.S. Pennings on furlough. B.L. & J.B. Draper on leave of absence.

Year						
1964	§H. Doorenbos °M.H. Doorenbos		§W.H. Storm §I.P. Storm §J. Veldman +H. Staal °H.V. Staal •LaD.M. Teumer §M.M. Heusinkveld §E.C. Heusinkveld +R.E. Weiss °A.B. Weiss §E. Veldhuizen (LS) °C Veldhuizen (LS) +H.S. Vogelaar (LS) §N. Vogelaar (LS)	§W.W. Thoms °•§E.S. Thoms +J.W. Dunham °J.D. Dunham +J.R. Kapenga °M.U. Kapenga §°A.R. De Young §A. Vander Zwag •C. DeJong M. DeJong °J. Garden §N.N. Garden	§L.R. Scudder II §D.B. Scudder §G.H. Nykerk °R.W. Nykerk +R.L. Vander Aarde °M. Vander Aarde +L. Vander Werff °P.J. Vander Werff	M.A. Holmes on furlough. J.H. Boersma on furlough. M.B. Allison on furlough.
1965	¢K. Warren •M. Warren §F.H. Richards (interim appointment)	§H. Doorenbos (LS) (Q1) °M.H. Doorenbos (LS) (Q1)	§M.B. Allison	§W.W. Thoms °•§E.S. Thoms §J.H. Boersma +J.W. Dunham °J.D. Dunham +J.R. Kapenga °M.U. Kapenga §°A.R. De Young §F.H. Richards (Q4)	§L.R. Scudder II §D.B. Scudder	D.R. & E. Mac Neill requested to resign Dec. 31.
1966	§D. Van Etten Mrs. Van Etten ¢K.R. Warren °M.M. Warren	§H. Doorenbos (LS) °M.H. Doorenbos (LS)	§M.B. Allison +J.W. Dunham °J.D. Dunham §D. Van Etten (Q1) Mrs. Van Etten (Q1) ¢K.R. Warren (Q1) M.M. Warren (Q1)	§W.W. Thoms °•§E.S. Thoms §J.H. Boersma §H. Doorenbos (Q3) °M.H. Doorenbos (Q3) +J.R. Kapenga °M.U. Kapenga §°A.R. De Young	§L.R. Scudder II §D.B. Scudder	
1967	+L.R. Scudder III (LS - Lebanon till 1973) °N.G. Scudder (LS - Lebanon till 1973)		§M.B. Allison +J.W. Dunham °J.D. Dunham	§W.W. Thoms °•§E.S. Thoms §J.H. Boersma §H. Doorenbos °M.H. Doorenbos +J.W. Dunham °J.D. Dunham +J.R. Kapenga °M.U. Kapenga §°A.R. De Young	§L.R. Scudder II §D.B. Scudder	R. P. Johnson is reposted to West Pakistan by Presby. Ch., resigns as Arabian Mission Field Rep. M.M. Heusinkveld assassinated in Matrah, Oman, Sept. 13. J. Veldman retires.

Yr.	Appointments	Basrah	Bahrain	Oman	Kuwait	Amarah	Absence/Change
1 9 6 8		Basrah Station closed when the School is taken by the Iraq Government.	§M.B. Allison	§W.W. Thoms °§E.S. Thoms §J.H. Boersma §H. Doorenbos °M.H. Doorenbos +J.W. Dunham °J.D. Dunham +J.R. Kapenga °M.U. Kapenga §°A.R. De Young	§L.R. Scudder II §D.B. Scudder		
1 9 6 9			§M.B. Allison	§W.W. Thoms °§E.S. Thoms §J.H. Boersma §H. Doorenbos °M.H. Doorenbos +J.W. Dunham °J.D. Dunham +J.R. Kapenga °M.U. Kapenga §°A.R. De Young	§L.R. Scudder II §D.B. Scudder		K.R. & M.M. Warren leave the field; posted in New York as Middle East Area secretary.
1 9 7 0			§M.B. Allison	§W.W. Thoms °§E.S. Thoms §J.H. Boersma §H. Doorenbos °M.H. Doorenbos +J.W. Dunham °J.D. Dunham +J.R. Kapenga °M.U. Kapenga §°A.R. De Young	§L.R. Scudder II §D.B. Scudder		M.B Allison retires W.W. & E.S. Thoms retire. W.L. & A.S. Lee resign (Q2). K.R. Warren resigns. E. Sluiter resigns (Q2). G.J. & L.E. Holler resign (Q2)
1 9 7 1	§M.B. Allison (returns)			§M. Bruins Allison §J.H. Boersma §H. Doorenbos °M.H. Doorenbos +J.W. Dunham °J.D. Dunham +J.R. Kapenga	§L.R. Scudder II §D.B. Scudder		W.W. Thoms dies in Oct.

Year	Personnel	Scudder family	Absence/Change
1972	§M.B. Allison §J.H. Boersma §H. Doorenbos °M.H. Doorenbos +J.W. Dunham °J.D. Dunham +J.R. Kapenga °M.U. Kapenga §°A.R. De Young	§L.R. Scudder II §D.B. Scudder	
1973	§M.B. Allison §J.H. Boersma §H. Doorenbos °M.H. Doorenbos +J.W. Dunham °J.D. Dunham +J.R. Kapenga °M.U. Kapenga §°A.R. De Young	§L.R. Scudder II §D.B. Scudder +L.R. Scudder III °N.G. Scudder	
1974	§M.B. Allison §J.H. Boersma §H. Doorenbos °M.H. Doorenbos +J.W. Dunham °J.D. Dunham +J.R. Kapenga °M.U. Kapenga §°A.R. De Young	§L.R. Scudder II §D.B. Scudder +L.R. Scudder III °N.G. Scudder	
1975	§M.B. Allison §J.H. Boersma §H. Doorenbos °M.H. Doorenbos +J.W. Dunham °J.D. Dunham +J.R. Kapenga °M.U. Kapenga §°A.R. De Young	§L.R. Scudder II §D.B. Scudder +L.R. Scudder III °N.G. Scudder	H. & M.H. Doorenbos reassigned to Ethiopia when Oman re-entry refused. L.R. Scudder II dies in Kuwait April 3.
1976	§J.H. Boersma +J.W. Dunham °J.D. Dunham +J.R. Kapenga °M.U. Kapenga §°A.R. De Young	§D.B. Scudder +L.R. Scudder III °N.G. Scudder	L.R. & N.G. Scudder (furlough followed by leave of absence)

Yr.	Appointments	Basrah	Bahrain	Oman	Kuwait	Amarah	Absence/Change
1977				§J.H. Boersma +J.W. Dunham °J.D. Dunham +J.R. Kapenga °M.U. Kapenga §°A.R. De Young	§D.B. Scudder		
1978				§J.H. Boersma +J.W. Dunham °J.D. Dunham +J.R. Kapenga °M.U. Kapenga §°A.R. De Young	§D.B. Scudder		
1979				§J.H. Boersma +J.W. Dunham °J.D. Dunham +J.R. Kapenga °M.U. Kapenga §°A.R. De Young	§D.B. Scudder		
1980	§J.W. Hill ¢J.V. Hill		§J.W. Hill ¢J.V. Hill	§J.H. Boersma +J.W. Dunham °J.D. Dunham +J.R. Kapenga °M.U. Kapenga §°A.R. De Young	§D.B. Scudder		
1981	+G.L. Robinson M.B. Robinson +L.R. Scudder III (returns) °N.G. Scudder (returns)		§J.W. Hill ¢J.V. Hill +L.R. Scudder III °N.G. Scudder	§J.H. Boersma +J.W. Dunham °J.D. Dunham +J.R. Kapenga °M.U. Kapenga §°A.R. De Young	§D.B. Scudder +G.L. Robinson M.B. Robinson		
1982			§J.W. Hill ¢J.V. Hill +L.R. Scudder III °N.G. Scudder	§J.H. Boersma +J.W. Dunham °J.D. Dunham +J.R. Kapenga °M.U. Kapenga §°A.R. De Young	§D.B. Scudder +G.L. Robinson M.B. Robinson		A.R. De Young retires.
1983			§J.W. Hill ¢J.V. Hill +L.R. Scudder III °N.G. Scudder	§J.H. Boersma +J.W. Dunham °J.D. Dunham +J.R. Kapenga	§D.B. Scudder +G.L. Robinson M.B. Robinson		J.R. & M.U. Kapenga retire.

Year						Notes
1984		§J.W. Hill ¢J.V. Hill +L.R. Scudder III °N.G. Scudder	§J.H. Boersma +J.W. Dunham °J.D. Dunham	§D.B. Scudder +G.L. Robinson M.B. Robinson		J.W. & J.H. Dunham retire.
1985	+J.A. Zandstra °J.L. Zandstra	§J.W. Hill ¢J.V. Hill +L.R. Scudder III °N.G. Scudder	§J.H. Boersma	§D.B. Scudder +G.L. Robinson M.B. Robinson +J.A. Zandstra °J.L. Zandstra		G.L. & M.B. Robinson retire. J.W. & J.V. Hill retire.
1986		+L.R. Scudder III °N.G. Scudder	§J.H. Boersma	§D.B. Scudder +J.A. Zandstra °J.L. Zandstra		J.H. Boersma retires.
1987	¢E.A. Ryan §P.A. Ryan	+L.R. Scudder III °N.G. Scudder		§D.B. Scudder +J.A. Zandstra °J.L. Zandstra		L.R. & N.G. Scudder resign.
1988		¢E.A. Ryan §P.A. Ryan		§D.B. Scudder +J.A. Zandstra °J.L. Zandstra		
1989		¢E.A. Ryan §P.A. Ryan		§D.B. Scudder +J.A. Zandstra °J.L. Zandstra		
1990		¢E.A. Ryan §P.A. Ryan		§D.B. Scudder +J.A. Zandstra °J.L. Zandstra		D.B. Scudder on vacation in July. J.A. & J.L. Zandstra on furlough (Q2)
1991				+J.A. Zandstra (Q1) °J.L. Zandstra (Q1)		D.B. Scudder dies July 10 in the USA.

Bibliography

As I took up the task of writing this study, what quickly became evident was that the so-called histories of the Arabian Mission which have appeared up to now—prominently those of Mason and Barny, Dorothy VanEss's supplement to that, and the pamphlet written by Stanley Mylrea - had as their object the promotion of the mission. In itself that is not an ignoble objective, but it is not one which, strictly speaking, intends to produce a history. Too many details are missing. The difficult passages in the story are never examined with the kind of candor a history demands, or they are given only light treatment. Even some of the very best passages are passed over. Personal foibles and interesting correlations go unrecorded. There is a lack of dimension to these works that cannot satisfy the historian's mind. The broader context in which the mission lived and worked is also given short shrift. In the case of both Mylrea and Van Ess this is remarkable, because they were individuals with extremely broad interests and vision, but this observation only serves to reenforce the assertion that what they were intentionally producing was public relations literature. Since that is all that has been available for public consumption, I fear that the true value of the Arabian Mission's experience has never really been perceived, never really having been revealed. In all candor, when I first toyed with the idea of working on an "intellectual history of the Arabian Mission" for a Ph.D. dissertation topic, a few superficial probes into the literature, caused me to back away feeling that it would be far too shallow a topic. In the past months, however, I have found a whole new world that I never knew existed and to which I now call the attention of serious scholars.

The deeper I plumbed the mass of untried documentation, the more massive the task grew until it became evident that I would have to include at the end of the study a tentative guide to further research. In a research task such as lies behind this book, to stop before one has touched each relevant document involves almost a physical pain of withdrawl. It is all so potentially revealing. And there were sources to which I never even got near. The CMS archives at the University of Birmingham and the various colonial and British-India governmental archives in London have, for reasons of brutal economy both of time and money, been bypassed. State Department archives in Washington, D.C., hold promise of even more material. The archives held in Hartford, Connecticut by the Duncan Black MacDonald Institute of the Hartford Seminary Foundation contain strong files on both Samuel Zwemer and Edwin Calverley. And there are personal collections of letters and papers which are only now beginning to find their diverse ways into archival collections.

What is evident is that the topic of the Arabian Mission is not to be summarized in one effort such as this. There are biographies to be found by the score, each of magnetizing interest. Zwemer, for instance, really needs fresh study, and with the recent appearance of his early diaries the prospects are exciting. Someone must write a biography of John Van Ess . And Paul Harrison is due for a frank reappraisal which does not begin under his charismatic spell. There are other personalities worthy of study—Stanley Mylrea, Lewis Scudder (Sr.), Harold Storm, Sarah Hosman, Everdine DeJong, the Jackson sisters,... many. There are area studies which ought to be undertaken, and closer examinations of specific incidents that could yield fresh insights. A "micro-history" of the closure of Amarah station would yield fascinating material. A close examination of the closure of Kuwait Hospital and its repercussions would also be extremely valuable as a study in the evolution of missiological policies. Some of these have only been indicated in this present study. Certainly there is a fertile field here for scholars and authors which will not be exhausted for a long time.

The following bibliography is neither complete nor highly selective. The majority of entries are either writings which have been directly cited in the text of this study or they are writings which have had an influence upon the author. The entries have been grouped into four classifications: (1) General works, (2) Periodical literature, (3) Reference works, and (4) Books and Articles by Arabian Mission personnel. In this latter classification no attempt has been made to list all the books written, nor has an exhaustive library search been undertaken to find all the articles penned by Arabian Mission authors. But the important books have been listed (and some of the unimportant too).

For those who wish to see an exhaustive bibliography of the writings of Samuel Zwemer, the most prolific of Arabian Mission authors by far, there exists a research paper which is composed almost entirely of such a listing in forty pages: Richard "D" Hight II, A Selected English Language Bibliography of Dr. Samuel Marinus Zwemer (1867-1952) (Fort Wayne, Indiana: Concordia Theological Seminary, a research report for a course leading to an M.Div. degree, 1979); a copy is found in Sage Library at New Brunswick Theological Seminary, New Brunswick, New Jersey. This listing omits all non-English writing, and Zwemer enjoyed writing in Dutch and published also in Arabic. Many of his titles were also translated into a variety of languages. For the writings of other Arabian Mission figures there exists no comparable study as far as I know.

It will be noted in the footnotes of the text that rather extensive citations are from original papers, documents, and interviews. Many of these are in the author's own possession, six file boxes of which were left in the keeping of the Reformed Church Archives in New Brunswick, New Jersey. Others were found in the Joint Archives of Holland in Holland, Michigan (Larry Wagenaar, Archivist), and at the Archives of the Reformed Church in America in New Brunswick, New Jersey (Russell L. Gasero, Archivist). For the assistance of the two archivists and of the library staffs at the two seminaries—Western Theological Seminary in Holland, Michigan, and New Brunswick Theological Seminary in New Brunswick, New Jersey—I am deeply grateful.

General works

Abeel, David, *The Missionary Convention at Jerusalem; or an Exhibition of the Claims of the World to the Gospel* (New York: John S. Taylor, 1838).
Abu Hakima, Ahmad A., *History of Eastern Arabia, 1750-1800, The Rise and Development of Bahrain and Kuwait* (Beirut: Khayyats, 1963).

Abu Hakima, Ahmad A., *The Modern History of Kuwait, 1750-1965* (London: Luzac & Company Limited, 1983).

Aharonian, H. P., *The Armenian Evangelical Church on the Crossroads* (Beirut: MECC, 1988).

Allen, Roland, *Missionary Methods: St. Paul's or Ours - A Study of the Church in the Four Provinces* (New York: Fleming H. Revell Company, 1913).

———, *The Spontaneous Expansion of the Church and the Cause Which Hinder It* (London: World Dominion Press, 1926) (fourth edition: 1960)

Antonius, George, *The Arab Awakening: The Story of the Arab National Movement* (Beirut: Khayats, 1938).

Arnold, Sir Arnold T. *The Persian Gulf: An Historical Sketch from the Earliest Times to the Beginnings of the Twentieth Century* (London: George Allen & Unwin Ltd., 1928).

Atiya, Aziz S., *A History of Eastern Christianity* (London: Methuen & Co., Ltd., 1968).

Basetti-Sani, Giulio, *The Koran in the Light of Christ* (Chicago, Illinois: Franciscan Herald Press, 1977)

Belgrave, James H. D., *Welcome to Bahrain,* (8th edition) (Manama, Bahrain: Augustan Press, 1973).

———., *Welcome to Bahrain: A Complete Illustrated Guide for Tourists and Travellers* (Stourbridge, Worcestershire, England: James H. D. Belgrave, 1953).

Bell, Richard, The *Origin of Islam in its Christian Environment* (London: Frank Cass & Co., Ltd., 1968 [originally published in 1926]).

Belyaev, A. E., *Arabs, Islam, and the Arab Caliphate in the Early Middle Ages* (translated from Russian) (New York: Frederick A. Praeger, Inc., 1969).

Betts, Robert Brenton, *Christians in the Arab East* (Athens: Lycabettus Press, 1975).

Chandy, Jacob, *Reminiscences and Reflections: The story of the development of the Christian Medical College and Hospital, Vellore, in the healing ministry of the Indian churches* (Kottayam, Kerala, India: The C.M.S. Press, 1988).

Chisholm, Archibald H. T., *The First Kuwait Oil Concession Agreement: A Record of the Negotiations 1911-1934* (London: Frank Cass, 1975).

Cooper, Ann (compiler), *Ishmael My Brother: A Biblical Course on Islam* (Bromley, Kent, England: STL Books [Operation Mobilization], 1985).

Cragg, Kenneth,

Kenneth Cragg is an extremely prolific writer in the field of Muslim-Christian relations, and had a deep influence upon Arabia missionaries. He is still producing. We note here those titles which had the greatest impact upon Arabia missionaries:

° *Sandals at the Mosque: Christian Presence Amid Islam* (New York: Oxford University Press, 1959);

° *The Call of the Minaret* (New York: Oxford University Press, 1964); and

° *The Dome and the Rock: Jerusalem Studies in Islam* (London: S.P.C.K., 1964).

Daniel, Norman *The Arabs and Medieval Europe* (London: Longman, 1975).

Dickson, H. R. P., *Kuwait and Her Neighbors (London: George Allen & Unwin Ltd., 1956).*

————, *The Arab of the Desert* (London: George Allen & Unwin, Ltd., 1949).

Dickson, Violet, *Forty Years in Kuwait* (London: George Allen & Unwin, Ltd., 1971).

Doughty, Charles M., *Travels in Arabia Deserta*, 3rd ed. (with an introduction by T. E. Lawrence) (New York: Random House, 1921).

Forman, Charles, *A Faith for the Nations* (Philadelphia: The Westminster Press, 1957)

Freeth, Zahra, *A New Look at Kuwait* (London: George Allen & Unwin, Ltd., 1972).

Geren, Paul, *New Voices, Old Worlds* (New York: Friendship Press, 1958).

Hartshorn, J. E., *Oil Companies and Governments: An Account of the International Oil Industry in its Political Environment* (London: Faber and Faber, 1967).

Her [Britanic] Majesty's Government, *Muscat and Oman* (London: F. Mildner & Sons, 1962).

Hodgson, Marshall G. S., *The Venture of Islam*, 3 vols. (Chicago: The University of Chicago Press, 1974).

Hoge, Dean R., Johnson, Benton, and Luidens, Donald A., *Vanishing Boundaries: The Religion of Mainline Protestant Baby Boomers* (Louisville, Kentucky: Westminster/John Knox Press, 1994).

Hopkins, C. Howard, John R. Mott, 1865-1955: *A Biography* (Grand Rapids, Mich.: William B. Eerdmans Publishing Company, 1979).

Howarth, David, *Dhows* (London: Quartet Books, 1977).

Khadduri, Majid, *Independent Iraq: A Study in Iraqi Politics from 1932 to 1958* (London: Oxford University Press, 1960).

————, *Republican 'Iraq: A Study in 'Iraqi Politics since the Revolution of 1958* (London: Oxford University Press, 1969).

Landen, Robert Geran, *Oman Since 1856* (Princeton, N. J.: Princeton University Press, 1967).

Lewis, Bernard, *The Middle East and the West* (Bloomington, Indiana: Indiana University Press, 1964).

Lipsky, George A. et al, *Saudi Arabia: Its People, its Society, its Culture* (New Haven, Conn.: HRAF Press, 1959).

Longrigg, Stephen Hemsley, *'Iraq 1900 to 1950: A Political, Social, and Economic History* (Beirut: Librairie Du Liban, 1953).

————, *Four Centuries of Modern 'Iraq* (London: Oxford University Press, 1925).

McLean, Archibald, *Epoch Makers of Modern Missions* (New York: Fleming H. Revell Company, 1912).

Marlowe, John, *Arab Nationalism and British Imperialism: A Study in Power Politics* (London: The Cresset Press, 1961).

————, *The Persian Gulf in the Twentieth Century* (London: The Cresset Press, 1962).

Miller, William M., *A Christian's Response to Islam* (Wheaton, Illinois: Tyndale House, 1976).

Mott, John R. (editor), *The Moslem World of To-Day* (New York: George H. Doran Company, 1925).

Mott, John R., *The Evangelization of the World in This Generation* (New York: Student Volunteer Movement for Foreign Missions, 1900).

Moucarry, Chawkat Georges, *Islam and Christianity at the Crossroads* (Tring, Herts, England: Lion Publishing, 1988).

Neill, Stephen, *A History of Christian Mission* (New York: Penguin Books, 1964).

————, *Colonialism and Christian Missions* (New York: McGraw-Hill Book Company, 1966).

Nevakivi, Jukka, Britain, *France and the Arab Middle East: 1914-1920* (London: The Athlone Press, 1969).

Nijim, Basheer K., *American Church Politics and the Middle East* (Belmont, Mass.: Association of Arab-American University Graduates, Inc., 1980?).

Monroe, Elizabeth, *Britain's Moment in the Middle East: 1914-1956* (London: Chatto & Windus, 1964).

Owen, Roderick, *The Golden Bubble: Arabian Gulf Documentary* (London: Collins, 1957).

Paget, Julian, *Last Post: Aden 1964-1967* (London: Faber and Faber, 1969).

Palmer, Michael A., *Guardians of the Gulf: A History of America's Expanding Role in the Persian Gulf, 1833-1992* (New York: The Free Press, 1992).

Phillips, Wendell, *Oman: A History* (Beirut: Librairie Du Liban, 1971).

————, *Unknown Oman* (Beirut: Librarie Du Liban, 1971).

Runciman, Steven, *A History of the Crusades*, 3 vols. (Cambridge: Cambridge University Press, 1951- 1954 incl.).

Said, Edward, *Orientalism* (New York: Random House, 1978).

Sanmiguel, Mgr. V.[ictor], *Christians in Kuwait* (Beirut, Lebanon: Beirut Printing Press, [1970]).

————, *Pastor in Kuwait: 1966-1978* (Kuwait: Bishop's House, 1978).

Scudder, Dorothy Jealous, *A Thousand Years in Thy Sight: The Story of the Scudder Missionaries of India* (New York: Vantage Press, 1984).

Searight, Sarah, *The British in the Middle East* (London: Weidenfeld and Nicolson, 1969).

Sergeant, R. B., *The Portuguese off the South Arabian Coast: Hadrami Chronicles* (London: Clarendon Press, 1974).

Semaan, Wanis A., *Aliens at Home: A Socio-Religious Analysis of the Protestant Church in Lebanon and its Background* (Beirut: Librairie du Liban, 1986).

Severin, Tim, *The Sindbad Voyage* (London: Hutchinson, 1982).

Smith, George, *The Life of William Carey, D. D., Shoemaker and Missionary* (London: John Murray, 1885).

Southern, R. W., *Western Views of Islam in the Middle Ages* (Cambridge, Massachusetts: Harvard University Press, 1962).

Tibawi, A. L., *American Interests in Syria 1800-1901* (Oxford: Clarendon Press, 1966).

Winstone, H. V. F., *Captain Shakespear: A Portrait* (London: Jonathan Cape, 1976).
Zeine, Zeine N., *The Emergence of Arab Nationalism: With a Background Study of ArabTurkish Relations in the Near East* (Beirut: Khayats, 1966).
————, *The Struggle for Arab Independence: Western Diplomacy and the Rise and Fall of Faisal's Kingdom in Syria* (Beirut: Khayats, 1960).

Books and Articles by Arabian Mission personnel

Allison, Mary Bruins,
Memoirs of Mary Bruins Allison (rough typescript, copy available in the Archives of the Reformed Church of America, New Brunswick, NJ - dated around 1989). This is the document to which reference is made in this text, but the memoirs have now been edited and published:
Doctor Mary in Arabia: Memoirs by Mary Bruins Allison, M.D. (Austin, Texas: University of Texas Press, 1994).

Badeau, John S., *The American Approach to the Arab World* (New York: Harper & Row, Publishers, 1968).
————., *The Lands Between* (New York: Friendship Press, 1958).
————, *The Middle East Remembered* (Washington, D. C.: The Middle East Institute, 1983).
Boersma, Jeanette, *Grace in the Gulf: The Autobiography of Jeanette Boersma, Missionary Nurse in Iraq and the Sultanate of Oman* (Grand Rapids, Michigan: Wm. B. Eerdmans Publishing Co., 1991).
Calverley, Edwin Elliot, *Islâm: An Introduction* (Cairo: The American University of Cairo, 1958).
————, *Worship in Islam: Being a Translation, With Commentary and Introduction, of Al-Ghazzâlî's Book of the Ihyâ' on Worship* (Madras, South India: The Christian Literature Society for India, 1925) [Calverley's doctoral dissertation].
Calverley, Eleanor T., *My Arabian Days and Nights* (New York: Thomas Y. Crowell Company, 1958).
Dalenberg, Cornelia (with David De Groot), *Sharifa*, No. 11 in The Historical Series of the Reformed Church in America (Grand Rapids, Michigan: Wm. B. Eerdmans Publishing Co., 1983).

Harrison, Ann M., *A Tool in His Hand: the Story of Paul W. Harrison of Arabia* (New York: Friendship Press, 1958).

Harrison, Paul W., "Christ's Contribution to the Moslem," in John R. Mott, ed., *The Moslem World of To-Day* (New York: George H. Doran Company, 1925), pp. 323-337.

———, *Doctor in Arabia* (New York: John Day, 1940).

———, *The Arab at Home* (New York: Thomas Y. Crowell Company, 1924).

———, "The Medical Missionary," in Jesse R. Wilson, ed., *Men and Women of Far Horizons* (New York, Friendship Press: 1935), pp. 3-8.

Johnson, R. Park, *Middle East Pilgrimage* (New York: Friendship Press, 1958).

Mason, Alfred De Witt, and Barny, Frederick J., *History of the Arabian Mission* (New York: The Board of Foreign Missions, Reformed Church in America, 1926).

Mylrea, C. Stanley G., *Kuwait Before Oil: Memoirs of Dr. C. Stanley G. Mylrea, Pioneer Medical Missionary of the Arabian Mission, Reformed Church in America* (mimeographed typescript circulated privately in limited edition by Dorothy F. Van Ess of the original manuscript owned by Mrs. Elizabeth Zwemer Pickens and edited by Samuel M. Zwemer; original written between 1945 and 1951).

———., *The Story of the Arabian Mission After Fifty Years, 1889-1939* (New York: The Board of Foreign Missions, Reformed Church in America, [1939]).

Staal, Harvey, *Codex Sinai Arabic 151: Pauline Epistles (Rom., I & II Cor., Phil.), Part I (Arabic Text) and Part II (English Translation)*, in J. Geerlings, ed., *Studies and Documents, Vol. XL* (Salt Lake City, Utah: University of Utah Press, 1969).

Storm, Harold W., *Whither Arabia? a Survey of Missionary Opportunity* (New York: Dominion Press, 1938).

Storm, Ida Patterson, *Highways in the Desert* (New York: Broadman Press, 1950).

Van Ess, Dorothy, *History of the Arabian Mission, 1926-1957* (Mimeographed text privately produced and circulated, copy available in the Gardner A. Sage Library, New Brunswick, N.J. nd.

———, *Pioneers in the Arab World*, No. 3 in The Historical Series of the Reformed Church in America (Grand Rapids, Michigan: Wm. B. Eerdmans Publishing Co., 1974).

Van Ess, John, *Living Issues* (Beirut: The John Van Ess, Jr. Memorial Fund, no date).

———, *Meet the Arab* (New York: The John Day Company, 1943).

Vander Werff, Lyle L., *Christian Mission to Muslims: The Record: Anglican and Reformed Approaches in India and the Near East, 1800-1938* (South Pasadina, California: William Carey Library: 1977).

Wherry, E. M., Zwemer, S. M., and Mylrea, C. [S.] G. (editors), *Islam and Missions: Being papers read at the Second Missionary Conference on behalf of the Mohammedan World at Lucknow, January 23-28, 1911* (New York: Fleming H. Revell Company, 1911).

Zwemer, S. M., *Arabia: The Cradle of Islam* (New York: Fleming H. Revell Company, 1900).

———, *Islam: a Challenge to Faith* (New York: Student Volunteer Movement for Foreign Missions, 1907).

———, *Raymund Lull: First Missionary to the Moslems* (New York: Funk & Wagnalls Company, 1902).

———, *The Cross Above the Crescent: the Validity, Necessity and Urgency of Missions to Moslems* (Grand Rapids, Michigan: Zondervan Publishing House, 1941).

———, *The Disintegration of Islam* (New York: 1915).

———, *The Early Diaries of Samuel M. Zwemer* (unedited personal diaries in the Archives of the Reformed Church in America in New Brunswick, New Jersey).

———, *The Moslem Christ* (London: Oliphant, Anderson & Ferrier, 1912).

———, *The Moslem Doctrine of God* (New York: 1905).

———, *The Moslem World* (New York: Young People's Missionary Movement of the United States and Canada, 1908).

———, *The Ship that Sailed and the Keel that Never Kissed the Sea* (New York: Board of Domestic Missions, Reformed Church in America, [1931]).

Zwemer, Samuel M., and Cantine, James, *The Golden Milestone: Reminiscences of Pioneer Days Fifty Years Ago in Arabia* (New York: Fleming H. Revell Company, 1938).

Zwemer, S. M., Wherry, E. M., and Barton, James L. (editors), *The Mohammedan World of To-Day: Being papers read at the First Missionary Conference on behalf of the Mohammedan World held at Cairo, April 4th-9th, 1906* (New York: Fleming H. Revell Company, 1906).

Zwemer, Samuel M., and Zwemer, Amy E., *Moslem Women* (New York: 1926).

Books and Articles about the Arabian Mission

Al-Tameemi, Abdul Malek, *The Arabian Mission: A Case Study of Christian Missionary Work in the Arabian Gulf* (Durham, England: Doctoral Thesis, School of Oriental Studies, University of Durham, 1977).

at-Tamîmî, 'Abd-ul-Mâlik Khalaf, *at-tabshîr fî mintaqat-il-khalîj il-'arabî: dirâsah fî ittârîkh il-'ijtimâ'î wa is-sîyâsî* [*Evangelism in the Region of the Arabian Gulf: a Study in Social and Political History*] (Kuwait: Sharikat-il-Kâzimah li in-Nashr wa it-Tarjamah wa it-Tawzî', 1982). [An adaptation in Arabic of the Doctoral Thesis noted above.]

Beatty, Jerome, *Americans All Over* (New York: John Day, 1938).

Bergman, H. J., *The Reformed Church in America's Mission in Iraq 1890-1957* (Seattle, Wash.: University of Puget Sound, masters thesis, 1963).

Clarke, Angela, *The American Mission Hospital, Bahrain: Through the Changing Scenes of Life 1893-1993* (Bahrain: The American Mission Hospital Society, 1993).

Hallock, Constance M., *Desert Doctor* (Paul Harrison of Arabia) (New York: Friendship Press, 1950).

Jessup, Henry Harris, *The Setting of the Crescent and the Rising of the Cross, or Kamil Abdul Messiah: A Syrian Convert from Islam to Christianity* (Philadelphia, Pennsylvania: The Westminster Press, 1898).

Wilson, J. Christy, *Apostle to Islam: A Biography of Samuel M. Zwemer* (Grand Rapids, Mich.: Baker Book House, 1952).

———, *Flaming Prophet: The Story of Samuel Zwemer* (New York: Friendship Press, 1970).

Winder, R. Bayly, "Education in Al-Bahrayn," pp. 283-335 in *The World of Islam: Studies in Honour of Philip K. Hitti* (James Kritzeck & R. Bayly Winder, editors) (London: Macmillan & Co. Ltd., 1959).

Zeigler, H. Conway, *A Brief Flowering in the Desert: Protestant Missionary Activity in the Arabian Gulf, 1889-1973* (Princeton, New Jersey: masters dissertation, Near Eastern Studies, Princeton University, 1977).

Periodical literature

Khoury, Paul, *Paul d'Antioche, Eveque Melkite de Sidon (xii s)* (Beyrouth: Imprimerie Catholique, 1964).

Corbon, Jean, "Middle Eastern Churches and the Ecumenical Movement," MECC *Perspectives,* no. 6/7, October 1986 (Middle East Council of Churches, Limasol, Cyprus), pp. 46-49.

Daniel, Norman, "Some Recent Developments in the Attitude of Christians Towards Islam," in E. J. B. Fry and A. H. Armstrong - eds., *Rediscovering Eastern Christendom: Essays in Memory of Dom Bede Winslow* (London: Darton Longman & Todd, 1963), pp. 154-166.

Hageman, Howard G., "The Golden Age of New Brunswick," New Brunswick Theological Seminary *Newsletter,* vol. 8, no. 3, March 1979 (New Brunswick, New Jersey).

Hunsberger, George R., "Sizing Up the Shape of the Church," *Reformed Review,* vol 47, no. 2, winter, 1993-1994 (Holland, Mich.: Western Theological Seminary), pp. 133-144.

MECC Staff, "Middle Eastern Churches' Life and Witness," MECC *Perspectives,* no. 6/7, October 1986 (Limasol, Cyprus: Middle East Council of Churches), pp. 30-42.

———, "The Middle East Council of Churches (M.E.C.C.)," MECC *Perspectives,* no. 6/7, October 1986 (Limasol, Cyprus: Middle East Council of Churches), pp. 50-51.

———, "Who are the Christians of the Middle East," MECC *Perspectives,* no. 6/7, October 1986 (Limasol, Cyprus: Middle East Council of Churches), pp. 8-22.

Nemeth, Roger J., and Luidens, Donald A., "The RCA in the Larger Picture: Facing Structural Realities," *Reformed Review,* vol 47, no. 2, Winter, 1993-1994 (Holland, Mich: Western Theological Seminary), pp. 85-112.

Said, Edward W., "The Phony Islamic Threat," *New York Times Magazine* Sunday, Nov. 21, 1993 (New York Times, Inc.), pp. 62-65.

Stamoolis, James, "Eastern Orthodox Mission Theology," *International Bulletin of Missionary Research,* vol 8, no. 2, April 1984 (Ventnor, N.J.: Overseas Ministries Study Center), pp. 59-63.

Books and Articles by Reformed Church in America authors

Chamberlain, Mrs. W. I. *Fifty Years in Foreign Fields: China, Japan, India, Arabia* (New York: Woman's Board of Foreign Missions, Reformed Church in America, 1925).

————, "The Church in Foreign Lands," *Tercentenary Studies*, 1928, Reformed Church in America (New York: Reformed Church in America, 1928).

Cobb, Henry N., *A Century of Missions in the Reformed Church in America: 1796-1896* (New York: Board of Foreign Missions, 1896).

Corwin, Charles E., *A Manual of the Reformed Church in America* (New York: Board of Publication and Bible-School Work of the Reformed Church in America, 1922).

Gasero, Russell L., *Historical Directory of the Reformed Church in America, 1628-1992*, no. 23 in The Historical Series of the Reformed Church in America (Grand Rapids, Michigan: Wm. B. Eerdmans Publishing Co., 1992).

General Program Council, the Reformed Church in America, *The Ad Hoc Report on World Mission* (New York: Reformed Church in America, 1980).

Heideman, Eugene, *A People in Mission: The Surprising Harvest* (New York: Reformed Church Press, 1980).

————, *A People in Mission: Their Expanding Dream* (New York: Reformed Church Press, 1984).

Hoff, Marvin D., *The Reformed Church in America: Structures for Mission*, No. 14 in The Historical Series of the Reformed Church in America (Grand Rapids, Michigan: Wm. B. Eerdmans Publishing Co., 1985).

Vandenberge, Peter N., *Historical Directory of the Reformed Church in America, 1628-1978*, No. 6 in The Historical Series of the Reformed Church in America (Grand Rapids, Michigan: Wm. B. Eerdmans Publishing Co., 1978).

Wichers, Wynand, *A Century of Hope 1866-1966* (Grand Rapids, Michigan: William B. Eerdmans Publishing Company, 1968).

Reference Works

Arabian Mission, *The Arabian Mission Field Reports* (#1, January 1-April 1, 1892 to #26, April 1-June 30, 1898); *The Arabian Mission Quarterly Letters from the Field* (#27, JulySeptember, 1898 to #40, October-December, 1901); *Neglected Arabia: Missionary Letters and News Published Quarterly by the Arabian Mission* (#41, January-March, 1902, to #215, Winter 1949); *Arabia Calling* (#216, Spring 1949, to #250, March 1962).

Arabian Mission, [Annual] Statement [of the Board of Trustees], #1 (1889) to #22 (1910) in The Joint Archives of Holland, Michigan.

The Middle East Council of Churches, MECC *Perspectives*, No. 6/7, October 1986 (Middle East Council of Churches, Limasol, Cyprus).

Horner, Norman A. *A Statistical Survey of Christian Communities in Cyprus, Egypt, Ethiopia, Iran, Iraq, Jordan, Lebanon, Sudan, Turkey* (Beirut: published in mimeograph by the author, 1972).

Lorimer, J. G., *Gazeteer of the Persian Gulf, 'Omân, and Central Arabia* (Calcutta: Superintendent Government Printing, India, 1915).

Reformed Church in America, *Acts and Proceedings of the General Synod of the Reformed Church in America*, Vols. I-IX inclusive (New York: Board of Publication of the Reformed Dutch Church, 1738-1860).

Index

570